The Founding of the Roman Catholic Church in Melanesia and Micronesia

1850–1875

Princeton Theological Monograph Series

K. C. Hanson and Charles M. Collier, Series Editors

Recent volumes in the series:

Philip Harrold
*A Place Somewhat Apart: The Private Worlds
of a Late Nineteenth-Century University*

John A. Vissers
The Neo-Orthodox Theology of W. W. Bryden

Caryn D. Riswold
Coram Deo: Human Life in the Vision of God

Sam Hamstra, editor
The Reformed Pastor by John Williamson Nevin

Bonnie L. Pattison
Poverty in the Theology of John Calvin

Paul S. Chung, Veli Matti Karkkainen, and Kim Kyoung-Jae, editors
Asian Contextual Theology for the Third Millennium

Stephen Finlan and Vladimir Kharlamov, editors
Theōsis: Deification in Christian Theology

Richard Valantasis et al., editors
The Subjective Eye: Essays in Honor of Margaret Miles

Christian T. Collins Winn, editor
*From the Margins: A Celebration of the Theological Work
of Donald W. Dayton*

The Founding of the Roman Catholic Church in Melanesia and Micronesia

1850–1875

Ralph M. Wiltgen

☙PICKWICK *Publications* · Eugene, Oregon

THE FOUNDING OF THE ROMAN CATHOLIC CHURCH IN MELANESIA
AND MICRONESIA, 1850 TO 1875

Princeton Theological Monograph Series 84

Copyright © 2008 Society of the Divine Word. All rights reserved. Except for brief quotations in critical publications or reviews, no part of this book may be reproduced in any manner without prior written permission from the publisher. Write: Permissions, Wipf and Stock, 199 W. 8th Ave., Suite 3, Eugene, OR 97401.

Pickwick Publications
A Division of Wipf and Stock Publishers
199 W. 8th Ave., Suite 3
Eugene, OR 97401

ISBN 13: 978-1-55635-209-6

Cataloging-in-Publication data:

Wiltgen, Ralph M., 1921–2007.

    The founding of the Roman Catholic Church in Melanesia and Micronesia, 1850 to 1875 / Ralph M. Wiltgen with a Preface by Charles W. Forman and a Foreword by William R. Burrows.

    Princeton Theological Monograph Series 84

    xvi + 580 p.; 25 cm.

    ISBN 13: 978-1-55635-209-6 (alk. paper)

    Includes bibliographical references (p. 551–56) and index

    1. Catholic Church—Melanesia—History. 2. Catholic Church—Micronesia—History. 3. Catholic church—missions. 4. Missions—Melanesia. 5. Missions—Micronesia. I. Burrows, William R. II. Forman, Charles W. III. Title. IV. Series.

BV3675 .W5 2008

Manufactured in the U.S.A.

Contents

List of Illustrations vii

Foreword by William R. Burrows ix

Preface by Charles W. Forman xv

1 Supriès, a French Carthusian, Interests Lombardy Clerics in Micronesia (1845–47) 1

2 Pope Pius IX Approves Lombardy's Seminary for Foreign Missions (21 February 1850) 19

3 Melanesia and Micronesia Vicariates Are Reduced to the Status of Missions (11 August 1850) 32

4 Fransoni Offers the Melanesia and Micronesia Missions to Lombardy's Foreign Mission Seminary (16 January 1851) 46

5 Pope Pius IX Suggests Training in a Nearby Mission (21 August 1851) 60

6 Fransoni Sternly Reprimands Prefect Apostolic Reina (7 February 1852) 80

7 French Marists Decide to Remain at Woodlark (29 June 1852) 103

8 Rome Grants Numerous Faculties to Melanesia Missionaries (1850–53) 114

9 Reina Decline Fiji and Chooses Melanesia and Micronesia (7 August 1852) 131

10 Is Reina or Frémont the Prefect Apostolic of Melanesia? (24 February 1853) 148

11 Sickness, Language Study, and Customs at Rooke and Woodlark (1852–55) 170

12 Mazzucconi Urges Reina and Marinoni to Abandon Rooke and Woodlark (6 January and 20 April 1855) 191

13 Reina Abandons Rooke and Woodlark and Awaits New Orders in Sydney (10 May and 10 July 1855) 212

14 Gazelle Massacre at Woodlark (September 1855) 230

15 Cuarterón, a Spanish Sea Captain, Offers to Reestablish Reina in Melanesia (9 August 1855) 265

16 Polding, Pompallier, and Bataillon Compete for the Milan Missionaries (27 July 1856) 312

17 Reina and Cuarterón Meet in Manila to Discuss Plans (1 October 1856) 330

18 Reina Leaves Labuan for Dorei Bay in New Guinea (25 February 1858) 344

19 Reina Reaches Singapore en route to Dorei Bay (6 March 1858) 360

20 Why Barnabò Sends Reina to Hong Kong (1850–58) 367

21 Barnabò Suppresses the Melanesia-Micronesia Mission (11 December 1858) 389

22 Decline of Cuarterón and His Labuan Mission (21 October 1859) 407

23 Bataillon Tells Barnabò: Send Elloy to Micronesia (1 May 1870) 429

24 Picpus Missionaries Refuse Melanesia and Micronesia (22 September 1873) 459

25 Marists Refuse Micronesia for the Third Time (18 June 1875) 468

26 Raimondi Becomes Vicar Apostolic of Hong Kong (4 October 1874) 485

27 Mill Hill Will Attempt to Reach New Guinea via Labuan (4 June 1878) 522

Abbreviations 549

Bibliography 551

Index 557

List of Illustrations

Vital statistics of Carthusian Father Thaddée Supriès 2

Explanation of the vital statistics of Father Thaddée Supriès 4

Bishop Angelo Ramazzotti, founder, Foreign Mission Seminary of Milan 22

Father Guiseppe Marinoni, first director, Foreign Mission Seminary 26

Decree naming Paolo Reina as Prefect of the Missions 92

Map of Rook (Rooke) Island 142

Medical Report about life on Rooke and Woodlark Islands 176

Map of Woodlark Island 250

Title page of position paper for the beatification
    of Father Giovanni Battista Mazzucconi 260

Father Giovanni Battista Mazzucconi 262

Encyclopedia article on Don Carlos Cuarterón 266

Letter of Cardinal Prefect Barnabò to Superior General Rouchouze 462

Letter of Cardinal Prefect Barnabò to Superior General Bousquet 466

Title page of Volume 50 of Mansi's Sacrorum Conciliorum 472

Excerpt of the address given by Bishop Elloy 474

Excerpt about the meeting of Superior General Arnold Janssen
    with Prefect Apostolic Raimondi of Hong Kong 508

News account of the meeting of Janssen and Raimondi 510

Bishop Raimondi, Prefect Apostolic of Hong Kong 516

Saint Arnold Janssen, founder of the Society of the Divine Word (S.V.D.) 520

Letter of Sister Mary Thais to Father Peter Benoit 542

Foreword

Ralph Wiltgen's Life and Work

WILLIAM R. BURROWS

I FIRST MET FATHER RALPH WILTGEN WHEN I WAS A HIGH SCHOOL STUDENT AND CANdidate for membership in the Roman Catholic Society of the Divine Word at East Troy, Wisconsin, in 1958. In March 2001—43 years later and also at East Troy, where he was now retired—I began a conversation with him about this book. By that time Ralph's health was failing. But as we discussed his life-long work on the book you hold in your hands, he came alive. I volunteered my services to help him wrap things up and bring the book to publication. Between 1958 and 2001, our paths crossed several times, most notably in Rome, where I was studying theology between 1969 and 1972. I always admired him, even when we disagreed. He was a man of enormous sincerity, intelligence, and energy, all of which he put to the service of God, the church, and the Society of the Divine Word. It was a great honor to be entrusted with that job by the Society's superiors as Father Wiltgen's health deteriorated further.

Born in Chicago in 1921, Ralph Michael Wiltgen entered the SVD (the popular name of the Society of the Divine Word and its members, an acronym taken from the official Latin name of the Society, *Societas Verbi Divini*) in 1938 at East Troy and was ordained at the Society's major seminary in Techny, Illinois, on 19 May 1950. Sent to Rome to study missiology that same year, Wiltgen obtained a doctorate at the Gregorian University in 1953 and returned to the United States in 1953, where he published his dissertation as *Gold Coast Mission History, 1471 to 1880* (Techny, Illinois, 1956). The Gold Coast of his thesis was a British colony on the West African Gulf of Guinea. After World War II it became a major mission of the SVD and obtained its independence in 1957 as Ghana.

In 1958 Wiltgen was assigned to the New Guinea "Region" (as its missions were called then) of the SVD to found the first Catholic weekly newspaper. Although the newspaper never got off the ground, Father Wiltgen came to love the country and the people. He was not destined to stay there long, but out of that period came the realization that there was no comprehensive history of the missionary efforts of either the SVD or other missionary societies that had been active on that island. It is not clear whether he requested to write that history or he was requested by superiors to do so. A trip through SVD archives shows a diligent, creative Father Wiltgen spotting an opportunity for work he could and wanted to do. Not long thereafter another portfolio would have been added to his list of duties. What is clear is that Wiltgen's work in public relations came to the attention of Father Johannes Schütte, SVD, a former China missionary and, like Wiltgen, one of the few doctors in missiology in the Society. Schütte was elected superior general of the SVD on 28 March 1958 and called Wiltgen to Rome to set up a professional public relations office for the Society. This assignment began the longest chapter in Father Wiltgen's life, since he was assigned to Rome from 1959 through 1995.

During this period, Father Wiltgen completed three books, including one best-seller, and managed the SVD generalate's efforts to facilitate communication with the ever-widening English-speaking constituencies of the Society as English began overtaking German as the SVD's common language. When the Second Vatican Council began in 1962, he realized that there was no balanced, truly informed source of news and perspective on the Council's deliberations. He grafted the Council News Service onto his responsibilities for Divine Word News Service. Soon DWNS was a sideline, and by the end of the fourth session of the Council, CNS was providing twice-weekly bulletins to 3,147 paying subscribers in English, French, German, Spanish, Portuguese, Hindi, Arabic, Japanese, Indonesian, and Chinese editions. By 1964, when his Council News Service was judged universally to be a success, Wiltgen wrote the following about the secret of that success. "We take no sides. We let both sides, the progressives and the conservatives, speak for themselves." When he wrapped up CNS after the Council's last sessions in late 1965, he was happy to present the superior general with a substantial check, "for the work of the missions."

Out of his interviews with hundreds of cardinals, bishops, superiors-general, and *periti* (experts in specialized areas of research, advisors to the council fathers) that had filled his news releases during the Council there was a book waiting to be written, and soon Father Wiltgen was writing it. Published by Hawthorn Books in 1967, *The Rhine Flows into the Tiber: The Unknown Council*, was a great achievement. Redemptorist Father Francis Xavier Murphy (who used the *nom de plume* "Xavier Rynne" for his famed dispatches from Rome published in *The New Yorker*) once told me that it was the single best book after the Council and that, although many liberals didn't like it, "Wiltgen's judgment on what *had* occurred was sounder than theirs." It was followed in 1970 by *The Religious Life Defined*, in which Wiltgen tried to counteract liberal reformers, whom he believed were misinterpreting the Vatican Council's teaching on religious life.

During this entire period, the archives show that he knew he was supposed to be devoting major efforts to writing the history of the SVD in New Guinea. Somehow, though, Wiltgen the journalist with a story to tell won out over Wiltgen the missiologist and historian. When I first got to know him personally in the fall of 1969, he had shifted attention almost totally to the New Guinea project, but he explained to the superiors that one could not legitimately start in 1896, when the first German SVDs set foot in Kaiser Wilhelmsland, as the German colony in North East New Guinea was known. "You have to go back to catch what the Congregation of the Propagation of the Faith and the various missionary congregations were thinking and doing in the seventy years of Catholic mission history that preceded the arrival of the SVDs." After a feast day dinner in the spring of 1970, Ralph invited me to the room in which he kept the records of his research in the archives of Propaganda, and missionary societies such as the Pontifical Missionary Institute of Milan, the Paris Foreign Mission Society, the Marists, and the SVDs. He had floor to ceiling index files, transcriptions of archives that he had consulted and taken notes from before photocopying became cheap, and in other places photocopies of documents that he had been able to make as technology advanced. I realized that the journalist was truly a scholar with enormous respect for facts and original research.

Out of this prodigious research came *The Founding of the Roman Catholic Church in Oceania, 1825–1850*. It was published by the Australian National University Press and received very positive reviews. Work on that book and this one, *The Founding of the Roman Catholic Church in Melanesia and Micronesia, 1850–1875* had been conducted at the same time. He hoped then to finish the Melanesia-Micronesia background history and begin what he hoped would go much quicker, the history of post-1875 missions of the Missionaries of the Sacred Heart (the MSCs) and Marists. Although the SVD was destined to provide the largest number of Catholic missionaries in New Guinea, Wiltgen knew that their work followed the MSCs and Marists, whose efforts he greatly respected. Ralph was always clear that this and the volume to follow it were preludes to the history of the SVD in New Guinea. Scholarship is immensely poorer for his not being able to get beyond 1875.

In later years, Wiltgen seemed to realize he would never get to the work that the superiors had assigned him. He told me that he was embarrassed when New Guinea missioners asked him about progress on the SVD history in New Guinea (Ralph never fully adjusted to the change in name to Papua New Guinea in 1975 when the distinct "territories" of Papua and New Guinea gained independence as Papua New Guinea). Whatever the case, he never finished his lifework, testimony to Martin Marty's adage that historians need to be careful about where they begin that lifework since the need to understand what precedes it often becomes an archival treasure trove out of which they never find their way. The richness of this volume should make us grateful that Ralph Michael Wiltgen, SVD, spent his time so profitably in the 1825 – 1875 archives.

Over the past several years, it has been my great pleasure to work intimately with Dale Irvin, President of New York Theological Seminary, and Scott Sunquist, Professor of World Mission and Evangelism at Pittsburgh Theological Seminary. Dale and Scott are authors of Orbis's two-volume *History of the World Christian Movement*. They have been assisted by over forty historians and missiologists from every major confessional group in world Christianity. We've learned several things, among which is the limitation of histories that focus on missionaries and in which local peoples are mostly background characters in a story dominated by the heroic deeds of missioners. The second is the need to integrate "mission" history with "general" Christian history, and the third is the importance of telling Christian history in the context of both world historical currents and the local history of a given people. If these are criteria for good Christian history, Father Wiltgen's book does not meet them. His interest is in ecclesiastical matters. Nevertheless, I commend this book to the reader and believe it should be assigned in graduate level courses in both general Christian history and mission studies. Why? Because there is no book like it to unfold the inner workings and thought of several generation of Catholics whose work yielded an enormous harvest. Wiltgen does not whitewash problems or gloss over character flaws. They are there for us to learn from, and when more comprehensive histories are written, the resources that Ralph Wiltgen brings into relief in this volume will be essential to telling those stories. If there were more historical research of the quality Wiltgen achieves in this volume, our understanding of both the past and present would be much richer. It has indeed been an honor to help Ralph and the talented people who have assisted him bring this treasure into the light.

This book is Ralph Wiltgen's from first page to last, but a number of people have collaborated to polish the style, run down missing pieces of documentation, and check facts and sources. The first and most important of those collaborators is Leona Foley, who worked as Father Wiltgen's assistant for sixteen years. Two of those years were spent on the previous volume, fourteen on the second. Of her work, she writes, "I felt privileged to assist in this important endeavor, bringing to light the never-before-told story . . . I arrived in Rome just when Pope John Paul was elected in October 1978 and remained there working with Father Wiltgen until he returned to the United States in 1995."

Others who assisted in the final stages of preparing the manuscript include Professor Charles Forman, who gave us a sense of the rare value of Father Wiltgen's work for the scholarly history of mission; Father Ray Quetchenbach, SVD, who preserved files, computer diskettes, and early copies of the manuscript when the author's health began to fail; Father Roger Schroeder, SVD, professor of missiology at Catholic Theological Union, who more than anyone else kept the project alive when it could have faltered; he later identified and placed the illustrations, as well as ran down details in bibliographic references; provincial superiors Father Thomas Krosnicki, SVD, and Father Mark Weber, SVD, who offered moral support and assured that the necessary financial resources were available; Thomas Artz at the SVD Chicago Province Center, who kept prodding us to meet deadlines and handled immense amounts of practical work; Marcia Stein of the SVD Chicago Province Center Archives, who helped run down information on the U.S. side of Wiltgen's life; Bob Land, who copy-edited the entire volume and created the index; Mary Ocasek, librarian at Catholic Theological Union, who helped with references and bibliographic details. In Rome at the Divine Word Generalate special thanks are due to five SVD priests: superior general Anthony Pernia, who urged us to complete the good work of an esteemed confrere; Franz Bosold and Herbert Scholz of the Society's archives, who assembled materials to help us understand better the career of Father Wiltgen, and his many unsung accomplishments; Friedrich Forster and Timothy Lenchak, who did so much to make my stay in the generalate and work in the archives both pleasant and productive.

Finally, thanks are due to the extraordinary individuals who make up the Wipf and Stock publishing team. Led by Jim Stock and Jim Tedrick, these men and women are dedicated to bringing important scholarly books into print and then keeping them there when publishers following conventional models and wisdom do not. Their competence, commitment, and good humor are an inspiration to all who know them.

Maryknoll, New York
Pentecost 2007

☙ REST IN PEACE ❧

As fate or Providence would have it, Ralph Wiltgen was destined never to see this 1850-1875 history in print. He died on 6 December 2007 a few days short of what would have been his 87th birthday, and one month before this book was to be printed. He was buried at Techny, Illinois, among hundreds of his Divine Word Missionary confreres and Holy Spirit Missionary Sisters.

The day after Father Ralph Wiltgen's death, I received word from Jan Szweda, Provincial Superior of the SVD in Papua New Guinea, that the provincial council had accepted my proposal to finish what Ralph began. Over the next several years, accordingly, I will be using the information collected by the late Father Wiltgen to write a history of the Society of the Divine Word in Papua New Guinea. I hope that my work will have the same reverence for facts that Ralph's did. I also hope than my continuation of his work will both present the history of the Society's efforts and offer insights (1) into the interaction of SVD priests and brothers with their Melanesian hosts in places like Ambunti on the Sepik, Mingende in the Chimbu, Pompabus in Wabag, and Mt. Hagen, as well as (2) into the translation process whereby Melanesians understood the Christian message in their own categories and worked to reshape their world in the light of their new insights.

W.R.B.
December 2007

Preface

A Perspective on Ralph Wiltgen's History of Catholic Origins

Charles W. Forman, Professor Emeritus of Missions, Yale University

THIS VOLUME BY RALPH WILTGEN TAKES A SPECIAL PLACE ALONGSIDE OTHER SCHOLARLY histories of Pacific missions. These histories are not numerous, for the field has not been widely explored until recently. When it comes to Roman Catholic mission histories, the following are all we have. The first writer of Catholic mission history in the Pacific was André Dupeyrat, writing on the fiftieth anniversary of the establishment of his mission in *Papouasie: Histoire de la Mission, 1885–1935*, published in Paris in 1935. Four years after Dupeyrat came a pioneer work on Kiribati by Ernest Sabatier, *Sous l'Equateur du Pacifique: Les Isles Gilbert et la Mission Catholique, 1888–1938* (Paris, 1939). This work proved to be a treasure for Kiribati history and was eventually translated into English.

A continuation of Dupeyrat's work was provided on the hundredth anniversary of his mission by Georges Delbos, *Cent Ans chez les Papous: Mission accomplie?* (Issoudun, 1984), which was also published in English within a year. Fiji had its fifty-year history with *La Croix dans l'Archipel Fidji (de 1894 à nos jours)* by Cyprien Destable and J. M. Sédès (Paris, 1944), and Vanuatu had its centenary volume with Paul Monnier's *Cent Ans de Mission, L'Eglise Catholique au Vanuatu, 1887–1987* (Port Vila, 1987). In accord with the bilingual character of the country, that book was published simultaneously in English. Micronesia waited longest for a history, Francis Hezel's *The Catholic Church in Micronesia: Historical Essays* (Chicago, 1991).

All these works have been by missionaries writing about their own missions. The only historical work by an academic historian is *Marists and Melanesians: A History of Catholic Missions in the Solomon Islands* by Hugh M. Laracy (Canberra, 1976). And there is the academic study that covers the whole of Catholic history in the Pacific as well as that of the Protestants, John Garrett's trilogy: *To Live Among the Stars* (Geneva, 1985), *Footsteps in the Sea* (Geneva, 1992), and *Where Nets Were Cast* (Geneva, 1997).

Standing among all the others, yet different from them all is Father Wiltgen's *The Founding of the Roman Catholic Church in Oceania, 1825–1850* (Canberra, 1979). That volume, of course, is the companion and predecessor to the study you now hold in your hand. In it and the present volume, Wiltgen concentrates on the beginnings of missions to an extent that is not found in any of the other studies. Both volumes deal only with the incipient stages of Catholic mission work. The dates they cover, 1825–1850 and 1850–1875 respectively, are prior to the work of the other Catholic histories we have mentioned. In the case of this volume on Melanesia, they are also dealing with dates prior to those covered in most Protestant mission histories. The first Protestant missionaries to New Guinea arrived in 1874 in the case of the London Missionary Society and in 1875 in the case of the Methodists. Anglican work in the Solomon Islands started earlier, but only in the form of visits that did not result in settlement. Only in the last quarter of the nineteenth century did Anglicans shift their center to the Solomons. Only on the fringes of Melanesia in Vanuatu and the Loyalty Islands was there an establishment of Protestant mission work before the period covered in this volume. So we have here, in effect, an introduction to Melanesian missions of *all* types and especially to the problems that missions were getting into when they entered Melanesia.

More notably, Wiltgen presents his story in a detail and with a thoroughness that no other Pacific historian has attempted to match. As year proceeds to year and sometimes month to month, the reader follows the course of mission life in a way that is not possible in the other, more cursory histories. Reading Wiltgen we wish that we could be as well informed about other times and places.

Furthermore, he provides insights into the inner workings of mission sending agencies that is not found elsewhere. We see how people with different ideas make their impact on the Catholic missions. We see how unexpected actors change the course of events. We see the details of policy making and how policies are related to specific persons. Nowhere else in Pacific mission history can one get this wealth of insight into the people behind the missions as well as into the minds of the missionaries themselves.

All this is a monumental work, one that will provide a great resource for historians of the future.

New Haven, April 2007

1

Supriès, a French Carthusian, Interests Lombardy Clerics in Micronesia

1845–47

IN EARLY JULY 1843 A FRENCH CARTHUSIAN MONK, FATHER THADDÉE SUPRIÈS (1800–1888), clashed with Giacomo Filippo Fransoni (1775–1856), an Italian cardinal twenty-five years his senior. The monk was vicar to the prior of the Carthusian monastery attached to the Basilica of Saint Mary of the Angels in Rome. The cardinal was prefect or director of the Congregatio de Propaganda Fide, a branch of the Roman Curia founded in 1622 by Pope Gregory XV to supervise and direct Roman Catholic missionary work around the world.[1] They clashed over Northern Oceania, better known as Micronesia, in the cardinal's office in Palazzo "de Propaganda Fide" near the Spanish Steps in Rome.

More precisely they clashed over the rank that Supriès was to receive on being placed in charge of missionary work in Micronesia. He had suggested to Fransoni on 6 April 1843 that the vast expanse of islands in the Pacific Ocean north of the equator and south of Japan, between Hawaii and the Philippines, should be made an independent mission called Northern Oceania. This was no idle dream of a pious monk. Paul-Laurent-Marcel Supriès was a veteran missionary of the Paris Foreign Mission Seminary, having served for almost ten years in India, Siam (now Thailand), and the Nicobar Islands. When later he became a Carthusian monk at La Grande Chartreuse in France on 29 June 1839, his Christian name was changed to Thaddée. Fransoni seemed ready indeed to give him the rank of prefect apostolic over Micronesia, which meant that he would be in charge of the mission as a priest. But Supriès insisted on being named vicar apostolic with the rank of bishop, since otherwise he would not have enough prestige to attract personnel, he said.

---

1. The Congregation for the Propagation of the Faith (*Congregatio de Propaganda Fide* in Latin) was founded by Pope Gregory XV in 1622. Because the word "propaganda" took on negative connotations in the mid-twentieth century, it was renamed "Congregation for the Evangelization of Peoples" (*Congregatio pro Evangelizatione Populorum*) by Pope John Paul II in 1982. In this volume it will be referred to as "Propaganda Fide" or "Propaganda," as it is in most historical writing.

153. Dom Thaddée SUPRIÈS.

Fréjus.
Né le 2o octobre 18oo à Cotignac (Var) diocèse de

Prêtre séculier, puis
Missionnaire des Missions étrangères de Paris.
Ordonné prêtre à Fréjus

CHARTREUSE: 68.	Novice:	28 juin 1838		
	G. Profès:	29 juin 1839		
Calabre:	Administrateur:	2o juil 184o	–	28 juil 1841
Rome:	Hôte:	28 juil 1841	–	1 nov 1841
	Vicaire:	1 nov 1841	–	1o août 1843
Pavie:	Hôte:	1o août 1843	–	185o
	Vicaire:	185o	–	1o avril 1851
	Procureur:	1o avril 1851	–	31 déc 1851
	Coadjuteur:	1 janv 1852	–	2 sept 1852
	Recteur:	2 sept 1852	–	1o mai 1855
	Prieur:	1o mai 1855	–	CG 1869

Définiteur aux CG 1856, 1863 et 1869.

Convisiteur de la Grande Chartreuse au CG 1856.
Visiteur des Maisons d'Italie aux CG 1856, 1863 et 1866.

" VP. Priori domus Papiae fit mia, et eligitur Prior
" domus Romae."   Charta CG 1869

Rome:	Prieur:	CG 1869	–	CG 1877

" VP. Priori domus Romae fit mia, et vadat ad domum
" S. Mariae de Mougères."   Charta CG 1877

Mougères:	Hôte:	CG 1877	– ob	2o nov 1888

Il meurt à Mougères le 2o novembre 1888, dans la 89ème année de son âge et la 5oème de profession.

" Obiit D. Thaddaeus Supriès, sacerdos, professus Car-
" tusiae, Antiquior domus S. M. de Mougères, alias Visitator provin-
" ciae Italiae, Prior, Rector et Vicarius domus Papiae necnon Prior
" et Vicarius domus Romae. Obiit aetatis suae anno 89; professionis
" vero 5o. Habens Missam de Beata per totum Ordinem in quo laudabi-
" liter vixit."

Charta CG 1889

Vital statistics of Father Thaddée Supriès, the Carthusian monk who inspired Milan seminarians with interest in foreign missionary work. He himself had served earlier in the Nicobar Islands as a member of the Paris Foreign Mission Seminary. Source: CART: *Catalogue des Religieux*, 148.

Some two weeks after his clash with the cardinal, Supriès wrote from his monastery in Rome telling Fransoni that he no longer experienced "some repugnance . . . at being named a prefect apostolic," because "Divine Providence has given me personnel for the mission of Northern Oceania in an altogether unexpected way." But by that time Fransoni had a new problem: he had to find quickly an alternative territory for Bishop Jean-Baptiste-François Pompallier (1801–71), vicar apostolic of Western Oceania with headquarters in New Zealand. Because of his French nationality, Pompallier was being threatened with expulsion by the British, who were fast taking over New Zealand.

The Vicariate Apostolic of Micronesia (or Northern Oceania) was created one year later on 16 July 1844, exactly as Supriès had suggested, but Rome did not entrust it to him. It was entrusted instead to a missionary group in France called Marists, officially known as the Society of Mary (S.M.), with headquarters in Lyon. Fransoni instructed the Marists, who supplied all of Pompallier's staff, to hold the new vicariate in reserve for the bishop in case he and his men should be expelled from New Zealand by the British. As for Supriès, Fransoni showered him with praise for having suggested the Micronesia Vicariate, but gave him no other role than "to recommend this important affair to the Lord."[2]

The Order of Carthusians (O. Cart.) transferred Supriès on 10 August 1843 from Rome to the Certosa di Pavia in northern Italy, extolled as the most celebrated religious monument in Lombardy.[3] This Carthusian monastery, founded in 1396 by Gian Galeazzo Visconti, is somewhat north of Pavia and about fifteen miles southwest of Milan. Clerics from Milan and Lombardy came to enjoy its beauty and stillness and to spend days of prayer and recollection called retreats. They all met Supriès, who had been put in charge of retreats.

"When I arrived in this part of Italy," Supriès later wrote to Cardinal Fransoni, "I was really grieved at finding so little interest among the clergy in taking up holy missionary work." He tried to understand why among so many priests in the province of Lombardy "not one could be found generous enough to abandon his homeland and cross the seas with the aim of bringing the knowledge of the name of Jesus Christ to nations without faith." He shared this disappointment "with some good priests" who visited him, and he examined the problem deeper with those who arrived "at various times to make here the spiritual retreats of which I am in charge."[4]

---

2. PF: SC Oceania vol. 2 (1842–45, Part I), f. 464r–465v, Supriès to Fransoni, 6 April 1843; ibid., f. 504rv, Supriès to Fransoni, 18 July 1843; PF: LDB vol. 329 (1843, Part I), f. 303v–304r, Fransoni to Supriès, 27 April 1843. Abbé J. F. M. Guérin collaborated with Supriès in presenting on 24 May 1843a more detailed plan for the Micronesia vicariate. For further details on the Supriès-Guérin proposals and on the founding of the Vicariate Apostolic of Micronesia, see Ralph M. Wiltgen, *The Founding of the Roman Catholic Church in Oceania, 1825 to 1850*, 267–310. Carthusians have priors, not abbots.

3. CART: "Catalogue des religieux," 148 no. 153, Dom Thaddée Supriès. This data on Supriès was supplied on 23 July 1987 by D. Luc Fauchon, archivist at La Grande-Chartreuse.

4. PF: SC Missioni vol. 21 (1844–46), f. 974r, Supriès to Fransoni, 6 April 1846.

La Grande-Chartreuse,
le 23 juillet 1987.

D. Luc Fauchon
(archiviste)
La Grande-Chartreuse
F-38380 St Laurent-du-Pont.

Mon Père,

En réponse à votre demande de renseignements sur D. Thaddée SUPRIES, je vous envoie son "curriculum vitae". C'est tout ce que j'ai trouvé. Je ne puis donc pas justifier, comme vous le désirez, ses dates de naissance et de décès.

D'autre part, nous ne possédons aucun écrit provenant de lui.

Voici quelques explications sur le vocabulaire de la feuille ci-jointe :

Administrateur: La chartreuse de Calabre venait d'être récupérée. Il n'y avait pas encore de communauté.

Hôte: C'est le titre que l'on donne à un religieux séjournant dans une maison dont il n'est pas profès et où il ne remplit aucune charge.

Vicaire: Chargé de présider en communauté, en l'absence du prieur. Il n'a alors aucun pouvoir sur le temporel.

Procureur: Chargé de la direction des Frères et du temporel.

Coadjuteur: Procureur chargé des personnes étrangères à l'Ordre.

Recteur: Titre que porte le supérieur lorsqu'il est à la tête d'une maison où l'on ne mène pas la vie régulière. On nomme aussi certains moines recteurs, avant de les nommer prieurs, quand on doute de leurs aptitudes à gouverner une maison.

Prieur: Titre du supérieur d'une chartreuse. Il n'y a pas d'abbés en Chartreuse.

Définiteur: Les définiteurs sont un groupe de prieurs qui, pendant la durée du chapitre général, dispose de tous les pouvoirs nécessaires pour régler les affaires de l'Ordre. Ce sont eux qui jugent si le Révérend Père (ministre général) et les prieurs doivent rester en charge ou non.

Pendant qu'il était prieur à Rome, D. Thaddée était aussi procureur général de l'Ordre. Cette charge était alors attachée à celle de prieur de Rome (jusqu'à l'abandon de la chartreuse de Rome, en 1884).

Je vous prie, mon Père, de bien vouloir agréer l'assurance de mon religieux dévouement en N.S.,

These explanations of the vital statistics of Father Thaddée Supriès were supplied on 23 July 1987 by Father Luc Fauchon, Archivist of La Grande-Chartreuse Monastery at St. Laurent-Du-Pont in France.

Seminarians studying philosophy and theology in Lombardy also found their way to the monastery, especially during the summer holiday period from June to September. They felt attracted by its prayerful atmosphere. Meeting Supriès was a treasured experience, and they quickly became enamored of this man whose eloquence set their hearts afire with new purpose. He described for them his experiences in the mission field and explained the organization of the Paris Foreign Mission Seminary to which he had once belonged. He also awakened their interest in the Vicariate Apostolic of Micronesia that he had envisioned, but for which he had volunteered in vain. The province of Lombardy ought to have a foreign mission seminary of its own, he told the young men, and its mission field ought to be the Vicariate Apostolic of Micronesia.[5]

One of the many seminarians inspired by Supriès was Giovanni Battista Mazzucconi (1826–55) from Rancio di Lecco in the Archdiocese of Milan. He was nineteen and had completed his first year of philosophy at the Monza seminary when he accompanied some seminarians to the Carthusian monastery during the summer vacation of 1845. Like others, he began corresponding with Supriès. Those with a budding interest in foreign missionary work found in this monk a wealth of information and inspiration; he was also a champion for their cause. In clerical circles the Certosa di Pavia fast became known as a nucleus of missionary animation. At the core of it all was the director of retreats, Father Supriès.[6]

Federico Salvioni, a theology student at the Milan major seminary, also visited the Carthusian monastery in the summer of 1845. When Supriès learned that he and a fellow seminarian were going to Switzerland on business, he prevailed upon them to extend their journey to Lyon in France and to spend a few days there at the Marist headquarters. He wanted them to learn more about Micronesia and other Marist missions in Oceania and so "imbibe the true apostolic spirit." Supriès, then forty-five, wrote a letter of introduction for Salvioni and his companion to fifty-five-year-old Father Jean-Claude Colin (1790–1875), the founder and superior general of the Marists.

By the time Salvioni and his friend were ready to leave for Switzerland and France, another seminarian had joined them. On reaching Lyon they found Colin engrossed in giving his society members their annual retreat, which lasted from 12 to 19 September. Colin therefore delegated the provincial superior of France, thirty-four-year-old Father Pierre-Julien Eymard (1811–68), to be one of their hosts. (This was the same Eymard who would be declared a saint on 9 December 1962 by Pope John XXIII.) On their return to Milan they were "full of admiration for what they had seen and heard" and "even more

---

5. See ibid., f. 944rv, Supriès to Buratti, 20 March 1846; ibid., f. 974r, Supriès to Fransoni, 6 April 1846.

6. Carlo Suigo, *Pio IX e la fondazione del primo instituto missionario Italiano a Milano*, 77; *Beatificationis seu Declarationis Martyrii Servi Dei Ioannis Baptistae Mazzucconi sacerdotis Pontificii Instituti pro Missionibus Exteris in odium fidei, uti fertur, anno 1855 interfecti Positio super introductione causae et super martyrio ex officio concinnata*, 60, 63, 430.

eager" to take up a missionary vocation. This made Supriès believe that the Lyon visit had produced "excellent results."⁷

Salvioni wrote to Colin from the Milan major seminary on 16 January 1846, nine months before his ordination to the subdiaconate. After reminding Colin of his visit the previous September, he explained that a reputable religious journal edited in Milan now wished to publish for the edification "above all of the clergy," the information that he and his two friends had obtained from the Marists. He asked Colin's consent to publish this material and requested additional data to complement and correct what had been learned by word of mouth from several Marist priests. Questions "of particular interest to us," he said, "are these: How did the Society of Mary begin and what is its present status? With what spirit and for what purpose was it founded? What are its principal rules, particularly those for the novitiate? In what pious works is it engaged? Where do foreign missions fit in among these works?" Hopefully Colin would answer these questions, Salvioni said, because such an article published in Italy could be "a seed that would be able to bear fruit in due time."⁸

Colin gave great importance to Salvioni's letter and asked Eymard, his closest collaborator, to answer it. Eymard explained how a handful of seminarians began meeting periodically in 1815. In late 1816 they were allowed to hold their meetings in a hall of the Lyon major seminary. There were "delays, refusals, contradictions and humiliations of every kind" that had to be endured for twenty years before the Society of Mary received papal approbation. When it was formally approved by Pope Gregory XVI on 29 April 1836, the society had only twenty priests, Eymard said. But by 1846, the current year, it already had ten foundations in France and had sent ninety of its priests and brothers to Oceania. Four priests had been made bishops by Rome and were in charge of vicariates in New Zealand, Central Oceania, New Caledonia, and Melanesia-Micronesia.

The letter ended with Eymard admitting that a wish had constantly filled his heart while he was composing the letter. "And now I dare to tell you about it," he said. The wish was that "you may become the instrument of Providence for transplanting the Society of Mary to your beautiful Italy which is so Catholic and so filled with devotion to the Queen of Heaven." Eymard said he would pray to the Virgin Mary "so that my wish may be fulfilled."⁹

Milan at this time was part of the Lombard-Veneto kingdom ruled by Austria. Since 1818 it had had an Austrian-born archbishop, then seventy-six-year-old Karl Gaetan Cardinal Gaysruck (1769–1846). This cardinal had forbidden the founding of new religious

---

7. PF: SC Missioni vol. 21 (1844–46), f. 974r, Supriès to Fransoni, 6 April 1846; SM: 436, Salvioni to Colin, 16 January 1846. Supriès, not aware of Salvioni's second companion, tells Fransoni incorrectly that two students of theology went to Lyon. Salvioni writing to Colin reminds him that they were three in number. See also n. 11.

8. SM: 436, Salvioni to Colin, 16 January 1846.

9. PIME: AME 28:747–50, Eymard to Salvioni, 8 February 1846. For extracts from this letter see *Origines maristes (1786–1836)*, J. Coste and G. Lessard, eds., 4:62–67. See also n. 11.

organizations in his archdiocese, a ban that extended to missionary organizations as well. Eager to go abroad as missionaries, but hindered by the archbishop's ruling, three young priests and a deacon instinctively turned to Supriès. He could not help them, he said, since what they needed was support from Cardinal Prefect Fransoni of Propaganda Fide. Vivid memories of his clash with the cardinal three years earlier made him believe that he was excluded from the cardinal's good graces. Yet the clerics gave Supriès no rest; month after month they persisted in asking that he intercede for them with Rome. After all, who would help them if he did not? And why had he been stirring up foreign mission interest in their breasts, if no missionary from Lombardy could go overseas?

Encouraged perhaps by Eymard's letter to Salvioni, which reached Milan on 14 February 1846, Supriès finally gave in and wrote to Rome on 20 March. But he did not write to Fransoni. Nor did he write to Fransoni's secretary, Archbishop Giovanni Brunelli. He wrote instead to Father Clemente Maria Buratti, a *minutante* or clerk in Fransoni's office. Supriès had come to know and trust him when making his 1843 proposals for the founding of the Vicariate Apostolic of Micronesia. Explaining why he was not writing directly to the cardinal, he said "a certain timidity—or let me rather say a kind of indescribable fear—hinders me from doing so." This fear was caused by "the remembrance of some past events, which you can well recall." He urged Buratti to show his "customary goodness" and hear him out, since his request was not for himself, but for others. The request was "very important" and, if realized, would "greatly benefit" the foreign missions. Supriès then told Buratti that two priests from the Archdiocese of Milan and also a priest and a deacon from the nearby Diocese of Lodi had been begging for many months "that I make it possible for them to become missionaries." Their spiritual directors had tested their vocations thoroughly and had found them to be "genuine." The two from Lodi could easily obtain the necessary permission from their bishop, but the two from Milan anticipated "great difficulties."

Since all four were from Lombardy and had become close friends during seminary days, they wanted to work together in the same mission. By reading the Italian edition of the famous French magazine known in English as *Annals of the Propagation of the Faith*,[10] they had become acquainted "with Oceania's great need for missionaries" and had learned "how well disposed" those peoples were toward Christianity. For this reason they wanted to have "Micronesia, for example," as their field of apostolic activity if it did not yet have missionaries, or else "any other place in that abandoned area."

Wanting their project to endure, the four clerics "had formed the plan of uniting themselves in a congregation named after and protected by Saint Francis Xavier." Such an organization would provide openings for mission work "for the many priests of Lombardy

---

10. The Italian edition, *Annali della propagazione della fede*, was published in Naples, Italy, and appeared in monthly installments. The twelve issues of 1846 totaled 721 pages and included reports on Oceania from Australia, Marquesas Islands, Melanesia, New Caledonia, New Zealand, Tonga, and Wallis.

who wish to go to the missions, but who cannot do so because no openings exist." The four pioneers were convinced "that companions will quickly join them, because many students of theology are excellently disposed to embrace this state of life."

But founding such an organization in Milan was out of the question at the moment, Supriès said, because the present archbishop would never give his approval. It was therefore proposed that the Congregation of Saint Francis Xavier exist formally only in those countries to which its missionaries would be sent. "After a change of circumstances," the congregation could be established formally in Milan. Since this city was a good source of missionary vocations and of financial assistance, it was considered an ideal location for the congregation's headquarters. As for necessary services in Milan, like those of a correspondent, supplier of goods, recruiter of personnel, and collector of funds, "a good priest has already volunteered to provide these services for the group." This priest, Supriès said, "would like to go to the missions himself, but he is hindered because of various assignments."

Supriès wanted "to do nothing else" but follow Buratti's advice. He therefore inquired whether he should write about this matter to Fransoni, or perhaps to the cardinal's secretary, Brunelli. "What should I say? Be frank and tell me if the project seems impractical! Should I give it no further thought? Or should I keep encouraging them?" Supriès asked for a speedy reply because "these good gentlemen do not have much patience" and "they maintain that much delay could give rise to new obstacles."[11]

Buratti's reply must have been both speedy and enthusiastic because Supriès wrote a four-page letter to Cardinal Prefect Fransoni seventeen days later on 6 April 1846. It was the third anniversary of the letter written by Supriès in Rome in which he had suggested to Fransoni the founding of an independent mission for Micronesia.[12] After describing for the cardinal what he had done to stir up mission interest in Lombardy since his arrival at Pavia, he said that four priests and a deacon[13] were persistently asking him "to provide them with the means" of going to the foreign missions. "They have felt themselves called by God to this walk of life for several years." The deacon and two of the priests were from the Diocese of Lodi. Since their bishop was "very zealous regarding mission work," they would have no difficulty in obtaining his permission to leave. But the other two priests were from the Archdiocese of Milan, he said, and "will have great obstacles to overcome." They therefore hoped "that the Sacred Congregation will kindly take some action with His Eminence, the Archbishop of Milan, to obtain his consent for their departure."

---

11. PF: SC Missioni vol. 21 (1844–46), f. 944rv. See also chap. 2, n. 10.

12. Wiltgen, *Oceania*, 267–68. Buratti's letter has not been located. But seventeen days was time enough for an exchange of correspondence between Pavia and Rome. The letter of Salvioni to Colin mentioned above, for example, was postmarked 17 January 1846 in Milan and on arriving in Lyon, France, was postmarked 20 January. Eymard's reply to Salvioni was postmarked 11 February in Lyon and on arriving in Milan was postmarked 14 February.

13. Supriès had mentioned three priests and a deacon when writing to Buratti on 20 March, but by this date (6 April) another priest had joined the group.

Supriès then explained under three headings "the project which they after mature examination desire to submit to Your Most Reverend Eminence":

1. The five clerics wished "to unite themselves in a congregation called 'The Missionaries of Saint Francis Xavier' and to found in Milan a mission center or seminary." But because of Archbishop Gaysruck's prohibition the formal establishment of the congregation in Milan would have to be postponed. The congregation would formally exist in those places, however, to which its missionaries might be sent. Meanwhile a chargé d'affaires or two, based in Milan, would recruit candidates, collect funds, write letters, and so on. "Two excellent priests full of zeal and possessing great influence" had already volunteered to perform these services for the congregation.

2. "They wish to be entrusted with a particular mission exclusively for themselves, which could be called a Milan mission, or better still a Lombard mission." The reasons favoring this "seem very strong to them," Supriès said, since then the province of Lombardy would want to support it, favor it, and regularly provide it with new missionaries and supplies. This might not happen "if they were to be interspersed with missionaries from other countries" or if the Lombard missionaries "were not all together in the same country." They believed that having a mission field "exclusively for themselves" would also be an excellent help for them "to preserve better the spirit of union, peace, fraternal charity and fervor, since they have been united by the closest bonds of friendship for a number of years already." They also believed "that this will be a very strong inducement for other Lombards to join them," something that would "make the new association stable and give it a large membership."

3. "Made aware of the great need for missionaries in Oceania by what they were able to read in the *Annals of the Propagation of the Faith*, and knowing also the favorable dispositions of those islanders to embrace the faith, they are hoping that this will be the area destined for their apostolic activities." Supriès added, however, that they wanted to do nothing "but the will of God" and that they were therefore ready and eager "to conform to whatever the Sacred Congregation might propose."

In his letter to Buratti, Supriès had specifically mentioned Micronesia as the mission desired by the young priests; in this letter to Fransoni he mentioned Oceania, not Micronesia. Perhaps Buratti had advised him to ask for some Oceania mission in general or for "whatever the Sacred Congregation might propose." Or perhaps Supriès, in view of his earlier falling out with Fransoni over Micronesia, preferred not to mention it in this first letter to the cardinal.

Supriès added that Deacon Cesare Mola expected to be ordained a priest on Trinity Sunday, 7 June 1846. He listed the names of all five clerics and added some information that he thought might interest the cardinal:

Clerics	Age	Place of Origin	Ordained a Priest
Paolo Faré	24	Milan Archdiocese	17 May 1845
Pompeo Beretta	25	Milan Archdiocese	17 May 1845
Vincenzo Cassinelli	24	Lodi Diocese	17 May 1845
Giovanni Vistarini		Lodi Diocese	
Deacon Cesare Mola	22	Lodi Diocese	

"It is true that they are rather young" to be entrusted with a mission of their own, Supriès admitted, "but this difficulty could perhaps be remedied by adding to their number some missionaries of mature age and experience." All five candidates were hoping that Rome would send a speedy and favorable reply "so that they can begin taking the necessary steps with both church and civil authorities." Supriès promised to supply at once any further information that might be needed by the cardinal.[14]

Before describing how "The Missionaries of Saint Francis Xavier" would be organized, Supriès said that the clerics were submitting the project to Fransoni "after mature examination." Now if the project had stemmed from the clerics, as has been maintained in literature,[15] there would hardly be need for them to examine it. As drafters of the project they would have been well aware of its contents. But if the project had been drafted for them by someone else, it then would have been necessary that they examine it before submitting it to Rome for approval. Who, then, was the originator of this project for a Lombardy seminary for foreign missions? No one else comes into question but Supriès. As he told Fransoni in his letter, the four priests and the deacon had come to him "in order that I might provide them with the means" of going to the foreign missions. "The means" that Supriès devised was the proposed missionary congregation of Saint Francis Xavier.

The choice of name for the missionary congregation was easy to understand. In northern Italy at this time there was an organization for those interested in praying for, learning about, and contributing to the foreign missions. It was akin to the Association for the Propagation of the Faith in France and was called the Company of Saint Francis Xavier. Mazzucconi, the seminarian who corresponded with Supriès, had been a member of this organization from his childhood. His father Giacomo had enrolled his entire family. As Supriès told Fransoni when explaining the name of the missionary congregation, members "will have no other aim but to imitate the holy apostle of the Indies, the great

14. PF: SC Missioni vol. 21 (1844–46), f. 974r–975v. The summary at the end of Supriès's letter made by an official of Propaganda Fide erroneously states that 'some priests of France" were inspired by Supriès "to found in Milan a congregation of missionaries called Saint Francis Xavier to go from there to the missions, specifically to Oceania." Ibid., f. 975v. See also chap. 2, n. 10.

15. *Beatificationis Positio*, 60, speaks of "the project of a missionary institute, which was the idea of some young priests." Giovanni B. Tragella in *Le missioni estere di Milano nel quadro degli avvenimenti contemporanei*, 1:19f, describes "the plan of a group of Lodi and Milan priests, in which a former French missionary, then Vicar of the Certosa di Pavia, figures as one who was consulted and as a counsellor." He also speaks of "their missionary ideal which—who knows how?—had already taken shape as a definite plan."

Francis Xavier, and will dedicate their entire lives to preaching the gospel in the midst of idolatrous nations."[16]

In addition to the above reasons, which credit the experienced French Carthusian with originating and developing the project and not the young and inexperienced Italian clerics, still another reason points toward the leading role played by Supriès. When presenting to Fransoni three years earlier his ideas on founding a mission in Northern Oceania or Micronesia, he made himself responsible for getting personnel if the mission should be entrusted to him. He told the cardinal that he would "lay the foundations for a new Congregation of Missionary Priests which will be established in Paris at the Church of Our Lady of Victory." The congregation was to be "modelled after the [Paris] Foreign Mission Seminary" to which he had earlier belonged.[17] For three years Supriès had harbored this idea; now he had found a way to have it realized in Lombardy.

Fransoni answered Supriès's letter of 6 April 1846 on 2 May, praising the project highly and expressing delight over this unexpected source of missionary personnel "so much needed at the present time." Because there was no new mission "that could be entrusted exclusively" to the Lombardy clerics at the moment, the cardinal offered another solution, "at least for now." If the young priests should agree, he would send them to an already existing mission to work under a capable prelate whose staff of veteran missionaries was rapidly dwindling. In this way they could gain missionary experience on the spot, while back in Lombardy their members would be increasing. When those abroad had sufficient experience to take charge, the mission would be turned over exclusively to them and they could choose its superior from their own ranks. "In your wisdom you will agree," the letter said, that their working under an experienced superior and side by side with veteran missionaries "is very fitting and even necessary," since the candidates "are still too green in age and too inexperienced" to be placed completely in charge of a territory at once.

Supriès had mentioned "the great need for missionaries in Oceania," but Fransoni pointed out that "the missions of Oceania are already taken care of, having been divided among two societies, the Marists and the priests called Picpus."[18] He added that "the Sacred Congregation would be pleased," however, if it could assign the Lombard priests to "some important missions in the Indies," where it wanted to have "Italian missionaries exclu-

---

16. PF: SC Missioni vol. 21 (1844–46), f. 974v–975r, Supriès to Fransoni, 6 April 1846; *Beatificationis Positio*, pp. XXXIX–XL, 62.

17. PF: SC Oceania vol. 2 (1842–45, Part I), f. 465r, Supriès to Fransoni, 6 April 1843; see also Wiltgen, *Oceania*, 268–69. When Supriès told Buratti on 20 March 1846 that the four clerics "have formed the plan of uniting themselves in a congregation named after and protected by Saint Francis Xavier," his words must be understood in the context of the entire letter to Buratti and also in the context of his letter to Fransoni. He told Buratti in his letter that the clerics had been begging for months "that I make it possible for them to become missionaries." PF: SC Missioni vol. 21 (1844–46), f. 944r.

18. For details on the Marists, officially known as the Society of Mary (S.M.), and on the Picpus Fathers, officially known as the Congregation of the Sacred Hearts of Jesus and Mary (SS.CC.), see "Marists" in Wiltgen, *Oceania*, 597, and "Picpus Fathers," ibid., 601.

sively" and where "priests are very scarce" in proportion to the immensity of the terrain. "Indies" was used by Propaganda Fide at this time for "India" and other nearby countries.

Fransoni's wish was that Supriès continue nurturing the missionary vocations of these young priests and that he inform them of Rome's suggestion. "If they are disposed to go along with this proposal, as I hope they will be," the cardinal said, "urge them to begin studying English right away since it is an altogether indispensable language in the regions referred to." In this mission they would "also have to learn the local language of the inhabitants."

The problem caused by Cardinal Gaysruck, the archbishop of Milan, was not overlooked by Fransoni. He told Supriès "to assure the priests, who ought to be praised again and again, that the Sacred Congregation in this matter will easily and efficaciously take the steps needed to remove the obstacles and iron out the difficulties that seem to hinder some of them from being sent abroad." The young missionaries were to make arrangements with the two Milan priests, who had volunteered to serve as chargés d'affaires for the new congregation, regarding the type of assistance that they were to provide. Propaganda Fide at the same time was to be kept informed of these arrangements until a house or seminary could be founded in a suitable place. Meanwhile Fransoni would await additional reports from Supriès, because "on the basis of these it will be possible for me to take further steps." He promised to keep Supriès abreast of all decisions made and ended his letter "with affectionate praise for your zeal."

Fransoni sent a second letter to Lombardy on 2 May, the same day on which he wrote to Supriès. But instead of writing a letter of blame to Archbishop Gaysruck of Milan, he wrote a letter of praise to seventy-seven-year-old Bishop Gaetano Benaglia (1768–1868) of Lodi. Knowing of your zeal and desire to help the missions, the cardinal began, "I do not hesitate to approach you in confidence in order to have news and information about some priests of your diocese." Without mentioning that it was Supriès, the cardinal said that "through a religious of distinction they have made known to me their desire to go and propagate the Gospel in places where there are infidels." The cardinal asked for an impartial appraisal of their qualities and said he would await the bishop's reply.[19]

Supriès passed on the information received from Fransoni to the five Lombard clerics and told the cardinal on 18 May 1846 that they were "most grateful" to him for granting their wishes. They recognized "the will of God in the commands of the Sacred Congregation" and were "ready to go to whatever mission is designated for them." Supriès added that all five clerics had already received the necessary ecclesiastical and civil permissions. Whenever Fransoni wished, they could leave for Rome to be "reunited there in the presence of Your Eminence in the course of the coming month of June."[20]

---

19. PF: LDB vol. 333 (1846, Part I), f. 451v–454r, Fransoni to Supriès; ibid., f. 462v–463r, Fransoni to Benaglia.

20. PF: SC Missioni vol. 21 (1844–46), f. 998r.

It greatly pleased Fransoni to learn that the five clerics had accepted his proposal. And when three of them arrived unannounced in his office—Fathers Faré, Cassinelli, and Vistarini—he received them "with pleasure" and found lodging for them in the Pontifical Greek College. But on learning that Beretta and Mola were planning an early trip to Rome as well, he quickly wrote on 11 June to Supriès, urging him "to tell them, if this gets to you on time, that they should not undertake the journey to Rome until they receive positive word to that effect." There was no room for them in Rome "at the moment." Instead they were "to keep practicing English in some way" in Lombardy, as their companions were doing in Rome, until such time "when they can later join their companions in Rome, so that all of them can be sent to the mission together."

Fransoni thanked Supriès again for his tireless zeal "in promoting the greater good of the missions." He likewise urged the monk to continue his efforts and to keep providing counsel, since this was "contributing toward the realization" of the proposed missionary congregation. He added that "all further news on this project" would make him happy.[21]

Before Supriès could reach Father Beretta to tell him to stay in Milan, he had left for Rome. Mola, now a priest, was still in Milan because his request for a passport had to be sent to Vienna. Supriès feared that the paperwork connected with this "may take months, even years," so he asked Fransoni on 30 June what he should do about it. Meanwhile Mola "was waiting patiently and was continuing his study of English."[22]

Prior to their departure from Milan for Rome between 18 May and 11 June 1846, Fathers Faré, Cassinelli, and Vistarini had visited the Seminario Filosofico at Monza to take leave of its superiors. Mazzucconi, who was completing his second year of philosophical studies there, was eager to see the missionaries. After waiting in a doorway for the longest time, he managed to get a glimpse of them. In May of that year he had received from Father Pietro Tacconi (1808–68), his spiritual director at Monza, the go-ahead for his own missionary vocation. During the June–August summer vacation he returned to the Certosa di Pavia to make a ten-day retreat and be with his friend, correspondent, and advisor Father Supriès. Like the missionaries destined for the Indies, he too began studying languages, especially English.[23]

In September 1846 the three Lombard priests from the Lodi diocese left Rome for Ceylon (now Sri Lanka), the mission chosen for them by Fransoni. Vistarini would remain there all his life. Mola would return to Italy in 1855 and go back to Ceylon in 1858, and Cassinelli would spend seven years in Ceylon. This foreign mission involvement by clerics of the Lodi diocese had an impact on clerics in the rest of Lombardy. It proved concretely that Lombards could be successful as foreign missionaries. Fathers Faré and Beretta from the Milan archdiocese decided not to go to Ceylon. They returned to Milan and gave up

---

21. PF: LDB vol. 334 (1846, Part II), f. 628rv.
22. PF: SC Missioni vol. 21 (1844–46), f. 1018r.
23. *Beatificationis Positio*, 35, 60, 63, 430, 433–34, 436, 443.

their missionary vocations. Did they become disillusioned on learning in Rome that the Ceylon mission entrusted to them was torn by schism and division?[24]

Death plays an important role in fashioning the course of human events. Cardinal Gaysruck, the Austrian archbishop of Milan, died at the age of seventy-seven on 19 November 1846. Thus the obstacle standing in the way of founding a foreign mission seminary in Lombardy was removed. It was not until 10 April 1847 that Emperor Ferdinand I of Austria proposed Carlo Bartolomeo Romilli (1795–1859) as Gaysruck's successor. Pope Pius IX (1792–1878) ratified this choice, making Romilli the new archbishop of Milan on 14 June 1847.[25]

One month after Gaysruck died, Supriès learned in the December 1846 issue of the Italian *Annals of the Propagation of the Faith* about the death of the Marist bishop, Jean-Baptiste Epalle. The bishop was in charge of the two vicariates of Melanesia and Micronesia, was attacked in the Solomon Islands on 16 December 1845, and died from his wounds three days later.[26] There were a few surviving missionaries in his Vicariate Apostolic of Melanesia, but there were none and never had been any in his Vicariate Apostolic of Micronesia. Supriès no doubt surmised that now there was greater likelihood of Rome entrusting Micronesia to the missionary priests of Lombardy.

Mission interest among the clerics of Lombardy continued to grow. Salvioni, who during his theological studies had visited the Marists in Lyon at the suggestion of Supriès, was ordained a subdeacon on 25 October 1846 and wanted by all means to become a missionary. His friend, Paolo Reina (1825–61), even before becoming a seminarian, had written to Bishop (now Blessed) Eugène de Mazenod of Marseille, France, the founder of the Oblates of Mary Immaculate (O.M.I.), and asked whether he could join that missionary order. But he was told to wait. Antonio Marietti had visited Supriès during the summer vacation of 1847 and announced that he would be joining the Marist missionaries in Lyon, France, to whom he then applied several times. When he was not accepted, he decided to seek admission to the proposed Lombardy mission seminary. Father Pietro Pontiggia, spiritual director at Milan's Canonica seminary, was also well aware of the project being promoted by Supriès. When Mazzucconi during his first year of theological studies (1846–47) approached Pontiggia for advice on what mission society he should join, Pontiggia said, "Within three years a house for the foreign missions will arise here in our midst."[27]

---

24. Tragella, *Missioni estere*, 1:21–22. The activity and success of the Lodi priests shows that Tragella errs when he says of Supriès: "The attempt that he made with a group of Lodi and Milan priests failed." Ibid., 1:25. The mission work of the Lodi priests in Ceylon, desired and required by Fransoni, was the first concrete step in the realization of the project.

25. Suigo, *Pio IX*, 42, 47.

26. *Annali della propagazione della fede* (December 1846), 703–21. For further details on the death of Epalle, see Wiltgen, *Oceania*, 336–41.

27. *Beatificationis Positio*, 39–40, 63–64, 443, 445; Tragella, *Missioni estere*, 1:23, 25; Suigo, *Pio IX*, 40; PIME: AME 13:893, Marietti to Marinoni, 12 June 1851. Tragella in *Missioni estere*, 1:25, cites this 12 June 1851 letter of Deacon Marietti to Marinoni as his source for saying that Marietti confided his desire to become a Marist

The developments of 1846 and 1847, as well as Supriès's unflagging concern for the establishment of what he called "a mission seminary in Lombardy,"[28] make it clear that certain words of his addressed to Cardinal Prefect Fransoni on 30 June 1846 are not to be taken seriously. Reacting to news received from Lombard priests in Rome about the Ceylon mission being convulsed by schism and other divisions, he told Fransoni that this news had "cooled off very much" the interest of those in Milan who had volunteered to help. "In fact, it has made them lose all their courage." As for getting further personnel, "it is very easy to foresee that young priests will not feel any attraction for such a mission. It grieves me to say that I therefore consider the project as having in fact vanished."[29]

Did Supriès really feel that the project had "in fact vanished"? Such a grandiose idea, germinating for several years in so many young hearts, certainly could not vanish overnight. His words were nothing but a hasty judgment reflecting a moment of discouragement. Or did he intend them rather as a ruse, a way of telling the cardinal that he should not have assigned the young priests to Ceylon, but instead ought to designate Micronesia as a mission field exclusively for the priests of Lombardy?

Since Supriès was both a Frenchman and a religious order member, it was not to be expected that he should become the founder of a foreign mission seminary for Italian secular clergy in Lombardy. Being a monk, however, he was able to back up all his efforts with a vast amount of prayer and divine assistance. He was an influential man, he had contacts in Rome and abroad, and he knew how to work through others and with others. He had succeeded in interesting young priests and seminarians of Lombardy in going overseas as missionaries, and he had managed to convince Fransoni of Lombardy's potential for supplying missionary personnel. But what he still needed was someone in Lombardy with ecclesiastical authority to take action.

In 1847, a year in which central Europe was filled with political unrest, thirty-seven-year-old Bishop Jean-Félix-Onésime Luquet (1810–58) journeyed from Rome to Switzerland on a papal mission.[30] While en route he made an unannounced stopover in

---

to Supriès, and that Supriès stopped him from going to the Marists. But Marietti does not mention Supriès. He says that the Certosa di Pavia contributed to his missionary vocation and that he applied to the Marists for admission several times, but was not accepted. Suigo, in *Beatificationis Positio*, 445 n. 7, also cites the same Antonio Marietti letter (writing p. 892—it is blank—for p. 893) as his source for stating that Antonio Riva [sic] received a reply similar to that given by Pontiggia to Mazzucconi. But Riva is not mentioned in the Marietti letter, nor is anything said about a new Lombard seminary to be founded in a few years.

28. PF: SC Missioni vol. 21 (1844–46), f. 1018rv, Supriès to Fransoni, 30 June 1846.

29. Ibid., f. 1018v. Tragella in *Missioni estere*, 1:22, says that the project "was destined to fail" and that "every practical step for the conceived foundation was halted." Suigo in *Pio IX*, 21, copying much from Tragella here, speaks of "the complete collapse of the proposed seminary."

30. When liberalism and radicalism became dominant in many cantons of Switzerland in 1845, the seven Catholic cantons rallied to defend their religious liberty and formed the Sonderbund. In July 1847 the Federal Diet ordered them to dissolve this alliance, but they refused. A civil war broke out in which the Catholic cantons were defeated. Cardinal Giuseppe Bofondi, Vatican secretary of state, said that the immediate purpose of the "extraordinary mission entrusted by the Holy Father" to Luquet was "to procure religious peace for

Milan between 11 and 24 November to visit the city's newly installed archbishop.[31] Not finding Romilli at his residence and learning that he was making his annual retreat at the nearby Collegio of the Missionary Oblates in Rho, Luquet went there.

As if directed by Supriès to say his lines, this French bishop told Archbishop Romilli that Pope Pius IX was eager to see founded in Lombardy a mission seminary modeled after the Paris Foreign Mission Seminary. The abundance of clergy in the Milan archdiocese and in its suffragan sees had attracted the pope's attention and had prompted his proposal. Missionary candidates were to be drawn from the clergy of Lombardy, and it was hoped that all the bishops of Lombardy would collaborate. It was the pope's wish, in fact, that there should be a Universal Seminary for Foreign Missions. That was Luquet's message.

And what was Romilli's reply? "I cast myself at the feet of His Holiness! All that he need do is make his wishes known to me and I shall surely carry them out."[32]

Who was Luquet? He was a Frenchman born in Langres on 17 June 1810. After obtaining a doctorate in architecture he quit the secular world, became a priest, joined the Paris Foreign Mission Seminary in 1841, and was sent to the Vicariate Apostolic of Pondicherry in India in 1842. Two years later he was sent to Rome, where on 17 February 1845 the cardinals of Propaganda Fide accepted the proposal that he championed for dividing the Pondicherry vicariate into three vicariates. The same cardinals rejected on 10 March 1845 a plan that he had helped prepare for dividing Western Australia into three ecclesiastical territories. But Pope Gregory XVI (1765–1846), a former prefect of Propaganda, overruled the decision of the cardinals and accepted Luquet's plan on 4 May 1845. Two weeks later on 19 May the cardinals decided to ask the pope to make Luquet a bishop. The pope agreed, and Cardinal Prefect Fransoni himself was the ordaining prelate on Sunday, 7 September 1845, in Rome's Church of Santa Maria in Vallicella, better known as Chiesa Nuova. Archbishop Brunelli, secretary of Propaganda Fide, was one of the two co-consecrators.

The Paris Foreign Mission Seminary further made Luquet its procurator at the Holy See by letter of 26 January 1846. He helped Bishop Pompallier draw up his plan of 8 December 1846 for establishing the hierarchy in Western Oceania, and he helped Father Colin, superior general of the Marists, to prepare a revised plan for the Western Oceania hierarchy dated 15 May 1847. Luquet was Colin's trusted advisor and accompanied him on 15 June 1847 during his private audience with Pius IX. Luquet also provided counsel for Bishop Guillaume Douarre, the first Marist bishop of New Caledonia, with whom he conjointly submitted a proposal to Pius IX on 10 August 1847, suggesting that New Caledonia

---

the Catholics of Switzerland and to discover ways and means of remedying the damage done to religious and church interests by the unfortunate war." Suigo, *Pio IX*, 46f; René Roussel, *Un précurseur: Monseigneur Luquet (1810–1858) des missions étrangères de Paris*, 43f.

31. The exact date of Luquet's visit is not known. The dates given here have been established by Suigo, *Pio IX*, 48.

32. Tragella, *Missioni estere*, 1:26f; Suigo, *Pio IX*, 48–51; *Beatificationis Positio*, 60; Gerardo Brambilla, *Il pontificio istituto delle missioni estere e le sue missioni: Memorie*, 1:7, 14.

be made a papal colony. Three months later this man of great vision and extraordinary influence was knocking at Archbishop Romilli's door.[33]

The visit of Luquet to Romilli in November 1847 prompted a publication to announce four years later that Pope Pius IX "must be credited with getting the first idea for this seminary."[34] The information, however, cannot be correct because Supriès and Fransoni were exchanging correspondence on the first steps to be taken in launching a foreign mission seminary for Lombardy as early as April and May 1846. Pius IX was not yet pope at that time.

A few days before Pius IX was elected on 16 June 1846, the first three priests from Lombardy, who had been in contact with Supriès, arrived in Rome where they were given lodging by Cardinal Prefect Fransoni. In one of his many audiences with the new pope, the cardinal no doubt mentioned these priests, adding that many more missionaries would come from Lombardy, if it had its own foreign mission seminary. Thus Fransoni easily could have won the pope's support for this project. Being in close contact with Luquet, Fransoni could have asked him to stop off in Milan to inform Romilli about the pope's wish regarding the foundation of a foreign mission seminary in Lombardy.

Nor is it improbable that Luquet, prior to knocking at Romilli's door, knocked at the door of Supriès. It would seem that this is what happened, because the project suggested by Luquet to Romilli was identical to the one that Supriès suggested to Fransoni. The Certosa di Pavia, where Supriès lived, was about fifteen miles southwest of Milan, and since Pavia was the capital city of Pavia province, Luquet's carriage must have passed through that city on its way to Milan.

Luquet and Supriès had a number of things in common to bring them together. They were both French. Both had worked in India in Pondicherry. Supriès had earlier been a member of the Paris Foreign Mission Seminary, and Luquet was now its highest official outside Paris, having been named its procurator general at the Holy See. Luquet and Supriès were both well acquainted with Cardinal Fransoni, and both had been in contact with Colin, superior general of the Marists. Except for Propaganda Fide officials, Luquet knew more about Oceania than anyone else in Rome. He therefore may have known about Supriès's role in the creation of the Vicariate Apostolic of Micronesia and about his efforts to have Micronesia entrusted to a foreign mission seminary to be founded in Lombardy.

---

33. Wiltgen, *Oceania*, 370f, 374, 408f, 428, 432f, 436; Roussel, *Un précurseur*, 31f.

34. Giuseppe Marinoni, first superior of the Lombard foreign mission seminary, made the statement in *L'Amico Cattolico* (November 1851). See Suigo, *Pio IX*, 49. The following authors write in a similar vein: Suigo, *Pio IX*, 44–51; Tragella, *Missioni estere*, 1:26f; Alfonso Bassan, *Da avvocato a patriarca: Cenni biografici di Mons. Angelo Ramazzotti (1800–1861)*, 52; Brambilla, *Pontificio istituto*, 1:14; *Beatificationis Positio*, 60. As is evident from their works, these authors were unaware of Luquet's important roles in the organization of the church in Oceania and of Supriès's role in founding the Vicariate Apostolic of Micronesia. They were also unaware of, or underestimated the significance of, the early correspondence between Supriès, Fransoni, and Buratti on the founding of a foreign mission seminary in Lombardy.

Like other travelers, Luquet may also have wanted to see Pavia's gem of Italian architecture, the Certosa di Pavia, especially since he happened to have a doctorate in architecture.[35]

Developments in Europe in 1847 seemed to indicate that Lombardy's foreign mission seminary would soon become a reality. In the South Pacific there were developments too. Successor to the late Bishop Epalle was thirty-one-year-old Bishop Jean-Georges Collomb (1816–48), a French Marist. Writing from Kororareka, New Zealand, in May 1847, the new vicar apostolic of Melanesia and Micronesia spelled out for Rome his strategy in developing his territory. All of his surviving missionaries were located on San Cristóbal Island at the southern end of the Solomon Islands. He planned to transfer some of them to Buka, an island at the northern end of the Solomon Islands, and others to Woodlark Island (now Murua) between the Solomon Islands and New Guinea. Within a year he hoped to visit additional sites for mission stations in New Ireland and New Britain, and also on the northern coast of New Guinea. By examining these locations in advance, he said, he could better provide for newly arriving personnel.

Collomb's letter describing these plans for Cardinal Prefect Fransoni stated explicitly that he had more than enough to do in Melanesia. "We earnestly desire that the Holy See should separate the Micronesia Vicariate from the Melanesia Vicariate as soon as possible." With equal earnestness he asked that the extensive Melanesia vicariate be divided "into several other vicariates."[36]

Because Bishop Collomb did not want to keep Micronesia, and because Archbishop Romilli was ready to do what he could toward founding a foreign mission seminary, it began to appear that missionaries from Lombardy might go to Micronesia after all, just as Supriès had wished.

---

35. Luquet's biographer, René Roussel, has found "absolutely nothing" in the personal papers and letters of Luquet regarding his proposing a seminary for Lombardy to Romilli. See his letter to Tragella of 16 August 1960 on this matter in PIME: AME 35-01 Giacomo Scurati, *Memorie dell'Istituto*, inside front cover. This strange silence by Luquet leaves open the possibility, or even the probability, that in this instance he was acting on his own authority or in accordance with the wishes of Supriès.

36. PF: SOCG vol. 970 (1848), f. 295rv, Collomb to Fransoni, 31 May 1847.

2

Pope Pius IX Approves Lombardy's Seminary for Foreign Missions

21 February 1850

ITALY BEGAN ITS WAR OF INDEPENDENCE AGAINST AUSTRIA ON 18 MARCH 1848 WITH A battle called the Five Days of Milan. In the previous month there had been a revolution in France, which had sparked revolutions against Austrian rule in Bohemia, Croatia, Hungary, and even in Austria itself. The arrival of this news in Milan between 16 and 17 March prompted its citizens to take courage the next day and start a revolution of their own.

Demanding arms and new reforms, crowds marched toward government buildings on Saturday, 18 March, waving the tricolor of Italy and shouting, "Long live Italy! Long live Pius IX!" A shot was fired, barricades were set up, and that first day thirty died. By evening of the third day the insurgents had the upper hand. Twice they refused to grant an armistice to eighty-one-year-old Field Marshall Graf Joseph Radetzky (1766–1858), commander of the Austrian troops. By evening of the fifth day, 22 March, the citizens had captured the last Austrian stronghold, forcing Radetzky and his troops to flee around 9 p.m. At dawn on 23 March the city gates were thrown open, and Milan joyously celebrated its liberation from Austrian rule.[1] The fervor of the revolution caught up in its path all young men of Milan, including seminarians, causing some of them to join the battalion of students in the Piedmont army of King Charles Albert (1798–1849). In fact, the battalion's fourth company was made up entirely of seminarians from various parts of Lombardy. One of the soldier-seminarians was Carlo Salerio (1827–70). While in action at Mantova on 14 July 1848, he was serving as standard-bearer when the king passed by to inspect his troops. Stopping before Salerio, the king gave him a pat on the shoulder and said, "You [seminarians] are the angels of my army." In the same battalion was Subdeacon Reina, friend of Salerio, who earlier had written to Bishop de Mazenod in France about going to the foreign missions. During the Five Days of Milan, Reina had been involved in putting

---

1. Antonio Monti, "Le cinque giornate di Milano," in *Enciclopedia italiana di scienze, lettere ed arti*, 23:289–91.

up barricades in the city. A month later, when a committee of theologian seminarians volunteered their services to Italian authorities, his name appeared second on the list. These volunteers became the "company of seminarians" in the "battalion of students."[2]

But liberty for Milan was short-lived, because on 6 August 1848 Radetzky and his troops reconquered the city. On 23 March 1849, the first anniversary of Milan's liberation, the Piedmont forces of King Charles Albert were defeated at Novara. The king had decided to fight against Austria single-handed, even though other European powers had advised against the war. On 6 August 1849, the first anniversary of Radetzky's triumphant return to Milan, he forced the Piedmont plenipotentiaries to sign a treaty of peace with Austria. By this time Charles Albert had gone into voluntary exile to Portugal; there he died three weeks after the treaty was signed.[3]

Radetzky had requisitioned the seminary buildings in both Milan and Monza on 6 August 1848 for lodging his troops. When the refectory of the seminary in Milan was left unoccupied, church authorities used it for giving a semblance of classes in the daytime to seminarians living in the city. Those living beyond the city limits received private tutoring and spiritual direction from their parish priests. When the seminary buildings were returned by Radetzky in July 1849, Archbishop Romilli of Milan informed the seminarians that regular classes would resume on 20 November.[4]

Meanwhile in the latter half of 1848 the seminarian patriots had returned home. Among them was Reina, who then completed his theological studies and was ordained a priest on 2 June 1849. For several years his spiritual director had been Father Angelo Taglioretti (1811–99), with whom he had often discussed his desire to go overseas as a missionary. Like other seminarians Reina too was acquainted with the movement to found a foreign mission seminary for Lombardy. He gave Taglioretti no rest, maintaining that the proposed seminary could now be founded because peace was gradually being restored.[5]

Taglioretti belonged to an association of priests known as the Congregation of the Missionary Oblates of Rho. They were secular priests of the Milan archdiocese who devoted themselves to preaching retreats for the clergy and religious communities; they also conducted parish missions. A collegio at Rho near Milan was their headquarters, and the superior of the community was Taglioretti's closest friend, Father Angelo Francesco Ramazzotti (1800–1861), a native of Milan. Archbishop Romilli of Milan was making his annual retreat at this collegio in November 1847 when he was visited by Bishop Luquet from Rome. Being greeted upon arrival by Father Superior Ramazzotti, Luquet told him that he had come to communicate to the archbishop the wish of Pope Pius IX that a foreign

---

2. Suigo, *Pio IX*, 43, 56f; Tragella, *Missioni estere*, 1:33–40 *passim*.

3. "Radetzky, Joseph, Graf," in *New Encyclopaedia Britannica, Micropaedia*, 8:372f; Niccolò Rodolico, "Carlo Albertó," in *Enciclopedia italiana*, 9:59–62.

4. *Beatificationis Positio*, p. XXXIX, 43f; Suigo, *Pio IX*, 56.

5. Suigo, *Pio IX*, 57, 79; Tragella, *Missioni estere*, 1:39.

mission seminary be opened in Lombardy. The archbishop invited Ramazzotti to be present during his talk with Luquet.[6]

Ramazzotti had studied law at the University of Pavia, receiving his doctorate degree with highest honors on 10 August 1823, one week after his twenty-third birthday. He was practicing law for two years when his father died in October 1826, making him heir to the immense family property at Saronno, some twelve miles northwest of Milan. One month later, Ramazzotti gave up his practice of law and entered the seminary. He was ordained a priest on 30 June 1829 and joined the Missionary Oblates of Rho the following year. When a cholera epidemic in the summer of 1836 left numerous orphans in its wake, he opened an orphanage and an oratory on his property in order to provide lodging and education for them.[7]

Taglioretti considered Ramazzotti's property at Saronno ideal for a foreign mission seminary and so talked to him about Reina, broaching the subject like this: "You had in mind converting your house into a residence for good priests, as you explained to me on several occasions. Would you not be able to take Reina into your house and also others with similar ideas and thus launch a mission institute?" The Saronno property contained San Francesco Monastery as well as a church by the same name and an extensive orchard. This property had belonged to the Order of Friars Minor (O.F.M.), or Franciscans, until it was confiscated by the Cisalpine Republic on 6 October 1797. When sold at public auction, it was purchased by the Ramazzotti family.[8]

Confronted repeatedly by Taglioretti's proposal, Ramazzotti was gradually won over by it. After all, he had a great devotion to Saint Francis Xavier, a missionary par excellence. He often wrote his sermons and retreat conferences before an image of the saint. He had even imagined himself as an Oceania missionary at times. And while giving spiritual direction and retreats to clerics throughout Lombardy, he had become aware of their great and growing interest in foreign missionary work. There was also the wish of Pope Pius IX for a Lombardy mission seminary, about which he had learned from Bishop Luquet. All of this in addition to the proposal coming from Father Taglioretti, his closest friend, prompted Father Ramazzotti to consider seriously offering his house at Saronno for the proposed mission institute. But he wanted to pray about it first and to take counsel with his superiors and with others.[9]

---

6. Suigo, *Pio IX*, 31, 47–50; PIME: AME 35-01 Scurati, *Memorie dell'Istituto*, 12. Ramazzotti often signed his Christian name "Angiolo" instead of "Angelo."

7. Suigo, *Pio IX*, 32–35, 100.

8. Ibid., 100; Tragella, *Missioni estere*, 1:40.

9. Suigo, *Pio IX*, 39, 47.

Bishop Angelo Ramazzotti is the founder of the
Foreign Mission Seminary of Milan (P.I.M.E.).
Source: *Beatificationis Positio*, TAV. IV.

Ramazzotti's third and last term of office as superior at Rho ended on 7 October 1849. His successor, Father Gaetano Ravizza, declared himself in favor of the Saronno project. Ramazzotti then decided to discuss the matter with Supriès, who had stirred up so much mission interest in Lombardy and had served in foreign missions himself. But never having visited the Carthusian monastery in Pavia, he asked Father Giuseppe Prada (1821–84), secretary to Archbishop Romilli and a close friend of Supriès, to accompany him. Prada had long been pressing for the foundation of this new mission seminary as proposed by Supriès.

Prada may well have been the unnamed priest mentioned earlier by Supriès as volunteering to serve as chargé d'affaires in Milan for Lombardy missionaries. Supriès had said that this "good priest" had wanted "to go to the missions himself," was "full of zeal and possessed great influence." but was "hindered because of various assignments." These descriptions fit Prada perfectly.

When Ramazzotti and Prada reached the monastery late on Sunday afternoon, 11 November 1849, it was already dark. Supriès welcomed them and took them to his cell.[10]

On hearing that Ramazzotti was prepared to turn over his house at Saronno as a center for training foreign missionaries, Supriès was overjoyed. The ensuing conversation was not recorded verbatim. In broad outline it went like this: "But I am merely providing the building and there is no one to take charge." Ramazzotti said. "Take charge yourself," Supriès urged. "But I cannot," came the answer, "because I belong to a religious house." "Drop the lesser good in favor of the greater," Supriès insisted, meaning that Ramazzotti should give up membership in the Missionary Oblates of Rho to become founder and director of the new foreign mission seminary. "Such a decision depends on my superior," Ramazzotti replied. "When your superior hears about it," Supriès assured him, "he will at once give his approval." Ramazzotti also had questions about foreign mission work and about the kind of training to be given to candidates. The monk and his visitors talked for several hours and later prayed together far into the night. Ramazzotti did not manage to sleep that night.

Before leaving for Milan the next morning, Ramazzotti and Prada consulted with the prior of the monastery, Father Charles-Marie Saison (1806–77). He had spent two years (1842–43) in Vienna negotiating with the emperor to have the Pavia monastery returned to the Carthusians. Saison advised Ramazzotti to incorporate the new seminary in the Congregation of Oblates of Saints Ambrose and Charles, at least initially, in order to facilitate its foundation. This congregation included the Missionary Oblates of Rho, the organization to which Ramazzotti belonged.[11]

---

10. Ibid., 58f; Tragella, *Missioni estere*, 1:40f; PIME: AME 28:141f, Supriès to Prada, 14 March 1850. The chargé d'affaires is described in PF: SC Missioni vol. 21 (1844–46) f. 944v, Supriès to Buratti, 20 March 1846; PF: ibid., f. 974v, Supriès to Fransoni, 6 April 1846.

11. Suigo, *Pio IX*, 58f, 61; Tragella, *Missioni estere*, 1:40f. It is clear that Prior Saison is the one who suggested incorporation. See Suigo, *Pio IX*, 59, 61. But when referring to these pages in his own text, Suigo mistakenly

Ramazzotti returned to Rho on 12 November and a day or two later received a letter in which Prada, secretary to Archbishop Romilli of Milan, described what he had done. He had presented the Saronno plan to the archbishop, who expressed his warm approval at once. Prada had also presented the plan to Canon Raffaele Bertinelli, who was enthusiastic about it as well. Father Bertinelli, a professor at the University of Rome and also its vice rector, was currently in Milan. He represented Lombardy in its dealings with the Roman Curia and now promised to obtain the necessary permissions from the Holy See for founding the new seminary.[12]

When sending word on 14 November to Superior General Angelo Molteni in Milan about his visit to the Carthusian monastery, Ramazzotti said that Supriès "told me that I ought to take charge of the project." A day or so later he visited his superior general to talk about it. Finding him favorably disposed, Ramazzotti asked whether he should mention the project to Archbishop Romilli. "Yes, go and tell him about it." Molteni said. On the way Ramazzotti met Prada, who urged him to see Canon Bertinelli as well. The archbishop not only approved, but also arranged for Ramazzotti to meet Bertinelli that very same evening. Bertinelli was deeply interested in the project. He promised Ramazzotti to take all necessary steps in Rome to obtain the papal brief needed for the seminary to open officially, but for this he had to have the facts in writing. He therefore asked Ramazzotti to draw up a formal request in his own name addressed to the pope. On receiving it, Bertinelli could then draw up a second more formal request for the pope, testifying that Archbishop Romilli of Milan had also supported the project.[13]

After receiving Ramazzotti's memorandum for Pope Pius IX, Bertinelli left for Rome. By this time barely two weeks had passed since Ramazzotti and Prada had visited Supriès. Everyone in Lombardy had played his part well, and now it was up to Bertinelli to take the next step in Rome. In view of the papal message transmitted by Luquet to Romilli at Rho in November 1847, the pope's approval could be foreseen. And in view of Bertinelli's influential position and his recognized finesse in dealing with the Roman Curia, his success in reaching the pope with the project was also guaranteed.

If Rome responded favorably, Ramazzotti was prepared to found and direct Lombardy's foreign mission seminary. "I can say that this idea has received universal approval," he had

---

says that it was Supriès who suggested incorporation. See ibid., 106 nn. 157, 113.

12. The author did not see Prada's letter, but learned of its contents from Ramazzotti's 14 November 1849 letter to Father Angelo Molteni. See Suigo, *Pio IX*, 60–61.

13. Ibid., 60–65; Tragella, *Missioni estere*, 1:40–42. Suigo and Tragella are aware of only the second more formal request whose authorship they mistakenly ascribe to Ramazzotti. However, there were "two memorandums" relative to this affair, according to both Cardinal Fransoni and Secretary Barnabò. Evidently the shorter and less formal one was written by Ramazzotti and polished for curial style by Bertinelli. The longer and more formal one, containing nearly all of the shorter one, was written by Bertinelli. See PF: Udienze vol. 111 (1850, Part I) f. 93Br–93Ev; PF: CV vol. 43, f. 149rv, Fransoni to Barnabò, 26 February 1850; PF: LDB vol. 339 (1850) f. 230rv, Barnabò to Fransoni, 7 March 1850. NB: Folio 93 in Udienze vol. 111 (1850, Part I) is followed by seven unnumbered folios, which for the sake of reference the author has called 93A to 93G in nn. 13, 26, 27, 28, and 30.

written to Superior General Molteni on 14 November. "There will be great difficulties, I know. But if the Lord makes manifest that it is his will to have this project realized, the difficulties will be overcome."[14]

Father Ravizza, Ramazzotti's immediate superior, heard some extraordinary news while in Milan on 29 November. He returned to Rho, rushed to Ramazzotti's room, and told him to meditate for half an hour on resignation to the will of God. He then handed Ramazzotti an official letter which said that Emperor Francis Joseph I (1830–1916) of Austria had chosen him to be the new bishop of Pavia. "Oh, my God!" Ramazzotti exclaimed. And for six or seven minutes he stood there silent and motionless.

The news placed him in a quandary. If he accepted the office of bishop, as Ravizza said he should, he could not be the director of the foreign mission seminary. On the other hand his being bishop of Pavia, which was one of the dioceses of Lombardy, would certainly prove beneficial to the venture. The emperor's nomination still needed papal approval. Nineteen-year-old Francis Joseph I had ascended the throne in 1848 in the midst of the revolutions. He appointed Ramazzotti on 11 November 1849, which was the day on which Ramazzotti and Prada had gone to Pavia to visit Supriès.[15]

Although Ramazzotti was shocked by the news of his episcopal appointment, he decided to accept it. The next day he chose Father Giuseppe Marinoni (1810–91), born in Milan, to become seminary director in his stead.[16] Marinoni was currently pastor at San Michele a Ripa Church in Rome. Attached to his church was the Apostolic Hospice of San Michele a Ripagrande, which contained a correction home, a school for arts and crafts, and homes for orphans, wayward women, and the aged.

Since seminary days Marinoni and Taglioretti had been very close friends. Ramazzotti therefore asked Taglioretti to convince Marinoni to accept the office. Taglioretti wrote on 30 November 1849, giving the news about the episcopal appointment and explaining that Ramazzotti "just in these days" had launched the founding of a foreign mission seminary. A good-sized building had been contributed by the new bishop for the project, two candidates had formally requested admission, and there were enough funds at hand to start.

But more important, he said, was the approbation already granted by the archbishop of Milan and his chancery office, by the bishop of Mantova, the superior general of the Congregation of Oblates of Saints Ambrose and Charles, the local superior of the Oblates at Rho, and by professor Bertinelli of the University of Rome. As for the Carthusian Fathers, "who seem to have been sent to the Certosa di Pavia to keep alive among our young clerics this spark of enthusiasm, they feel that the spark has now finally burst into a towering flame that will carry blessings and charity beyond the seas and beyond this hemisphere."

14. Suigo, *Pio IX*, 60–61.

15. Ibid., 49, 59, 67.

16. Marinoni was ordained a priest in 1834 and had taught in two minor seminaries in Lombardy. In 1837 he joined the Society of Jesus (S.J.) in Rome, but left after several months. He applied for admittance to the Order of Carthusians (O. Cart.), wanting to become a contemplative, but was not accepted because of poor health. He then joined the Society of the Catholic Apostolate (S.A.C.), or Pallottines, but left this group by 1841 because of ill health and other reasons.

Father Guiseppe Marinoni became the first Superior General of P.I.M.E.
Source: *Beatificationis Positio*, TAV. IV.

Taglioretti urged Marinoni to pray that the project might be crowned with success, adding that he could help "both from a distance and perhaps also, if God wills, right on the spot." He enclosed a report so that his friend could see "how far it has developed up till now." But what they needed in Milan was an envoy "from the Holy See" with a mandate from the pope "to lay the first stone for this edifice and to provide it with a program and a rule." Taglioretti asked Marinoni point blank: "Could you not be that envoy from Rome?"

And before his friend could say no, Taglioretti added: "Listen to me. If the pope were to tell you to go to Milan for one or two months as his envoy in this affair; and if you were to come to us after gathering all possible news, information, rule books, experience, advice from old missionaries, and sacred words of Pius IX; and if you were to make suggestions here and help get things organized; and if you together with others and also with me were then to found—supposing of course that obedience were to require it—the House of Saints Ambrose and Charles for the Foreign Missions; now, if all this were to come about, could you not do it all under the condition that afterwards you were to return to your orphans, etc.?

"And if afterwards the Archbishop of Milan, the pope, and God were to say: Look, at last we have found a position in the archdiocese that is carved out for Marinoni, namely, being superior of the House for Foreign Missions! Would you not then consider this as that clear and solemn voice being manifested to you, without which you feel forbidden to change your location? Think, pray, and write back immediately."

Taglioretti ended by saying that Ramazzotti "soon may have to leave for Rome for his consecration." In that case Marinoni and Ramazzotti could discuss the whole matter in Rome.[17]

On the following day, 1 December 1849, Ramazzotti met with Superior General Molteni. They discussed the proposal of Saison, the Carthusian prior, that the seminary should become part of the Congregation of the Oblates of Saints Ambrose and Charles. The meeting resulted in the archbishop of Milan and his suffragan bishops ordering Molteni to found a new community in the house offered by Ramazzotti at Saronno. The new community's task would be "to establish a Seminary for the Foreign Missions" and "to direct and perpetually assist" the missionaries trained there. Taglioretti had anticipated this decision on the previous day when he wrote to Marinoni and called the new seminary "the House of Saints Ambrose and Charles for the Foreign Missions."[18]

Ramazzotti moved from Rho to Saronno in order to supervise better the immediate preparations for founding the mission seminary. On 13 December he wrote Taglioretti that he was to give a conducted tour of the grounds and buildings that day or the following day

---

17. Suigo, *Pio IX*, 67, 69f; Brambilla, *Pontificio istituto*, 1:19; Tragella, *Missioni estere*, 1:48–50. Brambilla says that Taglioretti was "certainly commissioned by Ramazzotti" to write the letter to Marinoni. Suigo, the most recent of the three authors cited, says that Ramazzotti "turned" to Marinoni when looking for a director, but it was Taglioretti's task "to convince him to accept the office."

18. Brambilla, *Pontificio istituto*, 1:22f; Suigo, *Pio IX*, 71, 113–14.

to Prada and to the two Carthusians, Saison and Supriès. When he and these three men had met at the Certosa di Pavia on 11 and 12 November, they had together envisioned a mission seminary. Now, only one month later, they were already meeting within its walls! A qualified director had also been found, although he still had to be won over. And two priest candidates, Reina born in Saronno and Alessandro Ripamonti (1815–72), assigned to Saronno, had formally requested admission. All that was lacking was the pope's approval, and this was expected from Bertinelli within a couple of weeks.[19]

But January 1850 brought no news from Rome. Nor did February, the month in which Ramazzotti gave a retreat attended by Mazzucconi and Salerio a week prior to their ordination as subdeacons. Mazzucconi, the friend of Supriès, profited from this occasion by discussing with Ramazzotti his eventual acceptance into the mission seminary.[20]

On 14 March 1850 Supriès must have recalled that it was three months since his tour of the Saronno property and four months since Bertinelli had promised to take prompt action in Rome. But there was still no word from Rome. Had something gone wrong? Supriès picked up his pen and wrote that day to Prada. "How anxiously I am waiting to get a letter from you telling me that this great enterprise, desired so much by you for six years . . . , has finally been launched." Rome "must want it earnestly too," he said, but the news "never comes" and "I keep waiting in vain." He asked Prada kindly to write him something about it, "because I have this affair very much at heart."[21] What was causing the delay in Rome?

The length and breadth of Italy and most of Europe had been ablaze with revolution in 1848. The states of the church called papal states, which stretched across central Italy from sea to sea, were also affected. In an effort to reconcile liberal and conservative tendencies among his own subjects and throughout Italy, Pope Pius IX had appointed a layman, Pellegrino Rossi (1787–1848), as his prime minister on 16 September 1848. But when Rossi arrived at the chamber to present his government's program on 15 November, he was stabbed to death by a member of the revolutionary party. Anarchy followed, and the Quirinal Palace, residence of the pope, was besieged and cannonaded the following day. Cannon shot reached the courtyard and meeting rooms, and the secretary of the pope was killed.

Assisted by the French and Bavarian ambassadors, Pius IX on 24–25 November 1848 fled in disguise to Gaeta, a port city south of the papal sin the kingdom of Naples. King Ferdinand II (1809–59) gave his palace in Gaeta to the pope as a residence and provided for his needs. Here the pope lived and conducted church affairs until 4 September 1849,

---

19. Suigo, *Pio IX*, 69; Tragella, *Missioni estere*, 1:43–44; PIME: AME 4:9.

20. Suigo, *Pio IX*, 78. See *Beatificationis Positio*, XXXIX, 48, 50–51, 452. The ordination dates for major orders received by Mazzucconi as given in the chart on p. 48 of this work must be correct, because ordinations were regularly held on Saturday and 23 February (subdiaconate), 16 March (diaconate), and 25 May (priesthood) in 1850 all fell on Saturday. The dates 23 February and 16 March on p. 452 n. 28, and 23 February and 25 May on p. 50, are therefore correct. But 22 February (Friday) on p. XXXIX and 15 March (Friday) on p. 51 are incorrect.

21. PIME: AME 28:141–42.

when he moved to Portici at the foot of Vesuvius on the Bay of Naples. After seventeen months in exile Pius IX returned to Rome on 12 April 1850, thanks to European diplomacy and a French expeditionary force that occupied Rome as early as 2 July 1849.[22]

It was in the latter half of November 1849 when Bertinelli reached Rome with Ramazzotti's memorandum, so he had to work with ecclesiastical officials located in various places. The pope was in Portici. Fransoni, the cardinal prefect of Propaganda Fide, resided in Naples throughout the pope's exile. And Father Alessandro Barnabò (1801–74), the secretary of Propaganda, was in Rome.

Three choices were open to Bertinelli. One was to give the two memorandums to Secretary Barnabò, who in Fransoni's absence was directing Propaganda "alone and independently." Or Bertinelli could go to Naples and present the memorandums to Fransoni. Or he could go to Portici, six miles south of Naples, and present them personally to the pope.[23]

Bertinelli combined all three methods. First he discussed the project with Barnabò in Rome.[24] Next he went to Naples and discussed the project with Fransoni.[25] And finally, together with Fransoni he was received in audience by Pope Pius IX at Portici on 21 February 1850. After Fransoni presented Ramazzotti's memorandum, Bertinelli presented the memorandum that he had prepared in the name of the archbishop of Milan.[26]

---

22. Pietro Pirri, "Pio IX, Papa," in *Enciclopedia Cattolica*, vol. 9, col. 1514; Ivor F. Burton and Douglas Woodruff, "Pius IX, Pope," in *New Encyclopaedia Britannica, Macropaedia*, 14:483; Suigo, *Pio IX*, 76; Robert Forest Harney, "Rossi, Pellegrino," in *New Catholic Encyclopedia*, 12:681.

23. Josef Metzler, "Präfekten und Sekretäre der Kongregation im Zeitalter der neueren Missionsära (1818–1918)," in *Sacrae Congregationis de Propaganda Fide memoria rerum 1622–1972*, vol. 3, part I, p. 42.

24. Since Barnabò was conducting Propaganda's business "alone and independently" in Rome, as Metzler says in ibid., it is inconceivable that Bertinelli, who lived in Rome and was expert in Roman Curia procedure, would not first discuss the matter with Barnabò.

25. It is clear that Bertinelli went to Naples and was in contact with Fransoni, because on 26 February 1850 Fransoni writes to Barnabò from Naples that he is entrusting to Bertinelli many official papers meant for Barnabò that deal with matters recently brought to his and to the pope's attention, including the Ramazzotti and Bertinelli memorandums. See PF: CV vol. 43, f. 149rv, Fransoni to Barnabò.

26. Protocol gives precedence to a cardinal over a priest, and so Fransoni presented his memorandum first. Fransoni's signed statement on the back of Ramazzotti's memorandum says that the pope during an audience on 21 February 1850 granted the petition that was presented "for" the priest Angelo Ramazzotti of Milan. Its being signed by Fransoni is proof that he is the one who presented it. PF: Udienze vol. 111 (1850, Part I), f. 93Cv. Writing on 26 February 1850 to Archbishop Romilli of Milan, Fransoni said, "I reported on the project to the Pontiff in the audience . . . of 21 February." See the full letter in Suigo, *Pio IX*, 81. A note on the back of Bertinelli's memorandum states that it was presented "by" the priest "Raffaele Canon Bertinelli to His Holiness, Pope Pius IX, in the name of the Archbishop of Milan, for erecting a Mission House in Saronno." PF: Udienze vol. 111 (1850, Part I), f. 93Ev. In his memorandum Bertinelli says, "His Excellency [the Archbishop of Milan] charged the writer to express humbly and orally to Your Holiness this request, and to have the petition of Father Ramazzotti presented to you through His Eminence Fransoni." Ibid., f. 93Dv–93Er. It is not at all surprising that Bertinelli should have been admitted to this papal audience with Fransoni. The Lombardy foreign mission seminary was the concern of all the bishops of Lombardy, and Bertinelli was their procurator or official representative at the Roman Curia. Tragella, unaware of the archive material cited here, says "we do not know"

As is usual, the memorandums were written in the third person. Ramazzotti's memorandum said that "for a long time" he had "nourished the desire of establishing in the Archdiocese of Milan a mission house in order to bring together there those priests who give signs of having a vocation for missionary work among the infidels." For that purpose he had offered "his own house in Saronno to his own superior, the Most Reverend Archbishop of Milan, expecting from Providence additional means for launching the enterprise." Some funds had already been guaranteed because Cavalier Giovanni Vimercati promised to apply to the institute a legacy of Count Mellerio.

Ramazzotti's house in Saronno had an orphanage attached that contained youths who were "far removed from the dangers and vain desires of the world" and who were being "trained in the spiritual life." Some of them might have lay missionary vocations and so could become "collaborators, catechists, farmers, artisans or servants, depending upon their abilities and the needs of the mission." Ramazzotti assured the pope that he accepted all the conditions laid down in the memorandum of the archbishop of Milan, like the kind of training to be given to priests by the new institute and also its dependence upon Propaganda Fide. He ended his memorandum by asking the pope for a word of encouragement and for his apostolic blessing.[27]

Bertinelli then presented his own memorandum, which had two parts. First it credited Father Ramazzotti for suggesting to Archbishop Romilli "the erection of a house for the foreign missions." And although few had as yet requested admission, "It could be hoped that many would do so, once this house has become a reality." The studies were to be adapted "both to the aim of missions in general and to that mission in particular which might be assigned" to the house. Propaganda would naturally be asked to indicate "not only the norms for determining the course of studies to be followed." but also the rules and methods to be used "in forming that ecclesiastical spirit which one looks for in good missionaries."

The second part of the memorandum pointed out how greatly the archbishop of Milan esteemed Ramazzotti, how favorably he regarded the project, and how urgently he wanted authorization from Pius IX "to erect the above-mentioned house."[28]

Cardinal Prefect Fransoni wrote on 26 February 1850 to Archbishop Romilli about the audience, referring to the proposed foundation as "a Foreign Mission College dependent upon and in the service of" Propaganda. Pius IX had manifested great pleasure on learning of Ramazzotti's project, had praised his zeal, and had also praised the archbishop

---

whether Bertinelli "personally" brought the matter to the pope, or whether it was brought "by others." See Tragella, *Missioni estere*, 1:41. Suigo, also unaware of the archive material cited here, states incorrectly in *Pio IX*, 79f, that Bertinelli presented his request to the pope in an audience sometime after mid-February and that Fransoni presented the request in a separate audience on 21 February.

27. PF: Udienze vol. 111 (1850, Part I), f. 93Br–93Cv.
28. Ibid., f. 93Dr–93Ev.

"for having taken such lively interest" in seeing the project realized. Fransoni said that the pope had also given the project "the seal of his apostolic approval."[29]

A copy of the rescript, that is, the formal statement of the pope's decision, was eventually sent to Romilli. The original was signed by Fransoni, was dated 21 February 1850, and read as follows: "His Holiness kindly grants the petition of the Reverend Father Ramazzotti, nominated bishop for the See of Pavia, for the erection of the College referred to in his written request, according to the conditions explained in it, and enjoins the Reverend Secretary to conduct negotiations with the Archbishop of Milan until everything has been finalized."

When Supriès wrote to Prada, wondering why Rome had not yet taken action, it was 14 March 1850. Three weeks earlier, on 21 February at Portici, Pope Pius IX, Cardinal Fransoni, and Professor Bertinelli had already taken action. And five days after Supriès penned the words that the news "never comes," Barnabò sent Archbishop Romilli of Milan the rescript by Fransoni containing the pope's seal of approval for Lombardy's mission seminary.[30]

---

29. Suigo, *Pio IX*, 81. The complete letter is reproduced here.

30. PF: Udienze vol. 111 (1850, Part I), f. 93Cv. Fransoni sent the rescript to Barnabò, who in turn sent a copy of it to Romilli. See PF: LDB vol. 339 (1850), f. 239v–240r, Barnabò to Romilli, 19 March 1850.

3

Melanesia and Micronesia Vicariates Are Reduced to the Status of Missions

11 August 1850

POPE PIUS IX CREATED THE VICARIATE APOSTOLIC OF NEW CALEDONIA ON 27 JUNE 1847 and at the same time named thirty-six-year-old Bishop Guillaume Douarre, a French Marist, its first vicar apostolic. But three weeks later his missionaries, who were already in New Caledonia, were attacked by local tribesmen near Port Balade. One was killed and the rest, being put to flight, escaped to Sydney, Australia.[1] Douarre tried again in 1849 to make a foundation in New Caledonia. But when plans became known for massacring him and his entire staff, he sent nine of his missionaries to Sydney and settled with the remaining ten on the Isle of Pines about thirty miles southeast of New Caledonia.

Convinced of the impossibility of achieving anything in New Caledonia, Douarre on 6 January 1850 described his difficulties for Superior General Colin and sent to France his pro-vicar, Father Claude-Marie Bernin (1810–56), to deliver his message personally. He urged Colin to request that Rome assign him to a new mission, one that would be "less difficult and less costly." He excluded areas like Micronesia, Melanesia, and Fiji, because "difficulties of every kind" were connected with them, and he had "no courage to begin a mission in any of these lands." Nor did he care to go to New Zealand.

His preference was for some mission in either North or South America, as he informed Colin through Bernin, and he wanted to go there with all of his missionaries. But if this proved unfeasible, he was ready to take over the Navigators (Samoa) Islands as a vicariate apostolic. He was aware, however, that "such a dismemberment" of the Central Oceania vicariate, in which the islands were located, would be painful for its vicar apostolic, Bishop Pierre Bataillon (1810–77), a fellow Marist. Consequently Douarre would accept the Navigators vicariate only if Rome gave him "a formal order" to take them.[2]

---

1. For details on the New Caledonia Vicariate's foundation and on the expulsion of the missionaries, see Wiltgen, *Oceania*, chaps. 27 and 30.

2. PF: *Udienze* vol. 112 (1850, Part II), f. 763rv, Douarre to Colin, 6 January 1850; SM: Lettres du Procureur

Pro-Vicar Bernin reached Lyon in five months' time and delivered Douarre's letter to Colin, who then wrote to Cardinal Prefect Fransoni on 12 June 1850. News of the premature death on 16 July 1848 of Bishop Collomb, second vicar apostolic of Melanesia and Micronesia, had hardly arrived in Lyon, Colin said, "when other letters came from New Caledonia informing us that the second attempt to get this mission established had completely failed." Colin himself "would be pleased with a mission in America," since "many requests have already come to us from various places in that part of the world. . . ." But he knew that Rome would hardly be interested in so costly and time consuming a venture as recalling to Europe from Oceania a large number of missionaries and then sending them to a distant mission in North or South America.

Colin therefore suggested that Fransoni "name one or two prefects apostolic for Woodlark and the surrounding islands, including New Guinea." He would then "try to engage" some of Douarre's missionaries to go there.³ This proposal sprang partly from Colin's concern for a handful of sick Marists on the island of Woodlark, the only mission with personnel in his society's extensive vicariates of Melanesia and Micronesia.

On the following day, 13 June 1850, Colin wrote to Father Jean-Louis Rocher (1809–94), who was in charge of the Marist supply center in Sydney. "Do not forget the missionaries at Woodlark," he said. "It is possible that we shall engage some of the missionaries of New Caledonia to go and join them, but as yet nothing has been decided. . . ."⁴

And on the day after that, 14 June 1850, Colin wrote to Douarre, telling him that Bernin had left for Rome that very day and would negotiate with Propaganda Fide "in favor of a location in America according to your desires. But if he is unable to obtain from the Holy See a suitable place in that country, I have instructed him to request conditionally that they make you the Vicar Apostolic of New Caledonia, Melanesia and Micronesia." Explaining why he had made this proposal, Colin said it would be "disagreeable" for the Society of Mary "to abandon these three vicariates in Oceania at once with everybody being right there on the spot." His proposal, if accepted by Rome, would make it possible for Douarre "to take over" in the three vicariates "those places which prove to be more suitable."⁵

Douarre was in Sydney when he received this letter from Colin. He answered on 9 November 1850 that he would have to buy a ship if his territory were expanded to include the vicariates of Melanesia and Micronesia, "since I would be obliged to visit not only Woodlark, but also Ascension Island. And if I may judge from what I have heard on every side, it would be important to found a mission on this latter island without delay." Ascension Island or Ponape, which was in the Caroline Islands of Micronesia, had come

---

de Lyon (1845–56), p. 105, Colin to Douarre, 14 June 1850.

3. PF: vol. 112 (1850, Part II), f. 764rv.

4. SM: Lettres du Procureur de Lyon (1845–56), 104–5.

5. Ibid., 105.

to the attention of the Marists as early as 1837, but no missionaries had ever been sent there.[6]

It was also advisable, Douarre said, that he occupy some of the New Hebrides Islands,[7] an archipelago that was part of his New Caledonia vicariate, "since they are inhabited by Polynesians who are far less savage than the majority of inhabitants in New Caledonia. Because these islands are small in extent, they have the added advantage of being very healthful according to assurances that were given me." He felt certain that the Catholics of Sydney would give him funds to purchase a ship, if only they were urged to do so by their archbishop, John Bede Polding.[8]

In Rome, three months earlier, decisions had been reached regarding the Douarre-Bernin-Colin proposals. They were first discussed by Cardinal Prefect Fransoni and secretary Barnabò on 8 August 1850. Two days later Fransoni informed Colin that Propaganda had agreed to "the designation of two prefects apostolic for the mission of Melanesia and Micronesia . . ." The additional request "to designate another prefect apostolic" for New Caledonia had also been granted. Fransoni enclosed letters patent and faculties for all three prefects apostolic, leaving them blank as Colin had requested, but asking that he later submit the names of the candidates chosen so that Propaganda might complete its records.[9]

On the following day, Sunday, 11 August 1850, secretary Barnabò presented an eleven-page "Report on Western Oceania" to Pope Pius IX. It described the catastrophes that had struck the three vicariates of Melanesia, Micronesia, and New Caledonia, and it proposed how missionary work there should be reorganized. As expected, Fransoni and Barnabò had ruled out transferring the New Caledonia missionaries to North or South America, but both were in favor of creating a new vicariate in Western Oceania as suggested by Douarre and proposed him for the office of vicar apostolic. After hearing the report the pope confirmed the nomination of two prefects apostolic for Melanesia and Micronesia, one for New Caledonia, and he also created the "Vicariate Apostolic of the Samoa or Navigators Archipelago," naming Douarre its first vicar apostolic.

Hereby Pope Pius IX reduced Melanesia and Micronesia from the status of vicariates apostolic to the status of missions. It was 11 August 1850.[10] On the previous day Fransoni had anticipated this papal decision in his letter to Colin.

---

6. For details on this early interest in Ponape and for additional references to Ponape, see Wiltgen, *Oceania*, 138–39, 602.

7. An earlier New Hebrides mission at Aneityum was abandoned in 1849. See ibid., 512.

8. SM: ONC/418/1, Douarre to Colin, 9 November 1850.

9. PF: LDB vol. 339 (1850), f. 702rv, Fransoni to Colin, 10 August 1850.

10. For additional details on Barnabò's report to Pius IX, see PF: *Udienze* vol. 112 (1850, Part II), f. 762r, 762 (1r–10v), 767r; Wiltgen, *Oceania*, 517–19. Pro-Vicar Bernin while in Rome had learned another reason that a transfer of Douarre and his missionaries to America was impossible. "At their last council the two ecclesiastical provinces of the North," he said, "had requested the Roman Curia not to name for their district any bishop who had not already worked in that country and who was not presented [as a candidate] by the council." See SM: 410/SCPF, Douarre to Vidal, 14 August 1850.

In Western Oceania, where this news was not yet known, Bishop Douarre and his missionaries were making unexpected progress on the Isle of Pines, which was part of the Vicariate Apostolic of New Caledonia. When the fifty-eight-ton schooner *Mary Ann* happened to stop at that island en route from Futuna to Sydney, Douarre took passage on it to purchase supplies for his mission. He arrived in Sydney on 20 October 1850.[11]

Douarre was still in Sydney three months later when he wrote to Fransoni, signing himself "Vicar Apostolic of the Navigators Islands." He was making preparations for returning to New Caledonia, he said, "when the bulls reached me by which His Holiness named me Vicar Apostolic of the Navigators Islands. I would have preferred to have been left free to choose between the former and the new vicariate." After stating that he had bowed his head as a sign of acceptance, he quickly added: "But I did so with a repugnance that Your Eminence will find hard to imagine. All my affection centers on New Caledonia. And in spite of its inhabitants being extremely cruel, I love them. . . ."

Although Douarre himself had asked for a new vicariate and had suggested that Rome create it by removing the Navigators Archipelago from the Central Oceania vicariate of a Marist bishop, he now gave reasons against accepting it. "I know that the Most Reverend Bataillon must establish himself there," Douarre explained. He was also convinced that he himself was not the man to be put in charge of the Navigators Archipelago, since he was forty and therefore was "too old" to learn the language of those islands.

He added that approximately sixty New Caledonians had been transported aboard two vessels to Futuna, including the troublemakers who originally had forced him and his missionaries to flee. So now it would be possible for him to return to Port Balade with safety to revive missionary work there.

What really disturbed Douarre was his leaving New Caledonia "at the moment when it is menaced with being invaded by Anglican ministers." Six Anglican bishops at a meeting in Sydney on 25 October 1850 had decided that two of their number, one from New Zealand and the other from New Holland (now Australia), should be placed in charge of the Solomon Islands, New Hebrides, Loyalty Islands, and New Caledonia. They were to start with missionary work "in the place last mentioned." The bishops had appealed to the generosity of all Anglicans in Sydney, and the report was that sufficient funds had been promised to purchase a ship. No longer having authority to counteract these Anglican plans because of his latest orders from Rome, Douarre "with extreme repugnance" decided to transfer to the Navigators Islands. But before doing so he wanted to help the new prefect apostolic get started in New Caledonia.

This letter to Fransoni was written on 16 January 1851.[12] By coincidence it was the same day on which Fransoni wrote to Archbishop Romilli in Milan and to Bishop Ramazzotti in

---

11. SM: ONC/418/1, Douarre to Colin, 25 October 1850.

12. PF: SC Oceania vol. 4 (1848–52), f. 584r–585v. For details on the Anglican mission, see David Lockhart Hilliard, *God's Gentlemen: A History of the Melanesian Mission 1849–1942*.

Pavia, stating that Melanesia and Micronesia were both being reserved as mission fields for the Lombard mission seminary.[13]

On the day before writing to Fransoni, Douarre had informed Colin that he had bought a 140-ton schooner. Although it needed repairs, he hoped that it would be ready in two weeks' time to transport to the Isle of Pines food supplies and a prefabricated house for his missionaries. He had chosen thirty-three-year-old Father Pierre Rougeyron (1817–1902) for the office of prefect apostolic in New Caledonia, he said, using faculties that he had received from Rome. At this time Rougeyron and another priest were in Futuna giving religious instruction to the New Caledonians transferred there temporarily. Douarre told Colin that he would personally direct the mission at the Isle of Pines until Rougeyron's return from Futuna. After installing Rougeyron as prefect apostolic of New Caledonia, he would leave for his new Vicariate Apostolic of the Navigators Archipelago.[14]

But repairs on Douarre's schooner took much longer than anticipated, and two months later he was still in Sydney. During this interval he had done much thinking, and on 13 March 1851 he submitted a formal request to Pope Pius IX through Cardinal Prefect Fransoni to be reassigned to the Vicariate Apostolic of New Caledonia. Leading up to his request he told Fransoni that a French warship had visited Port Balade and that its commandant, the officers, and one of his missionary brothers aboard had sent him letters. These letters had removed all of his doubts about "the benevolent dispositions of the Balade inhabitants." A letter had also arrived from Futuna with much good news about the New Caledonians being instructed there. "Those not yet baptized will have this joy on Easter Sunday [20 April]," he said. Among those under instruction were "several chiefs and the majority of our former enemies."

Douarre again told Fransoni of his deep concern over the proposed Anglican mission for New Caledonia. Since the best harbor in New Caledonia was at Port Balade, it was "important" for him to arrive there before the Anglicans, even though his missionaries had had to flee from that spot twice before. He had therefore decided not only to continue the Isle of Pines mission, but also to reopen immediately the Balade mission and to assign three priests there.

From Port Balade he intended to sail to the island of Futuna to visit Father Rougeyron, the prefect apostolic of New Caledonia, who was not yet aware of his appointment. He also planned to visit Vicar Apostolic Bataillon who resided at Wallis (or Uvea) Island. From there he would sail with one priest and four brothers to his own Vicariate Apostolic of the Navigators Archipelago. "And when the ship that I have purchased will have made the circuit of my islands, I shall pick up the Christians" of New Caledonia now at Futuna "and bring them back to their country." Douarre was convinced that his actions "shall receive

---

13. PF: LDB vol. 340 (1851), f. 40r–42r.
14. SM: ONC/418/1, Douarre to Colin, 15 January 1851.

approval from His Holiness, since it seems to me that the glory of God, the interests of the Church and the honour of Catholic missionaries demand that I take this course."

Douarre's letter ended with this plea: "May His Holiness kindly give back to me my former title of Vicar Apostolic of New Caledonia. For an instant I renounced it, never thinking I could possibly hold out in the midst of a people which in the past had given me nothing but proofs of its cruelty. . . . In giving my title back to me, His Holiness will be giving a father back to his children."[15]

That same day, 13 March 1851, Douarre wrote to Colin and enclosed this letter for Fransoni, leaving it open for Colin to read.[16] He told Colin much the same, but added the names of the priests whom he intended to assign to various missions. He also confided to Colin that the more he thought about his appointment as vicar apostolic of the Navigators Archipelago, the more convinced he became that Rome could not have appointed a worse candidate. "Nevertheless I am making preparations for my departure and hope to be able to set sail at the end of this month." He told Colin that after transferring the new prefect apostolic from Futuna to New Caledonia, he would sail to Sydney, hoping to find there "a letter authorizing me to return to my first vicariate, or else announcing that I have a successor . . ."[17]

To make sure that Colin would receive his 13 March letter, Douarre repeated its contents in another letter on 24 March, adding solid reasons that the Navigators Archipelago ought to remain under the jurisdiction of Bishop Bataillon. "The welfare of the Navigators Mission requires someone who speaks the language very well," he said. "This is a condition for success. The man fitted for this is Bishop Bataillon. . . . He speaks their language and also knows their customs, since these are the same as those at Wallis." Further, Bataillon had recently sent a ship to Sydney with the news that on its return he intended to transfer his headquarters to the Navigators Archipelago.

By the process of elimination Douarre showed Colin that "the Navigators Islands," as he always called them, were the only suitable headquarters for Bataillon. Futuna, Rotuma, and the Tonga Islands, although within his territory, were out of the question. The same was true for the Fiji Islands, because there Bataillon "would have to learn a difficult language." If plans were afoot to make the Fiji Islands an independent vicariate apostolic, it would seem more advisable "to send someone new there, or better still to name [as vicar apostolic] one of the veteran missionaries already there." Consequently the only place left in Bataillon's vicariate that could serve as his headquarters was "the Navigators Islands."

---

15. PF: *Udienze* vol. 114 (1851, Part II), f. 975 (11rv, 16r), Douarre to Fransoni, 13 March 1851. The archive materials referred to in this note and in nn. 20, 23, 31, 32 and 39 consist of unnumbered folios between f. 975 and f. 975A. Folio 975r begins with the words: "Eminentissimo Principe. Dalle lettere in cui . . ." For the sake of clarity the author refers to f. 975r as f. 975 (1r) and continues this sequence to f. 975 (16r), because sixteen folios are concerned.

16. The reason that the letter to Fransoni was left open is mentioned in SM: ONC/418/1, Douarre to Colin, 24 March 1851.

17. Ibid., Douarre to Colin, 13 March 1851.

If on the other hand Douarre were to be in charge of these islands, he could do nothing more for them than to provide supplies. But for New Caledonia he could do very much more "because conditions there have completely changed." In fact, he was so confident that Rome would reassign him to New Caledonia that he had decided "not to leave Bishop Bataillon uninformed about my asking to be allowed to return to my first vicariate . . ."[18]

Douarre was wise in confiding like this in Colin. He may have been aware that Rome generally granted the wishes of an overseas bishop, if those wishes were supported by the superior general of the bishop's mission sending society.

This letter to Colin was hardly dispatched when out of the blue Douarre received a solution to his problems. The correspondence came from Colin and arrived on 4 April 1851. It had been written on 29 November 1850, approximately one month before Douarre learned of his appointment as vicar apostolic of the Navigators Archipelago.[19] In it Colin pointed out that Propaganda Fide would not at all be displeased if the bishop were to return to New Caledonia and take charge of missionary work there, should a change of circumstances require this or even permit it. Douarre believed, however, that his appointment as vicar apostolic of the Navigators Archipelago had automatically deprived him of jurisdiction over the Vicariate Apostolic of New Caledonia. If his thinking was correct, it would mean that he no longer had authority over New Caledonia.

But Colin had a solution for this problem. He pointed out that in Douarre's possession were letters patent supplied by Rome for designating a prefect apostolic for New Caledonia. Now since Rome had authorized Colin—who in turn had authorized Douarre—to pick out a candidate and write his name in the blank space provided, Douarre himself could take on that office for New Caledonia by simply writing in his own name. Then, while waiting for new powers to come from Rome, he could use in New Caledonia the faculties and jurisdiction granted to the prefect apostolic, which office he would now hold.[20]

Douarre knew that there would be no embarrassment for Father Rougeyron, originally chosen for this office of prefect apostolic, since that priest was in Futuna and was not yet aware of his appointment. Douarre therefore went along with Colin's proposal and once again became the ecclesiastical head of New Caledonia, but with the lower rank of prefect apostolic. From then on he was recognized locally as prefect apostolic of New Caledonia and vicar apostolic of the Navigators Archipelago.[21]

---

18. Ibid., Douarre to Colin, 24 March 1851.

19. Ibid. See the postscript dated 5 April 1851.

20. The contents of Colin's letter of 29 November 1850 to Douarre were learned from Douarre's letter of 6 April 1851 to Fransoni, in PF: *Udienze* vol. 114 (1851, Part II), f. 975 (11rv, 16r).

21. Since Douarre legally became prefect apostolic of New Caledonia in April 1851, Jaspers is incorrect in saying that "Douarre was no longer in charge of New Caledonia" when "he returned there in May 1851" and so his "return . . . naturally had to be legalized" by Propaganda Fide. See Reiner Jaspers, *Die Missionarische Erschliessung Ozeaniens: Ein quellengeschichtlicher und missionsgeographischer Versuch zur kirchlichen Gebietsaufteilung in Ozeanien bis 1855*, 278.

On the following day, 5 April 1851, Douarre began a letter to Cardinal Prefect Fransoni. All his preparations for the Navigators Islands had been finished, he said, and he was on the point of leaving for that mission filled with repugnance, "when only last evening a letter arrived from the Reverend Father Colin . . . which put me greatly at ease." After describing its contents and saying that he was delighted with the solution offered by Colin, Douarre assured Fransoni that "the Navigators Islands will be taken care of by Bishop Bataillon. I am sending him my powers so that he can act canonically until you assign to His Excellency an archipelago where he can establish his headquarters. . . ."

Explaining briefly his New Caledonia plans, Douarre said that he would assign three priests and three brothers to the Isle of Pines. "I myself shall settle at Balade with two priests and four Brothers. And when the two missionaries return, who are now instructing some sixty very fervent New Caledonians at Futuna, I shall probably open a second foundation for another tribe near Balade."[22] In closing his letter he no longer called himself vicar apostolic of the Navigators Islands, as he had done when signing previous letters to Fransoni, nor as vicar apostolic of New Caledonia, but simply as the bishop of Amata, which was the name of his titular see.[23]

True to his word, Douarre informed Bishop Bataillon that he would not be going to the Navigators Archipelago. Instead he was leaving them in Bataillon's care and was delegating to Bataillon all the powers over them that he himself had received from Rome.[24]

Nearly six full months after leaving the Isle of Pines, Douarre was still in Sydney. He told Colin on 9 April 1851 that repairs on the ship belonging to the New Caledonia and Central Oceania vicariates "have detained us much longer than we had anticipated." The ship was now scheduled to sail on 12 April, or at the latest on 14 April. After listing the names of the six priests and seven brothers whom he was assigning to the Isle of Pines and to Balade, he said that he might open another mission at Poébo after his two priests in Futuna returned.

He also wanted to open a mission "at Tikopia, an island in New Hebrides." Protestant missionaries had not yet arrived there, and the island was inhabited "by 3000 or 4000 Futuna natives who are extremely hospitable according to reports which I have been able to obtain." He planned to assign Fathers Gilbert Roudaire (1813–52) and Jean-Baptiste Anliard (1814–52) to Tikopia. Roudaire was eager to go there "because he loves the Polynesians and speaks their language." If the two priests succeeded in opening a mission,

---

22. In a postscript of 5 April 1851 in his letter to Colin of 24 March 1851, Douarre named this second mission Poébo. See SM: ONC/418/1.

23. PF: *Udienze* vol. 114 (1851, Part II), f. 975 (11rv, 16r). Although Douarre's letter to Fransoni is dated 6 April 1851, internal evidence shows that it was begun on 5 April, the day after Douarre received Colin's letter of 29 November 1850. At this time it was not customary to date letters at the top, when they were begun, but rather at the bottom, when they were finished.

24. The contents of Douarre's letter to Bataillon were learned from Bataillon's letter of 15 June 1852 to Fransoni. See PF: SC Oceania vol. 4 (1848–52), f. 924r.

Brother Michel Anliard (1819–52), the younger brother of Father Anliard, would be sent there as well.[25]

When Douarre finally returned to the Isle of Pines, he found his missionaries in good health and on the best of terms with the chiefs and people. A school had been opened, and among the pupils was the successor to the highest-ranking chief. "These eight pupils are an expense for us," he told Colin on 17 May 1851, "because we are obliged to keep them at our house and we must feed them." Nevertheless he wanted his missionaries "to open a schoolhouse in each of the principal villages and to build there a small lodging for themselves." This would make it possible for them "to spend two days a week at each place, conducting school and teaching catechism . . ." Douarre intended to leave the Isle of Pines on 19 May and sail to Port Balade in New Caledonia, he said. This would be his third attempt to found a mission there.[26]

The reception at Port Balade was much better than what Douarre had anticipated. Nor did his missionaries have any trouble in resettling at Baïaoup near Port Balade where they had had their previous mission station. In fact, Douarre on 20 October 1851 was able to tell Colin: "We have no complaints to make about our natives for the four months during which we have been residing at Baïaoup. . . . We have also baptized some in danger of death and among these was the murderer of Brother Blaise Marmoiton." The brother had been killed on 18 July 1847.[27]

Since the two priests at Futuna were expected to return in one or two months with the New Caledonia Christians, "We did not lose a moment in erecting buildings for ourselves," Douarre said. "We now have a wooden dwelling for the missionaries, a very ample kitchen, and also a large shed containing a forge, workshops for our carpenters and masons, and two rooms as well. In another month or six weeks we shall have finished a large schoolhouse, partly wood and partly stone, which . . . will serve as a church until a suitable one can be built. Our garden is also making great progress, thanks to the care given to it by our Father [Benoît-Jean] Forestier [1821–1906], who has already provided our table with good vegetables." Fields for cultivating yams were being set aside for the New Caledonia Christians arriving from Futuna, and it was hoped that they would do the cultivating themselves. In time the mission also hoped to acquire some livestock.[28]

Bishop Bataillon was making a circuit of his island missions in June 1851 when he received Cardinal Prefect Fransoni's letter of 14 August 1850. It gave numerous reasons that Pope Pius IX had removed the Navigators Archipelago from the territory of his Central Oceania vicariate and had erected it into an independent vicariate apostolic entrusted to Bishop Douarre.[29] This was a great blow for Bataillon, because on completing the inspection

25. SM: ONC/418/1.
26. Ibid.
27. For details on Marmoiton's death, see Wiltgen, *Oceania*, 465–68, passim.
28. SM: ONC/418/1.
29. PF: LDB vol. 339 (1850), f. 711r–712r, Fransoni to Bataillon, 14 August 1850.

of his missions he had intended to transfer his headquarters from Wallis to the Navigators Islands, thus making them the central point of his vicariate. Now this letter from Rome would force him to cancel those plans.

However, at the very same time, Douarre's letter arrived, stating that he was not going to the Navigators Islands after all and that instead he was delegating all his powers over those islands to Bataillon. This caused Bataillon to ignore Fransoni's ten-month-old letter, and he continued to administer the Navigators Archipelago just as before, transferring his headquarters there as originally planned. He bought a piece of land for building a house and also a stone church, which was "meant above all for the colony of Europeans that is beginning to form in this place."[30]

By the following month, July 1851, Douarre's formal petition to be reassigned to the New Caledonia vicariate had reached Cardinal Fransoni in Rome. The cardinal at once requested Superior General Colin to submit his views on the matter. Colin supported Douarre and urged Fransoni on 20 July 1851 to restore to Douarre "his title as Vicar Apostolic of New Caledonia and to permit him to make a new attempt on this island in person." He warned the cardinal, however, that Douarre and his missionaries "probably will be inclined to return to Europe, if this new attempt should fail." To prevent their return Colin suggested that it would be "opportune to keep the Navigators Archipelago for some time under the jurisdiction" of Bishop Douarre. Then if he and his missionaries "should be repulsed in New Caledonia," they could still find in the Navigators Archipelago "an asylum where they would establish themselves." Colin judged that such a proviso was in order, because "the position of vicars apostolic and of missionaries in the midst of these savage peoples is so uncertain, that one cannot prudently order a fixed and determined procedure."[31]

As a result of Colin's letter secretary Barnabò approached Pope Pius IX on Sunday, 10 August 1851. It had not been necessary to bring up this matter at a general meeting of the cardinal members, Barnabò told the pope. The reason was that neither by letter nor by papal brief "had it been stated in any way that the administration of the Vicariate Apostolic of New Caledonia was being removed" from the jurisdiction or authority of Bishop Douarre, even though "a provision had been made" for naming a prefect apostolic "in case the need arose." Strictly speaking, therefore, it was unnecessary to bring this matter to the pope's attention, Barnabò said. "Nevertheless the Most Reverend Douarre believed that his jurisdiction and authority over New Caledonia had come to an end when he was entrusted with the government of the new vicariate." Because of this he wanted "to have confirmation of his powers over the mission in question, or to have the powers returned to him..."

Barnabò reminded the pope that Pro-Vicar Bernin of New Caledonia one year earlier had come to Rome to request in both Douarre's and Superior General Colin's names, that the Navigators Archipelago be given to Douarre. But the earlier distressing news from New Caledonia, which had prompted this request, had given way to high hopes accord-

30. PF: SC Oceania vol. 4 (1848–52), f. 924rv, Bataillon to Fransoni, 15 June 1852.
31. PF: *Udienze* vol. 114 (1851, Part II), f. 975 (13r–14r), Colin to Fransoni, 20 July 1851.

ing to two recent letters received from Douarre. Barnabò told the pope that Colin was in favor of Douarre getting back his original vicariate of New Caledonia and retaining the Navigators vicariate as well. Barnabò explained, however, that Douarre's jurisdiction over the Navigators vicariate would be temporary and would cease automatically once he succeeded in establishing himself firmly in the New Caledonia vicariate.

Pius IX sanctioned these proposals that same day, 10 August 1851, which was one day less than a year since the same pontiff had created the Vicariate Apostolic of the Navigators Archipelago and had entrusted it to Douarre at his request.[32] The decree of 20 August 1851, which announced the pope's decision, reflected what was said by Barnabò during his audience with the pope on 10 August and also what was said by Colin to Fransoni in his letter of 20 July.[33]

Cardinal Fransoni explained these various transactions in a letter to Bataillon on 22 August 1851 and gave the reasons behind them. He did not reveal, however, that the one who had suggested that Douarre be allowed for the time being to retain jurisdiction over the Navigators Archipelago, was Colin. Instead he let Bataillon believe that the suggestion had come from Douarre. Fransoni assured Bataillon, however, that this time it seemed Douarre would indeed succeed in New Caledonia and that consequently the administration of the Navigators vicariate would "either remain in your hands or return to you shortly . . ." Fransoni asked Bataillon, however, whether it might be in the interest of religion for one of his missionaries to be made vicar apostolic over the Navigators Archipelago, or whether such an appointment should be deferred.[34]

When Bataillon arrived in Sydney on business in May 1852, he found Fransoni's letter of the previous August waiting for him. He replied on 15 June 1852 that Douarre had sent him delegated faculties for the Navigators vicariate twelve months earlier. Since that time he himself had governed the new vicariate and had also transferred the headquarters of his Central Oceania vicariate to the Navigators Islands, something that he had been planning to do for a long time. In giving this explanation Bataillon was brief. But when answering Fransoni's question on whether or not a new vicar apostolic should be placed in charge of the Navigators Islands, he replied at great length.

The total population of his Central Oceania vicariate, he began, "amounts to more than 300,000 souls. This population is divided into two quite distinct races that have completely different languages and customs. The Polynesian race inhabits the Navigators and Friendly [now Tonga] Archipelagoes and numbers 100,000 souls. The black race inhabits the large Fiji Archipelago which alone contains more than 200,000 souls. Now if the Central Vicariate must be divided, it is desirable that the division be made according to the demarcation of races and languages. And after the division has been made," he continued, "I should prefer to retain for myself that part of the vicariate containing the Polynesian race

---

32. Ibid., f. 975 (7r–10v).
33. PF: LDB vol. 340 (1851), f. 633r–634r.
34. Ibid., f. 616r–617r.

with which I have worked up to this time and whose language I know." He did not want to be "relegated" to the Fiji Islands, a part of his vicariate "which is not yet cultivated and whose language I do not know."

If the Navigators Islands were made an independent vicariate, this would deprive him of almost all of his Polynesian population, he told Fransoni. The only other Polynesians within his Central Oceania vicariate were those in the Friendly or Tonga Islands, but their population was "hardly more than 20,000 souls." Having so few Polynesians under his jurisdiction would not warrant his remaining among them. He would be obliged to move to the Fiji Islands and there learn a new language, he said, "something that is hardly easy or agreeable."

But his principal reason for not wanting to go to the Fiji Islands was "that the Society of Mary apparently no longer wants to supply priests for that archipelago. Instead it wishes to limit its activities to the Navigators Islands and to the Friendly Islands." This placed him in a dilemma. If he went to the Fiji Islands, he would be there without priests from the Marist Society to which he belonged. And if he went to the Friendly Islands, he would be there with only twenty thousand Polynesians, a mere fraction of the three hundred thousand people within the original boundaries of his Central Oceania vicariate. This was "equivalent to taking away from me the whole of my vicariate," he said.

The bishop therefore suggested a division that he believed to be "more fitting and more advantageous for the welfare of our missions." Let the Navigators Islands remain part of the Central Oceania vicariate, just as they previously had been. But cut off the Fiji Islands, make them an independent vicariate apostolic, and entrust them to another missionary society. This would be a more balanced division, he said, since then there would be two hundred thousand souls in the Fiji Islands vicariate and one hundred thousand souls in the Central Oceania vicariate. Each vicariate would have "a population of the same race and with the same language." This solution would leave him with Polynesians, the kind of people with whom he had begun his missionary work. It would also leave him with members of the Marist Society to which he belonged and from which he did not wish to separate himself. "As for the new vicar apostolic" to be appointed for the Fiji Islands, "it can make no difference to him whether he begins in one place or in another. . . ."[35]

As Bataillon wished, no territory was removed from his control at this time. The Fiji Islands, which he did not want, were removed from his jurisdiction in 1863, when they became a prefecture apostolic. The Vicariate Apostolic of the Navigators Archipelago was removed from his jurisdiction in 1872. Until then he continued directing missionary work there as administrator apostolic. He remained in charge of the Central Oceania vicariate until his death in 1877.

As was hoped by Superior General Colin and Cardinal Prefect Fransoni, Bishop Douarre's mission actually did take root in New Caledonia and began to prosper. Then it came time for Douarre to expand to the island of Tikopia in New Hebrides. As planned,

---

35. PF: SC Oceania vol. 4 (1848–52), f. 924r–926v.

Father Roudaire was placed in charge. He left Sydney aboard *Arche d'Alliance* on 6 November 1851, was joined at the Isle of Pines by Father Anliard, and reached Tikopia on Friday evening, 12 December. On the following morning the two priests, while accompanied by an armed landing party, reconnoitered the island for two hours. They then went aboard ship to tell Captain E. Cazalis that they would stay. The remainder of the day was spent unloading their supplies.

The captain went ashore with the last boatload of boxes and judged the population of the island to be about 450. Douarre had earlier told Colin that he had heard the population was "3000 or 4000."[36] Two venerable patriarchs, the principal chiefs of Tikopia, had assured the captain "that a house would be given to the missionaries, that each day they would be supplied with food, and that they would be given full protection." To seal the pact Captain Cazalis gave gifts to the chiefs. But he had to take leave of them abruptly and hasten aboard ship when the skies began to threaten. Not having found a suitable anchorage, he had been obliged to keep his ship under sail. When he asked the missionaries whether "the presence of *Arche d'Alliance*" could be of further use to them, Roudaire replied that the warm welcome given to him by the people had dispelled all his fears. The captain should therefore feel free to leave whenever he wished. At about six o'clock that evening *Arche d'Alliance* headed out to sea on its way to Shanghai. It was Saturday, 13 December 1851.

Six and a half months later, on 29 June 1852, Brother Michel Anliard left New Caledonia aboard Bishop Douarre's schooner, *Étoile du Matin*, to join the two priests and bring them supplies. He should have arrived at Tikopia within a week, but six months later his ship had not yet returned to New Caledonia nor to Sydney.

Had something gone wrong? The Marists in Sydney chartered a seventy-seven-ton schooner called *Chieftain* and assigned Father Jean-Xavier Montrouzier (1820–97), a veteran Melanesia missionary, to investigate. He left Sydney on 18 January 1853 and reached Tikopia on 27 February—one year, two months, and two weeks since Fathers Roudaire and Anliard had arrived in Tikopia, and seven months and two weeks since Brother Anliard was scheduled to arrive—but none of the three missionaries could be found. Nor did Montrouzier find any of their belongings when he visited the village and its surrounding area. Using interpreters he interviewed the people and concluded that *Étoile du Matin*, the ship carrying Brother Anliard and new supplies for the mission, must have suffered shipwreck before reaching Tikopia.

According to the same informants, Fathers Roudaire and Anliard, having received no word and no supplies for a year and having become sick, requested passage to Sydney aboard a whaling vessel. They had sailed off with all their possessions only two months before Father Montrouzier arrived. In their company were four young men from Tikopia, including the son of the local chief. Montrouzier trusted his informers and said that he did not have "the least suspicion that the natives had done any violence" to the missionaries.

---

36. SM: ONC/418/1, Douarre to Colin, 9 April 1851.

Since Fathers Roudaire and Anliard may have intended to instruct the four Tikopians in New Caledonia, Montrouzier stopped there on 8 March 1853. But he did not find them, nor did he find them in Sydney when he arrived back there on 29 March. To this day no one knows what happened to Roudaire and the two Anliard brothers. It is likely that they died at sea on two different ships, but the wrecks of these ships have never been found.[37]

Repeatedly Bishop Douarre had said in letters to Superior General Colin that he wished to resign as vicar apostolic of New Caledonia.[38] Not being able to learn languages, he said that he would be happy to work as an ordinary priest under a new bishop. Fearing that Rome might accede to Douarre's request, Colin begged Cardinal Prefect Fransoni on 20 July 1851 not to do so. He "is zealous and has a special talent for winning the hearts of others and for preserving peace among his missionaries," Colin said. This was "a quality which is as precious as it is rare."[39]

When matters began to run smoothly at Balade in New Caledonia, however, Douarre changed his mind about wanting to resign. "I wish to have a successor more than ever," he told Colin on 20 October 1851, "but not immediately, since I believe that my presence will be useful in New Caledonia for some time to come. I believe in all sincerity that I do not have what it takes to be in charge of others. . . ." Forty-year-old Douarre suggested that his successor might well be thirty-year-old Father Forestier, whom he considered ideal in many respects. "He is knowledgeable, pious, zealous, and he can learn languages easily. If you should decide in favor of his nomination, you could give him to me as my coadjutor." Douarre would leave that part of the world, he said, "when I come to believe that my presence is useless for New Caledonia."[40]

Colin wrote to Fransoni again on 6 June 1852, saying that the latest letters from Oceania had given him reason to hope that Bishop Douarre "this time will probably become established in New Caledonia. However, that holy bishop continues to manifest a desire to have a successor for his mission. I do not think it is time yet to give in to his wishes, suggested as they are by his modesty. . . ."[41]

Less than one year later Douarre was dead. He had cared for the sick during an epidemic and had contracted their disease. He died at Balade mission on 27 April 1853 at the age of forty-two.[42]

---

37. Hugh M. Laracy, "The First Mission to Tikopia," in *Journal of Pacific History* 4 (1969): 105–9.

38. Douarre told Fransoni this on 16 January 1851. See PF: SC Oceania vol. 4 (1848–52), f. 585rv.

39. PF: *Udienze* vol. 114 (1851, Part II), f. 975 (13r–14r).

40. SM: ONC/418/1.

41. PF: SC Oceania vol. 4 (1848–52), f. 918v.

42. Colin told Fransoni on 17 December 1853 that Douarre died on 27 April 1853. See PF: SC Oceania vol. 5 (1853–57), f. 355r. The same date is contained in SM: Index Defunctorum et Necrologium Generale, 25. Jaspers in *Erschliessung Ozeaniens*, 281, uses the above 17 December 1853 letter as his source, but mistakenly gives the date of death as 23 April. C. M. Léopold Verguet mistakenly gives the date 26 April in *Histoire de la première mission catholique au vicariat de Mélanésie*, 306.

Colin's 17 December 1853 letter to Fransoni announcing Douarre's death is incorrectly dated 15 December in the handwritten file copy in SM: Epistolae Variae Generalium, 1:64, no. 110.

4

Fransoni Offers the Melanesia and Micronesia Missions to Lombardy's Foreign Mission Seminary

16 January 1851

POPE PIUS IX HAD APPROVED OF BISHOP-ELECT RAMAZZOTTI'S PROJECT FOR A LOMBARDY mission college on 21 February 1850. But Cardinal Prefect Fransoni's letter with this news, written in Naples on 26 February, did not reach Archbishop Romilli in Milan until the end of March.[1] The reason for the long delay was that everything had to go through the hands of Secretary Barnabò in Rome.[2] When forwarding Fransoni's letter of 26 February, Barnabò added his own of 19 March, inviting Romilli to begin negotiations for founding the mission college and promising his "full cooperation."[3]

Having the enthusiastic support of Rome and of the archbishop of Milan, Ramazzotti was now eager to win the active support of the bishops in charge of the dioceses of Lombardy. The ecclesiastical province of Lombardy included the metropolitan or archiepiscopal see of Milan and the eight dioceses or suffragan sees of Bergamo, Brescia, Como, Crema, Cremona, Lodi, Mantova, and Pavia. Since Ramazzotti was bishop-elect of Pavia, he found it relatively easy to approach the bishops. In April 1850 he began contacting them personally and suggested that the college be a mission institute for the entire province of Lombardy. He also invited the bishops to be its cofounders and superiors. By 5 May,

---

1. Suigo, *Pio IX*, 81–82.

2. The delay was exceptionally long in this case because Barnabò on 7 March had to write back to Naples for the two memorandums that Fransoni had failed to include in the dossier. See PF: LDB vol. 339 (1850), f. 230rv, Barnabò to Fransoni, 7 March 1850. Fransoni had written to Barnabò on 26 February that he was sending many papers back to Rome with Bertinelli. See PF: CV vol. 43, f. 149rv, Fransoni to Barnabò, 26 February 1850.

3. PF: LDB vol. 339 (1850), f. 239v–240r. Tragella incorrectly says that Fransoni wrote to Romilli on 9 March (in his text) and on 19 March (in his note), and he attributes to Fransoni parts of Barnabò's letter to Romilli of 19 March 1850. See Tragella, *Missioni estere*, 1:42.

one month later, he had contacted all except the bishop of Bergamo and had won their support.[4]

In May 1850 developments followed in rapid succession: On 1 May, Ramazzotti wrote to Archbishop Romilli that candidates were eager for the mission college to open "in my house at Saronno." On 7 May, Romilli and Ramazzotti met at Rho to discuss the matter. Father Taglioretti then joined Ramazzotti at Saronno, and together they began working out concrete details. After mid-May, Ramazzotti visited the Milan major seminary to announce that the mission college would soon open and invited interested candidates to apply. Deacons Mazzucconi and Salerio requested admission on 20 and 24 May, respectively; they were to be ordained priests on 25 May. Father Marinoni, the thirty-nine-year-old priest in Rome chosen by Ramazzotti to become director of the mission college, arrived in Milan for a month of recuperation toward the end of May and accepted the office of director.[5]

Negotiations with Austrian officials also got under way in May. Archbishop Romilli wrote to Lieutenant Schwarzenberg, representative of the Austrian government in Milan, on 2 May.[6] He enclosed a copy of the 1 May letter received from Ramazzotti stating that "the bishops of the province" had praised and approved the desire of "some priests of the diocese" to begin training for foreign missionary work at Saronno.[7] Romilli's own letter said that Ramazzotti was promoting "an association of secular priests to propagate the Christian faith in foreign missions." What was "novel and indeed of special importance" in this project was that these missionaries would obtain their training in "a diocesan mission house dependent upon their own bishop." Consequently they "would not have to separate themselves from their own diocese and from their own country" in order to dedicate themselves to the foreign missions. Neither would they "have to go elsewhere to find the education needed for so sublime a ministry," nor would they "have to join for this purpose some [religious] family or some other foreign institute."

Since Ramazzotti's project was nothing but "a private gathering of five or six priests living in community and busy with ecclesiastical studies and pious practices, there would be no need to request approbation from public authorities." Romilli nevertheless wanted to pass on this information, convinced that Schwarzenberg would draw satisfaction from it. Romilli asked Schwarzenberg to remove any obstacles blocking the project and urged him personally to support Ramazzotti. After all, Austria would benefit from the project, he said, since its flag would protect the far-off Lombardy missions. This in turn would cause

---

4. Suigo, *Pio IX*, 83f.

5. Ibid., 77, 88f; Tragella, *Missioni estere*, 1:44.

6. Lieutenant Schwarzenberg is not to be confused with Austria's prime minister, Felix, Fürst zu Schwarzenberg (1800–1852). There were two Schwarzenbergs in Milan in 1850: Karl and Friedrich. It is not clear with which of these two Romilli corresponded, since the letters were signed simply "Lieutenant Schwarzenberg."

7. Suigo, *Pio IX*, 85.

Austria to "become more respected and dear" in those places. He added that "the Supreme Pontiff has already been approached . . . and has deigned to express his full support and supreme satisfaction."[8]

Schwarzenberg forwarded Romilli's letter to Field Marshall Graf Radetzky, the new governor general of Lombardy-Veneto. Radetzky answered on 29 May that he wanted clarification and further details on the scope and statutes of the organization.[9]

Meanwhile Pope Pius IX had ratified Ramazzotti's appointment as bishop of Pavia on 20 May 1850.[10] When Ramazzotti left Milan on 9 June to be ordained a bishop in Rome, Archbishop Romilli gave him a letter for Secretary Barnabò of Propaganda Fide. In it Romilli asked Barnabò to deal with Ramazzotti "as if you were dealing with me personally, since I am conferring upon him very extensive faculties so that he can represent me in all that concerns my jurisdiction" over the mission college.[11]

Ramazzotti reached Rome on 15 June, saw Cardinal Prefect Fransoni several times, and was ordained a bishop by him on Sunday, 30 June 1850, in San Carlo Church on Via del Corso. Two days later he obtained for Father Marinoni the formal release from his pastorate at San Michele a Ripagrande Church in Rome.[12]

One of the many things that Ramazzotti had to discuss in Rome was the assignment of a particular mission to his seminary. But when he followed the suggestion of Supriès and requested Micronesia, Cardinal Prefect Fransoni replied that a particular mission for the group would be chosen later.[13] Ramazzotti was asked, however, "to provide one excellent priest, or better two, to serve in Hong Kong as procurator of the Sacred Congregation de Propaganda Fide for the missions of China." The procurator's task was to transmit to religious order missionaries working in China the spiritual powers and financial aid dispensed by Propaganda in Rome. The priest chosen was also to be named ecclesiastical superior over Hong Kong "with the rank of prefect apostolic."[14]

---

8. Ibid., 86–88.

9. Ibid., 89.

10. Suigo cites the pertinent source material in the Secret Vatican Archives and gives the date in two different places as 20 May 1850. Tragella cites no source material and so would appear to be mistaken when he gives the date as 29 May. See Suigo, *Pio IX*, 49, 91; Tragella, *Missioni estere*, 1:42.

11. Suigo, *Pio IX*, 91–92; PF: Udienze vol. 111 (1850, Part I), f. 93Frv, Romilli to Barnabò, 5 June 1850. See chap. 2, n. 13.

12. Suigo, *Pio IX*, 70, 72–74, 91–93. Suigo gives many details on Ramazzotti obtaining Marinoni's release from seventy-three-year-old Antonio Cardinal Tosti, the protector-benefactor of the gigantic social undertaking known as the Apostolic Hospice of San Michele a Ripagrande.

13. Suigo gives trustworthy sources like Giacomo Scurati and Angelo Taglioretti as saying that Ramazzotti asked for "Micronesia." But Supriès, when thanking the same Taglioretti for his latest news, says, "I rejoice that the Most Reverend Bishop of Pavia asked Propaganda for the Carolines." Since the Caroline Islands are the principal island group in Micronesia, Supriès may have been using the part for the whole. See Suigo, *Pio IX*, 92; *Beatificationis Positio*, 73; PIME: AME 28:144, Supriès to Taglioretti, 25 July 1850.

14. *Beatificationis Positio*, 92–94; Tragella, *Missioni estere*, 1:258.

Bishop Ramazzotti arrived back in Milan on 14 July and the next day went to his house in Saronno with Fathers Marinoni and Taglioretti. They made immediate preparations for the seminary's opening day, which was set for 30 July 1850. Archbishop Romilli informed Ramazzotti in writing that he had "expressly authorized the Reverend Priests Alessandro Mornico, Alessandro Ripamonti, Giovanni Mazzucconi, Paolo Reina and Carlo Salerio" to enter the seminary on 30 July and begin "preparing themselves for foreign missionary work according to the plan and the rule that has already been presented to me . . ." Father Giuseppe Marinoni had also been "specially delegated" by him to direct the new seminary, he said.[15]

Taglioretti sent Father Bertani to the Carthusian monastery in Pavia to deliver a letter to Supriès with the latest news and to invite him for the opening of the seminary. Supriès wrote back on 25 July: "So Tuesday, 30 July, will be the beautiful day destined for launching such a holy task!" He wished that he could be "a witness to it," but monastery duties prevented him from attending. "Let me know how many candidates are received, who they are, and what hopes there are for the future! And if dear Mazzucconi is among the chosen, I shall be highly pleased. . . ." Supriès referred to Micronesia as "that promised land which they will have to water with their sweat and perhaps also with their blood." And he called the inhabitants of the Caroline Islands "certainly the mildest and most peaceful people in all of Oceania."

From Taglioretti's letter Supriès also learned that the Marists had asked Rome to be relieved of Micronesia.[16] This made him optimistic again: "Now that the greatest obstacle has been removed—and by this I mean the Marists—I have no doubt at all that this interesting mission will be entrusted to the nascent congregation of Saronno."[17]

Micronesia and Melanesia had become vicariates apostolic on 16 July 1844, and both were entrusted to the Society of Mary (S.M.) or Marists.[18] But these missionaries had concentrated on Melanesia, and so three and a half years later the Marist headquarters in Lyon, France, asked Propaganda to give Micronesia to someone else. Since the Clerics Regular of Saint Paul (C.R.S.P.), better known as Barnabites, had asked for a mission, Rome offered them the Micronesia vicariate on 23 June 1848. But one week later they declined the offer.

When the Melanesia vicariate became a graveyard for many young missionaries, including two bishops, the Marist headquarters asked to be relieved of that vicariate as well. Rome turned to the Congregation of the Sacred Hearts of Jesus and Mary (SS.CC.), known also as the Picpus Fathers, and offered them the two vicariates of Micronesia and Melanesia on 14 May 1850. But three weeks later they also declined, saying, "The same reasons which

---

15. Suigo, *Pio IX*, 96–98. Romilli's letter to Ramazzotti was dated 27 July 1850. For the entire text, see ibid., 97f.

16. Taglioretti's letter was not found, but its contents are evident from Supriès's reply.

17. PIME: AME 28:143–44, Supriès to Taglioretti, 25 July 1850.

18. For details on the creation of the Micronesia and Melanesia vicariates, see Wiltgen, *Oceania*, chap. 17.

oblige the Marists to abandon it, hinder us from taking charge of it." They were experienced missionaries, having worked in the islands of eastern Oceania since 1827.

Cardinal Fransoni was in the midst of these negotiations when Ramazzotti arrived in Rome on 15 June 1850 and asked for Micronesia as a mission field for his seminary. Since Fransoni was trying to find an experienced mission-sending society that would accept both Micronesia and Melanesia, he had told Ramazzotti that no decision could yet be made on Micronesia. Then on 25 June, five days before Fransoni ordained Ramazzotti a bishop, the cardinal offered the Micronesia and Melanesia vicariates to the Oblates of Mary Immaculate (O.M.I.), another order with missionary experience. But one month later the head and founder of the order, sixty-seven-year-old Bishop de Mazenod of Marseille, wrote to Fransoni that he found himself "forced to refuse... because I do not have enough personnel. And even if I did have enough, I would still refuse, not being able to flatter myself that I would succeed where the Marists had not succeeded." His letter was dated 25 July 1850.[19]

By coincidence it was also 25 July 1850 when Supriès wrote to Taglioretti about the islands of Micronesia and said, "I have no doubt at all that this interesting mission will be entrusted to the nascent congregation of Saronno."[20] Supriès was well aware of the difference between head-hunting Melanesia in the South Pacific, where numerous Marist missionaries had lost their lives and where no other missionary order wanted to go, and Micronesia in the North Pacific which contained clusters of tiny islands that reportedly were healthy and safe. Micronesia consisted of the Caroline, Mariana, Gilbert (now Kiribati), Marshall, and Palau islands.

As early as 1843 when still in Rome, Supriès had received particularized information on one of the Caroline Islands which some called Ponape and others called Ascension. Father Jean-Baptiste Epalle (1809–45), a French Marist from New Zealand who was in Rome on business, had supplied the information. He told about a Scots Presbyterian named James Hall who had traveled for six months on a whaling vessel from the Caroline Islands to New Zealand in search of Roman Catholic priests for Ponape.

According to Epalle, who had discussed the matter in great detail with Hall, the Caroline Islands were the best place to start missionary work in Micronesia. Epalle also stressed how important it was to place the mission headquarters at Ponape, because this island was located "in the center of the Archipelago of the Carolines" and had "a population of about 8,000 souls." The suitability and also the healthfulness of the location were confirmed by the fact that many European settlers had taken up residence there, having been attracted "by the beauty and fertility" of Ponape and "by the peacefulness and friendliness of its inhabitants."[21]

---

19. For details on the negotiations of Propaganda with the Marists, Barnabites, Picpus Fathers, and Oblates of Mary Immaculate, see Wiltgen, *Oceania*, 522–39.

20. PIME: AME 28:143–45, Supriès to Taglioretti.

21. Epalle gave these details in writing on 14 July 1843 to Abbé J. F. M. Guérin, whose confidant was Supriès.

From this it is clear that Supriès was no religious fanatic eager to send off young and inexperienced missionaries to certain death. He was instead a well-informed mission strategist who wanted to fill an appalling vacancy in Micronesia, which by 1850 still had no Roman Catholic missionaries. That vacancy, once filled, could augur only success, he believed.

The opening day of the Saronno mission seminary arrived. On the afternoon of 30 July 1850, priest candidates Mazzucconi and Salerio joined Bishop Ramazzotti at Rho and rode with him in a horsedrawn carriage to Saronno. On the outskirts of the town they stopped at a shrine of the Blessed Virgin Mary to pray. Arriving at the old Franciscan monastery destined to house the new seminary, they found director Marinoni, priest candidates Ripamonti and Reina, and other priests from the vicinity waiting for them. The inauguration ceremony was simple; it consisted of prayers and an invocation to the Holy Spirit. On the following day Mazzucconi had the honor of celebrating the solemn mass. Supriès and Taglioretti, both of whom had contributed so much to the project, were unable to attend.[22]

Prior to the opening day Bishop Ramazzotti, director Marinoni, and Father Taglioretti had drawn up preliminary drafts of the rule and of the daily order. Candidates Mazzucconi, Salerio, and Ripamonti, the first ones to take up residence in the seminary, were invited to discuss these drafts with Marinoni and to suggest changes. At Marinoni's invitation Taglioretti joined the study group for nine days in August.[23]

The month was not yet over when Lieutenant Schwarzenberg in Milan sent Archbishop Romilli an official government communication on 30 August. Since it concerned the mission seminary, Romilli's office sent a copy to Ramazzotti that very same day. Seeing the contents Ramazzotti at once called director Marinoni and candidates Mazzucconi, Salerio, Ripamonti, and Mornico to the chapel.[24] Standing before the altar Bishop Ramazzotti read the document in a voice filled with emotion.

The document stated that the minister of cult in Vienna by dispatch of 2 August had declared "that he finds no difficulty in approving the Institute of Missionary Priests for distant regions, as envisaged by the Bishop of Pavia," provided that these missionaries "observe existing regulations regarding passports, name a legal representative, etc." Furthermore, "The State Administration must never have to contribute any sum whatsoever for the maintenance of that Institute." On the contrary, the minister of cult said, one might well expect "that those considerable sums which are being sent to other similar Institutes abroad, will now be directed toward this [new] Institute."

Both Guérin and Supriès were collaborating at this time in persuading Propaganda to found the Vicariate Apostolic of Northern Oceania or Micronesia. See Wiltgen, *Oceania*, 276f.

22. Suigo, *Pio IX*, 99–101; Tragella, *Missioni estere*, 1:55–56.
23. Suigo, *Pio IX*, 102–3.
24. Mornico had arrived on 13 August.

Schwarzenberg added some words of his own, urging Archbishop Romilli "to take all necessary steps to have the proposed Institute become a reality." He asked that Romilli assure Ramazzotti "in the name of the Imperial Government of its most lively interest in the success" of this project "which gives promise of so much good for the Church and for the State." Furthermore, Romilli was to advise Ramazzotti of "the full recognition extended by the Government itself" for his "distinguished zeal for the Propagation of the Faith." When Ramazzotti finished reading Schwarzenberg's letter, he asked those present to join him in prayers of gratitude to God.[25]

Taglioretti informed Supriès that Mazzucconi was among the candidates admitted on the opening day,[26] and that the Austrian government had officially approved the new seminary. Thanking him on 7 September, Supriès said that now his chief preoccupation was "that the beautiful and very interesting mission of Micronesia, so neglected and so abandoned to this very day, may be entrusted to the care of this nascent congregation." And even if Micronesia "should be entrusted to some other society of missionaries," its vastness gave him "high hopes that it could easily be divided into two or three parts so that a small corner would be left over for the Lombards."[27]

Some six weeks later on 16 October 1850 Supriès again wrote to Taglioretti, wondering why Rome "has not yet taken a stand regarding the area to be assigned to the new missionaries." Concerned that Micronesia "might once again be forgotten," he urged Taglioretti "to keep Rome abreast of what is happening in order to attract their attention and get them to write some letters."[28]

Ramazzotti had meanwhile received the official ecclesiastical documents via Vienna, authorizing him to take possession of the Diocese of Pavia. After bidding farewell to all at Saronno on 28 September 1850, he moved to Pavia. Then on the following day, Sunday, he was solemnly installed as bishop of Pavia. He could now use the influence of this office on behalf of the new mission seminary. And at the same time, being so close, he could keep a watchful eye over it.[29]

Archbishop Romilli on 19 September had sent an invitation to all the bishops of Lombardy to attend a five-day episcopal conference starting on 27 November 1850. Replying to this invitation two days before he moved from Saronno to Pavia, Ramazzotti mentioned Marinoni's wish that the mission institute be on the agenda because "it was erected specifically in the name and under the auspices of all the Bishops of Lombardy." The bishops "would then be able to make those decisions on its behalf which they consider the most wise, and at the same time they could sanction the Rules that have been proposed

---

25. Suigo, *Pio IX*, 106–8, 118.
26. The contents of Taglioretti's letter are evident from Supriès's reply. See PIME: AME 28:147f, Supriès to Taglioretti, 25 August 1850.
27. Ibid., 151, Supriès to Taglioretti, 7 September 1850.
28. Ibid., 156, Supriès to Taglioretti, 16 October 1850.
29. Suigo, *Pio IX*, 108, 117.

for guiding the Missionary Candidates." Ramazzotti promised that director Marinoni, well in advance of the meeting, would provide each of the bishops with a copy of the rules and a copy of all documents concerning the new foundation.[30]

With the help of Taglioretti and the student body, Marinoni prepared packets of documentation for the archbishop of Milan and for the bishops of Bergamo, Brescia, Como, Crema, Cremona, Lodi, Mantova, and Pavia, enclosing also a letter for each. Taglioretti personally delivered the first packet on 5 October to Archbishop Romilli, who replied that the norms and rules could be implemented immediately.[31]

In the midst of this early October excitement the Austrians in local government circles began criticizing the seminary. There may have been some connection "with the Oblates of Rho," they said, "even though the reply given to a query on this matter stated that there was no such connection at all." And they accused the seminary of being "a gathering of priests hostile to the government," because some of the candidates had fought against Austria during the 1848 revolution.[32]

There was no denying that three of the five candidates had joined in the fray against Austria during the revolution. Mazzucconi and Salerio had had their roles as well as Reina, who entered the seminary on 31 August 1850. But their act of patriotism in 1848 did not mean that now they were actively hostile to the government, as the accusation implied. As for the other charge, Prior Saison of the Carthusian Monastery in Pavia did suggest that the new seminary initially should be affiliated with the Missionary Oblates of Rho. And Molteni, superior general of the Missionary Oblates, had made an arrangement to this effect with Ramazzotti. But this arrangement was never implemented. It was considered inadvisable that the mission seminary, which was seeking state recognition, should be affiliated with the Missionary Oblates of Rho, who had been refused state recognition.[33]

In arranging the mission institute's course of studies Marinoni sought advice from others, including Supriès, who had worked in the East Indies from 1829 to 1838.[34] "If I were to know" that the members "are to be assigned to Oceania," Supriès told Marinoni on 18 November 1850, "my advice would be for them to study the Malay language, since it is a universal language. On all those shores one can easily find at least some individuals who speak it. By having a knowledge of this language they could then make use of interpreters right from the start, which would be a very great advantage for them." In Paris one can easily obtain a grammar and a dictionary and so learn the language "without a teacher because, like the Italian language, it is pronounced in the same way in which it is written. Printed books also have the same kind of characters as your other books have."

30. Ibid., pp. 116, 121.

31. Ibid., 117, 119–20.

32. Candidate Ripamonti informed Taglioretti of these two accusations on 7 October 1850. See ibid., 106.

33. Tragella, *Missioni estere*, 1:33; Brambilla, *Pontificio istituto*, 1:22f; Suigo, *Pio IX*, 56f, 59, 113f. Suigo, in *Pio IX*, 59, describes Saison's proposal, but on 106 and 113 he incorrectly attributes this proposal to Supriès.

34. For details on the missions in which Supriès worked, see Wiltgen, *Oceania*, 273–75.

Supriès felt that it would also be advantageous for the young priests "to learn something about astronomy" and, if possible, to make a thorough study of geography. "I might add that some branches of natural history could prove useful for them as well, or at least serve as a pleasant recreation, like minerology, ornithology, a knowledge of shells, etc., etc." He also mentioned "the art of embalming birds, which are very beautiful in certain parts of Asia and excite great curiosity in Europe." And he urged Marinoni, as he had previously urged Taglioretti, "to engage in a bit of correspondence" with Cardinal Prefect Fransoni, "letting him know what you are doing at Saronno and what hopes you have for the future."[35]

During November letters arrived from church authorities in Ceylon requesting missionaries from the newly founded seminary. The candidates discussed the matter, but Micronesia remained their unanimous choice as a mission field. And since the meeting of the bishops of Lombardy was to take place in late November, Marinoni and the five candidates drew up a list of petitions on 26 November 1850 for consideration by the bishops.

They asked the bishops (1) to found the mission seminary formally, (2) to obtain confirmation from Propaganda for Marinoni's appointment as director, (3) to urge Propaganda to designate a specific mission field and preferably the archipelagoes of Micronesia, (4) to request Propaganda to recommend that the seminary receive a grant from the Paris and Lyon Central Councils of the Association for the Propagation of the Faith, (5) to determine whether Milan was a better location for the seminary than Saronno, and finally (6) to recognize the missionary candidates as remaining juridically and forever incardinated in their own dioceses.

The conference began as scheduled on Wednesday morning, 27 November 1850, and on the following day the six petitions were read, discussed, and voted upon. Archbishop Romilli and Bishop Ramazzotti were delegated to decide whether or not the seminary should be transferred to Milan, something that actually took place in June of the following year. The five other points were all adopted, except the designation of Micronesia as the mission field; this was made dependent upon Rome's decision in the matter. Being the one best informed about the new seminary, Ramazzotti was delegated to draw up the necessary documentation in the name of all.

Then on 30 November, the fourth day of the conference, he read out "the Act of Foundation of the College for the Foreign Missions, that has been erected in the name and with the consent of all the Bishops of Lombardy." He also read out the text of his letter addressed to Cardinal Prefect Fransoni of Propaganda containing the various requests voted upon two days earlier. All the bishops attending the meeting signed the Act of Foundation on Sunday, 1 December 1850, the closing day.

Bishop Carlo Gritti Morlacchi of Bergamo, giving ill health as his reason, did not attend the conference and did not sign the Act of Foundation. He did not believe in regional conferences of bishops, a modern idea for Italy at that time, and he also was not in favor of

---

35. PIME: AME 28:158.

a regional seminary. There was too little certainty that such a vast project could succeed, he said. However, he altered his position sixteen months later and gave the seminary his support.[36]

Ramazzotti wrote to Fransoni on 5 December: "In the name of the Archbishop of Milan and my fellow Bishops of the Province of Lombardy, I have the pleasure of presenting to Your Eminence the Act of Foundation of the Seminary for Foreign Missions. . . ." He devoted the largest amount of space—an entire page—to giving reasons that it was necessary for Rome to designate a specific mission field without delay.

"Since foreign mission fields are immense," he explained, "and since their climates, customs, languages, prejudices, errors and stages of culture, as well as the characteristics and inclinations of the peoples to be evangelized are all so diverse, it is necessary to select a specific mission in good time. Then preparatory studies can be better organized, useful advance correspondence can be initiated, and more suitable reading material can be procured. We therefore request Your Most Reverend Eminence kindly to indicate for us where you would consider it more opportune for our missionaries to carry the light of the holy gospel."

As Ramazzotti continued, he echoed the words of Supriès and the wishes of the five priest candidates: "If in this matter it is permitted to express the wish of the students already enrolled in the new seminary," and of others wanting to join, "they would like to have some virgin territory, a people that has not yet heard the name of Christ. As the Apostle [St. Paul] says: *My constant ambition has been to preach the gospel where the name of Christ was previously unknown* (Romans 15). Our candidates would like to found a mission all their own, so that they could have greater attachment to it and could more easily enkindle love for it among all their countrymen.

"Their compassion has been singularly aroused by the unfortunate state of those peoples who until now have not been reached by . . . the gospel because they live in most remote lands. The idea of discomforts, dangers and the worst possible difficulties that must be overcome in order to realize their goal, instead of making the candidates fearful, makes them courageous and enkindles within them to the highest pitch the fires of charity. The Archipelagoes of Micronesia, to which the venerable Congregation of Marists has not been able to dedicate itself except in part, is a very vast field for new missions and would be the land which the said students would like to water with their sweat and also—should need be—with their blood. . . ."

Since Archbishop Romilli and the other bishops wanted to obtain as speedy a reaction from Rome as possible, they decided to have director Marinoni personally present their letter to Fransoni. The cardinal could thus become better acquainted with Marinoni and at the same time could receive from him a firsthand report on the seminary. It was 6 December 1850 when Marinoni left Saronno for Rome.[37]

36. PIME: AME 35-01 Scurati, *Memorie dell'Istituto*, 457; Suigo, *Pio IX*, 121–25.

37. See PF: CV vol. 43, f. 157r–158v, Ramazzotti to Fransoni, 5 December 1850. Ramazzotti's sentence on

While Marinoni was en route to Rome, Propaganda Fide was trying to locate missionaries for the Vicariate Apostolic of Colombo in Ceylon. Its Italian vicar apostolic, Gaetano Antonio Mulsuce, had written to Rome urgently requesting "some European missionaries," and his only condition was that they be "Italians or at least Italian-born." He wanted four and hoped that they could be at their posts by June of 1851.[38] At this time Prior Saison of the Carthusian Monastery of Pavia happened to be in Rome on business. Knowing of his close association with the new mission seminary in Lombardy, Cardinal Fransoni asked whether that seminary could immediately send mature personnel to the Colombo vicariate. Saison quickly forwarded this news to Saronno on 9 December.

About this time Archbishop Romilli received an urgent letter from Bishop Giuseppe Maria Bravi (1813–60) of the Order of Saint Benedict (O.S.B.), the Italian coadjutor bishop of the Colombo vicariate. Bravi said that the vicariate would surely collapse if it did not receive additional personnel immediately. Taglioretti had been given some authority over the Saronno seminary in the absence of director Marinoni. Confronted now with Cardinal Fransoni's and Bishop Bravi's requests, he decided to convoke a meeting of the student body to discuss this new and pressing matter. He went to Saronno on 2 January 1851, held the meeting, and on 4 January sent the results to Marinoni in Rome.

Taglioretti assured Marinoni that the young priests were ready to go wherever Roman authorities might wish to send them. However, they did consider receiving Micronesia as something vital, something absolutely indispensable for the life and growth of their institute. And if the decision was up to them, they could in no way give up the idea of going to Micronesia. An eventual assignment to Ceylon would be only temporary, they hoped, a kind of preparation for their taking up missionary work in Micronesia.

The choice of the students had been most explicit in their "Petition" to the bishops of 26 November. Taglioretti reminded Marinoni that they had asked for Micronesia alone and that the bishops of Lombardy had supported this choice unanimously. Micronesia was the mission always intended by Father Supriès, he added. And it was likewise the choice of Father Pietro Tacconi, who as confessor and spiritual director at the Milan major seminary was "well informed of the secret wishes of those aspirants already admitted and of those still to be admitted."

After giving these arguments in favor of Micronesia, Taglioretti urged Marinoni to inquire in Rome whether the Colombo vicariate needed missionaries who were mature. If so, this would exclude the Lombardy candidates from further consideration, because the Saronno seminary had been founded only recently, he said.

Candidate Salerio had earlier prepared a nine-page memorandum entitled, "Whether Ceylon is suitable as a field of activity for the missionaries of the new Lombard seminary."

---

sweat and blood is taken almost verbatim from Supriès's letter of 25 July 1850 to Taglioretti. See n. 17.

38. See PF: LDB vol. 339 (1850), f. 997v, Barnabò to de Mazenod, 15 November 1850. Bishop de Mazenod, founder and head of the Oblates of Mary Immaculate, was also invited to provide the desired personnel. Details concerning the request from Ceylon were obtained from this letter.

Taglioretti had therefore invited Father Salerio to read this report at the 2 January meeting and had urged the student body to discuss it. After ruling out Ceylon as a suitable mission, Salerio gave numerous reasons that Micronesia or some other part of Oceania ought to be the mission field of the Lombard mission seminary. The candidates "had all agreed that the memorandum expressed the sentiments shared by each one," Taglioretti told Marinoni. He also enclosed a copy of the memorandum in his letter and urged Marinoni to read it "slowly and thoughtfully."[39]

On the opening page of his report Salerio said that if anyone examined the origins of the new Lombard seminary, he would find that it was Father Supriès, "the Venerable Vicar of the Certosa di Pavia," who had made "the first proposal for a Lombard mission." And "his proposal was Micronesia in Oceania." Fathers Cassinelli, Vistarini, and Mola, who very early had been in touch with Supriès, had been sent by Propaganda to Ceylon. But the reason for this was that no missionary organization had as yet been established for sending Lombard priests on a regular basis to a particular mission. And since Rome had sent the first three Lombard missionaries to Ceylon, where they were still working, church authorities in Ceylon learned from them that a mission seminary was being founded in Lombardy. Consequently the first request for missionaries had come to the Lombard seminary authorities from Ceylon, Salerio said.

"It is true that Ceylon needs missionaries," he admitted. "But this is no less true of the Americas, China, Africa and Asia." Oceania, however, "is practically abandoned and Micronesia is abandoned. Therefore the needs of Oceania and Micronesia are much more serious." We want to go there, he said, precisely because they are so far away, because they are so abandoned, because their "cry" reaches no one else.

Giving statistics from Adriano Balbi's *Compendio di geografia*, which was widely read at that time in both France and Italy, Salerio said that Ceylon had 830,000 inhabitants, whereas Oceania had over 20 million. The gospel had reached Ceylon three centuries earlier, and its people were being served by over thirty missionaries in two vicariates apostolic. The 20 million Oceanians, however, were being served by only three vicariates apostolic.

After presenting numerous arguments to show that Micronesia and Oceania each had greater needs than Ceylon, Salerio asked: Since our own bishops have manifested their approval, may we not hope that our superiors in Rome will also approve and will send us the good news that "the evangelization and regeneration of Oceania, at least in part, is being entrusted to us.... This we hope for, this we desire, this we request."[40]

The wishes of the candidates were unexpectedly fulfilled even before the reports of Taglioretti and Salerio were mailed to Rome. Marinoni wrote from Rome on 3 January

---

39. PIME: AME 4:337–544, Taglioretti to Marinoni, 4 January 1851; Suigo, *Pio IX*, 92, 135f; *Beatificationis Positio*, 74.

40. PIME: AME 4:338, Taglioretti to Marinoni, 4 January 1851; PIME: AME 11:1383–91, passim, Carlo Salerio's Memorandum on Ceylon. Balbi's figure of 20 million inhabitants was far from correct, as later statistics showed. For details on Balbi's works, see Wiltgen, *Oceania*, 281, 350, 568 n. 4.

1851 that Propaganda had promised to entrust to the Lombardy mission college not only Micronesia, but also Melanesia. Taglioretti replied to Marinoni on 17 January saying, "The students are overjoyed at seeing their hopes confirmed by your latest letter."[41] They had received the two missions because no one else could be found who wanted them.

Cardinal Prefect Fransoni wrote his long-awaited official letter to Archbishop Romilli and the rest of the bishops of Lombardy on 16 January 1851. "I would like to assure Your Excellencies" that the wishes of those in your mission college "will be completely fulfilled. In fact, circumstances at the present time make it possible to designate at this moment already, and for them exclusively, the desired and vast Missions of Melanesia and Micronesia. For lack of personnel the Marists of Lyon are asking to be exonerated of them. Therefore as soon as your seminary is able to furnish a small group of tried and tested priests, they will be sent quickly to the coveted regions mentioned. And in addition to these, there will always be available for the zeal of these same students other vast regions that have been lying abandoned up to now. No matter how large the number of sacred ministers that the seminary is able to supply, there will never be lacking a field to be cultivated by them."

Fransoni also assured the bishops of Lombardy that their choice of Marinoni as seminary director had received "the full approbation" of Propaganda. But for the future, after the seminary was well established and had many years of missionary experience, he asked the bishops to make it a norm to choose the spiritual directors and other directors from among the alumni of the seminary. The bishops were to recall from the missions for these offices "some of the older and more meritorious members who will have distinguished themselves" in the performance "of their sacred duties" in the missions.

As for receiving funds from the Association for the Propagation of the Faith in France, Fransoni said that Pius IX himself had intervened. Eager to give proof of his fatherly interest in the new seminary, the pope had ordered Propaganda to write in his own name and without delay to the nuncio apostolic in Paris. This official was instructed "to take action in the most efficacious way with the two Central Councils" of this fund-collecting agency, "in order to obtain at least for some years a regular and copious subsidy for the nascent seminary of Saronno."

Nor would Archbishop Romilli have trouble imagining, Fransoni said, "the satisfaction and pleasure which the Holy Father ... experienced on learning that such a pious and useful foundation has already been launched, one which he had so ardently wished to see realized ..." Romilli was asked to convey to the other prelates "the benevolent affection and pleasure of the Holy Father" and "to urge them to promote ever more the holy work that has been started ..." Fransoni concluded his letter by assuring Archbishop Romilli "and all your respectable colleagues of my deep concern and my readiness to cooperate in every way that is possible for me ..."[42]

---

41. Suigo, *Pio IX*, 136; *Beatificationis Positio*, 74.
42. PF: LDB vol. 340 (1851), f. 40v–42r.

This lengthy letter for Archbishop Romilli of Milan was enclosed in a letter of the same date for Bishop Ramazzotti. Fransoni said that he considered it proper to address his formal reply to the archbishop of Milan, but nevertheless he wanted Bishop Ramazzotti to know its contents. "And so I am sending it to you with the request that after reading it, you have it sealed and give it to the prelate. . . ."[43]

Director Marinoni after completing his work in Rome returned to Saronno. En route he stopped off at Pavia to deliver to Ramazzotti the two letters from Fransoni and to give a report on his successful mission.[44]

Why did the seminary in Lombardy receive both Micronesia and Melanesia, when it had requested only Micronesia? When Micronesia became a vicariate apostolic on 16 July 1844, it was made part of a double vicariate containing both Micronesia and Melanesia. A peculiar political circumstance had prompted Rome provisionally to unite the two vicariates under one vicar apostolic. Superior General Colin of the Marists accepted this arrangement in 1844 with the understanding that he would soon be relieved of responsibility for Micronesia.[45]

By 1850, however, Colin was insisting that he be relieved of responsibility for Melanesia as well.[46] Unaware that the two vicariates had been reduced to the status of missions, the missionaries from Lombardy believed that Rome was offering them two vicariates.

But what about the young and inexperienced missionaries from Saronno? Could they succeed where the Marists had failed? Did they not realize that Melanesia was one of the most difficult missions in the world? The odds against any lasting success were astronomically high, even for seasoned missionaries. Rome knew well that the task was difficult, but offered it to Lombardy's fledgling mission seminary nevertheless, intending to take all necessary precautions. The candidates and the bishops of Lombardy accepted the mission with joy, and Father Supriès rejoiced with them. His dream of 1843 was fast becoming a reality and soon Micronesia would be abandoned no longer. So he thought.

43. Ibid., f. 40rv.
44. See PF: CV vol. 43, f. 165r, Ramazzotti to Fransoni, 13 February 1851.
45. See n. 18.
46. Wiltgen, *Oceania*, 531.

5

Pope Pius IX Suggests Training in a Nearby Mission
21 August 1851

DEATH OFTEN VISITED THE VICARIATE APOSTOLIC OF MELANESIA. WITHIN THE FIRST three years it claimed two Marist bishops and four Marist priests. This reduced the staff of the vicariate to two priests and one brother at Woodlark (or Murua) and to one priest and one brother at Rooke (or Umboi), two islands in eastern and northeastern Papua New Guinea, respectively. In an effort to recoup their strength and reconsider their strategy, the survivors at Rooke temporarily abandoned that island on 17 May 1849 and went to Our Lady of Seven Sorrows Mission at Guasopa Harbor in Woodlark. Here they found two newly arrived Marist priests, thirty-six-year-old Pierre Trapenard and twenty-nine-year-old Eugène-Joseph Ducrettet, bringing their number to five priests and two brothers.[1]

But by June 1851 the "young and impressionable" Ducrettet, a Savoyard, was back in France. His missionary work had not lasted two full years, and now he told Superior General Colin that he wanted nothing more to do with Melanesia. The discontent and friction among the Woodlark missionaries had caused him to leave, he said. Thirty-year-old Brother Optat Bergillon, a gardener by trade, had left Woodlark with Ducrettet; in Sydney he had boarded a ship en route to the Americas, where he intended to remain. The departure of these two missionaries reduced the Marist staff in Melanesia once again to five (four priests and one brother), and all five were at Woodlark.[2]

One of the many letters that Ducrettet brought along for Colin was from Father Pierre-Jean Frémont in Woodlark, the acting provincial superior. Writing on 7 September 1850 he said that there was not yet any noticeable tendency toward Christianity at Guasopa where the Marists had their principal foundation. A second mission station had been opened in 1849 farther north at Uaman (or Waman) in the center of Woodlark by Fathers Joseph Thomassin and Pierre Trapenard, but it had to be closed in August 1850. Food supplies

---

1. For details on the closure of the Rooke Mission, see Wiltgen, *Oceania*, 484–86.

2. SM: Epistolae Variae Generalium, 1:43–45, no. 79, Colin to the Woodlark missionaries, 23 June 1851; SM: OMM/208, Frémont to Rocher, 24 June 1849.

could be brought there only with great difficulty, and the few people living there were not well disposed toward the mission. But at Guasopa there was sufficient food, clothing, and shelter for all five missionaries, Frémont said. Nevertheless all wanted to receive explicit orders from Colin on whether they were to remain at Woodlark or leave.

Brother Optat "told me some time ago that he does not want to be a religious any longer," Frémont added, "and he wanted me by all means to free him from his vows." He also "threatened to go native and probably would have done so, except for Brother Gennade's surveillance." The year had been quite peaceful, however, "except for some tests which the good God permitted, no doubt for our greater good."[3]

"You desire a formal decision from us on whether you should remain at Woodlark or leave," Colin wrote back to his missionaries on 23 June 1851. "This is a delicate question and can be a matter of conscience, since the decision concerns the eternal destiny of these people. I can do nothing but leave you free. Since you are on the spot, you can decide better than anyone else what is fitting for you to do." If they were forced to leave Woodlark, he said, they could join the Marists in New Caledonia or those in Central Oceania. He reminded them also that "Ponape or Ascension Island in Micronesia has been asking for missionaries for a long time."

Colin wanted his missionaries to divide their time between study and prayer, "but do not neglect prayer." They were to pray, "and pray without ceasing," for the conversion of these people. "Man and his knowledge are of no avail in converting anyone," he said. "Grace and conversion are the fruit of prayer. . . ."

The heavy losses of personnel in Melanesia, Colin added, had obliged him to inform Rome that the Society of Mary "could henceforth provide no more priests for the Vicariates of Melanesia and Micronesia." Consequently Propaganda Fide "recently entrusted these two vicariates to Italian priests. When they shall leave [Europe], or where they shall settle, I do not know. This measure, however, is completely to your advantage and will not derogate from the title of prefect apostolic sent to you by Rome and which undoubtedly you will have received by the time this letter arrives. If you do become established somewhere, our society will be able to support you."[4]

Meanwhile Bishop Luquet in Rome had sent a warning note to Bishop Ramazzotti in Pavia. Speaking from his own "practical knowledge of missionary work," he said that a mission "in Micronesia and Melanesia will not produce . . . abundant fruit. It will also cost much more in money and missionaries than would be the case if the very beautiful mission offered in Ceylon had been accepted." Ramazzotti's priests after reaching Ceylon could branch out to "the center of Buddhism" in central Ceylon and also to the Maldives and the Seychelles, two archipelagoes which had no priests. A mission in Ceylon would also provide a steppingstone to additional missions overseas, he said. Correspondence

---

3. SM: OMM/208. Brother Gennade in civilian life was Jean-Pierre Rolland (1817–98). Bishop Collomb spelled his name "Genade." See Wiltgen, *Oceania*, 478. On Frémont's Christian names, see chap. 6, n. 2.

4. SM: Epistolae Variae Generalium, 1:43–45, no. 79.

could be sent via Ceylon and Singapore to Australia, for example, "where Aborigines in the interior have not yet been evangelized." In the case of Ramazzotti's seminary which was "just beginning," these advantages ought to be given particular consideration, especially if one realizes "how many losses there will otherwise be in Missionaries, in effort, in money, in everything . . ." All too frequently, he warned, losses like this serve no purpose.[5]

Alarmed by Luquet's remarks and wondering whether Micronesia and Melanesia should be accepted after all, Ramazzotti sent the letter to Father Supriès for his comments. The Carthusian's reply was immediate and unequivocal. "I would have no inclination to send them to Ceylon where so many different missionaries are found mixed together." By no means should Ramazzotti "renounce taking up work in Micronesia," he said. Nor should the Lombardy missionaries be trained in some other mission, but rather in Micronesia itself.

Eager that Micronesia should remain Ramazzotti's choice, Supriès volunteered to order for him from Paris one of the volumes of *Univers pittoresque*. This work of sixty-seven volumes contained a "history and description of all peoples, of their religions, morals, customs, etc." Its last three volumes with 310 plates treated Oceania and sold for eighteen francs [sic]. One of them contained an extensive report on the Caroline Islands, which according to Supriès "constitute Micronesia properly so-called." The description of its peoples showed clearly "what good and excellent dispositions they have for becoming Christians," Supriès said. And he found the report so well written and so convincing that it would surely move the bishop to tears. "I can assure you that they are the peoples most worthy of receiving the gift of faith." He said it would be "a misfortune if the Protestants should arrive there before us!"

On the day before writing this letter, Supriès had received a visit from Cavalier Giovanni Vimercati, who earlier had promised to assist the Lombardy seminary with a legacy from Count Mellerio. Vimercati had won his case in court and was now ready to bestow the legacy. But was the seminary starting out on the right foot? Since its purpose was to train foreign missionaries, he said, "the good success of the new seminary" required that it be entrusted "to persons with experience both in conducting missionary work" and in forming and inspiring missionary candidates. Vimercati and Supriès had both discussed this matter "with lively interest for at least a solid hour-and-a-half." In the end both were convinced that the only solution was "to affiliate this nascent Lombard congregation with some other congregation," one whose merits "are already universally recognized and which is still in its first fervor."

After explaining all of this in his letter to Ramazzotti, Supriès by way of example suggested affiliation with "the Marists of Lyon in France. They have three vicariates apostolic

---

5. Luquet to Ramazzotti, 24 January 1851, in Brambilla, *Pontificio istituto*, 1:102f. The original of this letter was not found by PIME archivist Father Francesco Frumento. Luquet had received firsthand information on Australian Aborigines from Father John Brady, vicar general of Archbishop Polding of Sydney, in Rome in February 1845. See Wiltgen, *Oceania*, 370–71, 374.

and very flourishing missions in Central Oceania and Melanesia and they do so much good in France" in favor of religion. "They would be most pleased to make a foundation in Italy and particularly in Milan," he said, "something that they had stated several years ago to certain clerics from Milan who went to visit them in Lyon." Their coming would also be "an enrichment for Lombardy," since foreign missionary work was not their only type of work. And because Supriès knew personally "the Superior General, the Reverend Colin, who is the founder himself," he volunteered to write in Ramazzotti's name and get things moving, "if no obstacle stands in the way."[6]

But Ramazzotti did not invite Supriès to begin negotiations with the Marists. Nor did he ask Cardinal Fransoni to take back Micronesia and Melanesia and give his seminary the Ceylon Mission.

As is clear from this letter and many others of Supriès, he recommended consistently that the Lombardy missionaries should do missionary work in Micronesia. He never showered praise on Melanesians, nor did he advocate that Lombardy's missionaries should go to work among them, as some historians maintain.[7]

Seven weeks passed without Supriès receiving any further word from Ramazzotti. He therefore asked director Marinoni on 9 April 1851 whether the first missionaries would be sent to Oceania or to Ceylon. "Is it true that they must go to Rome? And when?"[8]

Marinoni visited Supriès, gave him the latest news, and left behind a sheaf of documentation for him to read. Included was the seminary's book of rules. Later Supriès told Marinoni that he had read the rules "with indescribable pleasure" and had found them to be "full of exquisite prudence and charity." They also manifested "a great knowledge of the human heart" and "experience in mission affairs."[9]

---

6. PIME: AME, 28:159–62, Supriès to Ramazzotti, 16 February 1851. Federico Salvioni was one of the Milan clerics who went to Lyon. And Father Pierre-Julien Eymard, provincial superior of the Marists in France, was eager for his society to be founded in Italy. See chap. 1.

Supriès errs, however, in saying that the Marists had "three vicariates apostolic." At this time they were still responsible for six vicariates: Western Oceania (1836), Central Oceania (1842), Melanesia (1844), Micronesia (1844), New Caledonia (1847), and the Navigators Archipelago (1850). See Wiltgen, *Oceania*, chaps. 6, 14, 17, 27, and 34.

Univers pittoresque was the cover title of the work. The actual title was, *L'Univers; histoire et description de tous les peuples, de leurs religions, moeurs, coutumes, etc.* It contained *Océanie o cinquième partie du monde; revue géographique et ethnographique de la Malaisie, ecc., ecc.* [sic], par G. L. Domeny de Rienzi. Thanks to Father James Artzer, S.V.D., for locating this title and many other bits of bibliographic information.

7. Brambilla is such a historian. Since the Lombardy missionaries decided to work in Melanesia, where they met with disaster, he says of Supriès: "The facts have unfortunately shown how much he was deceived!" But Supriès never praised the Melanesians, nor did he ever advocate Melanesia as a mission. Also in this letter he speaks of "Micronesians." Brambilla misquotes him as saying that he highly praised "his beloved Oceanians," which includes Melanesians. Compare Brambilla's extracts in *Pontificio istituto*, 1:105, with the original letter in PIME: AME, 28:159-62, Supriès to Ramazzotti, 16 February 1851.

8. PIME: AME 28:163.

9. Ibid., 165, Supriès to Marinoni. This letter was not dated by Supriès. Someone has added in pencil the date 3 May 1851, which is the date given to the letter by Brambilla, *Pontificio istituto*, 1:69. A copy of the rule

Cardinal Prefect Fransoni as early as 11 January 1851 had given special instructions to the nuncio apostolic in Paris, Archbishop Pietro Antonio Garibaldi (1797–1853), on behalf of Lombardy's mission seminary. This was five days before he informed Archbishop Romilli that the "Missions of Melanesia and Micronesia" were being designated exclusively for that seminary. Pope Pius IX and Propaganda Fide, Fransoni told the Nuncio, "wish to foster and promote the formation and foundation in Italy of some mission colleges for the Secular Clergy similar to those commendable organizations that have been founded in France." For some years at least, he said, the mission seminary in Lombardy would need "a large subsidy," since the bishops could not cover all the costs. But since Fransoni feared that "simply a letter or a recommendation" from himself to the Association for the Propagation of the Faith in France "would not produce the desired results," he asked the nuncio kindly to handle the matter with his usual "expertise and delicacy." The nuncio's success, Fransoni said, would prove "particularly satisfying for the Holy Father."

Nuncio Garibaldi on 7 June 1851 was able to inform Fransoni that the association's councils of Paris and Lyon had decided to give "the considerable sum of two thousand scudi" as their first contribution.[10] Archbishop Romilli of Milan thanked Fransoni for the donation and at the same time submitted a report on the seminary prepared by Marinoni.[11]

The report said that the seminary had meanwhile been transferred from Saronno to Milan according to the wishes of Archbishop Romilli and Bishop Ramazzotti. The archbishop had assigned the Blessed Virgin Mary Shrine of San Calocero in Milan to the seminary, causing authorities in Rome to refer to it as Collegio di San Calocero. The student body started with five priests, now numbered ten, and others were seeking admission. Students were obliged to study French, which they knew fairly well, and English. As for the languages of "the islands in Oceania to which they shall go," these "can best be learned on the spot," Marinoni said.

In moral theology the seminary was following the teachings of Saint Alphonsus Maria Liguori (1696–1787). For reviewing dogmatic theology the textbooks of Father Giovanni Perrone (1794–1876) were being used "in order to be safe." This Jesuit's nine-volume work, *Praelectiones theologiae dogmaticae*, had been published in Rome in 1835–42. It was universally praised for its clarity, conciseness, methodology, and use of patristic sources.[12]

Acknowledging the receipt of this progress report on 19 July 1851, Fransoni told Marinoni that he was now looking forward to the day which would bring him "the joyful

---

as presented to Rome in December 1850 (thirty-five pages plus a Table of Contents of two pages) is in PF: CV vol. 43, f. 126r–144r.

10. PF: LDB vol. 340 (1851), f. 26rv, Fransoni to Garibaldi, 11 January 1851; PF: CV vol. 43, f. 167r, Garibaldi to Fransoni, 7 June 1851.

11. PF: CV vol. 43, f. 173rv, Romilli to Fransoni, 8 July 1851.

12. Ibid., f. 174r–175r, Marinoni to Fransoni, 8 July 1851; Celestino Testore, "Perrone, Giovanni," in *Enciclopedia Cattolica*, vol. 9, col. 1197–98. The San Calocero Shrine was assigned to the seminary on 26 April 1851 and the transfer from Saronno to Milan took place in June. See Suigo, *Pio IX*, 122 n. 38. The shrine and adjoining seminary were destroyed by bombs during World War II.

news" that the first missionaries "have completed their training." They could then "be sent off" like "a team of chosen agriculturists to reap the abundant harvest assigned to them."[13]

When Marinoni discussed Fransoni's letter with Romilli and Ramazzotti, they decided that the time had come to offer Rome "at least" six priests. Marinoni informed Fransoni of this on 29 July 1851, the day on which the seminary's first class completed one full year of preparation for missionary work. "Wise and very pious persons," he said, had advised him to wait no longer before sending the first missionaries "to the designated islands of Micronesia." The six priests "are young men and are new in this arduous missionary career." But he hoped that their solid and unadulterated piety, their zeal for the salvation of souls and their other qualities, "will supply what is missing in age."

Fathers Reina and Salerio were being sent to Rome immediately to manifest the respect and submission of all, Marinoni said. They were "ready to sail with four companions to Oceania whenever it should please Your Eminence." That same day, 29 July 1851, Marinoni petitioned Secretary Barnabò to obtain an audience for Reina and Salerio with Pope Pius IX. The two priests then left for Rome.[14]

Meanwhile through Giovanni Maria Alfieri, an Italian priest friend in Lyon, Marinoni had requested information from the Marists on Melanesia and Micronesia.[15] The provincial superior in Lyon sent Marinoni two letters with information, and then Superior General Colin himself on 30 July 1851 answered five specific questions as follows:

1. If they wished to begin their missionary work in Melanesia, they could go "via Batavia" to the Malaquel (?) Coast in the Gilolo Strait, or "via Sydney" to the Solomon Islands. To enter Micronesia they would have to go "via Valparaíso." But in all three ports it would be necessary to charter a ship to take them to where they wanted to go in Melanesia or Micronesia.

2. "In the numerous islands of Melanesia and in Oceania in general, the inhabitants are ordinarily almost nude. It is therefore essential for you to take along a complete wardrobe and all other items that you might need. Locally you will find nothing but yams, taros, etc. From Europe we have regularly sent what our missionaries need for religious worship and also their clothing, since it costs us less [in France] than in Sydney."

3. Not having "sufficient knowledge of the places," Colin could not give advice on where to go to accomplish the greatest good. "Ponape or Ascension Island in Micronesia asked for Catholic missionaries long ago," he said. "Perhaps this island

---

13. PIME: AME 1:35–36.

14. PF: SC Oceania vol. 4 (1848–52), f. 644r-646r. Since Reina and Salerio carried to Rome these two letters of 29 July, they must have left Milan near the end of July, not "about the middle of July 1851," as Suigo says in *Pio IX*, 136.

15. Father Giovanni Maria Alfieri was a member of the Hospitaller Order of Saint John of God (O.H.), known in Italy as Fate Bene Fratelli (F.B.F.).

would offer more security to your missionaries than many others. We have regretted for a long time that Bishop Epalle did not begin work on the Coast of Gilolo in 1844 or 1845.¹⁶ Recently our missionaries at Woodlark in Melanesia wrote that they have not yet been able to achieve anything. The people there have avoided them and do not want to hear them talk about religion. I do not know whether they will be able to become established there and do some good as time goes on."

4. "Two bishops had been named Vicars Apostolic of Melanesia and Micronesia by the Holy See. But they hardly arrived in these islands when one was massacred with some of his missionaries and the other died there as a result of exhaustion and sickness."¹⁷

5. As for transportation from Europe, ships enough could be found "sailing from the ports of France and above all from the ports of England to Valparaíso, Sydney or Batavia." But it would be advisable for one of the Milan missionaries "to make a trip to Paris and London to obtain the appropriate information." Colin did not know whether ships sailed from the Italian port of Genoa to ports in the Southern Hemisphere. "Transportation costs from Le Havre or from London to Sydney could amount to 1,500 or 2,000 francs per person." However, it would be difficult to say how much money the missionaries should take along, "because it all depends upon the place where you will be going." Colin warned that "sometimes it may take many years to communicate with Europe."¹⁸

While Colin's letter was en route to Marinoni in Milan, Reina and Salerio were en route to Rome. On arriving there in early August the two priests were received by Cardinal Prefect Fransoni and Secretary Barnabò, but they were given no immediate orders regarding Oceania. In fact, Reina was called into a meeting on China and was asked in the presence of both Fransoni and Barnabò whether he was ready to go to Hong Kong. He answered that he would go wherever Propaganda wanted to send him. Then on 21 August he and Salerio were granted a private audience with Pope Pius IX, who made them feel right at home. For

---

16. Colin is confused here and surely meant to say "on the Coast of Waigeo in 1845." Bishop Epalle sailed from London only on 2 February 1845 and so could not have made a foundation in Oceania "in 1844." Gilolo (now Halmahera) was one of the Moluccas or Spice Islands. Although Bishop Epalle on 2 January 1845 had said that Gilolo was at the northwestern boundary of his Vicariate Apostolic of Melanesia, this vast island was listed neither by him nor by Cardinal Fransoni as one of the islands within his vicariate founded on 16 July 1844. Both he and the cardinal, however, did list Waigeo as one of the islands within his vicariate. Furthermore, when Epalle wrote to Colin from Sydney on 17 August 1845, he made special mention of Waigeo and described the advantages of founding his vicariate there. See Wiltgen, *Oceania*, 290, 302, 309, 330f.

17. For details on these two bishops, see "Collomb, Bishop Jean-Georges" and "Epalle, Bishop Jean-Baptiste," in ibid., 589, 592. Epalle was mortally wounded on 16 December 1845 and died three days later. Three of his missionaries were killed on 20 April 1847. Contrary to what Colin says, Epalle was not massacred "with" them. Collomb died on 16 July 1848. See ibid., 336–41, 474f, 484.

18. PIME: AME 28:717–19.

a good half hour the pope spoke leisurely with them about church affairs in Lombardy, in Oceania, in Greece, and about the controversial professor of philosophy, Father Antonio Rosmini Serbati (1797–1855), whom the pope and Salerio admired.

On hearing Pius IX express concern repeatedly over the lack of priests in Corfu (also Corcyra, now Kérkira), a Greek island with numerous Italian immigrants, Reina and Salerio wondered whether he wished them to go there instead of to Oceania. Corfu was hardly the foreign mission of their dreams, however, being no more than sixty miles from the heel of Italy. They were about to volunteer to go, when the pope dropped the matter, saying that he would discuss it with Propaganda on Sunday, 24 August, three days later. The two priests were left in suspense, wondering whether they would be sent to "poor Oceania" or now perhaps to Corfu.[19]

Unknown to Reina and Salerio, Fransoni and Barnabò at this time were occupied with reorganizing the New Caledonia, Samoa, and Central Oceania vicariates. This was necessary because Bishop Douarre wanted to be reassigned to the New Caledonia vicariate just one year after he had requested and received in its place the Samoa vicariate. It was 10 August 1851 when Pius IX sanctioned the reorganization proposed for these three vicariates. The corresponding decree was issued by Propaganda on 20 August.[20]

On the following day, 21 August, Reina and Salerio had their audience with the pope. Later that same day Cardinal Prefect Fransoni wrote at great length to Superior General Colin about Melanesia and Micronesia, reminding him of their recent correspondence. Sixteen months earlier, he said, Colin had pointed out that his Society of Mary was "not in a position to continue caring for the missions of Melanesia and Micronesia." Fransoni had then asked Colin to keep his personnel at their posts long enough to train new missionaries. Colin subsequently surprised Fransoni by saying that his few missionaries at Woodlark ought not be forced to leave, if newcomers should arrive. To this Fransoni agreed.

Colin had also requested that the Marist missionaries be allowed to choose one or two prefects apostolic for the two missions of Melanesia and Micronesia, saying that he would try to persuade some of the banished New Caledonia missionaries to go there. "I adhered with true pleasure to your request for designating the two prefects apostolic for the two missions," Fransoni said, "and I concurred fully in your wise observations. . . ." The cardinal was particularly pleased with Colin's proposals because they would make possible the training of new personnel and would contribute toward the "reestablishment or reactivation" of the Melanesia and Micronesia missions.

If Colin's priests should decide to continue working "in one of the two missions," something that would make Fransoni "very happy," they could choose Melanesia or

---

19. Suigo, *Pio IX*, 137–41. Here Suigo reproduces two letters, each dated 22 August 1851, one by Salerio to Tacconi, 137–39, and the other by Reina to Marinoni, pp. 140f. The letters describe their audience with the pope. For the part on Hong Kong see PIME: AME 11:300, Reina to Marinoni, 7 October 1856; PIME: AME 16:491, Reina to Barnabò, 13 March 1858.

20. See chap. 3, pp. 42–43.

Micronesia as their mission. Whichever they did not want, the cardinal said, would be given to the newcomers. A Marist prefect apostolic was to supervise the training of the new missionaries and was also to decide when they were experienced enough and numerous enough to take charge of a mission by themselves. Fransoni promised to inform Colin well in advance of their being placed in charge, so that those members of his society working in the territory to be entrusted to the new group "could freely transfer" to the mission chosen by the Marists.

At this point and without being specific Fransoni informed Colin that he had made many unsuccessful attempts to find missionaries.[21] But now "the Lord has deigned to offer me personnel through means of the recently founded Seminary for Foreign Missions in Milan," he said. He was aware that Colin had been in touch with this seminary (through Father Alfieri), and he told Colin that two of the five or six who would be going to Oceania were currently in Rome making arrangements for departing within a few months. "The Sacred Congregation has suggested to them that, before returning to Milan, they should go to Lyon—something that they themselves had intended to do—to confer with Your Reverence." Colin was to give them "all the instructions, counsel and information" that they might need to reach their destination, "since no one else is in a better position" to do so. And Colin was to be as interested in these new missionaries "as if they were your own alumni and members of your own society."

In a postscript Fransoni summarized a report that had been submitted to Propaganda Fide "many years ago." It told how "the Island of Ponape or Ascension" in Micronesia had requested from New Zealand some Catholic missionaries, "but who, it is believed, were never sent." If that island should still be as favorably disposed as it was previously, Fransoni said, "it would be advisable" to entrust that mission "to the new priests from the Milan seminary. They could begin missionary work there and from there branch out to other islands which form that immense archipelago."[22]

Fransoni's letter to Colin, which was meant to serve as a letter of introduction for Reina and Salerio, was given to them unsealed for their information and for delivery (after being sealed) to Colin in Lyon. They sent director Marinoni a copy for his information.

From Civitavecchia, the port of Rome, they sailed by steamer as far as Marseille on their way to Lyon. They were pleasantly surprised to find Thomas Grant (1816–70) aboard. Just a few weeks earlier on 27 June he had been named bishop of Southwark in Greater London and had received his episcopal ordination on 6 July. Since he had been a student at the Venerable English College in Rome, he could speak Italian with them. They would meet again in London one year later.

---

21. Fransoni had requested personnel in vain from the Barnabites, Picpus Fathers, and Oblates of Mary Immaculate. See Wiltgen, *Oceania*, 524–39.

22. PF: LDB vol. 340 (1851), f. 608v–610v, Fransoni to Colin, 21 August 1851. The report to which Fransoni refers in his postscript was drawn up by Father Epalle in Rome on 14 July 1843, and its contents were repeated almost verbatim by Epalle in a letter on 1 August 1843. See Wiltgen, *Oceania*, 276–77, 291. See also "James Hall," in Wiltgen, *Oceania*, 594.

In a letter to Marinoni of 22 August, Reina had described his audience with Pope Pius IX. Salerio had done the same for Father Tacconi, his former spiritual director in Milan. According to Reina, the pope had remarked that priests and missionaries were leaving "for distant countries, whereas we have need of missionaries at the portals of Italy." He was deeply concerned about the Diocese of Corfu in Greece, for example. This haven for Italian immigrants had become what the pope called "a poor abandoned Mission" in great need of priests.

Salerio, who had written the long paper on why Micronesia or some other Oceania mission was more suitable than Ceylon for their seminary, said that he had never felt so ready to make the supreme sacrifice of giving up the Oceania mission, as when he listened to the pope. "I was ready to obey without reserve, if he should issue a formal invitation" for us to go to Corfu, he said.

Reina also wanted to tell the pope: "Give the order, for we are ready. . . ." And he would have done so, he said, "if it had not been for the fact that I am a member of a congregation, and it is not up to one person alone to decide for a congregation." From Propaganda, Reina said, he would learn "the Will of God, that is, what God wishes from us . . . To tell the truth, we are ready for everything. Now it is up to them. . . ."[23]

Reina's letter about the pope indicating Corfu as a possible mission puzzled Marinoni so much that he mailed the letter to Father Taglioretti, a cofounder of the mission seminary, requesting his advice. Taglioretti replied on 29 August 1851, saying, "I see that the Holy Father wants to have our candidates for the little Mission of Corfu. Let us go there, then, with the blessing of God. . . . And what about Micronesia? I do not believe there is any reason to abandon it." Four or five priests going to Corfu "would not empty the seminary," he said. And besides they would be "those who are less able to face more difficult ventures." The others going to Oceania "could get some training at Corfu, even though it would not be proportionate" to the task awaiting them in Oceania. But that training would still be "more useful than what they are receiving in Milan."

Some days after receiving Taglioretti's reply, Marinoni was again perplexed, this time at seeing the "Brief" sent by Pius IX on 30 August 1851 to Archbishop Romilli of Milan. This was in reply to the archbishop's letter carried to Rome by Reina and Salerio. Marinoni then asked Bishop Ramazzotti to send him immediate instructions on what to do about his

---

23. On the papal audience, see n. 19 above. On the voyage, see Giuseppe Marinoni, P.I.M.E., *Scritti vari del defunto Mons. Giuseppe Marinoni*, 276. On Bishop Grant, see Remigius Ritzler, O.F.M. Conv., and Pirminus Sefrin, O.F.M. Conv., *Hierarchia Catholici Medii et Recentioris Aevi, vol. 8, 1846–1903*, 525. Colin told Fransoni that he had received the cardinal's 21 August 1851 letter from Reina and Salerio. See PF: SC Oceania vol. 4 (1848–52), f. 681r, Colin to Fransoni, 28 September 1851. Fransoni had given Reina and Salerio this 21 August 1851 letter unsealed for Colin. They had sent a copy to Marinoni, and he in turn had sent a copy to Ramazzotti. This is surely what happened, because Marinoni and also Ramazzotti's secretary Origo in separate letters refer to the contents of the cardinal's 21 August 1851 letter to Colin. Compare PF: LDB vol. 340 (1851), f. 608v–610v, Fransoni to Colin, 21 August 1851; PIME: AME 4:183f, Origo to Marinoni, 10 September 1851; SM: 436, Marinoni to Colin, 10 September 1851.

three enclosures: the pope's letter to Romilli, Fransoni's letter to Colin, and Reina's letter on the pope and Corfu.

By coincidence Supriès was at the bishop's office when the three letters arrived, and so Ramazzotti shared them with the Carthusian monk. Ramazzotti had his secretary, Father Spirito Origo, write back to Marinoni that same day, Wednesday, 10 September 1851, saying that he and Supriès were both "satisfied indeed" with the latest news about the seminary. And Supriès was "highly pleased" with Fransoni's letter to Colin, "principally because of the postscript" which referred to Ascension (or Ponape) Island "as the place where the new Institute ought to begin its work. Father Supriès believes, too, that this ought to be their first field of activity," Origo said, "and the bishop desires it as well."[24]

From this letter and that of Taglioretti it was clear to director Marinoni and to the candidates of his seminary that Fransoni, Ramazzotti, Taglioretti, and Supriès all favored Micronesia as the seminary's first mission in Oceania.

But what particularly disturbed Ramazzotti and Supriès was the "Brief" from Pope Pius IX to Archbishop Romilli. "We applaud . . . your efforts and those of the other bishops," the pope said, "in founding a Seminary or Congregation of priests" to bring "the beautiful light of the holy Gospel" to far-off lands. The services of those trained at the seminary would prove advantageous, he said, "also for those regions not so far away from our own, for whose needs it is very important to provide relief and assistance."[25] With those final words it seemed like the pope was saying that he wanted the Milan missionaries to go to Corfu or to some other nearby mission in addition to Oceania.

"It would be well to answer the Pope along the lines of the Brief," Ramazzotti replied. Thank him for approving the foundation of the seminary, "and at the same time declare to him that the Institute is also ready to evangelize whatever places His Holiness might wish." Ramazzotti and Supriès were in agreement that an easier mission, like Corfu, "could prove opportune for those members of the Institute" who might be unsuited for more remote missions. As Supriès pointed out, "Ordinarily someone over thirty years of age is no longer suitable for those Missions where it is necessary to learn languages."

Secretary Origo's letter containing Ramazzotti's instructions of 10 September 1851 reached Marinoni that same day. But he did not write to Rome at once, nor did he write directly to the pope.[26] He had asked for immediate instructions from Ramazzotti because

---

24. PIME: AME 4:417, Taglioretti to Marinoni, 29 August 1851; PIME: AME 4:183f, Origo to Marinoni. Origo mistakenly dated his letter 10 August 1851. August cannot be correct because the letter comments on Fransoni's letter to Colin dated 21 August 1851 and also on the brief of Pius IX dated 30 August 1851. The correct date is 10 September 1851, as indicated by the postmark on the envelope: "10.9.51. Pavia." In Europe the sequence of dates is day, month, and year.

25. Suigo, *Pio IX*, 142f. Romilli's letter was dated 28 July 1851. See Suigo, *Pio IX*, 142.

26. PIME: AME 4:183f, Origo to Marinoni, 10 September 1851. Reacting to Ramazzotti's instructions, Marinoni wrote to Fransoni on 4 November 1851. See PF: SC Oceania vol. 4 (1848–52), f. 689rv. Brambilla knew that Marinoni wrote to Fransoni, but he could not locate the letter. See Brambilla, *Pontificio istituto*, 1:127.

he wanted to rush off a letter to Colin, hoping that it would reach Lyon before Reina and Salerio had left. That same day, 10 September, he wrote to Colin. Since it was now clear that Fransoni, Colin, Ramazzotti, and Supriès all agreed that Ponape in Micronesia was the place for his first group of missionaries to start, Marinoni no longer doubted. "We ourselves want it," he told Colin, "since it is located very close to Ualan Island [now Kusaie] and to many other islands, which seem to offer numerous possibilities for obtaining the abundant harvest which we desire."

Regarding "the time and the conditions of apprenticeship" for Milan missionaries serving under the Marists, Marinoni urged Colin "to determine these matters in advance in such a way as to prevent every possible dissension from arising between our two congregations . . . , which have to work side by side for the same purpose." He asked Colin to indicate for Reina and Salerio the best time and place for their departure and to give them "all the information, counsel and instructions" that he judged conducive to a better organization of the seminary at Milan and its mission in Oceania. In return for these services Colin would "have a right to the gratitude" of the Milan missionaries "in perpetuity."[27]

Mid-September was a most inopportune time for Reina and Salerio to visit the Marist headquarters in Lyon. Every year the Marists gathered there in large numbers for their annual retreat, which lasted a week and always began on 12 September. This was the feast of the Most Holy Name of the Blessed Virgin Mary, patroness of the Society of Mary. Writing back to Marinoni on 27 September, Colin said that he had had "the honor of seeing and entertaining" the two priests. But he regretted not having been able to offer them hospitality because of the annual Marist retreat, "which obliged more than thirty of our Fathers to take their lodging outside the house."

Colin assured Marinoni, however, that "there is no reason to fear that difficulties or conflicts will arise between your missionaries and ours in Oceania." Since the death three years earlier of Bishop Collomb, the second vicar apostolic of Melanesia and Micronesia, Colin had "discontinued sending missionaries to those Vicariates. And each day we realize more and more how necessary it is for us to limit our feeble efforts to the Vicariates of Central Oceania and New Caledonia. Nothing, therefore, can hinder the Sacred Congregation from assigning to your Institute both Melanesia and Micronesia in their entirety."

Currently there were five Marist missionaries at Woodlark in Melanesia, Colin explained. He hoped that they would leave the island "upon the arrival of your missionaries, go to New Caledonia, and place themselves at the service of the Vicar Apostolic of that island. . . ."[28] But since the prospects at Woodlark by that time could change, he did not want to order his missionaries to give up their posts immediately. "We intend to leave them free to judge what action would be best to take for the greater glory of God and the salvation

---

27. SM: 436. Almost in a straight line to the southeast of Ponape are, in sequence, Mokil Atoll, Pingelap Atoll, and Kusaie (formerly Ualan Island).

28. Pope Pius IX had reconfirmed Douarre, a Marist bishop, as vicar apostolic of New Caledonia on 10 August 1851, six weeks before Colin wrote this letter.

of souls," he said. If they should be "enjoying some success in Woodlark," or if they should have "some basis for hoping that they would be able to plant the faith solidly in this island, then we would even order them to stay there until the missionaries of your Institute or of some other congregation are in a position to replace them."

It was "essential," Colin told Marinoni, that the Milan missionaries "receive from the Holy See independent powers for both Melanesia and Micronesia and be free to establish themselves in whatever place seems most suitable to them." He suggested that they sail from London for Oceania via Sydney. The Marists at Sydney would give them all the necessary information, help them find a ship that would take them to Woodlark, and provide them with whatever additional services they might need. On reaching Woodlark the Milan missionaries could discuss matters with the Marists "and from there they could go to Ascension Island or Ponape, if they decided to choose that place for beginning their apostolic ministry."[29]

On 28 September 1851, the day after writing to Marinoni, Colin wrote to Fransoni and tried to excuse himself from having Marists train the Milan missionaries going to Micronesia. In the summer of 1850, he pointed out, the Holy See had issued letters patent "for two of our missionaries to be designated prefects apostolic locally by their colleagues, one for New Caledonia and the other for Melanesia." This "pontifical act" had made him believe that "our missionaries no longer have jurisdiction over Micronesia." It would therefore be necessary for the Holy See "to provide for the needs of that part of Oceania without our collaboration."[30]

It is difficult to understand how Colin could write in such a garbled way to Rome, trying to exonerate himself of responsibility for Micronesia. Actually Fransoni had told him on 10 August 1850 that all his wishes had been "favorably received by the Sacred Congregation," including "the designation of two prefects apostolic for the mission of Melanesia and Micronesia" and the designation of a third prefect apostolic, if warranted by circumstances, for New Caledonia. Fransoni had enclosed letters patent and faculties to be forwarded to the new prefects apostolic. And Colin himself was authorized to choose the new prefects and to insert their names on the letters patent and on the lists of faculties enclosed.[31]

Colin did not choose the prefects apostolic himself. Instead he subdelegated Bishop Douarre to choose a prefect apostolic for New Caledonia, and he subdelegated the surviving missionaries at Woodlark—by his letter to them of 25 August 1850—to elect by secret ballot one prefect apostolic for Melanesia and Micronesia. The election took place on 18 June 1851, three months and ten days before Colin sent his garbled letter to Rome. Frémont was elected unanimously as "Prefect [Apostolic] of the Mission of Melanesia and Micronesia

---

29. PIME: AME 28:721–23, Colin to Marinoni, 27 September 1851. There is a copy of this letter in PF: SC Oceania vol. 4 (1848–52), f. 690r-691r.

30. PF: SC Oceania vol. 4 (1848–52), f. 681r-682r.

31. PF: LDB vol. 339 (1850), f. 702rv, Fransoni to Colin, 10 August 1850.

according to the faculty granted by the Holy See," as he himself later informed Fransoni.[32] From this it is clear that Colin erred—although Fransoni did not take the trouble to correct him—in saying that Micronesia had been removed from the jurisdiction of the Marists.

Wanting to be freed as well from the obligation of training Milan missionaries who might go to Melanesia, and hoping to prevent the possible dissensions feared by Marinoni, Colin told Fransoni that the Italian missionaries in no way should be made dependent upon the Marist prefect apostolic in Melanesia. Instead they ought to be given "independent powers over both Micronesia and Melanesia," since "it is difficult for them to foresee with certainty in what part of these diverse archipelagoes they will be able to establish themselves. If they do not have extensive and independent powers" over the two vicariates, he said, "they could easily find themselves in an embarrassing situation."

Although Melanesia and Micronesia had been reduced to the status of missions by Rome on 11 August 1850, Colin continued to refer to them as vicariates in the letter of 28 September 1851.

His five missionaries in Melanesia, he told Fransoni, had asked him several times already whether they should abandon the Woodlark mission. His answer had been that they were "completely free" to do what they judged best. However, he did impose upon them the obligation "of remaining at Woodlark, if at all possible, until the arrival of the new missionaries." But his own preference—and here he repeated for Fransoni what he had told Marinoni the day before—was that the Woodlark missionaries "should join their colleagues in New Caledonia, especially since prudence seems to be obliging us to restrict our collaboration to the two Vicariates of New Caledonia and Central Oceania."

Colin insisted that the best way "to maintain good harmony" between the two groups, "and to avoid every dispute," was for Fransoni to grant complete autonomy over Melanesia and Micronesia to the Milan missionaries, just as he had granted to the Marists complete autonomy over Woodlark in the event that they should decide to stay there.[33]

Fransoni did not agree with this policy, however, and he told Colin so on 12 November 1851. "In the beginning—and in this I am certain you will agree with me—the priests in question cannot be left abandoned and by themselves without any guidance and direction. Consequently it will be absolutely necessary that your missionaries" remain in those places "as I have requested." Fransoni said that the Marists were to stay, not only "until the arrival of the new missionaries," as Colin had stated in his letter, "but rather as long as these latter are not capable of conducting the sacred ministry by themselves." The Marists were "already acquainted with the language and the customs of those areas." They also possessed "that experience and those other gifts" which the Milan missionaries "cannot have and could not acquire" unless they received assistance from the Marists. Colin's priests would

---

32. Regarding Douarre, see chap. 3, n. 20. Colin's letter of 25 August 1850 is mentioned by Frémont in SM: OMM/411, *procès-verbal*, 18 June 1851. For Frémont's title see PF: Udienze vol. 117 (1853, Part I), f. 271r, Frémont to Fransoni, 29 June 1852.

33. PF: SC Oceania vol. 4 (1848–52), f. 681r–682r, Colin to Fransoni, 28 September 1851.

therefore have to "direct them, support them and help them in every way, at least for some time."

Propaganda Fide would also do its share, the cardinal promised. It would give the Milan missionaries "those faculties and those instructions which Your Reverence points out to me as opportune for the purpose intended." Once the newcomers "become capable of conducting the evangelical ministry by themselves, they will begin preaching the Faith in Micronesia or in Melanesia, that is, in the place where your missionaries will not be able to take charge."

Making the Milan missionaries completely independent of the Marists as suggested by Colin, or releasing them prematurely from training under the Marists, "could achieve nothing but their ruin," Fransoni said. "Or at least it would force them to return home." Official instructions from Propaganda were indispensable, and the cardinal assured Colin that such instructions would be issued to the Milan missionaries before they set sail for Oceania. Fransoni promised that Colin would see those instructions as well. He in turn was to send a copy of them to his own priests in Woodlark. Fransoni told Colin he could not imagine that "the zealous and experienced [Marist] missionaries would refuse to collaborate with and lend their support to these new and inexperienced missionaries and thus abandon them to fate."[34]

Meanwhile Fathers Reina and Salerio had returned from France, arriving in Milan on 19 September 1851. While in Lyon they had visited the offices of the Association for the Propagation of the Faith, wisely becoming acquainted with the officials of this fund-collecting agency. From Lyon they had gone to Paris in order to profit from the 190 years of missionary experience of the Paris Foreign Mission Seminary.[35] When informing Fransoni on 4 November 1851 that the two priests had returned from France, Marinoni said they were "in great expectation over what Rome will decide as a result of their conferences with the Reverend Colin." He listed the names of his six priests who were ready to leave for Oceania: Paolo Reina, Carlo Salerio, Giovanni Mazzucconi, Timoleone Raimondi, Alessandro Mornico, and Angelo Ambrosoli. And he enclosed for the cardinal's information a copy of the 27 September letter that he had recently received from Colin.

Since Bishop Ramazzotti of Pavia was the principal founder of the Foreign Mission Seminary of Milan, director Marinoni sent him a copy of his 4 November 1851 letter to Fransoni. In it Marinoni spoke of the pope's "long conversation" with Reina and Salerio. He also thanked the cardinal "for having listened to them so often and for having answered

---

34. PF: LDB vol. 340 (1851), f. 825v–826v.

35. Tragella, *Missioni estere*, 1:80; PIME: AME 5:433, Marinoni to Barran, 20 September 1851. In this letter to Barran, director of the Paris Foreign Mission Seminary, Marinoni says: "Yesterday I finally had the good fortune to embrace my two missionaries after returning from their journey which lasted more than two months." Actually, the journey lasted less than two months, because Reina and Salerio left Milan for Rome with letters of introduction dated 29 July 1851, and returned to Milan on 19 September. Marinoni's words, "more than two months," must be what prompted Suigo to state that Reina and Salerio left Milan for Rome "about the middle of July"; he calculated backwards "more than two months" from their return to Milan. See n. 14.

their multitude of questions." Then he mentioned the letter sent by the pope to Archbishop Romilli of Milan. In that letter, he said, the pope "cherishes the hope of gathering copious fruit [through the Milan seminary] not only for very remote regions shrouded in the darkness of paganism, but also for those which are nearer, since it is important to provide also for their spiritual needs. May the Lord fulfill the wishes of his Vicar, so that our personnel may live up to the expectations conceived for them."[36]

This was Marinoni's response to the instructions received from Ramazzotti eight weeks earlier. In those instructions Ramazzotti had said that Marinoni should "thank the Holy Father" for having given his approval to the founding of the Milan seminary for foreign missions, "and at the same time declare to him that the Institute is also ready to evangelize whatever places His Holiness might wish." Ramazzotti reasoned that these words would include Corfu implicitly, in case Pope Pius IX actually wanted to send the Milan missionaries there.[37]

When Ramazzotti saw the copy of Marinoni's letter to Fransoni, however, he considered it a breach of his orders and became furious. He wrote back to Marinoni on 11 November 1851, saying that his reply had been "tardy" and that it should have been sent "directly to the Supreme Pontiff." Nor did it state that "the Institute is also ready to evangelize whatever places His Holiness might wish." Was there perhaps someone at the seminary "interested in going rather to one place than to another"? And was Marinoni afraid "to contradict him"? Was this why Marinoni in his reply "felt that he must take a middle road, which leaves someone the hope of arriving where he wants to go, rather than where he ought to go"? Ramazzotti insisted that Marinoni must speak out "clearly" and tell the candidates at the seminary "that they must listen to the Supreme Pontiff and leave him completely free in the choice of missions" for them.[38]

One of the reasons that Ramazzotti had chosen Marinoni as director of the Milan mission seminary was his absolute loyalty and dedication to the Holy See. Marinoni was therefore puzzled, grieved, and offended over this sharp letter from Ramazzotti. There was no question of his readiness or that of his missionary candidates to go wherever the pope might wish to send them, even though they happened to have their hearts set on Micronesia. Nor could Marinoni help but wonder why Ramazzotti should want him to write directly to the pope in answer to a letter that the pope had addressed to the archbishop of Milan.

Marinoni nevertheless sat down immediately and composed a letter to Pope Pius IX, stating that the seminary now numbered sixteen priests and laymen. Six of the priests and two of the lay missionaries "are already prepared to leave. They await only a sign from Your Holiness and they will go voluntarily wherever you may be pleased to send them." Not only these priests, but "the entire House for Foreign Missions" was being placed in the pope's

---

36. PF: SC Oceania vol. 4 (1848–52), f. 689rv. For Ambrosoli's birthday see PF: CV vol. 43, f. 291r; for those of the other five priests, see Suigo, *Pio IX*, 77–79.

37. PIME: AME 4:183f, Origo to Marinoni, 10 September 1851.

38. Ibid., 63f, Ramazzotti to Marinoni, 11 November 1851.

hands. "We ask that you dispose of it entirely according to your sovereign good pleasure and that you consider it a House that is all your own."

The letter also informed the pope that the Austrian government by its communication of 31 October 1851 had granted state approval to the seminary, which meant that it now enjoyed "all those rights and privileges which are granted to institutions protected by the state." Preferring to have Archbishop Romilli sign the letter, Marinoni brought it to him that very evening. The letter, dated 12 November 1851, was mailed the following day.[39]

Convinced that he had now fulfilled Ramazzotti's wishes, Marinoni sent him a copy of the letter along with his apologies. Ramazzotti had asked him, "Why did you write to the Prefect of Propaganda Fide? Has not the Supreme Pontiff said: I am the Superior of Propaganda Fide?"[40] Marinoni's enclosed message said, "I shall tell you frankly that I wrote to His Eminence, Cardinal Fransoni, because it seemed to me that I had no business directing correspondence to the Holy Father without using the customary channels, which in affairs regarding Foreign Missions are Propaganda Fide."[41]

Unaware of the misunderstanding that had arisen between Ramazzotti and Marinoni, Cardinal Fransoni replied to Marinoni's letter of 4 November 1851 on 22 November, enclosing for Marinoni's information a copy of the 12 November letter that he, the cardinal, had sent to Colin. He wanted Marinoni and his six priests going to Oceania to read it, since the norms that it contained were meant for them as well. In fact, when preparing the "instructions, faculties, patents and other matters" for the six missionaries, he intended to abide by the norms indicated in this letter to Colin. He had written in this way, he said, "so there would be no misunderstanding regarding my directives on the most important matter of assistance and guidance, which are so indispensable at the beginning of this enterprise." Without help from Colin's veteran and capable missionaries, he said, the six new missionaries from Milan "either would be sacrificed or their mission would be rendered useless and would have no results."

Fransoni wanted Marinoni to inform him "who among the six by age, prudence, doctrine and other moral qualities ought to be the person chosen as superior or Prefect of the mission." He was particularly interested in Archbishop Romilli's choice.

He also asked Marinoni to indicate "in detail the total costs" for sending the six missionaries to their destination. Since two thousand Roman scudi had already been allotted by the Association for the Propagation of the Faith, Fransoni now wanted to know "whether for the missionaries in question you have available other assistance as well, and what kind, so that I may be able to determine how much Propaganda will have to provide for them in order to complete the total amount." Upon receipt of "this detailed and precise

---

39. PIME: AME 27:553–54, Romilli to Pius IX, 12 November 1851; Suigo, *Pio IX*, 141; Brambilla, *Pontificio istituto*, 1:128–29.

40. PIME: AME 4:63f, Ramazzotti to Marinoni, 11 November 1851.

41. Brambilla, *Pontificio istituto*, 1:129, Marinoni to Ramazzotti, 16 November 1851.

information I shall lose no time in providing you as quickly as possible with the definitive arrangements, thus hastening the desired departure of your zealous priests."[42]

In his reply of 12 December 1851, Marinoni praised Fransoni for the guidelines and directives contained in his letter to Colin of 12 November. Previously Marinoni had been uneasy about the outcome of the mission, he said, since his missionaries were "still inexperienced in the apostolic ministry and ignorant of the language, customs and prejudices of the peoples of Oceania." But since the cardinal had decided to entrust them "to the friendly direction of the Reverend Marist Fathers, whose wisdom and zeal is well known," he now enjoyed "peace of mind" and was convinced that the mission would be a success.

The unanimous choice for the office of superior or prefect of the mission, Marinoni said, was Father Paolo Reina, who possessed "excellent qualities" for the task. He then listed the transportation costs: 150 francs per person for the journey from Milan to London; 1,500 francs per person for the voyage from London to Sydney; and 4,000 francs to charter a ship for about two months to take the missionaries from Sydney to various parts of Oceania. Since the six priests were to be accompanied by two lay missionaries or catechists, also members of the Milan seminary, the total estimated cost for the eight missionaries was 17,200 francs.[43]

It was 30 December 1851 when Fransoni informed Marinoni that twenty-six-year-old Reina had been chosen "to be superior" of the missionaries because of recommendations received from Archbishop Romilli and Bishop Ramazzotti. There was no mention of the office of prefect apostolic. Reina had been ordained a priest on 2 June 1849 and had entered the mission seminary on 31 August 1850, a month after it had opened.

The cardinal was pleased with the news that a deceased pious priest had left 1,331 Roman scudi to the seminary. This amount, Fransoni said, plus the 2,000 Roman scudi already received from the Association for the Propagation of the Faith in Lyon, was equivalent to approximately 18,000 francs and was more than enough to "cover the cost of the voyage." The surplus of almost 1,000 francs could be used for "furnishings, sacred vessels and other expenses connected with founding the mission." For these latter categories of expenses he assured Marinoni that further funds would be forthcoming from the Association for the

---

42. PF: LDB vol. 340 (1851), f. 853v–854v. Suigo in *Pio IX*, 141, incorrectly says that in this letter of 22 November 1851 to Marinoni, Fransoni (1) "communicated the official designation of Melanesia and Micronesia as a mission field for the institute" of Milan and (2) also fixed "March 1852" as the departure date. Actually Fransoni assigned to the institute "Micronesia or Melanesia" (in that order), whichever the Marists might decide not to keep. And the cardinal did this not in his 22 November 1851 letter to Marinoni, but in his 12 November 1851 letter to Colin, a copy of which he enclosed for Marinoni to read because of the "norms" that it contained for the French Marists in Oceania and the Italian missionaries, who soon would join them. This can hardly be called the "official designation" of a mission to an institute. Nor is the date March 1852 to be found in the 22 November letter. It is in Fransoni's letter to Marinoni of 30 December 1851. See PF: LDB vol. 340 (1851), f. 826r, 959r.

43. PF: SC Oceania vol. 4 (1848–52), f. 724rv. It was obligatory to inform Propaganda of the names of priests being sent to a mission, because they needed ecclesiastical jurisdiction. But this was not true for lay missionaries, and therefore Marinoni does not mention their names here.

Propagation of the Faith in Lyon prior to the departure of his missionaries. Fransoni suggested March as the date of departure, unless Colin had a counterproposal, "since spring seems to be the most propitious time for sailing."[44]

On the same day, 30 December, Fransoni wrote to Baron Antoine de Jessé, president of the Lyon Central Council of the Association for the Propagation of the Faith. "Six priests and two lay catechists" shall be leaving for "the missions of Melanesia and Micronesia in Oceania," he said, perhaps no later "than this coming March." Once sufficiently trained they would take over "one of these extensive missions, or perhaps both, depending upon the circumstances in which the Marists find themselves . . ." Fransoni asked President de Jessé whether it might be possible for him to provide these missionaries "with a subsidy of about two thousand francs" for sacred vessels, furnishings and basic needs of the new mission. He added that Reina was to be "superior of the missionaries and prefect apostolic of the mission."[45]

On hearing that Reina and Salerio were back from their journeys, Supriès wrote to Marinoni on 16 October 1851 that he hoped "to have the pleasure of seeing them soon at this Carthusian Monastery and of spending a long time with them."[46] They visited him on 14 November, and he was "profoundly edified by their fervor and their most ardent desire to be good and holy missionaries." His only wish, as he told Marinoni that same day, was that God would allow him "to see the Micronesia Mission get started on the right road. With a full heart I shall then say my Nunc Dimittis."[47] These two Latin words at the beginning of Simeon's canticle (Luke 2:29–32) express readiness to die after one's last wish has been fulfilled.

Archbishop Romilli of Milan was highly pleased with Rome's concern for what he looked upon as his Seminary for Foreign Missions. And so on 27 December 1851 when sending best wishes to Cardinal Prefect Fransoni for the New Year, he said: "I must give you special thanks" for all your help this past year. The seminary was making excellent progress, it was "getting new and élite candidates" all the time, and it was fast winning favor "among the clergy and also among the people" in the province of Lombardy.[48]

Cardinal Fransoni, too, must have been pleased with the smooth and rapid progress being made. One year ago Bishop Ramazzotti had written to him announcing (1) that the seminary had been formally established on 1 December 1850 and also (2) that the seminary hoped to receive "the Archipelagoes of Micronesia" as its mission field. Now, twelve months later, the Micronesia mission was almost ready to be launched. Fransoni needed only to issue the letters patent, faculties, and special instructions, and to provide some ad-

---

44. PF: LDB vol. 340 (1851), f. 959r–960r. Reina's biographical data is in Suigo, *Pio IX*, 79.

45. PF: LDB vol. 340 (1851), f. 956r–957v. The exchange rate derived from Fransoni's figures is 5.4 francs for 1 Roman scudo. Fifteen years earlier the rate was also 5.4 to 1. See Wiltgen, *Oceania*, 130.

46. PIME: AME 28:169.

47. Ibid., 171.

48. PF: CV vol. 43, f. 177r.

ditional funds. Once this was done, Reina and his seven companions could leave Italy for Oceania. Then after a period of training they would become successors to the Marists in Micronesia, or in Melanesia, or perhaps even in both of these vast areas, should the Marists decide to abandon them altogether.

And so 1851 ended happily for the officials in Rome, for the promoters of the Foreign Mission Seminary in Milan, and for the Marist superior general in Lyon. The new year began just as happily when Fransoni's letter of 30 December 1851 reached the Milan mission seminary on 5 January 1852, the eve of Epiphany, a great missionary feast in the Roman Catholic Church. Excitement mounted as the news spread that Reina had been chosen superior of the seminary's Oceania mission and that Rome's remaining paperwork for founding the mission was almost done. The coincidence of the news arriving on the vigil of Epiphany was looked upon by the enthusiastic young missionaries as a special sign of God's blessing upon them, upon their work, and upon their mission field in Oceania.[49]

Did Fransoni believe that he finally had succeeded in conciliating the wishes of all interested parties? If so, he was mistaken.

49. PF: SC Oceania vol. 4 (1848–52), f. 763r, Marinoni to Fransoni, 15 January 1852. Here Marinoni says that the cardinal's letter of 30 December arrived on "the vigil of the great feast of the Calling of the Gentiles," his expression for Epiphany, which fell on 6 January. Evidently Brambilla, *Pontificio istituto*, 1:105f, was unaware of Fransoni's 30 December letter, its contents, and the exact time of its arrival, because he says incorrectly that Rome arranged matters in such a way that on Epiphany itself the candidates received their appointments as missionaries apostolic along with "the most ample faculties." However, Fransoni's letter of 30 December 1851 merely announced that the appointments and faculties would soon arrive. They were dated 11 January 1852 and eventually did arrive with Fransoni's letter to Marinoni of 14 February 1852. Suigo in *Beatificationis Positio*, 108f and 463, attempting to explain why Scurati erroneously said that Mazzucconi received his appointment as missionary apostolic along with faculties on 5 January 1852, supposes that some related information must have been received in Milan from Rome in early January. He was not aware of Fransoni's letter to Marinoni dated 30 December 1851; neither was he aware of its contents, nor that it had arrived on 5 January 1852. Other writers add to the confusion. Nicholas Maestrini in *Mazzucconi of Woodlark: Priest and Martyr*, 79, incorrectly says that Reina's appointment "as the Superior of the mission" arrived on 2 December 1851 along with "the official papers from Rome assigning part of Melanesia as the new mission field of P.I.M.E." However, Marinoni had submitted Reina's name to Fransoni as a possible candidate for that office only on 12 December that year. Maestrini on the same page mistakenly says that the young priests received their individual appointments as "Apostolic Missionaries" on 6 January 1852. Piero Gheddo in *Mazzucconi di Woodlark: Un martire per il nostro tempo*, 120, also speaks of "the official designation of a mission field in Melanesia-Micronesia by Cardinal Fransoni," which he says was received in Milan on 2 December 1851.

6

Fransoni Sternly Reprimands Prefect Apostolic Reina
7 February 1852

FATHER ROCHER OF THE MARIST SUPPLY CENTER IN SYDNEY CHARTERED THE *BRIDE*, a sixty-five-ton schooner with Captain Dalmagne in charge, to deliver mail and supplies in 1851 to the handful of Marist missionaries at Woodlark. The ship sailed from Sydney on 27 May[1] and by 17 June was at Guasopa Harbor. In the mail pouch were official documents from Rome forwarded by Father Colin, who had preferred not to name a prefect apostolic for Melanesia and another for Micronesia, as he had requested and as he had been delegated to do by Cardinal Prefect Fransoni. Instead Colin, by his accompanying letter of 25 August 1850, subdelegated all surviving Marist priests in the Melanesia-Micronesia mission to assemble and elect from their number by secret ballot one prefect apostolic for the Melanesia-Micronesia mission.

The entire mission of Melanesia and Micronesia had only four Marist priests at that time, and all were in Woodlark. After recommending the matter to God and to the Blessed Virgin Mary, "We each celebrated Mass for this same intention," Frémont said. On 18 June 1851, "after invoking the name of God, all four placed in an urn their ballots, which the Reverend Father Frémont—named to verify the ballots—then opened." According to the minutes of the election, "The Reverend Father Pierre-Jean Frémont was elected unanimously by receiving the three votes of his three colleagues, in testimony of which we have drawn up this present official report." It was signed by Frémont, Thomassin, Montrouzier, and Trapenard. Frémont thereby became the prefect apostolic of the Mission of Melanesia and Micronesia.[2]

---

1. John Hosie, "The French Mission: An Australian Base for the Marists in the Pacific to 1874," 416.

2. SM: OMM/411, *procès-verbal*, 18 June 1851; SM: OMM/208, Frémont to Colin, 22 June 1851. In both places Frémont is called simply "Prefect Apostolic." But in his letter of 29 June 1852 to Fransoni, he gives his office as "Prefect of the Mission of Melanesia and Micronesia." See PF: Udienze, vol. 117 (1853, Part I), f. 271r.

In the *procès-verbal* Frémont's Christian name is given as "Pierre-Jean," which must be the correct form because Frémont signed this document. When presenting him earlier as candidate for coadjutor bishop in the Melanesia-Micronesia vicariate, Colin had said his name was "Jean-Pierre" in PF: SOCG vol. 965 (1844),

Captain Dalmagne told the missionaries that his ship would be in their vicinity for a few days, and he offered to mail letters for them on his return to Sydney. Four days after his election Frémont wrote to Superior General Colin, but could report only little success at the Woodlark mission, which had been founded nearly four years earlier.[3] "Up to now we do not even have a single catechumen," he said. "Since the founding of the mission we have baptized 132 persons, but most of these were tiny babies and the rest were adults in danger of death. Fifty-three of those baptized have meanwhile died and of this number, thirty-eight were infants in their baptismal innocence. There are seventy-nine Christians still living." Father Montrouzier, he said, had begun baptizing all infants at birth for fear that otherwise they might die without Baptism.

It was comforting, Frémont added, that in the preceding weeks some young men had begun asking to be accepted as catechumens, and so he was going to try something new that might help his mission gain a better foothold in Woodlark. Since the *Bride* was returning empty to Sydney and so had room for passengers, he had decided to send along several young men from the island. Father Montrouzier was in need of recuperation in Sydney and would accompany them. "Everyone agrees that this is our only means of dissipating their stupid and gross pride and of dispelling at the same time their false ideas," he said. Montrouzier's departure reduced the Marists at Woodlark to four: Fathers Frémont, Thomassin, and Trapenard, and Brother Gennade.[4]

It was about this time that Father Montrouzier wrote to Father C. M. Léopold Verguet, who had quit missionary work in Melanesia four years earlier and was now living in France. "We are still sowing in tears," he said. "And to this day we have had no other consolation but that of suffering and of doing the will of God. . . . Our people resist grace and, although we do not refuse labor, we find ourselves without work." Rome had authorized them to elect a prefect apostolic, he said, but this gave no assurance that they would be keeping the mission. This "nevertheless gives the mission more stability and has encouraged us all."[5]

The letter to Verguet was in stark contrast to the glowing letter written by Montrouzier to his family three years earlier. "That which gives us the greatest encouragement and consolation at Woodlark," he had said, "is the large number of children that we find here, their good dispositions and their intelligence. The entire future rests upon the youth." Therefore, he said, "we are working zealously at training them to be catechists. Who knows if later we might be able to realize the wishes of the Holy See and train some of them to be priests." In that way the Catholic Church would "become naturalized" in this area, he said.[6]

---

f. 457r–458r, Colin to Fransoni, 8 May 1844, the source cited by Wiltgen in *Oceania*, 299, for that form of his name.

3. The Woodlark mission was founded on 15 September 1847. For more details, see Wiltgen, *Oceania*, 475–78.

4. SM: OMM/208, Frémont to Colin, 22 June 1851.

5. Verguet, *Vicariat de Mélanésie*, 294. Verguet does not give the date of Montrouzier's letter.

6. SM: OMM/208, Montrouzier to his parents, 25 April 1848.

The Marists at first had "quite a bit of trouble" finding youths who wanted to sail to Sydney, Thomassin told his parents. But they persevered and eventually found five candidates. The priests were convinced that "the sight of this large town with its prosperity resulting from civilization, and with its religious benefits, would favorably impress" them. Seeing Sydney would also make these young men "compare their own living conditions with those which Christianity has produced for us," the missionaries thought, and would help them "decide to embrace the faith."[7]

But before returning to Sydney, Captain Dalmagne wanted to see the wreck of the British whaler *Mary*, which was lying on a reef at the Laughlan or Nada Islands. This island group was located some forty miles to the east of Woodlark. The British ship had run onto a reef during a tropical storm at 4 a.m. on 22 November 1843. Seven of the crew perished in the shipwreck, and nine months later Captain Stein and six of his crew were killed by the Laughlan inhabitants. The surviving twenty-two crew members fled to Woodlark in a whaleboat. But the Woodlark inhabitants were soon joined by those from Laughlan, and together they killed all survivors but Valentine, who managed to escape. He was rescued by the brig *Tigress*, which happened to stop at Woodlark for fresh water.[8]

The population of the Laughlan Islands was "about 200." Although Montrouzier had never been there before, he was known to some men from there who had seen him at Woodlark. Each year during March and November the Laughlan islanders would fill their seagoing canoes with coconuts and sail to Guasopa Harbor where they traded them for taros. They carried on this trade for a month and so met the missionaries. Because of these earlier contacts Montrouzier was able to persuade three Laughlan youths to go with him to Sydney.[9]

The *Bride* reached Sydney on 3 August 1851, and four days later Montrouzier informed Colin that he and the eight young men had arrived safe and sound. "In my opinion this project can result in very much good and can bring about a revolution" in the thinking habits of our people, he said.[10]

Frémont's letter of 22 June prompted Colin to write to Fransoni on 22 December 1851. The only positive development in the mission at Woodlark, he told Fransoni, was that "eight children or young men" had been taken to Sydney where they could be instructed more easily and where they could broaden their horizons "by becoming acquainted with

---

7. Ibid., Thomassin to his parents, 12 October 1851.

8. "Laughlan," *Salem Observer* (9 May 1846), in *American Activities in the Central Pacific 1790–1870: A History, Geography and Ethnography Pertaining to American Involvement and Americans in the Pacific Taken from Contemporary Newspapers, etc.*, vol. 4, R. Gerard Ward, ed., 8f. See also OMM/208, Montrouzier to Colin, postscript of 7 August 1851 in his letter of 21 June 1851.

9. SM: OMM/208, Thomassin to his parents, 12 October 1851.

10. Ibid., Montrouzier to Colin, postscript of 7 August 1851 in his letter of 21 June 1851; Hosie, "French Mission," 416. Hugh Laracy, "Roman Catholic 'Martyrs' in the South Pacific, 1841–55," *Journal of Religious History* (December 1976): 200, incorrectly says it was 1852 when this "party of Muruans" was sent to Sydney. Murua is another name for Woodlark.

a society of civilized people." This step, Colin said, "will probably bring about in time the conversion of this island." He also informed the cardinal that Frémont had been unanimously elected prefect apostolic and that Montrouzier for health reasons had been obliged to leave the mission.

Colin used this occasion to reply to Fransoni's forceful letter of 12 November 1851, in which the cardinal for the second time had insisted that Colin must keep his missionaries in Melanesia to train the new personnel coming from Milan.[11] The news about the eight young men, Colin said, would help Fransoni in drawing up his instructions for the Milan missionaries. They ought to know, he said, that Woodlark was not a large island, that it did not have a considerable population, and that therefore "it would perhaps be useless for all of them to settle at Woodlark." They should also know that "each of these numerous islands usually has a different language. Consequently our missionaries cannot be of any use to them in learning a language, except for those who might settle in Woodlark itself."

The Marist superior general emphasized that Bishop Collomb, the second vicar apostolic of Melanesia and Micronesia, "had hoped to penetrate New Guinea . . . and had advanced along the coast of this considerable and important island. Perhaps Divine Providence led our missionaries to Woodlark and to Rooke, where Bishop Collomb died, in order to prepare the way for [other] missionaries to enter New Guinea . . . , which seems like a continent." If Catholicism could first penetrate this island, he said, "it would be easier to bring the light of the Gospel to the numerous and less important islands surrounding it."

Colin promised once again to order his missionaries to remain at Woodlark, as Fransoni wished, in order to give the Milan missionaries all possible assistance. But since there was now hope that the Woodlark youths by going to Sydney might bring about the conversion of their island, he had a special request. "If our missionaries should be inclined to remain at Woodlark, I would like to leave the decision up to them," he said. "It seems important and also proper to me not to force them to surrender this post to the new missionaries." Should they be forced to do so, it would be a repetition of "the measures taken by the Sacred Congregation in similar circumstances for New Zealand" in 1848,[12] a policy that Colin blamed for having enervated and discouraged his missionaries in the whole of western Oceania.

He also suggested that the Milan missionaries should have their own supply center "which could see to it that every year or two they would be visited [by a ship] and would receive the necessary provisions." Such an arrangement was indispensable because

---

11. For the full text of Fransoni's letter, see PF: LDB vol. 340 (1851), f. 825v–826v.

12. Here Colin mistakenly wrote 1847 for 1848. He is referring to Rome's decision of 4 June 1848, which created the two dioceses of Auckland and Port Nicholson (now Wellington), and also to Rome's corresponding provisions of 30 June 1848. At that time Propaganda Fide gave to Bishop Pompallier the Diocese of Auckland, an area already well developed by the Marists. Those Marists, who were discontent with Pompallier, were allowed to transfer to the Diocese of Port Nicholson (now Wellington). But this area was altogether undeveloped at that time. See Wiltgen, *Oceania*, 505, 508.

"commercial ships have hardly yet penetrated" the area. Without this service the new missionaries would be isolated for years at a time, "receiving no news from Europe and being exposed to every need as regards clothing and whatever is required for the Holy Sacrifice of the Mass."

The most striking news in Colin's letter was contained in a postscript. Recently he had received several letters from Bishop Bataillon, vicar apostolic of Central Oceania, and from other Marist missionaries working there. These letters, he said, had informed him that "an almost general movement toward Catholicism has set in, chiefly in the Navigators [now Samoa] and in the Viti or Fiji archipelagoes." Fiji was an important and well-populated archipelago, and the few Marists there were requesting more personnel and also a bishop. "But the Society of Mary cannot supply all these needs," Colin said, "and it intends to limit its aid to the Navigators and Tonga archipelagoes and to the islands of Wallis, Futuna and Rotuma."

For the last four years Colin had been urging Bataillon to request priests from Propaganda for Fiji. "Would it not be in place," he now asked, "to make the Fiji Archipelago a vicariate apostolic and to send the Milan missionaries or some other missionaries there with a bishop in charge?" In Fiji, he said, "they would probably be successful more quickly than in Melanesia and Micronesia."[13]

On 23 December 1851, the day after writing to Cardinal Fransoni on Fiji, Colin wrote to Director Marinoni in Milan. He cordially invited Marinoni to have his missionaries lodge at the Marist house in Lyon on their journey to London, where they planned to start their sea voyage. He would show as much interest in their work and welfare, he said, "as if they were members of the Society of Mary, since we all have the same goal and we are all working in the vineyard of the same Father . . ." However, he added, "I do not know what services we shall be able to render to your excellent missionaries. . . . If we can be useful to them in any way, we shall grasp the opportunity with real pleasure. And we shall recommend them to our missionaries in a special way."[14]

Earlier Marinoni had been elated over the precise and stern orders regarding collaboration issued by Fransoni to Colin. But now he was alarmed by Colin's words, which he considered nothing but a vague and generic promise of assistance. On New Year's Day 1852 he therefore rushed off to Fransoni a copy of Colin's letter, saying that "from it Your

---

13. PF: SC Oceania vol. 4 (1848–52), f. 685r–686v, Colin to Fransoni, 22 December 1851. Jaspers in *Erschliessung Ozeaniens*, 279 n. 33, incorrectly says that the Fiji Islands proposal was contained in Colin's letter to Fransoni of 28 September 1851.

Bishop Bataillon on 15 August 1844 went to Lakemba Island in Fiji to install Fathers Bréhéret and Roulleaux with Brother Donnet. They found Wesleyanism widespread, met opposition, went to Namuka Island, and returned to Lakemba Island. Ovalau mission, now a diocese, was founded in 1851, and Rewa mission was founded in 1852. See the report on Fiji of 9 October 1855 by the Marist Procurator General C. Nicolet in PF: SC Oceania vol. 15 (1885–86), f. 508r, 510r.

14. PIME: AME 28:725f, Colin to Marinoni, 23 December 1851. This letter is a reply to Marinoni's of 12 December 1851.

Eminence will be able to see the terms by which he intends to assist our missionaries in their ministry. And so I renew my request that the Sacred Congregation recommend as ardently as possible to the kind concern of the Marist Fathers this first expedition of ours. If it proves successful, so very much good will result for the unfortunate peoples there, and so very much growth will result for our new seminary here."[15]

Reacting at once to Marinoni's request, Fransoni told Colin on 10 January 1852 that Marist cooperation in Oceania was absolutely indispensable for the successful outcome of the Milan mission. If such cooperation should be lacking, the cardinal said, he would be "filled with the most grave fears." Nor could he stress enough the necessity of "assistance and support" for the new missionaries as long as they "had not acquired all the knowledge necessary . . . for so difficult an undertaking." He then extended his "affectionate gratitude" to Colin "for the interest which you are showing on behalf of the good missionaries from Milan, graciously supporting my own concern that this expedition, now being planned, may have excellent results."

Colin had sought assurance that his own missionaries might stay in Woodlark, if they so wished, even if the missionaries from Milan should decide to go to Melanesia. Referring to this request of Colin, Fransoni promised to keep the matter in mind. He would issue special *Instructions* for the Milan missionaries, he said, which would make them aware of whatever arrangements Propaganda had previously made with Colin. These *Instructions* were to serve as a norm of conduct for the newcomers, and Colin himself was to receive a copy for his "complete peace of mind."

The purpose of these *Instructions* was "to provide for any possible emergency that might arise" and "to exclude completely the danger of any clashes or unpleasantness" for the Marists. Only after the new missionaries were trained could they take over that mission "which your own missionaries will want to entrust to them or give to them."

Fransoni liked Colin's Fiji Islands proposal very much and said that he would mention it in the *Instructions*. "Therefore if the enterprise in Micronesia is not feasible, and if Bishop Bataillon . . . should wish to take advantage of the new missionaries "and have them care for the [Fiji] archipelago . . . , thus preparing it to become a new vicariate, and if they reach an agreement with this Prelate, and if for the present they dedicate themselves exclusively to that mission, Your Reverence can rest assured that nothing will happen unless it is done in full accord with, and unless it is pleasing to, either Father Frémont and his companions or Bishop Bataillon. Neither will the peace of the Marists, nor the places where they reside and which they are able to care for, be disturbed in any way."

Colin had also suggested that the Milan missionaries should immediately set up their own supply center, but Fransoni did not agree to this. "In the beginning and for some time to come," he said, the Marist supply center in Sydney should "provide the same assistance for the missionaries of Milan that it regularly provides for the Marists." The reason for this was that the new seminary was not able to manage everything at once. However, the new-

---

15. PF: SC Oceania vol. 4 (1848–52), f. 746r.

comers would open a supply center of their own "as soon as possible after deciding upon a location and after obtaining the necessary advice from your members in Sydney...."[16]

Fransoni sent a copy of Colin's letter containing the Fiji Islands proposal to Archbishop Romilli of Milan, saying that it contained "some pertinent observations and remarks which, I believe, will be helpful to your missionaries." He requested Romilli to pass on the letter to Director Marinoni and to inform him that Propaganda Fide, when drawing up its *Instructions*, would "keep in mind all that is mentioned in this letter. It will also make provisions for each and every case and for possible alternatives indicated in the letter, particularly in the postscript...."[17]

In addition to passing on a copy of Colin's letter to Marinoni, Archbishop Romilli of Milan sent a copy to Bishop Ramazzotti of Pavia, whom he called "the particular promoter and protector" of the mission seminary in Milan. He wanted to give Ramazzotti the opportunity to express his personal views "regarding the place where the first mission should be."[18]

Ramazzotti sent his views to Romilli on 24 January 1852. It was evident from Colin's letter, he said, "that recently one of the Reverend Marist missionaries was named Prefect Apostolic of Micronesia and Melanesia" and also that the Marists "would be remaining in their mission at Woodlark—insofar as one can judge—also after the arrival of the missionaries from Lombardy. Now since they have jurisdiction over those islands, they will also be the superiors of the Lombard missionaries when these are sent to Micronesia and Melanesia." But this could be "an obstacle to the progress of the Lombard mission," because it would "extinguish, or at least diminish, that commitment which is so helpful for and needed by the seminary." Ramazzotti therefore believed it "to be our duty to make the Most Eminent Prefect of Propaganda Fide aware of these fears of ours." However, Fransoni was to be assured "that the Lombard missionaries very promptly will go" wherever he might wish to send them, "since he speaks in the name of the Most Holy Father."[19] There was not a single word about Fiji in Ramazzotti's letter.

Romilli enclosed Ramazzotti's letter when he answered Fransoni on 26 January 1852. He said that he himself, as well as Ramazzotti, Marinoni, and the missionary candidates, begged the cardinal in his wisdom "to designate a mission field in such a way as to obviate all future dangers whatsoever, even involuntary clashes." However, the Lombard seminary did wish to be given a mission territory in which "it could expand gradually without finding it necessary to transfer itself elsewhere because the initial field was too restricted."[20] Romilli's letter, like Ramazzotti's, contained not a word about Fiji.

---

16. PF: LDB vol. 341 (1852, Part I), f. 24v–26v, Fransoni to Colin, 10 January 1852.
17. Ibid., f. 28r–29r, Fransoni to Romilli, 10 January 1852.
18. See PF: SC Oceania vol. 4 (1848–52), f. 765rv, Romilli to Fransoni, 26 January 1852.
19. Ibid., f. 767r, Ramazzotti to Romilli, 24 January 1852.
20. Ibid., f. 765rv, Romilli to Fransoni, 26 January 1852.

Cardinal Prefect Fransoni was greatly annoyed by Romilli's and Ramazzotti's letters and immediately suspected that their misgivings had originated with Fathers Reina and Salerio. When these two priests were in Rome, he recalled, they had presented the very same objections. Consequently when a letter arrived about the same time from Reina regarding a legacy, Fransoni decided to reply himself, even though it was addressed to secretary Barnabò.[21] After briefly answering Reina's question about the legacy, Fransoni said, "I wish that you and your companions would put out of your minds completely those doubts and fears, which seem to return from time to time, and which are contrary to the clear and precise explanations that were given to you in Rome."

Fransoni then told Reina how he had sent a letter from Colin to Archbishop Romilli to be given to director Marinoni. Romilli had meanwhile sent a reply, the cardinal said, and from it,

> I can see that the letter of the Marist Superior which I passed on, instead of serving you as a norm containing fitting directives for future needs, has given rise to new misunderstandings, oversensitiveness and distrust. These have also had an effect on the renowned Prelate.
>
> However, I should like you to convince yourself once and for all that this Sacred Congregation has paternal concern for you; that it cannot permit your inevitable ruin and a most unfortunate outcome for the expedition, something that certainly would follow if the Sacred Congregation were to allow you to be there by yourselves, abandoned, without support, help and guidance. These aids are all indispensable for you, both during the voyage and in the initial period after your arrival in the mission. Nor can the Marists manifest their benevolence toward you in a more favorable way than by assisting you to learn the language, first during the voyage, and then at your destination, giving you their loving support on every occasion. In this way you will become capable of practicing the ministry fruitfully by yourselves in the mission that is destined for you.

Fransoni minced no words. He told Reina that he "must not confound preliminary instructions with later practice of the ministry, nor temporary directives with a badly understood dependence upon, or being mingled with, other missionaries. You and your men will have a distinct and separate mission, once you are prepared to take care of it. Nor will you experience any other dependence except dependence upon Propaganda, that is, upon the Holy See."

From the *Instructions*, which Reina would soon receive, he would see "very clearly the benefit and the wisdom of these guarantees," the cardinal said. "They have no other purpose but to produce better results for the expedition and to procure great advantages for you, which later will make you very happy...."[22]

---

21. Ibid., f. 771rv. Reina's letter to Barnabò was dated 27 January 1852; Romilli's to Fransoni, 26 January; and Ramazzotti's to Romilli, 24 January.

22. PF: LDB vol. 341 (1852, Part I), f. 171v–173r, Fransoni to Reina, 7 February 1852.

Quickly and humbly on 13 February 1852, Reina answered Fransoni's "precious letter of the 7th," which had brought him "the voice of a Father who corrects and loves." He begged the cardinal "not to fear any sinister impression in the mind of our excellent Archbishop, because this most worthy Prelate has the highest esteem and veneration for Your Eminence and Propaganda Fide. I believe that I would inflict wounds too bitter for the sensibilities of his heart, if I were to communicate to him what Your Eminence has written to me, words which certainly were meant only for my welfare and that of my companions. This excellent Prelate would see in these words a tacit reproof for himself, something which no doubt is contrary to the intention expressed by Your Eminence...."

Fransoni had truly shown himself so kind and good in Rome, Reina said, "that we cannot doubt that whatever Your Eminence in your wisdom might have decided upon, would be the best possible arrangement for us. So if we have added some considerations, we did not do so because we doubted what Your Eminence said, but rather because it appeared to us that our Superior wanted to have our personal feelings in this matter. We believed it was our strict duty to say simply what our mind and our heart suggested. For the rest we accept with profound submission and with sincere affection and gratitude the paternal admonitions which Your Eminence has directed toward us. They shall be for us an unalterable norm in the future."

Reina and his companions felt obliged to thank Fransoni, Reina said, "because you do not wish to abandon us, young and inexperienced as we are, to difficulties and dangers whose magnitude is unknown to us. We shall also be most grateful to those excellent [Marist] missionaries who are to perform such a great act of charity on our behalf."[23]

Three days after sending his letter of reprimand to Reina, Fransoni also wrote to Archbishop Romilli of Milan. Going straight to the point, he said:

> From Your Excellency's letter of 26 January and the enclosed letter of the Bishop of Pavia, it seems clear to me that the fine and good missionaries of your Seminary destined for Oceania have not yet banished their unfounded fears, which during their stay in Rome could not be dispelled by even the clearest of explanations. In addition they have managed to influence even Your Excellency and the praiseworthy Bishop [of Pavia] to such an extent, that the very communication of the letter of the Marist Superior, which was intended to give them more courage and confidence, has been the cause of new perplexities and doubts. Although I have just written to the Reverend Prefect Apostolic Elect Paolo Reina on this subject . . . , I nevertheless believe it opportune to provide here for Your Excellency a brief account of the thinking of Propaganda on this particular matter. Hopefully it will assist you in removing completely from their minds every ill-conceived apprehension.

Repeating some of the ideas contained in his letter to Reina, Fransoni stressed the arduousness of the enterprise and the futility of leaving the missionaries completely to themselves. "In fact," he said, "how could they possibly succeed in this cause without an

---

23. PF: SC Oceania vol. 4 (1848–52), f. 790rv.

extraordinary outpouring of the omnipotence of God, since they are ignorant of the language, the customs, the character, etc., of those barbarous tribes, having neither knowledge of nor experience about the area or anything else?" The veteran Marist priests on the other hand, "who have worked in those missions for a long time," could provide "complete and most loving assistance, support, guidance and help." Consequently "all their needs will be cared for, and in a short time they shall become capable of practicing the ministry, since they will also have learned the language and will have acquired all the knowledge necessary to work well in the future."

But the young missionaries from Milan, Fransoni insisted, "have confused, and still are confusing, this first temporary assistance and guidance—which is no less useful than it is indispensable—with an imaginary and perpetual dependence upon the foresaid Marists. They presuppose that Propaganda Fide wants to keep the two groups joined with one another. But this would be just as displeasing to the missionaries of Milan as it would be troublesome for the Marists themselves." Fransoni insisted that as soon as the Milan priests would be instructed by the Marists and could work by themselves, "They shall obtain a distinct and separate mission...."

Some agreements had already been reached with the Marists, however, and Propaganda would stand by them, Fransoni said. "If the Marists should [decide to] retain Melanesia, then the priests from Milan would take over exclusively the other mission of Micronesia as soon as they were qualified, or vice versa...." The Marist missionaries might even surrender both Melanesia and Micronesia to the Italians, if they "were obliged to go to the aid of the Central Mission, or of Wellington, or of some other mission in their care which also might need reinforcements."

Fransoni then called Romilli's attention to "the vast Central Oceania Vicariate," saying that some islands there could be assigned to the priests of Milan. A mission in those islands, he said, "would certainly be much easier and would offer far greater hope of success." In fact, he said, the Milan priests "can choose this easier mission right now . . . Then when their numbers have increased, and when they are able to extend their activity elsewhere, without leaving this mission [in Central Oceania] they could take up work in Melanesia or in Micronesia. . . . By that time, too, the obstacles to introducing the Gospel would be fewer there." The cardinal said that Romilli would appreciate more and more as time goes on "the precautions" adopted by Propaganda Fide "for the greater good" of his priests and "for preventing the most grave and certain dangers to which they otherwise would be exposed." He felt confident that Romilli would "know how to reassure the vacillating minds of those good priests, who can hardly doubt the lively interest shown in them and in their success by Propaganda Fide." And he concluded by saying that hopefully his presentation had clarified whatever doubts the archbishop might have had.[24]

---

24. PF: LDB vol. 341 (1852, Part I), f. 187v–190r, Fransoni to Romilli, 10 February 1852. One wonders why Fransoni in this letter refers to Reina as "the Reverend Prefect Apostolic *Elect*," even though Fransoni and Barnabò as early as 11 January 1852 had signed the decree naming Reina the prefect apostolic. See the official

On receiving Fransoni's letter Archbishop Romilli at once called together Reina and the other priests and told them what the cardinal had said. Hurriedly he wrote back on 17 February 1852, saying that Reina and his companions had accepted the reprimand "not only with sentiments of humble docility, but even with true gratitude." They were now "perfectly disposed to accept the mission destined for them by Propaganda and precisely in the manner which Your Eminence has indicated to me . . ." Romilli had meanwhile seen a copy of Reina's letter to Fransoni and said, "I hope that Your Eminence will be satisfied with it."

Romilli then defended himself, saying that the young missionaries had not at all "succeeded in inspiring me with distrust toward the most worthy Marists, and much less toward the benevolence and protection shown by Your Eminence and by the Sacred Congregation for this young institute." In his previous letter to Fransoni he had called attention to "the genuine sentiments of these missionaries" in order to obtain from Rome "an authoritative statement on these matters." He knew that "it would prove to be so much the more reassuring and efficacious" for the missionaries, "the less it would appear to come from me. Thanks be to God, the result corresponds to my expectations."

To show that it "certainly was not the intention of the Missionaries of Milan to withdraw themselves from the guidance of other missionaries," he quoted chapter 3, section 1, of the mission seminary's rule, which he and his suffragans had provisorily approved. Members going to a new mission field, the rule said, should first be sent to some adjacent mission "so that under the guidance and benevolent assistance of some other congregation of missionaries, they might make their necessary noviceship. Once they are well experienced, they may transfer to their own mission field."[25]

On Sunday, 11 January 1852, the day after Fransoni had sent Romilli a copy of Colin's letter on Fiji, secretary Barnabò petitioned Pope Pius IX to grant Reina "all those faculties customarily given to vicars apostolic in Oceania, including that of confirming, but excluding those which require the episcopal character . . ." It was two days before Reina's twenty-seventh birthday. Barnabò said that Reina had been chosen to be "the Prefect Apostolic of Melanesia, or of Micronesia, or of some other mission in Oceania, depending upon the circumstances and in accord with the *Instructions* to be given on this matter to the said prefect and his missionaries." The pope replied that Fransoni was authorized to grant the faculties if he saw fit.[26]

---

decree in PIME: AME 1:59. Similarly when writing to Reina on 7 February 1852, Fransoni does not use his new title of prefect apostolic, but addresses him simply as "Don [or Father] Paolo Reina." See PF: LDB vol. 341 (1852, Part I), f. 171v. The reason for the difference is that the official decree had not yet been sent to Reina (it was mailed only on 14 February 1852), and therefore it had not yet been published. No one in Milan knew that in the previous month Reina had already been named prefect apostolic. From the point of view of Rome, therefore, he was already prefect apostolic. But from the point of view of those in Milan, and according to protocol, Fransoni referred to him correctly as prefect apostolic *elect*.

25. PF SC Oceania vol. 4 (1848–52), f. 794r–795r.
26. PF: Udienze vol. 115 (1852, Part I), f. 58v–59r.

Also on that day, 11 January 1852, Cardinal Prefect Fransoni and secretary Barnabò signed a decree of Propaganda Fide whereby Reina was named "the Prefect of the Missions of Melanesia, or of Micronesia, [or of some other mission] in Oceania in accord with the *Instructions* . . ." In this decree the words here given in brackets were omitted through an oversight.[27]

On Saturday, 14 February 1852, Fransoni sent director Marinoni a letter with numerous enclosures: the decree of 11 January naming Reina as prefect apostolic, the list of faculties granted to him by Pius IX, rescripts, the *Instructions*, a letter in Latin for the French Marist missionaries in Oceania, and a letter for Colin. There were also letters patent issued on 11 January, which named Fathers Salerio, Mazzucconi, Raimondi, and Ambrosoli "Missionaries Apostolic in Melanesia or Micronesia, or for some other mission of Oceania in accord with the *Instructions* . . ."[28]

The Instructions for the Prefect Apostolic and the Missionaries of the Seminary of Milan Going to Oceania was the longest enclosure in Fransoni's letter to Marinoni. It was dated 9 February 1852, was signed by Cardinal Prefect Fransoni and by Secretary Barnabò, and consisted of "both general and specific instructions recommended for full observance." In the "most energetic way possible" the Lombardy missionaries were exhorted "never to let it escape their minds that assistance, counsel and direction were not only fitting and opportune, but also absolutely necessary in the beginning of their enterprise." They were to manifest this kind of attitude toward the priest in charge of the Marist supply center at Sydney, who would help them decide where to open a supply center of their own, once they were firmly established in their own mission. Until that time he would provide for all their needs.

---

27. PIME: AME vol. 1, p. 59. This is the original decree of Propaganda naming Reina a prefect apostolic. For Reina's full title, see Barnabò's words to Pius IX on 11 January 1852 in PF: Udienze vol. 115 (1852, Part I), f. 58v–59r, and the introductory paragraph of the faculties granted to Reina by Pope Pius IX and Fransoni, also on 11 January, in PIME: AME 1:53–56.

For confirmation that Reina's title must read prefect apostolic "of Melanesia, or of Micronesia, or of some other mission in Oceania," see the correspondence of Fransoni of 10 January 1852 with Colin and Romilli, and Fransoni's subsequent correspondence with Romilli and Marinoni, as presented in this chapter.

Numerous authors have spread the mistaken notion that Reina already at this time was named the prefect apostolic of Melanesia *and* Micronesia, whereas the official documents all say Melanesia *or* Micronesia *or* some other mission in Oceania. For example, Tragella in *Missioni estere*, 1:93, says that Reina was named "the prefect of the missions of Melanesia and Micronesia, or of some other mission . . ." Suigo in *Beatificationis Positio*, 107, calls Reina the prefect apostolic "of the mission of Melanesia and Micronesia or of some other mission." Suigo once again in *Pio IX*, 79 n. 67, like Jaspers in *Erschliessung Ozeaniens*, 279, and like Gheddo in *Mazzucconi*, 120, says that Reina was named the prefect apostolic of "Melanesia and Micronesia." See also chap. 5, n. 42.

28. PF: LDB vol. 341 (1852, Part I), f. 210r–210v; *Beatificationis Positio*, 108. Suigo in this latter work, 107, says that the *Instructions* were sent to Reina in January 1852. However, they bear the date 9 February 1852 and were actually sent to Marinoni for Reina and his missionaries with Fransoni's letter of 14 February 1852.

DECRETUM

S. CONGREGATIONIS DE PROPAGANDA FIDE.

REferente *R. P. D. Alexandro Barnabò Secretario* Sacra Congregatio Praefectum Missionum *Melanesiae seu Micronesiae in Oceania, juxta instructiones ad suum beneplacitum* — declaravit *R. D. Paulum Rojna Presb. Sem. Mediol. Miss. ad Exteros* cum auctoritate ea exercendi, quae ad earumdem Missionum regimen pertinent ad praescriptum decretorum Sacrae Congregationis et facultatum eidem concessarum, et non alias nec alio modo

Datum Romae ex aedibus dictae Sacrae Congregationis die *11 Januarii 1852*.

J. Ph. Card. Fransoni Praef.

This decree issued by the Propaganda Fide on 11 January 1852 names Paolo Reina "the Prefect of the Missions of Melanesia, or of Micronesia, in Oceania in accord with the *Instructions*. . . ." The document is signed by Cardinal Perfect Fransoni and Secretary Barnabò.
Source: Archives PIME: AME Vol. 1, p. 59. (see fn 230)

Throughout their entire training period, the *Instructions* said, the missionaries from Milan "must not consider themselves as a separate or distinct body, nor may they make use of the faculties granted to the Prefect of the mission." They were free to use the faculties only after their training had been completed and when they "have undertaken on their own the task of preaching the Gospel in the place or places assigned exclusively to them. Here the new missionaries will be dependent upon their own Prefect and their own Superior, who in turn will depend directly upon the Sacred Congregation for the Evangelization of Peoples."

Much space was devoted to the place or places where the Lombardy missionaries were to take up work. "Although they are assigned to the Missions of Western Oceania in a general way," the precise place was to be "dependent upon various circumstances," and consequently it had been "found necessary" to issue the following directives:

Since Propaganda Fide did not wish to take away from the Marists "that mission which they can or would like to retain and develop," the Milan missionaries would eventually receive a mission from the Marists "according to the understanding already reached on this matter" by Propaganda and the Marist superior general. If the Marists should decide to keep Melanesia, "It is understood that Micronesia will be entrusted to the missionaries from Milan." If the Marists were to keep Micronesia, the Milan missionaries would receive Melanesia. And if the Marists decided to keep neither, then both Melanesia and Micronesia would be entrusted to the missionaries from Milan.

But "there seem to be serious obstacles at present," which make missionary work impossible in both Melanesia and Micronesia, the *Instructions* said. For although the Marists had made "very great sacrifices of personnel and funds" in this area, all their efforts "have proven quite useless." In the entire mission only three priests were left, and they were "nearly paralyzed" by obstacles. Consequently "the moment chosen by Divine Providence does not seem to have arrived as yet" for Melanesia and Micronesia.

The *Instructions* then pointed out that "an easier field is available," one just as large, but "in some other islands." This was especially true, the document said, "for the large archipelagoes of Fiji, of the Navigators [now Samoa], and of others as well," located in the Central Oceania vicariate. The inhabitants there had "the most favorable dispositions for receiving the light of the gospel." Because Vicar Apostolic Bataillon had requested more missionaries than the Marist headquarters could supply, Superior General Colin had suggested that "perhaps the most suitable arrangement would be to send [there] the missionaries from Milan." Bishop Bataillon could then supervise their training, and "afterwards they could be put in charge" by him and "be given the government of the Fiji Archipelago." Later this archipelago "would be erected into a separate vicariate apostolic."

Because Propaganda considered this proposal of Colin "most prudent," it gave all necessary "faculties to the missionaries of Milan" for taking up work in the Central Oceania vicariate, "if this should please them more than going to the missions of Micronesia and Melanesia." Nor would their starting in the Central Oceania vicariate exclude their receiving the missions of Micronesia and Melanesia at a later date, when circumstances there had improved and after their numbers had sufficiently increased "to extend their field of activity."

In any event, if they did go to the Central Oceania vicariate, these *Instructions* drawn up for the missions of Melanesia and Micronesia would also be in effect there. Their training would be supervised by Bishop Bataillon, and when completed, "They would be able to take over the proposed Fiji Islands mission, which would be assigned to them and administered by them in dependence upon their own Prefect [Apostolic]...." With this precise case in mind, it was pointed out, the letters patent for Melanesia and Micronesia had been amended to read: "*or for some other Mission*, as indicated in the present *Instructions*."

Propaganda Fide actually considered the Fiji mission "preferable because it is a much easier task for this first contingent of new missionaries, and because the Central Vicariate offers much greater possibilities for training." But since it was impossible "to foresee all the reasons which might counsel" the new missionaries to make a different choice, and since the Sacred Congregation "at the same time does not wish to set limits to their zeal," it decided to abstain from ordering them to take the Fiji Mission rather than Melanesia and/or Micronesia. "It gives them freedom of action, assuring them that it will be completely satisfied and will approve whatever decision they make, provided that they follow the advice of the Marist prelates and priests...."[29]

Since these *Instructions* were written in Italian, and since they were also meant for the French Marist missionaries in Oceania who knew no Italian, Fransoni had written an additional letter in Latin meant for them. It was to be given to the Marists in Melanesia, or to Bishop Bataillon of the Central Oceania vicariate, depending upon where the Milan missionaries might go. This particular letter, Fransoni said, could be used "for every other need" as well.[30]

In his accompanying letter to Marinoni, Fransoni said that he was "confident" that now "all matters have been clarified" and that the young missionaries would be "satisfied with the beneficial and necessary measures taken by the Sacred Congregation on their behalf." Hoping "that they will be ever more reassured of this by attentively reading and pondering over" the pages of the *Instructions*, Fransoni concluded by promising "to refrain from bringing up the same subject again."[31]

When Marinoni on 20 February 1852 acknowledged the receipt of all the letters and documentation, he thanked Cardinal Fransoni especially for having named Father Reina the prefect apostolic. "Perhaps you were pleased with the ... submission with which he accepted the recent admonitions from Your Eminence. I can assure you that he made them with all the sincerity of his heart." Marinoni also thanked Fransoni for "the most wise

---

29. PF: LDB vol. 341 (1852, Part I), f. 173r–179v, *Instructions*, 9 February 1852.
30. Ibid., f. 210rv, Fransoni to Marinoni, 14 February 1852.
31. Ibid.

Instructions," saying that they would promote the welfare of his first missionary group and would be an unchangeable norm for them to follow.[32]

Prefect Apostolic Reina and his companions also wrote to Fransoni that same day and each of them signed the letter. They promised His Eminence that in choosing their particular mission, they would be guided by the *Instructions* received from the cardinal, by Colin in Lyon, by the head of the Marist supply center in Sydney, and by the vicar apostolic of Central Oceania. "And for our part we shall do as much as we can to obtain the Fiji Archipelago as our mission, thus satisfying the wishes manifested by the Sacred Congregation with such great and delicate reserve." They planned to leave for Oceania in the first week of March, if the government created no obstacles in granting their passports.[33]

Optimistic about the rapid growth of his seminary, Marinoni had told Fransoni as early as 15 January 1852 that by the end of the current year he hoped to have ready for departure "at least once again as many missionaries" as were in his first group. They could assist the pioneers who had "such a vast field to evangelize."[34]

On being informed of the departure date Father Supriès, the Carthusian monk at Pavia, wrote to Marinoni that he was filled with happiness on learning that "the angels of peace" would be leaving in March "for those innumerable islands waiting for them." His own mission was now accomplished, he said, since he was convinced "that the Lord wanted nothing more from me than to use my weakness in order to give the first impulse to this gigantic edifice." The results had far exceeded his expectations. "Now there is nothing more for me to do but pray in the silence of my cell and accompany them in all their holy enterprises with my heartfelt and warmest good wishes." He asked that Marinoni kindly keep him abreast of all developments since any news concerning this project, "to which I have been able to make a tiny contribution, will always stir up in me the most lively interest." He wanted the young missionaries to know that "I do not cease to remember them before the Lord and I carry them in my heart."[35]

As the date of departure drew near, the Milan missionaries became more conscious of the costs for founding a mission in distant Oceania. Using estimates that Colin had sent, Marinoni on 12 December 1851 had told Fransoni that his six priests and two lay missionaries would need 17,200 francs to reach their mission.[36] The cardinal on 30 December 1851 then informed Marinoni that he had allocated 17,000 francs for the journey and 1,000 francs for "furnishings, sacred vessels and other expenses connected with the founding of the mission."[37]

---

32. PF: SC Oceania vol. 4 (1848–52), f. 803r.

33. Ibid., f. 801rv, Reina to Fransoni, 20 February 1852.

34. Ibid., f. 763rv, Marinoni to Fransoni, 15 January 1852.

35. PIME: AME 28:175f, Supriès to Marinoni, 19 January 1852. Supriès mistakenly wrote 1851 when dating this letter.

36. PF: SC Oceania vol. 4 (1848–52), f. 724v.

37. PF: LDB vol. 340 (1851), f. 959v–960r.

But before this news reached Marinoni, he asked the cardinal for a larger grant on 1 January 1852, basing his request on a new estimate received from Colin. His request read like this:

For eight persons	French Francs
Journey from Milan to London:	1,600
Voyage from London to Sydney:	12,800
Voyage from Sydney to Woodlark:	10,000
Living expenses for about two years (600 francs per person per year):	9,600
Six portable altars for the priests (360 francs each):	2,160
Extraordinary costs:	3,840
Total	40,000

Since the 40,000 French francs were equivalent to 2,000 Neapolitans of gold, and since the exchange rate was 3.72 Roman scudi for one Neapolitan of gold, the amount being requested was equivalent to 7,440 Roman scudi.[38]

On receiving this new request from Marinoni, and on learning two weeks later that five priests instead of six would be in the first group going to Oceania, Fransoni passed on the estimate to an accountant for verification.[39]

After sending this request to Rome, however, Marinoni began to wonder whether he had asked for too much or too little. In addition to paying their passage, he had to provide his missionaries with medicine, clothing, furniture, building materials, and school supplies. There would also be shipping costs for these items, their books, and other personal property. Marinoni therefore wrote again to Colin on 7 January 1852, asking whether 40,000 francs was an unwarranted amount.

Colin replied on 18 January that the sum did not seem unwarranted at all. "On the one hand it is impossible to tell whether something might go wrong, thus causing unforeseen expenses," he said. "On the other hand there is no way of knowing at what future date additional aid from Europe might reach the missionaries. Therefore it would not seem imprudent to me that they carry the sum of 60,000 francs. . . ."[40]

---

38. PF: SC Oceania vol. 4 (1848–52), f. 746rv, 748r. Colin on 23 December 1851 sent the following figures on transportation costs in reply to Marinoni's inquiry of 12 December: 150 to 200 francs per person for the journey from Milan to London, 1,500 to 1,600 francs per person for the voyage from London to Sydney, and 6,000 to 10,000 francs for hiring a vessel in Sydney to take the missionaries to Woodlark. Marinoni used the larger figure in each instance. See PIME: AME 28:725f.

39. Marinoni wrote on 15 January 1852 that Father Alessandro Morino had to postpone his departure. See PF: SC Oceania vol. 4 (1848–52), f. 763v. For the accountant's report, see PF: SC Oceania vol. 4 (1848–52), f. 746/Ar.

40. PIME: AME 28:727, Colin to Marinoni, 18 January 1852. Marinoni's letter of 7 January 1852 has not

On receiving the completed report from his accountant on the proposed budget of 40,000 francs, Fransoni wrote to Marinoni that he would have liked to provide a subsidy "so large that it would be equivalent to the highest figure indicated by you." But the amount actually being granted was 3,331 Roman scudi, or the equivalent of 17,921 French francs, he said.

> Emergencies in other missions have imposed proportionate restrictions and limitations on our financial resources, and these prevent me from giving as much as I would like for this cause. Nevertheless I have gathered together all that I could . . . and I am adding a check in the amount of 2,000 Roman scudi. This means that the missionaries . . . will have for the needs of their voyage the equivalent of 5,331 Roman scudi all told. I would not say that this amount is abundant, but possibly it will suffice for the seven individuals mentioned, provided that they are discreet and parsimonious when using it.

The 5,331 Roman scudi received by Marinoni were equivalent to 28,680 French francs. Although there was now one fewer priest in the group, this amount was still 7,960 francs less than what Marinoni needed. Fransoni therefore suggested that this difference could be provided by Archbishop Romilli of Milan, by Marinoni himself, or by others who might wish to contribute funds to the missionaries at their departure.

The cardinal assured Marinoni, however, that Propaganda Fide had taken energetic action with the Lyon Council of the Association for the Propagation of the Faith in order to have it assign "a generous annual subsidy in the future for the subsistence of the missionaries . . . and also for the needs of that mission which would be assigned exclusively to them." His postscript announced that he had just been informed by the Lyon Council that it would give the departing missionaries 2,000 additional francs for purchasing sacred vessels and liturgical vestments, and that it would also provide the requested annual subsidy.[41]

The departure date was finally set for Tuesday, 16 March 1852. Archbishop Romilli of Milan celebrated the solemn Mass that morning in the chapel of the mission seminary. As he gave the mission cross to each one, he called it "your support in danger, your unfailing comfort in life and in death." The large group of priests and people at the departure ceremony included the seminary's founders: Bishop Ramazzotti, director Marinoni, Father Taglioretti, and Father Supriès.

The ages of the five priests ranged from twenty-five to twenty-eight years, and each had received from eleven to nineteen months of training in the mission seminary. The lay mission helpers, Giuseppe Corti and Luigi Tacchini, had been in training for four months and eight months, respectively. The two laymen and five priests all came from the Archdiocese of Milan.

---

been found, but is mentioned here by Colin.

41. PF: LDB vol. 341 (1852, Part I), f. 211rv, Fransoni to Marinoni, 14 February 1852. See also Fransoni's letter of thanks of the same date to Baron Antoine de Jessé, president of the Lyon Council of the Association for the Propagation of the Faith, in ibid., f. 208v–209v.

During the ceremony one priest continually shed tears. He was Father Federico Salvioni, hindered from becoming a missionary because of poor health. Under the prodding of Supriès he had traveled with two fellow seminarians to see Colin at the Marist headquarters in Lyon as early as mid-September 1845. Supriès had wanted him and his companions to learn more about Micronesia and other Marist missions so that they might "imbibe the true apostolic spirit." Salvioni was now a professor at the diocesan minor seminary of San Pietro Martire near Milan, and had remained one of the closest friends of the mission seminary. He was also a writer, and three days after the ceremony he published in the newspaper *Cattolico* an article titled, "The Departure of the Lombard Missionaries for Oceania." Later that year he became secretary to Bishop Ramazzotti of Pavia.[42]

After the church ceremony Marinoni and his seven missionaries paid a visit to the nearby Shrine of Our Lady of Saint Celso before boarding a stagecoach for their journey to France. When they stopped to change horses at Sedriano, they were surprised to find Bishop Ramazzotti, Father Taglioretti, Father Supriès, and other priests and friends waiting to bid them a last adieu. On the following day, 17 March, they reached Turin and then crossed the Alps. Since the Moncenisio Pass was covered with ice and snow at this time, they and their baggage were transferred to horse-drawn sleds. On Friday morning, 19 March 1852, they reached Lyon and were warmly received at the Marist headquarters by Superior General Colin.[43]

Marinoni and his missionaries spent three days with the Marists. One of the first things they did was to give Colin the 14 February 1852 letter addressed to him by Fransoni, which they had hand carried from Milan. It said that the Milan missionaries were being sent to Colin "to reach more precise agreements, to receive more precise information," and to obtain "whatever instructions, suggestions and assistance" Colin might still wish to offer. Reina had been chosen "prefect apostolic of the expedition and future mission," he said, and would show Colin for his "information and peace of mind" the *Instructions* that the Sacred Congregation had provided "as a norm and guideline." In them Colin would find mentioned "the wise suggestions" that he himself had made. And he would see "what confidence" Fransoni had placed in his ability to make "all the more successful" the expedition of the Italian priests.[44]

Describing this visit for Cardinal Fransoni on 22 March 1852, Marinoni said that he and his missionaries had been received "with all charity and benevolence" by the Marist

---

42. PIME: AME 9:615, Ripamonti to Marinoni, 17 March 1852; PF: CV vol. 43, f. 203r; Suigo, *Pio IX*, 143; Tragella, *Missioni estere*, 1:101f. See also chap. 1, n. 6. *Annales de la propagation de la foi*, vol. 24 (1852): 310–17, when describing the departure ceremony, gives incorrect dates and information. It quotes a 6 March (for 16 March) story from Milan as its source and says the departure took place "on Tuesday, the 2nd day [for 16th day] of this month" for missionaries "going to San Cristóbal in Micronesia to replace the Marists." There was no plan to send the Milan missionaries to San Cristóbal, nor were there Marists on the island at this time. Further, San Cristóbal is in Melanesia, not Micronesia.

43. Tragella, *Missioni estere*, 1:102.

44. PF: LDB vol. 341 (1852, Part I), f. 207v–208r.

Fathers. "We spoke with the Very Reverend Colin on the choice of a mission and we gave him the *Instructions* which Your Eminence had kindly given us. . . . We have abandoned our own views completely in favor of the decisions and the wishes of this Very Reverend Father, a true man of God. He himself will convey to Your Eminence in a letter of his own his wishes and proposals. . . ."[45]

Eight days later Prefect Apostolic Reina also wrote to Fransoni. The wish and mind of Colin, he said, was "that we should take over the mission of Micronesia and Melanesia, because he cannot bear to abandon those missions which have cost the Marist Society so much effort, such great cost, and so much blood. He expressed this most earnest wish repeatedly in reply to our questions." Wanting "to conform to the wishes of Your Eminence" as perfectly as possible, director Marinoni also approached Colin on the same matter "in private conversations" and received the same answer.

Reina said that his own decision and that of his missionaries, as to whether or not they should accept both Micronesia and Melanesia, would depend upon a number of factors. First of all it was necessary to wait and see how Fransoni himself would reply to Colin on this matter. Then, too, Reina had to conform to what the Marist Fathers in Sydney "will judge to be most opportune." The Marists there would meanwhile have "become acquainted with the wishes of Propaganda Fide and with those of their superior." And they would also be aware "of current conditions in the available missions." Reina assured Fransoni that he and his men were "ready to accept whatever mission might be considered the most opportune."[46]

Father Colin on 22 March 1852, the same day on which Marinoni had written to Fransoni, described for the cardinal the proposals that he had made to Reina and Marinoni. The Lombardy missionaries, he said, were "full of zeal, courage and confidence in God, completely prepared to give their blood for the unfortunate peoples of Oceania." Reina had duly shown him the *Instructions*, and Colin had found them "full of wisdom." They would "help maintain good relations among the missionaries of the two organizations," he said.

"I have believed it my duty," he told the cardinal,

> to counsel these missionaries to go via Sydney to Woodlark in Melanesia. I also suggested that they found a second station immediately at Rooke. Bishop Collomb and one of our members died here and were buried on this island, which is very close to New Guinea. Our members in Woodlark are acquainted with this island and some of them have lived there. They have at least an imperfect knowledge of the language. I am asking Reverend Father Frémont, the prefect apostolic, to send one of his companions to Rooke with these new missionaries in order to share their dangers and their labors. The Reverend Father Frémont would remain at Woodlark with his other companions and with the other missionaries from Milan.

---

45. PF: SOCG vol. 970 (1848), f. 841r.
46. Ibid., f. 842v, Reina to Fransoni, 30 March 1852.

When giving Fransoni the reasons that had induced him to suggest this procedure, Colin said: "In the designs of Providence it would seem to me that one cannot abandon islands already sprinkled by the blood of several martyrs. It is true that up to now these islands have remained sterile in spite of the labors of our missionaries. But our missionaries in these islands do not seem to be in any imminent danger. Perhaps the providential moment has come for these people. The recent brief sojourn in Sydney of eight youths from Woodlark [and Laughlan][47] may have proven beneficial for them. And when they return to their island[s], they will probably be able to win favor for the missionaries among their relatives." The islands "of Wallis, Futuna, Fiji, and others as well, had manifested the same difficulties and the same resistance to the grace of God in the first years [of contact]. But they were converted eventually and, without a doubt, the same will happen to Woodlark and Rooke."

For Colin it was "of the greatest importance that New Guinea be entered" as quickly as possible. "Now in order to achieve this," he said, "the most efficacious way (if God in his goodness should deign to bless this enterprise)," is to have a mission on Rooke Island, since it borders on "this important island" of New Guinea. It also seemed prudent to him "that the missionaries should make foundations on two different islands simultaneously. Then if they should find themselves in danger on one of them, or if they should discover that their activity is fruitless there, they would have the possibility of transferring to the other island."

These new proposals, Colin said, did not exclude the Fiji Islands. Since all of the Lombardy missionaries would go first to Woodlark Island, they could discuss the current situation with the veteran Marist missionaries there. "If the obstacles appeared insurmountable" at Woodlark, "by common accord they could then go to Fiji, where they would be received with open arms." And if Cardinal Prefect Fransoni should not be in agreement with these proposals, Colin said, he would still have time to contact the Milan missionaries by letter, since they were not to embark from London until 10 April.[48]

Colin's report on Woodlark and Rooke and on the great importance of New Guinea makes one wonder why these very same reasons were not valid for his retaining these missions for his own Society of Mary. His letter to Fransoni, however, must be seen as his latest in a long series of attempts to unburden his society of responsibility for Micronesia and Melanesia. Ever since 12 February 1848 he had been trying to get rid of Micronesia, a mission to which he had never sent any personnel. And ever since 6 July of that same year he had been asking Rome to free the Marists from responsibility for Melanesia as well.[49]

---

47. Colin, having incomplete information, mistakenly says all eight came from Woodlark. Actually, five came from Woodlark and three came from Laughlan. See SM: OMM/208, Thomassin to his parents, 12 October 1851.

48. PF: SC Oceania vol. 4 (1848–52), f. 811r–812r.

49. See Wiltgen, *Oceania*, 523, 527–28.

Officially Reina and his companions had assured Fransoni on 20 February 1852—one month before meeting Colin in Lyon—that they would do all in their power to obtain the Fiji Islands as their mission, "thus satisfying the wishes manifested by the Sacred Congregation with such great and delicate reserve."[50] But privately they were not at all enthusiastic about the Fiji Islands. In fact, at one of their meetings prior to leaving the Milan seminary for Lyon, they had decided that the Fiji Islands were "little suited" to their needs.[51]

Colin must have noticed in his discussions with these exuberant young men that their hearts were set on receiving both Micronesia and Melanesia, and that they had no interest in Fiji. They may even have told him so. Therefore, in dealing with them he pushed his Fiji Islands proposal into the background. This was a technique used regularly by Propaganda itself: what one group did not want, it would give to another that wanted it. Now Colin did not want Micronesia and Melanesia, and the Milan missionaries did. And so in Lyon there was a speedy and happy meeting of minds.

From the facts it would appear that both Reina and Colin were guilty of intrigue, conniving in an attempt to outwit Fransoni. The cardinal had wanted Colin's group to keep either Melanesia or Micronesia; he had also wanted Reina's group to start work in an easier mission like Fiji. Hence Colin was no more responsible—and also no less—than were Reina and his mentor Marinoni in determining the fateful choice of a mission field for the missionaries from Milan.

From Lyon on 23 March 1852, the day after Colin had sent his proposals to Fransoni, Reina sent a hasty note to treasurer Ripamonti at the Milan mission seminary. "We have found the Marist Fathers and particularly Father Colin so favorable in our regard, that it was really a mercy of God!" By this date Colin had also described in separate letters to Father Rocher, head of the Marist Center in Sydney, and to the few Marists left in Woodlark, the proposals that he had sent to Fransoni. Colin furthermore had given copies of these two letters to Reina, who in turn sent copies along with his letter of 23 March to Ripamonti in Milan.[52]

From Lyon the Milan missionaries moved on to Paris, where they lodged at the Paris Foreign Mission Seminary. While there they made an eight-day retreat, which ended with visits to the Shrine of Our Lady of Montmartre and Our Lady of Victory Church. Marinoni, still concerned about funds, received from the two councils of the Association for the Propagation of the Faith at Paris and Lyon on 3 April an additional grant of twenty thousand francs for his departing missionaries.[53] In Lyon, Marinoni and his missionaries had been introduced by the Marists to Baron Antoine de Jessé, president of the Central Council of the Association for the Propagation of the Faith.

50. PF: SC Oceania vol. 4 (1848–52), f. 801r.
51. This information is contained in a 28 July 1852 entry in Reina's diary. See PIME: AME 11:75.
52. Ibid., 63.
53. See PF: Udienze vol. 115 (1852, Part I), f. 843r, Marinoni to Fransoni, 4 April 1852.

The Italian missionaries left Paris on the Tuesday before Easter and from Boulogne sur Mer took an overnight steamship. After crossing the strait, they entered the mouth of the Thames and went up the river about eight hours "to that vast city of London," where they stayed at Hotel Ford. Their mailing address, however, was that of their bank: c/o Monsieur de la Villesboisnet, 4 Dorset Street, Manchester Square, London. This man had been "most helpful and kind," Marinoni said. He had drawn a check for thirty-five thousand francs on a bank in Sydney, Australia, "charging only two-and-one-half percent interest," whereas other banks were charging "four or four-and-one-half percent."[54]

Fransoni had requested Colin to send along one of his veteran missionaries in order to teach the Italians the language of their mission en route. But Colin had no priest to send. However, he did entrust to them Solomon Huinima, a Wallis youth brought to France by Commandant Auguste Marceau of *Arche d'Alliance*. But since Huinima's language was used neither in Woodlark nor in Rooke, the missionaries could profit little from studying his language.[55]

The date of departure from Europe had finally arrived, Holy Saturday, 10 April 1852. The *Tartar*, a seven-hundred-ton ship under Captain M. Davies, was to carry the missionaries to Sydney, Australia. Marinoni and his missionaries went by rail from London to the Thames and by steamboat to Gravesend. It was "one of the most beautiful spring days," Marinoni said. He accompanied his missionaries aboard the *Tartar*, said some final prayers with them and then parted. On Easter Sunday morning, now alone, Marinoni wrote Cardinal Prefect Fransoni that his missionaries had sailed from Gravesend "yesterday at about 4 P.M."[56]

Besides being a fine speaker, Mazzucconi was also an excellent writer. His colleagues had therefore chosen him to compose a letter in the name of all for their relatives, friends, and benefactors, which Marinoni took back to Milan. It read in part: "After the Lord has led us safely to new lands, our first and chief goal ... will be to form a church ... founded on the people living there.... Perhaps on those shores the Lord has already prepared some boy who will grow up side by side with a missionary and be introduced by him to literature and to the sciences. And perhaps, too, he will become the first teacher and priest among his people...."[57]

---

54. Ibid., f. 846r, Marinoni to Fransoni, 11 April 1852; SM: 436, Reina to Colin, 5 April 1852; Marinoni, *Scritti vari*, 270, 274.

55. SM: 436, Reina to Colin, 5 April 1852; PF: SOCG vol. 970 (1848), f. 845r, Marinoni to Fransoni, 11 April 1852; PIME: AME 11, *Notizie Sull'Istituzione del Seminario delle Missioni Estere Eretto dai Rev. Vescovi di Lombardia nel 1850: Partenza e Prime Lettere dei Missionari Giunti in Oceania*, 35. This is the only copy of *Notizie* known to exist; it is a 142-page book.

56. Marinoni, *Scritti vari*, 277; PF: SOCG vol. 970 (1848), f. 845r, 846r, Marinoni to Fransoni, 11 April 1852.

57. Tragella, *Missione Estere*, 1:105.

7

French Marists Decide to Remain at Woodlark
29 June 1852

THE *TARTAR* WITH THE SEVEN MILAN MISSIONARIES ABOARD BELONGED TO THE HOUSE of Green, which had some thirty ships on the high seas. This particular vessel had three masts, twenty-four sails, and a maximum speed of ten to ten-and-a-half knots.[1] Its crew and list of passengers numbered about 130, even though the ship was no longer than seventy paces and no wider than fourteen or fifteen.

Captain Davies was thirty-five years of age, a tall Scotsman and an admirable officer. Although belonging to a different faith, he showed himself most kind to the Roman Catholic missionaries from the very beginning. For the benefit of his passengers he went to the salon at noon each day and indicated on a map that part of the voyage which had been completed in the past twenty-four hours. He also posted the ship's latitude and longitude. Father Salerio faithfully copied this data into his tiny notebook each day, making it possible for posterity to trace the route of the *Tartar* as it sailed from Gravesend to Sydney.[2]

Salerio was a handyman, and on Easter morning, 11 April 1852, the day after they had sailed from Gravesend, he made an altar in the largest of the cabins occupied by the missionaries. That day and on the following days when weather permitted, all five priests celebrated Mass one after the other at that altar.

On Easter Monday the *Tartar* was still sailing along the coast of England, when Captain Davies sent a sailor up the main mast to unfurl a square sail. The sailor made his way to the end of the spar, and as he unlatched the cord, a gust of wind blew the sail with great force into his face, toppling him into the sea. Passengers shrieked, a lifeboat was lowered, but the sailor was never seen again. He was the first of three who would be lost at sea.

When the missionaries awoke on Tuesday morning, 13 April, their ship was anchored in the port of Plymouth on the southwestern tip of England, their only scheduled stop

---

1. PIME: AME 11, *Notizie*, 45, 49, 54.

2. *Beatificationis Positio*, 136–37, Mazzucconi to his family, 6 August 1852; *Beatificationis Positio*, 125–27, Marinoni to Ripamonti and Colleagues, 10 April 1852. For the log of Carlo Salerio, see "Giornale di Viaggio," in RIP: R B-N.2, N.1.

before Sydney. George Errington (1804–86), who had been named bishop of Plymouth the previous June, invited the missionaries to be his guests during the time that their ship was in port. He had earned a doctorate in theology in Rome and therefore could readily converse in Italian with his visitors.[3]

When they went aboard ship again on the evening of 15 April, they found not only more passengers, but also some four hundred fowl and animals. There were hens, chickens, ducks, geese, thirty rams, thirty young pigs, and a caged cow for providing fresh milk daily for morning and evening tea. Fresh water had been taken aboard, as well as salted meat, fish, biscuits, preserves, flour, and butter. Except on days when the sea was rough, they always enjoyed "fresh meat, freshly baked bread, excellent milk and water in abundance," Mazzucconi said.[4]

Following an earlier suggestion made by Colin, Marinoni while in Lyon had written from there to Fransoni requesting that he recommend to Archbishop Polding of Sydney the young Italian missionaries soon to arrive.[5]

The *Tartar* was still at Plymouth when Fransoni wrote to Polding on 15 April 1852. He said that Father Reina, along with priests and laymen from Milan, were being sent "by His Holiness" to work in "Micronesia or Melanesia as assistants to the priests of the Society of Mary." Fransoni recalled how Polding regularly had shown special concern for all missionaries headed for that area of the Pacific, receiving them and looking after them "very lovingly." But he asked the archbishop "to be even kinder" toward this latest group, "showing them every courtesy," since it was "the first small contingent of missionaries produced by the newly founded Seminary for Foreign Missions in Milan . . ." They were consequently in need of "more help than is usually offered." And whatever Polding "might give to those beloved priests, or whatever he might do for them," would be "most pleasing to this Sacred Congregation." In return for Polding's expected goodness toward them, the cardinal asked that God bestow upon him "a long and prosperous life."[6]

On Sunday, 18 April, two days after the *Tartar* left Plymouth, a Catholic Irishman died at 11 a.m. At the request of Captain Davies, Fathers Mazzucconi, Raimondi, and Ambrosoli conducted a brief burial service the next day about 9 a.m. The man's body, sewn in a sack, was then dropped into the sea.[7]

The *Tartar* crossed the equator into the southern hemisphere on 10 May 1852. Since the ship had a daily order of its own, the missionaries had to accommodate their own daily

---

3. *Beatificationis Positio*, 133–34, Mazzucconi to his family, 13 April 1852; *Beatificationis Positio*, 104f, "Introduction"; Marinoni, *Scritti vari*, 278. On Bishop Errington, see Ritzler and Sefrin, *Hierarchia Catholici Medii et Recentioris Aevi*, vol. 8, *1846–1903*, 460, 597. Errington was named bishop of Plymouth on the same day when Thomas Grant was named bishop of Southwark.

4. PIME: AME 11: 1153, 1155, Carlo Salerio to Giovanni Salerio, 6 August 1852; *Beatificationis Positio*, 137, Mazzucconi to his family, 6 August 1852.

5. PF: Udienze vol. 115 (1852, Part I), f. 841v, Marinoni to Fransoni, 22 March 1852.

6. PF: LDB vol. 341 (1852, Part I), f. 421r–422r.

7. *Beatificationis Positio*, 155, Ambrosoli to Della Longa, 10 August 1852.

order to it. Food was served six times a day: Tea was served with bread and butter at 5.30 a.m.; breakfast with beef and cutlets at 9 a.m.; and there was a snack with bread and wine at noon. Dinner with beef, pudding, and beer was served at 3.30 p.m.; tea with bread and butter at 7 p.m.; and then bread and wine at 9 p.m. "These meals might seem a bit excessive," Mazzucconi said apologetically, "but I really must say that we get very little to eat each time. . . ."

The missionaries did not take the first and last meals, since they rose at 5.30 a.m. for morning prayers, meditation, and Mass, and at 9 p.m. they recited the rosary in common. The rest of their day was filled with study, more prayers, recreation on deck, spiritual reading, and gathering in one of their cabins to chat and sing. There were "weeks and weeks of clear skies and excellent winds," Mazzucconi said. In fact "entire weeks pass by in which we pray, study, eat and sleep, without hardly realizing that we are at sea."[8]

The *Tartar* sailed in the general direction of Rio de Janeiro, Brazil, in order to catch a wind there that would blow it across the southern Atlantic Ocean toward the Cape of Good Hope. When the *Tartar* reached a point southeast of Rio de Janeiro at about twenty-six degrees south latitude and thirty-seven degrees longitude, the passengers noticed numerous ships sailing in many directions. On Sunday night, 23 May, the sky was dark and cloudy, and visibility was almost nil. Passengers were sound asleep in their bunks when the *Tartar* suddenly lurched and changed its course sharply. The missionaries ran up to the deck but could see nothing. They learned that the lookout in the crow's nest had seen a gigantic shadowy object moving toward the *Tartar* on a collision course, but only at the last moment. He shouted desperately to the helmsman who spun the wheel, changing the ship's course. A much larger vessel en route from Africa to the Americas slid by them so close that the two commanding officers were able to shout angry greetings to one another.[9]

Eleven nights later on Thursday, 3 June 1852, the missionaries had all retired for the night when overhead at 10 p.m. there were shouts of "Fire! Fire!" They jumped up from their bunks, opened their cabin doors, and were at once engulfed in dense clouds of smoke. A Frenchman was screaming, "We are lost!" With others they ran upstairs and helped carry water and throw burning beds and tables overboard. Some young officers had left a lighted candle near a fluttering curtain in their cabin, which had caused the fire. Two sailors were also badly burned in the blaze. On the following day Captain Davies praised

---

8. Ibid., 133, Mazzucconi to his family, 13 April 1852; ibid., 136, Mazzucconi to his family, 6 August 1852; Giovanni Mazzucconi, *Scritti del Servo di Dio: P. Giovanni Mazzucconi*, 221, Mazzucconi to a friend, 8 August 1852; Gheddo, *Mazzucconi*, 131.

9. *Beatificationis Positio*, 136, 140, Mazzucconi to his family, 6 August 1852; PIME: AME 11:1159, 1161, Carlo Salerio to Giovanni Salerio, 6 August 1852; Gheddo, *Mazzucconi*, 133. Gheddo in *Mazzucconi* says mistakenly that this incident took place while the *Tartar* was rounding the Cape of Good Hope. Maestrini in *Mazzucconi*, 105, mistakenly says that it occurred on the coast of South Africa. And Suigo in Mazzucconi, *Scritti*, 25, mistakenly dates the episode as 27 May instead of 23 May.

the missionaries for the rapidity and calmness with which they had reacted and said, "You are always merry and wise."[10]

The *Tartar* rounded the Cape of Good Hope on the southern tip of Africa without incident on 12 June 1852.[11]

In Sydney just three days later Bishop Bataillon, the Marist vicar apostolic of Central Oceania, wrote to Cardinal Prefect Fransoni about the Fiji Islands. Sending a tardy answer to the cardinal's query of 22 August 1851 on whether his extensive vicariate should be divided at once or later, Bataillon suggested that Rome "cut off the Fiji Islands, make them an independent vicariate apostolic, and entrust them to another mission society." There would be "200,000 souls" of the black race in the Fiji Islands vicariate, he said, and approximately one hundred thousand souls of the Polynesian race in Samoa and Tonga, the islands that he wanted to keep in his Central Oceania vicariate. The two vicariates would then each contain "a population of the same race with the same language." Bataillon did not want to be "relegated" to the Fiji Islands, he said, a part of his Central Oceania vicariate "which is not yet cultivated and whose language I do not know."[12]

The *Tartar* was only eight days en route when Colin, who had received no word from Fransoni, urged Marinoni on 18 April 1852 to contact the cardinal himself. "If Propaganda Fide should not approve of sending your missionaries to Woodlark," Colin said,

> you would still have time to write to them in Sydney, where they certainly will be obliged to stay for some time. I must admit that the letters which I have very recently received from our missionaries stationed on that island are not encouraging. The obstacles to the reception of the Catholic faith would appear considerable. If Propaganda should indicate that your missionaries ought to go elsewhere, I ask you kindly to let me know. In that case I would write to our missionaries in Woodlark, telling them to leave immediately for New Caledonia. . . . [13]

Had Colin meanwhile forgotten what he had told his men at Woodlark only ten months earlier on 23 June 1851? The decision on whether they should remain at Woodlark or leave, he had said, rested with them and not with him, because they were right on the spot and therefore could make the better judgment.[14]

---

10. RIP: R B-N.2, N.1, Carlo Salerio, "Giornale di Viaggio," 3 June 1852; *Beatificationis Positio*, 140f, Mazzucconi to his family, 6 August 1852; PIME: AME 11:1161, Carlo Salerio to Giovanni Salerio, 6 August 1852; Gheddo, *Mazzucconi*, 134. Gheddo in *Mazzucconi*, and Maestrini in *Mazzucconi*, 105, give the date of the fire incorrectly as 4 June.

11. *Beatificationis Positio*, 136, Mazzucconi to his family, 6 August 1852.

12. PF: LDB vol. 340 (1851), f. 616r–617r, Fransoni to Bataillon, 22 August 1851; PF: SC Oceania vol. 4 (1848–52), f. 924v–925r, Bataillon to Fransoni, 15 June 1852.

13. PIME: AME 28:729–30, Colin to Marinoni, 18 April 1852.

14. For more details on Colin's letter, see chap. 5, pp. 60–61.

The *Tartar* was still one month away from Sydney when this 23 June 1851 letter of Colin reached Frémont. It had been en route for one year. When Frémont answered it on 25 June 1852, he had already been serving as prefect apostolic of the Mission of Melanesia and Micronesia for one year and seven days.[15] "On learning that you leave us free to depart from Woodlark or to remain, we decided unanimously to remain," he told Colin. "We are resolved... not to abandon this post at all, unless we are ordered to do so, or if some major calamity should occur which we cannot foresee, or if Propaganda should order others to take our place."

Frémont then listed details about their work which might assist Colin in making his own judgment about their staying. "The masses have not yet been converted, nor do they manifest as yet dispositions toward early conversion," he said, continuing:

> But the spirit of the people and their opinion of us have been altered considerably to our advantage. We now have complete liberty of speech, we may circulate everywhere, and we may do whatever we wish, except convert souls. A good portion of the population... attend catechism lessons very faithfully. There is interest, there is involvement, there is something that motivates and attracts them. But what it is, neither they nor I know. They sense it themselves. Whatever it is, they are receiving instructions imperceptibly. The moment will perhaps come when those who do not see, will see, and when those who do not believe, will believe....

A catechumenate program had been launched, that is, an organized preparation for baptism. "Everyone is invited" to join the lowest class, Frémont said, "and in it we limit ourselves to explaining the dogmas and precepts of natural law. From there they advance to the second class which contains those in whom we notice more perfect dispositions. These receive a more specialized course of Christian instruction, but nothing on the mysteries of the Holy Eucharist and Confession.... We have only sixteen people in this class now, but a goodly number are seriously requesting admission." Those in the second class who become "well instructed and well disposed, will be promoted to the third class, whose aim will be a proximate preparation for the reception of holy Baptism. We do not have anyone in this class yet. But, please God, perhaps it will not be long before some are admitted."

Several reasons had prompted them to divide the catechumenate into three sections or classes, Frémont said. It would make the people strive to equal or excel one another, and their time of preparation would not seem so long. They could also be instructed more thoroughly in the law of Christ, and it would be possible to prepare them to receive the sacrament of baptism more worthily and to their greater personal advantage. "And because young unmarried people find themselves in the most critical circumstances and encounter the greatest danger for their moral lives, we shall be opening a kind of retreat house" for

---

15. Colin's letter was delivered by the chartered schooner *Jessie*, which left Sydney for Woodlark in May 1852. See Hosie, "French Mission," 417.

young men. Those "who are determined to live good lives" could go there at the end of the day.[16]

Frémont on 29 June 1852, the feast of Saints Peter and Paul, wrote to Cardinal Prefect Fransoni for the first time, saying that he had been elected "Prefect of the Mission of Melanesia and Micronesia according to the faculty granted by the Holy See." He admitted being tardy in submitting a report on his mission, but the reason was that he had been waiting to see what developments might take place.

"Our losses in material goods and in personnel, as well as the sterility of our ministry which we have experienced for about the past seven years," have had a serious effect on Superior General Colin, he said. And truly, the Melanesia and Micronesia mission had proven to be difficult and fruitless. But Father Colin

> does not dare simply to recall us, for he is not so bold as to pass sentence on these unfortunate people regarding what he rightly refers to as their eternal salvation or damnation. Ultimately he leaves it up to us, saying that we are free either to remain in these places or to leave, after we have prayed over the matter and given it deep thought. However, it seems advisable to us to refer this matter to Propaganda for a decision, and this is what we are doing now.
>
> Having stated this, let us next say that we agree unanimously—to a man—that we should stay here until such time as we may be removed, either by orders, or by successors, or because of some grave and unforeseen reasons.

Numerous reasons had prompted them to remain, Frémont said. "Instead of being expelled by the local people, we are [now] being requested to stay, not indeed because of a pure love for religion, but rather because of temporal advantages that result for them. . . . There is also sufficient money to pay for our necessary expenses. And we are as healthy as if we were in Europe." The attitude of the people had changed so much, he said, that "now we can speak, work and go on a journey with complete liberty and safety." He also described the catechumenate program for the cardinal, saying that "some are already asking for Baptism."

Without intending to do so, Frémont proved how fit he was to be superior of the mission. "Even if here and now there should be no conversions, no positive declarations in favor of the faith, no shining hope, it is not yet time to despair," he said. "What are five years in these missions, where all human means are lacking, like books, interpreters, and so on? We are barely beginning to become acquainted with the ideas, the customs, the languages, etc., of these people. So how could we earlier have been able to instruct their minds, so blinded, so undisciplined, so corrupt?" Only if God were to multiply miracles could the gospel message be accepted immediately on every side, he said. "But we must expect that through our concern and our labor, through much patience and long-suffering, God will

---

16. SM: OMM/208.

give life to those who are dead. . . . He will pity them, granting his mercy to those who do not know him, to those who do not seek him."[17]

Meanwhile top authorities of Propaganda in Rome, of the Society of Mary in Lyon, of the Foreign Mission Seminary in Milan, and even the pope himself were busy complimenting one another on the settlements reached.

Cardinal Fransoni's reply to Colin's proposal that the Milan missionaries should go immediately to Woodlark and Rooke islands, and from there try to get into New Guinea, was warm and positive. The cardinal's aim all along had been to establish a harmonious working relationship between the French and Italian missionary groups, something that now seemed guaranteed. So he told Colin on 6 May 1852, almost four weeks after the *Tartar* had left Gravesend, "I must give you my approval and I must thank you for what you have done for the Milan missionaries, for the assistance and various counsels that you have given to them, and for everything else that you have mentioned in your letter."[18]

On reading these words Colin was overjoyed, because they meant that finally he was beginning to rid himself and his society of responsibility for Micronesia and Melanesia. "The approbation kindly given by Your Eminence to the measures which we have taken conjointly with the excellent missionaries of Milan for their establishment in the mission," he said, "has been a great consolation for me."[19] Four years earlier, when Colin began pleading to be relieved of Micronesia and Melanesia, he had told Fransoni that these missions had "cost the Society of Mary eighteen missionaries." Five of these had lost their lives, and many of the others had been "forced to withdraw for reasons of health."[20] Would the missionaries of Milan have a similar fate?

By writing letters to Rome from Lyon, Paris, and London, Marinoni had kept Fransoni abreast of all that was happening to his missionaries during their last three weeks in Europe. The cardinal replied that he could do nothing "but praise the loving concern that you have manifested toward your missionaries by what you have done for them in Lyon, Paris and London . . ." Marinoni had said in his letter of 4 April 1852 from Paris, "If Your Eminence approves, I would plan to send another six priests and two catechists this coming spring." Surprisingly, Fransoni did not react to this offer in his reply. It was the second time that Marinoni had offered the cardinal additional personnel.[21]

Archbishop Romilli of Milan, the ecclesiastical authority responsible for the Foreign Mission Seminary, sent Father Colin a letter of "thanks" and "admiration" for the "wise

---

17. PF: Udienze vol. 117 (1853, Part I), f. 271rv.

18. PF: LDB vol. 342 (1852, Part II), f. 542r.

19. PF: SC Oceania vol. 4 (1848–52), f. 918r, Colin to Fransoni, 6 June 1852.

20. Ibid., f. 94r–95r, Colin to Fransoni, 6 July 1848. For more details on this letter, see Wiltgen, *Oceania*, 527f.

21. PF: LDB vol. 341 (1852, Part I), f. 477r, Fransoni to Marinoni, 29 April 1852; PF: Udienze vol. 115 (1852, Part I), f. 843r–843v, Marinoni to Fransoni from Paris, 4 April 1852. Marinoni's first offer of additional personnel was made on 15 January 1852. See p. 95.

counsel, instructions and assistance" given to the young priests from the "newly founded Institute of Lombardy."[22] Colin replied in equally gracious terms.[23]

When Pope Pius IX sent a brief about the new missionaries to Archbishop Romilli of Milan, the *Tartar* was at 125 degrees longitude below the Great Australian Bight, following an eastward route between 44 and 47 degrees south latitude. The pope had read "with great pleasure" a report of the March departure ceremony, which he called "a very auspicious beginning" for the Foreign Mission Seminary of Milan. He congratulated Archbishop Romilli and Bishop Ramazzotti, and gave "everlasting thanks to the Lord, hoping that he will send laborers into his harvest, so that these uncultured peoples may be enlightened by the Gospel and thus multiply the sons and daughters of His Holy Church." The pope promised "to implore God earnestly that he graciously bless" the efforts of the Milan missionaries "and that he incessantly assist them, so that they may gather a very great harvest from their Evangelical Mission. . . ." He signed the brief "in Rome at Saint Peter's on the tenth day of July in the year 1852, the Seventh Year of Our Pontificate."[24]

The missionaries from Milan had already rounded Tasmania and were sailing north out of the Tasman Sea toward Sydney, when Marinoni sent a copy of the pope's letter to Father Taglioretti, one of his early collaborators. "The Lord has been pleased to give us a bit of consolation to confirm us even more in our sincere desire to serve Him," Marinoni said. "The consolation could not be more authoritative, coming as it does from the lips of the Vicar of Jesus Christ. Nor could it have arrived at a more opportune time. Read this Brief and draw joy from it yourself."[25]

Marinoni sent a copy of the brief also to Father Supriès. "In a word," the Carthusian monk replied, "you are moving forward with Rome. Rome approves and blesses what has been done and also what you wish to do. Therefore everything is moving along well, everything is holy, and you ought to proceed without any fear at all. You can rightfully say: *God wills it*."[26]

On Friday, 23 July 1852, the *Tartar* was three hundred miles off the coast of Australia, moving at ten knots per hour with the help of a stiff wind.[27] That evening the wind became much stronger, coming from the Australian coast on the west and tipping the ship so much

22. SM: 436, Romilli to Colin, 27 April 1852.
23. PIME: AME 28:733f, Colin to Romilli, 9 May 1852.
24. Suigo, *Pio IX*, 144.
25. Ibid., 145, Marinoni to Taglioretti, 22 July 1852. Suigo here writes 1851 for 1852.
26. Tragella, *Missioni estere*, 1:124, Supriès to Marinoni, 4 August 1852.
27. In *Beatificationis Positio*, 142, and in Mazzucconi, *Scritti*, 210f, Mazzucconi tells his family on 6 August 1852 that the episode described took place "on the evening of 25 July, which was a Friday." But 25 July in 1852 was a Sunday. For proof that the correct date was 23 July, a Friday, see RIP: R B-N.2, N.1, Carlo Salerio, "Giornale di Viaggio," 23 July 1852, where Salerio notes in his log that the two masts were lost on 23 July. And on 24 July he says in "Giornale di Viaggio" that a gigantic wave broke open a hole in the side of the ship. Suigo in Mazzucconi, *Scritti*, 203, says that the original of Mazzucconi's letter is not to be found, so it cannot be consulted.

that it sailed on its starboard side as it headed north. Nearly all twenty-four sails were unfurled, and Captain Davies kept a watchful eye on them.

At 9 p.m. the missionaries went down to their cabins to recite the rosary as usual. They were beginning their prayers when they heard a report like a thunderclap. Immediately the ship righted itself, stood still, and all was silent. Thinking that a beam had sprung loose, Reina, Mazzucconi, and Salerio rushed to the deck. The passengers "had become pale and mute and did not dare to move," Mazzucconi said. "I asked what had happened and one of them pointed outside."

On opening the door "We were astonished to see that only the lower half of our main mast was still standing! All the rest of the mast, along with spars and sails, had been pitched into the sea." The broken topmast was held fast by the rigging, and the thickest part of the mast pressed down on the starboard side of the ship. The motion of the waves made the mast twist and turn with a grinding effect. Like an anchor it kept the ship from moving. "We looked at the mast up front, and it was intact," Mazzucconi said. "We then looked at the mast in the stern of the ship, and it too was broken in half, but it hung suspended in the air by cords and was dancing in the wind, threatening the heads of those below. Meanwhile sailors and officers stood silently by awaiting orders."

Reina and his two companions went back to their cabins to pray the rosary for God's help, and afterwards they went up on deck again. By this time one sail and half of another were still unfurled on the front mast; they could not be lowered because the pulleys were jammed. The broken main mast was still twisting and turning on the bulwark, which soon collapsed under the weight. "Then the expected order came to cut the rigging and abandon to the sea those things which could no longer be saved and were endangering the rest of the ship," Mazzucconi said. "You cannot believe how many blows of the sailors' cutlasses were needed to sever those huge cords suspended in the air."

There was an additional danger, however, and all were aware of it. Once the broken mast with its spars and sails would be cut loose and abandoned to the sea, the waves could turn it into a battering ram for hammering away at the ship and perhaps causing it to sink. But in spite of this possibility, the sailors continued slashing away at the rigging. When finally "that part of the mast which was athwart the bulwark slid into the sea," there was deathly silence. "But the ship slowly withdrew [from the spot] and we were freed," Mazzucconi said.

While some of the sailors had been cutting free the main mast from the ship, a task which took until 11 p.m., others were salvaging the dangling mizenmast spars and sails, lowering all carefully onto the deck. "Shortly afterwards," Mazzucconi noted, "the wind began to blow quite strongly once again. Our ship was off balance because of the two missing masts and it rolled frighteningly." Because of the loud wind, the wild sea, and the battered condition of the ship, hardly anyone slept that night.

Then at daybreak on Saturday, 24 July, a tremendous blow struck the side of the ship. "We jumped to our feet, hearing cries of terror overhead," Mazzucconi said. "Intermixed with these cries was the gurgling of water pouring into our ship. The stairway nearby became a chute down which the water streamed into our corridor...." It seemed like the ship was sinking. In a few minutes, however, they learned that a powerful wave had broken through the wall of a cabin above theirs. Since the breach was above the water level, it was not dangerous and not too difficult to repair. The sailors patched it within an hour, even though the force of the wave had pierced three layers of wood covered with copper plates. That day, with the help of only three of its original twenty-four sails, the battered *Tartar* continued its course northward toward Sydney.

On the following day, Sunday, 25 July, land was sighted for the first time since leaving Plymouth. It was 9 a.m. "You can imagine how happy we were," Mazzucconi said. "At midday we saw the port and wanted to enter, but the wind drove us back.... At midnight we were close once again, but the wind blocked us. We signaled to those in the lighthouse, requesting that the city send a steamboat to tow us in. But there were no steamboats available." One hour after midnight the *Tartar* was forced to head out to sea again.

At six o'clock on Monday morning, 26 July 1852, "We were so far away that we could hardly see land," Mazzucconi said. But there was an excellent wind. Flying two half-sails held together with nails and cords, their ship came into view of Port Jackson, Sydney's port, at 10 a.m. By 12 noon they were close enough for a pilot to go aboard. The *Tartar* then entered Port Jackson at 2 p.m., dropped anchor before Sydney with its fifty thousand population[28] at 4 p.m., and at 5 p.m. some passengers began to disembark.

The *Tartar*'s entry into the harbor had been humbling. Whereas other oceangoing vessels entered with twenty or twenty-two sails flying, "We had only one mast and on it were only two sails," Mazzucconi said. That afternoon Fathers Reina and Salerio went to the cathedral to pay their respects to Archbishop Polding. But he was in Perth at the opposite end of Australia on business, and so Bishop Henry Charles Davis, O.S.B., of Maitland, Polding's coadjutor, received them. He welcomed them to Australia and invited the entire group to join him for breakfast on the following day. Monday night they slept aboard ship for the last time. They had spent over one hundred nights aboard since leaving Gravesend on 10 April.[29]

They rose very early the next day, Tuesday, 27 July 1852, and each celebrated a Mass of thanksgiving. By 7 a.m. they disembarked and had breakfast with Bishop Davis and Father Rocher of the Marists, who at midday took them by steamboat to Tarban Creek, seven leagues from Sydney, where the Marist center was located. There the missionaries found Bishop Bataillon, in whose Central Vicariate the Fiji Islands were located. With him were thirteen young men from various islands in his vicariate, including some Fijians.

---

28. Mazzucconi's figure of fifty thousand population is approximate. The 1851 census gives the population for the City of Sydney as 42,240, and for its suburbs as 9,684, or a total of 51,924.

29. Both PIME: AME 11, *Notizie*, 45, and Maestrini in *Mazzucconi*, 103, state that the voyage lasted 105 days. To obtain this figure, the writers omitted the 3 days, 13 to 15 April, when the *Tartar* lay at anchor in Plymouth.

Reina and his companions also met here Father Montrouzier, the Marist missionary formerly assigned to Woodlark, who had accompanied to Sydney the eight young men from Woodlark and Laughlan islands in 1851.[30]

The stage was now set, and the consultations desired by Cardinal Fransoni and called for by the *Instructions* could begin. The Milan missionaries would have to decide whether they should go to the Fiji Islands, as Cardinal Fransoni had warmly suggested; or whether they should go to Woodlark and Rooke islands in Melanesia, and then to New Guinea, as Father Colin had suggested when they visited him in Lyon; or whether they should go to Micronesia, as Father Supriès had been suggesting since 1845 when he first met Mazzucconi.

Several nights later at the Marist residence in Tarban Creek, Mazzucconi wrote a lengthy letter to his family. "I want to spend this evening entirely with you," he said, and he did so by giving his family numerous details on his voyage to Sydney. He reminisced on crossing the equator, saying that he was "particularly struck by the heat, the calm and the disappearance of our North Star." He recalled having observed that star so very many times in the seminary garden back home. During the voyage, he said, "We gazed up at it every night while seated on the poop deck. But we noticed that it was always getting lower on the horizon. Then one evening we looked for it in vain."[31] Mazzucconi would discover a whole new firmament in the Southern Hemisphere. Little was he aware that he would never see the North Star again.[32]

---

30. *Beatificationis Positio*, 142–47, Mazzucconi to his family, 6 August 1852; PIME: AME 11:1175–83, Carlo Salerio to Giovanni Salerio, 6 August 1852; PIME: AME 11:507, Ambrosoli to Della Longa, 10 August 1852; RIP: R B-N.2, N.1, Carlo Salerio, "Giornale di Viaggio," 23 to 27 July 1852; PF: SC Oceania vol. 4 (1848–52), f. 978rv, Reina to Fransoni, 27 August 1852.

31. *Beatificationis Positio*, 136, 139, Mazzucconi to his family, 6 August 1852.

32. For some of the nautical terminology in this chapter the author is indebted to C. J. Ware, Reader's Services Section, National Maritime Museum, Greenwich, London.

8

Rome Grants Numerous Faculties to Melanesia Missionaries 1850–1853

IN ORDER TO MAKE PREPARATIONS FOR THEIR VOYAGE TO SYDNEY, FATHERS SALERIO AND Mazzucconi had left Paris for London a few days before the others. At 8 o'clock one morning they had boarded a steamer at Boulogne sur Mer on the French coast, had crossed the Strait of Dover, and had arrived about 11 a.m. at Folkestone on the English coast. From there they left by train at 6 p.m. and arrived in London at 10.30 p.m.

They paid a visit to Nicholas Patrick Cardinal Wiseman (1802–65), the archbishop of Westminster, on Tuesday, 6 April 1852. Wiseman first spoke English with his guests, then French, but switched to Italian on learning who they were. He had been informed by Archbishop Romilli of Milan of their coming. The two priests, perhaps unaware that Wiseman had spent some twenty-two years in Rome, marveled at his fluency in Italian. He gave them "all the faculties" that they needed, Mazzucconi said, "for blessing marriages, performing Baptisms or receiving [people] into the church, and for hearing confessions aboard ship and in distant places, where it might not be possible to reach the local bishop." The Holy See had empowered the archbishop of Westminster and the archbishop of Dublin to give these faculties to missionaries leaving by ship for service overseas.[1]

The "faculties" received by Salerio and Mazzucconi from Wiseman were rights or powers granted to a subordinate in order to perform certain ecclesiastical functions. In granting a faculty the superior extends the exercise of his own jurisdictional power by sharing it with another. Not having a required faculty makes the performance of a function by a subordinate either invalid or illicit.[2]

On Easter Sunday morning, 11 April 1852, the day after the *Tartar* sailed from Gravesend on its way to Sydney, director Marinoni wrote from London to Cardinal Prefect Fransoni that the "only sorrow" experienced by his missionaries on leaving was that "they

---

1. *Beatificationis Positio*, 129f, Mazzucconi to his brothers and sisters, 8 April 1852; *Beatificationis Positio*, Documento VI, Introduzione, 104.

2. See John Joseph McGrath, "Faculties (Canon Law)," in *New Catholic Encyclopedia*, 5:786–87; A. James Quinn, "Faculties, Decennial" and "Faculties, Quinquennial," in *New Catholic Encyclopedia*, 5:787.

did not receive the promised letter from Your Eminence with faculties." The archbishop of Westminster, Marinoni said, "had granted them the faculties which were necessary for the voyage, like hearing one another's confessions and those of others."³

Fransoni wrote back on 29 April, saying that he did indeed receive Marinoni's letter of 22 March from Lyon, the one containing the request for faculties. But he did not answer immediately, because the letter "did not reach me on time to get a reply back to you" at the forwarding address indicated. Moreover, the requested faculties had to be obtained from the pope, and there had been "a lack of [papal] audiences." In the future, Fransoni said, "It would be fitting for you to take action in due time by anticipating emergencies. Then there would be a considerable latitude making it possible to provide for any need."⁴

Marinoni's letter of 22 March 1852 from Lyon had asked Fransoni whether his missionaries could follow the liturgical calendar used in the Roman Rite instead of the calendar peculiar to the Ambrosian Rite of Milan, to which they were accustomed. (A rite is the manner in which liturgical worship is carried out and includes ceremonial observances.) And if no particular feast was prescribed by the Roman calendar for a particular day, Marinoni requested that his priests be allowed on those days to pray the Divine Office of the Most Blessed Sacrament, of the Passion of Jesus Christ, of the Immaculate Conception, or "of saints for whom they have a special devotion."⁵

Secretary Barnabò brought this request to the attention of Pope Pius IX on Sunday, 18 April 1852. The pope granted the desired faculties for a period of three years.⁶ (This happened to be the day on which the Irishman had died aboard the *Tartar*.)

Earlier that same year on 15 January, after learning that Fransoni was preparing faculties for his missionaries, Marinoni had written to ask that the cardinal send the faculties as soon as possible. This would make it possible for his missionaries to embark at once and thus "avoid the cold of the Cape of Good Hope, where there is winter during our summer." In addition Marinoni had requested for Father Reina, the superior, "all the faculties already granted to Bishop Epalle when he was designated Vicar Apostolic of Micronesia and Melanesia."⁷ Epalle, in fact, had been ordained a bishop in Rome on Sunday, 21 July 1844, by Fransoni himself. That same day Father Brunelli, secretary of Propaganda Fide, had obtained from Pope Gregory XVI for Epalle the faculties usually granted "to the vicars apostolic of those far-distant regions," plus a few more that Epalle had specifically requested.⁸

Marinoni's request for "all the faculties already granted" to Bishop Epalle was not unusual. Propaganda knew that the ecclesiastical superiors in Oceania would all have similar problems and consequently would need similar faculties. The practice of conferring

---

3. PF: SOCG vol. 970 (1848), f. 845r.
4. PF: LDB vol. 341 (1852, Part I), f. 476v–477r.
5. PF: Udienze vol. 115 (1852, Part I), f. 841rv.
6. Ibid., f. 802r, 805v–806r.
7. PF: SC Oceania vol. 4 (1848–52), f. 763rv.
8. Wiltgen, *Oceania*, 304–5. Brunelli later became an archbishop, on 23 May 1845.

similar faculties had a long history and started with Bishop Pompallier, vicar apostolic of Western Oceania. When Father Angelo Mai, then secretary of Propaganda, approached Pope Gregory XVI to request faculties for newly ordained Bishop Pompallier on 10 July 1836, he asked for "the same faculties granted by Your Holiness to the Most Reverend Rouchouze, Bishop of Nilopolis and Vicar Apostolic of Eastern Oceania." The pope granted the faculties without hesitation.[9]

Bishop Pompallier and his missionaries were waiting for their ship to sail from Le Havre, France, when secretary Mai again approached Gregory XVI on 20 November 1836. He said that Pompallier "requests the faculty for himself and for his missionaries of being dispensed from using wine in the two ablutions at Mass in view of the exorbitant price of wine and the difficulty in obtaining it in that very remote vicariate." The pope also granted this faculty.[10] The law for bishops and priests everywhere at this time was to purify the chalice twice at Mass after having consumed the consecrated wine, using first unconsecrated wine and then water along with unconsecrated wine.

When Marinoni wrote to Fransoni on 15 January 1852, asking that Epalle's faculties be granted to Reina, he could therefore expect to have his request granted. But Propaganda had more foresight than Marinoni realized and had anticipated his request by four days. On 11 January, a Sunday, Reina had been named "Prefect Apostolic of Melanesia, or of Micronesia, or of some other mission in Oceania. . . ."[11] That same day secretary Barnabò had approached Pope Pius IX and had requested for the priest Reina, "all those faculties customarily given to vicars apostolic in Oceania, including that of confirming, but excluding those which require the episcopal character. . . ." The pope, however, did not grant the faculties directly. He reminded Barnabò that earlier he had delegated these faculties to Cardinal Prefect Fransoni, and that consequently the cardinal was authorized to subdelegate the faculties to whomsoever he wished.[12]

Fransoni subdelegated the faculties to Reina that same day, 11 January 1852, and he was more than generous. He granted thirty faculties for the exceptionally long period of fifteen years. At the end of that period they could be renewed upon request.

The first fifteen faculties were dispensations—that is, acts that remove an obligation imposed by law. Faculty number one authorized Reina "to dispense from any irregularity whatsoever, also that resulting from voluntary homicide, provided that in this latter case no scandal arises because of dissension."

An "irregularity" is an impediment resulting from church law that renders it unlawful for a person to receive ordination and forbids the exercise of orders already received. The impediment can be removed only by dispensation. An irregularity is not a penalty, but rather a means of safeguarding the dignity of the clerical state and office by excluding

---

9. Ibid., 126.
10. Ibid., 134.
11. See chap. 6, nn. 26 and 27.
12. PF: Udienze vol. 115 (1852, Part I), f. 58v–59r.

those who are unqualified for the service of the altar. Granting this power to dispense was Rome's way of encouraging Reina to start training candidates for the priesthood as soon as possible, even though one or the other might have killed someone in a tribal war. (After World War II there were European candidates for the priesthood, actively engaged in combat during that war, who later requested and obtained this same dispensation before becoming priests.)

Reina was likewise authorized to dispense from all oaths whatsoever, from restitution being made by poor people in certain cases, and from numerous marriage impediments. He could grant a dispensation from the disparity of cult impediment, for example, whereby a baptized man could validly enter marriage with an unbaptized woman, and a baptized woman could validly enter marriage with an unbaptized man, under certain conditions. A similar dispensation regarding the impediment of mixed religion allowed Reina to authorize marriages between Roman Catholics and Protestants. He could also allow newly baptized men, who possessed several wives prior to baptism, "to retain whichever one of these they preferred, if the chosen one also joined the faith. But if the first wife wished to convert," she was to be recognized as the lawful wife. This was an enlargement of the Pauline privilege. All of these dispensations from marriage impediments were to be granted by Reina "completely gratis."

Faculties numbered sixteen through eighteen gave Reina the authority to absolve those who had fallen into heresy, those who had apostatized, those who were schismatics, those who had been excommunicated, and those who had been inflicted with any kind of ecclesiastical censure and penalty, even if the censures and penalties may have been reserved to the Holy See by some ecclesiastical constitution.

Faculty number nineteen allowed Reina to consecrate chalices, patens, and portable altars, provided that he used oils blessed by a bishop. Faculty number twenty allowed priests, "whose eyesight had become defective or who were afflicted with some other infirmity, to celebrate a votive Mass of the Blessed Virgin Mary or a Mass for the deceased, if they could not read the particular Mass formulas assigned to each day of the year by the rubrics of the Roman Missal." Faculty number twenty-one allowed Reina "to retain and read heretical books, or those of pagans dealing with religion, in order to confute them."

Faculty number twenty-three empowered Reina to administer the sacrament of confirmation to both sexes, but without wearing pontifical robes, and provided that he used chrism blessed by a Roman Catholic bishop, even if the chrism had been blessed two, three, or four years previously. Faculties numbered twenty-four to twenty-six authorized him to bless rosaries, crosses, and medals; to erect the Way of the Cross; and to found confraternities of the Most Holy Rosary, of the Most Sacred Heart of Jesus, of the Propagation of the Faith, of the Scapular of the Blessed Virgin Mary, and others as well that had been approved by the Holy See. At the same time he was authorized to apply to these confraternities "each and every indulgence and privilege, which the Supreme Pontiffs [or popes] have granted to the confraternities mentioned." The same was true for the Way of the Cross.

Faculty number twenty-seven not only extended the area in which Reina was free to use his numerous faculties, but also authorized him to extend the area in which his missionaries could make use of the faculties that he had subdelegated to them. He and they could "use these faculties validly and licitly in any lands or islands whatsoever, to which by force or by necessity [he or] they may have to translocate, and for the amount of time that [he or] they must remain in those places, provided that no other missionary is there, and that the said lands or islands are not under the jurisdiction of someone else."

Faculty number twenty-nine gave Prefect Apostolic Reina the power to name a pro-prefect, if circumstances required this. Reina, and in his absence also his pro-prefect, were authorized "to subdelegate in whole or in part the previously mentioned faculties to other missionaries." Furthermore, Reina was authorized by faculty number thirty to subdelegate all of his faculties "in whole or in part to his pro-prefect and to other missionaries within his district in such a way, that they in turn could subdelegate the faculties to other missionaries subject to them."[13] After examining his thirty faculties, Reina decided to write to Rome for several more. Hesitant about sending his request to Fransoni, from whom he had just received the thirty faculties, he wrote instead on 27 February 1852 to Father Bertinelli, the spokesman in Rome for the bishops of Lombardy. Reina asked for himself and for his missionaries the faculty to hear one another's confessions while en route to their mission. This faculty was indeed among the thirty that he had received, but he was not allowed to use any of the thirty until he reached his own mission territory and until he had been authorized to use them by the Marists.

Reina also requested authorization to delegate Marinoni in such a way that Marinoni could subdelegate to new missionaries leaving Italy the faculties that they would need in Reina's mission. Reina explained to Bertinelli that he might well be in some remote place at the time of their arrival in his mission. The new missionaries would then have to wait until his return in order to obtain the necessary faculties. Superior General Colin of the Marists, he said, had been granted a faculty like this for the benefit of his missionaries leaving for Oceania. Reina also wished to have the faculty of using oil in place of candles during Mass, because "those countries have no wax."[14]

On its way to Rome at this very time was another request for the faculty of using oil in place of wax. It had been prepared by Prefect Apostolic Frémont on 16 October 1851 at Woodlark in Melanesia and was addressed to Colin in Lyon,[15] who forwarded it to Fransoni on 3 May 1852. "I was puzzled," Frémont's letter said,

> at not finding anywhere in the pages regarding the Prefect Apostolic, the faculty to use oil in place of wax at Holy Mass. For some time now we have been finding ourselves forced to make use of this dispensation, or else not celebrate Mass at all. But since this dispensation ordinarily is granted, and since our deceased Vicar Apostolic

13. PIME: AME 1:53–56. See n. 42 on the Pauline privilege. Need full information for AME.
14. PF: CV vol. 43, f. 179r.
15. SM: OMM/208.

[Collomb] had it among his faculties, we presume that it is the intention of Holy Church rather that we say Mass using oil, than that we abstain from Mass.... But to be in order, I ask that you obtain this dispensation for us from Rome, since we shall be obliged to make use of it, perhaps often, if we remain in these lands.[16]

The oil to which both Reina and Frémont referred was whale oil. It had been used as fuel for lamps since the 1600s and continued being used until the 1860s, when kerosene became plentiful. Whale oil was produced by boiling blubber, the strip of fat lying beneath the skin of whales. Since the whaling industry at this time was flourishing, and since whaling vessels were frequent visitors to the islands of Melanesia, whale oil became the least expensive and most readily available source of light for the missionaries there.

Frémont's request was presented to Pius IX by secretary Barnabò on Sunday, 16 May 1852. The faculty ought to be granted to Frémont, the pope said, "in the form and in the terms of the concession granted to the deceased Vicar Apostolic [Collomb]." He added that "a decree should be transmitted on animal wax."[17]

When sending the decree to Colin on 22 May 1852 for forwarding, Fransoni said that Frémont's request had been unnecessary. "This faculty, in fact, ought not to have been understood as being granted to the person of the deceased Prelate," he said, "but rather to the mission, as long as the lack of wax persisted. Oil could therefore have been used without any hesitancy." But "for their greater peace of mind," the matter had been presented to the pope, "who kindly decided to renew" for the missionaries and missions of Melanesia and Micronesia "the faculty *in the form and in the terms of the concession granted* to the deceased Vicar Apostolic."[18]

Propaganda Fide could have given Frémont this faculty also in virtue of a decree that had been issued twenty months earlier by the Sacred Congregation of Rites, today called the Sacred Congregation for the Sacraments and Divine Worship. During a regular meeting of that congregation on 7 September 1850 in the Vatican, secretary Barnabò of Propaganda had presented a request to use whale oil for beeswax while celebrating Mass. The request came from the missionaries of Oceania, he said. They could not get beeswax or vegetable oil for candles or lamps, but they could easily obtain the purified oil or fat of whales. When purified, this oil "gives a bright, pure and good light," he said. The missionaries wished to use this oil, "since they do not want to celebrate Mass without light."

After hearing the report of Barnabò, the cardinals of the Rites Congregation discussed the matter and formulated two statements: (1) The missionaries would be granted the faculty of using whale oil, "if it is impossible for them to obtain beeswax for the candles used at divine services." (2) "And if they cannot obtain oil," it would be permissible for them to celebrate divine services "without any light." The vote taken on these statements was affirmative, "provided that their requests coincide with the truth." The Rites Congregation then

16. PF: Udienze vol. 115 (1852, Part I), f. 1153r.
17. Ibid., f. 1154v.
18. PF: LDB vol. 342 (1852, Part II), f. 572r.

issued a decree dated 7 September 1850 containing all of this information. It was signed by Luigi Cardinal Lambruschini, prefect of the Sacred Congregation of Rites, and by his secretary, Monsignor Giuseppe Gaspare Fatati.[19]

As new needs arose, mission heads in various parts of Oceania submitted requests for new faculties. Father Montrouzier of Woodlark Island, the Marist pro-vicar of the Melanesia and Micronesia vicariates, had requested eight faculties from Cardinal Prefect Fransoni on 22 June 1849. "I humbly present the following difficulties to the judgment of your Sacred Congregation for a solution," he said.

Of his eight queries, only three fell within the competence of Propaganda Fide, namely:

> (2) Are two priests and one lay brother at the same mission station a large enough number for receiving permission to preserve the Most Holy Sacrament of the Eucharist, supposing that all other requisites are fulfilled? If the answer is negative, how many missionaries must there be, so that the foresaid faculty may be granted to them?
>
> ... (5) All infants because of their frailty are in danger. Would this be a sufficient reason for baptizing indiscriminately and by private Baptism, all newly born infants whom we find on our weekly or near weekly visits? Although the parents refuse to bring them to church because of the distance, there is reason to hope that these children will be educated as Christians.
>
> ... (8) In view of there being such a great variety of authors on rubrics, could someone choose with a safe conscience one of these works and not deviate from it, for example, *Manuel des cérémonies romaines*? Or is each one bound to select sections from all the different authors?[20]

---

19. PF: SC Oceania vol. 4 (1848–52), f. 523r. The author has not learned who among the Oceania missionaries prompted this decree. However, the initiative may well have come from Father Bernin, pro-vicar of the New Caledonia vicariate. During his stay in Rome in August 1850, he was constantly in contact with Fransoni and Barnabò. As Bishop Douarre's and Father Colin's representative, he discussed with Fransoni and Barnabò numerous problems of the Marist vicariates (Central Oceania, New Caledonia, Melanesia and Micronesia, and the Navigators Archipelago).

The request for the use of whale oil by missionaries in Oceania may well have come up during these discussions. In fact, the printed decree of the Rites Congregation dated 7 September 1850 is attached to that page of Propaganda's archives, which is preceded by a 10 August 1850 letter of Bernin to Barnabò and is followed by a 25 September 1850 letter of Colin to Fransoni. The dates and the placement of the three documents tend to indicate a close and most likely causal connection between them. See PF: SC Oceania vol. 4 (1848–52), f. 521r–526r. Furthermore a note on the rear of the sheet to which the decree is attached, f. 523v, says: "Decree on stearic wax for the distant missions." For Bernin's activities in Rome at this time, see Wiltgen, *Oceania*, 512–19, 539–42, 544.

20. PF: SC Oceania vol. 4 (1848–52), f. 461r. The manual referred to by Montrouzier was no doubt the newly corrected and expanded edition of *Manuel des cérémonies romaines: tiré des livres romains les plus authentiques, et des écrivains les plus récens et les plus intelligens en cette matière*. This two-volume work (384 pp. in vol. 1 and 368 pp. in vol. 2) was published by Fischer-Joly et Compagnie in Avignon, France, in 1840, five years before Montrouzier and twelve other Marists left London for Melanesia with Bishop Epalle, who was the first vicar apostolic of Melanesia and Micronesia. See Wiltgen, *Oceania*, 330.

It was Montrouzier himself who had introduced the practice of "baptizing indiscriminately and by private Baptism, all newly born infants," for fear that they might die without baptism, as Frémont later told Colin.[21] And so Montrouzier by this query was seeking justification for a practice that he himself had introduced into the mission. His view, it seems, was not shared by all the Marists at Woodlark mission.

Fransoni answered Montrouzier on 14 March 1850, repeating in full his three queries and giving Propaganda's reply to each. As for number two, he said, "The grounds for reserving the Sacrament of the Most Holy Eucharist do not depend so much upon the number of missionaries living together, as upon the safeness of the place and its being out of danger, provided that all other conditions are fulfilled."

Regarding number five on the baptism of newborn babes, he said: "If you mean baptizing the infants of pagans, we judge that the answer must absolutely be negative. For you must know that the words *in danger of death*, or rather *at the moment of death*, are to be taken strictly. Consequently they do not imply any kind of danger, or remote danger, but rather a proximate critical moment."

As for number eight on rubrics, Fransoni said: "We inform you that one must adhere to those rubrics—and thus one acts safely—which are contained in the *Roman Ritual*, in the *Missal*, and in the *Ceremonial*. Also, uniformity is to be diligently preserved in this area."

Fransoni sent the above explanations to Montrouzier and added that five of his queries had been sent to the "Supreme Inquisition." This sacred congregation, officially known as the Holy Roman and Universal Inquisition, was also called the Holy Office. Today it is known officially as the Sacred Congregation for the Doctrine of the Faith. The primary task of this body has always been to assist the pope in examining questions from around the world concerning faith and morals in order to safeguard Roman Catholic doctrine. Fransoni promised to forward the replies of this body to Montrouzier as soon as they reached his office.[22]

On 9 March 1850, a Saturday, the day after secretary Barnabò forwarded the five queries of Montrouzier to the Holy Office, he himself "in virtue of extraordinary faculties kindly granted to me by His Holiness, Pope Pius IX," issued some faculties in response to still further requests received from Montrouzier. Had the pope been in Rome, the requests would have been presented to him personally by Barnabò. But since the pope was in exile

---

The bibliographic record was located for the author among the 13 million entries in the Online Union Catalog of the Online Computer Library Center (OCLC), Dublin, Ohio, U.S.A., by the Reverend Doctor James J. Artzer, S.V.D., of Rutgers University, New Brunswick, New Jersey. The only library listed as holding the work at the time of the search (9 June 1986) was the College of Saint Thomas in Saint Paul, Minnesota. Bibliotheca Pagesiana at the Marist Generalate in Rome has an edition published in Paris in 1717 (vol. 1: xiv + 491 pp.; vol. 2: viii + 492 pp.).

21. SM: OMM/208, Frémont to Colin, 22 June 1851.

22. PF: LDB vol. 339 (1850), f. 197v–199r.

at Portici south of Naples, he had delegated Barnabò to reply in his name and with his authority.[23]

One of the requests made by Montrouzier was that the missionaries of Melanesia and Micronesia "be dispensed from using copes, as well as palls interlaced with gold or silk, and wine cruets made of glass, since all that we now have are broken through use." Glass cruets held the wine and water needed for Mass. The cope was a capelike liturgical vestment open in front, fastened at the chest, and reaching almost to the feet; it was used in processions and other ceremonies.

Montrouzier had also asked "that the missionaries of Melanesia and Micronesia be granted permission to practice medicine on one another and on the local people, as well as to cauterize under the usual conditions. The reason for the latter request," he said, "is that very many of the local people in these regions suffer from open sores which frequently cannot be cured except by searing." Montrouzier had requested further that this privilege "be granted to me personally in case I should be sent to other regions by my Superiors."[24]

The faculty regarding copes, palls, and cruets was granted by Barnabò "as requested."[25] But before deciding what to reply regarding the practice of medicine and cauterizing, Barnabò had some investigation done on previous positions taken by his Sacred Congregation on this matter. He then based his decision on the results of that study.

"Generally speaking," the prepared report said, "the faculty of practicing medicine and surgery has been denied except in particular cases. Thus in 1665 Capuchin missionaries in Georgia [on the Black Sea] asked Propaganda kindly to grant them the permission to practice the arts of medicine and surgery in those places where pious missions were being preached. Propaganda felt that the requested dispensation could be granted, provided that the following conditions were fulfilled: the missionary priest, namely, had to be skilled in the art of medicine and surgery; he had to perform his services gratis; and he was not allowed to make incisions or to cauterize. Moreover, the faculty could be used only if there were no lay doctors where the missionary resides." This decree was issued by Propaganda on 23 November 1665, during the reign of Pope Alexander VII.

The report went on to say that "this same Propaganda sent a request from the Vicar Apostolic of China to the Sacred Congregation of the Council. His question was: What must missionaries in these regions do when it becomes necessary to cut away one of the principal parts of the body on behalf of someone who is suffering and in evident danger of death? The Sacred Congregation of the Council replied on 9 February 1669: In case of necessity one may have recourse to incisions. On 27 June 1701 faculties were granted to

---

23. PF: Udienze vol. 111 (1850, Part I), f. 167r.

24. PF: SC Oceania vol. 4 (1848–52), f. 461r, Montrouzier to Fransoni, 22 June 1849. Montrouzier's Latin was not perfect, but from the sense of his request regarding the practice of medicine, and from Rome's reply, it is clear that he wanted faculties for practicing it on missionaries and on the local people. His Latin text reads: "sive pro seipsis sive erga indigenas."

25. PF: Udienze vol. 111 (1850, Part I), f. 165r.

the Prefect [Apostolic] of Nubia and Burno for practicing medicine and also for surgical operations, like making some small incisions, cauterizing, applying burning cotton, drawing blood, and similar operations."

A commission of theologians deputized by Propaganda "gave this reply on 28 November 1641: If it is a case of necessity, missionaries do not need a dispensation and may licitly engage in healing." The report then gave modern examples of missionaries practicing medicine, like "the case of 19 February 1837, when four missionaries in the East Indies were granted permission to practice medicine and surgery, to draw blood, and to open tumors. Also on 2 June 1833, three professed priests of the [Hospitaller] Order of Saint John of God were granted the faculty to practice medicine *in general*, and in cases of necessity also surgery, provided that no payment was accepted. When this faculty was granted to a certain Father Liguorino in March 1827, the [restrictive] clauses *without cauterizing* and *without incisions* were omitted."

The report concluded with this observation: "If a missionary obtains faculties like this for the benefit of others, it seems even more logical that he should be able to make use of them for himself. However, no example of this has been found."

Using the extraordinary faculties delegated to him by Pius IX, Barnabò authorized the missionaries of Melanesia and Micronesia to practice medicine on one another and on the local people, as well as to cauterize. But they could do this "only in cases of necessity and without accepting payment, provided that all due measures be taken, especially with regard to propriety when curing open sores. They must abstain, however, from curing open sores of women." Contrary to Montrouzier's wish, he was not given these faculties personally. He was told to apply again in case he actually should be transferred to some other mission.

Barnabò granted these faculties in Rome on 9 March 1850.[26] And on 14 March Fransoni, who was in exile in Naples, sent them to Montrouzier through Colin along with his own replies to Montrouzier's three queries, numbers two, five, and eight.[27]

It was 8 March 1850 when Secretary Barnabò sent the five difficulties of Montrouzier, which were not within the competence of Propaganda, to Father Tommaso-Giacinto Cipolletti of the Order of Preachers (O.P.), who was commissary of the Holy Office.[28] Montrouzier wanted to know,

(1) How should we conduct ourselves, when it is necessary for us to land on a new island inhabited by uncivilized people? Should we persuade the sailors—or at least permit them—to show themselves ready for battle? And here is a much greater

---

26. Ibid., f. 164r, 165r, 167r, 172r–173r. For further details on medical practice and surgery being authorized for missionaries, see Metodio Carobbio da Nembro, "La Missione Etiopica nel secolo XVIII," in *Sacrae Congregationis de Propaganda Fide Memoria Rerum: 350 Years in the Service of the Missions 1622–1972*, vol. 2, *1700–1815*, 465 nn. 8 and 9. He cites passages from PF: Acta vol. 71 (1701), f. 149rv, 169r–170v.

27. PF: LDB vol. 339 (1850), f. 197v–199r, Fransoni to Montrouzier, 14 March 1850; PF: LDB vol. 339 (1850), f. 199r, Fransoni to Colin, 14 March 1850.

28. Ibid., f. 232r.

difficulty for us: If these uncivilized people attack, may we join the laymen [sailors] in repelling force with force, regardless of whether we be the bishop, or other missionaries and lay brothers in temporary vows?

(3) When receiving catechumens, is it the mind of the Holy Roman Church: (a) that certain rituals and certain prayers are to be used? (b) What are these ceremonies and words? (c) And in case the rituals and prayers prescribed by the Roman Ritual for Baptism are used [in the ceremony for receiving catechumens], should these be repeated when eventually the sacrament [of Baptism] is administered?

(4) There is a vague suspicion that our local people, who ordinarily are plagued with many superstitions, will attribute to Baptism itself the death of infants who are baptized when they are dying. They do this because they see special water being used. Would we be allowed in this case to use water that has not been blessed, until we become better acquainted with the thinking of our local people?

(6) What stand must we take on marriages in Woodlark? There is no man born here, or almost none, who has not deserted his first wife for at least some months. Are these marriages to be considered real marriages?

(7) What is to be done in case the first wife asks for Baptism? Must we insist that she leave her husband, if he refuses to give up his concubines?[29]

When submitting the five queries of Montrouzier to the Holy Office on 8 March 1850, Barnabò had said: "I shall await your reply."[30] He waited a year and two months before Monsignor Prospero Caterini, assessor of the Holy Office, sent him a reply on 16 May 1851.[31] Two days earlier, on 14 May, the cardinal members of the Sacred Congregation of the Holy Office had discussed the five queries of Montrouzier. Their decision on number one regarding self-defense was: "Affirmative in all of its points." Their answer to number three regarding catechumens was: "Consult the *Roman Ritual* on the Baptism of adults." Their reply to number four on the use of unblessed water for baptism was: "It may be used in this case." These decisions were all approved by Pope Pius IX.[32]

Caterini pointed out in his letter to Barnabò that only three of the five queries had been answered, because "the lack of necessary clarifications" had rendered it impossible to answer numbers six and seven, the two questions on marriage. Before a reply could be

---

29. PF: SC Oceania vol. 4 (1848–52), f. 461r. An abbreviation for "Holy Office" in the margin, "S. Of.," indicates which of the eight queries were sent to that body.

30. PF: LDB vol. 339 (1850), f. 232r.

31. PF: SC Oceania vol. 4 (1848–52), f. 598r.

32. This information was copied from the archives for the author by Father Giuliano Geppetti of the Order of Friar Servants of Mary (O.S.M.), a scribe in the Sacred Congregation for the Doctrine of the Faith, formerly known as the Holy Office.

given to them, he said, the petitioner would have to "specify in a detailed way the customs of those peoples regarding marriage."[33]

Fransoni sent a copy of this 16 May 1851 letter from the Holy Office to Colin on 24 May, asking that he forward it to Montrouzier along with the other decisions already reached by the Holy Office. He hoped that the replies "might serve as a norm" for the missionaries of Melanesia and Micronesia. He also asked Colin to have the missionaries there "send me the information that is requested by the Holy Office."[34]

Colin forwarded the documents to his missionaries in Woodlark on 23 June 1851,[35] but it took one year for his letter to arrive in Woodlark. By that time Montrouzier was in Sydney, and Frémont had been prefect apostolic for a year. The faculties, therefore, did not go to Montrouzier, but to Frémont, who sent the desired information on local marriages to Cardinal Fransoni by return mail on 29 June 1852. This information was included in a further request for faculties which read as follows:

(1) With regard to marriages, nearly all men follow the local custom of contracting several marriages. They do not wait until after their first wives are dead, but dismiss them for the slightest reasons in order to marry another. The women do the same. Sometimes they will recall one who has been dismissed earlier, and dismiss the one married later. . . . They seem to contract marriage only under the condition—which at least is tacit and often expressed—that they will live together and be bound in marriage until it pleases one of them to dismiss the other. Having stated this, I ask whether in this mission of ours we could follow the apostolic indult of 28 December [1837] regarding the marriage of infidels. It was granted by Pope Gregory XVI of happy memory to the missionaries of Eastern Oceania and I have a copy at hand. It seems to me that our difficulties are the same. The reasons for doubting the validity of the marriage also seem to be the same."

(2) Since very often we do not have new oils on the Saturdays before Easter and Pentecost, what are we to do? Is it better to use water [for Baptism] that has been blessed in the previous year and wait for new oils? Or should we use old oils and obtain a faculty to bless new (baptismal) water on the days mentioned?

(3) If it pleases His Holiness, I most humbly request that the number of feast days for all the faithful living in this mission be limited according to the privilege granted by Pope Paul III [1468–1549]. Kindly add, however, these feasts: Conception of the Blessed Virgin Mary, Blessed Michael the Archangel, Blessed Joseph, the Nativity of Saint John the Baptist, and All Saints Day.

---

33. PF: SC Oceania vol. 4 (1848–52), f. 598r, Caterini to Barnabò, 16 May 1851. The Doctrine of the Faith Congregation's archive copy is in DF: Minutario (1851), 160. Need description of DF.

34. PF: LDB vol. 340 (1851), f. 377r.

35. SM: Epistolae variae generalium, 1:43 n. 79.

(4) Supposing that we should remain, and if His Holiness judges my request expedient, I as prefect apostolic humbly ask for the faculty of confirming under the usual conditions those who have recently been baptized.

(5) The faculty of dispensing from interrogation of the pagan party is requested, if there should be opposition and provided that the usual conditions are fulfilled.

(6) When the husband is disposed for Baptism, but the wife not as yet, and vice versa: Is it better to dispense [from the impediment of disparity of cult] by using the procedures already laid down by Propaganda, or [is it better] to defer baptizing [the one disposed] until the other is also disposed? In case the first is better, I most humbly request this faculty [of dispensing].

(7) Kindly grant the faculty for erecting the pious practice known as the Way of the Cross, for blessing scapulars of the Immaculate Blessed Virgin Mary, and for granting the corresponding indulgences.

(8) In the page of faculties one reads: It is licit [for the superior] to subdelegate these faculties to the priests of his mission and also to other priests, for all places contained within his mission. I graciously request authorization to grant [to the priests of my mission] the faculties for hearing confessions of all the faithful—especially those traveling on ships—in every place where there are no ordinaries and, if recourse [to an ordinary] is difficult, also to other priests, if there should be need.[36]

An "ordinary" is someone empowered with ecclesiastical jurisdiction over an area in virtue of his office.

Secretary Barnabò presented three of Frémont's requests (number three on feast days, number four on confirming, and number five on interrogation) to Pope Pius IX on Sunday, 6 February 1853. All three were granted. As for number three, however, Frémont was told to retain as well the feast of Saints Peter and Paul. Number two on baptismal water and number seven on the Way of the Cross and on scapulars were granted by Propaganda itself.[37]

Barnabò had still another audience with Pius IX on 20 February 1853 at which he presented Frémont's request number eight about hearing confessions. These faculties were also granted by the pope as requested by Frémont.[38]

At this same audience of 20 February, Barnabò presented a request to the pope on behalf of director Marinoni of the Milan mission seminary, who was in Rome at the time. For the members of his seminary Marinoni wished to receive the following faculties:

---

36. PF: Udienze vol. 117 (1853, Part I), f. 271v–272v. The "tacit and often expressed" condition mentioned in number one would indicate that true matrimonial consent did not exist. Number five about interrogation would seem to be a case of the Pauline privilege. See also n. 42 below.

37. Ibid., f. 246r, 271v–272v.

38. Ibid., f. 344r.

(1) Of being allowed to celebrate Holy Mass at sea, also aboard a ship that is not anchored, provided that the prescribed caution is always used.

(2) Of being able to go to confession during the voyage and of administering the Sacrament of Penance to their own catechists and also to others, when they are aboard ship and also when they are on the coasts of very extensive dioceses, provided that it is not easy to reach the local ecclesiastical authority.

(3) Of being able to obtain on the day of their departure [for the missions] a plenary indulgence (provided that they go to confession, receive Communion and pray for the Propagation of the Faith), and that this be granted also to those who, on the occasion of their departure, go to Holy Communion in order to recommend them to God on this occasion.

(4) Of being able to bless rosaries, medals, etc., beginning with the day of their departure from Milan, in order to satisfy the devotion of their relatives, friends, etc.

(5) Of being able to say Holy Mass from two hours before sunrise up to two hours after midday.

(6) Confirmation is desired for what was kindly granted orally by the Holy Father to the Director of the Missionaries of Milan, namely, the indulgence of a privileged altar for those missionaries who at present belong to the above mentioned seminary, and also for those who will belong to it in the future.

He had requested the privilege "three times a week and under the condition that nothing beyond the customary offering [for Mass] be received because of this privilege."

Pope Pius IX granted all of Marinoni's requests.[39] Fransoni lost no time and wrote to Prefect Apostolic Frémont on 24 February 1853. "As you will see from the attached rescript," he said:

> We took care of obtaining for you from our Most Holy Father the faculties requested in your letter. The two questions that you proposed on the marriages of those inhabitants, however, have been sent to the Supreme Inquisition [or Holy Office] for a solution. We shall send you the answers as soon as they come to hand. Lastly, as regards your question on what should be done if fresh Holy Oils are not available for blessing baptismal water on the Saturdays before Easter and Pentecost, know that you should use old oils [to bless new water], rather than use water blessed in the previous year. . . .[40]

Twelve days before Cardinal Prefect Fransoni wrote to Frémont, Secretary Barnabò had sent Frémont's requests in numbers one and six on marriages to Monsignor Caterini at the Holy Office, saying that he was enclosing "two queries proposed by the Prefect Apostolic

---

39. Tragella, *Missioni estere*, 1:129.
40. PF: LDB vol. 343 (1853, Part I), f. 119r.

of the Melanesia Mission in Oceania" for a solution or for advice.⁴¹ His calling Frémont in this official letter the prefect apostolic "of the Melanesia Mission" shows that he was already taking it for granted that the Marists would be remaining in the Melanesia mission.

Frémont's request number one with regard to local marriages had to be sent to the Holy Office because he was asking that an apostolic indult along with the corresponding faculties—which fifteen years earlier had been extended to include the missions of Eastern Oceania—now be extended to include as well the missions of Melanesia and Micronesia in Western Oceania. This apostolic indult had a 266-year-old history that embraced the West Indies, Canada, and the Gambier Islands. As early as 2 August 1571, Pope Saint Pius V (1504–72) had issued a decree stating that men in the West Indies with more than one wife "on being baptized may remain with the wife who is baptized with them, as with their legitimate wife, after the others have been dismissed."

Archbishop Joseph Signay (1778–1850) of Quebec, Canada, in whose archdiocese polygamy was widespread among Indian tribes, approached the Holy See with a problem that was discussed by the Holy Office in 1836. According to faculty number eleven of the twenty-nine faculties granted to him and to other bishops by an extraordinary indult, "infidels having several wives are bound after their conversion and Baptism to keep the first wife, if she should want to be converted."

But this obligation, the archbishop pointed out, was a great obstacle to the conversion of his people. His missionaries had therefore been requesting insistently that such men "be permitted to choose from among their wives the one whom they prefer (who is usually the youngest of all) and then according to the rules of the Church marry her, if she agrees to this, instead of their being obligated to choose the first wife." The decree of Pius V of 1571, the archbishop maintained, made "no mention of the first wife having to be taken as the legitimate wife, but only of a wife who is baptized with them."

When discussing this matter, the cardinals of the Holy Office made this distinction:

(1) For polygamous men who in their pagan culture had intended to enter a true marriage, that is, a marriage contract with one woman for life, "there can be no doubt that after their conversion they must retain their first wife, if she also receives Baptism, or if she at least agrees to live with him [peacefully] without offense to the Creator."⁴²

(2) If there is a serious doubt, however, about the marriage having been a true marriage in the pagan culture, then "an infidel on becoming a convert can choose after his conversion whomsoever he wishes among his former wives, supposing that she

---

41. Ibid., f. 141rv, Barnabò to Caterini, 12 February 1853.

42. The Pauline privilege, partly referred to here by the Holy Office, is based on 1 Cor. 7:12–15. For current church law on this matter, see Canon 1143 in *The Code of Canon Law*, 202.

also converts to the Catholic religion, receives Baptism, and expresses matrimonial consent in words. Or he can enter marriage with any other woman."[43]

Pope Gregory XVI gave his approval to the decisions of the Holy Office on 8 June 1836, thereby making them applicable within the vast territory included in the Archdiocese of Quebec.

Missionaries of the Congregation of the Sacred Hearts of Jesus and Mary (SS.CC.) in the Gambier Islands of the Eastern Oceania vicariate had the same problem regarding polygamous men as the missionaries in the Archdiocese of Quebec. During a trip to Europe in 1837, Father François-d'Assise Caret of the Gambier Islands went to Rome to find a solution. As a result Pope Gregory XVI ordered that "the *Instruction* issued for the Most Reverend Archbishop of Quebec regarding polygamous infidels converting to the Catholic religion, in view of a decision taken by the Sacred Congregation of the Universal Inquisition and approved by himself on 8 June 1836," should be observed as well "in the missions of Eastern Oceania." He likewise extended the faculties granted on 8 June 1836, "as indicated in the rescript attached to the same *Instruction*, to the missions of Eastern Oceania." His papal decree was issued on 28 December 1837.[44] This was the privilege that Frémont wished to have extended to his Melanesia and Micronesia mission, but he had to wait until the Holy Office would give its reply.

Meanwhile Father Montrouzier, the French Marist formerly in Woodlark, had sent a letter from Sydney to Father Colin in Lyon on 16 June 1852, requesting still another faculty. This was two days before the first anniversary of Frémont's election as prefect apostolic of the mission of Melanesia and Micronesia. Referring to the time when he was still pro-vicar, Montrouzier said, "I always forgot to ask Propaganda for permission to use the local language for singing at all church services." The local language, he maintained, had been "banned by the Constitution 'Annus quo' of Pope Benedict XIV on 19 February 1749 and by a decree of the Congregation of Rites on 24 March 1653." He pointed out, however, that songs in the vernacular were "very helpful for embellishing the ceremonies" and that "they captivate the local people for the church." Missionaries of China, however, had received permission to use songs in the vernacular during liturgical functions. "I think that permission would also be granted to us if we were to request it," he said. "I think that I am not going against the wishes of Father Frémont if I ask Father Poupinel to send a request on this matter to Propaganda."[45] Whether Poupinel, an official at the Marist headquarters in

---

43. Since the presumption in this case is that none of the marriages were true or valid, the man never had been married to anyone. Consequently he was free to enter a Christian marriage with whomsoever he wished.

44. See the papal decree of 28 December 1837. Father Amerigo Cools, archivist at the Rome Generalate of the Congregation of the Sacred Hearts of Jesus and Mary, sent the author a copy of this decree on 12 May 1986. The details in the text are from this decree.

45. SM: OMM/208. Montrouzier's letter is not dated, but bears a 16 June 1852 Sydney postmark.

charge of foreign missions, actually submitted Montrouzier's proposal to Rome, or whether Rome reacted, cannot be ascertained.

At this time when Rome was granting so many faculties to both the French Marists and to the Milan missionaries, no one in Europe knew what decision Reina had taken regarding his mission field. Surely the pope along with the cardinal prefect and secretary of Propaganda must have presumed, in view of Frémont's encouraging report about Woodlark and the unanimous decision of his missionaries to remain there, that he and his staff would keep the Melanesia mission in which Woodlark was located. And so the Italian missionaries naturally would be taking up work in Fiji or perhaps even in Micronesia.

Fransoni's letter of 24 February 1853 to Frémont announcing that certain faculties had been granted could easily have reached Sydney by 20 August of that year. It would then have been delivered by the 124-ton schooner *Supply*, which left Sydney on 21 August to visit the three Marist missionaries still based at Woodlark and Rooke islands. Frémont and his two companions, however, would have had little time to make use of the faculties, because the three of them were aboard the *Supply* when it left Rooke and Woodlark for Sydney.[46]

After reaching Sydney the French Marists did not return to their Melanesia and Micronesia mission. Their faculties, however, were transferable. Consequently the missionaries from another country, who meanwhile had taken charge, were able to make use of them.

---

46. Ibid., Frémont to Colin, 9 January 1854; Hosie, "French Mission," 417.

9

Reina Declines Fiji and Chooses Melanesia and Micronesia
7 August 1852

THE MOMENT OF DECISION FOR THE MISSIONARIES FROM LOMBARDY HAD NOW ARRIVED. According to their *Instructions* received from Rome, they were given the choice of various missions in Oceania. But they were to make that choice only after consultations with the Marist superior general in France and after further consultations with other Marists in Oceania. Since Prefect Apostolic Reina had to report on the matter to Cardinal Prefect Fransoni and also to director Marinoni, he kept a careful record of the negotiations.

On Wednesday, 28 July 1852, the day after reaching the Marist Center at Tarban Creek on the outskirts of Sydney, twenty-seven-year-old Reina consulted with forty-three-year-old Father Rocher, the Marist in charge there. Superior General Colin had favored Melanesia, Reina said, but Fiji was also a possible choice. Surprised at the mention of Fiji, Rocher urged Reina "not to discuss it" with Bishop Bataillon. According to Rocher, Bataillon on his own initiative was seeking priests for Fiji, since "Father Colin is not sending him any more personnel and he has great need of them." In fact, the bishop had already sent a priest to Fiji contrary to Father Colin's wishes.

Pondering over Rocher's remarks, Reina wrote into his diary: "But is it good to keep silent [about Fiji]?" His *Instructions* clearly stated that his choice was to be made "with the consent and counsel of the prelates and the Marist priests." Since Bataillon was the prelate in charge of Fiji, Reina felt obliged to discuss it with him.

On the following day thirty-one-year-old Montrouzier, the former pro-vicar of Melanesia and Micronesia, gave Reina "very many notes" on Woodlark for copying into his notebook. Montrouzier "was most eager to return there, or at least to accompany us," Reina said. According to him the Marists "had not been able to accomplish much," because they thought "that they might be obliged to abandon that mission." Reina told Montrouzier that if the Marists should wish to remain in Woodlark, he would make no difficulties whatsoever for them, "since this was the understanding reached with Father Colin." Montrouzier took it for granted, however, that the Marists at Woodlark would be replaced by the Italians.[1]

Colin had sent along a letter with Reina for Montrouzier, asking him to be as helpful to the new missionaries as possible. "I placed myself completely at their service," Montrouzier replied. "Fraternally I shared with them all my notes on the language, on the customs of our natives, on the country and on the material needs of the missions. . . ."[2]

While in Lyon, Reina had given Colin his Italian copy of the *Instructions*, as he had been told to do by Fransoni. Colin at once had the document translated into French for his personal study and intended to send a copy of this French translation to Rocher. This was wise, because the *Instructions* spelled out clearly Rome's position in this delicate matter, and the French missionaries knew hardly any Italian. But Rocher failed to find "the *Instructions* which Colin had translated into French" in the packet of correspondence sent with Reina.[3]

On Friday, 30 July 1852, Reina decided to give his Italian version of the *Instructions* to Rocher. After reading it, Rocher realized that it was necessary for him to inform Bataillon of the contents. And here the confusion began, because the French missionaries understood pitifully little of the Italian nuances in this long document.

On Saturday, 31 July, Rocher had business in Sydney and so there were no discussions. Then on Sunday the Italian missionaries celebrated a Mass of Thanksgiving for their safe arrival. The choir was made up of thirteen young men from various islands in the Central Oceania vicariate, whom Bishop Bataillon had brought to Sydney.

Monday, 2 August 1852, was an important day in the decision-making process. Rocher on that day presented Bataillon with the Italian *Instructions* and with the Latin letter from Fransoni to the Marists in Oceania.[4] Fransoni's letter said that a shortage of personnel had prompted Superior General Colin "repeatedly and insistently" to ask Propaganda Fide to reduce the extent of the Marist Society's responsibilities in Western Oceania and to send other missionaries into areas cared for by them. Colin had pointed out, Fransoni said, that "either the Melanesia Mission or the Micronesia Mission" could be given to the new missionaries, "or some part of the extensive Central Vicariate" of Bishop Bataillon.

In fact, Fransoni went on, "a most opportune place for spreading the Catholic faith," according to Colin, was to be found "especially in the Viti or Fiji Archipelago or in other islands" of the Central vicariate. If the Italians were to take over one of the areas of Bishop Bataillon, then he and his priests could better manage the rest of their territory, Fransoni

---

1. PIME: AME 11:75f, Reina to Marinoni, 8 August 1852.

2. Montrouzier's reply to Colin's letter of 21 March 1852 in SM: OMM/208 is undated, but it was certainly written by 15 September 1852, as is clear from internal evidence.

3. The handwritten translation of the *Instructions* into French is in SM: 436. It covers six full pages.

4. Reina must be incorrect when he writes in his diary that Rocher gave "the bull in Latin" to Bataillon. See PIME: AME 11:75. A bull is a papal letter. The Latin letter from Rome was not from the pope, but from Cardinal Prefect Fransoni, and was dated 14 February 1852. See PF: LDB vol. 341 (1852, Part I), f. 213r–216r.

said. He insisted, however, that the Italians were to make their choice only after taking counsel with the French missionaries. And no matter where the Italians might go, the Marists were to "receive them kindly, foster fraternal charity, instruct them and aid them, until they are found capable and ready to take on their sacred duties" and until "they can manage and govern the mission by themselves."

Fransoni had considered the possibility that the Marists might decide to remain in Melanesia, and that the Italians might prefer a Central Oceania mission to one in Micronesia. In that case, the cardinal said, "the Fiji Archipelago or some other region" would be assigned and given to them by Bishop Bataillon. And once their numbers had increased and religion had begun to spread, their territory would be "erected into a distinct vicariate apostolic." Then as time went on, the cardinal said, this new vicariate apostolic "would perhaps be able to provide assistance for the Micronesia Mission."[5]

This letter of Fransoni written on 14 February 1852 must have stunned Bataillon because *four months later*—on 15 June 1852—Bataillon himself had written to Fransoni suggesting that the cardinal "cut off the Fiji Islands" from his Central Oceania vicariate, "make them an independent vicariate apostolic, and entrust them to another mission society." Those islands, Bataillon had said, were a part of his vicariate "which is not yet cultivated and whose language I do not know."[6] When Bataillon was writing his letter to Fransoni, Reina strangely enough was sailing aboard the *Tartar*, hand carrying the cardinal's precocious "reply" to Bataillon.

Fransoni's anticipation and approval of Bataillon's requests before they were even made were remarkable. And since seven young and healthy missionaries had come to Bataillon's very door seeking an Oceania assignment, it was only natural that he should offer them Fiji and that they should accept. But this did not happen.

"The bishop called me to his room," Reina wrote in his diary. He began the conversation "by telling me that he had no active vote in this decision. But he did desire our welfare and so he had a word of advice for us." Reina then explained to the bishop how he was bound by the *Instructions* to discuss the matter with him, because according to the wishes of Rome the decision was to be made by the Marists alone. Bataillon replied that he wished "to have no part in this affair," because it dealt with an issue that concerned him personally. "He therefore had nothing but advice to give us," Reina said.

Bataillon's advice, however, was more a warning than a counsel. "I know that the Woodlark missionaries have received instructions from Father Colin to remain there as long as the mission prospers," he said. "The mission, therefore, either is prospering or it is not. If it is, they will stay there and your help will be of no avail, because there are enough of them for that island. But if the mission is doing badly, they will leave. In that case how can you be bold enough to go there? If the Marists in spite of their good spirit become

---

5. PF: LDB vol. 341 (1852, Part I), f. 213r–216r, Fransoni to Marist missionaries in Oceania, 14 February 1852.

6. PF: SC Oceania vol. 4 (1848–52), f. 924v–925r, Bataillon to Fransoni, 15 June 1852.

discouraged, how can you succeed?" Bataillon said it would be well for Reina to know that the missions of Melanesia "are the most difficult missions in Oceania. It could be that the Marists went there thinking that the missions were easy. They may have had some preconceived plan, but the plan could not work, because it did not take into consideration the difficulties which they were bound to find there."

Reina told Bataillon that he and his missionaries were aware of these difficulties and that from the beginning Father Colin had written to them "in the most clear and forceful terms" about the obstacles to be found in those missions. "Precisely because they were abandoned and difficult," Reina said, "we wanted them." To this the bishop replied: "Think it over well and pray. Pray much!"

It would seem that by this time Reina had already made up his mind to choose the Melanesia Mission, because he gave Bataillon a number of reasons in its favor. "I told him that Propaganda had always spoken to us about this mission; that the Fiji idea was inserted subsequently because of a postscript by Father Colin; that during a conference held in our seminary the judgment was reached that the Fiji Mission was little suited to our needs; that Father Colin had submitted his ideas on Melanesia to Rome; and that we are ready for everything in obedience to our superiors." When Reina enlarged on these points, Bataillon told him to conduct all further business in the matter with Fathers Rocher and Montrouzier.

That night Reina entered these observations on Bishop Bataillon in his diary: "It does not seem that he wants us for Fiji...."[7] Instead he spoke at length about the difficulties of the Melanesia mission, stressing "our own good" in order "to have something to say to Propaganda." Reina clearly indicated by what he wrote that his mind was made up: "We shall go to Woodlark. And after the necessary introductory period we shall try to enter New Guinea. Or we shall go to Rooke accompanied by some Marists." This was the plan to which Colin had agreed in Lyon, and also the one that he had submitted to Rome. For Reina the die was cast. He and his companions would let Micronesia slip into the background. They had their hearts set on the larger and more difficult mission of Melanesia with its vast and unknown island of New Guinea.

Meanwhile Reina's companions had been translating the *Instructions* into French as well as they could. On Tuesday morning, 3 August 1852, Reina presented them to Bataillon. After the midday meal he heard Rocher and Bataillon engaged "in a lively discussion," and so that evening he went to Rocher's room to ask what the bishop had said. "His Excellency does not want to make a decision," Rocher told Reina, "because the matter is delicate and important." But the bishop had spoken at great length with Rocher and this is how Reina summarized Rocher's version of what the bishop said:

---

7. Tragella in *Missioni estere*, 1:153, says that Bataillon "had a secret desire that the new recruits should be directed toward the new mission" to be carved from his Central Oceania vicariate. But if Bataillon's desire was "secret," how did Tragella know about it? He gives no documentary evidence for his statement.

I have received no instructions from my superior, nor has he told me what decision I ought to make.... On the one hand there are five priests, two laymen, and an entire seminary at stake. Now if the seminary is to prosper, it needs good initial reports. Because if word got around that one of them had died and that another had been murdered, there would be a big drop in the number of vocations. On the other hand I have no precise data on Melanesia and so I cannot give them good directions. They also need a safe place for establishing their general headquarters, and I lack the knowledge for pointing this out to them. All of this weighs heavily on my shoulders. So what am I to do? I would suggest Melanesia. But this is merely a suggestion and not a decision meant to determine their fate....

Although Reina was inexperienced, he was very sure of himself. In fact he had answers for all of Bataillon's anxieties. Believing that the bishop was referring to Colin when he said that he had received no instructions from his superior, Reina told Rocher that he himself was well aware of Colin's thinking from various letters received from Colin "and from what he had decided together with us in Lyon." Nor did Reina admit that misfortune could be counterproductive for his seminary, "since difficulties often serve as incentives."

Earlier Reina had discussed the Melanesia mission with Montrouzier and now he suggested to Rocher that Montrouzier be invited to supply information that might help in reaching a more firm and relaxed judgment on the choice to be made. Montrouzier was then called in and was advised of the situation. His first questions were: What would be most advantageous for the Milan seminary? What was Propaganda's initial proposal? And what was the thinking of Father Colin? After receiving the answers, Montrouzier said that the Italian missionaries "would be safe at Woodlark" and added that he himself had "high hopes for that island, even though the people there are really bad." Here the interview ended.

On that same day, 3 August, Reina acquainted his companions with the progress of his negotiations. They then pointed out to him "how clear it was from the *Instructions* that the proposals made by Father Colin and by Procurator [Rocher] were merely consultative and that we also could have a part in the deliberations." So Reina decided to mention all of this to Rocher on the following day "and come to a decision." He also asked himself: "Where did we ever get this idea that the decision rests entirely with them? Had we not read the *Instructions* many times in Milan? I see that the reprimand sent to me by Propaganda has produced in me a sense of utter submission, so much so that it also made me understand the *Instructions* in this way."[8]

The *Instructions* were very clear indeed about the role of the Milan missionaries in the decision-making process. The text read: "Propaganda ... will approve that decision which they will make in accord with the counsel of the Marist prelates and priests, either during their voyage or after they have reached their adopted place."[9]

---

8. PIME: AME 11:75f, Reina to Marinoni, 8 August 1852.
9. Ibid., 1:73, *Instructions*, 9 February 1852.

On Wednesday, 4 August 1852, Bataillon gave back to Reina the French translation of the *Instructions*. In them the bishop had read that Propaganda "gives to the missionaries of Milan full faculties" to go to the Central vicariate and take up work in the Fiji Islands. Subsequently they "will be put in charge by the same bishop and be invested with the government of the Fiji Archipelago, which later will be erected into a distinct vicariate apostolic." This was to happen if the new missionaries chose Fiji as their mission.[10]

On receiving the *Instructions* back from Bataillon, Reina once more asked the bishop for his opinion on the mission that he should choose. Again the bishop said that he had no opinion in the matter. Reina then asked the bishop kindly to advise him privately, for his personal guidance, as to what choice he should make after having heard "the opinions of Father Colin, the Procurator, and Father Montrouzier." It seemed to the bishop "to be the will of God that we should take Melanesia," Reina wrote in his diary. "I also asked him what place we ought to choose in case the Woodlark missionaries should be forced to leave Woodlark, and he suggested the island of Ponape."

That evening Reina mentioned all of this to Father Rocher and learned that it was also "his opinion that we should go to Melanesia." When informing Marinoni of this, Reina assured him that he had "explicitly mentioned" to Rocher that he "should not be concerned about our desires, but should simply make his choice according to what he believes is best before God."[11]

It seems unfortunate that the Milan missionaries did not want the Fiji mission and that Bataillon did not try to persuade them to accept it. Four years earlier in 1848, and again in 1849, Colin had urged Bataillon "to provide himself with other missionaries for the numerous islands of the Fiji or Viti Archipelago." Nor did time change Colin's resolve. For the remainder of his term of office as superior general, which ended with his resignation on 9 May 1854, he sent no new missionaries to Bataillon nor to any other mission in Oceania.[12] Perhaps Bataillon's merit consists in his having tried to dissuade the Italians from accepting Melanesia.

On Saturday, 7 August 1852, Reina sent Cardinal Fransoni the results of his consultations with the Marists. In obedience to the directives received, he said, "We presented the pages of *Instructions* to the Reverend Father Procurator [Rocher], to Bishop Bataillon and to Father Montrouzier. We left it completely up to their views and judgment to determine which mission we ought to choose. Father Procurator [Rocher], in view of letters received from his superior general and helped by information obtained from Father Montrouzier about the Woodlark Mission . . . , expressed himself in favor of that mission." According to

---

10. Ibid., 72f.

11. PIME: AME 11:76, Reina to Marinoni, 8 August 1852. Commenting here on Bataillon's mention of Ponape, Reina says that this was "the first idea of Cardinal Fransoni." Reina errs, because the original offer of Fransoni made on 16 January 1851 was "the desirable and vast Mission of Melanesia and Micronesia." See Wiltgen, *Oceania*, 546.

12. Wiltgen, *Oceania*, 543, 547.

Montrouzier, "Everything has given reason to hope that a fine beginning at last has been made in the Melanesia Mission." And Reina added that Woodlark was "the best center for reaching the very numerous islands to which one could quickly bring the light of the Gospel, if there were an abundance of personnel."

As for Bishop Bataillon, he at first abstained from expressing a preference, Reina said. "Without concealing the difficulties" of the Melanesia mission, the bishop nevertheless had said that "it appeared to him to be the will of God that we should direct our poor efforts to Melanesia and Micronesia." Reina therefore had decided to go along with "this unanimous counsel" and had chosen the missions of Melanesia and Micronesia. He told Fransoni that now he hoped to receive "the approbation of the Sacred Congregation," promising at the same time that this same congregation "in every case will always have for its orders our prompt and absolute obedience, no matter what the cost."[13]

On the following day, 8 August, a Sunday, Reina sent numerous extracts from his diary in a letter to Marinoni. He called this letter "the history of how we chose our mission." Following "the advice and instructions of Bishop Bataillon, of Father Rocher and of Father Montrouzier," he said, "we have decided to choose Melanesia and Micronesia."[14]

Enclosed for Marinoni's information and for forwarding was Reina's letter of the previous day addressed to Cardinal Fransoni. "I have read this letter to Father Rocher . . . , and he was completely satisfied with it," Reina said. "And so the matter rests. Now what do you have to tell me? My conscience does not bother me at all. . . . But woe to me if this was not the will of God! If you write to Propaganda, tell them—also in my own name—that they should recall me from the mission, if they wish to do so. Pray much for me and for these companions of mine, who really are so good. . . ."[15]

Four days later Reina wrote to Superior General Colin in Lyon: "According to your advice and that of His Excellency and of the two priests, we have chosen the mission of Melanesia and Micronesia."[16] All three Marists—Bataillon, Rocher, and Montrouzier—had advised Reina to wait in Sydney for the return of the forty-four-ton schooner *Jessie*, which

13. PF: SC Oceania vol. 4 (1848–52), f. 1025r–1026r.

14. PIME: AME 11, *Notizie*, 65.

15. Ibid., 76, Reina to Marinoni, 8 August 1852. In *Missioni estere*, 1:152, Tragella states that Propaganda "in the last analysis had left every decision" up to the Marist superior general, Father Colin. But in view of the directives in the *Instructions*, in view of the decision taken against Fiji by Reina and his men while still in Milan, and in view of Reina's weeklong negotiations in Tarban Creek, one cannot accept Tragella's statement as correct.

16. SM: 436, Reina to Colin, 12 August 1852. A Vatican document of 1983 incorrectly states that "the Mission of Melanesia and Micronesia" had already been assigned to the Italian missionaries when they left Milan for Oceania on 16 March 1852. See "Beatificationis seu declarationis martyrii Servi Dei Ioannis Baptistae Mazzucconi, sacerdotis Pontificii Instituti pro Missionibus Exteris, in odium Fidei a. 1855 interfecti. Super Dubio," in *Acta Apostolicae Sedis: Commentarium Officiale*, 76:332–37. According to the *Instructions* the assignment of the mission took place automatically after the Milan missionaries had consulted with the Marists and at the time when they made their choice.

had gone to Woodlark and was expected back in August with the latest news about that mission.[17]

The *Jessie* arrived in Sydney on Monday, 23 August 1852,[18] bringing good news about Marist progress in Woodlark. Three days later Father Raimondi wrote to his priest brother Carlo in Italy: "We shall go to Woodlark on this same ship within a few days, arriving there in three weeks." There were three French priests at Woodlark, he said, who had arrived there four years ago.[19] "After much patience they are now beginning to see some results. . . ." Raimondi said that his group would not remain at Woodlark for long, but with the help of a French missionary would try to open a mission "on some other island, most probably Rooke. It is the doorway to New Guinea, the place toward which all our efforts are directed."

He told his brother that Rome had entrusted to their seminary "the evangelization of two parts of Oceania," Melanesia and Micronesia.[20] "We shall begin with Melanesia because it is closer to the center of Oceania and it is also more populous and more needy. Then if we get the chance to enter New Guinea, we shall have personnel nearby to move in. God has begun this work! He will also continue it and bring it to completion." In another letter Raimondi said that New Guinea was "an island as large as France with numerous inhabitants."[21]

On 27 August 1852—four days after the *Jessie* had returned from Woodlark—Reina sent Fransoni a copy of his 7 August letter, inserting a new paragraph about "the good progress being made" at Woodlark, which was consoling for all of them. "Providence is thus preparing for us a safe station from which we can spread out and evangelize the numerous surrounding islands. . . . The ship is now being readied and will transport us to the spot. We shall head directly for Woodlark in order to begin our mission on that island, or on some other island, according to the judgment of the Reverend Father Frémont and under the guidance of the Fathers there."[22]

---

17. SM: 436, Reina to Colin, 12 August 1852; Hosie, "French Mission," 417.

18. In SM: OMM/208, Montrouzier's undated letter to Colin says that the *Jessie* arrived on 22 August. However, this date must be inexact, because Reina, Raimondi, and Hosie all give the date as 23 August 1852. Raimondi even says that the ship arrived "this past Monday, 23 August." That date in 1852 fell on a Monday. See PF: SC Oceania vol. 4 (1848–52), f. 1025r–1026r, Reina to Fransoni, 27 August 1852; PIME: AME 11, *Notizie*, 84–86, Timoleone Raimondi to Carlo Raimondi, 26 August 1852; Hosie, "French mission," 417.

19. Brother Gennade, a Marist, was also there with the priests Frémont, Thomassin and Trapenard. See SM OMM/208, Frémont to Colin, 16 October 1851.

20. Since their consultations were completed and they had made their choice, the "two parts of Oceania" now were entrusted to them. See note 16. Propaganda Fide, however, was always free to decide otherwise, and actually did so, entrusting only the Melanesia mission to Reina as is shown later in this chapter.

21. PIME: AME 11, *Notizie*, 84–86. Timoleone Raimondi to Carlo Raimondi, 26 August 1852; PIME: AME 11, *Notizie*, 87, Raimondi to the pastor of Annone, Italy, 8 August 1852.

22. PF: SC Oceania vol. 4 (1848–52), f. 979r.

It seems very strange that Reina never refers to Frémont as "prefect apostolic" and that he never calls him the "prefect apostolic of Melanesia and Micronesia." He surely knew that this was Frémont's title. Did he somehow feel that by using it for Frémont, he might forfeit it for himself? Because he had told Fransoni on 7 August and again on 27 August that he had followed "unanimous counsel" in choosing "Melanesia and Micronesia" as his mission, he had every reason to expect that Rome would name him prefect apostolic of Melanesia and Micronesia."

About the time when Reina wrote to Fransoni on 27 August 1852, Montrouzier told Colin that the visit to Sydney of the eight young men from Woodlark and Laughlan islands in the preceding year had been responsible for the good results that the Marists currently were enjoying at Woodlark. These young men, who were in Sydney no longer than two months, had returned to their islands aboard the *Bride* in September 1851 with Captain Dalmagne.[23] Prior to their return from Sydney, Frémont had written: "We do not yet have even one catechumen."[24] But now, one year later, Montrouzier could report enthusiastically that there were "two classes of catechumens" in Woodlark. This good news had been brought by the *Jessie*.

"The first class is made up of those who are more advanced, and it contains sixteen natives," Montrouzier said. "Among them are six couples of whom the majority were in bad repute because of their debauchery or attachment to superstition. . . ." When he passed on this news to the Italian missionaries, he told Colin, "They concluded that our Fathers would want to keep Woodlark and would be handing over [to them] the rest of Melanesia along with Micronesia." In that case they would go to Rooke Island on the northeast coast of New Guinea. And if Frémont gave up only Micronesia, they would go to Ponape. Montrouzier added that the newcomers had "wisely" pointed out that these were only provisional plans, "and that it would be necessary for them to go to Woodlark in order to make definite plans." Their ship was scheduled to sail "about 15 September," he said.

Montrouzier then told Colin what the Milan missionaries had said about him. They said "that you had told them that foreign missions no longer are one of the principal aims of our society." And Bishop Bataillon had said "that you are inclined to believe that our missions are not suitable for a religious community and that one by one you will abandon all the mission posts that we now occupy."

Gravely Montrouzier continued: "What you are threatening to do—and I hope that it is not yet irrevocable—has no doubt been inspired by good reasons." But if those reasons were faults on the part of the missionaries, he said, many of them could be obviated if the missionaries were provided with a Mission Rule. This would indicate, among other things,

---

23. The eight young men arrived in Sydney on 3 August 1851 and returned home in the following month. See the 7 August 1851 postscript in SM: OMM/208, Montrouzier to Colin, 21 June 1851; SM: OMM/208, Frémont to Colin, 16 October 1851; Hosie, "French Mission," 416.

24. SM: OMM/208, Frémont to Colin, 22 June 1851.

all the rights of a bishop and all the rights of a local representative of a mission sending society.[25]

Meanwhile Reina was kept busy gathering the many supplies needed to keep his group alive for a year. He also continued his studies of English and attended Montrouzier's classes on the Woodlark language. This Marist had produced the first Woodlark dictionary (fifteen hundred words) and the first grammar. He taught his class how to read and write Woodlark and acquainted them with the customs of the island's people. Montrouzier said, however, that their language was "not at all similar to the language of New Guinea." Reina's group nonetheless felt that they should learn at least "the general nature" of that language, even though they found it "really quite strange."[26]

"In Melanesia every island, no matter how small, has its own language," Raimondi reported. "But these languages cannot be called poor, because they contain words which refer to the slightest details of an object. The language of New Guinea is still unknown, but it is believed to be a branch of the Malaysian language." Father Ambrosoli found Woodlark grammar simpler than English grammar. But its verbs were very rich, "because the least modification of an idea calls for a different verb form." The fact that they were applying themselves to learn the Woodlark language, he said, did not mean that they had "forgotten about Ponape or Ascension, which has so often requested missionaries without ever receiving any . . ."[27]

Raimondi had told his brother on 26 August that he would be leaving for Woodlark aboard the schooner *Jessie* "within a few days." The Australian gold rush, however, changed those plans. As Ambrosoli said, "It is not hard to get a ship, but it is hard to get sailors. In Sydney they are all deserting their ships now to go to the gold mines in the Blue Mountains about one hundred miles southwest of Sydney . . . , where they hope to make a great fortune."

Raimondi told his brother about gold being discovered some six hundred miles from Sydney. These various mines were attracting people from everywhere, especially Englishmen. "As a result manual laborers have become very expensive and ships due to leave for Europe are forced to remain behind for lack of sailors," he said. In fact, the wages formerly paid to a captain "are now paid to a sailor."[28]

The Australian gold rush of 1851–52 was closely linked to the California gold rush of 1849. Among the eighty thousand prospectors who arrived in California in the United

---

25. Ibid., Montrouzier to Colin, no date. Internal evidence shows that Montrouzier's letter was written between 22 August and 15 September 1852.

26. PIME: AME 11, *Notizie*, 65, Reina to Marinoni, 8 August 1852; PIME: AME 11, *Notizie*, 78, Mazzucconi to his family, 6 August 1852; PIME: AME 11, *Notizie*, 84, Timoleone Raimondi to Carlo Raimondi, 26 August 1852.

27. Ibid., 86, Timoleone Raimondi to Carlo Raimondi, 26 August 1852; ibid., 61, 63, Ambrosoli's undated report. Raimondi writing in Italian uses "Malese," which the author has translated as "Malaysian."

28. Ibid., p. 59, Ambrosoli's undated report; ibid., p. 84, Timoleone Raimondi to Carlo Raimondi, 26 August 1852.

States of America in 1849, some eight hundred were Australians and many times that number arrived in the following year. One of these was Edward Hargreaves. Noticing that the gold-bearing country of California was very similar to land that he knew well in Australia, he hurried back to Sydney and on 12 February 1851 washed alluvial gold from a creek near Bathurst. His discovery soon became public, causing prospectors to stream over the Blue Mountains making new discoveries. Then on 8 August 1851 at Ballarat in the vicinity of Melbourne another goldfield was discovered, which at one time was probably the richest alluvial goldfield known in the world.[29] Lured by the hope of making a quick fortune, sailors understandably abandoned their ships in droves.

Nearly a month passed before a crew could be recruited for the Milan missionaries. "We are to depart on the twenty-first of this month," Reina told Marinoni on 18 September 1852, "and we have chartered a ship to take us to Woodlark for four hundred pounds sterling. If we need to go elsewhere, something that might well happen, we must pay two hundred pounds per month, counting from the day on which we leave Woodlark until our return there." Reina was fortunate in obtaining Dalmagne, a seasoned captain, for commanding the 114-ton *Jeune Lucie*, the ship that he eventually chartered. Besides being Catholic and French, Dalmagne was well acquainted with the reefs and harbors of Woodlark and other islands. In fact, during 1850–52 he had been captain four times on ships chartered by the Marists for their voyages to Woodlark.

Describing the vessel for his family, Father Mazzucconi called it a "very beautiful ship" with two masts, "flying the banner of our country and the banner of our [beloved] Milan. It shows the standard of our religion: the red cross of charity on a white field of faith. The ship is completely encircled with a mesh of barbed wire in order to hold off the boats of the local people in those areas, who usually like to come aboard because of their great desire for goods."[30]

Among the supplies taken aboard by the missionaries were "medicines, all of the more needful kitchen utensils, tools for woodworking and for cultivating the soil." They also bought large quantities of food, including dried meat, biscuits, yellow and white flour, wine, vinegar, lard, salt, and rice. They took aboard seeds and plants. The seeds were placed in bottles, which were then well sealed. The plants were put in wooden boxes and their roots were covered with soil; straw was used to support and protect the plants. Grapevines and a fig tree were also taken aboard, as well as numerous pieces of iron. The iron was highly appreciated in the islands by the local people as a trade item.[31]

---

29. P. F. Connole, *Australia and the Near North: The Commonwealth in the Modern World*, 2:23, 40f, 48f.

30. PIME: AME 11:83, 85, Reina to Marinoni, 18 September 1852; Mazzucconi, *Scritti*, 224, Mazzucconi to his family, 19 September 1852; Hosie, "French Mission," 416f. Hosie (417) calls the *Jeune Lucie* a 98-ton schooner, but Reina's letter to Marinoni and Mazzucconi's to his family both give the figure as 114 tons in their letters.

31. PIME: AME 11:187, Reina to Marinoni, 3 December 1855; PIME: AME 11, *Notizie*, p. 139, undated letter of Ambrozoli.

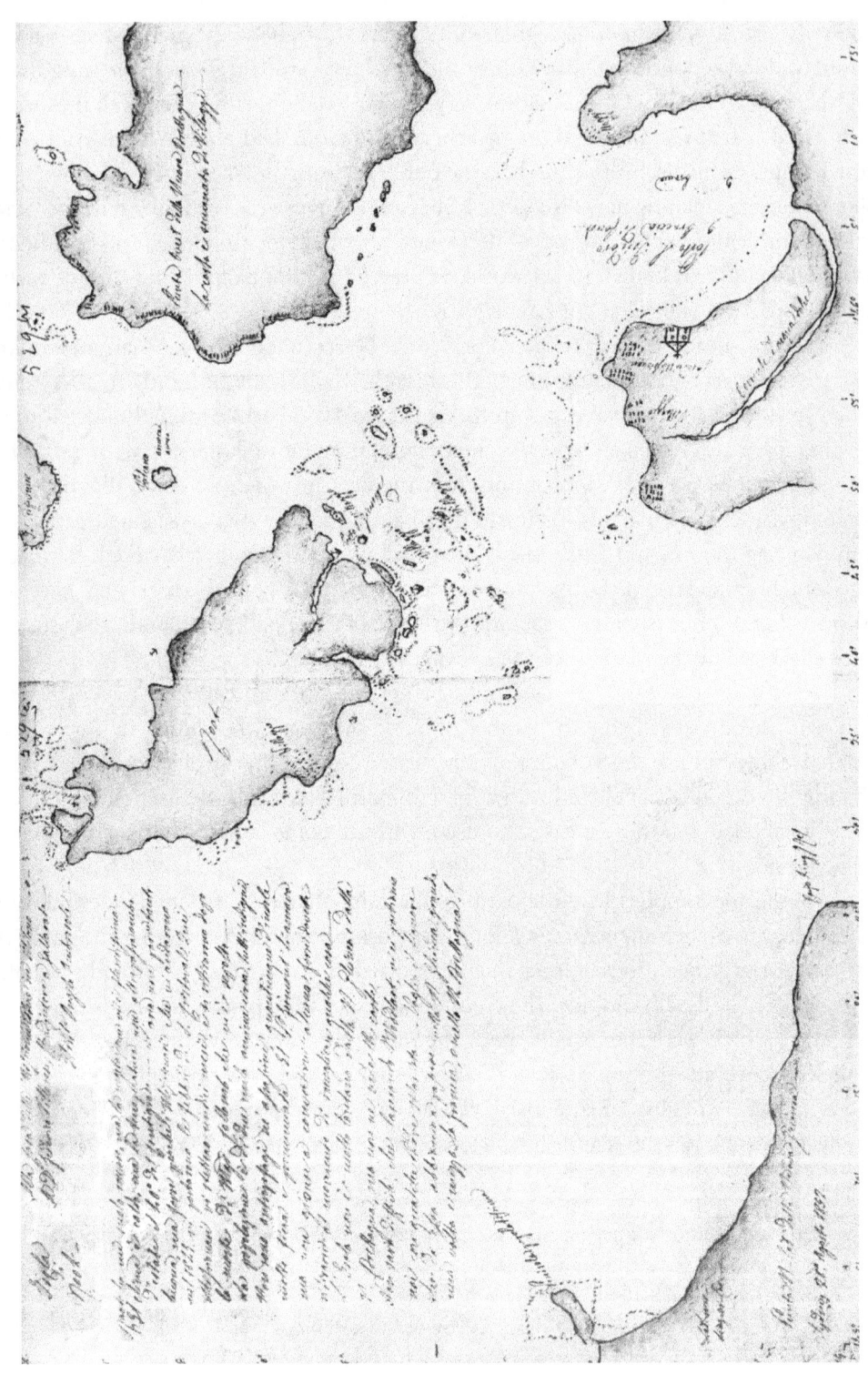

This map of Rook (Rooke) Island was drawn by Ambrosoli.
Source: Archives PIME, AME 11, 529.

Colin on 21 March 1852 had told Montrouzier that he was free to accompany the Milan missionaries to Rooke, "especially if they themselves desire it and on condition that Father Rocher does not have to be alone." Since Bishop Bataillon was now at Tarban Creek, he could be Rocher's companion, serve as confessor, and take charge of the Marist Center if Rocher should die, Montrouzier replied. In addition, the Milan missionaries expressed the desire of being accompanied by Montrouzier.

His own thinking, which he shared with Colin, was that it would be "imprudent" for Frémont or Thomassin to leave Woodlark and go to Rooke to introduce the new missionaries to the natives there. These plans, of course, presupposed that the Marists would remain in Woodlark and that Reina's group would go to Rooke and from there to New Guinea. So Montrouzier told Colin, "I am certain that if you were here, you would send me back to Woodlark." Nor was Father Rocher opposed any longer to his going. But when the hour of departure arrived, Reina wrote to director Marinoni in Milan, "We had hoped that Montrouzier would go with us, but he cannot go."[32]

Ambrosoli explained to friends back home that the traveling time between London and Sydney was rapidly diminishing because steamships were replacing sailing vessels on that route. This reduced the voyage by several weeks. Such a steamship had brought the news while he was in Sydney that England "was preparing a fleet at Valparaíso, Chile, to reconnoiter all of Oceania. In seven years time this fleet will visit all of these islands," he said. And he was pleased that such an expedition would show the people of those islands "that whites are powerful." Otherwise local people "would think that they alone possess knowledge and riches, and they would feel that someone coming to live in their midst is coming to live off of them."[33]

Ambrosoli liked cartography. Using information received from Father Montrouzier, he sketched maps of Rooke and Woodlark on 28 August 1852 and sent them to Father Federico Villoresi in Italy. These maps showed the entire islands and included close-ups of the areas where the Marists had founded their principal mission stations. Ambrosoli may have wanted Villoresi to see how these islands could serve as stepping-stones to New Guinea.[34]

Captain Dalmagne had told Reina that *Jeune Lucie* would be sailing for Woodlark on Tuesday, 21 September 1852, and that he and his missionaries should board the ship that morning. Bishop Bataillon, Fathers Rocher and Montrouzier, and the thirteen young men from the Central Oceania vicariate accompanied the five Italian priests and two catechists aboard. One of the thirteen young men had become so fond of Salerio that he cried in

---

32. SM: OMM/208, Montrouzier to Colin (for the date see n. 25); PIME: AME 11:83, Reina to Marinoni, 18 September 1852.

33. PIME: AME 11, *Notizie*, 61–62, undated extracts from Ambrosoli letters.

34. PIME: AME 11:526–27, 529 bis, 529 ter.

desperation all morning, begging the priest not to go to Woodlark Island "because the people there are bad and will eat you."³⁵

Father Ambrosoli somehow found time that same day to write one last letter to his family. "After two months of rest in Australia, I am once again setting out to sea. This time I am going to Woodlark Island, where we hope to arrive in three weeks or a month.... Here in our vicinity [in Australia] much gold has been discovered and everyone is rushing there to get it. And we? We are distancing ourselves from the gold. It is not something that attracts us, because we are interested in souls. Yes, these souls are indeed a greater good than gold! The winning of a single one is a far greater gain than acquiring all the gold in the world."³⁶

Captain Dalmagne waited all day for the wind to blow, but it never did. The visitors left, the missionaries slept aboard, and on the following morning they heard sails fluttering in the wind. The *Jeune Lucie* with her cargo of missionaries and mission supplies was gently being blown out of Port Jackson and onto the high seas. One more lap of the long voyage to their Oceania mission had begun. It was Wednesday, 22 September 1852, six months and six days since they had left Milan.³⁷

This handful of missionaries was in no way adequate for evangelizing the extensive territory of Melanesia and Micronesia with which they wanted to be entrusted. A continuous stream of personnel would be needed to develop the entire area. Director Marinoni was well aware of this and had been thinking of a second expedition even before the first one had left Europe. In fact, he had written to Fransoni from Paris on Palm Sunday, 4 April 1852, that he planned on sending to Oceania "another six priests and two catechists this coming spring, if Your Eminence approves."³⁸ This was six days before Reina had set sail from Gravesend for Sydney, and it was the second time that Marinoni had announced this second expedition to Fransoni.

After waiting eight months for word from Fransoni about his offer, Marinoni brought up the subject a third time on 6 December 1852. The Association for the Propagation of the Faith in Lyon and in Paris, he said, had informed him that they were granting twenty thousand francs toward the expenses of "the six priests and two catechists who are to leave

---

35. PIME: AME 11, *Notizie*, 93–94, Salerio to his parents, December 1852.

36. Brambilla, *Pontificio istituto*, 1:60, Ambrosoli to his family, 21 September 1852.

37. PIME: AME 11, *Notizie*, 93f, Salerio to his parents, 4 December 1852. Here Salerio says, "We embarked on the morning of 21 September.... We had to wait all day, since there was no breeze to blow us out of port until the next morning...." In his carefully kept log Salerio also gives 22 September as the date on which the *Jeune Lucie* left Sydney. See RIP: R B-N.2, N.1, Carlo Salerio, "Giornale di Viaggio," 22 September 1852. Mazzucconi was therefore incorrect when over a month later he told his family, "We left Sydney on the feast day of Saint Matthew...," which was on 21 September, the day on which he boarded the ship. Evidently using Mazzucconi's inexact letter as his source, Tragella says that the missionaries left Sydney "on 21 September" and in his next paragraph that they left on the feast day of Saint Matthew. Compare Mazzucconi, *Scritti*, Mazzucconi to his family, 31 October 1852, 228; Tragella, *Missioni estere*, 1:153.

38. PF: Udienze vol. 115 (1852, Part I), f. 843v.

in the beginning of this coming spring." But if thirty-two thousand francs were not considered sufficient for the first group of seven missionaries, he wondered how the smaller sum of twenty thousand francs could be considered sufficient for this second group of eight missionaries.[39]

The six priests in this second group were Father Angelo Curti from the Diocese of Lodi and Fathers Francesco Pozzi, Antonio Marietti, Antonio Riva, Giulio Sciomacher, and Ignazio Borgazzi, all from the Archdiocese of Milan. The two catechists were Luigi Invernizzi and Giovanni Longoni.

Just nine days later, on 15 December 1852, Reina's first letters from Sydney reached Marinoni.[40] Among them was that of 8 August 1852 for Marinoni himself containing extracts from Reina's diary, showing why he had chosen the Melanesia and Micronesia missions. The packet also contained his letter to Cardinal Fransoni of 7 August 1852, which Marinoni was to read and forward. In it Reina said that following the advice of Bataillon, Rocher, and Montrouzier, he had decided to choose the missions of Melanesia and Micronesia. In this letter he requested approbation from Propaganda Fide for his decision.

Losing no time Marinoni wrote to Fransoni two days later, on 17 December 1852, saying that he did not want "to delay one moment in forwarding the Prefect Apostolic's letter." That of Reina and those of the other missionaries asked that the second group of missionaries leave soon because "the harvest is great" and they were in need of "numerous workers." The members of the second expedition "are waiting for a sign from Your Eminence authorizing them to leave," Marinoni said, "just as those who have already left are waiting for approval from Propaganda for what they have agreed upon with the Reverend Marist Fathers and with Bishop Bataillon."[41] This was the fourth time that Marinoni had brought up the matter of a second expedition.

Not waiting for Fransoni's reply, Marinoni wrote to Colin on 5 January 1853, informing him that "someone [it was Reina] has written that I should send my missionaries as soon as possible in order that they can be in Sydney before the second half of June, since that is the best time for sailing to Melanesia." Marinoni asked whether he might take advantage of Marist hospitality once again, since he would be sending "six priests and two catechists" through Lyon in February on their way to London. But this time it would be only an overnight stop, since they would be leaving Milan just a few days before their ship was scheduled to sail from England.

Marinoni told Colin that the Association for the Propagation of the Faith in Lyon had granted him only twenty thousand francs for this second expedition. He therefore asked Colin "kindly to use your good offices with the respectable Administrators of the Association . . . in order to obtain, like last year, an increase in subsidies for this second ex-

39. PF: SC Oceania vol. 4 (1848–52), f. 1023r.
40. Ibid., f. 1024v, Marinoni to Fransoni, 17 December 1852; Tragella *Missioni estere*, 1:126.
41. PF: SC Oceania vol. 4 (1848–52), f. 1024rv.

pedition." Colin earlier had been correct in pointing out that sixty thousand French francs would be needed by the first group, Marinoni said. Now this second group was even larger and had to bring along not only funds for itself, but also for the first group's second year in the mission.[42]

Hardly had Marinoni sent off this letter to Colin when he received Fransoni's reply to his two letters of 6 and 17 December. The cardinal was pleased to learn that the first group of missionaries had arrived safely in Sydney and that they were preparing to continue their voyage to Melanesia and Micronesia. "I must tell you, however, that I do not consider it opportune to send the second expedition until the first one has reached the place destined for it and has begun to cultivate the vineyard of the Lord."

Fransoni pointed out that Marinoni in time would be receiving additional news from Reina, and this would prove helpful to him in making proper arrangements for dispatching the second group. A bit of delay, he noted, would also make it possible for Marinoni to collect additional funds. "Now although it is my judgment that the departure of the new missionaries should be postponed somewhat, I do not mean by this that you should lessen your concern for making the necessary preparations."[43]

The cardinal's letter to Marinoni of 31 December 1852 was accompanied by one of the same date to Reina, who was addressed as "the Prefect Apostolic of Melanesia." It was the first time that Fransoni had used the title "prefect apostolic" for Reina. "I fully approve of the decision suggested to you by one and all of going to Melanesia," the cardinal said. But at the same time he pointed out that the *Instructions* still permitted Reina to change this decision if circumstances might warrant it.

Paternally the cardinal added: "How much I have at heart this undertaking entrusted to you and your collaborators. And when you reach Woodlark or some other port, I feel certain that you will send me further news for my peace of mind.... You will also provide me with new considerations to be kept in mind when sending out the second group of missionaries now being prepared...."[44]

It is clear from this letter that Fransoni considered Reina the prefect apostolic only of Melanesia, not of Melanesia and Micronesia, the missions which Reina said that he had chosen. The cardinal was evidently under the impression that the Marists at Woodlark intended to transfer to Micronesia. So he kept the Prefecture Apostolic of Micronesia in reserve for them.

Supriès, by this time rector at the Carthusian monastery of Pavia, was informed by Marinoni that Reina and his companions had arrived safely in Sydney. Replying on 30 December 1852, the monk said that this news had brought him great consolation, "because finally I see crowned my most ardent desires. Yes, I say it again, this is truly the work of

---

42. SM: 436.
43. PIME: AME 1:83f, Fransoni to Marinoni, 31 December 1852.
44. PF: LDB vol. 342 (1852, Part II) f. 1132rv.

God! And I am extremely happy, even proud, that the Lord wanted to use a poor hermit like myself for laying the first stone, so to speak, of that holy edifice. Glory be to God!"[45]

Nine days later Supriès joyfully informed Marinoni that he had received a letter of his own sent from Sydney by Mazzucconi in the name of all. He assured Marinoni that he was remembering these young missionaries daily at Mass and after praying his Little Office of the Blessed Virgin Mary. He also said a special prayer for them each night and promised to continue these pious practices on their behalf.[46]

Reina and his six companions finally had left Sydney for Woodlark. Would they ever return to Sydney? And if so, would they return as victors or as vanquished? The curtain was slowly rising on the drama of their lives in Melanesia. That curtain would quickly fall—after three short years—leaving two of them dead, others sick, and the rest dispersed.

---

45. PIME: AME 28:185.

46. Ibid., 187, Supriès to Marinoni, 8 January 1853. The Little Office is a shortened version of the Liturgy of the Hours honoring the Blessed Virgin Mary. It dates from about the middle of the eighth century.

10

Is Reina or Frémont the Prefect Apostolic of Melanesia?
24 February 1853

PONAPE, ALSO CALLED ASCENSION ISLAND, WAS BEST KNOWN OF ALL THE CAROLINE ISLANDS in Micronesia. It was here that Father Reina had planned to go with his missionaries in case Father Frémont decided to keep the entire Melanesia mission. But two weeks before Reina and his missionaries left Sydney for Woodlark, a Protestant mission was founded at Ponape by the Congregational Church. Its missionaries had been sent by the American Board of Commissioners for Foreign Missions and by the Hawaiian Evangelical Association.[1]

Captain Dalmagne did not sail directly to Woodlark when he left Sydney with the Italian missionaries on 22 September 1852. Instead he sailed to New Georgia in the Solomon Islands where *Jeune Lucie* dropped anchor about 10 p.m. on Sunday, 3 October, before two large islands. "Merchants go there regularly to barter for tortoises," Father Salerio explained, "because they are found there in extraordinary abundance." When local inhabitants came out to the ship by canoe the next morning, one of the missionaries said with surprise: "They are men like us!"

Describing the people for his family, Salerio said that their teeth "are very black and their mouth is a fiery red because they chew betel. This is composed of lime, nutmeg and an aromatic leaf, something which they consider delicious. . . ." What they chewed was betelnut, the green astringent seed or fruit of the betel palm, which is about the size of a large apricot. After years of betelnut chewing, teeth turn black.

New Georgia was only thirty leagues from Woodlark, but "quite badly indicated on maps." Father Mazzucconi said that the people "offered us the native fruits found in all these islands, namely coconuts, bananas, sweet potatoes, taro, excellent sugar cane, almonds, etc. In return they requested a piece of cloth, iron, glass, or something else from Europe."[2]

---

1. William E. Strong, *The Story of the American Board*, 232–33.
2. PIME: AME 11, *Notizie*, 94, Salerio to his family, 4 December 1852; PIME: AME 11, *Notizie*, 103, Salerio to Marinoni, 4 December 1852; PIME: AME 11, *Notizie*, 107, Mazzucconi to his family, 31 October 1852.

Jeune Lucie anchored at nearby Baniata on 4 October and at Simbo and Lunga on 5 October.[3] After finishing his business in New Georgia, Captain Dalmagne sailed southwest to Woodlark, an island covering about 430 square miles and consisting of a succession of hills and valleys covered by dense tropical forests. The missionaries in their letters consistently referred to it as Mujù, using the local name. Woodlark today is usually called Murua.

They reached the southeast coast of Woodlark on the morning of 7 October, Salerio said. "But during the night the current carried us to the north side of the island." Dalmagne tacked, working his way back south. The next morning at 7 o'clock *Jeune Lucie* entered Guasup (now Guasopa) Harbor and at 8 o'clock it dropped anchor before the small house of the French missionaries. "We could see the Fathers on the coast and made signs to them," Salerio said. The shore quickly filled with children, who the newly arrived missionaries thought were all baptized, but none of them were.

When the Milan missionaries set foot on land, it was exactly 9 a.m. on Friday, 8 October 1852.[4] On the beach they were embraced by the French missionaries of Father Colin. "The emaciated faces of these missionaries struck us," Mazzucconi said, "and confirmed at once the reports that we had heard about their great sufferings and their virtue." On Sunday, 10 October, the new missionaries sang a Mass of thanksgiving, and on that occasion the French Marists brought into church for the first time "seventeen catechumens, those who appeared closest to the grace of baptism." What they called a church, Mazzucconi observed, was "a low hut made of grass having a roof of leaves. That is all!"[5]

The emaciated Marists were Fathers Frémont, Thomassin, and Trapenard, and Brother Gennade. "These good missionaries received us as if we were sent by the Lord to continue their work," Mazzucconi said. "For several years already they have been asking to be allowed to join their colleagues in the very numerous islands of the Central Vicariate, which has so many Christians and such a great need of priests."[6]

Mazzucconi could not have been correct, however, in saying that the Marist missionaries wanted to leave Woodlark and go to the Central Oceania vicariate. As recently as 29 June 1852, one month before the Italian missionaries had reached Australia, Prefect Apostolic Frémont had written to Cardinal Prefect Fransoni of Propaganda Fide in Rome that the Woodlark mission was making progress and that he and his missionaries had voted unanimously to remain at their posts.[7]

---

3. RIP: R B-N.2, N.1, Carlo Salerio, "Giornale di Viaggio," 4 and 5 October 1852.

4. Ibid., 8 October 1852. Tragella in *Missioni estere*, 1:153, mistakenly says that the missionaries landed at Woodlark on 9 October.

5. PIME: AME 11 *Notizie*, 96, Salerio to his family, 4 December 1852; PIME: AME 11 *Notizie*, 108, Mazzucconi to his family, 31 October 1852.

6. Ibid., 108, Mazzucconi to his family, 31 October 1852.

7. PF: Udienze vol. 117 (1853, Part I), f. 271r.

Moreover, the Marists at Woodlark were greatly surprised when they saw *Jeune Lucie* come into port on 8 October 1852. They had not expected to see another ship for twelve or fifteen months after *Jessie* had sailed off to Sydney with Frémont's 29 June letter to Fransoni. "We were even more surprised at seeing seven missionaries set foot on land," Father Trapenard told Father Colin in Lyon. "The new arrivals are very reserved and tell us nothing but what is indispensable. And they attempt to conceal the wishes of their hearts. We on the other hand only want to know both the mind of Rome and their wishes so that we can comply fully. But it is impossible for us to get any precise information."

The letters that had been delivered to them, Trapenard said, had been read and reread. But they caused nothing but anxiety and vexation because "there is nothing decisive in them. They leave everything up to our conscience." In this uncertainty "all three of us [priests] came together to see what we should do. After carefully examining the situation we believe that we have no reason to abandon our post.... We shall give these gentlemen a part of our territory, shall fix the boundaries, and then shall submit all to Rome for approval."[8]

On the very day of his arrival at Woodlark, Friday, 8 October 1852, Reina began negotiations with Frémont, the prefect apostolic of the Missions of Melanesia and Micronesia. That night he wrote in his diary: "I presented the letters to Father Frémont, who in our presence silently read the one from Father Colin and then said to us: Father Colin orders us to remain at Woodlark because this is the desire of Propaganda. You will therefore be stationed elsewhere and I shall accompany you there."[9]

As a result of the meeting of the three Marist priests it was decided that Father Trapenard should leave with *Jeune Lucie* for Sydney, that Father Montrouzier should come to Woodlark, and that one Italian priest should remain at Woodlark with Father Thomassin and Brother Gennade. All the other missionaries from Milan were to accompany Frémont to Rooke Island where he would help them get established. Once they were trained he would return to Woodlark, and the Italian missionary left behind at Woodlark would join his companions in Rooke.[10]

This is precisely what Propaganda in Rome had hoped would happen—namely, that the two mission sending societies would divide the vast territory in such a way that each might become responsible for developing a part of it.

At first Frémont had been uncertain whether "he should take us to Rooke or to Ponape," Reina wrote in his diary on 9 October. "I gave him full liberty of choice because we have no particular preference." Eventually he decided in favor of Rooke "whose language he knew and still remembered well." Frémont intended to keep Woodlark for the Marists along with its adjoining islands and the Louisiade Archipelago. The rest of the Marist mission, Reina

---

8. SM: OMM/208, Trapenard to Colin, 23 January 1853. The three Marist priests were Frémont, Trapenard, and Thomassin. Brother Gennade, also a Marist, did not participate in the meeting.

9. PIME: AME 11:95, Reina to Marinoni, 31 October 1852.

10. SM: OMM/208, Trapenard to Colin, 23 January 1853.

said, would be handed over to him, but only after everything had been submitted to Colin for approval. Then on Sunday, 10 October, Frémont told Reina it was possible that the Marists "might be leaving the mission" altogether.

On Monday, 11 October, Reina held meetings with his missionaries to find out who might be willing to stay behind and work in Woodlark. One of his men, whom Reina did not name, was strongly opposed to anyone at all remaining behind. "Woodlark had been started wrongly," he charged, and must be discontinued. "But why abandon a good thing already begun?" Reina asked. "Faith was sold for the price of iron!" was the reply. "Yes, but there are now Catechumens, and these were not bought," Reina retorted. "But the purpose of the iron was to recompense them!"

Reina chose Father Salerio as future superior of the Woodlark mission, in case the Marists left, "because of his vision and his surprising activity." When Reina asked him whether he might want a companion, Salerio replied: "Rather than get someone who would stay here unwillingly, I would prefer to remain alone."[11]

Meanwhile Reina's companions had been making seemingly casual remarks that greatly distressed the Marists; they took careful note of them, examined them and compared them. As head of the mission Frémont was particularly concerned over their insinuations, and he confided to Trapenard his uneasiness and embarrassment. Trapenard in turn counseled Frémont to approach Reina for more details on Rome's intentions insofar as he might be aware of them.[12]

Frémont then asked Reina to go walking with him after Mass on Tuesday morning, 12 October. "He wanted me to give him a better explanation of the *Instructions*," Reina wrote in his diary. "I did so and then I asked . . . whether he could go to Rooke, remain there with us for fifteen days to install us, and then leave. This he would be able to do, he said, but it was the only assistance that he could offer. I answered that he should do it, if it pleased him, and I left it up to his conscience. . . ." Frémont replied: "I have prayed and I have read the letters of my Superior and also the other letters attentively. I believe that we must give up this mission. . . ." Frémont then left Reina and sought out Father Trapenard.

Half an hour later he was back. "These missions belong to you exclusively," he told Reina. "You are now the Superior and we are nothing but your helpers. I have decided that we shall withdraw, since this is the will of God. We Marists shall keep the Central Oceania Mission and your seminary will receive the western part."

What was Reina's reaction? "I told him not to hasten matters along, saying that we were agreeable to everything and that the Marists have a complete right to retain this mission, if they so wish. He said that it had been decided . . . , and that he realized it was good for his Society." Reina then asked whether it would be necessary for him to assign two

---

11. PIME: AME 11:95f, Reina to Marinoni, 31 October 1852.
12. SM: OMM/208, Trapenard to Colin, 23 January 1853.

Italian priests to Woodlark, as Frémont had suggested earlier. Frémont said yes, because that island, too, would now be given up by the Marists.[13]

Father Trapenard reported to Father Colin in Lyon what had happened. After Reina had given Frémont his latest explanation of the *Instructions* that Tuesday morning, Frémont had come to consult him. "The situation now appeared clear to us," Trapenard said. "After Father Frémont had informed me of everything, I saw that he was greatly inclined toward abandoning [the mission]. But he did not dare take any step or make any decision. I then explained to him the reasons which I believed were in favor of abandonment. These reasons seemed plausible to him and he then made his decision without reservations. The sacrifice has been made and it is complete."

It was at this point that Frémont had returned to Reina one half hour after leaving him, to announce that the Marists were pulling out of Melanesia and Micronesia for good, and that he was divesting himself completely and at once of his title, his office, and his power.

Father Frémont "has reserved for himself no title and no power at all," Trapenard told Colin. "We want to be completely dependent upon these gentlemen. Rome puts these gentlemen at our service and we, in order to conform to the spirit of our Society, put ourselves entirely at the disposal of these gentlemen. In order to fulfill Rome's wish that these new missionaries should not go alone into the midst of these savage peoples . . . , we have promised to help them with our feeble suggestions and our little experience. These gentlemen accept everything with joy and gratitude. We noticed quickly that we had done something very agreeable to our new guests. Their joy and contentment can be noticed in their words and actions. . . ."

The Italians should have been pleased indeed because the Marists, as Trapenard said, "went so far as to hand over to them" all the things that they possessed which could be of use to the mission. "We are keeping only a few books from our library which can be of no use to these gentlemen. We are giving them everything necessary for holding divine services in two different stations, like vestments, sacred vessels and linen. In addition to this the two stations which we are giving them contain all that they need, like food, kitchen utensils, houses, small furnished rooms, etc., etc."

In view of this new arrangement, Trapenard pointed out, Father Frémont and Brother Gennade would be going with four Italians to found the station in Rooke, whereas Father Thomassin and three Italians would remain at Woodlark. "I myself shall be leaving for Sydney where I am to await my colleagues who will come and join me with the first ship available. As for Father Montrouzier, he is receiving orders from Father Frémont not to come" to Woodlark.[14]

It was a blow for Salerio when eventually he received his definite appointment for Woodlark. When he asked Reina whether he would be assigned to that island forever,

---

13. PIME: 11: 95–96, Reina to Marinoni, 31 October 1852.
14. SM: OMM/208, Trapenard to Colin, 23 January 1853.

Reina promised to let him found a new mission if he could not get used to Woodlark. Reina also assigned Father Raimondi and Cathechist Tacchini to remain at Woodlark with Salerio.[15]

Frémont at once began making the necessary preparations for going to Rooke with four of the Italian missionaries. Present when Bishop Epalle was mortally wounded in 1845 in the Solomon Islands, he was wounded himself and became a cripple for life. Thomassin would remain at Woodlark to introduce the three other Italians to missionary work, teaching them the Woodlark language at the same time. He had been there since 15 September 1847. Like Frémont, he had also been in the first band of Marist missionaries to go to Melanesia and had assisted at the death of Bishop Epalle.[16]

As for Reina, he now had all that he wanted: a mission station at Woodlark and another soon to be opened at Rooke. And he told director Marinoni on 31 October 1852 that he was already thinking of founding a third mission station. "When the second group arrives," he said, "I plan to found a new mission either in New Britain or in New Guinea. . . . But we may have to wait eight years before getting a catechumen in that mission . . . , because their morals are extremely lax . . . and there is no grammar for their language. I am also keeping Ponape in mind. And I want Micronesia to remain the responsibility of our seminary as well. What do you think of that? Before taking this step, however, I shall await a decisive reply from you."[17]

It is difficult to understand how two mission heads, one so experienced and conscientious as Frémont and the other so inexperienced and amibitious as Reina, could have made such an unwise decision. It was diametrically opposed to the basic principle contained in the *Instructions* issued by Cardinal Prefect Fransoni—namely, that no authority whatsoever was to be given to Reina until such time as he and his missionaries had completed their training period and had been found capable of running the mission, which certainly could not be accomplished within fifteen days. Propaganda's authorities could well be pardoned for feeling indignant over such a decision. Up to this point these authorities had hoped that the veteran Marist missionaries would continue their fine work in Melanesia or at least in Micronesia. But now it was clear that the Marists would abandon the area, perhaps forever, as soon as the next ship arrived from Sydney.

The die had been cast, however, and mission work had to go on. Reina together with Fathers Ambrosoli and Mazzucconi and Catechist Corti were to accompany Frémont to Rooke. They boarded *Jeune Lucie* on Saturday, 16 October, together with a young man from Woodlark named Puarer. Frémont knew him well, trusted him, and had engaged him as a mission helper. For three days their ship was obliged to wait at Woodlark for lack of wind,

---

15. PIME: AME 11:95f, Reina to Marinoni, 31 October 1852.
16. PIME: AME 11, *Notizie*, 92, Reina to Marinoni, 31 October 1852; Wiltgen, *Oceania*, 340f, 477, 480.
17. PIME: AME 11:95–96, Reina to Marinoni, 31 October 1852.

but finally it set sail on 19 October 1852. Salerio was in tears at seeing his companions go. But Raimondi said good-humoredly, "One place or another is all the same to me."[18]

While en route to Rooke the young missionaries used Captain Dalmagne's spyglass to examine the northwest coast of New Guinea, "spread out alongside of us with its many high mountains reaching into the clouds," as Mazzucconi described it. He was reminded of the happy day when he and his priest brother Michael had studied a map of New Guinea and had told one another that this country "could become a beautiful field of activity for Catholic missionaries." At that time New Guinea had seemed "far, far away" Mazzucconi said. "But now that island is right here, so very close at hand."

In three days time they came in sight of Rooke Island, today called Umboi and locally considered one of the Siassi Islands. On nearing Rooke an officer, who had climbed up the mast, shouted an order on seeing their ship heading for a sandbank covered by a thin sheet of water. *Jeune Lucie* veered and bypassed the sandbank. "since our maps are always inexact," Mazzucconi said, "we marked the sandbank on the map and thanked the Lord for having saved us."

The next morning, Saturday, 23 October 1852, when their ship entered port, it scraped the tops of coral reefs four times, but suffered only slight damage. It was about noon when *Jeune Lucie* dropped anchor at Port Saint Isidore on the northwest end of Rooke Island.[19] The port and the adjoining village of Nurua had been named Saint Isidore by the first Marist missionaries who had arrived there on 15 May 1848, the feastday of Saint Isidore. Nowadays the port is known as Luther Anchorage.

Men from Nurua coming toward the ship in canoes recognized Frémont and shouted that his small house was still in good condition. When he and three other Marists had left Rooke Island on 17 May 1849, they had asked the villagers not to touch the house.[20] Actually, nothing had been taken away from it in the past forty-four months, not even the iron that the local people prized so highly. The doors and shutters were still closed and intact.

"In fact, they are in such great need of iron," Mazzucconi said, "that it arouses your compassion to see them cut down a tree and hollow out a canoe with no other instrument for cutting but a sharpened stone. . . . We gave them pieces of iron which they now use in place of stone, and you can imagine what noise they make as they work away feverishly." But only three weeks earlier one of these Italian missionaries, not named by Reina, had severely criticized the French Marists at Woodlark for having given iron to the people there. Now the Italians were doing the same at Rooke. The young missionaries were beginning to learn that they had to help raise the standards of their people, not only in spiritual matters, but for life in general.

---

18. Ibid., *Notizie*, 92, Reina to Marinoni, 31 October 1852.

19. Ibid., 108f, Mazzucconi to his family, 31 October 1852. Mazzucconi here says that they dropped anchor "at 1 P.M." and Reina in ibid., 92, writing to Marinoni also on 31 October 1852, says it was "at midday."

20. See Wiltgen, *Oceania*, 479f, 486.

One of the first things that they did on reaching shore was to visit the graves of Bishop Collomb and Father Villien. They prayed that the deceased bishop might continue to show concern over his former flock. The first two nights in port they slept aboard ship because their house was being readied for occupancy. Then on Monday, 25 October 1852, they took up lodging in the house "after having blessed it according to the Ritual and after having thanked the Lord and prayed to him to have mercy on these people and on us."[21]

Father Ambrosoli wrote that Rooke Island was twenty miles long and five or six miles wide. He had seen some seven or eight small islands adjacent to Rooke Island and said that three of them were inhabited. "There are about seventy villages scattered throughout Rooke Island with approximately one hundred inhabitants in each, making a total population of six or seven thousand," he said. "The reason why the graves of Bishop Collomb and Father Villien have been respected up to now," he explained, was that in the culture of the local people violating a grave "constitutes a serious crime" and one caught in the act "would be guilty of sacrilege and would be killed." Frémont had brought along a receptacle for collecting the remains of Bishop Collomb, but he refrained from using it precisely because the local people would look upon such an act as the violation of a grave.[22]

Mazzucconi could not get New Guinea off his mind. "Every time I look out to sea toward the west," he told his family,

> I see the tops of its mountains. When shall we be able to enter that land? There is a man here from New Guinea and we have already decided, once we have overcome our initial difficulties with the Rooke language, to have him come and tell us as many words as possible from the New Guinea language. We shall then draw up a small dictionary for ourselves in case God should wish to give us the grace of entering that land. It really is a *new* land and is so very large. But if Our Lord should wish to reserve this gift for others, then we shall give them the collection of words that we prepare.

Looking eastward from Rooke Island, Mazzucconi said, "We see New Britain, which is also very large. And if we may judge from what people tell us, it is less evil." He described an active volcano between New Britain and Rooke that poured forth smoke. "It *devours men*, as the local people say, and is perhaps the most powerful image of another fire which actually devours souls."[23] This volcano was Ritter Island, called Kulkul by some and Kurkur by others.

Wanting to send along a report with Captain Dalmagne, Reina wrote at length to director Marinoni on the last day of October 1852. He gave numerous details on leaving

---

21. PIME: AME 11, *Notizie*, 92, Reina to Marinoni, 31 October 1852; PIME: AME 11, *Notizie*, 108f, Mazzucconi to his family, 31 October 1852.

22. Ibid., 136–37, undated extracts from letters of Ambrosoli.

23. Ibid., 110–11, Mazzucconi to his family, 31 October 1852. The people of Rooke in 1966 still carried on trade like their ancestors with the villages of Sio, Kalasa, and Sialum in New Guinea and with the villages from Sag Sag to Arawi (near Arawe Island) in New Britain. See Letter, Willard Burce to Ralph M. Wiltgen, 12 January 1966.

Sydney, arriving at Woodlark, having discussions with Frémont, leaving behind three men to be introduced to missionary work by Father Thomassin at Woodlark, and going with three others to Rooke where Father Frémont would introduce him and them to missionary work and also teach them the local language. There was no more talk of Frémont leaving Rooke after only fifteen days; he would now remain until the next supply ship arrived from Sydney.

"So here we are in the midst of our children," Reina told Marinoni, continuing:

> As I write this, they are at the window calling me by name and saying that I am a good man, a *curáb jabóc*. But the Lord alone is good! Generally speaking, I have great hopes. True, things will go slowly and it will be a long ordeal for us. But if we should have to wait ten or even twenty years in order to make a beginning, I hope that with the Lord's help I shall not lose courage. We have no bodily sufferings, truly none. The martyrdom of charity, however, is also meritorious in the eyes of God; it is the basis for everything. Yes, please invoke charity upon us, your sons. Implore for us a spirit of continual prayer, of patience, of courage, of love. And place us in the hands of the Lord and of Mary Most Holy, under whose patronage we have placed this mission.[24]

When Captain Dalmagne arrived back at Woodlark, Salerio had been there a month and a half, during which time he had made a host of observations. He told his family that he had been assigned "to Mujù or Woodlark Island, as it was called by [Captain Grimes of] the ship [*Woodlark*] that discovered it in 1832." The women there were quite well covered, he said, all wearing a skirt three layers thick made of coconut palm leaves reaching from below the waist to the knees. "They like clothes very much and they ask for them avidly."[25]

Writing also to Father Marinoni that same day, 4 December 1852, Salerio said that Woodlark's population was "about two thousand." (Ambrosoli had estimated it to be "six or seven thousand.") He had not yet been able "to found a school for these people, who are eager to have one. It would be good if we could start a boarding school. Then, if we had several missions, we could transfer the children [from one school to another] and so keep them in closer contact with us. In this way we could train them better, shielding them at the same time from bad example." It would be ideal, he added, if he were able to send some of these children to the Marist Center at Sydney. "But this is all of little avail if we do not succeed, as time goes on, in establishing a native *Seminary* in some colonial city. We could then send there those youths who are suitable candidates for instruction and for the priesthood, once the Lord calls them."

He was planning to found an oratory where boys and men could meet on feast days for prayer, instruction, singing, and schooling. Here Salerio intended to combine recreation with development of the intellect and will. "I am convinced that this is one of the most efficacious means available for a missionary to form his people," he said. A start could

---

24. PIME: 11, *Notizie*, 92f, Reina to Marinoni, 31 October 1852.
25. Ibid., 96, Salerio to his family, 4 December 1852.

be made with the mission's few catechumens and with others who visit the missionaries at their residence on Sundays.

And what about the women? They would also need an oratory, Salerio said. "But to get it started, we need a holy woman like Madame [Francoise] Perroton at Wallis" in Central Oceania. This woman had come from France and had arrived in Wallis on 25 October 1846. According to Salerio the conversion of Wallis was due in no small measure "to her indomitable patience and firm character. But you do not find Madames Perroton everywhere! Nor has the time come yet for women from religious orders." But once the mission would be launched, and once the ideas of the majority would be changed, Salerio said, women from religious orders through the work they do "would become angels for these poor and ignorant peoples."

Salerio was also convinced that "all of the surrounding islands would soon experience great benefit," if in Woodlark the missionaries could "form a good nucleus of fervent Christians." Rooke Island was better situated to do this than Woodlark, he said. But Woodlark, too, had its contacts. Half a day away to the east were the islands of Nada and Laughlan. Although these islands had few inhabitants, there was "a most fervent catechumen" on one of them who had wives and sons. The Guavak and Trobriand islands, much more populated than Woodlark and in constant communication with it, were a day's voyage to the northwest.

"A little more than ten or fifteen leagues away to the west," Salerio said,

> are the very vast Massimme Islands, which are not indicated on maps.[26] These islands reach as far as New Guinea, with which they carry on trade in iron. Twice a year their boats also come to Woodlark for trade. These islands are confused with the Louisiade Archipelago and with the d'Entrecasteaux Islands, which Dumont d'Urville maintains are not separated from New Guinea. All of these islands have the advantage that one can travel there without ever losing sight of land. Therefore it will be easy to flit from island to island with a small boat, once those islands have been converted.

An added advantage, Salerio said, was that these island peoples had already been in contact with the Marist missionaries of Woodlark and consequently some of their ancient ideas and prejudices had already disappeared. The bit of civilization that had come to Woodlark had also served as a stimulus for them. "An even greater advantage is that all understand and speak" the language of Woodlark, "even though all have their own languages." These advantages definitely would be taken into consideration, Salerio said, if the mission began to spread from Woodlark to its immediate surroundings.

But it might be preferable to direct the preaching of the gospel to the Solomon Islands, he said, because they are more populous, are constantly being visited by ships, and as a result already have some degree of civilization. If they were to direct their work toward

---

26. The author has not been able to ascertain the spelling and location of the Guavak and Massimme islands mentioned by Salerio.

the Solomon Islands, Salerio suggested that a start be made at New Georgia, which was only thirty leagues distant from Woodlark. "It is quite badly indicated on maps," he said, "but merchants go there regularly to barter for tortoises, because they are found there in extraordinary abundance."[27] Salerio was convinced that "a missionary would be accepted there immediately." In fact, living in Woodlark "for over a year" was a man who had been born in New Georgia.

The daily life of the missionaries at Woodlark, Salerio assured Marinoni, was

> precisely like it was in the Seminary [at Milan]. We find that we are able to follow the daily order almost completely, as well as the manner of life and study proposed by our rules.... We get up at 5 o'clock and then have meditation and Holy Mass. At 7.30 we study and at 11.45 we have community prayers and examination of conscience, which are followed by dinner. At 2.30 we meditate in common and this is followed by study, etc., until 6.30, when we go to supper. At 8 we recite matins, followed by Ave Maris Stella, the rosary and examination of conscience. Here you have the daily order of your missionaries.

What they studied most of all was the Woodlark language, although they did practice some English and continued their studies in dogmatic and moral theology. "Rest assured that in these missions time will not be lacking for study," Salerio said. "Once the missions are flourishing and numerous, and after the villages are converted, a missionary no doubt will be busy and will have continual and varied work. But while the missions are only in their infancy, and especially in the stage in which this mission now finds itself, a missionary has the entire day free, if you exclude the two hours devoted to giving catechism lessons in the course of an entire week. At least Sundays will soon become busier."

For a long time, Salerio said, Marinoni would have to send missionaries to Melanesia "to sow, but not to reap; to irrigate with their sweat and perhaps even with their blood, but not to harvest." He was eager to impress upon Marinoni that supplies from Sydney were absolutely indispensable for the men in Woodlark, because a missionary was esteemed so little by the local people. "They refuse to give him even leftovers from their food; instead they throw them to the swine." This was ironic, he pointed out, because "swine were introduced by the missionaries, who brought them to this island for its benefit." Since the island was not only sterile, but also void of game, Salerio foresaw that he and his missionaries "would be in the greatest peril in time of famine."

Surprised when he found something about Trappists in the diary of the late Bishop Collomb, Salerio called it to Marinoni's attention. This former vicar apostolic of Melanesia and Micronesia had had in mind requesting the abbot general of the Trappists to send a number of his monks to Oceania. "This idea," the bishop wrote, "is an inspiration which stems from my conviction that I need help from those who practice penance in a rather

---

27. Tortoise shells were used for making combs, jewelry, and other articles.

extraordinary degree, in order to drive out demons from these islands. In addition it seems to me that Trappists are the persons best suited for inspiring others with a taste for work."

Salerio then touched upon the subject of catechists, referring particularly to Tacchini and Corti, the two laymen trained as missionaries at Milan who had come to Oceania with him. As long as there was no flourishing indigenous Christian community from which candidates for the role of catechist could be drawn, he said, "We shall need to have at least one [from Europe] for every station." These lay missionaries were to be endowed with a love for work and with a talent for being able always to find some task to keep themselves busy. "This foresight and industriousness," Salerio stressed, "is the principal characteristic after piety which they ought to possess." Gardening, carpentry, and masonry were tasks that could be performed by them only during the cooler parts of the day. As for midday occupations, the ingeniousness "of each one has to determine what he will do and what suits him best."

In his report Salerio also gave a thumbnail sketch of a missionary in Oceania. "An ardent zeal, a mania for work and a life brimful of activity along with all the best of intentions do not suffice for a missionary among these island peoples," he said. "The life of a missionary must be a life of patience: patience in bearing the most revolting humiliations; patience in waiting for his labors to bear fruit; patience in seeing frustrated his most perfect plans for reaching a goal; patience, courage and confidence in praying when his prayers for a long time go unanswered; patience in all things, while joyfully bearing all of them for the Lord." They had placed their mission under the protection of the Immaculate Heart of Mary, he told Marinoni, "hoping that the Lord will help us obtain solid conversions...."[28]

Whereas Salerio stressed the scarcity of food in Woodlark, Mazzucconi had stressed its abundance in Rooke just one month earlier when writing to his family. The people of Rooke "are infinitely poor and are deprived of everything except food," he said. "But because of the large fruit-bearing trees which God has raised up in these lands, and because of the very large number of fish and birds with which He has enriched their sea and their forests, they abound in food."[29]

It was 7 January 1853 when *Jeune Lucie* arrived in Sydney with Father Trapenard aboard. His departure from Woodlark continued the Marist exodus from the Melanesia mission. There were now only three Marists left, two priests and one catechist. They also intended to leave once the Italian missionaries had been trained. Trapenard's orders, in fact, were to wait for them in Sydney.[30]

Meanwhile back in Europe Reina's letters to Fransoni of 7 and 27 August 1852, announcing that shortly he and his missionaries would be leaving Sydney for Woodlark, had arrived just before the end of 1852. In them Reina told how the three Marists—Bataillon, Rocher, and Montrouzier—had all advised him to take up work in "Melanesia and Micronesia."

28. PIME: AME 11, *Notizie*, 100–106, Salerio to Marinoni, 4 December 1852.
29. Ibid., 109, Mazzucconi to his family, 31 October 1852.
30. SM: OMM/208, Trapenard to Colin, 23 January 1853; Hosie, "French Mission," 417.

And he expressed the hope of receiving "approbation from the Sacred Congregation" to commence work there.[31]

Replying on 31 December 1852, Fransoni gave assurance that because of a faculty included in the *Instructions*, Reina's choice of a mission had been approved at the time when it was made. "Nevertheless I tell you again that I fully approve of your decision to go to Melanesia as suggested to you by the others." Fransoni officially addressed Reina as "Prefect Apostolic of Melanesia."[32]

The cardinal, however, did not call Reina the prefect apostolic "of Melanesia and Micronesia," but only "of Melanesia," which meant that he was holding Micronesia in reserve. In view of the various possibilities foreseen in the *Instructions*, Fransoni must have believed that the Marists had chosen Micronesia.

Fransoni sent the letter for Reina to Marinoni, so that he could read and forward it. In an accompanying letter of the same date to Marinoni, Fransoni suggested that sending a second group of missionaries to Oceania at this time was inopportune. It would be better to wait until the first group had reached its destination and had taken up work. After receiving news of this, the cardinal said, Marinoni would be able to make proper arrangements regarding the destination of the second group. Meanwhile he could gather additional funds.[33]

On receiving news from Fransoni of Reina's appointment as prefect apostolic of Melanesia, Marinoni and his seminary rejoiced and the members of the second expedition became even more eager and impatient to leave. Marinoni therefore on 14 January 1853, ignoring what Fransoni had said about the departure, sent another list of reasons that he felt would surely convince the cardinal that the second group should leave at once. Among other things, he quoted Reina's statement that it was necessary, according to Father Rocher, for the new group to leave Europe at once in order to catch the ship sailing to Woodlark in the good season. If they missed that one, they would have to wait an entire year for the next one to leave.[34]

About this same time Superior General Colin of the Marists received a reply from Frémont to his letter of 23 June 1851, in which he had told his missionaries that they were completely free to remain in Woodlark or to leave it. Frémont's reply was dated 25 June 1852 and so was written one month before the Italian missionaries had arrived in Australia. In it he reported to Colin that the Woodlark mission finally was making progress and that he and his missionaries had decided unanimously to stay there.[35]

    31. PF: SC Oceania vol. 4 (1848–52), f. 978r–979r, 1025r–1026r.

    32. PF: LDB vol. 342 (1852, Part II), f. 1132rv.

    33. Ibid., f. 1132v–1133v, Fransoni to Marinoni, 31 December 1852.

    34. PF: SC Oceania vol. 5 (1853–57, Part I), f. 128rv, 131r.

    35. SM: OMM/208. Enclosed with Frémont's 25 June 1852 letter for Colin was a 29 June 1852 letter for Fransoni.

Also about this time Superior General Colin had received Reina's letter written at Tarban Creek on 12 August 1852, in which he said, "According to your counsels" and those of Bataillon, Rocher, and Montrouzier, "we have chosen the mission of Melanesia and Micronesia."[36]

Having learned from Frémont that he and his missionaries had unanimously decided to remain at Woodlark in Melanesia, and from Reina that he had chosen the Melanesia and Micronesia mission, Superior General Colin began to fear that a conflict might arise between his missionaries and those of Marinoni. He therefore wrote to Marinoni on 13 January 1853 as follows:

> Our Woodlark missionaries have written me that they now are full of hope because they no longer are being avoided so much by their poor savages. They even have several categories of catechumens whom they are instructing.... Our missionaries add that they wish to remain at Woodlark and they are writing about this to Propaganda. I do not know which portion [of the mission] the Reverend Prefect Apostolic of your missionaries will be taking.... One of our missionaries wrote to me that perhaps he would be going with them to Rooke.[37] Because of all this uncertainty, would it not be advisable for you to wait for word before you send out a second group of missionaries?

Colin suggested further that Marinoni might want to assign someone to Sydney "in order to provide all those services which your missionaries no doubt will be needing..."[38]

Marinoni had barely forwarded Fransoni's letter of 31 December 1852 to Reina, naming him prefect apostolic of Melanesia, when he received Colin's letter stating that the Marists at Woodlark were now successful and had decided to stay there—news that made him panic. In spite of his having already written five times to Fransoni in vain, trying to convince him that the departure of his missionaries for Oceania could tolerate no delay, he now envisioned as many additional steps that he and others could take to achieve that goal.

First he sent Fransoni a memo on the matter on 21 January 1853, saying that the Association for the Propagation of the Faith in Lyon had already promised him sixty thousand francs to cover the costs of the second expedition.[39] Then he rushed off a letter to Bishop Lodovico Besi (1815–72), his friend in Rome and confidant of Cardinal Fransoni, asking that he use his influence in trying to obtain authorization from Fransoni for send-

---

36. SM: 436.

37. The missionary vaguely referred to by Colin was Montrouzier at Tarban Creek. But it was Colin himself, not Montrouzier, who had suggested on 21 March 1852 that he go with the Italians to Rooke. When Montrouzier replied, he told Colin that he wanted to go with them to Woodlark. See SM: OMM/208, Montrouzier to Colin, n.d. Internal evidence shows that Montrouzier's letter was written between 22 August and 15 September 1852. Colin's letter of 21 March 1852 has not been found, but is mentioned in Montrouzier's reply.

38. PIME: AME 28:739f.

39. PF: SC Oceania vol. 5 (1853–57, Part I), f. 129rv.

ing the second group of missionaries to Oceania at once. Besi was originally from Verona, Italy, had been named administrator of the Nanking vicariate in China in 1838, and had returned to Europe in 1847.[40]

Besi wrote back on 8 February 1853, telling Marinoni that on a recent evening he had discussed the matter with Fransoni, but that the cardinal considered it inadvisable to send off a second group at once. In fact, Besi said, it was easy to tell from the cardinal's manner of speaking "that this is not only his personal view, but one that is shared by the entire Propaganda Fide." Those in authority considered it imperative "to wait and see what the outcome and results of the first expedition will be."[41]

Not waiting to receive Besi's reply, Marinoni decided to take even further steps. He would go to Rome and personally plead his case with Propaganda's authorities and with the pope himself. But first he wanted to prepare the way by obtaining help from others.

He asked the archbishop of Milan to assist him with a letter of recommendation. Romilli obliged by writing to Fransoni on 5 February 1853. "We have received the most consoling news" from the group that left last year, he said. He added that Father Marinoni, director of the mission seminary and bearer of his letter, would be visiting Rome "to arrange for sending off a new group of missionaries."[42]

Since Marinoni wanted to leave no stone unturned to guarantee the success of his mission, he also approached Bishop Ramazzotti of Pavia and asked him for a letter of recommendation. Ramazzotti obliged by writing to Fransoni on 6 February. "I recommend to you the reason" for which Marinoni is going to Rome, he said. "He is going in order to solicit the prompt sending of a second portion of missionaries from his college. Or, let me rather say, he is going in order to present our request that other missionaries be sent promptly . . . , but always in accord with the will of the Superiors of Propaganda. It seems to us that this is suggested by a number of good reasons."

Ramazzotti listed four: (1) This would make it possible for the Milan missionaries to take advantage of the next ship being chartered by the Marists in Sydney. If the second group were not sent, this would leave the first group "without aid for even more than a year." (2) Preparations could then begin immediately for sending a third group. (3) The sixty thousand francs granted by Lyon would be forfeited if the second group were not sent now. (4) In Milan "it will look bad" if there is further delay. And "the fervor of the possible recruits" will diminish. All of this, he added, would be explained much better by Marinoni. "But we accept your decision," no matter what it may be.[43]

---

40. Marinoni's letter to Besi has not been found, but its contents are evident from PIME: AME 27:11f, Besi to Marinoni, 8 February 1853. Some authors give "Ludovico" as Besi's first name, but he himself always writes "Lodovico."

41. Ibid.

42. PF: SC Oceania vol. 5 (1853–57, Part I), f. 153rv.

43. Ibid., f. 154rv. Since Marinoni was still in Milan when this letter of 6 February 1853 was written, Brambilla cannot be correct when he says in *Pontificio istituto*, 1:130, that Marinoni went to Rome "in the beginning of 1853."

Fransoni had meanwhile written on 1 February 1853 to Marinoni in Milan, answering his two letters of 14 and 21 January. The reasons that Propaganda had for postponing the departure of the second group, he said, outweighed those indicated by Marinoni for an immediate departure. The cardinal did agree with Marinoni, however, that the foundation of a supply center in Sydney should be postponed, since at the moment there was no news about the Milan missionaries other than that they had left Sydney in September 1852 for Woodlark.[44]

By the time Fransoni's letter reached Milan, however, Marinoni had left for Rome. From there he explained to Fransoni in still another letter on 16 February that his purpose in coming was "to communicate to you that information which might have some bearing on your decision regarding the opportuneness of sending off our missionaries promptly."

He was "altogether convinced," he said, that delaying their departure for another year "will undoubtedly produce a sinister impression" in various categories of people. In Oceania his missionaries would feel abandoned. In France the officials of the Association for the Propagation of the Faith would not give him the sixty thousand francs until they received firm assurance "of a definite [departure] date for the planned expedition." In Milan and in its surrounding dioceses unfavorable interpretations and insinuations would surely be made, because news of the proximate departure of the missionaries had already been published.

In the event that bad news about the first group should come from Sydney, he continued,

> would it not be better for new missionaries to have left Milan by that time, so that they can provide support for the first group, give them courage and take their places? How can I send anyone later, either to that mission or elsewhere, if I have the entire city [of Milan] at my back, and especially all the parents, insisting that it would be imprudent to make any new attempt? But if the news is good—as I hope it will be—the wisest thing would be to have the new missionaries join the others quickly, so that they can share the work of the others and its results.

Marinoni also called attention to "the excellent suggestion" made by Bishop Bataillon to Propaganda—namely, "that there be founded in Sydney a Procure House and a General Seminary for the Missions of Oceania." Reina could assign one or two priests in the second group to Sydney in order to have them trained as procurators at the Marist Center. Such training would prove helpful, Marinoni said, no matter what the ultimate destination of the group might be.[45]

This letter marked the tenth occasion within thirteen months that Marinoni personally or through others had approached Fransoni on this issue. Would Cardinal Fransoni

---

44. PIME: AME 1:87.
45. PF: SC Oceania vol. 5 (1853–57, Part I), f. 150r–151v.

and secretary Barnabò continue to be as adamant in postponing the departure as Marinoni was persistent in requesting it?

Meanwhile in January 1853, shortly after Fransoni had named Reina of Milan the "Prefect Apostolic of Melanesia," he received a letter from the Marist missionary Frémont dated 29 June 1852 stating that he had been elected by his colleagues "as Prefect of the Mission of Melanesia and Micronesia according to the faculty granted by the Holy See..." Frémont explained that Colin had said they were free to remain in the mission or leave it, because of its sterility and all the lives and property that had been lost "since we entered this Mission about seven years ago." Although he had been in office one year already, he had postponed submitting a report on his mission because he had wanted to see first how it would develop. He was now happy to report that Woodlark mission was progressing well. After listing the pros and cons for its continuance, he said, "We agree unanimously—to a man—that we should stay here until such time as we may be removed either by orders, or by successors, or because of some grave and unforeseen reasons."

In the same letter Frémont requested eight faculties. Fransoni could see from what he requested that Christianity was beginning to take root in Woodlark, thanks to the efforts, experience, and patience of the Marists.[46] So on 6 February 1853, and again on 20 February (when director Marinoni was in Rome), secretary Barnabò approached Pope Pius IX to obtain the faculties requested by Prefect Apostolic Frémont.[47] Because some of them had to be obtained through the Holy Office, Barnabò on 12 February wrote to assessor Caterini saying that he was enclosing "two queries proposed by the Prefect Apostolic of the Mission of Melanesia in Oceania...."[48]

In secretary Barnabò's letter to assessor Caterini, Frémont was called "Prefect Apostolic of the Mission of Melanesia in Oceania." And in Cardinal Prefect Fransoni's letter written six weeks earlier (31 December 1852), it was Reina who was called "Prefect Apostolic of Melanesia." From this it was clear that Propaganda at this time had two prefects apostolic for the same mission.

Who was to blame for this confusion? Frémont was not to blame because on 22 June 1851, just four days after his election as prefect apostolic of Melanesia and Micronesia, he had sent the details of his election to Colin. Nor was Colin to blame, because on receiving this news he immediately sent word of Frémont's election to Fransoni on 22 December 1851.[49]

---

46. PF: Udienze vol. 117 (1853, Part I), f. 271r–272v, Frémont to Fransoni, 29 June 1852. Colin had received this letter from Frémont (see n. 35) for forwarding to Fransoni.

47. Ibid., f. 246r, 344r. For the faculties requested by Frémont, see chap. 8, pp. 125–30 passim.

48. PF: LDB vol. 343 (1853, Part I), f. 141rv.

49. SM: OMM/411, *Procès-verbal* of 18 June 1851; SM: OMM/208, Frémont to Colin, 22 June 1851; PF: SC Oceania vol. 4 (1848–52), f. 685r, Colin to Fransoni, 22 December 1851.

Was Reina to blame? He may have been partly to blame for the confusion because he had told Fransoni in August 1852 that Bishop Bataillon, Rocher, and Montrouzier had all advised him to take up work in "Melanesia and Micronesia." Bataillon, however, had strongly advised him against going to Melanesia. In this connection it is surprising to note that Reina nowhere in his correspondence from Sydney uses Frémont's title of prefect apostolic. He calls Frémont only "the Superior of the Marists." Surely Reina had learned at Tarban Creek that Frémont was prefect of the Missions of Melanesia and Micronesia.

Naming Reina as prefect apostolic of Melanesia had been decided upon by Cardinal Prefect Fransoni and by secretary Barnabò, who was the mastermind of Propaganda at this time. Was Barnabò perhaps to blame for the confusion? It would seem so, because nowhere in the *Instructions*—which he no doubt conceived and composed—was it explicitly stated that the chief person with whom Reina ought to consult when choosing a mission in Melanesia and Micronesia was Frémont, the one actually in charge of that area. Reina had been told instead to consult with Colin in Lyon and with other Marists in Sydney. On the basis of his choice resulting from these consultations, Propaganda had named him the prefect apostolic of Melanesia.

But no matter who was to blame for the confusion, Fransoni and Barnabò had to extricate themselves from the impasse. All along they had been striving to find an additional working force for the vast missions of Melanesia and Micronesia. Now having named two prefects apostolic of Melanesia from two different mission sending societies, they began to fear that one society might well expel the other and that even both could be lost to the mission. The solution appeared quite simple to them, however. The French Marists could have their pick, keeping either Melanesia or Micronesia. The Italian missionaries would then receive what remained.

This solution was spelled out in a hurried letter drafted by Barnabò and signed by Fransoni on 24 February 1853. Replying to Frémont's letter of 29 June 1852, Fransoni called Frémont the "Prefect Apostolic of Melanesia or Micronesia in Oceania." The cardinal had been "very happy" to learn from Frémont's letter, he said, that the situation in Melanesia was now much more hopeful than it had ever been since the mission was founded. And although Propaganda had agreed to the repeated requests of Colin to reduce the burden for the Marists and to provide some personnel from the Milan mission seminary "to partake in your labors, still it was by no means our intention that we remove you from those regions or oblige you to leave them.

"What is more," he said, "according to the *Instructions* given to the Milan priests . . . , the Apostolic See transmits to them for development that part of those regions which you yourselves would like to entrust to them. Consequently, if it should please you to retain the Melanesia Mission, then they would receive the care of Micronesia, or vice versa. . . ." The transfer of authority to the Milan priests, Fransoni said, was to take place "as soon as they would be considered equal to the task of exercising the ministry."

All of this, Fransoni believed, must be "sufficiently clear to you from the documents presented by the same priests, and we trust that everything has already been properly arranged between you in the manner in which the Sydney Procurator [Rocher] together with Bishop Bataillon and Father Montrouzier have announced to us as being judged expedient. . . ."[50] Now since one of these two missions most happily is being retained by you, we took care of obtaining for you from our Most Holy Father the faculties requested in your above-mentioned letter, as you will see from the attached rescript. . . ." Fransoni earnestly recommended the Milan missionaries to Frémont and urged him to extend kind assistance to them in every possible area.

Fransoni explained further that "the personnel of the Milan mission seminary" were to have consulted with Colin in Lyon, with Procurator Rocher in Sydney "and with you" in making their choice.[51] The *Instructions* of 9 February 1852, however, do not say that prior consultation was to take place with the head of the Marist mission in Melanesia and Micronesia. Furthermore, Fransoni and Barnabò had named Reina the prefect apostolic of Melanesia on the basis of Reina's letter written at Tarban Creek before he had even met Frémont in Woodlark. This contradiction makes it appear that Fransoni and Barnabò were trying to shed responsibility for having caused the confusion.[52]

Cardinal Fransoni's letter to Reina of 31 December 1852 calling him "Prefect Apostolic of Melanesia" was quickly followed by a letter to Frémont of 24 February 1853 calling him "Prefect Apostolic of Melanesia or Micronesia in Oceania." Both letters would lie side by side for a long time in Sydney until they could be delivered by Captain Dalmagne to Reina and Frémont at Rooke Island. It was not until 21 August 1853 that Dalmagne sailed from Sydney aboard the *Supply* with the letters.[53]

Propaganda now had an additional reason for postponing the departure of Marinoni's second group of missionaries. It needed to learn who was the prefect apostolic of Melanesia: Reina or Frémont. Although Marinoni was in Rome for most of February 1853, he hardly would have been told by Fransoni and Barnabò that Pope Pius IX had granted faculties to Frémont, and that there was confusion over who was in charge of Melanesia.

---

50. In reality Rocher, Bataillon, and Montrouzier had "announced" nothing to Fransoni; he had obtained word about their opinions in the matter from Reina.

51. PF: LDB vol. 343 (1853, Part I), f. 118v–119r, Fransoni to Frémont, 24 February 1853. This official file copy of Fransoni's letter incorrectly refers to Frémont's letter as being dated 19 June 1852; it was dated 29 June 1852. For Frémont's original letter see PF: Udienze vol. 117 (1853, Part I), f. 271r–272v.

52. The *Instructions* stated that Propaganda "will approve whatever decision they [the Milan missionaries] make, provided that they follow the advice of the Marist prelates and priests . . ." Now Frémont was no prelate; he was simply a priest with the title "prefect apostolic." And from the letter sent by Reina and his companions to Fransoni on 20 February 1852 after receiving the *Instructions* in Milan, it is clear that they understood "Marist prelates and priests" to include no other Marists but Colin, Rocher, and Bataillon. See chap. 6, pp. 93–95.

53. For the sailing date see Hosie, "French Mission," 417.

Director Marinoni himself was granted an audience by Pope Pius IX in that month of February. But instead of the audience being a joyful and uplifting event, one that would provide inspiration for his seminary and his missionaries in the field, it greatly depressed him, his candidates, and all others intimately connected with his seminary.

During the audience the pope said that he would have preferred to see the Milan missionaries go to Corfu in Greece rather than to Oceania.[54] As Bishop Ramazzotti later told the other bishops of Lombardy, the pope had even complained, so to speak, that he had hardly found "that desirable, prompt and perfect obedience" which he had anticipated would be given to his wishes. The pope also said that he had wanted to profit from the seminary's personnel for the benefit of missions that were closer.

Marinoni was deeply disturbed by this audience, and on returning to Milan he made the pope's words known to everyone closely connected with his seminary. All were filled with anxiety. Automatically the idea of sending a second group of missionaries to Oceania was dropped, and the seminary began cross-examining itself. Morale went down, and the young priest candidates began to believe that Propaganda would never send a second group of missionaries to Oceania. All asked themselves whether they were on the right road, the one that the pope wanted, or perhaps on one dictated by their personal whims.

Like the student body, Marinoni became convinced that their every step had been in conformity with the *Instructions* and with the wishes of Rome. But Ramazzotti did not agree. He accused Marinoni of letting himself be guided by the personal wishes of the young priests, whereas the wish of the pope should be supreme. The young priests in turn began to fear that their mission seminary might be moved to Rome. Marinoni later described the period as "a real tempest, the worst that could have happened to the institute."

Bishop Ramazzotti decided to take matters in his own hands and early in April drew up a text addressed to the pope. But instead of signing it himself, he sent it to Marinoni with instructions for him to have Archbishop Romilli of Milan amend the text and sign it. Marinoni, however, did not find Ramazzotti's text factual and persuaded Romilli not to sign it.[55] Marinoni then drew up a text of his own and forwarded it to Cardinal Prefect Fransoni on 6 April 1853. Writing candidly on behalf of the seminary and in the name of its members already in Oceania, he described their embarrassing situation. He begged Fransoni to find out the mind of Pope Pius IX in this matter and to send back a word of comfort in their hour of trial.

Fransoni took the letter addressed to himself and read it to the pope. Then on 23 April 1853, Fransoni wrote Marinoni about what he had done, and said that the pope on hearing the contents had ordered him to write the following lines to Marinoni: "As he himself told you, he would have considered it fitting" that the missionaries sent to Oceania should have been "sent first to a mission that was less rugged and that was closer. This could have been the needy church in Corfu or some similar church."

54. Brambilla, *Pontificio istituto*, 1:130.
55. See Tragella, *Missioni estere*, 1:128–33.

However, the pope "did not thereby intend to disapprove the expedition already sent [to Oceania], nor did he mean to deny his most generous blessings to the missionaries sent abroad, nor to the institute itself." In fact, Fransoni continued, "he now lovingly imparts it to them once more. You can therefore expel from your heart the fear that you experience, since His Holiness wishes you to continue promoting with all possible zeal the progress of an institute which is very dear to his heart and from which he expects great help for the propagation of our Catholic religion. I have been ordered to tell you this, so that you may draw great comfort from it."

Surprised and delighted with Fransoni's reply, Marinoni rushed off a copy to Bishop Ramazzotti on 27 April 1853, saying that he could not possibly wish for "a more precise explanation of the mind of the Vicar of Jesus Christ. I am also happy over the consolation which, I hope, these words will bring to Your Illustrious Reverence, whose most loving heart must have suffered much in these past days. You can well imagine what great joy now fills the hearts of our priest candidates...."[56]

Fransoni's quoting the words of the pope and Marinoni's happy reaction to them, however, did not change Ramazzotti's heart. To Marinoni's great distress and that of the seminary's candidates, Ramazzotti remained unyielding and accused the candidates of being disobedient. Marinoni wrote to him on 21 May 1853, saying that his rigidity "in considering the position of our missionaries as irregular in the eyes of Rome," in spite of what Pope Pius IX had instructed Fransoni to tell them on 23 April, "greatly disturbs me and all the candidates." Tension and misunderstandings between Marinoni and Ramazzotti increased, however, until all was finally resolved when the seminary's candidates in June signed statements to the satisfaction of Ramazzotti.

Then during Ramazzotti's *ad limina* visit he personally assured Pope Pius IX on 29 September 1853 that the members of the Milan Seminary for Foreign Missions were prepared to go wherever the pope might want to send them. On that same day Father Salvioni, Ramazzotti's secretary, described the visit for Marinoni, saying that the pope was highly pleased even on hearing the name of the mission seminary. "And he accepted lovingly the offer made to him through the bishop by its missionaries of their complete and entire devotion for any mission whatsoever."

Before his audience with the pope, Ramazzotti had met Cardinal Fransoni, who told him that between the Milan missionaries and the Holy See there was "nothing disagreeable that needs healing." Fransoni also assured Ramazzotti that Propaganda wanted to see their mission in Oceania continue.[57]

---

56. Brambilla, *Pontificio istituto*, 1:132f; Tragella, *Missioni estere*, 1:133f. Tragella here quotes a document as saying "una scabrosa e più vicina missione" (134); Brambilla quotes it as saying "una non scabrosa e più vicina Missione" (132). The document however says: "una meno scabrosa e più vicina missione," that is, a "less rugged" mission. See PF: LDB vol. 343 (1853, Part I), f. 285v, Fransoni to Marinoni, 23 April 1853.

57. Tragella, *Missioni estere*, 1:134–43, passim; Brambilla, *Pontificio istituto*, 1:133.

Salvioni sent still further news to Marinoni on 8 October 1853, saying that Ramazzotti had had an opportunity to speak directly with secretary Barnabò, who likewise gave assurance of the benevolence and protection of the Holy See toward the Milan missionaries. "In addition the Oceania Mission will be continued and favored," Salvioni wrote. "And as regards the next expedition, they are only waiting for news to arrive from Oceania. With the help of this news the second expedition, which will be able to bring supplies for the first, can be better organized and directed."[58]

58. Tragella, *Missioni estere*, 1:142–43.

11

Sickness, Language Study, and Customs at Rooke and Woodlark
1852–55

It was Wednesday, 19 October 1853, when Captain Dalmagne guided his 124-ton schooner *Supply* into Port Saint Isidore at the north end of Rooke Island and dropped anchor near Nurua mission. This was the first ship seen by Prefect Apostolic Reina and his companions since their arrival on 23 October 1852. They were particularly distressed on learning that there were no new missionaries aboard. Reina received several letters from director Marinoni, but the most recent of these was already seven months old—and when he opened his mail from home, he learned that his dear mother had died.

On the following day, 20 October, Reina wrote his first letter to Marinoni in a year. "I remember telling you in my last letter that we had no physical sufferings, really none at all. And this was true. . . . We had hoped that we would be able to work energetically for these people. . . ." Fifteen days later, however, the French catechist, Brother Gennade, was attacked by severe fever, Reina said. "After two or three days the same happened to all of us, one after the other. These severe attacks of fever struck us down and for the first two months it was really an effort to get on our feet, to make our beds and to hang out in the sun our clothing, so soaked with perspiration. Our constant companions were extreme weakness, terrible pains in the head, swellings in our legs, constant lack of appetite and a continual feeling of being indisposed along with drowsiness of intellect and diminution of sight and hearing.

"But our Lord did not abandon us," Reina said. "Father Frémont and Brother Gennade, who had already suffered from the same fevers for more than a year and a half at San Cristóbal, took action immediately and helped us in all our needs. After about two months of treatment with quinine we were able to arrest the fever for some days. On these days the energy that we had lost was slowly regained. We continued like this for the rest of the year, taking quinine every eight or ten days. But at the beginning of August our quinine ran out and the ship [that arrived yesterday] brought us no new supply. May the Lord be blessed as we abandon ourselves even more completely to his holy will. This is how we spent our first year in this mission."

Reina told Marinoni: "The local people tell us that our God is evil, because we are always sick. They are not aware that we are the evil ones, that being humiliated is something good and that the real way to continue this mission is through suffering, since suffering obtains mercy." The missionaries kept praying and waiting for "the day of mercy," Reina said, "because there is no one else but God who can change the hearts [of these people]." For the past four nights he had slept little, he admitted, and even now he had a bit of fever. "I shall go to bed immediately after finishing this letter. . . . I would like to write more, but I am very tired. . . ."[1]

Father Mazzucconi, stationed on Rooke Island with Reina, wrote to his family on the same day, 20 October 1853, and confessed that his health was rather bad. "During my first days on this island," he said, "God gave me fever as a present. I had it all year and I still have a little." He decided to describe for them what fever in Oceania was like, thinking that they might like to know.

"First you feel some chills in your body. Then your hands and your fingernails become livid and white. Finally the chills spread everywhere, you shiver all over, and you have to go to bed." His companions would then cover him with whatever they could find.

> When you are buried like this under the covers, your teeth begin rattling without your wanting them to, and you shake for some hours until a hot fever sets in. Then your blood boils; your forehead becomes hot like fire; and if you have eaten anything, you vomit. Generally some moments of delirium follow, during which you speak all the languages which the Lord finds on earth. Then after some hours of abundant and even incredible perspiration, you say: Thank God, this too has passed! You pick up your cot and carry it out in the sun to dry. And you have an occasion to laugh with your companions, because your knees have become so weak—and often so swollen and painful—that they prevent you, not only from carrying a few blankets, but also from holding your body erect, even though it has lost so much weight.

Mazzucconi had suffered more than the others in the beginning, he said,

> perhaps because of a mistake that was a bit excusable. I believed that by not eating, I would get well. The hour when my fever was the highest was midday. I was taking a bit of food with my companions when I was assailed by chills the first time. I vomited and left the table. The following day at midday the same thing happened. So I believed that a perfect diet could make me well, and that eating nothing certainly could not make me sick. But there was another need that I had, since when the fever came, it found me weaker each day and it departed leaving me even weaker still. In short order I was unable to carry my cot out into the sun . . . . I then changed this system and began asking for something nutritious. In the beginning my stomach did not want to

---

1. PIME: AME 11, *Notizie*, 113–15, Reina to Marinoni, 20 October 1853. The missionaries from Milan consistently wrote "Rook" instead of "Rooke" or "Rooke Island," now also called umboi, one of the Siassi Islands. For Nurua one finds in their printed and manuscript sources various spellings like Nurna, Nurcia, etc. Ambrosoli in a letter of 5 July 1856 from Sydney points out that the proper spelling is Nurua. See his letter in PIME: AME 11, *Notizie*, 138.

> accept it and rejected it. But finally the Lord said to this wretched machine of mine that it should start grinding away again, and so I became stronger. As for the remedy, I am not ashamed to confess that generally I started and ended with water.
>
> Later we started taking quinine, of which we had a moderate supply. And here is how we took it: Being certain that an attack was over, we took doses of three or four grains of this powder at various times [during the day]. On the next day we did the same and on the day after that we did the same again. In this way we succeeded in stopping the fever for about seven days. On the eighth day it returned like it was on the first day, so again we took the medicine as we had done before. We kept this up all year, except that recently the fever began to subside for about fifteen days.
>
> The amusing thing for us was that our quinine ran out at the beginning of this month when we all had fever, but with no means of getting relief, not even for a few days.[2] And together with the quinine, our sea biscuits ran out. Although they were very hard and wormy, they did serve as our most substantial food. And since our small pieces of iron and of cloth had also run out, as well as whatever else we gave to the local people when they brought us their local produce, they also—as was just—ceased to bring us anything.

The *Supply* was expected and had arrived with new provisions at noon on 19 October 1853. "In all honesty I tell you that our shoes were worn out and that our shirts had turned to shreds, being constantly eaten away by perspiration day and night. And my two suits, perhaps discontented because they had to serve as a mattress, as a blanket and as clothing, were tired out and no longer wanted to hold together." The generosity of others had now provided them with too much, Mazzucconi said. "But we found no quinine, which we looked for so eagerly."[3]

Mazzucconi explained that he had written "at length about this sickness" to his family, so that they would know "with what the Lord had wanted to keep us occupied the most during this year." But he had another purpose as well.

> If you should happen to speak with a good doctor, you might be able to get some suggestions and some medicine for this sickness, which was identical for all of us with very few exceptions. Then, if you write and tell me this, you will be able to do something beneficial, not only for me, but perhaps even more so for those colleagues of mine who are still to come. It could be that this sickness is produced by swamps. But here near the equator the air generally is so pure and there is so much ventilation, that I am rather inclined to believe it is nothing else but severe overheating of our blood supply due to the rather extreme heat. But then, both fever and health are in the hands of God; he sends us one or the other, whichever *is better* for those whom he has chosen. . . .[4]

---

2. Reina reported that their supply of quinine ran out "at the beginning of August." Here Mazzucconi says that it ran out at the beginning of this month," that is, October, two months later.

3. Tragella in *Missioni estere*, 1:163, says incorrectly that a new supply of quinine did arrive at this time.

4. Mazzucconi, *Scritti*, 233–35, Mazzucconi to his family, 20 October 1853.

When the Marists were at Rooke Island five years earlier, from 6 July 1848 until 17 May 1849, they too had suffered from fever. Describing the island for Superior General Colin soon after they had left, Frémont said:

> One cannot doubt that fevers hold sway at Rooke, at least on the northwest coast where we were based. It is possible that the east coast would be more healthy, being less wooded and more exposed to the regular winds. Nevertheless the climate does not appear to be too murderous for the local people. From among a population of about six hundred which encircled us, we did not see more than six natives die. Four of these were old and decrepit and one was an infant of three days. . . . Several large rivers come down the mountainside causing unhealthy swamps along the shore.[5]

Mazzucconi reported as follows:

> On days between attacks when we were free from fever, we were able to busy ourselves completely with what then was our current obligation, namely, nothing else but learning the language well. And to accomplish this we had to do nothing else but go outside, sit down in the midst of the natives, listen to them speak and then write down the words one after another that we could grasp. At times I happened to fall asleep while I was speaking with them, because I was so weakened by fever.[6]
>
> If sometime you should like to come with the help of your imagination and look for your son or brother, look for him especially at the seashore in the open air, in the midst of a more or less numerous circle of people, always with pencil and paper [in his hand] and with someone nearby who asks: "Why do you not write down my word too?—Because I wrote it already.—And will that cloth (paper) then tell you the things well?—Yes, it repeats to me everything that I put down there, when I look at it." Someone in the group then says: "I must say, you are a fine man! Will you give me a piece of iron?"

While learning words and sentences, Mazzucconi also began learning Rooke grammar. "A characteristic of their language," he said, "is that a noun is declined to indicate, not the case (its relationship with a verb), but the possessive (its relationship with a person). For example . . . , my mouth is *kog*, your mouth is *kom*, his mouth is *kona*, and mouth in general is *kori*." Mazzucconi had also noticed this characteristic in the languages of some other islands in Melanesia.

"As for numbers they count up to fifty," he said. And "when they go beyond fifty, they clap their hands and shout *naul* (so many)." But "they have only five words for numbers. They reach fifty by saying five times the fingers of their hands. For twenty, however, they use a special word, *tomota*, which means an entire man, that is, twenty fingers and toes."

For the moment, he said, mission work consisted in "always being with them, learning their language and beginning to accustom them gradually to think a little like we do. Then,

---

5. SM: OMM/208, Frémont to Colin, 24 June 1849.
6. Mazzucconi, *Scritti*, 236, Mazzucconi to his family, 20 October 1853.

when the Lord wishes it, we shall speak to them about him."[7] But Rooke Island was more complicated linguistically than the missionaries had first imagined. It had three different peoples—the Nurua, the Cobai, and the Cabebe—and each had a completely different language. That first year they studied the language of the Nurua people among whom they were living. "If it should please the Lord," Mazzucconi said, "perhaps before long we shall be able to express in these various languages the dear truths of our religion."[8]

Mazzucconi's family had asked him to send a list of Italian words translated into various local languages. He picked out sixteen words: God, heaven, earth, sea, mountain, father, mother, husband, wife, son, food, hook, man, woman, older brother, younger brother. These he listed in one column in Italian and in eight parallel columns he gave the translations in Nurua, Cobai, and Cabebe, which were the three languages of Rooke; and in languages of New Britain, New Guinea, Woodlark, San Cristóbal, and Ponape. In a "Notice" accompanying these lists he pointed out some grammatical rules of the three Rooke languages. At the end he added, "I have about six hundred words of the Ponape language," collected earlier by Father Désiré-Louis Maigret, a Picpus father. "But they are written in such a manner that I can hardly understand a single one."[9]

The languages of these island peoples can be called poor "because they have few ideas," Mazzucconi said.

> But the ideas which they do have, and with which one must work, they dress up in so many different, strange and varied ways that no one would believe it, if he has not experienced it. For example, we have gathered many nouns of the Nurua language because they are easy to discover. But it is much more difficult to discover the verbs. Nevertheless we have collected more than nine hundred of them. And yet in this number many of the most important verbs are missing, like the verb to believe, for example. But for this verb we have found a circumlocution: *log pe battonga kion*. This means, "My spirit is in favor of what you say."[10]

In the forests Mazzucconi had found "large and surprisingly beautiful fruits without number." The rule for the missionaries was: "Do not eat those fruits which the natives do not eat. This is a good rule for preventing a catastrophe because it is known that many of them are poisonous." Mazzucconi went on:

> But it is also known that superstition and prejudice can greatly influence these poor people and perhaps they abstain from eating fruits that really are excellent. For example, one day while in the forest we came across some fruits that beyond a doubt I would have called lemons and oranges. When I went up to them, they shouted out: If you eat them, you will die. I picked some, opened them, and recognized that they were really lemons and oranges, which are so useful in the intense heat. In spite of

---

7. Ibid., 231, Mazzucconi to his family, 31 October 1852.
8. Ibid., 242, Mazzucconi to a friend, 20 October 1853.
9. Ibid., 237, Mazzucconi to his family, 20 October 1853. For the lists of words see ibid., 314f.
10. Ibid., 236–37, Mazzucconi to his family, 20 October 1853.

this I have not been able to induce anyone to taste them up to now. But we use them all the time. Who knows how many other harmless fruits become mature and rot away without being able to serve the purpose for which they were created . . . ?

There were "three great wonders" on Rooke Island that natives from far and near came to see: white men, *pat* or *gietra*, and *nakau*. "White men" were the missionaries. *Pat* or *gietra* were local names for a small statue of the Blessed Virgin Mary. "The third wonder is *Nakau*,"

Mazzucconi said, "that is, a music box kindly given to us by the Very Reverend Provost. . . . Imagine for yourselves how they shout: *Lom loco!*—Hold your breath!—on hearing the first sweet sounds" coming from this mechanism. "They love every sort of harmony so much."

Mazzucconi asked his family to send him a toy horse with a rider, or a toy cart "made completely of wood and drawn by an ox." Then he could provide the people of Rooke with some new ideas "and busy them for an entire day with something that is sinless. I would also like to have some wooden dolls to teach them how to understand painted figures a bit better. . . . Hopefully some day I shall be able to teach them the truths of faith with paintings. . . ."[11]

The people of Rooke had often asked Father Reina whether he and his missionaries came from heaven. "They doubted very much that we were human beings and thought that they were giving us pleasure by saying that we would become men with black skins, if we stayed at Nurua." White-skinned persons for them were not men, that is, not *curáb*, but something else. "They asked whether we were born small like they were; whether there were white women; and whether we die."

At Nurua the people believed that their missionaries had the power to cause earthquakes, Reina said. Each month Rooke Island experienced three or four of them. One occurred several minutes before sunset on Tuesday, 17 April 1855, while Fathers Reina and Ambrosoli were on the beach talking with the people. The earthquake moved from north to south and was followed by a second tremor even stronger than the first. It caused the windows of their house to fly open and they heard crashes inside. The statue of the Blessed Virgin Mary in the chapel fell and broke. "It was difficult for me to stay on my feet," Reina said. Then later "two prayer leaders came up and asked me to show them how I had caused the earthquake. . . ."[12]

---

11. Ibid., 240f, Mazzucconi to his family, 20 October 1853. Although Mazzucconi says "all'udire le prime voci soavi di questo strumento" (literally, at hearing the first sweet voices of this instrument), "voci" cannot be translated as "voices" here because the human voice was transmitted for the first time only in 1877 when Thomas A. Edison invented the phonograph.

12. PIME: AME 11, Reina, "study on the Island of Rooke," 429, 431, 433. This study covers forty-four pages.

loro rubicondo, e di un gusto sensibilissimo ed aggradevole; il quale dà vita e nuova energia nelle prostrazioni tanto facili in quei clima sì caldi. L'uso del bettel è universale, ed avidamente conservato. Ogni *gamagar* (giovinotto di primo sviluppo) va glorioso del suo *lagum* (zucca per la calce) ed ha grande premura di trovarsi ben provvisto d'ogni droga necessaria. Nei convegni, all'incontro di un amico, durante le conversazioni; è atto di pulitezza offrire del proprio bettel a masticare, e riceverne d'altrui. Rifiutarlo sarebbe un'offesa.

Si crede comunemente dai viaggiatori che sia l'uso di questa droga, che annerisca i denti degli indigeni. Ciò non è, al dire del sullodato Salerio, il quale fa notare che dessi, essendo ambiziosi della nerezza dei denti, stanno provveduti di vimini aventi la proprietà di tingere in nero. Sono legni di un umore acre, sortente sotto la masticazione, il quale in sulle prime corrode la patina lasciata dal bettel la quale è rossiccia e perciò disaggradevole ai loro occhi, e li pulisce; in seguito li fa neri.

Brevità della vita e malattie.

Riferisce il Salerio, che in Woodlark sulla massa della popolazione di 2,000 persone difficilmente se ne sarebbero contate 40 di età senile; e che la morte naturale avviene nel periodo del trentesimo al quarantesimo anno.

Le malattie, segue lo stesso, sono la febbre, la risipola, la lebbra, l'ulcera e qualche altra affezione diversa ma non comune. La febbre non è mai schivata dai forestieri. La risipola è universale ai bambini specialmente, ai quali credesi attaccaticcia. Io qui sarei indotto a diffidare che vi sia risipola attaccaticcia per sè, piuttosto crederei che si debba la diffusione pronta del male alla comune influenza aerea e termica, influenza che sulla pelle dei bambini fa naturalmente una impressione più facile ed alterante. La lebbra, si veste del carattere squamoso ed ulceroso; quest'ultimo è penosissimo.

Long before introducing the Italians to missionary work on Rooke, Frémont had noticed that the natives there "and all those in the vicinity practiced circumcision." It took place when boys reached eight years of age. "What meaning they attach to this practice, I cannot say," he said. "But the circumcision of their children is one of their biggest feasts. They prepare for it many days in advance by singing and dancing. And the parents must offer at least one pig for each child. These pigs are then eaten in common by the people of the village."[13]

Mazzucconi believed that the practice of circumcision was "something which these peoples preserve from the Jewish tradition." One day when such a ceremony was to be held, he told his family,

> the natives came, calling out to us in a loud voice that we should attend. Since we needed to know what it was like, we went. But there was no prayer, nothing resembling religion. The elders told me that once upon a time it was conducted with more pomp. But time had cancelled all of this. Nothing remains but the ceremony called *kaglia*, truly horrible and painful . . . for a child of eight years. Whoever is not circumcised here has little to say in the meetings. And to call someone uncircumcised is a great insult. I must confess to you that every time they insult me like this, the word always makes a deep impression on me. . . . It reminds me . . . of the time when those who were circumcised were the Lord's people.[14]

If a child should become sick, Frémont had reported, "It lives completely hidden, something which can last for several months. Once the child is well again, a great feast takes place. The child leaves its place of hiding and important people promenade through the village, where each one must give the child a small gift."

When in 1848 Frémont arrived in Rooke for the first time, he was surprised to see how much the people prayed. "They have specific prayers which they use for praying over the sick, for turning back a cloud, or when a wind is blowing against them," he said. "But I have not been able to find out to what divinity they pray. They do recognize spirits superior to men, whom they call *Mareaba*. And they attribute to them everything which appears to be a bit extraordinary. The existence and immortality of the soul is well known, but what happens to the soul after death they cannot explain. Some of them say that souls live on in the woods; others say that they go to join the rest of the *Mareabas*."

Commenting on other customs Frémont said: "We have found no trace of cannibalism among them. Nor do they make war on one another. All the tribes on this island trade with one another and with the islands nearby." As for village life, "The women are slaves here, more so than at San Cristóbal and Woodlark. They are the ones who carry all the burdens,

---

13. SM: OMM/208, Frémont to Colin, 24 June 1849. Circumcision continued to be part of the ritual of inducting young men into the clan, but by 1966 it was no longer practiced. See Letter, Willard Burce to Ralph M. Wiltgen, 12 January 1966, supplying information obtained from the Rev. Con Eckermann, an Australian Lutheran missionary who had lived and worked on Rooke Island for many years.

14. Mazzucconi, *Scritti*, 239–40, Mazzucconi to his family, 20 October 1853.

make the gardens, do the cooking, etc. The men busy themselves with constructing canoes, making nets, going fishing and cutting down the forest for making gardens."

The position of Rooke Island was "precious for the mission," Frémont said, "because its inhabitants have contact with the people of New Britain and New Guinea. And its soil appears to be fertile. One finds there an abundance of breadfruit and a hard almond called *kangar*, which is very good. There are also coconuts, taros, yams and many species of sweet potatoes, which make up the principal nourishment for the natives. Pigs run wild there and in great numbers; they are one of the animals which the people hunt. There are also different kinds of birds, especially very large pigeons, which fill the forests."

Frémont submitted these details when Superior General Colin had asked him to write an article for publication about the people of Rooke. "If we do not provide all the details that you desire, and that the members of the Association for the Propagation of the Faith [in Lyon] request," he said,

> the reason is prudence rather than ill will. In order to know an island, its products, etc., it is necessary to examine it closely and study it. And in order to know the habits, the customs, the religion, etc., of the savages, it is necessary to know their language, to observe them, to ask them questions and to study them with care. And one must do this for many years. It would be sad to give nothing but false or inexact information. We ourselves have already seen mistakes of this kind in periodicals and in geography books.[15]

The people of Rooke Island still have the hard almond that they call *kangar*. Traditionally these nuts served as small introductory gifts prior to the actual trading. As late as 1966 the people of Rooke were still using their large oceangoing outrigger canoes furnished with sails. The seasons for trading and visiting were April and May, the change-of-wind season, and from September to November, when prevailing winds made possible trips to the New Guinea mainland and New Britain.[16]

Ambrosoli, one of the four Italian missionaries at Rooke, also described the customs of the people in his letters. Cannibalism was abhorred there, he said, although it flourished on the nearby coast of New Guinea. "Here they do not steal like they do at Woodlark and San Cristóbal, where they are professional thieves."

The favorite foods of the people in Rooke, Ambrosoli said, were wild pig, "a species of dog that they themselves carefully breed," and tortoises and fish of various kinds. The mountain people in the interior of the island would bring their tobacco, taro, and other food to Nurua, where they received iron and fish in exchange. Rooke had two seasons, Ambrosoli said. There was wind and rain in the bad season from October to April, and there was good weather during the rest of the year. In the bad season the men made their boats and canoes, and in the good season they sailed to New Guinea and New Britain

---

15. SM: OMM/208, Frémont to Colin, 24 June 1849.
16. See Letter, Burce-Eckermann to Wiltgen, 12 January 1966.

to obtain bows, arrows, clay pots, teeth of fish, etc. "They plant gardens with taro, yams and many species of bananas," he said. "In order to make a garden they have to cut down enormous plants."

As for the many seeds and plants that Ambrosoli and the others had so carefully collected in Sydney, most had already rotted by the time they arrived at Rooke. The grapevines were planted near their residence, but the results were poor. They had brought along one fig tree and gave the first ripe fig to the captain of the ship.[17] But when the missionaries prepared the soil for making their own gardens at Rooke, their wrists and ankles broke out in boils.[18] Mazzucconi did not want to conceal from his family the dark side of his people at Rooke. "Imagine for yourself a people on fire with every passion, without a law, without authority, without punishment. Here a man can kill another man without a voice being able to say: You have done wrong! This is a place where fathers and mothers kill more than half of their children, and one cannot tell whether they experience even a fleeting moment of remorse over it. . . ."

After arriving at Rooke, Mazzucconi said,

> We learned one day that there was a baby in one of the huts very close to ours. Anxiously we asked if it was well and everybody told us yes. Feeling uneasy some hours later, we went to visit it. As soon as we stepped outside we met a woman and we asked whether the baby was healthy. "It is healthy," she answered, "but buried!" Not understanding well enough the strange usages of the language, we replied: "How is it possible that it can be healthy and buried?" To which she answered: "Look, there is the father filling a ditch." We went to the father who was alongside his hut and we asked: "Where is your son?" "I buried him." "Who killed him?" "His mother and I. Afterwards I carried him outside, dug a hole and buried him. Do you do the same in Italy?" "No, we do not do this in Italy."

The companions of Mazzucconi were so shocked that they could not speak, he said. "Later we learned that it was the custom to kill all the firstborn. And of those born after the firstborn, one is kept and one is killed." The woman by saying that the child was healthy really meant that it had no defects. By saying that it was buried, she meant it had been killed, "because people in Nurua are accustomed to talk like this." Mazzucconi believed that the people even said this proudly, 'since they want to convey that they—different from other tribes—bury their infants instead of eating them."[19]

When describing for Marinoni the practice of killing babies at Rooke Island, Reina said: "It is the mother herself who takes them and suffocates them, [destroying] that life which they have just received from her. We have tried using all sorts of reasons to dissuade them from practicing such great inhumanity . . . , promising gifts to the one who gives us a baby destined to die. But it was all in vain! We were able to save only one baby girl by

---

17. PIME: AME 11, *Notizie*, 136–39, undated letters by Ambrosoli.
18. Tragella, *Missioni estere*, 1:161.
19. Mazzucconi, *Scritti*, 237–38, Mazzucconi to his family, 20 October 1853.

practically snatching her from the hands of her mother, who had already begun to choke her. We were able to baptize the child and seven days later it died. So we buried little Maria in our garden...."[20] Ambrosoli reported that if the mother's strength was not sufficient to strangle "the fruit of her womb..., the father with a club smashes the head..." And he added, "You would not believe it unless you saw it with your own eyes."[21]

One day Mazzucconi was standing perfectly still, contemplating a huge rock in the sea. Noticing this, Father Frémont went up to him and said, "Do you want to infuse intelligence into that rock?" Laughingly Mazzucconi said no. "But you want to infuse religion, morality and grace into the hearts" of the people of Rooke. "This is an even more difficult task, because they are able to resist. But with the help of the Lord you can do everything."[22]

Reina complained that "these people in their ignorance ridicule everything that is outside the scope of their own experience and their own ideas." He blamed this on their "inconceivable limitation of ideas," which made them "disbelieve everything that you tell them, even what concerns the most simple natural truths, things that are unknown to them." Reina also called attention to their "changeableness of mind and heart," which he said was perhaps even more sad. "When listening at times to factual information they say to us in our presence that it is all true, and they seem to be convinced of it.... But a moment later, when they are hardly two steps away, they tell us that it is not true and they laugh at our simplicity."

He saw only two solutions to this problem. Either one must wait for the passage of time and for frequent visits from ships to arouse in the natives "at least the desire to comprehend." Or else the missionaries should take many of them on a mission ship to Sydney, "so they can feel with their hands" the truths being talked about. "But this expedient," Reina said, "would be too expensive and would have an uncertain outcome. It would also be difficult to do because of their extreme distrust toward strangers and because of their excessive attachment to this island...."[23]

Together with his long letter of 20 October 1853 from Rooke, Prefect Apostolic Reina sent director Marinoni a *Memorandum* on (1) relations between the Milan Mission Seminary and its foreign missions, (2) rules for missionaries in the field, and (3) suggestions regarding the kind of spirit that ought to permeate a missionary in his work. Treated in section three were suggestions on the type of contact that ought to exist between the local people of a particular mission and their missionaries. Nothing in the missionary was to offend or to alienate the local people, Reina said. He wanted his priests always to be united and in agreement on how they think and act, since they were always being observed by

---

20. PIME: AME 11:125–27, Reina to Marinoni, 22 January 1855.
21. PIME: AME 11, *Notizie*, 138, undated letter by Ambrosoli.
22. Mazzucconi, *Scritti*, 239, Mazzucconi to his family, 20 October 1853.
23. PIME: AME 11:125, Reina to Marinoni, 22 January 1855, PIME: AME 11, *Notizie*, 114f, Reina to Marinoni, 20 October 1853.

the local people. In addition he asked that they keep themselves in control and never show "anger in the presence of the natives, who are very clever at recognizing interior feelings."

The missionary, too, should never attempt to "dominate" in any way, nor should he insist on being respected and loved simply because of being a priest. The native people were not ready for this yet, Reina felt. For the present the missionary had to keep to himself this sentiment of his own dignity, externalizing it through the integrity of his life, but postponing for many years his desire for respect and affection. Finally, Reina said, it was necessary to maintain with the natives a certain "friendly reserve," which would attract them through love and ensure reciprocal respect. unity of action by his missionaries, he said, was "something very important in the mind of the indigenous people."[24]

Besides having health problems and social problems in Rooke, the Italian missionaries had serious financial problems in Sydney. As Father Rocher of the Marist Center wrote to Marinoni on 27 July 1853, the Australian gold rush had been responsible for increasing the prices of all goods whatsoever, and also the costs for chartering ships. It was becoming embarrassing for him, he said, since the funds of the Italians were very low. In fact, when the *Supply* left Sydney on 21 August 1853 with provisions for the Italians at Woodlark and Rooke, it carried enough for only half a year, because there were no Italian funds on hand to purchase more.[25]

En route to Rooke the *Supply* stopped at Woodlark to unload goods for the mission. Father Salerio, head of that mission, decided to accompany Captain Dalmagne to Rooke so that he could give a full report on his mission to Prefect Apostolic Reina. They sailed from Woodlark on 13 October 1853, reached Rooke Mission on 19 October, and Salerio was able to converse with the missionaries there until 24 October. Father Frémont and Brother Gennade, who had finished training the Italians at Rooke Island, accompanied Salerio to Woodlark, where they arrived on 7 November. There the two Marists were joined by their colleague, Father Thomassin, who had finished training Fathers Salerio and Raimondi and Brother Tacchini. Some days later the three French missionaries sailed with the *Supply* from Woodlark to Sydney, leaving the Melanesia mission completely in the hands of the missionaries from Milan.[26]

The *Supply* was still in Woodlark on 12 November 1853 when Salerio completed a detailed report for Marinoni on what had happened at his mission in the previous thirteen months. Most of these details he had already discussed with Prefect Apostolic Reina and the other missionaries at Rooke. Salerio told Marinoni that Woodlark "up to now has produced nothing but the thorns of a sterile and perverse terrain." Father Thomassin, the Marist who had trained them during that first year, was very good to the people of Woodlark, he said,

---

24. Tragella, *Missioni estere*, 1:164–65.

25. See PIME: AME 28:787, Rocher to Marinoni, 27 July 1853; PIME: AME 28:785f, Poupinel to Marinoni, 21 August 1854; Mazzucconi, *Scritti*, 251, Mazzucconi to Marinoni, 20 April 1855; Hosie, "French Mission," 417.

26. RIP: R B-N.2, N.1, Carlo Salerio, "Giornale di Viaggio," 13 October to 7 November 1853.

treating them "with a fatherly heart" and "even more, with maternal tenderness," using "all the means which his zeal and charity could suggest, sparing no sacrifice or expense," and reacting to "wrongs, insults and the blackest of betrayals with unconquerable patience."

God had shown his wrath and power that first year, Salerio said, when he struck the people of Woodlark "with a triple scourge" of famine, pestilence, and war. "The famine started at the beginning of the new year [1853] and afflicted them for six months." Salerio saw entire families with nothing to eat all day long except a small taro at nightfall. "They snatched it from one another's mouth, they wailed, and they died from hunger. Our own provisions we made available to the young people who approached us. Our aim was not to have them show gratitude toward us, but rather to have them open their hearts for God's grace." But this was something that "their pride could not allow."

The first scourge had hardly ended, Salerio said, when they were afflicted by another even more severe. It was "a sickness which in less than three months spread over the entire island and wiped out a good fourth of the population. It was a terrible disease causing within three days the death of two, three, and as many as six members of a single family." Even the most robust were struck down. Among those who died were "eleven members of the family of the chief who had done so much harm to the mission. Seven villages are still completely deserted." Others driven by terror and panic fled "to the forests and to the craggy coastline, going as far away as possible and abandoning their dear ones, yet dying on the way as they fled from death."

It was agonizing to see this, Salerio said, not only because of the anguish suffered by the people, but more so because not one of them drew any comfort from, or placed any trust in, the religious truths that they had learned. They believed that the malady had been inflicted by the God of the missionaries. "Tell your God to leave us in peace . . . ," they said. "You have your religion and we have ours, so what does it matter to him?" Their pride had been wounded and their spirit was battered down by fear, Salerio said, "but their obstinacy and blindness drove them on, making them take up their superstitious practices with the same frenzy as before."

The pestilence brought about a rift in relations between the people and the missionaries. As a result "that bit of esteem and authority, which we apparently had been acquiring, also came to an end," Salerio said. No one listened to them anymore.

Then came a third scourge, a civil war in which they began "murdering one another, as if the pestilence had not done enough." Salerio was wondering how it all would end, since the civil war was still raging. "Their hearts are disturbed, puzzled and exasperated. They cry out, they threaten, they fear, they are terrified! And God's minister, what can he do . . . ?"

One bright star had appeared on the horizon, Salerio said, when thirty young men decided to remain at the mission station day and night, "impatient to learn the prayers of a Christian, and wanting to leave their country in order to withdraw themselves from its sorry examples and so escape from the intimidations of their parents and of people in the village."²⁷ These thirty young men were smaller and bigger boys recruited by Father Thomassin, "who instructed and fed them all year long."

"The experiment progressed well as long as the needy period lasted and as long as the guarantee existed for them to acquire new pieces of iron. But when the famine passed and when the usual happy times and dances began, they all left, one after the other, stealing as much as they could from the house. As a result Father Thomassin saw himself abandoned by all of them a few months prior to his departure for Sydney."²⁸ Thomassin was crushed, Salerio said, at seeing "that even the best of them had left" and "that actually there is nobody here any more, not even a single one."²⁹

While everything in Woodlark seemed to be tumbling down, twenty-eight-year-old catechist Luigi Tacchini from Acquate in northern Italy was busy building up. Two days before Salerio wrote to Marinoni about the three scourges at Woodlark, Tacchini wrote to his mother. In his first year at Woodlark, he said, he had served as "blacksmith, carpenter, cook, laundryman and gardener." At present he was cutting boards "for building a new house, because the one which we have at present has suffered a bit." He had always enjoyed good health, he told her. And he said that she would be surprised to learn "that the natives know very well how to cheat European gentlemen."³⁰

Salerio described for his parents what the people of Woodlark believed about death. They say that when they die "they go to *Tum* where there are coconuts in large quantities, very many yams, taro and pigs, and now also very much iron." Their deaths, they believed, were caused by *Monokuaus*. These were witches who "eat the stomachs of men . . . Or they might stuff so much food into some poor fellow's stomach, that he is not able to digest it; this causes him to become bloated and to decompose. There are also some [witches] that put a *Buagan* or devil inside of you." But in reality, Salerio said, "These sicknesses come from the way of life here and from the climate, which produces the most frightful intestinal inflammations. This is the usual sickness in these lands and a number of missionaries have also died from them, like Bishop Collomb." The local people maintained, however, that "it is the *Monokuaus* who do this. And therefore as soon as they feel any indisposition, they drink a good quantity of sea water to expel all the *Buagan*. They then go and hide in the fields or in the woods, so that the *Monokuaus* cannot find them again." Salerio was an excellent observer and anthropologist and also described for his parents in detail how the people of Woodlark held a wake, how they buried their dead, and how they mourned.³¹

Father Raimondi of Woodlark did not enjoy such good health as Catechist Tacchini. Writing to his sister in Italy on 10 November 1853, Raimondi said that nearly all his companions in Melanesia "had fever for long periods," whereas he himself "suffered from open

27. *Beatificationis Positio*, 288–89, Salerio to Marinoni, 12 November 1853.
28. PIME: AME 11:157, Reina to Marinoni, 3 September 1855.
29. *Beatificationis Positio*, 288, Salerio to Marinoni, 12 November 1853.
30. PIME: AME 11, *Notizie*, 140, Tacchini to his mother, 10 November 1853.
31. Ibid., 97–98, Salerio to his parents, 4 December 1852.

sores on his feet and legs." At times these caused him much pain. "When my feet allowed me," he said, "I visited the villages. And when they did not allow this, I stayed at home and studied the language of the local people...."[32]

Salerio had a brother back home who was a medical doctor. Seeking help from him, Salerio described at some length the malady with which he was afflicted during his first year at Woodlark. Like Raimondi, he too had open sores on his legs that "took a long time to heal. Ever since December 1852, I have not been able to be out of the house for a walk longer than half an hour," he wrote in November 1853. There could be as many as thirty-three open sores on his legs at one time, he explained, eighteen on one leg and fifteen on the other. One sore would close, but two more would open. Although he used European and native medicines, it was to no avail. When the sores were nearly all healed, there were still four left that needed bandaging. "After six months the sores surrendered and retreated," he said. "But then they joined forces in a single open sore which was as bad as all the rest combined. And afterwards like fresh troops they once again swarmed over the devastated battlefield" of his two legs.

Raimondi "suffers no less than I," Salerio said, and up to the present time he is still confined to rest, not being able even to celebrate Mass." Salerio did not know the nature of these eruptions, but believed them to be altogether different from the mortal eruptions which afflicted the natives. He called the malady "an annoying tribute which is the price, I believe, that must be paid for acclimatization and for being spared other maladies like fever, which torments my most dear colleagues in Rooke so much. Here you see what I have been confronted with physically during this first year of my life in Oceania. . . . We live, we vegetate, we suffer, we laugh."[33]

The malady from which Salerio and Raimondi suffered was most probably yaws, called also Amboina pimple, frambesia, and tropical ulcers. It is a contagious skin disease occurring in tropical and subtropical countries caused by bacteria commonly found in water and sewage. Its name "frambesia" comes from a French word meaning raspberry, indicating the appearance of the excrescences.

The three Marists—Frémont, Thomassin, and Gennade—arrived in Sydney aboard the *Supply* on 19 December 1853.[34] This marked the end of Marist activity in the Prefectures Apostolic of Melanesia and Micronesia. Three weeks later Frémont wrote to Superior General Colin that they had come to Sydney because "we do not know what your inten-

---

32. PIME: AME 11, *Notizie*, 129.

33. Ibid., 135. The date of Salerio's letter is not indicated here, but probably was 10, 11 or 12 November 1853, because Tacchini and Raimondi wrote letters on 10 November, Salerio and Thomassin wrote letters on 11 November, and Salerio also wrote on 12 November. All of these letters written in Woodlark were taken by the *Supply* to Sydney. Salerio says in this letter that he had completed a year in Woodlark, and internal evidence shows that the letter was written after 7 November 1853.

34. Hosie says that the *Supply* reached Sydney on 20 December 1853, but Frémont writing to Colin three weeks after arrival says that the ship reached Sydney on 19 December. See Hosie, "French Mission," 417; SM: OMM/208, Frémont to Colin, 9 January 1854.

tions are regarding us." He preferred not to say anything at all "about the condition of the missions of Woodlark and Rooke, because all of this is still in such a precarious state that it is difficult to give exact information." The year with the Italian missionaries had passed peacefully, cheerfully, and charitably, he said. "I confess that the situation did not delay in becoming delicate. The knowledge that you have of these men will immediately provide you with a presentiment of the reason. Having priests from two nations, from two societies, joined together in one house, while working at one and the same task, and [especially] a task of this nature, will make you aware, my Reverend Father, that the devil of discord can find there enough for satisfying himself.

"But in spite of this," Frémont continued,

> I can say that we lived together like brothers. Prefect Apostolic [Reina] and his two colleagues,[35] with whom I was at Rooke, constantly showed themselves very affable in spite of the state of suffering to which fever had reduced them. And although I made every effort to efface myself and to keep out of all matters concerning the government of the mission, they did nothing without asking me for my advice, etc. And when I left them, their resignation to everything and their trust in God touched my heart. Merciless fever still held them in its crucible. What makes their misfortune even greater is the fact that their supply of quinine has been exhausted. It is the most efficacious and almost the only remedy [against fever] that they have. May God help them!

Frémont suggested that Colin relieve the Marist Supply Center in Sydney of responsibility for the Italian mission in Melanesia. "More than once in the course of the year I had occasion to think about this matter," he said. Meanwhile since his arrival in Sydney he had discussed it with Father Rocher and learned "that his position in regard to these gentlemen is very delicate. For no matter how qualified our procurator is and no matter how much good will he shows, it is difficult for him—not to say impossible—to do things in such a way as to satisfy everyone. They believe, namely, that he does not manifest toward them all the interest that he should, etc."

There was also a personal matter that Frémont wished to discuss with Colin, who had sent the following message to Rocher: "As Fathers Frémont and Thomassin tell me, they shall be going to [New] Caledonia." These words, Frémont wrote,

> caused my conscience some embarrassment, because on the one hand I wanted to obey you and remain faithful to the principle which I have adopted of not refusing anything and of not asking for anything. On the other hand I saw that your words are not at all a formal order, but seem to be rather a permission granted to a previous request. Now I have no recollection at all of ever having manifested the desire of going to [New] Caledonia. This is not all.

---

35. Frémont here refers to Reina and the two other clerics from Italy, Fathers Mazzucconi and Ambrosoli. He does not mention their companion, Catechist Giuseppe Corti, who was also there.

The state in which I see our Oceania missions makes me feel singularly detached from this work. Let me say without fear of lying, that I esteem and love the activity in itself, that it is neither the dangers, nor the labors involved, nor the climate and other things, which have brought about this estrangement in me. Far from that! . . . Let me further say that my special attraction, my very strong desire, is to be a religious Marist. It is within the Society, I believe, and no place else, that I must find happiness in my life and a guarantee for the salvation of my soul.

Now, my Very Reverend Father, in view of the present situation, I am not quite sure whether I shall be able to find the Society of Mary in the missions of Oceania. It is true, you can find priests who bear the name of Marists, priests—if you wish—who are virtuous and zealous, priests who perhaps will be faithful in following all the practices of piety found in our houses in Europe. But the spirit, the life, the government, the influence of our Mother Society, these, I believe, would be difficult to find. What is the reason for this? Will there be a remedy? What will the remedy be?

I set aside all of these questions, since they are none of my business. I merely call attention to what appears to me to be a fact, and I do so only with the purpose of letting you see what has been responsible for this change that has taken place in me regarding our missions. I believe, my Reverend Father, that you are sufficiently well aware of the state of the question. In taking this step I have wished both to learn the will of God and to put my conscience at rest. This twofold result I shall obtain through your decision, whether you send me back to the islands, whether you call me back to Europe, whether you make me stay at the Supply Center or someplace else, no matter where. I hope that God will give me the grace to be obedient. When I know that it is your will that I should be at a certain post, whatever that post may be, I shall consider myself to be a member of our Society at that place. I shall find my happiness in this act of obeying, and not in doing something that I have suggested. Through obedience I shall find God everywhere, and with God I shall always be happy. . . . Have no fear of disappointing me. I shall await your decision here."[36]

It was, in fact, Colin himself who had suggested New Caledonia as a possible destination in case Frémont and the other Marists should decide to leave Woodlark. In his letter to them of 23 June 1851 he had said that they were perfectly free to remain in Woodlark or leave it. And then he added: "If you are obliged to withdraw from Woodlark, and if you find no suitable spot [elsewhere in Melanesia], you could join the missionaries of New Caledonia or of Central Oceania." He also said that "Ponape or Ascension Island in Micronesia has been asking for missionaries for a long time."[37]

36. SM: OMM/208, Frémont to Colin, 9 January 1854.
37. SM: Epistolae Variae Generalium, 1:43f, no. 79. Laracy says that the Marists left Woodlark because by November 1853 they "had had enough." Tragella says that they left because "the Melanesia Mission did not produce the results that were expected in the previous year." The decision of the Marists to leave, however, was not made in November 1853. Nor was it made because they "had had enough," nor because—as Tragella indicates—the results foreseen by them in 1852 did not materialize in 1853. The Marist decision to leave was made by Frémont in Woodlark as early as 12 October 1852, the day on which he handed over to Reina complete authority for governing the Melanesia-Micronesia mission. Frémont's decision had resulted from letters received

In addition to having health problems and social problems in Melanesia and financial problems in Sydney, the Milan missionaries had political and theological problems at home. A plot to kill twenty-two-year-old Francis Joseph I (1830–1916), emperor of Austria (1848–1916), was discovered in Milan on 6 February 1853.[38] Charges were made that the members of the Foreign Mission Seminary in Milan had rejoiced on learning of this attempt on the emperor's life. This accusation along with others reached the desk of Cardinal Prefect Fransoni in Rome. He listed the charges and sent them to Bishop Ramazzotti of Pavia on 15 November 1853, instructing him to investigate the charges "reported to this Sacred Congregation on the internal state" of the seminary. He was turning to Ramazzotti, he said, because of the great interest shown by that bishop in having the mission seminary founded.

Fransoni, however, did not make these accusations his own. He simply indicated the charges that had been made and he asked Ramazzotti to reply to them.[39] Evidently some influential cleric or political figure, or a combination of these, had made the charges, and so Fransoni was obliged by protocol to give a reply.[40] He hoped to draw material for his reply from what Ramazzotti might tell him.

"It has been attested to Propaganda," Fransoni began, "that one notices in the lower ranks of the clergy in the Kingdom of Lombardy a profound aversion for the Imperial Austrian Government. This became evident from the zeal with which these same clergymen supported the latest revolution. At that time some young clerics in the [Milan] Archdiocesan Seminary carried out their idea of emigrating, instead of remaining perpetually subject to the Austrian Government." According to the charges made, it was "with this spirit of liberty and with the idea of finding opportunities for emancipating themselves in time, that the first candidates entered San Calocero," the Milan Foreign Mission Seminary. Among these candidates, the charge continued, "were some who had fought

---

from Colin and Fransoni and from the interpretation given to him by Reina of Propaganda's *Instructions*. See chap. 10, p. 152; Laracy, "Roman Catholic 'Martyrs' in the South Pacific, 1841–55," *Journal of Religious History* (December 1976):. 200; Tragella, *Missioni estere*, 1:167.

38. Both Fransoni and Ramazzotti wrote letters to one another in 1853. Fransoni's letter (15 November 1853) speaks of the attempt on the emperor's life being made "this past year," whereas Ramazzotti's reply of December 1853 says that the plot was discovered in Milan "on 6 February of this year." "This past year" in Fransoni's letter must therefore be understood as referring to 1853. Since forty-five weeks of 1853 had already passed, Fransoni must have allowed himself to refer to that period as "this past year." See PF; LDB vol. 344 (1853, Part I), f. 876rv, Fransoni to Ramazzotti, 15 November 1853; PF: CV vol. 43, f. 201r, Ramazzotti to Fransoni, [n.d,] December 1853.

39. Tragella in *Missioni estere*, 1:146, says that Fransoni "made these accusations his own" and presented them "always in an absolute way, as if they were facts." What Fransoni actually did was to list the charges for Ramazzotti's information in the absolute way in which they had been made. This is different from listing them "as if they were facts" and making them his own.

40. Tragella in ibid., pp. 1:146f, n. 62, gives reasons that Father Carlo Caccia, who became provicar of the Milan archdiocese in 1853, may have been the person who directly or indirectly was responsible for some or all of these charges reaching the desk of Cardinal Fransoni.

with the troops of the famous adventurer [Giuseppe] Garibaldi" (1807–82). And whereas "the honest citizens manifested their sadness" over the attempt made on the life of the emperor, "the candidates [of the mission seminary] did not know how to conceal their joy or how to keep in check their scornful laughter."

Another charge made against the Foreign Mission Seminary was that its members "are keeping close contact with those professors of the Archdiocesan Seminary who taught the doctrines of Tamburini." These charges, Fransoni said, had greatly distressed "Propaganda, which had been hopeful of finding help" from the Milan Mission Seminary "for the great task of conducting Catholic missionary work." If the charges were true, then Ramazzotti had to take steps "in order to have dismissed from that seminary those who are the cause of such great scandal." Further, he was to see to it "that healthy doctrines are taught and that the candidates be reminded of that spirit, which alone must animate them and make them worthy ministers of the Lord for promoting his greater glory, their own sanctification and the salvation of so many souls, who live in darkness and in the shadow of death in lands far distant from ours . . ."[41]

Father Pietro Tamburini (1739–1827), the one whose teachings were being questioned, was born in Brescia, Italy. He was a Jansenist theologian and therefore unorthodox. Although dead for twenty-six years, his views were still in circulation because he had written more than thirty published works and had become the mind and heart of Italian Jansenism. The theological opinions of this school, proposed and developed by Dutch Roman Catholic theologian Cornelis Jansen (1585–1638), had been condemned by various popes. But in spite of these condemnations, Jansenism lingered on.

Fransoni's letter shocked Ramazzotti. In the midst of his "pain and surprise," he decided to go to Milan "so that on the spot I could find out the truth from the mouths of the director and of the missionaries themselves." In his reply he mentioned the various charges and showed how each was groundless.

The spirit of liberty resulting from the 1848 revolution against Austria, according to one of the charges, had prompted candidates to enter the Foreign Mission Seminary of Milan so that they could free themselves from Austrian rule by taking up work in a foreign mission. "On this point," Ramazzotti said,

> I can assure Your Eminence that the first students . . . , who are now to be found in the mission field of Oceania, had conceived and manifested their ideas of dedicating themselves to the apostolic missions long before the 1848 turbulence. They had also taken counsel on this proposal with their spiritual directors and had spoken of it with the Venerable Father Supriès, now rector[42] and then vicar of the Carthusian Monastery in Pavia, and also with the Most Illustrious and Reverend Bishop Bettauhini of Ceylon [now Sri Lanka]. The date alone of these events should suffice

---

41. PF: LDB vol. 344 (1853, Part I), f. 876r–877r, Fransoni to Ramazzotti, 15 November 1853.

42. Supriès was rector from 2 September 1852 until 10 May 1855, when he became prior. The Carthusians have no abbots.

to prove that the 1848 revolution and the spirit of liberty springing from it were completely extraneous to the decisions made by those young men.

If they had been looking for a means to emancipate themselves from Austrian rule, Ramazzotti added, they did not need to join the Foreign Mission Seminary "and then go and bury themselves in an island of Oceania. Instead they could have gone much more easily to Piedmont or to Switzerland, or . . . they could have accepted the Corfu Mission which was offered to them, that asylum for refugees located at the very threshold of Italy."

Nor was it true that even a single candidate had ever belonged to the troops of Garibaldi, the bishop said. "It is true, however, that before receiving Sacred Orders some of them went to the camp of King Charles Albert [of Piedmont], but for the most part only to assist the wounded." Before admitting to the seminary those who had participated in the war in any way, Ramazzotti said, the archbishop of Milan "wanted superiors to conduct a rigorous examination of what their conduct had been like at that time. The result of this examination was that unworthy candidates were excluded from the priesthood. As for our candidates, however, they not only advanced to the priesthood with full approbation from their superiors, but they even distinguished themselves among their companions during the training period in the seminary by receiving those offices which customarily are given to the most meritorious."

Ramazzotti charged that a person must be "blind or malicious" to believe that "seminarians could be so perverted in mind and heart as to approve and rejoice over a crime so revolting" as the attempt on the emperor's life. "When this plot was discovered in Milan on 6 February of this year . . . ," he said, "many came to the seminary warning our seminarians to beware of the daggers of those in revolt, since the revolutionists had designated the seminarians particularly as targets for their vengeance. . . . So what could the seminarians have in common with the revolutionaries?"

Nor was it true, Ramazzotti said, that the seminarians were "in contact with professors teaching the doctrines of Tamburini," since his doctrines were never taught in any of the Milan seminaries. It might be a case of mistaken identity, he pointed out. Some of the students may have expressed a liking for the doctrines of Father Antonio Rosmini Serbati, whose philosophy had been taught at the seminary of Monza for many years. Although they believed that his philosophy was orthodox, they wanted to abide by whatever judgment the Holy See might make. Textbooks used in the mission seminary for other faculties were by authors beyond reproach, he said. The works of Father Giovanni Perrone, S.J. (1794–1876), were used for dogmatic theology, those of Saint Alphonsus Liguori (1696–1787) were used for moral theology, and those of Archbishop Giovanni Devoti (1744–1820) were used for canon law.

Ramazzotti assured Fransoni that he had known all of the candidates personally and had been in close contact with them for a long time. "I am altogether convinced that these young men . . . were moved to dedicate themselves to the missions, not because of political passion, but because of their zeal, their faith and their desire to save abandoned souls," he said. Nor can any authority whatsoever "alter this conviction of mine. I believe that the Lord may have permitted charges like these to be made, so that a bishop could speak out loudly in the presence of the Sacred Congregation and with the full force of his convictions, and in this way defend the most holy motives which urged on and supported these good missionaries in the midst of their great sacrifices."[43]

Fransoni was completely satisfied with Ramazzotti's defense. "Although your letter of this past December does not require a reply from me," he wrote on 7 January 1854, "I believe it is fitting for me to assure you of my pleasure over your having presented me with such valid arguments to quiet in me the fears which arose in connection with the topic known to you. I now see that in the future, no less than in the past, I can nourish every hope for the continued good conduct of that establishment. . . ."[44]

Frémont's letter of 9 January 1854 from Sydney, telling Colin about his leaving Melanesia with two other Marists and about his estrangement from missionary work, should easily have reached Lyon before 9 May 1854. On that day Colin's resignation as superior general was accepted by the Society of Mary. Since 1836, when he had become superior general, he had sent seventy-one priests and forty-five brothers of the Marist Society to the Oceania missions.[45] Describing for Cardinal Prefect Fransoni what his years in office had been like, he said, "Every day we learn that one cannot do good except by experiencing a thousand crosses and a thousand difficulties; we find no other consolation but that of abandoning ourselves to the hands of God."[46]

Like Colin in France, his missionaries in Melanesia had also experienced "a thousand crosses and a thousand difficulties." Would the story be any different for their successors from Milan?

---

43. PF: CV vol. 43, f. 200r–201r, Ramazzotti to Fransoni, [n.d.] December 1853; see also Tragella's commentary on this letter in *Missioni estere*, 1:146–49. Tragella on 148 establishes the date of Ramazzotti's letter to Fransoni as "23 or 24 December."

44. PF: LDB vol. 345 (1854), f. 8v.

45. *Centenaire*, 2.

46. PF: SC Oceania vol. 5 (1853–57), f. 355rv, Colin to Fransoni, 17 December 1853.

12

Mazzucconi Urges Reina and Marinoni to Abandon Rooke and Woodlark

6 January and 20 April 1855

Director Marinoni informed the bishops of Lombardy on 28 April 1854 that he had just received letters from his missionaries at Rooke and Woodlark written in October and November describing their open sores, fevers, lack of quinine, and lack of success. He concluded on an optimistic note, however, saying that one can hope for everything "from a mission that begins with the cross."[1]

Four days later Bishop Ramazzotti of Pavia wrote to Cardinal Prefect Fransoni that the Milan seminary had priests ready to leave for any foreign mission whatsoever. At the same time he begged the cardinal not to leave their missionaries in Oceania without reinforcements.[2]

Marinoni informed Superior General Colin of the Marists on 12 May that letters had finally arrived from his men in Melanesia. "I have written to Rome for instructions on what to do," he said. "And I hope that you have written to Rome as well, describing what conditions in those missions are like."[3] But on 9 May 1854, just three days before Marinoni wrote this letter, the Society of Mary accepted Colin's resignation as superior general. The founder of the Marists, now sixty-three years old, was succeeded in office by forty-one-year-old Father Julien Favre.[4]

Fransoni replied to Ramazzotti on 13 May 1854: "With true pleasure I received your letter of 2 May which brought me two letters of Father Paolo Reina. The one for the Holy Father has already been given to His Holiness. In the other letter the good Prefect gives me news about himself and his companions and he reports on the mission."

---

1. Tragella, *Missioni estere*, 1:174–75.

2. This letter of 2 May 1854 of Ramazzotti to Fransoni was not found; its date and contents were learned from Fransoni's reply of 13 May 1854. See PIME: AME 1:129.

3. SM: 436.

4. OM: 4:238, 275, 277.

The cardinal was consoled "by the excellent dispositions" of the missionaries. But he was filled "with just as much displeasure on learning of the sufferings in which they find themselves . . . and on noting the discouragement which they nevertheless are trying to overcome . . ." Yet he was still opposed to sending more personnel to Melanesia at this time, since "increasing the number of missionaries would have no other effect but to increase the suffering and embarrassment of those already sent."

It would be better to send new personnel to a "less dangerous" place. "From there with the help of reinforcements they could extend their work and their operations." And although there was hope that "the fervent zeal" of the missionaries in Melanesia would "produce results," Fransoni wanted Ramazzotti to explain to them "how wise further delay in the departure of other missionaries will be." As for the priests awaiting a mission assignment, Fransoni asked "whether some of them might be willing to go—at least for the moment—to some other less difficult and less dangerous mission, like Eastern India, for example." The remaining priests would then constitute "the second expedition to Melanesia, as soon as . . . news arrives that conditions there have become more stable."[5]

In reply Ramazzotti sent Fransoni the names of ten priests on 22 May 1854, indicating that they were ready to leave at once for a mission assignment. Seven were from the Milan archdiocese and three from the dioceses of Lodi, Trent, and Ivrea. Ramazzotti gave assurance that they would go wherever Propaganda Fide might wish to send them. Two lay catechists were also prepared to join them. He added that Fransoni would "do the seminary and me the greatest favor," if he were to dispose of the Milan Mission Seminary "as though it belongs to the Holy Father and to Propaganda."[6]

Fransoni expressed great satisfaction on 3 June over Ramazzotti's assurance that his candidates would go "with pleasure wherever the Sacred Congregation might send them" and that the Milan seminary would not fail "to assist the Oceania Mission with other personnel as soon as the right moment arrives."

Two requests had arrived from bishops in India, Fransoni said. One was from Bishop Daniel Murphy, vicar apostolic of Hyderabad, who needed the assistance of at least two priests temporarily. The other was from Bishop Patrick Joseph Carew, vicar apostolic of West Bengal and Calcutta. His territory was so vast that he had been suggesting for a long time that part of it should "be made first a Prefecture Apostolic and afterwards a separate Vicariate." Fransoni had in mind sending to Bishop Carew "four or five of the good priests named" by Ramazzotti "together with the two lay Catechists . . ." Since the catechists were artisans they would "prove most helpful in building and servicing the proposed new Mission or Prefecture." Fransoni asked Ramazzotti to indicate who among the priests was "gifted with such eminent qualities" that he could "assume the office of Superior or Prefect of this Mission, and likewise be able to govern it as Vicar Apostolic when the time comes." The new priests "for some period of time would be supported, directed and assisted by the

---

5. PIME: AME 1:129.
6. PF: CV vol. 43, f. 204r, Ramazzotti to Fransoni, 22 May 1854.

excellent and most kind Prelate of [West Bengal and] Calcutta, so that they could become acquainted with the places, customs, languages and other matters." They would then "take over the management of the Mission itself, once the Prelate judges that they no longer have need of further assistance. Your Excellency realizes that in the beginning such assistance will be as indispensable for them as it was in the case of the missionaries for Oceania. . . ."

Propaganda also wished to send two or more priests to Bishop Murphy, the vicar apostolic of Hyderabad, "in order to satisfy in this way his urgent requests . . ." Fransoni assured Ramazzotti that this new mission was "less difficult and not dangerous." He also suggested that having men in India would no doubt prove beneficial "for that very difficult and problematical Mission of Oceania." In fact, the new mission in India "will be able at times to provide some priests more suited and better trained for your other mission [in Oceania]." Thus could be avoided the risk "of assigning missionaries to Oceania as a first assignment, immediately after they leave the seminary in Milan." Fransoni promised to inform Ramazzotti as soon as he received confirmation that the two bishops were pleased with the arrangement.[7]

Bishop Antonio Novasconi of Cremona and Bishop Giovanni Corti of Mantova were in Rome for their *ad limina* visit in June–July 1854. Like Ramazzotti they were bishops of Lombardy and had helped bring the Milan Mission Seminary into existence. Ramazzotti wrote asking them to approach Fransoni in his name and in the name of Archbishop Romilli with the request that the cardinal send at least two of their new priests to Melanesia.[8]

The two bishops visited the cardinal at once, and he expressed deep regret over the unhappy results experienced by the pioneers due to the nature of the climate and the character of the people. "But if we send others there, they will suffer the same fate," the cardinal said, "and we accomplish nothing but to keep increasing the number of victims. The prudent thing to do is to refrain from increasing the gravity of the losses and instead to assign [available] personnel to more useful tasks." And if no good news should arrive from the mission at all, Fransoni said, then "the proper thing to do is to send" the missionaries who are there "to other harvests." Bishop Corti hurriedly sent off this news to Bishop Ramazzotti on 12 July 1854.[9]

That same day Canon Raffaele Bertinelli—liaison officer in Rome for the bishops of Lombardy—informed Marinoni that his seminary and his missionaries were esteemed and loved by Rome. He was replying to three letters received from Marinoni in the past six weeks. As for Marinoni's fears that Fransoni and Propaganda were dissatisfied with his seminary, Bertinelli insisted that such fears were groundless.

However, the cardinal "was always of the opinion" that in Melanesia or Micronesia "they would have much suffering, little success and great hardships." Explaining why criticism had come from Milan, Bertinelli said it was prompted by a similar principle, but un-

---

7. PIME: AME 1:133–35, Fransoni to Ramazzotti, 3 June 1854.
8. See ibid., 4:121–23, Ramazzotti to Reina, 7 August 1854.
9. Ibid., 27:511–12.

der a different aspect. It was said that the missionaries "at less expense could have proved more useful in the Ionian Islands, [where Corfu is located and] where the Holy Father had wanted to send them, than at the world's frontier." Fransoni, however, "reasoned differently and said they are full of zeal, full of excellent spirit and ready to obey. Therefore Propaganda is happy to have [in them] an extra helping hand."

Further, the fact that Propaganda, "wanting to be indulgent to their wishes, has assigned them to a mission producing few results, cannot be held against them, since they had the consent of the Sacred Congregation. They are also gathering experience for themselves from this first step, which will prove of value to them in other Missions, in which Propaganda will want them to take up work without showing the least resistance to it." Bertinelli added that Cardinal Fransoni "has been undecided for some time as to whether he should send them to China. However, I am of the opinion that once the situation in that Empire has quieted down, those being sent to India will be transferred from there either to China or to Japan. But you must not say a word about this to anyone," Bertinelli warned, "since this is an opinion of mine which I have deduced from conversations that I have heard."[10] Clerical friends then began sending the Melanesia missionaries a flood of correspondence to keep up their courage. Father Taglioretti told Reina and his men on 26 July 1854 that their faith had rendered their sufferings sacred and "accepted by the Lord." Yet "orders are issued in *Rome* which suspend sending any more missionaries to help you." Rome also said no to the proposal that "a visitator be sent" to comfort them. And "in *Milan* some wickedness hopes to discredit your generosity and the spirit of the Institute." This caused the candidates at the mission seminary "to long all the more to be with you, to suffer and die with you," Taglioretti said.

Still, Taglioretti continued, "Rome sends complaints instead of encouragement, basing its judgment on news and reports which perhaps are inexact, but which according to the thinking of the Sacred Congregation come from persons worthy of all respect. . . . Therefore the first missionaries disobeyed the Holy Father. And those coming after them are not docile, are highly suspect, have bad intentions, manifest spurious virtue, etc. . . . Nevertheless in the midst of all this obstructionism caused by human judgments, God gives his blessing, the Vicar of Jesus Christ gives his blessing, the Bishops are favorable . . . and give their blessing, and the Institute keeps growing stronger. . . ." Taglioretti said that the old building was being expanded, restorations were being made, "candidates are applying from dioceses near and far and from Rome the most consoling news has come of the esteem which Rome has for the Institute. . . ."[11]

---

10. Ibid., 29:101f, Bertinelli to Marinoni, 12 July 1854. Bertinelli writes "Melanesia or Polynesia," which the author has changed in the text to Melanesia or Micronesia. Polynesia is evidently an oversight, because it never came into question as a mission field for the Milan seminary. See also chap. 20, n. 36.

11. Ibid., 4:541–44.

Marinoni on 7 August 1854 sent Reina a comforting letter.¹² On that same day Ramazzotti told Reina that he had anticipated his official visit to Rome "in order to inform the Holy Father and Propaganda of your most sincere and most complete compliance to their desires and in order to speak on behalf of sending a second group." He had accepted Rome's decision "not only with becoming resignation," he said, "but also with the complete conviction that Rome knows what it is doing." The decision nevertheless had caused him "great pain because of the abandonment" in which they were left.¹³

Father Supriès, now rector at his monastery, also tried to restore the courage of the abandoned missionaries and sent them seven pages of spiritual exhortations on 24 August 1854. "Remember your old friend at the Carthusian Monastery," he urged. He reminded them of Christ's example, "doing well to all, evangelizing all." And he recalled for them how the Apostle Paul had told the Galatians that he was "like a Mother enduring birthpangs until Christ be formed in them." Closing his long letter he called himself, "Your most humble and most affectionate servant and friend in Our Lord."¹⁴

Pius IX, in a papal brief addressed to Bishop Ramazzotti on 29 July 1854, spoke of "the letter which you enclosed from our dear priestly son, Paul Reina, written to us from Rooke in Oceania." In reply he encouraged Reina "to be at peace and in good spirits" in his service of the Holy See. The pope added that he was "very happy" to learn from Ramazzotti that there were candidates at the Milan seminary "who are ready and willing to evangelize whatever region we choose."¹⁵

All this time Father Alfieri at the Tiber Island generalate of the Hospitalers of Saint John of God in Rome had been conducting official business for director Marinoni in an unofficial capacity. Finally on 10 September 1854, Marinoni drafted a letter in which he officially and earnestly requested Alfieri "to serve when needed as our liaison person in Rome at Propaganda and elsewhere, in order to explain our position better and to inform us from time to time of what may be of interest to us."¹⁶

Four weeks later on 7 October 1854, Alfieri reported to Marinoni the results of a meeting with Cardinal Prefect Fransoni that day. "He wishes to assure you and all of your members of his esteem and affection . . . ," Alfieri said. "As regards your Oceania Mission the cardinal persists in his view, wishing that you send no personnel until there are satisfactory results. He thinks that no one will be able to succeed there unless they take natives from that island, train them and make them priests."¹⁷

---

12. Writing to Marinoni on 25 September 1855, Reina mentions having received the 7 August 1854 letter from Marinoni, but no copy of it has been found. See ibid., 11:167.

13. Ibid., 4:121–23, Ramazzotti to Reina, 7 August 1854.

14. Ibid., 28:191–97. See Gal. 4:19.

15. Ibid., 8:965f. Tragella in *Missioni estere*, 1:178, n. 14, mistakenly dates the brief 29 *August* 1854.

16. PIME: AME 5:823f.

17. Ibid., 10:63. Brambilla in *Pontificio istituto*, 1:144, mistakenly dates Alfieri's letter 8 October.

Director Marinoni replied at once on 30 July 1854 after receiving a letter of 24 May from Father Rocher, head of the Marist Center at Sydney. "You are surprised at my delay" in sending you "the necessary funds for our missionaries at Woodlark and Rooke," he said. The reason for the delay was the hope that some new missionaries might take along these funds and other supplies to Melanesia. "But Propaganda has judged it better to await more assuring news on the success of our Oceania Missions before exposing additional personnel almost uselessly to the danger of such great sufferings."

Within a few days, Marinoni said, he would be sending a shipment of clothes, books, and other items. In his letter he sent two foreign bills of exchange, one for seven hundred pounds sterling and another for four hundred. "I hope that this is enough for the current year. If the mission is to be continued, I shall very promptly send you all that is needed for the coming year."

After explaining that Propaganda had assigned some of his personnel "to the missions of Calcutta and Hyderabad, very close to Madras," he requested Rocher to provide him with all possible information "on the contacts which could be established between Eastern India and our Oceania missions." He thought of possibly transferring his projected supply center for Oceania "to India, thus perhaps reducing the costs." Not knowing how to thank Rocher sufficiently for his continued concern for the Milan missionaries, Marinoni told him that "God alone" could do so.[18]

As always when writing to Marists in Oceania, Marinoni sent his letter to their headquarters in Lyon for forwarding. The reply that he received by return mail was brusque. It came from Father Victor Poupinel, procurator at Lyon for Marist missions since 1841. To all appearances Poupinel had not read the letter addressed to Rocher.

He told Marinoni that the newly elected superior general, the provincial superior, and Father Colin were all out of town. Father Rocher in Sydney "wrote to us last 23 May," he continued,

> about the very great embarrassment in which he finds himself regarding your worthy missionaries. After paying the expenses for the schooner [*Supply*], which visited your Woodlark and Rooke Missions toward the end of last year, there were no additional funds on your mission's account at Father Rocher's disposal other than 331.15.7 pounds sterling.
>
> Now here is the embarrassment in which he finds himself: The months of September, October and November are the only ones, more or less, when ships can prudently be sent to the shores where your missionaries are located. He is convinced that it is necessary for a ship to visit them this autumn [1854] and take them provisions for a year. But he cannot do this with the funds still available, since all food supplies are extremely expensive in Sydney. Chartering a schooner costs 200 to 250 pounds sterling a month at present. Each day he has been waiting impatiently for some letters and some funds to arrive from you, providing him with the means to

18. PIME: AME 5:817f.

have your beloved sons visited and assisted. Now since he had the honor of writing to you twice, I hope that meanwhile he will have received the letter of credit for which he is waiting.

Poupinel was not particularly suave in his use of words and betrayed his impatience as he continued:

> I use this opportunity, Reverend Superior, to say that Father Rocher has once again charged me to ask you insistently to place at Sydney without delay one or two of your sons who can look after affairs there for their colleagues. We have been very happy to be able to render some slight services to your worthy missionaries and to your young seminary. But you must know, Reverend Superior, how painful it is to have to conduct the affairs of others and to answer for their money. Our members ask insistently that they be discharged of this responsibility. They have also made the same request of His Eminence, the Cardinal Prefect of Propaganda.[19]

On receiving word from Bishops Carew and Murphy of India that they were delighted over Rome's offer of priests from Milan, Fransoni hastened to inform Marinoni of this on 22 November 1854.[20]

In far-off Woodlark, which had been struck by a triple scourge in 1853, the Milan missionaries had managed to survive. But Salerio, head of the mission, had decided upon new tactics for 1854. Instead of going out to the people, as he had formerly done, he would now stay at home, hoping that this would make the people come to him. He also had a grandiose plan. He decided to build a completely Christian village to be called Saint Michael's Village. He, Raimondi and Catechist Tacchini, a carpenter by trade, built the village all by themselves, dedicating their energies to the task on such days in 1854 when they were well enough to work. They built a house for themselves inside the village.

The people of Woodlark were amazed to see this village grow before their eyes. Meanwhile the missionaries tried to recruit a nucleus of responsible families for it, but progress in recruiting was slow. By the end of 1854, when the village was finished, only three families of catechumens had been accepted. Saint Michael's Village was solemnly blessed and inaugurated on 8 December 1854. A well-organized course of instructions was launched, and religious festivities and banquets were sponsored by the missionaries, who in this way wanted to adopt local customs. Baptism for the three pioneer families was scheduled for Easter Sunday, 8 April 1855. "Our aim," Salerio said, "is to detach them from their old villages and from their former contacts and practices." These practices were superstitious, he said, and suffocated whatever interest his people had in religion. "This in turn paralyzed all our efforts."

Of the three families that moved into Saint Michael's Village, the one that held out the highest hopes was Pakò's. Salerio considered him to be "far superior in talent and in

---

19. Ibid., 28:785–86, Poupinel to Marinoni, 21 August 1854.
20. Ibid., 1:141–42.

knowledge to all his fellow countrymen." Pakò had spent more than five months in Sydney and recognized "the superiority of Europe and the dignity of a priest," Salerio said. "While in Sydney he had been showered with all possible concern and affection. And on the island [of Woodlark] he was always given preference by all the missionaries from whom he had received privileges of every kind."

Pakò and his wife both came from the Laughlan Islands southeast of Woodlark. In fact, Salerio had to pay a high price to induce Pakò to move to Woodlark, where Salerio then supported him for many months and built him a house in the new village as large as the house of a chief. Pakò had a daughter eighteen months old who was extraordinarily precocious and good. "Whenever she could slip out of her mother's arms, she ran to the house of the missionaries," Salerio said. And because she heard the words "Ave Maria" so often, she began to repeat them herself. Salerio hoped that in her he would have an outstanding Christian leader some day.[21]

But right after Christmas 1854, hardly three weeks from the day on which the village had been blessed, the little girl's parents were on the point of returning with her to the Laughlan Islands. Worried lest she be lost to the mission forever, Salerio rushed to the boat and managed to prevent her departure by threatening her father, who was greatly indebted to him. Since Pakò was the chief in Saint Michael's Village, it would have collapsed if he had left.

Salerio's dream of providing a Christian environment through Saint Michael's Village lasted three months, until March 1855, when the boats returned from the Laughlan Islands. By this time Salerio could tell that Pakò had changed and was not sincere in wanting to become a Christian. "We saw them brazenly return to their superstitions," he said. And they "promised one another to keep the matter concealed from us." But since none of them could keep a secret, Salerio was able to follow them and assist at their gatherings unobserved. "I saw it all with my very own eyes and became convinced that there was not the least shadow of remorse in their hearts," he said. "These facts forced me to realize that we were still very far from being able to have any effect upon their minds and hearts." Furthermore, Pakò "let me know that this time any resistance on my part would be in vain."

Relations worsened between Salerio and Pakò when his little girl took sick. She responded to none of the medicines provided by Salerio, "becoming neither better nor worse." Her mother then insisted on leaving Woodlark "in order to remove her from the influence of witches and sorcerers among whom, naturally, we were also included," Salerio said. Then on the very day of departure from Woodlark the little girl suffered severe and repeated convulsions and fell into a coma. Running to the spot and finding her at death's door, Salerio privately administered baptism, giving her the name Maria. "Shortly afterwards our little Maria was already in God's embrace," he said. She died in Saint Michael's Village on Monday, 19 March 1855, the feast of Saint Joseph.

21. *Beatificationis Positio*, 293–95, Salerio to Marinoni, 24 September 1855; Tragella, *Missioni estere*, 1:159, 170; Brambilla, *Pontificio istituto*, 1:118.

Present at Maria's death were her father's stepmother and her mother's brother, both of whom insisted that "all their superstitious ceremonies should be performed over the dying child." This was subsequently done, Salerio said, "in the midst of our village itself and before our very eyes in the presence of the two other families of the village, who became incensed over it." Later that same day Pakò's stepmother died and also the brother of Maria's mother after a fit of apoplexy. Salerio called Pakò "the most deceitful, laziest and most ungrateful man that one could imagine." The numerous privileges and endless acts of kindness showered upon him by the missionaries had served no other purpose, he said, "but to foster his pride and greediness and to make him . . . a more heinous impostor."[22]

The missionaries at distant Rooke, of course, had no idea of what was happening at Woodlark. In his survey covering the year 1854, Reina wrote: "The Lord has not yet been pleased to free us from attacks of fever, which break out at various periods and have continued up to the present time. Although I cannot say that I had fever all year long, I can say that I had it every time when I did something the least bit strenuous. I was also plagued with sores on my legs, one of which is still festering."

Father Ambrosoli had a bit less fever, Reina said, "but he suffers most severe stomach pains which last for periods of three to four days." Catechist Giuseppe Corti had suffered from fever all year

> and for the past two months [December 1854–January 1855] all parts of his body have become so swollen, that he must remain in bed and cannot move. . . . Because he was unable to breathe he had such an abundance of convulsions—and they were so severe—that we had to give him the Last Sacraments of the Church. We now fear constantly that soon we shall be deprived of him. Father Giovanni Mazzucconi has been indisposed almost continually by a mild fever. To this has been added in the last few months what I believe to be an inflammation of the lungs. His body is also beginning to puff up all over, something which threatens to reduce him to the state of our poor Corti. In addition to our being sick like this, we are deprived of many necessities of life. . . .[23]

By Epiphany, 6 January 1855, Fathers Reina, Ambrosoli, and Mazzucconi and Catechist Corti had been on Rooke Island for two years, two months, and two weeks. During that time it had become more than evident to Reina "that the islands of Melanesia are unhealthy," and consequently that it was imprudent to send personnel there. At least it was demanding too much from them. Reina reasoned, however, that such a conclusion "loses all its force, if instead of judging the matter according to the laws of human prudence, one judges according to the principles of faith and in the spirit of Jesus Christ, who loved his brethren so much that he laid down his life for them." These thoughts "rushed through my

---

22. *Beatificationis Positio*, 293–95, Salerio to Marinoni, 24 September 1855. In view of Salerio's description, Maestrini in *Mazzucconi*, p. 170, cannot be correct when he calls Pakò "the head man of the tribe" and says that "his influence extended over the entire island" of Woodlark.

23. PIME: AME 11:126, Reina to Marinoni, 22 January 1855.

mind at Rooke during those moments when I saw nothing around me but languor and sickness," he said. "Then the sad thought suggested itself that we could not retain these islands...." There was also this consideration: "If these missions are so slow in producing results, would it not be better to abandon them?"

Reina and his three companions at Rooke, however, had never succumbed during 1854 "to any thoughts of this kind," he said. "In fact, we fought them off like a temptation. But then right on the feast of Epiphany [6 January 1855] there was someone who began to put these ideas into words for us and to propose them as a subject for reflection." That "someone," Reina said, was Father Mazzucconi, whose "virtues and talents" he admired.

Mazzucconi insisted

> that the hour of grace had not yet come for these peoples; that the expenses and sacrifices for these missions were being made in vain; that currently there were so many peoples elsewhere ready for conversion, needing nothing else but ministers of the gospel; that Bishop Collomb himself, according to what Father Frémont had told us, had planned on beginning in the Gilolo area [of northwest New Guinea] with those islands which are in contact with more civilized peoples, intending to descend gradually from there to these islands. And if cannibalistic peoples had been converted, and even others more ferocious than they, the reason was that such peoples had fallen so low, forcing nature itself to erect a barrier to preserve their lives, which had become so bestial. Thus nature had forced them to adopt whatever method of salvation was presented to them.

The reason that the people of Rooke showed no promptness in receiving the gospel, Mazzucconi claimed, was that they had fallen so low. But they had not yet fallen low enough, "since they must descend to the very depths of misery and they must feel its whole weight before sensing the need for a change and voluntarily embracing the gospel, when it is presented to them." This might well be true for some peoples, Reina said, but not necessarily for all, since there were exceptions.

Nevertheless Mazzucconi had made such a forceful presentation of his arguments, that "it appeared our missions would have to be abandoned," even if the climate had been healthy. But Reina could not agree to this. "If these missions had made even slow progress," he said, "or if there had been some hope of success . . . , I would not judge that they have to be abandoned. . . ." His missionaries were sick, and the people of Rooke were slow to become Christians. But "we could very well have withdrawn from the spot where we were and also, if necessary, from the island of Rooke," Reina said. "We could have moved to New Britain or to New Guinea, choosing less swampy locations for making another attempt. The local people themselves told us that in New Guinea, where the mountains reach out to the sea, there are villages without swamps."

One of Reina's missionaries—whom he did not name—had said that it was useless to try to convert the people of Rooke, "because they do not want to be converted. We have seen and experienced that reasoning has no power over their customs, that we are despised for doing good to them, that in their eyes we are people who have no country, and that all of our efforts to win over their youth have been in vain." In reply, Reina said:

> All this is true. But no one can maintain that these defects result from their incapacity; they derive rather from their corruption. Nor can one say that they are stupid, because in everything regarding the sixth commandment they show sufficient intellectual advancement. Nor can they be called fickle, because they are not like that when we treat of matters which affect them deeply, or when a question comes up concerning their customs and their ideas. They are flighty when we try to oblige them to reflect on ideas odious to them or contrary to their passions, since no one likes to condemn himself.

No one can deny, Reina maintained, "that fundamentally they are competent and they show an intellectual development which causes wonder even in us." For Reina the logical conclusion was "that the great obstacle to conversion is not the inherent character of the race to which they belong, but rather their character as deformed by passion. Their passions themselves are the obstacle. And how does one fight against and conquer passion?" Priests engaged in pastoral work in Europe faced the very same problem, Reina said. As he saw it, the job of the missionary was the conversion of his people. That is, he must "turn their wills—this faculty which is so free and so hidden—toward God and toward what is good."

Still another consideration that came up at Rooke on Epiphany, 6 January 1855, was that "nobody knows how many years we might remain here without having any results." Reina admitted that he had no statistics for Rome on the number of catechumens or on the number of baptized in his mission. "We have nothing but expenses and hopes," he said, "hopes based on the children and on the youths around us." Any possible results, as far as he could see, were still in the hands of God, since "the poor missionary has nothing but suffering for his lot." Still, we "ought to try everything, trusting in the grace of God, which will manifest itself in due time and in such ways as are pleasing to him. . . ."

And what might the situation in Rooke be like after twenty years? "Some doubt that even in that amount of time we could succeed in having a small Christian community sufficiently stable," Reina said. They believe "there might well be one or the other Christian, but the mass of the population will still be indifferent or even hostile, because they are so bad." Reina again disagreed, defending the people of Rooke: "Although brutalized, they do have intelligence and they have a heart like ours. They need to see the beauty of virtue. Once we have won their hearts, we can be certain of success.

"You say they are bad? Yet what do you do to make them good? What spirit of humility and gentleness do you show them? You say they are not capable of appreciating the beauty of virtue? But why does no one ever say that we practice too little virtue, that the virtue manifested by us is suspect, that we do not enjoy the peace which we preach, that the graces prepared by God for these peoples have been kept at a distance because of our sins?" Reina was referring to no specific mission or missionary, he said, but rather "to that sentiment which all of us ought to have regarding our own defects." Reina also asked his tiny group: "If an attempt to found these missions cannot be made now, when will it be made?" The answer was: "Wait until the whites come to them, making them more civil and thus preparing the road for us missionaries...." Reina admitted that commerce or contact with whites "will contribute toward the culture of the savages." But the culture of whites "is not embraced with love by the natives, because whites use violence and force," he said. "Besides it is most evident that very many savage peoples, in spite of being in contact with whites for a long time, still preserve their unhappy customs."

Then Reina asked: "If it is true that one of the roads leading to civilization is commerce with whites, why should not contact with missionaries be even a better road? Will not the goodness of the missionary instruct, will it not render these souls more pliable" than the presence of other whites in their midst? "And what about the sufferings and the prayers of the missionaries? Will they not draw down upon these peoples greater graces than the scandals and evil lives of whites?" Furthermore, if one follows the principle that whites and commerce must arrive before the missionaries, then those islands and those peoples will be forever abandoned "that provide no outlet for commerce or that cannot be visited by whites because they are unhealthy."

A further consideration was proposed: If personnel and funds are so limited that it is impossible to provide sufficiently for two places, then "either one or the other must be abandoned. Preference obviously should be given to the one which is more promising." Reina insisted, however, that "there are sufficient means available for all missions, but the needs and hopes indicated by some are perhaps a bit exaggerated." All of the missions in Oceania, he said, even the most recent ones,

> although they may not have sufficient personnel for all of their needs, have nevertheless been launched and are already growing. Their administration is also stable and organized and they have facility in communicating. It is likewise probable that they shall obtain good catechists and also indigenous priests, as well as those additional advantages which spring from a printing press.... All of this expedites the propagation of the gospel and renders more far-reaching and fruitful the work of the missionary. The needs which a mission has, are greatly diminished by such advantages. It also seems to me that the continual sending of missionaries would suffice for the requirements of the populations concerned.

Over and above the advantages mentioned, Reina hoped that some day there would be "one and the same language, a vast and united country, bustling contacts between the inhabitants and avidity for novelties." He foresaw "a people initiated in civility, even though still pagan, as well as indigenous priests working with much success, causing needs to diminish even further." Consequently "it does not appear just to me," he said, "that you have to abandon completely one mission, for which very little has been done, in order to make an already existing mission run better. All of these savages are sons of the Church...."

The reasoning of Reina was in favor of continuing the two missions of Rooke and Woodlark and also in favor of opening additional missions in Melanesia once new personnel had arrived. His feelings, however, ran counter to his reasoning, he said. "Remaining in these missions, which are difficult under all respects and to the utmost degree," meant that he would have to continue bearing "the weight which has never left me in peace."

By "weight" he must have meant the responsibility for having made the decision of taking his men to Melanesia in spite of advice to the contrary received from Cardinal Fransoni and from Bishop Bataillon. If he were to go with his missionaries to some other place, he said, he would be freed from this burden. And he added, "I must force myself to think no longer about these questions."[24]

Was it a mere coincidence that this heated and lengthy discussion between Fathers Reina, Ambrosoli, and Mazzucconi on abandoning Rooke and Woodlark should have taken place on Epiphany, the important missionary feast commemorating the manifestation of Christ's divinity to mankind? Three years earlier on the eve of Epiphany, Reina had received at Milan his appointment as superior of the Oceania mission. Now only three years later he and two priest members of his pioneer group had seriously discussed the abandonment of their first two mission stations at Woodlark and Rooke.

As each new day dawned Reina and his missionaries scanned the horizon for a sail in the wind, some harbinger of hope. Would their mail, their reinforcements, their supplies for the new year ever come? They had been without quinine for over a year, and it was their only remedy for malaria.

Like the missionaries at Rooke, those at Woodlark also scanned the horizon day by day. Then late in December 1854 they sighted a ship, but it disappeared as quickly as it had appeared. Three times on three successive days it appeared and disappeared. Was the captain lost? They recognized the ship as the 114-ton schooner *Jeune Lucie*, now converted into a steamer, which had brought them to Woodlark two years and three months earlier. Thinking that the captain was new and fearing that he did not recognize their port, they went looking for him and found him down the coast engaged in trade. His name was Captain Blair, and the missionaries guided him to their port.

But Captain Blair's ship brought them neither mail nor personnel. "Good God! What a sacrifice! Thy will be done . . . ," Salerio said. He had been promised by the captain of the *Supply* that another ship would arrive "in five or six months," because the *Supply* had brought provisions for only half a year. The waiting period, however, had lasted thirteen and a half months.[25]

---

24. Ibid., 173–77, Reina to Marinoni, 19 October 1855 [probable date]; ibid., 257, Reina to Marinoni, 15 June 1856.

25. Salerio is inexact when he tells Marinoni on 31 December 1854 that the interval between ships was "fifteen months." See PIME: AME 11:1279. Brambilla also says it was "fifteen months" in *Pontificio istituto*, 1:118. The *Jeune Lucie*, however, had reached Woodlark by 31 December 1854, when Salerio wrote the above letter. And the previous ship, *Supply*, had not yet left Woodlark on 12 November 1853, the date on Salerio's letter to Marinoni, which was carried to Sydney by the *Supply*. See *Beatificationis Positio*, 288f. The interval from

The three missionaries at Woodlark—Salerio, Raimondi, and Tacchini—learned from Captain Blair that the Crimean War (1853–56) was in progress and that Great Britain, France, and Turkey had joined forces against Russia. They believed this to be the reason that they received no mail and no new personnel.

Since Salerio was in charge of Woodlark mission, and since he had been out of contact with Prefect Apostolic Reina for over a year, he decided to go with Captain Blair to Rooke to discuss with Reina the future of his mission. To his dismay, however, he learned that Captain Blair would not return to Woodlark after dropping off supplies at Rooke, but would follow the northern coast of New Britain, circumnavigate its northern tip, and then continue along the eastern coast of the Solomon Islands, conducting trade at every port en route. From there he would proceed directly to Sydney. This left Salerio no alternative but to remain at Woodlark and write to Prefect Apostolic Reina about what had happened in the past thirteen and a half months.[26]

Captain Blair's route should have made it clear to Salerio that Father Rocher's funds in Sydney for the Italian mission were so low that he could not afford to charter the *Jeune Lucie* for the Italian missionaries. The agreement reached by Rocher and Joubert, the owner, was that the *Jeune Lucie* would simply deliver goods to the missionaries at Woodlark and Rooke for a fixed price. The voyage itself was a business venture for Joubert. Since his ship was now a steamer and no longer dependent upon the winds, he wanted Blair to stop for trade at whatever villages he could find en route, also at those on the coasts of Woodlark and Rooke.[27]

The *Jeune Lucie* left Woodlark mission about New Year's Day 1855 and after further trading reached Rooke on 19 or 20 January. This was four or five days less than fifteen months since the Rooke missionaries had seen the *Supply* sail out of sight, their last contact with the outside world.[28] Like the missionaries at Woodlark, those at Rooke, on seeing *Jeune Lucie* arrive, hoped that it would have new personnel aboard. Seeing none, and noting that no one from Woodlark was aboard, Reina and his men felt discouraged and abandoned after waiting for new personnel for fifteen months. Nor did Captain Blair have even a single letter for them from Europe. Originally Reina had planned to send both Corti and Mazzucconi with Captain Blair "to Woodlark, a healthier island, where they could recover." He and Ambrosoli had intended to accompany them. But then Reina learned

---

12 November 1853 to 31 December 1854 is thirteen and a half months.

26. PIME: AME 11:1277–79, Salerio to Marinoni, 31 December 1854. For Blair's route see PIME: AME 11:126, Reina to Marinoni, 22 January 1855.

27. See ibid., 28:811–12, Rocher to Marinoni, 6 April 1855.

28. Salerio says that the *Supply* left Rooke on 24 October 1853. See RIP: R B-N.2, N.1, "Giornale di Viaggio." Reina tells Marinoni on 15 June 1856 that the *Jeune Lucie* arrived "on 19 January 1855." See PIME: AME 11:257. Mazzucconi writing to his family on 20 April 1855 says it arrived on 20 January 1855. See Mazzucconi, *Scritti*, 247. The interval from 24 October 1853 to 19 or 20 January 1855 is fifteen months minus four or five days. Maestrini in *Mazzucconi*, 158, when referring to this visit of the *Jeune Lucie*, incorrectly says that "the ship was not coming from Woodlark" and that "[it] could not give them the slightest help."

that this would be impossible because the steamer was en route to Java for commerce. This news excited Mazzucconi, who at once repeated his proposal of Epiphany, namely, that they abandon Rooke and Woodlark and start in another more civilized place like Java. Because of Mazzucconi's poor health Reina decided to let him accompany Captain Blair to Java. "But when we told the captain that Mazzucconi wanted to go along [to Java], he explained that his ship was not going to the European colony of Java [in the Dutch East Indies], but instead to Tonga-Java, a group of islands . . . with numerous coconut palms, where he hoped to take on oil."[29]

What Captain Blair called "Tonga-Java" was an atoll group five degrees south of the equator and due east of Rooke, lying about 160 miles north of Santa Isabel Island in the Solomon Islands. It had been named Ontong Java by Tasman in 1643 and was renamed the Lord Howe Group by Captain Hunter in 1791. The local name is Luangiua.[30]

When Mazzucconi learned to which Java Captain Blair was referring, and that he did not expect to reach Sydney for another three months, he no longer talked of leaving Rooke. But Reina insisted that he was free to take the three-month voyage, and even urged him to do so for his health. When Mazzucconi consented, Reina instructed him to remain in Sydney until he was completely cured and then return immediately with provisions for Woodlark and Rooke. And since Captain Blair would be stopping for trade all along his route, visiting many islands in Melanesia entrusted to Reina, Mazzucconi was asked "to gather information on the location of ports, on the customs [of the people] and on the climate." He was urged also to take note of whatever else he found of interest, "because those lands are hardly known."

Reina was convinced that Mazzucconi on his return voyage from Sydney would be bringing new personnel for both Woodlark and Rooke. "I gave him a signed note," Reina said, "authorizing him to do whatever he wished at Woodlark, either keep the mission or have our missionaries abandon it. . . . He was to act as if he himself were the superior."[31] Reina's note was addressed to the missionaries of Woodlark and read as follows: "I have given to Father Giovanni Mazzucconi full powers to deal with individuals and with the Woodlark Mission as he thinks best and according to what I told him orally. . . . I approve of all that he will do. . . ." The note was dated 23 January 1855.[32]

That same day Reina wrote to Bishop Ramazzotti. "When our new companions arrive," he said, "I would like to open a mission in New Guinea. It is certain that in time either the English, or the French, or the Dutch, or some other nation will attempt to colonize this

---

29. PIME: AME 11:257, Reina to Marinoni, 15 June 1856.

30. *Pacific Islands Year Book and Who's Who*, 429.

31. PIME: AME 11:126, Reina to Marinoni, 22 January 1855; ibid., PIME: AME 11:257f, Reina to Marinoni, 15 June 1856; PIME: AME 11:797, Mazzucconi to Marinoni, 20 April 1855.

32. Ibid., 129.

vast land of New Guinea. And if they do—rather than trying to enter new places—they will choose to follow in the footsteps of missionaries."[33]

Writing to director Marinoni on the previous day, 22 January 1855, Reina had said that he was sending Mazzucconi to Sydney "while he was still strong enough to make the voyage alone and without assistance . . ." Corti was incapable of making such a long sea voyage and would have to stay behind. Nor had it been possible to send the two men to Woodlark to recuperate, Reina said, because Captain Blair "told me . . . that his voyage was routed to the north of New Britain and to the east of the Solomons, and that from there he would return to Sydney."

Reina was nevertheless "rather confident that this voyage will prove advantageous for our mission," because it would be an easy matter for Mazzucconi "to visit the coasts of New Britain and the principal islands in the Solomons. Then on his return he will be able to give us some good advice to help us in deciding where to make a new foundation, if the Lord decides to send us new companions."[34]

When Mazzucconi boarded the ship at Rooke in late January 1855 for the voyage to Sydney, he was a very sick man. Earlier that month at Reina's suggestion he had made his last will and testament because death seemed very close. "I took along my cot and the few clothes that I still had," he said. But others carried everything aboard for him, because he was too weak to do so himself. Several days later some of the ship's officers said: "On seeing you come aboard we believed that you could never survive a sea voyage of three months. But now we are beginning to have hope." Mazzucconi told his family that "from the first moment when I set foot aboard ship, I no longer had the slightest fever. But during the voyage I had some sores on my feet, which were like purgatory for me. . . ."[35] And his teeth, he said, "were black like my cassock."[36]

Of all the places that Mazzucconi visited, he chose Ontong Java (also Lord Howe Group) to describe for his family. It was made up of "twelve tiny islands close to the equator," he said. "Here we found people who have no idea at all of sweet water, our drinking water. . . ." Their islands "consist of nothing but coral sand and therefore any rainwater dries up in a moment. Instead of giving them water, Providence has given them so many coconut palms that, calculating roughly, I would say that within a year they do not consume one-fortieth of the nuts produced there annually. They get their drink and their food from these coconuts. And during the many days that we were there, I also drank from them and ate them. . . . As we left I looked back from my spot high up on the ship and thought: Goodness

---

33. Ibid., 133.

34. Ibid., 125–27. Reina's precise description of Captain Blair's intended route excludes the circumnavigation of New Ireland, which was erroneously included as part of the route by the designer of the map facing p. 160 in *Beatificationis Positio*.

35. Mazzucconi, *Scritti*, 247, Mazzucconi to his family, 20 April 1855.

36. Ibid., 254, Mazzucconi to his family, 12 May 1855.

knows when a missionary will arrive in these islands! They are so far away, so segregated from all the other islands!"³⁷

Captain Blair's estimate of three months for the return voyage from Rooke to Sydney could not have been more exact. He had reached Rooke on 19 January 1855, and he dropped anchor at Sydney on 19 April.³⁸

During his voyage of three months Mazzucconi made copious notes on ports, customs, and climate, as Reina had wanted him to do. He also acquired some new friends, one of whom was Captain Blair, "a businessman and a Protestant with whom I departed from Rooke. He respected me from the beginning, then liked me and finally chose me as a friend, a brother," Mazzucconi said. "Seeing that I lacked everything, he provided all, even superfluous things. And when we reached Sydney, he would take no money, neither for the voyage nor for the meals during the previous three months. . . . He left immediately for a port in Asia and probably I shall never see him again. But I shall always feel obliged to pray for him and I shall also feel comforted when doing so."³⁹

On his arrival in Sydney on Thursday afternoon, 19 April 1855, the first thing that Mazzucconi wanted to know from Father Rocher was whether new personnel or mail had arrived. The last mail that he had received from Europe had reached him at Rooke Island on 19 October 1853, a year and a half ago.

Rocher told Mazzucconi that no new personnel had arrived and that according to a letter received by him from Marinoni, Rome was waiting for "more assuring news" from the Melanesia mission "before exposing additional personnel almost uselessly to the danger of such great sufferings." In that same letter Marinoni had promised to send funds promptly for the needs of the coming year of the Melanesia mission, "if the mission is to be continued." Rocher also knew from this letter that Rome lately had given to the Milan seminary new missions in Eastern India, something that was making Marinoni consider the advisability of establishing his planned supply center for Oceania in India, where costs presumably would be lower than in Australia.⁴⁰

On hearing this news Mazzucconi was stunned and became convinced that superiors both in Rome and in Milan were now doubtful about continuing the Melanesia mission. How else could one explain their sending new missionaries to India instead of to Oceania?

As for mail, Rocher had none for Mazzucconi. He explained that none at all had arrived from Europe for any of the Italian missionaries during the fourteen-month period between 21 August 1853 when the *Supply* left with mail for Woodlark and Rooke, and 19 October 1854 when the *Jeune Lucie* left for those same islands. Mazzucconi must have found it hard to believe that a year and two months could pass without family, friends, or

---

37. Ibid., 247f, Mazzucconi to his family, 20 April 1855.
38. See Hosie, "French Mission," 418, for the arrival date in Sydney.
39. Mazzucconi, *Scritti*, 269, Mazzucconi to Marinoni, 16 August 1855.
40. See PIME: AME 5;817f, Marinoni to Rocher, 30 July 1854.

superiors in Rome and Milan sending any one of them a letter! But within a month after the *Jeune Lucie* had left Sydney, mail did arrive and Rocher entrusted all of it to Captain Dalmagne, who sailed out of Sydney on 14 November 1854 in command of the 140-ton brig *Phantom*.

Both the *Phantom* and the *Jeune Lucie* were owned by Joubert and were expected to cross paths en route. At that point Captain Dalmagne would hand over to Captain Blair the mail for the missionaries at Woodlark and Rooke. But the two ships never met. Mazzucconi concluded that the *Phantom* had probably been lost at sea. When informing Marinoni of this, he said that "the three coffers of money, however, which you in your charity sent us, are safe here in Sydney."

During his first full day on land Mazzucconi discussed his ideas at great length with Rocher on abandoning Rooke and Woodlark in favor of some more hopeful mission elsewhere in Melanesia. That same evening, 20 April 1855, he wrote to director Marinoni, saying that he was a soldier sent back from the front as an invalid, but "I feel obliged to write you a letter which can greatly influence the continuation of these poor missions of ours in Rooke and Woodlark. I shall tell you everything...."

He enclosed a letter from Prefect Apostolic Reina that showed "how sickness in this third year continues to be more or less the same, how it has brought Catechist Corti almost to death's door, and how I was so afflicted that he [Reina] believed it necessary to send me to Sydney in order to save me." On arriving in Sydney the previous evening, Mazzucconi said, he had learned from Rocher "that the companions for whom we have been waiting so long are not coming, that our Seminary has received other assignments, and that our missions here are also being called into question."

In Reina's letter and in one written by Salerio, Marinoni would find some details on how the Woodlark and Rooke missions were developing, Mazzucconi said. "But I believe it is an obligation of mine to take the liberty of calling attention to facts and ideas which are not contained in their letters.

"Various messages seem to indicate that Father Salerio truly has been reduced to a state of quasi-helplessness. Insistently he asks that he be substituted by another superior since, as he says, he thinks of nothing but dying. As for Father Reina, he told me that the Rooke establishment must be transferred elsewhere. And although he in his heart is ready to die, he cannot bear the thought of submitting his companions to that same trial." As for the native population, Marinoni could see what they were like from the letter addressed by Reina to the bishops of Lombardy. "They are really base," Mazzucconi said, "and we have not yet done any direct missionary work [among them]."

He then presented the proposal that had been nagging him since Epiphany. "My heart fills with tears at the thought of abandoning even temporarily so many peoples living in those islands," he said. The ideal situation would be to have the means and the personnel needed to care for everyone. "But if charity is forced to make a choice, if it must pick out one people and abandon another, then every man filled with zeal for religion and for the

Lord will say that it would be best to choose peoples who are a bit closer to being civilized, who are closer to producing some results and who do not require such enormous outlays." If it is necessary to choose, he continued, one ought to choose an area where the obstacles, humanly speaking, are less. Marinoni could well see to what kind of decision these thoughts would lead. "But this very serious decision," he said, "we place entirely in the hands of our Reverend Superiors."[41]

In effect Mazzucconi was saying that his group ought to receive an easier mission. Was he aware that in the name of all he was now accepting the sound advice given earlier by Bishop Bataillon, who had asked how the young and inexperienced group could expect to succeed where the Marists had failed? Was he aware that now he was echoing the wisdom of Cardinal Prefect Fransoni, who had urged the group to begin work in an easier mission, like Fiji, and only later—after having acquired experience and having grown in numbers—to take up work in Melanesia and Micronesia?

But there was "another decision" which had occupied Mazzucconi's mind that entire day, one that he had also discussed with Father Rocher. "I am writing to you about it this evening," he said, "because tomorrow the steamship leaves for Europe and it is very important that I receive a reply from you quickly."

Within a month or six weeks, he said, "we shall be sending a ship to Rooke to inform" Prefect Apostolic Reina "of the new situation in which our Seminary finds itself and to invite him to consider whether it might not be best for all of us to gather here in Sydney to await your orders." If Propaganda intends to keep up "these poor missions of ours," we would first need much money and healthy men. When we are restored to health, we could all go to a healthier place [in Melanesia] and make a foundation there."

But should Propaganda not intend to keep up the Melanesia mission, "then it would be better to avoid the expense of buying the new supplies" that would have to be purchased, if the Woodlark and Rooke missions were to continue for another year. Continuing those missions, he stressed, "will require much money, because these islands of ours are never visited by a ship." Prices in Sydney were also exorbitant, he said. "Yesterday when I landed," for example, "I had no shoes and was obliged to hand out about twenty francs for a pair of miserable lightweight shoes."

With the increase of mission stations, he said, "we must be ready to hand out no less than twenty thousand francs for chartering a ship. And this is over and above the cost of providing the missionaries with food. . . ." In Central Oceania and in New Zealand it was possible to obtain food locally, he said, but not so in Woodlark and Rooke, "because these islands are poor and a missionary cannot survive there."

Mazzucconi said that he "would certainly like to receive a reply" to his letter before sending a ship to Woodlark and Rooke. "But you will understand the situation in which we find ourselves." Woodlark and Rooke had received from the *Jeune Lucie* enough provisions "for only six months because there were no more funds at hand [in Sydney]. By this time

---

41. Mazzucconi, *Scritti*, 249f, Mazzucconi to Marinoni, 20 April 1855.

three months have already passed! Furthermore, it would take eight months for your reply to reach me. Then it would take one more month to fit out a ship and still another month for it to arrive there, if all goes well. This makes a total of ten months." The missionaries would therefore be out of supplies again "for at least seven or eight months," if it were necessary to wait for Marinoni's reply before sending a ship.

"Furthermore the house at Rooke is collapsing and they do not have the strength needed to repair it," he said. "We would have to buy a [prefabricated] house here, but they are so expensive! In addition to this Corti was dying when I left, Father Salerio was reduced to extremes and the two [priests] at Rooke were sick. You will agree that they cannot be left for so long time in such great distress waiting for a reply from you, which—it seems to me—will perhaps say that we ought to withdraw. And if it should say that we ought to stay, we would be ready to obey with greater alacrity and strength, if meanwhile we had regained our health."

Mazzucconi's mind was evidently made up: he would accompany a ship to Woodlark and Rooke and persuade the missionaries there to return with him to Sydney to recuperate. "By the time you receive this poor letter of mine," he told Marinoni, "you can take it for granted that your sons will all be gathered together here in Sydney." And so by the time Marinoni's reply would arrive, he said, "we shall be ready, I hope, to go wherever your new orders will send us: either back to the islands or off to larger lands." When explaining that his voyage from Rooke to Sydney had lasted three months and that Prefect Apostolic Reina had wanted him to take copious notes wherever he went, Mazzucconi said, "I actually had plenty of time to do this because the ship stopped everywhere. It is impossible, however, for me to transcribe from my diary all of this information tonight. But I tell you about it, my good Superior, because if you were to consider it opportune, I would gladly send you not only this long letter, but also my entire diary."

Before closing Mazzucconi admitted that his health was "not very good, but of late it is better than fair. And they take such good care of me here that in a few days I shall be completely restored to health." He hoped to write again within a month, he said, but more calmly. Therefore he suggested that Marinoni might want to refrain from taking action on his proposals until after receiving his next letter.[42]

Mazzucconi had completed only two months of his three-month voyage to Sydney when Catechist Corti died at Rooke. Corti had begun having severe stomach pains and diarrhea on Tuesday, 13 March 1855. By Friday he became calm, Reina said,

> but he was extremely weak. At 3 A.M. on the 17th [Saturday] he lost consciousness and I noticed that his tongue was swollen. Then for a short time around 8 A.M. he regained consciousness, so I took advantage of these moments to tell him of his danger. I also called to mind some pious thoughts for him. Right after that he fell back into unconsciousness, perspiring profusely, but with an immobile expression on his face. At 2 P.M. we gave him the Sacrament of the Last Anointing and the Papal Blessing.

42. Ibid., 249–53.

He died as we were reciting the final prayers. It was impossible to give him the *Holy Viaticum* because he was always unconscious. But we were consoled by the thought that he had received the Sacraments on the previous Sunday. We had to ask the natives to help us bury him, because he was so extremely swollen that we were not able to carry him.

That same day Reina and Ambrosoli had fever attacks.[43]

Corti's death certificate still exists in a Roman archive and reads as follows: "The undersigned priest attests that Giuseppe Corti from Aquate in the district of Lecco, Province of Como, a Catechist of the Lombard Missionaries, died of dropsy on this Island of Rooke on the seventeenth of March 1855 at 3:00 in the afternoon." It is signed by "Paolo Reina, Prefect Apostolic," and is dated "Rooke Island, Nurua Village, 18 March 1855." Corti died at the age of thirty-seven.[44]

The Roman Catholic mission to Rooke and Woodlark was dying out.

43. PIME: AME 11:155, Reina to Marinoni, 3 September 1855.
44. Ibid., 143.

13

Reina Abandons Rooke and Woodlark and Awaits New Orders in Sydney

10 May and 10 July 1855

FAITHFUL TO HIS WORD, FATHER MAZZUCCONI WROTE WITHIN A MONTH TO DIRECTOR Marinoni from Tarban Creek. "I was quite surprised," he said on 12 May 1855, to learn that all the Marists here "are convinced that the best thing to do is not to abandon those peoples and those missions for good, but *to withdraw from them for the time being*. Meanwhile we should try to obtain reliable information on the status of the natives in northwest New Guinea." They suggested that we start among peoples "who are beginning to rise to some degree of culture. From such peoples our work could gradually be extended" to the peoples of Rooke, Woodlark, and vicinity. Mazzucconi then listed for Marinoni the reasons given by the Marists for their proposal.

First of all the missions of Rooke and Woodlark "are too costly at present." In fact, they "are the most costly missions in the whole Catholic Church." Over and above the long voyage from Europe, missionaries must charter a ship and fit it out in a port "where everything is extremely expensive." Food supplies and a wooden house "must be purchased for the missionaries and transported a great distance." Nor is any other solution possible, "because those islands are never visited by other ships. The people there are poor and a priest cannot survive, if he does not obtain food elsewhere. He also needs some structure which is at least suitable for hiding his provisions from the cupidity of the savages."

All of the Marists agreed that costs were enormous, but thought that in less than half a century these might be reduced to small amounts. "In fact, if commerce continues to spread like it has, and if New Caledonia remains a French colony," the islands of Rooke and Woodlark "after a short period will no longer be the most distant shores in the world! Instead ships will be visiting them frequently, helping them become prosperous; and the local people being prompted to work somewhat harder, will have food available for themselves and also for others. This will reduce a missionary's transportation costs. And perhaps he might even be able to survive there without having to import foreign foods."

The second reason given by the Marists for abandoning Woodlark temporarily was that "these peoples at present really are in a very low state." In view of precise information received from Marists who are active in Central Oceania and in New Zealand, Mazzucconi said, "I have to admit that our islands in almost all respects are immeasurably more backward than the others. . . ." If humanly speaking a priest's words are to produce some results, he said, it is necessary for him to exercise some authority over the natives. "But for him to have a bit of authority, the natives must begin at least to understand that whites, too, are human beings and that they can have at least as much knowledge as the blacks. Although this notion has not yet reached our peoples, it is found in all those islands where European ships arrive with some frequency."

European commerce, Mazzucconi said, was "a school of the sword, of oppression and of blood, but nonetheless a school. And the Lord," who knows how to draw good out of "the decadence caused by sin, makes use of this school to reach and to rouse the hearts of those, who would hardly allow themselves to be moved by simply benevolent and harmless words. It might be better to allow them to pass through this school first and then evangelize them. By that time they would be able to recognize love. Finally, as far as all extreme forms of wickedness and corruption are concerned," Mazzucconi said, "our savages cannot learn anything new at all from the Europeans. Sad to say, they know it all and do it all from their childhood."

The third and last reason given by the Marists was identical with the one that Mazzucconi had championed in Rooke. He paraphrased it like this: "If there were so many priests and missionaries that the needs of all peoples could be satisfied at least sufficiently, if not abundantly, I would then beg my good Superior to take no heed of expenses, of uncertainty regarding success, of sicknesses or even of death. I would beg him to let me stay among a people who might be the only abandoned people, no matter what the cost. But if there should be many abandoned peoples, and if there should be need to make a choice, then it is our obligation to keep in mind all circumstances, to economize on means and to begin with those peoples who, in view of their very location, seem to be placed by God closer to the truth." Mazzucconi hoped that these three reasons with their accompanying considerations would be of value to Marinoni in reaching a decision. "If not, then push them aside," he said. Meanwhile he had done some research on the peoples of northwest New Guinea.[1] It appeared that they, too, had few contacts with Europeans. "But in any event," he said, "it is certain that in the port of Sydney there are very many ships which pass through the Torres Straits, hugging those shores as they go on their way to ports in Asia." In fact, a ship was leaving Sydney that very day for Calcutta, he said.

"Perhaps it would be neither difficult, nor excessively costly," he continued, "for missionaries located in such [Asian port] cities to be put into contact with other missionaries

---

1. Mazzucconi, *Scritti*, 258. This printed copy of Mazzucconi's letter of 12 May 1855 to Marinoni reads "northeast New Guinea." It should read "northwest New Guinea" like the original letter in PIME: AME 11:801.

who might be settled on the coasts of northwest New Guinea or on nearby islands." In that case their supply center could be located "in that Asian port which would have more commerce and better contact with those islands. Prices here in Sydney are appalling and it seems that the Marists themselves are doubtful as to whether they should remain here."

Mazzucconi added that Bishop Collomb, the Marist who had founded the missions of Rooke and Woodlark, "had wanted to go to the other side [of New Guinea] closer to Java, Sumatra, etc., where he had hoped to find more advanced peoples." He was thinking of the island of Amboina, Mazzucconi said, when he died at Rooke on 16 July 1848.[2]

Father Rocher on 24 October 1854 had written to director Marinoni in Milan, saying that for fifteen months he had received neither letters from him nor money "to provide for the needs of your missionaries in Oceania." With only 331 pounds sterling left on their account, Rocher "for this time only" had nevertheless been able to send them with the schooner *Jeune Lucie* on 19 October "provisions for about six months, thanks to the collaboration of our agent in Sydney, Mr. Joubert." The cost for chartering the schooner was 500 pounds sterling. Rocher gave Joubert 100 pounds, using the balance of the 331 pounds on Marinoni's account for purchasing supplies. Joubert's condition was that he receive the remaining 400 pounds "as soon as possible." Furthermore, in view of his not being paid the full amount at once, Joubert stipulated that the *Jeune Lucie* would engage in commerce at Woodlark and Rooke as well as elsewhere en route.

Rocher urged Marinoni to send him some word, "and above all send me the money, because without it the Procure cannot function... If I receive nothing from you, I shall be forced to my great displeasure to leave your missionaries at the mercy of the natives." The 400 pounds sterling owed to Joubert, he said, were equivalent to 10,000 [French] francs. He added that it would be necessary to send supplies to the missionaries again in May.[3]

Marinoni's letter of 30 July 1854 finally reached Rocher on 13 November with two bills of exchange, one for 700 pounds sterling and another for 400 pounds. "It will no doubt surprise you," Rocher told Marinoni one week later, "when I say that I shall not be able to touch the 1,100 pounds sterling that you sent me until after about nine months. The two bills are payable to a bank in London and I was obliged to send them to that address." It would have been possible to cash them at a bank in Sydney, he said, but if something unforeseen were to happen, he would be obliged to reimburse the Sydney bank for the total amount plus a fee of 25 percent to cover interest and charges. He asked that Marinoni in the future send such bills of exchange to the London bank concerned, which would then credit Rocher's account at the Sydney bank.

A second packet from Marinoni dated 7 August 1854 also arrived on 13 November containing numerous letters for the missionaries at Woodlark and Rooke. "These letters arrived just in time," Rocher told Marinoni, "because on the following day I was able to

---

2. PIME: AME 11:799–801, Mazzucconi to Marinoni, 12 May 1855.
3. Ibid., 28:803–5, Rocher to Marinoni, 24 October 1854.

send them with a brig, [the *Phantom*], which is to meet the schooner *Jeune Lucie* in the vicinity of Woodlark."[4]

Mazzucconi had learned from Rocher of the difficulty with the bills of exchange and told Marinoni on 12 May 1855 that he and Rocher were still waiting for a reply from the London bank. "If the money arrives, we shall have the pleasure of satisfying Mr. Joubert, who loaned us money for hiring the services of his ship last year. We shall also be able to fit out a ship for the current year." This meant, however, that nearly all the London money would be spent by the time it arrived. "For the coming year we shall need more," Mazzucconi said. "Our good Father Rocher says that he would be pleased to receive 1,200 pounds sterling, that is, 30,000 [French] francs."

Waiting for news from Marinoni, which would "make us aware of our situation, is the reason why we are postponing the fitting out of a ship . . . ," Mazzucconi added. But he could not wait much longer, because the missionaries at Rooke and Woodlark had "received provisions for only six months, and more than four of these months have already passed . . . So in two or three months I hope to be able to return to the islands. . . ." Prefect Apostolic Reina "will be greatly surprised at seeing me arrive all alone," Mazzucconi said, "and will ask me: 'Where are your companions?' And I shall answer: 'My companions are in Madras or in Calcutta.' I shall then give him the advice of the Reverend Marist Fathers, namely, that it would perhaps be best for us to assemble in Sydney and there await orders. . . . The purpose would be to gain a year's time, to restore our health and to avoid the great expense of having the ship come a second time, probably to take us away."[5]

Meanwhile the missionaries in Woodlark had seen relations between themselves and their people become steadily worse. They were blamed for deaths and the plagues that had afflicted the island. Raimondi wrote that he had become a living corpse, just like Salerio and Tacchini. Because all three were famished and in need of food, they approached a family considered to be their special friends. The missionaries merely asked for a simple vegetable called taro. But "they refused to give us some, even though they had taros in abundance," Raimondi said. And when the local people "saw us sick, they kept far away from us, as if we were people who had been struck by the vengeance of their gods."[6]

Beyond the boundary of Saint Michael's Village, Salerio said no one could be found "who would come near us . . . And in our very presence they practiced deceit, dissimulation, flattery and fraud to promote their own interests and greed. Their conversations were filled with mockery, rude expressions and derision. In their opinion we were people without parents, without friends, having neither a roof over our heads nor a home. We were merely hungry vagabonds. Even in the open they would steal as much as they could [from us]. And their insults were so revolting, you could hardly believe it! This is the relationship that we have had with them. . . ."

4. Ibid., 807f, Rocher to Marinoni, 20 November 1854.
5. Ibid., 11:799–801, Mazzucconi to Marinoni, 12 May 1855.
6. *Beatificationis Positio*, 296, n. 34, Raimondi to Gioachino Olivares, 20 December 1855.

Because the people of Woodlark could not keep a secret, Salerio was aware that "they had consulted among themselves and more than once had made up their minds" to annihilate the missionaries. It was also common knowledge that Salerio was waiting for new missionaries to arrive from Europe. So "the chiefs along with the important men and the boldest warriors on the island had conspired to take possession of the ship on its arrival."

The plan had been carefully worked out, Salerio said. One group was "to attack those of us who were on land" and simultaneously "to attack crew members on shore busily unloading our freight. At the same time a second group was to attack the rest of the crew on board. In case of difficulty this group was to make holes in the vessel and sink it! They hoped that the new companions whom we expected would be aboard ship," Salerio said. "By simultaneously killing all of us they felt that no news would find its way to those who knew us and so nobody would come to take revenge. I myself heard them discussing the opportuneness and nature of their operations," Salerio said. "And I heard them incite one another by saying that it was easy to do and highly profitable."

This was the climate in which Salerio, Raimondi, and Tacchini were living in late April 1855 when the 140-ton brig *Phantom* under command of Captain Dalmagne glided into Guasopa Harbor. "On the afternoon of the day on which the vessel arrived in port," Salerio said, ". . . the brother of the Chief was in a frenzy trying to induce some visitors from the d'Entrecasteaux Islands and from New Guinea . . . to lend their support. But they did not want to do so. Two rifle shots, which were fired from the vessel by chance at that very moment, filled all with such fright that they fled into the woods."[7]

The *Phantom* had reached Woodlark with letters for the missionaries before the end of April 1855, the very month in which Mazzucconi had written to director Marinoni that the brig with all of their mail had "probably" been lost at sea. Dalmagne gave the missionaries their long-awaited letters that had been written in Europe in August 1854. But he had no news for them about further personnel. Salerio was especially pleased that Dalmagne, his old friend, was in command of the *Phantom*. It was he who had brought Reina and the others to Woodlark and then to Rooke aboard the *Jeune Lucie* back in 1852. In 1853 he had returned with the *Supply*, and now he was back in 1855 with the *Phantom*.

Salerio, superior of the Woodlark mission, had been out of touch with Prefect Apostolic Reina for eighteen months. He noticed that in the bundle of mail going to Rooke there were letters for Reina from Cardinal Prefect Fransoni,[8] from Bishop Ramazzotti, and from director Marinoni.[9] Believing that they contained attitudes on their mission work in Oceania, and being eager to discuss mission strategy and the mission's future with Reina, he wanted to accompany Captain Dalmagne, who was taking the mail to Rooke. At first Dalmagne hesitated, since no return trip from Rooke to Woodlark was scheduled for the

---

7. Ibid., 295–97, Salerio to Marinoni, 24 September 1855.
8. See PIME: AME 11:151, Reina to Fransoni, 3 September 1855.
9. See ibid., 167, Reina to Marinoni, 25 September 1855.

Phantom.¹⁰ His orders were to sail from Rooke to New Britain, to the Solomon Islands and to New Georgia for trade, and then return to Sydney. But Dalmagne had a soft spot in his heart for these young men whom he himself had brought to these ends of the earth. Taking matters into his own hands, Dalmagne agreed to take Salerio to Rooke and promised to return him to Woodlark, where Raimondi and Tacchini would await his return.

The *Phantom* sailed from Woodlark on 1 May 1855, and on 3 May it sighted the southern coast of New Britain just west of Awio Bay. On 4 May it sailed westward along the New Britain coast and that evening entered Dampier Strait, which separates New Britain from Rooke Island. It was 9 p.m. when the brig passed Ritter Island. At 9 o'clock the following morning, Saturday, 5 May 1855, the *Phantom* entered Nurua Harbor at Rooke.¹¹

Seeing the brig with Salerio and Dalmagne aboard, Reina and Ambrosoli rejoiced, but they were disheartened at seeing no new personnel. They told their visitors of Corti's death and of Mazzucconi's departure aboard the *Jeune Lucie* in late January for Sydney. Reina and Ambrosoli then received their first mail from Europe in eighteen and a half months.¹² The enclosed official letters from Cardinal Fransoni, Bishop Ramazzotti, and director Marinoni, however, all told the same story: no new personnel would be sent to them until the Oceania mission had become established and had started to produce results.

Up to this time Reina and Ambrosoli had been living peacefully at Rooke, experiencing bouts of fever, "but not so strong as in the first year," Reina said. "Nor did we meet any opposition; the reason was that we had adopted a negative method, not speaking of anything except natural truths. We did this by holding conversations, but without referring to morality except in cases so repugnant to nature that the people themselves understood it, like killing babies, burying sick people who had not yet died, and so on."

Reina and Ambrosoli were convinced that "few of the present generation will be converted without a miracle of grace." They had ransomed a baby girl and a baby boy, both of whom would otherwise have been killed by their parents. Three more babies had been promised to them. "Our hopes were all founded on the babies that we could save," Reina said, since "according to a custom on the island they would become our children unconditionally." The families, however, did not give up these children "in deference to our principles, but only to make themselves our friends and so obtain a bit more iron."

To this difficulty of making progress with the people, Reina said, there "must be added our state of constant sickness. We had decided to move our house to a place somewhat farther away from the swamps. But the effort was too great a burden for us, since we were so easily subject to fever." Had they asked for help, the local people "would have despised

---

10. Reina told Marinoni that Captain Dalmagne "did not intend to go back to Woodlark" with the *Phantom*, "if Salerio had not been aboard." See ibid., 155, Reina to Marinoni, 3 September 1855.

11. RIP: R B-N.2, N.1, Carlo Salerio, "Giornale di Viaggio," 1–5 May 1855. New Britain came in sight when the *Phantom* was at 149°55′ east longitude.

12. The previous mail was brought to Rooke by the *Supply* on 19 October 1853; Dalmagne was also captain of that ship.

us for having shown need of them," he said. Reina also wondered about the advisability of new personnel arriving, "since they would almost certainly be exposed to very severe sicknesses. And if none should arrive, how can we continue the mission?"[13]

It was Salerio's arrival that "persuaded me to leave Rooke," Reina said, "since there were only two of us. We were both sick and there was no hope of getting additional personnel.... We were also exposing ourselves without reason." Salerio wanted Reina to see the Woodlark mission for himself "and judge whether it should be abandoned ..." But he himself "did not want to be responsible for this decision in the sight of God," Reina said. "He left the whole burden to me."[14]

Salerio told Reina how the natives at Woodlark "more than once" had threatened to kill him and the other two missionaries, and how from the time of their arrival in Woodlark on 8 October 1852, they had constantly been plagued with open sores, particularly on their legs. They had considered themselves fortunate, however, not having to suffer from fever like the missionaries at Rooke. But to their great surprise after a two-year reprieve, they began having severe fever attacks as well.[15] It was this news from Woodlark, Reina said, as well as the absence of Mazzucconi, the death of Corti, the state of his own health and that of Ambrosoli, "which made me decide to take advantage of the ship that had to return to Woodlark. In this way we could reunite our forces there. The presence of two more of our men at Woodlark made us hope that this would prove a salutary jolt for the natives there."[16]

Arrangements were made by Reina with Captain Dalmagne to take him and Ambrosoli along with Salerio to Woodlark. They went aboard on Wednesday, 9 May 1855, but there was a calm that day and the brig could not sail.[17] "We left Rooke on 10 May," Reina said. "The natives showed some displeasure, but nevertheless promised to keep our house intact, since we could not take it along. As we painfully bade farewell to these people, we asked God to bless them, since they should have been our first children."[18]

Since the *Phantom* was not chartered by the Milan missionaries, it took a roundabout way from Rooke back to Woodlark, engaging in commerce wherever it went. From 11 to 16 May it sailed along the northwest coast of New Britain, and on 17 May it headed for Saint George's Channel between New Britain and New Ireland. By 20 May it was in the vicinity of Port Praslin (now Gower Harbor) at the southwestern tip of New Ireland. It reached the northern cape of Buka in the Solomon Islands on 22 May, was kept at a standstill there for

---

13. PIME: AME 11:155f, Reina to Marinoni, 3 September 1855.

14. Ibid., 167, Reina to Marinoni, 25 September 1855.

15. See *Beatificationis Positio*, 291, Reina to the Association for the Propagation of the Faith in Lyon, 3 September 1855.

16. PIME: AME 11:152, Reina to Fransoni, 3 September 1855.

17. RIP: R B-N.2, N.1, Carlo Salerio, "Giornale di Viaggio," 9 May 1855.

18. PIME: AME 11:156, Reina to Marinoni, 3 September 1855.

almost five days because of a calm, and sailed along the coasts of Buka and Bougainville on 29 May.

On 30 May the *Phantom* began its voyage from the Solomon Islands across the Solomon Sea to the Trobriand Islands and then toward Woodlark, which it almost reached by 7 June. But on that day a storm blew the *Phantom* back across the Solomon Sea toward Bougainville, which came in sight on 8 June. By Sunday, 10 June, the *Phantom* had again traversed the Solomon Sea and sighted Madau Island alongside Woodlark. But Captain Dalmagne ran into "very strong and always contrary winds" on the northern coast of Woodlark, and it took him an unbelievable seven days of constant battling with the winds simply to get to the southern side of the island and into Guasopa Harbor. It was nighttime on Sunday, 17 June 1855, when he guided the *Phantom* into the harbor. As Salerio noted in his journal, the ship scraped bottom on entering.[19]

This was at least the tenth time since 1850 that Dalmagne, coming from Sydney or from Rooke, had entered Guasopa Harbor as captain of a ship.[20] The harbor was treacherous, as Salerio pointed out on a map that he later published. It abounded in low-lying and extensive coral reefs, sandbars, and large breakers. The passages giving access to the harbor were shallow and dangerous, and there was a barrier reef on the west end of the harbor. So even an experienced captain like Dalmagne could find himself in difficulty, particularly with a 140-ton brig like the *Phantom*.[21]

Captain Dalmagne could not have known that he was running a race with time and that he was losing. In the Solomon Islands he had lost five days because of calms; in the Solomon Sea and at Woodlark he had lost ten more days because of storms.

During the thirty-nine days that it had taken the *Phantom* to get from Rooke to Woodlark, Reina had much time to discuss mission strategy with Salerio, who was convinced that Woodlark should also be abandoned. "There were moments when I myself was persuaded to abandon it . . . ," Reina said. During the voyage, however, he made no decision either way. "In fact, there were days when I was determined beyond the slightest doubt to remain at Woodlark, if for no other reason but to make one last attempt. And, what is more, I wanted to see for myself whether that mission should, in fact, be abandoned. You see, I was afraid that the fevers, which for the past three months had afflicted the men at Woodlark," may have deprived them of sound judgment in the matter. They might "too easily have been inclined to judge that all hope was lost."

Reina had to admit, however, that there were days during the voyage when he was very much in doubt about remaining at Woodlark. The thought would suddenly come to him: "Would it not be better for us to go to Sydney to regain our health and so be better prepared to obey," if our superiors "might want to send us elsewhere"? Explaining his

19. RIP: R B-N.2, N.1, Carlo Salerio, "Giornale di Viaggio," 9 May to 17 June 1855.
20. See Hosie, "French Mission," 416–18.
21. Salerio's map was originally published in *Petermanns Geographische Mitteilungen* in 1862 (pp. 341–44) with German legends. It was reprinted by Tragella in *Missioni estere*, 1:304 (adjoining plate).

dilemma later to director Marinoni, Reina said: "I read and reread your letter of 7 August 1854[22] as well as that of Bishop Ramazotti and also the copy of those considerations which you kindly sent me. In view of the circumstances in which we found ourselves, I did not know whether I would fulfill the will of my superiors better by retreating to Sydney or by remaining at Woodlark. The idea of withdrawing seemed more reasonable to me, but at the same time it was a bold act. I feared that this stand was perhaps due to my own capriciousness—I might even say resentment—over no one wishing to send us additional personnel. . . ." At times the thought also came to mind "of the bad impression that our retreat would create in Europe."[23]

The firm resolve of continuing the Woodlark mission, which Reina had on leaving Rooke, was considerably undermined after discussing the matter repeatedly with Salerio during the thirty-nine days when they were en route to Woodlark. On reaching Woodlark, he asked Fathers Salerio, Raimondi, and Ambrosoli to offer Masses and to pray to God for the grace of making a wise decision on whether or not Woodlark should also be abandoned. He wanted Salerio and Raimondi particularly to reflect well "on the state of their mission in order to be able to give a definitive answer" when the time came for requesting their views.

Salerio and Raimondi had sufficient time to make up their minds, because Captain Dalmagne "had to remain for fifteen days or more" at Woodlark "in order to make some necessary repairs on his ship," which had suffered severe damage from the ten days of winds and storms. When Reina finally asked "whether we should abandon this mission," both Salerio and Raimondi "stated forcefully that it ought to be abandoned. No matter how much I tried to oppose them," Reina said, "the reasons that I gave were always refuted victoriously by them."

The two missionaries did not insist, however, that Woodlark had to be abandoned at once. They were prepared to continue working there with Catechist Tacchini until a decision arrived from authorities in Europe. One of their reasons for saying that the mission "had to be abandoned" was that "the money and effort being put into it were all of no avail. Actually, if I may judge from what I myself was able to observe during our sojourn there of three weeks," Reina said, "I found that the people there were different from the people at Rooke only in externals, being more civil and polite. But as for cupidity and immorality they were the same." Added to this was "their affected character and their duplicity. They also had a really strong contempt for whites, which made them so bold that one really had

---

22. There is no copy of this letter of 7 August 1854 in the PIME Archives. See Letter, Father Francesco Frumento to Wiltgen, 8 October 1985.

23. The anxiety expressed by Reina in this paragraph shows that Maestrini in *Mazzucconi*, 163, is misinformed when he says that Reina decided "to follow Rome's suggestion to leave Woodlark and return to Sydney. . . ." Had such a suggestion come from Rome, Reina would have had no reason for being filled with such great anxiety over his decision to return to Sydney. Maestrini repeats the misinformation on pp. 169 and 170.

to fear for his life. These qualities had not yet manifested themselves at Rooke and had not yet become the dominating spirit of our people."

Numerous other reasons prompted Prefect Apostolic Reina to abandon Woodlark. First of all the Marists had been unsuccessful with their various mission methods at Woodlark over a period of six years. Salerio and Raimondi told Reina that "the Marists had begun their mission with extensive gift-giving, caring for all the needs of the natives and enduring great fatigue by going to various parts of the island to give them instructions. They did this for the first three years. Seeing that this brought no results and observing how the natives sought nothing but their own profit at every turn, experiencing also the contempt in which they were held by the natives, they sent some boys to Sydney who returned worse than they were before." Father Thomassin then opened a school at Woodlark for thirty boys where he taught and fed them for an entire year. This experiment went well as long as the hunger period lasted "and as long as there was a guarantee of having new pieces of iron." But later all left, one after the other. When Thomassin left Woodlark for Sydney in November 1853, he told Salerio and Raimondi "that he would have no doubts of conscience in abandoning that mission. Father Frémont repeated the same thing."

When Salerio was head of the Woodlark mission, "He tried for some time the method of not speaking about religion anymore and not giving the people much iron." In this way, Reina said, he hoped "to be able better to recognize those who through conviction—and not through self-interest—approached the missionaries. But this attempt, as well as Saint Michael's Village, had both failed."

Added to this was the public derision inflicted upon the missionaries, the constant vexing to which they were subjected, and the plotting on the part of the people to kill them. "To all appearances the matter was serious," Reina said, "because all the chiefs were also against them." The people became even more impudent when they saw the missionaries sick and when they succeeded in massacring with such great facility those who were shipwrecked here, as Salerio has written to you." Reina told Marinoni that "these reasons seem to be more than sufficient for our decision to abandon Woodlark."

Reina found even further support for his decision to abandon Woodlark in the letters given to him by Dalmagne. From them it appeared that Rome was "ready to withdraw" the pioneers, "rather than expose them to death from so much suffering, unless there was more assuring news about the probable progress of these missions." In fact "from these letters it seemed almost certain that we were to be recalled from Oceania," Reina said.

Since Salerio and Raimondi definitely wanted to abandon Woodlark, Reina asked whether it might be wise to remain there until Mazzucconi arrived with a ship from Sydney "and then have it transport us to another part of our vicariate"[24] for launching missionary work anew? Or "would it be better to take advantage" of the *Phantom* already at Woodlark "and go to Sydney to restore our health"? Salerio and Raimondi pointed out that it could

---

24. Reina incorrectly refers to his territory as a vicariate; five years earlier, on 11 August 1850, it had been reduced to mission status. See chap. 3.

take several months for Mazzucconi's ship to arrive. And meanwhile what would they do in Woodlark? It was useless to teach religion to the people, because they wanted to hear nothing at all about it. And so the only thing that one could do while waiting in Woodlark would be "to give them iron to keep them quiet."

The missionaries had heard from Captain Dalmagne that the *Phantom* would be visiting New Georgia on its return voyage to Sydney. "Since we had to pass it, we even got the idea of making a foundation in New Georgia," Reina said. "But making a new foundation there while we were in such bad health seemed to me far too premature an action to take. It also appeared to be a step that was not conformable to the will of our Superiors, who—as we knew—were in doubt as to whether or not they should leave us in these lands." All sensed the gravity of these questions, Reina said, "and for some days we were in doubt. We were abandoning the post assigned to us by our superiors and by Providence; we were anticipating a decision which Propaganda was on the point of making on whether we were to remain in these missions or not; and we were making ourselves the cause for the decline of our Seminary in public esteem."

But on the other hand, Reina continued, "we were leaving the vicariate[25] only temporarily for reasons of health. We also hoped that [in Rome] the decisions would already have been made by the time news reached Europe of the procedure that we had followed. We would also gain time if our orders were to reach us after our having some months of rest in Sydney, that is, after we had regained our health, God willing! If on the contrary a decision were to reach us while we were still in the islands, it would not be possible immediately to take up the assignment without our health first being restored to some extent."

Furthermore, Reina said, "We hoped to arrive in time to stop the ship which was supposed to bring Mazzucconi and our provisions, something that would save us a great deal of money. This was all the more true because the ship, which was to take us to Sydney, would not cost us any more than a few casks of salted meat which we had to give to the captain."

The day eventually came for taking the final vote: should they all sail with the *Phantom* to Sydney and, while recuperating there, await new orders? "We prayed to God," Reina said, "and we offered him the anguish and the doubts which filled our hearts. Our vote to leave was unanimous. May it all be for the glory of God." Reina told Marinoni: "I do not intend to convince you that what we did was done well. I merely wish to reassure you of the good intentions of my companions and of their lively desire to do the will of their Superiors."[26]

Salerio informed Marinoni that on the very day when he arrived back in Woodlark with the *Phantom*, "the old Chief died and left as his heirs a good number of minor princes, all of whom tried to get power and will end up destroying one another." Serious quarreling

---

25. See previous note.

26. The numerous deliberations given above on whether Woodlark should be abandoned or not are found in PIME: AME 11:155–58, Reina to Marinoni, 3 September 1855; PIME: AME 11:167–69, Reina to Marinoni, 25 September 1855.

started at once among Guasopa Harbor villages, which began waging war with villages in nearby Ravat Bay. This civil war made living on land so precarious for the missionaries that they boarded the *Phantom* on 1 July and lived aboard until they left Woodlark. The ransomed babies, of course, had meanwhile been returned to their families.

In addition to tiny Maria, who had died, there was another bright spot on the Woodlark horizon for the missionaries from Milan. It was a young man described by Salerio as "the best talented youth and the one with the most courteous manners, the same one who had gone to Sydney with Father Montrouzier and to Rooke with Father Frémont." His name was Puarer.[27] He had always lived in the house of the missionaries, Salerio said, and it seemed likely that one day he would "decide resolutely in favor of our religion." When this young man "learned that we would have to leave, he asked if he could come with us. He was despised by others on the island because he had lived with us so much. This annoyed him, causing him to become even more attached to us, and this made us believe that his request was sincerely meant. To refuse would have been both scandalous and detrimental. We spoke about it with the captain and he agreed to take him aboard, even giving the lad hope that he would be returned to Woodlark if he should become dissatisfied with remaining among Europeans."

Puarer joined the missionaries during the first ten days of July when they were already living aboard the *Phantom*. "But then secretly one morning, without his telling us goodbye, we saw him disappear aboard a canoe which had come to get him," Salerio said. Convinced that the young man was acting under pressure, Salerio that very same day asked Captain Dalmagne for the use of his whaleboat. "With it I went back to the village to find out for myself whether it was his decision to remain there. At the same time I provided him with the means to rejoin us, if what he had done was nothing else but giving in to pressure from his relatives. But he insisted that he did not want to join us and that he had never wanted to join us.... That same night his brother died."

Greatly disillusioned, Salerio returned to the ship wondering whether anyone could believe "that all the eagerness and happiness" manifested by Puarer "was nothing else but cunning pretense to steal from us a few presents for his relatives. Not even we could believe it...." Then toward evening on 10 July 1855 the *Phantom* weighed anchor, glided out of Guasopa Harbor, and headed for New Georgia in the Solomon Islands.[28]

"When we left," Reina said, "there was not even one who wished to follow us, not even one who said: 'How shall we save our souls?' Instead they all said: 'From now on we shall have no more iron!' Not one of the younger or older boys, whose education we mis-

---

27. Salerio does not name the youth. But when Frémont accompanied the Milan missionaries to Rooke, he took along Puarer from Woodlark. See chap. 10, pp. 153–54.

28. *Beatificationis Positio*, 295–98, Salerio to Marinoni, 24 September 1855. For the stay aboard ship and the departure, see RIP: R B-N.2, N.1, Carlo Salerio, "Giornale di Viaggio," 1 to 10 July 1855. Gheddo in *Mazzucconi*, 221, incorrectly says that the missionaries left Woodlark "on 17 July with a ship that happened to be passing by."

sionaries had taken so much to heart, not a single person of either sex who so very easily had been moved by the principal truths of our faith, no, not one of these uttered a word of regret."[29] Salerio's comment was: "And so we departed with the certainty that we were leaving behind not a single sad heart...."[30]

Thirty-one months earlier, after being in Woodlark for only eight weeks, Salerio had described his new mission for Marinoni as follows: "The field which the Lord has assigned to your sons, Beloved Superior, is a thorny one. It is full of poison and is under the control of seven demons.... Here the missionary enjoys neither the confidence, nor the love and still less the respect of the population. He is not recognized as a minister of religion. And to this very day, after five years and two months of missionary work [by the Marists], he would be butchered and driven away if he did not offer some hope of material advantages for the natives.... Although the people do not yet recognize a missionary as a minister of God, they at least say that the *Sinap* of the *Gumanum* is good...," that is, the Religion of the Men with Iron is good. The name used locally for missionaries was "Men with Iron."

Iron, Salerio said, "is the only reason" that the missionaries "have not been driven out or massacred on the many occasions when this question has been discussed." Despite the low opinion which they have of the missionary, he added, "They have an extraordinary fear of him and they are not able to say why. They refrain from committing many abuses and from practicing many superstitions simply because they fear the *Gumanum*...." In that early report Salerio warned Marinoni that "for a long time" he would have to send missionaries to Woodlark "to sow and not to reap, to water with their sweat and perhaps with their blood...."[31] Captain Dalmagne had beautiful weather and a good wind for his voyage to New Georgia, which came in sight on 12 July. His passengers may have recalled that their first voyage with him in 1852 from Sydney to Woodlark was via New Georgia and had lasted seventeen days.[32] If their present voyage in the opposite direction were to last that long, they would reach Sydney by 26 July.

As in the case of every voyage taken by Salerio, he faithfully indicated in his journal what islands and ports were visited, what the weather was like, what the latitude and longitude were at noon each day, and whatever happened of particular interest. From 13 to 20 July the *Phantom* sailed along the coasts of New Georgia, he said, visiting places like Vanunga, Simbo, and Baguatia. After stopping at Guadalcanal on 22 and 23 July, the brig headed southwest for Australia. On 25 July, the sixteenth day of the voyage, they were still in the Solomon Islands just west of Rennell Island, and on 31 July they were in the Coral Sea Basin opposite northern Queensland between Cooktown and Port Douglas.

On 4 August, when they were approximately at the latitude of Townsville, Salerio wrote, "The vessel has been leaking for some days." Then on the following day, Sunday, 5

---

29. PIME: AME 11:168, Reina to Marinoni, 25 September 1855.
30. *Beatificationis Positio*, 295–98, Salerio to Marinoni, 24 September 1855.
31. Ibid., 286f, Salerio to Marinoni, 4 December 1852.
32. See chap. 10, pp. 148–49.

August 1855, the *Phantom* ran into a calm, advancing southward no more than one degree and ten minutes in the next five days. It took two more days—until 12 August—for the *Phantom* to advance another degree.³³ (One degree is approximately 61 nautical miles, 70 statute miles, or 112 kilometers.) In Sydney on the following day, Monday, 13 August 1855, Father Rocher, head of the Marist Center, chartered the 153-ton brig *Gazelle* for the Milan missionaries. The cost for chartering this ship, Mazzucconi said, was "480 pounds sterling for going directly from Sydney to Woodlark and from Woodlark to Rooke." If he were to find all of his colleagues in Woodlark, having no need of going to Rooke, "the price will be only 410 pounds sterling." If on the other hand the missionaries at Rooke wanted to go to Woodlark, or if all the missionaries already were at Woodlark and wanted to go to Sydney, "the captain will have to take them there without additional payment."

Rocher had decided to charter the *Gazelle* on 13 August because he "was beginning to fear that he had delayed too long" in sending a ship to Woodlark and Rooke. In January the missionaries there had received supplies for only six months.³⁴ Rocher in October had told Marinoni that it would be necessary to send new supplies in May.³⁵

Mazzucconi's four-month stay in Sydney had restored him to excellent health, and his black teeth had begun to turn white again.³⁶ In those four months he had received only one letter. It came from director Marinoni, was dated 24 February 1855, and had arrived on 30 June with the mail vessel *Marco Polo*. It brought news about the departure of missionaries for various stations in Asia, about the hopes of the Milan Mission Seminary, and about the dogma of the Immaculate Conception being defined on 8 December 1854.³⁷ The *Marco Polo* of 30 June had also brought the bills of exchange that Rocher in November 1854 had sent to a London bank for rectification. "Thanks be to God, everything is now in order," Mazzucconi said.³⁸ He pointed out to Marinoni, however, that all the money sent from Europe for the current year had been used for chartering the *Gazelle* and for purchasing the provisions that he was taking to the missionaries of Woodlark and Rooke. And so "for the coming year we shall be in need of the same amount again," he said.³⁹

---

33. RIP: R B-N.2, N.1, Carlo Salerio, "Giornale di Viaggio," 10 July to 12 August 1855.

34. Mazzucconi, *Scritti*, 268f, Mazzucconi to Marinoni, 16 August 1855. Mazzucconi in *Scritti*, 269, calls the *Gazelle* a schooner, and so does Hosie in "French Mission," 418. But Rocher, who regularly chartered ships for the Marists and for the Milan missionaries, must have been better informed. He calls the *Gazelle* a brig. See PIME: AME 28:816, Rocher to Marinoni, 19 April 1856. It is also listed as a brig of 153 tons in the 1855 volume of *Lloyd's Register of British and Foreign Shipping* under G, No. 49.

35. See n. 3.

36. *Beatificationis Positio*, p. 292, Reina to the Association for the Propagation of the Faith in Lyon, 3 September 1855; Mazzucconi, *Scritti*, 254, Mazzucconi to his family, 12 May 1855.

37. Mazzucconi, *Scritti*, 265, Mazzucconi to Marinoni, 16 July 1855.

38. Ibid., 267.

39. Ibid., 269, Mazzucconi to Marinoni, 16 August 1855.

Bishop Bataillon, vicar apostolic of Central Oceania, had been at the Marist Supply Center in Tarban Creek since mid-July 1855.[40] Early during his stay he had asked Mazzucconi for news about the missions in Woodlark and Rooke, expressing deep interest in and great concern for what was happening there. In later conversations he repeatedly expressed his eagerness to have the missionaries of the Milan Seminary take up work in the Fiji Archipelago of his vicariate. "Then yesterday evening," Mazzucconi told Marinoni in a special letter on 16 August 1855, "when he realized that I would be leaving for Woodlark and Rooke within three or four days, he took me to his room and asked me to write to my good Superior about his desire of having our Missionaries in that Archipelago."

Two possible ways were suggested by Bataillon for realizing his proposal, and he left the choice up to Marinoni. First, the missionaries of the Milan Seminary could "come to the Fiji Archipelago for the present simply as assistants, and allow time and circumstance to determine the opportune moment for separating that Archipelago from the Central Vicariate. At that time it would become a mission entrusted exclusively to the Milan Seminary." In this case "Bataillon promises that the Italian Missionaries will enjoy the same conditions as the French Missionaries, since he will provide for their needs in equal measure."

The second method was for the missionaries of the Milan Seminary "to become established for the present in one of the two large islands which principally make up the [Fiji] Archipelago, namely, in that island of the two in which there are no Marist Fathers as yet." For this part of Fiji the Very Reverend Bishop "would grant full jurisdiction immediately and the Italian Missionaries there would remain completely independent."

The vicar apostolic "spoke to me from his heart, saying how much he would like to see this plan carried out because he wished to see these peoples instructed, because the number of his missionaries was too small, and because he would be giving support to an idea presented to him some years ago by the Reverend Superior General of the Marists." Bataillon added that he would prepare a letter on the subject in his own hand for Mazzucconi to give to Prefect Apostolic Reina.[41]

When writing to his family on 16 August, Mazzucconi took leave of his father, Giacomo; of his mother, Anna; and of his eight brothers and sisters by name. "We shall all see one another again up there on high," he said, "where we shall have stars as the flooring of our dwelling."[42]

"My departure is not far off," Mazzucconi told Marinoni that same Thursday, 16 August 1855. "Tomorrow I go aboard the . . . *Gazelle* and the day after tomorrow, Saturday morning, we shall be on the high seas." Everywhere he had met people who showered him

---

40. Ibid., 265, Mazzucconi to Marinoni, 16 July 1855.

41. Ibid., 272f, Mazzucconi to Marinoni, 16 August 1855. The first sentence indicates that this letter, restricted to Bataillon's invitation to Fiji, preceded the wide-ranging letter of Mazzucconi to Marinoni of the same date found in ibid., 268–71.

42. Ibid., 275.

with favors, he said. The Marist Fathers had received him like one of their own and had lavished care upon him. As for Father Rocher, he could not have been more concerned or more helpful. "And now, on the point of my departure, he does not allow me to reimburse his office for the expenses of my stay here," Mazzucconi said. So he asked Marinoni, when writing his next letter to the superior general of the Marists, kindly "to express my gratitude and that of all my companions for the generosity and the love with which their excellent Procurator Rocher cares for all of our needs, even though he is weighed down almost to excess by other responsibilities."

Mazzucconi could have complained to Marinoni, but he did not. "I have been waiting anxiously for the mail [vessel]," he said, "hoping that I might receive prior to my leaving the letters of our relatives, some cases and perhaps even the Companions whom you told me about in your last letter. But it arrived on Saturday and the Lord wishes that I should be happy over receiving nothing. May he be doubly blessed for this. Meanwhile the season moves on and our good Companions in the islands are already out of supplies, having received only enough for six months...."[43]

Like Bataillon, Rocher also gave Mazzucconi a letter for Reina. In it he explained that there was not enough money in Reina's account for maintaining two separate missions at Rooke and Woodlark. He therefore tried to persuade Reina to concentrate his personnel in Woodlark. This would reduce food costs by making necessary only one kitchen instead of two, and it would reduce the high costs for chartering ships.[44]

The hour for the *Gazelle*'s departure finally came, and Rocher gave Mazzucconi a farewell embrace, wishing him Godspeed. Much later when recalling what happened on this day, Rocher wrote, "The undersigned certifies that the Reverend Father Mazzucconi said to me on 18 August 1855, that in the event of his death he would give to Reverend Father Reina, Prefect Apostolic of Melanesia and Micronesia, the 67 pounds sterling and 18 shillings which he left on deposit at the Procure of the Marists in Sydney."[45]

Meanwhile Captain Dalmagne was bringing Fathers Reina, Salerio, Raimondi, and Ambrosoli and Brother Tacchini safely down the east coast of Australia to Sydney in the *Phantom*. On 16 August, when Mazzucconi was writing his letters to Marinoni and his family, they could see Moreton Bay in the vicinity of Brisbane. Then within the next twenty-four hours they had their best sailing day since leaving Woodlark, because they progressed southward two degrees and thirty-five minutes. This was a greater distance southward than they had covered in the seven days from 5 to 12 August.

---

43. Ibid., 268–70, Mazzucconi to Marinoni, 16 August 1855. Father Mazzucconi here (ibid., 269) calls the *Gazelle* a schooner. But actually it was a brig. See n. 34.

44. PIME: AME 11:159, Reina to Alessandro Ripamonti, 15 September 1855.

45. Ibid., 28:819, Certified statement by Rocher, 12 August 1856. In ibid., vol. 11, p. 260, Reina incorrectly tells Marinoni on 15 June 1856 that the amount was "about 80 English pounds." Reina's words are also printed in *Beatificationis Positio*, 341.

But on 17 August 1855, the day on which Mazzucconi was to board the *Gazelle*, they were caught in a tempest at 3 p.m. at the Solitary Islands and were mercilessly driven backwards up the coast.[46] Describing the voyage Salerio said, "We had only one good day, but we had to pay for it with another most violent one . . . which pushed us backwards ninety miles in a single night." The entire voyage from Woodlark to Sydney, he said, had been "like the flight of locusts" because we were "always sailing zigzag."[47]

The *Phantom* was near Trial Bay on 20 August, near Port Macquarie on 21 August, and near Port Stephens on 22 August. About midday on Thursday, 23 August 1855, it dropped anchor at Sydney.[48] It had been en route from Woodlark for the last twenty-two days in July and for the first twenty-three days in August, totaling forty-five days.[49] This was nearly three times as long as Reina and his colleagues had anticipated.

"You can easily imagine how we felt," Reina said, "when immediately upon our arrival we learned that Father Mazzucconi—perfectly restored to health—had left for Woodlark just five days earlier!" He explained that "a long and dangerous voyage with constant adverse winds, or rather Providence who governs events according to his designs unknown to the mind of man, had caused us to arrive in Sydney only on 23 August, although we had left Rooke on 10 May." Reina said, "It was our duty to submit to the designs of Providence."[50]

Captain Dalmagne and the *Phantom* had raced with time and lost. The cause was five days of calm in Buka and Bougainville, ten days of stormy weather in the Solomon Sea and off the coast of Woodlark, fifteen days and more that were needed to repair the *Phantom* in Guasopa Harbor. Added to this were the calms and contrary winds that had plagued the route from Woodlark to Sydney. Then, to culminate the fiasco, the *Phantom* and the *Gazelle* unwittingly passed one another at sea, perhaps during a storm, perhaps in the dead of night.

Very distraught, Reina wrote to Marinoni on 3 September 1855 that he and all of his missionaries had arrived in Sydney "only on 23 August, five days after Mazzucconi had

---

46. RIP: R B-N.2, N.1, Carlo Salerio, "Giornale di Viaggio," 5 to 12, 16 and 17 August 1855. The Solitary Islands were at 154°16′ east longitude and 27°30′ south latitude.

47. PIME: AME 11:1305, Salerio to Ripamonti, 25 September 1855.

48. RIP: R B-N.2, N.1, Carlo Salerio, "Giornale di Viaggio," 20 to 23 August 1855.

49. It would seem that the first and last days of the voyage, 10 July and 23 August, should be included in the total. Salerio writing to Ripamonti incorrectly gives the total as forty-three days and also incorrectly says that the voyage ended on 22 August. See PIME: AME 11:1305, Salerio to Ripamonti, 25 September 1855. Tragella, copying Salerio's error, also says the voyage ended on 22 August, but changes Salerio's total of forty-three days to forty-five days. See Tragella, *Missioni estere*, 1:171. Reina, however, tells Cardinal Prefect Fransoni that they reached Sydney on 23 August. See PIME: AME 11:153, Reina to Fransoni, 3 September 1855. Salerio's own precise log of the voyage—contrary to what he told Ripamonti—says that the *Phantom* "dropped anchor at Sydney about mid-day on 23 August." His log also says that the *Phantom* left Woodlark "toward evening on 10 July and headed for the island of New Georgia." See RIP: R B-N.2, N.1, Carlo Salerio, "Giornale di Viaggio," 10 July and 23 August 1855. Since 10 July and 23 August were sailing days, they should also be added to the total.

50. *Beatificationis Positio*, 292, Reina to the Association for the Propagation of the Faith in Lyon, 3 September 1855.

left in good health with our boxes, with our letters, with everything."[51] He was saddened over the great financial loss represented by the unnecessary voyage, because after paying the costs on the *Gazelle*'s return, "there will be nearly nothing left over for us on our account."[52]

Reina and his missionaries nevertheless had one consolation: they had thought of the possibility that Mazzucconi's ship might pass them by. So they had left behind letters at Woodlark instructing him to return to Sydney at once.[53] They took it for granted that he would return within a month or two, not realizing the depth of "the designs of Providence" to which they would have to submit.

---

51. PIME: AME 11:158, Reina to Marinoni, 3 September 1852.
52. *Beatificationis Positio*, 160, Reina to Ripamonti, 15 September 1855.
53. See ibid., 330, Salerio to Ripamonti, 20 September 1855.

14

Gazelle Massacre at Woodlark
September 1855

ALTHOUGH THE *PHANTOM* ON ITS RETURN FROM WOODLARK HAD DROPPED ANCHOR AT Sydney about noon on Thursday, 23 August 1855, it was about 10 a.m. of the following day before Reina and his missionaries disembarked. Boarding one vessel and then another, they went six miles up the Parramatta River to Tarban Creek, where they received lodging at the Marist Center.[1]

Reina and Salerio were having violent attacks of fever every two days, and Salerio also had severe pain in his right side, which resulted from what was later diagnosed as kidney stones. He was the only one in the group immediately confined to bed. While at Woodlark he had suggested that they remain in the mission "without a house, without provisions, without iron, simply placing ourselves at the discretion of the natives." Reina also had a leg wound which, he said, "gets worse when I am sick." Within a month Raimondi and Tacchini were also having fever attacks. The only one spared was Ambrosoli.[2] Reina told director Marinoni that his group had been received "with open arms" by Father Rocher, head of the Marist Center at Tarban Creek. "Here we have an abundance of everything that is needed to restore our health. . . . Hopefully we shall recover rapidly like Mazzucconi."[3] Three weeks later he wrote, "I do not know how to describe the charity, the concern and the goodness of Father Rocher here in Sydney."[4]

As head of the abandoned mission Reina had important and urgent letters to write. For example, he had to explain to authorities in Rome and in Milan why he and his missionaries had left Melanesia without their authorization.

---

1. RIP: R B-N.2, N.1, Carlo Salerio, "Giornale di Viaggio," 23 and 24 August 1855.
2. PIME: AME 11:169, Reina to Marinoni, 25 September 1855; PIME: AME 11:227, Reina to Marinoni, 30 January 1856; Tragella, *Missioni estere*, 1:215.
3. PIME: AME 11:158, Reina to Marinoni, 3 September 1855.
4. Ibid., 168, Reina to Marinoni, 25 September 1855.

By Monday, 3 September 1855, he felt strong enough and courageous enough to write to Cardinal Prefect Fransoni of Propaganda Fide. He told the cardinal how abandoned they had felt after getting no news from any superiors for approximately eighteen months, how he at Rooke and Salerio at Woodlark had been out of touch with one another for that same amount of time, how the people of Woodlark had threatened the lives of the missionaries working there, and how Salerio had managed to visit Rooke. In addition, he explained, Mazzucconi had been sent to Sydney to recuperate, Corti had died, and Reina's own health like that of Ambrosoli was poor. All of this had prompted him and Ambrosoli to go to Woodlark, but there they found "no hope at all of having any conversions." Nor did their health and funds allow them "to start a foundation in another place." As a result they had all sailed to Sydney to recuperate, hoping in this way to prevent Mazzucconi from departing for Woodlark with new supplies.

"We understand the gravity of the decision that we have made," Reina said, "and it was the fear that we were doing something displeasing to Your Eminence and to our Superiors which made us hesitant and uneasy for a long time. Please believe me when I say that we tried to act with a pure intention, since I was fully aware of the grave responsibility which was mine before God and man. Although our sicknesses are not yet cured, we hope to be vigorous in body and spirit after a short while and so be ready once again for some other assignment. We shall remain in Sydney to await further orders from you and from Propaganda."

Reina begged Fransoni to send them anywhere he might wish. "We have no particular desires," he said, and his companions as well wanted him to assure the cardinal of this. "Our only desire is to obey in every respect our Holy Father, Your Eminence and Propaganda." He urged Fransoni to "dispose of us and do with us as Your Eminence in your wisdom sees fit." He further gave assurance that he and his missionaries were eager "to heed your voice and your commands promptly without regard to our own ideas, which we manifested on other occasions and toward which the truly paternal heart of Your Eminence had wanted to be so indulgent."[5]

On the same day Reina told director Marinoni that he would conceal from him none of the reasons which he had discussed with his missionaries and which had prompted him to abandon Rooke and Woodlark.[6] Reina also enclosed his letter to Fransoni for forwarding. He said that from it Marinoni could see his attitude and that of his missionaries toward any new orders that might come from Rome. Reina's words sounded almost like a confession: "It would be a great displeasure for us" if the Roman authorities "were to make the choice depend upon us or upon our wishes, rather than give us precise and absolute orders," he said. "We have already done wrong in manifesting our desires [earlier regarding Micronesia and Melanesia] and perhaps God has chastised us. If now the opportunity

---

5. Ibid., 151–54.
6. For the reasons for abandoning Rooke and Woodlark see chap. 13, pp. 215–21 passim.

should come to remedy what we have done badly, we would thank Providence for it." Reina also urged Marinoni "to give us precise orders without concern for our weakness and our self-love. By the help of God we hope to be ready for anything anywhere."[7]

Fearing that he had not sufficiently explained to Marinoni why he had abandoned Rooke and Woodlark, Reina sent even further details: three pages on 25 September and five pages on 19 October.[8]

Father Ripamonti, treasurer general of the Milan Foreign Missionaries, had asked Reina whether he had gone to New Guinea. "We did not go there," Reina replied.

> Fever and also the obligation in conscience of not exposing ourselves to too many dangers by living in the midst of natives so shamelessly evil, is what prohibited this step. But we did speak with inhabitants from the [New Guinea] coast opposite Rooke Island. We also wrote a small dictionary of the languages in that area where practically every village has its own language. And, should you like me to admit it, it was my intention to set up a station there upon the arrival of new personnel.
>
> After New Guinea, I planned to try opening some stations in New Britain in the area closest to Rooke Island, that is, about sixteen miles away. In those villages they speak a language closely related to that of Rooke. You might call it a dialect. After starting in this way with a foundation, it should become possible to extend [our work] gradually along the coasts of those two great land masses. Attempts could also be made to reach the interior which, in view of what we were able to learn, must be inhabited by people who are more savage and depraved than those along the coast. Contact could be maintained between these various stations either by means of native canoes or, better still, by a vessel of eight or rather ten tons owned by the mission.

But to execute such a plan "both men and money are needed," Reina said, "and we had neither one nor the other. In fact, there was even too little money for our running expenses." Ripamonti being treasurer general was responsible for obtaining the funds needed by the Milan Mission Seminary's foreign missions. In his letter he had strongly suggested that Reina could reduce the expenses of his mission by gardening and by raising herds of domestic animals. "I do not know where you got those ideas," Reina said. "In any case I feel obliged to inform you that this was impossible in the missions where we were located. I would beg you to believe me, since going into detail would take much too long.

"Let me only say that the islands in the central part [of Oceania] are much richer than ours. (At Futuna and Wallis they kill up to four hundred pigs on big feasts, whereas at Rooke the maximum was two or three.) Only after those islands had been converted to some extent were the missionaries able to introduce herds. And they were able to do this

---

7. PIME: AME 11:155–58, Reina to Marinoni, 3 September 1855.

8. Ibid., 167–69, Reina to Marinoni, 25 September 1855; ibid., 173–77, Reina to Marinoni, 19 October 1855. The date 19 October does not appear on these five pages, which no doubt accompanied Reina's letter of that date to Marinoni. For that letter see ibid., 171–72.

because of the help received from the natives. This help they gave from their hearts because of the love which they had for their missionaries."

The high costs of his mission "must be shocking news for you as treasurer," Reina said. He was convinced, however, that Ripamonti would show his customary indulgent smile and "with your usual charity you will use every means possible to help us in the straits in which we find ourselves." He was really in difficulty, he said, "because when Father Giovanni Mazzucconi returns, and when the voyage for his ship is paid, there will be on our account nearly nothing left over for us."[9]

Meanwhile, back in Europe, Mazzucconi's first letter from Sydney dated 20 April 1855 had reached Marinoni about the beginning of August. It was accompanied by others, some written by Salerio and Raimondi in Woodlark and others written by Reina and Ambrosoli in Rooke. Marinoni at once took counsel with Bishop Ramazzotti. They both agreed that Mazzucconi's letter suggesting the abandonment of Rooke and Woodlark should be sent to Cardinal Prefect Fransoni with some of the others.[10] In an accompanying note Marinoni pointed out that Mazzucconi's letter "asks of me a prompt reply, which I entrust completely to the hands of Your Eminence." It was Saturday, 4 August 1855, when Marinoni sent these letters to Fransoni.[11] That was exactly two weeks before the *Gazelle* with Mazzucconi aboard was to set sail from Sydney for Woodlark.

Thirty-three days after the *Gazelle*'s departure from Sydney, Salerio wrote in a very serious vein to treasurer general Ripamonti: "The Reverend Mazzucconi is beginning to hold us in suspense by his delay.... He should have found our letters [at Woodlark] recalling him promptly to Sydney, but he has not yet returned."

Salerio continued with a touch of satire: "Could it be that my wonderful people of Woodlark wanted him to pay the debt, which they believed had been incurred by my fabulous personality? I do not believe so. But still they are so capable, so cold-blooded when it comes to atrocities, that should an occasion present itself to them for taking some action, I would not be surprised if they were to profit from it. But a more probable conjecture would seem to be this: Since the captain was new, he would not have dared to advance far into the large and very extensive bay. In that case those in Woodlark [to whom we entrusted our letters] certainly would not have inconvenienced themselves to the extent of taking our letters" out to the ship. Mazzucconi then "would have hurried off to Rooke to say some Requiem Masses for poor Corti. Now this means another good month of waiting."[12]

---

9. PIME; AME 11:159–60, Reina to Ripamonti, 15 September 1855.

10. See ibid., 5:885, Marinoni to Mazzucconi, 7 August 1855.

11. PF: SC Oceania vol. 5 (1853–57, Part II), f. 795r.

12. PIME: AME 11:1289, Salerio to Ripamonti, 20 September 1855. In this letter Salerio mistakenly says that Mazzucconi had left for Woodlark "two months ago"; he had left only thirty-three days before Salerio wrote this letter. It is difficult to follow Salerio's logic when he says that Mazzucconi must have gone to Rooke "to say some Requiem Masses for poor Corti." Corti was alive when Mazzucconi left Rooke in late January 1855. Therefore Mazzucconi could not have known that Corti meanwhile had died and was buried in Rooke.

Then on 24 September 1855, four days after writing to Ripamonti, Salerio detailed for director Marinoni, exactly as he had done earlier for Reina, the plot conceived by the people of Woodlark against the mission. They had expected the arrival of a ship with new mission personnel and had planned to kill the crew and all the missionaries as well.[13] Then one day later, 25 September, Reina wrote optimistically to Marinoni: "We expect Mazzucconi back any day now."[14] On 19 October, however, he told Marinoni: "Don Giovanni Mazzucconi has not yet arrived."[15] Eighty days after Mazzucconi's departure Reina again wrote to Marinoni saying that he had not yet arrived. "The average time for sailing to Woodlark and returning has already passed," he said. "But nothing is more uncertain than the duration of a voyage. Perhaps the winds coming from the south, which prevailed in these past days, have delayed him. For some days, however, the wind has been coming from the northeast and this would have been favorable for him."

This letter also contained some good news. Through the French consul residing in Sydney, Reina had received a letter in Latin from Pope Pius IX dated 29 July 1854. This was in reply to Reina's own letter to the pope of 23 October 1853 written from Rooke. The pope promised to pray "that God may protect you, Beloved Son, and also your Companions... May He also bless abundantly the activities and studies in which you are engaged to bring the light of the Gospel to those peoples." Reina told Marinoni that it was "such good fortune" to receive this letter from the pope.[16]

The pope's letter was "such good fortune" for Reina because it freed him from the guilt feelings that he had been experiencing since 5 May 1855. On that day at Rooke he had received letters from Milan delivered by the *Phantom*. From them it became clear, he told Ramazzotti soon after arriving in Sydney,

> that a blunder which I made when I was with the pope has become the chief basis for those who have submitted observations against our Seminary to Rome. It pains me to hear that the Seminary and its Superiors have been submitted to such a severe trial because of me and on my account. Was it not possible to avoid all this scandal by directing the blow to the guilty one, showing that the words were said by an individual and not by the group? Or was it not possible to go farther and cut me off in order to show that the Seminary did not subscribe to what I had done?[17]

Six weeks after writing this humiliating letter to Ramazzotti, Reina received the comforting letter from the pope.

---

13. *Beatificationis Positio*, 296. For details on this plot see chap. 13, page 216.
14. PIME: AME 11:169, Reina to Marinoni, 25 September 1855.
15. Ibid., 171–72.
16. Ibid., 183–84, Reina to Marinoni, 6 November 1855. Here Reina gives the full Latin text of the letter that he received from Pope Pius IX.
17. PIME: AME 11:161, Reina to Ramazzotti, 15 September 1855.

But further worries were on his mind, because he wondered what his superiors in Rome and Milan might think of his unilateral decision to abandon the missions of Rooke and Woodlark. It was about one month after receiving the pope's letter that a letter arrived from Marinoni addressed to Mazzucconi. In view of an agreement made by Reina with Mazzucconi, he now opened the letter. "You can imagine how happy I was on reading your first words," he told Marinoni on 3 December 1855. "In them I found your approbation for what we had done after so much hesitation."[18]

What Reina interpreted as approbation was Marinoni's introductory sentence to Mazzucconi: "I am writing only to you, although I am convinced that this letter will find all of our beloved missionaries reunited in Sydney with the excellent Prefect Apostolic." As for abandoning the mission, however, "I can give you no answer. I wrote immediately to the Sacred Congregation explaining the real state of affairs and implored a prompt decision."[19]

Marinoni had wanted to know from Mazzucconi how long their food supplies had lasted, so Reina gave the answers. "Meat lasted a year and two months, biscuits lasted three months and cornmeal lasted three or four months," he said. "Wine and vinegar lasted only a very short time. Lard, salt, white flour and rice always lasted until the next ship arrived with new supplies. But let me call attention to the fact that we do not eat everything, but only a good part of the flour, rice and biscuits. The reason is that insects of every kind penetrate everywhere and make holes even in wood." Reina said that the humidity was very high at Rooke and Woodlark, and this was also responsible for the deterioration of food supplies.

"As for Mazzucconi, his tardiness is beginning to make us uneasy," Reina said. "Three and a half months have passed and both Father Rocher and Mr. Joubert, the agent, tell us that the time is up. So what should we do now? It would be best to send a ship in search of him. And if I have no money, I can take out a loan, because I am certain that the relatives of Father Giovanni [Mazzucconi] will cover the costs, if our Seminary should not be able to do so."

But this brought up another question: "Is it a good idea to send a ship now? The bad season begins this month and it is really bad. There could be some weeks of good weather from December to March; but knowing when this would be, is pure chance. It is also useless to send a ship without a missionary aboard, because no one knows the language. And you cannot put much faith in captains, because they will engage in trade instead of conducting a search. And sending a missionary in this season would be risky and imprudent."

Mazzucconi either "has perished . . . or he has not perished," Reina said. And if he did not perish, "he could have with him a year's provisions for our two missions. In that case what should we do? After talking with Father Rocher at great length this idea came to me: On receiving new orders we shall go to India, or to where Father Riva is, or elsewhere. En

18. Ibid., 187–88, 387–88, Reina to Marinoni, 3 December 1855.
19. Ibid., 5:885, Marinoni to Mazzucconi, 7 August 1855.

route we shall go via Woodlark and Rooke. But I do not say for certain that we shall do this, since plans can change."

Reina explained that no matter what decision was taken, the initial supposition always would be "that there is money available either in the Seminary or in the Mazzucconi household. The case is not altogether desperate, however, and I still have hope." Reina did suggest, however, that "it would be well to keep silent about this for the present, in order not to cause disturbances ahead of time."

With his letter he enclosed a certificate "On the death of poor Corti." He explained to Marinoni that he had indicated dropsy as the cause of death "in order to put down something. In reality, however, I do not know what the cause was. I also said that he died *at three o'clock* in the afternoon. But I am not certain about this because we had no clock. When the sky was clear, we judged by looking at the sun. But when it rained, there was nothing to look at."[20]

Back in Milan at this time—it was early December 1855—director Marinoni had just received word from Reina that he and his missionaries had arrived in Sydney after leaving Rooke and Woodlark. When informing Cardinal Prefect Fransoni of this on 8 December, Marinoni said that Mazzucconi unfortunately had left Sydney "a few days" before the other missionaries had arrived. But he added, "There is reason to hope that Providence, always so wonderful in its proposals, will also draw profit from this."[21]

Writing to a priest friend in Italy on Christmas Day, which was 129 days after Mazzucconi had left Sydney, Ambrosoli said, "I maintain that he is alive and I hope that someone will still find him."[22] Then on 4 January 1856 Reina wrote to Marinoni:

> There is still no news about Mazzucconi and by now some misfortune seems certain. All agree that it would be difficult for the ship to be lost on the high seas, because it was in good condition. It must have foundered on the reefs with which the sea from New Guinea to Woodlark is strewn. These reefs make it very difficult to navigate in those areas, which are so little known. Many ships have already returned from that region a month ago and report that they had bad weather. If a ship founders on a reef, those aboard can easily save themselves.
>
> But if there are natives around, then new dangers arise. As for the natives of Rooke, we feel safe with them, because we are well acquainted with their dispositions. Those of Woodlark, however, would be more capable of a coup than those of Rooke. But both Salerio and Raimondi maintain that they would not attack, since Mazzucconi is known there. According to native custom this is a strong guarantee for one's safety.
>
> Nothing can be predicted, however, if they arrived at other lands. In general, however, it is most unlikely for natives to kill on an initial contact. They decide to do

---

20. Ibid., 11:187–88, 387–88, Reina to Marinoni, 3 December 1855.

21. PF: CV vol. 43, f. 247rv, Marinoni to Fransoni, 8 December 1855.

22. PIME: AME 11:600, Ambrosoli to Paolo Maestri, 25 December 1855. The extract from this letter as given in *Beatificationis Positio*, 333 n. 11, is not exact.

this only after the sailors have won their confidence and begin to be malicious. But Mazzucconi knows how to deal with natives very well and also knows how to win their affection. So even in such a situation there should be reason for hope. In any case we recommend him to God, who is Lord over all that happens.

When Reina inquired about chartering a ship to go in search of Mazzucconi, he was told that at this time all shipowners would refuse. "Just about all ships from the South Seas returned to port last month," he said. "And they shall not go back to those seas again until the month of March."[23]

The Sydney Morning Herald of 22 January 1856 carried a letter to the editor dated 16 January from "A Subscriber" who said there existed "a Roman Catholic Mission" in no inviting spot in a "chain of islands, all but connected to Papua . . . In a few of the large maps are some half dozen large dots representing them, and about the largest is Woodlark. . . . There is little to tempt the trader, and he seldom visits them." *The Empire* of 14 January, the writer said, had stated that, "to succour and relieve her servants, the *Gazelle* brig . . . was especially sent, and the Rev. Mr. Marruconi [i.e., Mazzucconi], a man of eminent piety and learning, sailed in her. Before sailing, she had undergone a most complete overhaul, under the inspection of our Surveyors, by an able shipwright, and her speed was well known—her master who was also part owner, a man well qualified to perform his voyage safely and speedily.

"Up to this date nothing has been heard of her, and fears are fast giving place to despair of ever seeing her again. There is now only a hope that her crew may, if alive, be on some of the islands, perhaps, slaves—and it behooves the Government to use every exertion to try and recover them. The *Torch* ought to be able soon to give an account of them, the distance being trifling, and if she is not used in these cases—of what earthly use is she?"[24]

Another letter to the editor dated 17 January entitled "The Lost Missionary" appeared in *The Empire*: "Since you mentioned the subject [of Mazzucconi] in your copy of the 16th, many are anxious to know if the Government means to do anything, and what that is." If it should take no action, then "the Roman Catholic clergy will, I have no doubt, find plenty to subscribe to a fund to send a small screw steamer after him." The *Gazelle* had to sail along the coast of New Guinea on going to Rooke and returning, the writer said. "And if by any chance she struck on a coral reef, there is little doubt her crew, if spared by the natives, are in slavery. Most of the crew of the brig have relatives in Sydney, and their minds must indeed be anxious." The author signed as "One Willing to Add His Mite to the Good Cause, if Requisite."[25]

23. PIME: AME 11:211–12, Reina to Marinoni, 4 January 1856.

24. *The Sydney Morning Herald* (22 January 1856). For the original clipping see PIME: AME 11, fig. op. p. 223. In this and other newspaper articles Mazzucconi's name is misspelled. In *Beatificationis Positio*, 334, the date of publication is given incorrectly as 16 January 1856; that was the date on the letter to the editor.

25. For this newspaper clipping see PIME: AME 11, fig. op. p. 222. The author has not been able to learn the date of *The Empire* issue in which the letter appeared.

Reina sent Marinoni the newspaper clippings. "Not knowing who was the author of the letters," he said, "we reasoned like this: If it is a friend of Mazzucconi, he should have first come to talk with us and see what we wanted to do. If it is some person interested in taking advantage of the Mazzucconi affair in order to get money from Catholics, it is prudent for us to keep quiet and let him go ahead." But he added, "It seems certain that the two letters have been written by the shipowner himself. . . ."

But Reina could not charter a ship to look for Mazzucconi, he said, because meanwhile he had run out of money. The appeal for funds in *The Empire* apparently had been unsuccessful. Nor did Reina feel that he could personally approach the people of Sydney for funds. He therefore intended "to take out a loan," if no funds arrived from the Association for the Propagation of the Faith in Lyon, France. But it would be up to Marinoni, he said, "to decide who has to pay for it." Although he realized that the Milan seminary was poor, he had meanwhile decided not to approach the family of Mazzucconi with a request that it sacrifice some of its money, "because this seemed being rather hard, in view of the family already having sacrificed one of its very dear members."[26]

In an overall report to Cardinal Prefect Fransoni, Reina said that Mazzucconi had met with "almost certain tragedy," because "his voyage should have taken two months," whereas more than five had already passed without any news about him. As for himself, Raimondi, Ambrosoli, and Tacchini, they had all suffered from fever and other maladies for three months after reaching Sydney. Now, however, they hoped that they had recovered completely. "But Salerio, formerly superior at Woodlark, instead of getting better, had only become worse." He had kidney stones, the doctor said, "a chronic and very painful ailment," and he was unfit for further missionary work. Reina had been doubtful for a long time about what to do regarding Salerio. But Bishop Bataillon, then at Tarban Creek, and all of Reina's companions had agreed that Salerio should return to Europe.[27] The doctor had also said that Salerio would receive much better care in Europe and that the cost would not be so great as in Sydney.[28]

After protesting, shedding tears, and pleading in vain, Salerio obediently boarded the *Waterloo* on 1 February 1856. In his luggage were Reina's two latest letters for Marinoni and Fransoni. On the following day the *Waterloo* was towed out of port and began its long voyage to Gravesend, the same port on the Thames near London from which Salerio had left for Oceania so happily less than four years earlier.[29]

When director Marinoni forwarded to Cardinal Prefect Fransoni on 4 August 1855 a packet of letters from Melanesia, including Mazzucconi's of 20 April suggesting the abandonment of Rooke and Woodlark, he had asked for a prompt reply. Fransoni reacted to the letters on 21 August: "I was flattering myself that they would contain some good news

---

26. PIME: AME 11:221–23, Reina to Marinoni, 29 January 1856.
27. Ibid., 213–15, Reina to Fransoni, 28 January 1856.
28. Ibid., 211, Reina to Marinoni, 4 January 1856.
29. RIP: R B-N.2, N.1, Carlo Salerio, "Giornale di Viaggio," 1 and 2 February 1856.

about the mission," he said. But on reading them he had learned of the insurmountable difficulties experienced by the missionaries, "at least for the present," and he had seen that they had "no results whatsoever to show for their indefatigable labors.

"From the letter of Father Mazzucconi," he said, "it is also apparent to what a serious plight they have been reduced, both those in Woodlark and the others in Rooke. One cannot but approve of the plan suggested by that same Missionary [Mazzucconi] of profiting from the ship which is soon to leave Sydney and using it to transport all those praiseworthy missionaries to Australia, in order to recover somewhat from the sickness and the infirmity which they have endured, and then wait there for further orders from the Holy See." Marinoni was asked to inform Reina in Fransoni's name "that the suggested departure is approved and that new instructions will be issued as soon as possible...".[30]

Marinoni sent Reina a copy of Fransoni's letter approving the temporary abandonment of Rooke and Woodlark. This news reached Reina in time for him to reply to the cardinal through Salerio. "Your Most Reverend Eminence kindly approved in advance the decision taken by us with such great uncertainty and with such great fear...," he said.[31] But how could Fransoni by his letter of 21 August 1855 have approved "in advance" Reina's decision of 10 July 1855?

Even director Marinoni found it difficult to follow Reina's logic when forwarding his letter to Fransoni on 8 December 1855. And so he simply said, "Although the decision of the Sacred Congregation had not yet been known to him, he did not err in anticipating it."[32] Indeed the decision had not yet been known to him; it had not yet been made.

Reina had taken it for granted that the owner of the *Gazelle* would send another ship to search for it. But when Father Rocher asked the shipowner "what he intended to do, his attitude was very cold and he said simply that his ship was insured."[33] Later, when asked whether he would at least divide the costs with Reina, he "coldly replied that we would be reimbursed by the families of those who were shipwrecked, if we brought them back to Sydney."[34]

The brig *Gazelle* was the joint property of Mr. W. T. Parkins, its captain, and Mr. Champion of Geelong, and nearly the entire crew consisted of men from Sydney. The 153-ton brig had been constructed in 1839 in Bremen, Germany, and had been insured for 1,300 pounds sterling at Mr. Metcalf's office in Sydney. Its cargo had been insured for 580 pounds sterling.[35]

---

30. PIME: AME 1:153, Fransoni to Marinoni, 21 August 1855.
31. Ibid., 11:213, Reina to Fransoni, 28 January 1856. See also chap. 13, p. 220, n. 23.
32. PF: CV vol. 43, f. 247rv.
33. PIME: AME 11:222, Reina to Marinoni, 29 January 1856.
34. Ibid., 239, Reina to Marinoni, 15 April 1856.
35. See the last paragraph in both "Loss of the Brig *Gazelle* and Murder of her Crew by the Natives of Woodlark Island" in *The Sydney Morning Herald* (14 June 1856), and "Wreck of the Brig *Gazelle* and Horrible Massacre of All on Board" in *The Empire* (Sydney, 14 June 1856). The first article gives the insurance as 1,880

Mr. S. Julien, an acquaintance of Father Salerio, visited Reina at Tarban Creek in late February 1856. He requested information on the lost brig *Gazelle*, "because he wanted to approach the Governor personally and induce him to send one of the two steamers lying idly in port" to search for the *Gazelle*. "We encouraged him," Reina told Marinoni, "and we told him that one of us who knew the local language was ready to go along. He made all of us hopeful and said that in a short time he expected to be able to give us a decisive answer." Reina moreover was confident that Julien would succeed, because the captain and sailors of the *Gazelle* "have their families in Sydney and therefore many people are pressing for action."

If Julien should succeed, many advantages would follow, Reina said. "Since the vessel in question is a steamer, it can go wherever it wants and without great danger. It can also return within three weeks time and so we would have a prompt reply. Financially it is also advantageous for us, because the amount required to send a ship at my own expense" would be twenty thousand francs. Withdrawing that amount from his account with Father Rocher, he said, would mean that he would not have enough money left over for himself and his missionaries to go to their next assignment.[36]

"For the rest of this month," Father Ambrosoli wrote on 19 March 1856, "we shall wait and see whether the Government replies favorably in any way to the request made for help." He was not optimistic, however, because the interest being shown in the coming elections for a new government was "reason enough for giving up all hope—if ever I had any—that the Government is thinking of providing . . . a ship to search for Mazzucconi." Ambrosoli's premonition was correct. The government answered that they were not "certain the brig was lost on Woodlark," and so they could not dispatch a government vessel "to ascertain the fate of the Crew of the *Gazelle*."[37]

---

pounds sterling on the ship and cargo; the second gives the insurance on the ship alone as 1,300 pounds sterling. Additional details on the *Gazelle* are also in *Lloyd's Register of British and Foreign Shipping* (1855), G, No. 49.

Again, the first article repeatedly calls the captain "Parkins" and the second repeatedly calls him "Parkin." The author has used "Parkins" because the first article is signed by Father Raimondi, Captain A. Barrack of the *Favourite*, and his mate J. Bennett, all of whom can be expected to have known the name and spelled it correctly. The form "Parkins" is also found in "The Late Shipwreck and Murder in the South Seas" in *The Sydney Morning Herald* (18 June 1856), evidently an editorial. "A Master Mariner" also uses "Parkins" in his letter to the editor titled "The Woodlark Murders" in *The Empire* (Sydney, 24 June 1856) 4. *The Empire* used "Parkin" only in its early issues. *Lloyd's Register of British and Foreign Shipping* does not give the master's name in its entry on the *Gazelle*. "Parker," used by Hosie in "French Mission," p. 418, must be incorrect.

36. PIME: AME 11:235, Reina to Marinoni, 28 February 1856. The elected head of government at this time was referred to as the colonial secretary, and he was under the imperially appointed governor. Today the elected head of government is the premier. Mrs. Lyn Love, honorary research officer of the Royal Historical Society of Queensland, informed the author that "many historians use the two terms interchangeably, though this is not strictly correct." See Letter, Mrs. Love to Wiltgen, 23 September 1988.

37. PIME: AME 11:607, Ambrosoli to Federico Villoresi, 19 March 1856; "The Woodlark Murders," *The Empire* (Sydney, 24 June 1856) 4.

Rocher at Reina's request then chartered the schooner *Favourite* "to go directly to Woodlark," the island to which Mazzucconi had been instructed to go. Since the entire voyage "will last about two months," Rocher said, "the price agreed upon was 380 pounds sterling."[38] The logical choice to accompany the search vessel was Father Raimondi. He had been based at Woodlark for thirty-three months and consequently knew the people and the language of that island better than any of the others. He also knew English better than any of the others and so was best suited for life aboard ship, where the entire crew was English-speaking.[39]

On the day before leaving Sydney to look for Mazzucconi, Raimondi told Marinoni: "I shall go and search out every nook and cranny. I shall make inquiries and conduct investigations. What I want to know for certain is at least—at the very least—where he went and what happened to him. However, I still have a bit of hope that I shall find him alive. Meanwhile tell his Relatives and assure them in my name, that I shall do everything in order to find him and shall spare no efforts.... Meanwhile do not stop praying and do not stop having others pray."[40]

Raimondi left Sydney for Woodlark aboard the seventy-six-ton schooner *Favourite* on 14 April 1856, four days less than eight full months since Mazzucconi had left aboard the *Gazelle*. Captain of the *Favourite* was Mr. A. Barrack, who had been mate of the *Supply* when it visited the Italian missionaries (including Mazzucconi) at Woodlark and Rooke in 1853. If Raimondi did not find Mazzucconi at Woodlark, the *Favourite* would take him to other ports on condition that he pay 190 pounds sterling per month over and above the basic fee of 380 pounds sterling for the round trip from Sydney to Woodlark. If Raimondi judged it necessary to go farther than Woodlark, Reina had told him, "he should do so without regard to the cost and should try to return as soon as possible." He was "not to stop

---

38. PIME: AME 28:815–16, Rocher to Marinoni, 19 April 1856. Rocher, who chartered the schooner, as well as Reina, Raimondi, and Ambrosoli, regularly spell its name "Favorite." They wrote the name as it would have been spelled in French and Italian, their mother tongues. The Italian missionaries regularly Italianized the names of ships. "Favorite" is also used in "Wreck of the Brig *Gazelle*" three times. The spelling "Favourite" appears in the introductory sentence of the carefully written "Loss of the Brig *Gazelle*," calling attention to the authenticity of the report by stating: "The following account is an extract from the log of the schooner *Favourite*...." *The Shipping Gazette and Sydney General Trade List* of 16 June 1856, reporting on the return of that vessel to Sydney in the preceding week, calls the schooner *Favourite*, as does also *Lloyd's Register of British and Foreign Shipping* (1856), F, No. 102.

39. PIME: AME 11:237, Reina to Salerio, 8 April 1856. Here Reina says that originally he had designated Ambrosoli to go in search of Mazzucconi because Raimondi—knowing English better than the rest—had been assigned assistant priest at the new parish of the Marists at Kissing Point. But subsequently Ambrosoli's health worsened, there was little for Raimondi to do as assistant priest, and Father Rocher stated "that the needs of the Mission had priority over everything else." Ambrosoli, in fact, had written to Federico Villoresi as late as 19 March 1856: "On April 10th or at the latest in mid-April, I shall again be on the sea en route to Woodlark and perhaps also to Rooke in search of Mazzucconi." See PIME: AME 11:607.

40. *Beatificationis Positio*, 337, Raimondi to Marinoni, 13 April 1856.

for trade in other islands," however, "even though Mr. Joubert had stated in the contract that half of the profits would be given to the mission."[41]

On 6 May 1856, three weeks after Raimondi had left for Woodlark, Captain Dalmagne returned to Sydney aboard the *Jeune Lucie* from a voyage of nearly seven full months. He had left Sydney on 11 October 1855—eight weeks after Mazzucconi's sailing date—and during his absence he had visited Simbo, New Georgia, Santa Isabel, Three Sisters (near San Cristóbal Island), Wallis, Futuna, Rotuma, and Spirito Santo. In all those ports, he told the Italian missionaries, he had met no one who had seen Mazzucconi.

This convinced Ambrosoli that Mazzucconi for some unknown reason had become stranded at Woodlark and would surely be found there alive. When presenting this idea to Marinoni, he pointed out that Captain Parkins of the *Gazelle* had never been at Woodlark in his life, whereas Captain Barrack of the search vessel *Favourite* "has been at Woodlark three times already and also at Rooke." Had Captain Barrack never been there, Ambrosoli said with tongue-in-cheek, "I would be keeping myself ready to go in search" of Raimondi. He assured director Marinoni on 17 May 1856—nine months after Mazzucconi had left Sydney—that Raimondi "in one more month can very well be here with that poor lost fellow."[42]

When Raimondi sailed out of Sydney's Port Jackson on Monday, 14 April 1856, a rather strong south wind drove him northward toward Woodlark, which lies on nearly the same longitude as Brisbane. "By the 22nd [of April] we were in the Coral Sea," he said. There he asked himself: "Who knows, was the poor *Gazelle* perhaps shipwrecked on these reefs? So there I was on the deck with my spyglass from morning till night, looking in every direction for some sign of a shipwreck. But no sign appeared! There was nothing else but sea, sky and eternal silence. . . ."

Rocher had said that the *Favourite* would be "going directly to Woodlark," and Reina had told Raimondi that he was "not to stop for trade in other islands." Nevertheless Captain Barrack headed for New Georgia in the Solomon Islands and arrived at Cape Du Pin on Sunday, 27 April. Perhaps he expected to find the *Gazelle* there en route to Sydney. Or perhaps he had to go there in order to catch the winds and currents that would take him to Woodlark. The *Favourite* reached Baniata early Monday morning; it reached Simbo on Tuesday; and that same evening—because no trace of the *Gazelle* or Mazzucconi could be found—it sailed southwest towards Woodlark. "Then on 1 May [Thursday] we saw Uaman

---

41. PIME: AME 11:239, Reina to Marinoni, 15 April 1856. Reina says here that Joubert is the owner and that Barrack is the captain. Barrack in "Loss of the Brig *Gazelle*" is one of the signatories and calls himself "Master," that is, captain, of the *Favourite*. Hosie in "French Mission," 418, incorrectly calls Barrack the owner and Coutts the captain. In PIME: AME 11:1009, Raimondi on 20 June 1856 tells Salerio that the *Favourite* was a seventy-five-ton schooner. The copy of this letter in *Beatificationis Positio*, 351, incorrectly gives the tonnage as 43. In PIME: AME 11:612, Ambrosoli says the tonnage was seventy-six, which is the figure also used by Hosie in "French Mission," 418. *The Shipping Gazette and Sydney General Trade List* of 16 June 1856 calls the *Favourite* a seventy-six-ton schooner.

42. PIME: AME 11:612.

Peak" on Woodlark Island, Raimondi said. "I was so happy and full of hope, imagining that I would find our colleague there."[43]

On Friday, 2 May 1856, the *Favourite* was close enough to the north coast of Woodlark for Raimondi to admire "the mountains of Surao and the long strip of land from Coadeo to Uaman. I thought that we would be entering port on the following day," he said, "but a contrary wind did not allow us to pass Nubar [Island at the northeastern end of Woodlark] until Sunday morning, 4 May."[44] By noon that day the *Favourite* was at 9 degrees 14 minutes south latitude and 153 degrees 27 minutes east longitude. At 1 p.m. a slight breeze from the east-northeast arose, and so all possible sails were set.[45] This breeze pushed the *Favourite* southward under Woodlark Island and then westward toward Guasopa Harbor.

"Then at 2 o'clock that [Sunday] afternoon," Raimondi said, "the captain cried out: 'Brig *Gazelle*! Brig *Gazelle*! There she is! There she is!' We all turned toward the spot on which his eyes were fixed and there we saw a brig lying on a reef with its masts cut in half." Describing the spot for Salerio, Raimondi said: "You know well the long stretch of coral reef which extends [westward] from Uatatol Point to the first of the three Reu Islands. Well, right there, very close to Reu, but on the side facing Uatatol, is where the poor *Gazelle* suffered shipwreck."[46]

Captain Barrack's log was less dramatic than Raimondi's report, but more detailed: "Discovered a wreck—apparently a brig—lying on her [starboard] beam-ends, the lowermasts and bowsprit standing, and lower-rigging swinging about. The wreck then bore about W.N.W., distant five miles. At 2.30 p.m., abreast of the wreck, then distant 2-1/2 miles, and made out that part of her stern was knocked away, and a portion of the copper torn from the port side, also several of the planks in her bottom gone, with the daylight showing through her."[47] Captain Barrack could confirm that what he had found was "a brig ..., in every respect a total wreck."[48]

"The brig was found! Now we had to look for our companion and the crew," Raimondi said. "It was my idea that we should not proceed into port before we were able to see clearly how the Woodlark natives had received those aboard the *Gazelle*." Raimondi therefore suggested to Captain Barrack that he not take the first passageway between Reu and Oviai

---

43. These and most of the details that follow regarding Raimondi's search for Mazzucconi are taken from his sixteen-page letter addressed to Salerio on 20 June 1856 and meant as an official report to Marinoni. Salerio was well acquainted with the many place names and personal names that it contains, and so Reina had asked him to give further explanations to Marinoni, as needed. The original letter of sixteen pages is in PIME: AME 11:1009-24. Nearly the entire letter, except for what happened between 14 April and 1 May 1856, can be found in *Beatificationis Positio*, 351-61. On various spellings for "Baniata" see p. 247, n. 57.

44. *Beatificationis Positio*, 352, Raimondi to Salerio, 20 June 1856.

45. "Loss of the Brig *Gazelle*."

46. *Beatificationis Positio*, 352, Raimondi to Salerio, 20 June 1856.

47. "Loss of the Brig *Gazelle*."

48. "Wreck of the Brig *Gazelle*." This report specified that the brig was lying on its "starboard" or right side.

islands, something that the small schooner could easily have done. Rather he should come in from the west, "taking the wide passageway and dropping anchor between Oviai Island and the mainland called Lavat in the vicinity of Boaiò." This would keep the *Favourite* at a good distance from the villages near the shore of the harbor and would make maneuverability possible in case of need.[49] Captain Barrack followed this suggestion as can be seen from his log: "At 4 p.m., off the entrance, hauled up for it, and stood in, when inside hove to . . ."[50]

"On entering the harbor," Raimondi said, "we saw afar a tiny craft coming toward us. At first I thought it was a rowboat, but afterwards it appeared to be a native canoe. Then I thought that I saw a white man in it. My heart began pounding with excitement and I was just about to yell, "They're alive and one of them is coming to bring us the news!' when I noticed that all were natives."

There were six young men in the canoe and Raimondi knew them all: Tatai, Ualabau, Butunveu, Mariash, Macavas, and Teitanau. Seeming afraid to approach the ship, they kept watching from a distance.

> I then shouted: "Aveiali?" My shouting this word in their own tongue was like a thunderbolt. All of them looked around straining to see, as if they were unable to believe that someone aboard had spoken their language. As they cupped their hands over their ears to make sure it was true, I shouted louder: "Aveiali shavo remi?" On saying this, I disclosed myself to them. As soon as they saw me they shouted [my name] joyfully and contentedly, "Timoleone, Timoleone," hitting their mouths with their hands [as a sign of great excitement].
>
> This cheerfulness and pleasure over seeing me, and the fact that meanwhile no white man had appeared, began to make me suspicious. When their canoe came close to the brig, I at once asked them whether there were any whites on land. With one voice they answered: "Not one of the whites is on land." "Then where did they go?" "Uh, uh, you see, Timoleone, they took the [ship's] boat and they went uh . . . , uh . . . , uh . . . , toward the west." Tatai then said, "They went to Rooke."
>
> While telling me this Tatai reached up a small packet of paper and said, "Ioanni [Giovanni Mazzucconi] anavualab, yes, it is the letter of Ioanni." Mariash handed me another tiny packet.

What Mariash handed over was indeed a letter, but not from Mazzucconi. It was instead the letter left behind for Mazzucconi which Salerio and Raimondi had written. Tatai's packet contained no letter, but instead about twenty calling cards with "*Gazelle*" written in pencil on the back of some of them.[51] Engraved on the front was "Mr. W. T. Parkins," captain of the ill-fated *Gazelle*.[52] Raimondi asked whether Mazzucconi had given them a letter for him. No, they said; they had no other letters.

49. *Beatificationis Positio*, 353, Raimondi to Salerio, 20 June 1856.
50. "Loss of the Brig *Gazelle*."
51. *Beatificationis Positio*, 353–54, Raimondi to Salerio, 20 June 1856.
52. "Loss of the Brig *Gazelle*."

Raimondi then cross-examined the group. "But the whites, did they go ashore before leaving?" Ualabau answered, "They came ashore and then they left." Tatai shouted "No" and reprimanded Ualabau for being misinformed. "This difference of views and there being no letter from Mazzucconi, increased my fears," Raimondi said. "I then turned to the captain, telling him that it would not be prudent at all to proceed into port and I asked that he drop anchor near Oviai. And so he did."

Meanwhile night had fallen, so Raimondi sent back to their villages all of the young men except Mariash, a catechumen who said that he was the only one still living in Saint Michael's Village built by the missionaries. When Raimondi asked why he and the others had come out to the ship, he said, "In order to see who was aboard and to learn why they had come." And why were bonfires now being lit along the shore of the harbor? Raimondi asked. "In order to keep awake," came the reply. "But why are they keeping guard?" "Because they are afraid of the ship." "And why are they afraid of our ship?" "Because they took everything that was aboard the *Gazelle*." Then Mariash added quickly: "But wait! Ioanni said that once they had departed, we could take all the boxes, but we were not to touch the ship. We were to leave it intact and not destroy it."

Thinking that he might learn the true story from Mariash, Raimondi took the youth to his cabin. "I laid on the table a beautiful string of pearls that I had purchased at New Georgia, as well as a tomahawk and some pieces of iron." Raimondi said: "Look, this is all yours, if you tell me the truth." But Mariash bargained for more in return for the truth, so Raimondi took some shields from his trunk, added them to the gifts on the table, and then invited the youth to tell the truth.

"You know well that I have joined your religion," Mariash began, "and that God forbids a person to lie. So do not fear that I might tell you lies. I want to tell you everything, yes, everything that I know. Now look, the ship of Ioanni arrived early one morning. As soon as we saw it, my brother Nit, Puarer, Gunemuadu [sic] and Uliveli went to the ship to deliver the letter of Father Carlo [Salerio]. They reached the ship and gave the letter to Ioanni. Immediately after this Nit noticed that the ship was too close to the reefs and he called out to the captain, "Captain, Captain, ship no good, plenty stones sit down." "Do not worry," the captain answered. "All is well! All is well!" But while he was giving this assurance, he felt the brig strike a reef and shouted an order to the helmsman to turn. But the brig did not turn."

Mariash said that the brig had gone onto a reef and began swaying dangerously. Some of the Woodlark youths had earlier boarded it, but now became terrified, jumped down into the water, got into their canoe and drew back from the scene. "The captain meanwhile had given orders to lower the boat and to put aboard everything necessary," Mariash said. "Then your companion [Mazzucconi] called out to Puarer to approach the lowered boat in his canoe, but the canoe capsized in the waves."[53]

---

53. *Beatificationis Positio*, 353–55, Raimondi to Salerio, 20 June 1856. On various spellings for "Gunemuadu," see this chapter, p. 249, n. 62.

Describing the incident in nautical terminology Captain Barrack said, "The brig *Gazelle* being close to the reef missed stays and went on shore."[54] That is, the brig was sailing to windward, missed some tacks, and went onto a reef.

Puarer and the others were meanwhile trying to reach the capsized canoe, Mariash said, when "the captain escorted Ioanni into the boat. But when he tried to get out, the captain held him back." Raimondi asked why, and Mariash answered: "Because the captain was enraged at having lost his ship and he said that it was because of Ioanni that he had come to Woodlark." The captain had said: "Ioanni, you must share my future misfortune." "Where did they go?" Raimondi asked. "They went toward Madao." (Madao, now Madau, is an island at the western end of Woodlark.) "But because their boat was overloaded," Mariash continued, "the captain put ashore two men on an island near Madao.

"The two were on shore eating coconuts when two canoes from Madao passed by en route to Uaman. The . . . white men were invited into the canoes and accepted the offer. But the canoe which they entered capsized because it was overloaded. The owner of the canoe then became angry, took his spear and killed them. Perhaps one of the two was your companion," Mariash said, "because the men from Madao told the people at Uaman that one of the two was dressed in black like the rest of you missionaries." "And where did the others go?" Raimondi asked. "They went toward Gau [an island northwest of Madao]. I believe that the people of Gau killed them because, when Gau people came to Woodlark, they told us that they had found on the beach two or three boxes belonging to white men."

"Behold what I was able to draw out of Mariash," Raimondi told Salerio. "But this account did not satisfy me at all and I immediately recognized it as a tale invented to cover up the massacre committed by them." The more Raimondi insisted that the Guasopa Harbor villages had massacred all aboard the *Gazelle*, however, the more offended Mariash pretended to be. "Do you not know that I have taken on your religion," he said, "that I alone have remained in the village [of Saint Michael] . . . , and that I alone have stayed there to recite my prayers regularly?" He begged Raimondi to come ashore and visit the poor Village of Saint Michael, because it pained him to think that "it no longer has a missionary." Since Raimondi could get no satisfactory information from Mariash on the fate of those aboard the *Gazelle*, he asked for some current local news. Mariash said that the three villages of Amanot, Guasup, and Derraquadi in Guasopa Harbor, as well as those at Uaman and some at Coadeo, had joined Tatai in the civil war currently being waged. Opposing Tatai were the villages of Cuvalevi Uasigug, which had entered an alliance with all of the Lavat villages. Tatai had been in the canoe which had come out to the *Favourite* that Sunday afternoon. Raimondi therefore urged the captain again to be on his guard during the night.[55]

---

54. "Loss of the Brig *Gazelle*." Did the *Gazelle* arrive at Guasopa Harbor in the course of a terrible storm or as one was just subsiding? If so, this could well explain why the upper halves of its two masts were broken off, why the captain had difficulty in navigating, why the brig swayed dangerously being buffeted by wind and waves once it was trapped on a reef, and why there were waves enough to capsize Puarer's canoe.

55. *Beatificationis Positio*, 355–56, Raimondi to Salerio, 20 June 1856. Raimondi regularly uses Madao for

According to Barrack's log the "very vague and unsatisfactory" answers of Mariash "made us think it not advisable to go up the harbour that night, and therefore we anchored near the entrance in 10 fathoms, sheltered from the eastward by an island. Loaded all the fire arms, and clewed the sails up; set a double anchor-watch, and the night passed off quietly. Large fires were seen on shore, which the boy said were lit on account of the natives being afraid we intended to burn the village."[56] Raimondi said that Barrack, "in addition to having a small canon and six cavalry rifles [ready], had placed on guard a sailor with a rifle and a Baniata native with a tomahawk. And then we went to bed."[57]

The next day was Monday, 5 May 1856, Raimondi's twenty-ninth birthday, and he was on deck early that morning. About 7 o'clock he saw Taionau arriving in his canoe. This young man had always kept him and Salerio well informed of what was happening in the village and so Raimondi had asked Tatai on the previous day to send Taionau to visit him. With Taionau were Nit (the brother of Mariash), Nit (the brother of Puarer), and Donerili. "I then took Taionau into my cabin and invited him to tell me the truth," Raimondi said. "But I could not obtain any more information from him than what I had learned from Mariash." And so he ended his questioning.

"Nit then asked me to request the captain to move his ship close to their village because the old men had many things taken from the brig [*Gazelle*], which they wanted to bring to him," Raimondi said. "The captain at once asked whether they had any gold on land and they answered yes. Then the captain told them that he would never come near their village unless they brought him the money that they had on land. The four then left with their canoe, promising to return at midday with the money." Raimondi had asked Nit why his brother Puarer had not come along. Nit said that he would tell Puarer that he was wanted.

At midday a canoe did arrive with Nit, Puarer, Ladbes, Grummeruli, and Tuab, each one carrying some money. The youths also brought aboard a bottle of brandy, two small saws, and some pieces of cloth.[58] The money had been found in a trunk in the *Gazelle*'s

---

the island in the Woodlark Group today called Madau. "Wreck of the Brig *Gazelle*" and "Loss of the Brig *Gazelle*" do not use the names Madao and Gau, which are used by Raimondi. They use instead Maddan, Tronbiea or Cape Denis, and Javonsee. These names were taken from Captain Barrack's log and probably came from nautical charts, whereas those used by Raimondi probably were the names used by the people of Guasopa Harbor. A comparison of details in the two newspaper reports and in Raimondi's report makes it appear highly probable that Maddan is another form of Madao; that Tronbiea or Cape Denis are equivalent to what Raimondi calls the vicinity of Madao or an island near Madao; and that Gau used by Raimondi is equivalent to Javonsee, an island in a group of islands called Guavag, located northwest of Woodlark. See also *Beatificationis Positio*, 345 nn. 33–35, and 348 nn. 44–46.

56. "Loss of the Brig *Gazelle*."

57. *Beatificationis Positio*, 356, Raimondi to Salerio, 20 June 1856. Raimondi uses Baugnata and Bagnata for Baniata. See *Beatificationis Positio*, 356, 360. Gerhard Kimmel of Neu-Isenburg, West Germany, informed the author by telephone on 17 November 1986 that he had consulted a firearms expert, who identified the "sei fucili cawelar" in Raimondi's text as 'six cavalry rifles,' which were in use at that time.

58. *Beatificationis Positio*, 356–57, Raimondi to Salerio, 20 June 1856.

cabin, they said, but it turned out to be only "eight shillings and six pence in silver and nine pence in copper, English coin," as Captain Barrack reported. "The old men at the village," he said, "had told the boys to ask us if we were angry? [sic] as they wished to trade in pigs and yams—wishing us to come near the village. This request we believed to be only a decoy, as none of the old men had come off, and no canoes, excepting the one alongside. Their real intent . . . ," Captain Barrack continued, "was to get us up the harbour, separate us from the ship by trading, and then take the vessel."[59]

Eager to locate Mazzucconi's diary, Raimondi asked whether they had any books on shore, but they said no. "I then questioned all of them together," he said, "to see whether I might be able to trap them in their replies. But I could get nothing out of them. However, they always spoke about eight sailors being on the *Gazelle*, whereas I knew that there were fourteen persons aboard. I scolded and threatened them, saying that if they would not tell me the truth, we would go and visit the *Gazelle* and then we could easily see whether they had killed those aboard or had let them go. This statement frightened them and Nit kept asking me: "But—but will you be able to tell by visiting the ship whether we killed them? But—but how will you be able to know?" These repeated questions increased my suspicions," Raimondi said.[60] At 2 p.m., however, Captain Barrack "got the boat ready to go to the wreck . . ."[61]

Meanwhile Raimondi had been looking for an opportunity to speak alone with Puarer, knowing that the youth would never give any information "in the presence of his companions." Eventually Raimondi did find him alone.

> I approached Puarer and addressed him like this: "Why do you not tell me the truth, since you are the one who usually told me everything that happened in the village?" While speaking to him in this way, I laid my hand on his shoulders, knowing how effective such acts of confidence with this young man were. He then looked up at me and smiled. From his smile I knew at once that he would talk and therefore I encouraged him further. He asked me: "When will you be leaving?" "Perhaps tomorrow." "Well then, I need to talk to you before you leave." "Why not talk now?" I then ordered the mate to allow none of the natives aboard to come near my cabin. I also told the others that I had brought along a gift for Puarer, which I wanted him to see, and I took Puarer with me. The minute he found himself alone with me inside my cabin, he told me: "They were all killed."

Puarer then told Raimondi the following story:

> As soon as I saw the brig appear, I set out for it with Nit [the brother of Mariash], Gunemmuiu [sic] and Uliveli. On arriving there I spoke with Mazzucconi and told him that you and the others had left and that Paulo [Reina] and Ambrosoli were with you. But we became frightened because the ship was swaying so very much. We then went back with the cloth goods that Mazzucconi had given us. As soon as we

---

59. "Loss of the Brig *Gazelle*."
60. *Beatificationis Positio*, 356–57, Raimondi to Salerio, 20 June 1856.
61. "Loss of the Brig *Gazelle*."

reached the village, the old men asked us whether the ship had dropped anchor out there. We said that it had gone onto a reef. Orighiamai then proposed that the men go and kill those aboard and take over the ship. All agreed, even though I told them not to do this.

A number of canoes then set out from Amanot, Guasup and Derraquadi [*sic*], but the men left behind their spears and shields in order not to arouse suspicion, taking only their tomahawks which they concealed under their loincloths. On reaching the ship they began displaying compassion for the poor whites, promising to help them.[62]

Puarer reported—as Captain Barrack wrote into his log—that they had done this according to "a plan already formed by the chief" and that "eight canoes went off to the ship, six men in each.... The crew of the *Gazelle*, at this time, had one boat out, and a second was being got over. In fact, all were employed about something when the natives boarded...."[63] Three sailors were already in the ship's boat that had been lowered into the sea for the rescue operation.

"The first one who tried to get aboard was Avicoar," Puarer said. "But the captain (being in great distress over the loss of his ship) tried to prevent him from coming aboard by striking him several times with a thick cord. Then, while the captain was occupied with Avicoar, Tanar tried to climb aboard from the other side. When the captain turned toward Tanar, Avicoar sprang onto the deck and went up to Mazzucconi to greet him and shake his hand. By this time many others had practically reached the deck from every side of the ship."

Puarer testified that "the signal was then given by Avicoar, who raised his large tomahawk and with a single blow struck down dead" Mazzucconi.[64] On hearing "a cry behind him," the captain had swung around fast enough to see "a native strike his tomahawk into the head" of the priest, and when the captain bent down to take a belaying pin from the rail to fell Mazzucconi's murderer, he himself "was struck in the neck by Tanar. At the first blow he fell to the deck and was finished off with a second blow." The rest of the crew were all tomahawked within a few minutes. The *Gazelle* was then "plundered of everything the natives fancied, and the rest destroyed," as Captain Barrack wrote in his log. "The dead bodies were left where they fell—but the boys who had no hand in this affair shortly after threw them overboard." The murderers had discussed "whether the bodies should be buried, but decided that they were not worthy of this."[65]

62. *Beatificationis Positio*, 357–58, Raimondi to Salerio, 20 June 1856. Raimondi writes Derraquadi, but Ambrosoli's map in *Beatificationis Positio*, fig. op. p. 304, has Darraquadi. Raimondi here writes Gunemmuiu for one of the three companions who accompanied Puarer to the *Gazelle*. But earlier in the same letter he calls this companion Gunemuadu. See *Beatificationis Positio*, 354, 357. It is not unusual for people to have more than one name or more than one form of the same name. See also this chapter, p. 245, n. 53.

63. "Loss of the Brig *Gazelle*."

64. *Beatificationis Positio*, 358, Raimondi to Salerio, 20 June 1856.

65. Ibid.; "Loss of the Brig *Gazelle*." What Raimondi calls "a long piece of iron" in *Beatificationis Positio*, 358, was recognized by Captain Barrack from Puarer's description as "a belaying pin," the term that he uses in "Loss of the Brig *Gazelle*."

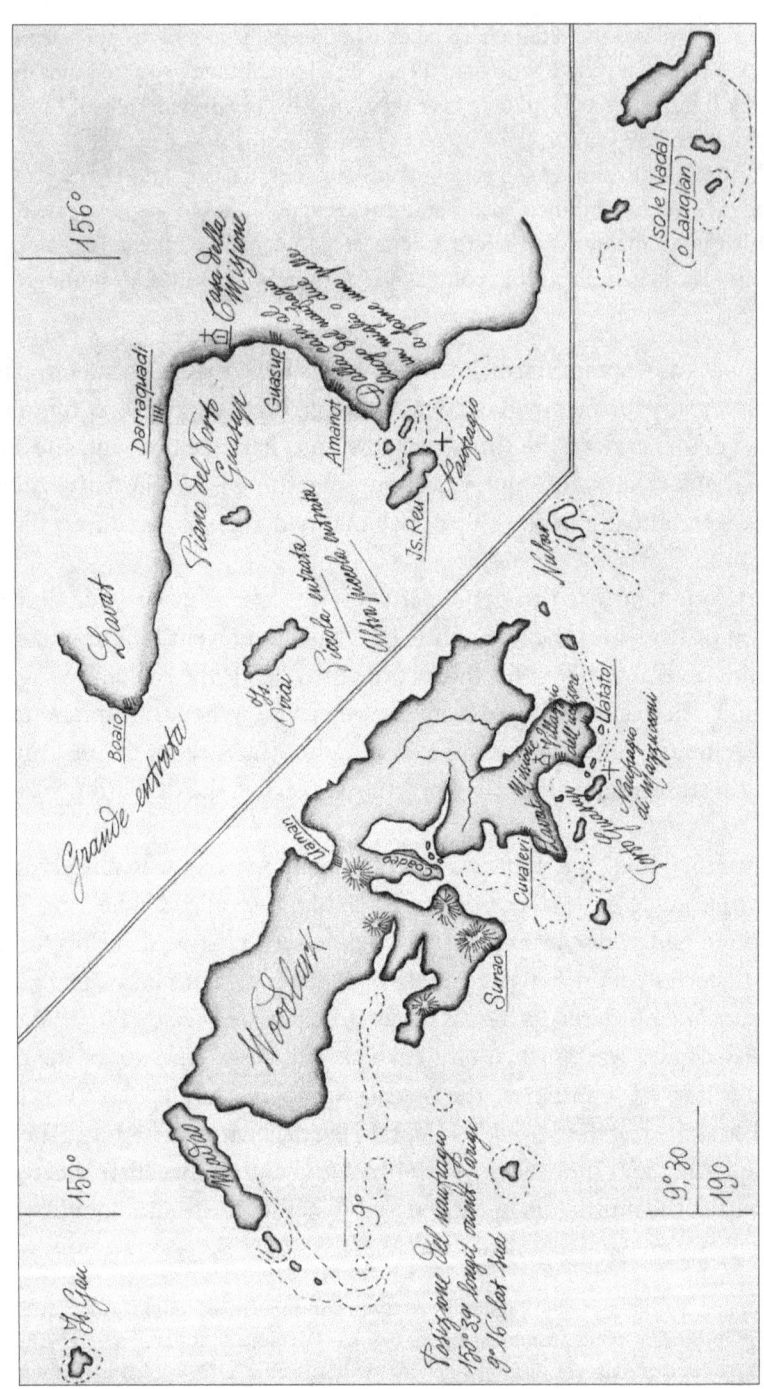

This map of Woodlark Island was drawn by Ambrosoli. The insert in the upper right indicates the place of the shipwreck (*naufragio*) and the site of the missionary residence (*casa della missione*), which are approximately one or two miles apart.
Source: Archives PIME: AME 11, 602.

Puarer knew the names of the murderers, probably because he had heard the individuals boast of their deeds of valor at village gatherings. "The three [sailors] in the boat were killed at the same time [as the captain] by Tasuasup, Techiau, and Maioquau," he said. "The others on deck were killed by Cumliuadeo, Manomam, Tobut, Tamudoli, Davao, Arague, and a man from Coadeo who had settled at Amanot." These ten men in addition to Avicoar and Tanar made a total of twelve assailants. Because customarily in such a massacre the number of assailants is equivalent to the number of victims, "two names were still missing," Raimondi said, "Since there had been fourteen men aboard the *Gazelle*. I believe that they were Gobeu and Sironam, but Puarer did not have the courage to tell me so."

And what was Raimondi's reaction to all of this? "Although I was already aware from the first day when we entered the harbor, that they had been killed, still on hearing those cruel words: All were killed, and on learning the despicable way in which they were massacred, shivers ran through me.... With all my heart I recited the De Profundis for the soul of my poor companion and I prayed for the murderers."[66]

After Puarer finished his report, Raimondi asked: "Why did the others say that the whites went toward Madao?" Puarer replied: "It was Orighiamai who invented all this nonsense. They were all killed aboard the ship; no one left it."[67] Captain Barrack said that Puarer's report "was corroborated by another boy. This prevented us from visiting the wreck, for when the boat was manned there would only have been two hands left on board the ship. Having now received all the information we could, we hoisted in the boat and made ready for sea."[68]

Raimondi was convinced that if the natives on shore were to learn

> that we knew everything, they would do all in their power to attack our ship and prevent it ... from bringing the sad news to Sydney. My fears of an imminent attack became greater when I saw a number of canoes patrolling our ship at a certain distance and going to the other side of Oviai Island. I recommended to the mate that he keep them under surveillance, since I feared that they would camp on the island and try to attack us during the night. At the same time I spied upon the youths aboard ship to learn what they had in mind. I noticed that they were inspecting the ship and studying how strong each one of us was. It was getting dark and I suspected that they might have become aware that Puarer had told me everything. Since I also suspected that they would go ashore to report on the sturdiness of the ship, on the number of

---

66. *Beatificationis Positio*, 358, Raimondi to Salerio, 20 June 1856. Raimondi's statement that "there were fourteen persons aboard" the *Gazelle*, which he even emphasizes in *Beatificationis Positio*, 357, shows that Gheddo in *Mazzucconi*, 220, is incorrect in giving the total of those massacred as: "Mazzucconi, the captain of the ship and his fourteen sailors." Raimondi takes it for granted that Salerio, to whom he is writing, will know why Gobeu and Sironam were suspects and why Puarer refrained from naming them.

67. *Beatificationis Positio*, 359, Raimondi to Salerio, 20 June 1856.

68. "Loss of the Brig *Gazelle*." From Raimondi's insistence in his letter to Salerio it is clear that no other youth gave a report anything like that of Puarer in accuracy, length, and detail. Captain Barrack must be referring to testimony given by a second youth that coincided in part with testimony given by Puarer.

whites, etc., I suggested to the captain that he send all of them down into the bilge and keep them locked inside all night. And this is what he did.

Additional precautions were taken as well. "Since we had some rockets aboard," Raimondi said, "we tried to launch them into the air that same evening to intimidate the savages. But they were too damp and the results were not good. We posted two guards and then I retired for the night. But I could not fall asleep because every minute I expected the canoes of the natives to arrive."

The next day was Tuesday, 6 May 1856. "Early in the morning we weighed anchor," Raimondi said. "We unfurled the sails, made the natives on board go down into their canoe—except for Puarer who wanted to come to Sydney, and sailed out of the harbor. But we had hardly left when the wind died down...." Ever so slowly the *Favourite* sailed eastward, just south of the wrecked *Gazelle*, and after two hours it had not yet passed Uatatol Point. "With a spyglass we could see the entire seashore covered with people and a number of canoes coming toward us," Raimondi said. "At that moment Puarer said to me: 'Look and see how many people there are at Uatatol Point; many are on the reefs.' The natives believed that we were going to visit the shipwrecked vessel in our boat, and they were waiting for a favorable occasion when they could find us divided and kill us.

"I then asked Puarer whether any plans had been made in the village to seize our ship. He told me that as soon as the *Favourite* appeared, Tanar had suggested that they lure us close to their village and kill all of us, while we were occupied receiving the various items which they had taken from the *Gazelle*." It was Tanar, in fact, who had killed Captain Parkins of the *Gazelle*.

"Because a calm was threatening, I suggested that the captain frighten them with a cannon shot," Raimondi said. "We tried, but it did not fire. We tried all the rifles, but not a single one fired. We finally succeeded in firing a shot from a small cannon and immediately we could see all the savages at Uatatol Point flee into the woods. The canoes, which had been dispersed, came together. We fired a second shot and the canoes withdrew. We then continued our route to Sydney" via "New Georgia, Simbo and Baniata..."[69]

Who was Puarer and of what value was his testimony? When the veteran Marist missionary Frémont left Woodlark on 19 October 1852 in order to train Mazzucconi and others for missionary work on Rooke Island, he took along Puarer from Woodlark. His choice of Puarer indicates how much he esteemed this young man. Puarer thus became closely associated with Mazzucconi at Rooke for a full year, that is, until Frémont and Puarer left Rooke on 24 October 1853 aboard the *Supply* to return to Woodlark. The mate on that fifteen-day voyage happened to be Mr. Barrack, now captain of the *Favourite*, and so he also knew Puarer well. Raimondi, too, became well acquainted with Puarer after he arrived

---

69. *Beatificationis Positio*, 359–60, Raimondi to Salerio, 20 June 1856. See p. 247, n. 57 on alternate spellings for "Baniata."

back at Guasopa Harbor in Woodlark on 7 November 1853. Both of them were in close contact until Raimondi left for Sydney with the other missionaries on 10 July 1855.[70]

The *Favourite* with Raimondi aboard arrived in Sydney on Friday morning, 13 June 1856. The very next day, 14 June, *The Sydney Morning Herald* ran a news story nine inches long with graphic details titled "Loss of the Brig *Gazelle* and Murder of Her Crew by the Natives of Woodlark Island." It was an extract from the *Favourite*'s log and was signed by Father Raimondi, Captain Barrack, and mate Bennett. On the same day *The Empire* of Sydney printed a story nine inches long titled "Wreck of the Brig *Gazelle* and Horrible Massacre of All on Board." Since Raimondi was the only one aboard who knew the Woodlark language and since he had done the interviewing, the details in Captain Barrack's log came principally from him. As Raimondi said, "I passed on all the information to the captain."[71]

On the same day, Saturday, 14 June 1856, Prefect Apostolic Reina drew up and signed the following death certificate: "I the undersigned attest that the priest, Reverend Giovanni Battista Mazzucconi, a native of Rancio, District of Lecco, Province of Como, was killed by the natives of Woodlark Island in the beginning of September of this past year 1855."[72] One of Captain Parkins's relatives on learning of the massacre visited immediately the elected head of the New South Wales government, Colonial Secretary Donaldson, and pointed out the necessity of sending a punitive expedition to Woodlark. The colonial secretary then invited Father Raimondi to come to his office and present a detailed report on his findings. Raimondi gave his report most probably on Saturday, 14 June, and certainly no later than Sunday, 15 June. He was accompanied to the government office by Reina and on the way they decided what to say, if the colonial secretary should ask whether Raimondi was prepared to accompany a warship on a punitive expedition. "Both of us," Reina said, "agreed that it was better to answer no, and also that we had done our duty, which was to look for our companion and not to avenge him."

"After having me describe the massacre," Raimondi said, the colonial secretary

---

70. See chap. 10, pp. 153–54; RIP: R B-N.2, N.1, Carlo Salerio, "Giornale di Viaggio," 24 October 1853, 7 November 1853, 10 July 1855; PIME: AME 11:239, Reina to Marinoni, 15 April 1856. John Rooney in *Khabar Gembira (The Good News): History of the Catholic Church in East Malaysia and Brunei (1880–1976)*, 20, says incorrectly that Puarer was "a native of Rook Island" who "had cooperated in the murder of Mazzucconi and, repentant of his crime, had decided to become a Christian and serve the fathers." Maestrini in *Mazzucconi*, 175, incorrectly calls Puarer "the Chief of a small village."

71. See *Beatificationis Positio*, 339, Reina to Salerio, 14 June 1856. For Raimondi's words on passing on information to the captain, see *Beatificationis Positio*, 359. In *Beatificationis Positio*, 343 and 346, the date of *The Sydney Morning Herald* should read 14 June 1856, not 15 June 1856. The original newspaper clippings are in PIME: AME vol. 11, fig. op. p. 619. See also the weekly issue of *The Shipping Gazette and Sydney General Trade List* dated 16 June 1856, which reports that the 76-ton schooner *Favourite* under Captain Barrack was currently in the Cove.

72. PIME: AME 11:253.

asked me whether we wished to have a warship go there. I replied that we did not wish to have the death of our companion avenged, since it was not our custom to take revenge for someone murdered, but to pray for the murderers. "But what about commerce? Do you believe it would be safe?" "It is the government's business to think about this, if it wants to keep commerce safe in those regions." "But this is not the first ship that they have taken. It is not the first and therefore they ought to be punished." "This is the government's business," I answered. "Let the government do what it believes to be its duty."

Then he asked me whether I would be ready to go aboard in case the government were to send a warship. "No," I answered, "I cannot. We had asked the government two months ago [*sic*] for a ship to go to Woodlark, not to avenge our colleague, but only to look for the *Gazelle*, since the ship was English and the crew was English. But the government refused. So we chartered a ship at our own expense and we now know that our colleague is no longer alive. We have done our duty. There is nothing more for us to do. If the government wants a pilot, it could call upon Captain Barrack, who was in command of the *Favourite* and knows the spot exactly." With this the Colonial Secretary appeared to be satisfied.[73]

The press during the entire week that followed was filled with further news on the Woodlark massacre and also with angry reactions. On Monday, 16 June 1856, *The Shipping Gazette and Sydney General Trade List* published on page 123 the identical news story that had appeared two days earlier in *The Sydney Morning Herald*, using the type received from that publication. That same day *The Empire* listed on page 4 "the names of the unfortunate crew of the *Gazelle* who were massacred by the savages at Woodlark Island." The ones listed were: William Thomas Parkins, Captain, a native of Deptford; Junius Parkins (his brother), chief mate, aged twenty-seven; Robert King, born at Norfolk, England, carpenter; Henry Gould of Chelsea, cook and steward, aged twenty; James Coffey of Liverpool, able seaman, aged thirty-two; Henry Wilson, born in the United States, able seaman, aged twenty-seven; John Gilligen of Boston, able seaman, aged thirty; Joseph Fullard of Maryland, able seaman, aged twenty-two; H. Bagust, of Chiswell, ordinary seaman, aged twenty; and a lad, a native of Sydney, fifteen years of age, named James Yates. Then followed this notice: "No second mate's name is on the articles; it is therefore probable that one of the able seamen acted in that capacity."[74]

---

73. *Beatificationis Positio*, 341, Reina to Marinoni, 15 June 1856; *Beatificationis Positio*, 360–61, Raimondi to Salerio, 20 June 1856. Since Raimondi returned to Sydney on Friday morning, 13 June, and since Reina's report about the meeting sent to Marinoni is dated Sunday, 15 June, the visit to the Colonial Secretary took place on 13, 14, or 15 June. Raimondi is incorrect in saying that the request for a ship was made "two months ago." The request was made by S. Julien in early March, that is, three months prior to the time when Raimondi spoke with the colonial secretary.

74. Raimondi said that the Woodlark youths "always spoke about eight sailors being on the *Gazelle*, whereas I knew that there were fourteen persons aboard." See this chapter, p. 248. The crew members listed by *The Empire* total ten, to whom Mazzucconi must be added. *The Empire*'s list is not necessarily complete. A letter to the editor from "A Master Mariner" published in *The Empire* of 24 June 1856, p. 4, says that "the poor little

On Wednesday, 18 June, *The Sydney Morning Herald* published an editorial titled "The Late Shipwreck and Murder in the South Seas." The writer insisted that "it is the duty ... of New South Wales to demand unequivocal and immediate redress for the several treacherous and unprovoked murders done lately upon many of its citizens in the South Seas." After describing how Father Mazzucconi and Captain Parkins were killed, the writer said that "the native boy who is now in Sydney, and who informed Mr. Raimondi, the missionary, of the circumstances of the murder, must know this man who killed Captain Parkins and also the name of the Chief who planned the treachery. No doubt Mr. Raimondi knows both those men; and now we say plainly to the people of Sydney, that those two men at least should die the death before the eyes of their friends and abettors...."

The editorial called for retribution and said that

> the Government of New South Wales must carry out some fixed resolve.... If this impunity in murder goes much farther, there will be no safety for white men in any of the islands about that of Woodlark.... As we are told, several wholesale murders have been done successively on Woodlark Island, and as punishment has followed none, so has the courage and the wish to do more evil increased.... Therefore let us have the courage in this case to teach a lesson from the leaves of justice, to be remembered with fear and trembling by any who may think the white man comes on shore shipwrecked only to be murdered and cast into a dishonourable and undug grave.

The article was signed D.P.[75]

On Friday that week, 20 June, *The Empire* published a letter to the editor from "Verax" with the title "Murder Will Out." The writer said that three months earlier when the missionaries had petitioned the government to send a vessel to search for the *Gazelle*, they were told it was not certain that the *Gazelle* was lost on Woodlark and therefore no vessel could be sent. But now, since Captain Barrack had found the *Gazelle* lying on "a reef some 10 miles from the entrance to the port" of Woodlark, there was no longer any doubt about where the vessel was. And there were three government vessels—the *Torch*, *Juno*, and *Spitfire*—lying in the harbor of Sydney "at an enormous expense, doing nothing." The government, had it so wished, "could have had a merchant steamer at a day's notice. But, no; the lives of poor missionaries and sailors, what are they?"

---

boy Ducie, a lad of twelve years," was also among those massacred. The chief mate, called Junius Parkin(s) in *The Empire*'s June 16 list of crew members, is called Julian Parkin(s) in *The Empire*'s story, "Wreck of the Brig *Gazelle*," published two days earlier (14 June 1856).

75. "The Late Shipwreck and Murder in the South Seas," *The Sydney Morning Herald* (18 June 1856). Here the author wishes to thank those who kindly supplied copies of the various newspaper stories as well as information regarding the numerous vessels mentioned in this chapter, namely: Eileen Dwyer, archivist, John Fairfax Limited, Sydney, letter of 5 November 1986; Lexie Steel, Research Service, Mitchell Library, Sydney, letter of 16 March 1989; Iain MacKenzie, Enquiry Services, National Maritime Museum, Greenwich, London, letter of 22 May 1989; William Foot, Search Department, Public Record Office, Kew, Richmond, Surrey, letter of 20 June 1989.

The ebony from Woodlark, "Verax" said, "is much prized and there is some tortoise shell." And although "we may oppose useless expenditure, yet that spent in protecting our commerce, or in punishing those that murder and insult our citizens, no one would grudge." He pointed out further that Captain Barrack had made a chart which, "if published, would be a very valuable addition to our meagre stock of charts of the islands."

But the people of Woodlark "delight in treachery" and are "always at war," he said. Since "they in cold blood murdered all hands . . . , the Government owe [sic] it to the community that such vile pests should be rooted out. Their crime committed in last September, which through gross neglect was long unknown, has at length come to light and demands punishment." Truly, he said, "the punishment they deserve is severe and ought to be speedy." The missionary was "a man highly gifted and much beloved by many; the captain [was] an able, good seaman, and one 'who would not hurt a worm'—the embodiment of good nature; and [there was] a fair crew, all gone. To those who, like the writer, knew them, as many in the city did, it seems hardly a reality." "Verax" did not advocate "indiscriminate punishment," yet he believed that "hanging those murderers before their villages is only what we have a right to expect . . . Are the men who have slaughtered four ships' companies in cold blood to go scatheless?"

On that very same day, 20 June, Raimondi finished a long letter to Salerio, giving a detailed report on what he had learned at Woodlark. Ending his letter he said, "Here in Sydney the relatives of the captain have caused quite a stir and in the newspapers they continue to write in large letters: Massacre of the *Gazelle*."[76]

On the following day, Saturday, 21 June, "some gentlemen had an interview" with Colonial Secretary Donaldson "to ascertain what steps the Government intended to take with reference to the late massacre at Woodlark Island." Mr. Donaldson stated

> that on the arrival of the *Juno* from Broken Bay, now hourly expected, a meeting of the executive would be convened to take into consideration the evidence that had already been given by Mr. Raimondi (the missionary who arrived lately from Woodlark Island) with a view to such steps being taken as may be deemed necessary for bringing the offenders to justice, and also for the purpose of ascertaining whether there are any survivors from the wreck. Mr. Donaldson stated that he was most anxious to do everything that would further the ascertaining of the fate of the wrecked people. He also stated that Mr. St. Julian, the Hawaiian Commissioner, had been most indefatiguable [sic] in affording information to the Government.

Sydney readers found these details in "The Late Massacre at Woodlark Island" in *The Empire* on Monday, 23 June. This news story irritated "A Master Mariner" who that same day, 23 June, dashed off a letter to the editor of *The Empire*. By this time ten days had already passed since the *Favourite* had arrived in Sydney with news of the murders. "I am much surprised," the writer said, "that up to this time no Government vessel has been

---

76. "Murder Will Out," *The Empire* (Sydney, 20 June 1856), 2; *Beatificationis Positio*, 360–61, Raimondi to Salerio, 20 June 1856.

despatched to ascertain the fate of the Crew of the *Gazelle*." Since the "fact has been determined" that "the brig was lost on Woodlark," he wondered why Mr. Donaldson was waiting for the *Juno*, when he knew well that "ten lines in one of the daily papers . . . would procure a steamer, and the whole [also the voyage to Woodlark and back] would not occupy three weeks."

He pointed out that Captain Barrack, because of the smallness of his crew and the nature of his vessel, had been able to ascertain only the loss of the *Gazelle*. "But a man-of-war piloted by him, and in possession of what he has elicited, might do much more." He quoted Captain Barrack as having stated "that the long continued absence of our power to punish, despite their frequent atrocities, leads them to believe that we have neither the ability nor power to punish. The presence of a man-of-war, the hanging of the principal murderers before their own people, in particular Tanar, the largest of them . . . , would prevent any further murders." Tanar, he said, seemed to glory "in the murder not only of Captain Parkins, but [also of] the poor little boy Ducie, a lad of twelve years . . ." The master mariner's letter was published under the title "The Woodlark Murders" in *The Empire* on the following day, Tuesday, 24 June.[77]

After the statement by Colonial Secretary Donaldson appeared in *The Empire* on Monday, 23 June, people expected that the *Juno* would "hourly" arrive in Sydney, coming from Broken Bay only fifteen miles away, to be sent to Woodlark. But two weeks passed and the *Juno* did not appear. Another warship named *Electra* was anchored at Sydney, but it could not be sent because—as the officials said—one warship always had to remain on duty in the harbor. When the *Juno* finally did arrive, the *Electra* had to leave for Plymouth, England, within a few days, making it necessary for the *Juno* to remain at Sydney. When reporting all of this to Marinoni, Ambrosoli said that he believed no action would be taken by the government at all. "Will anyone still know after some fifteen years," he asked, "that those aboard three ships were killed" by the Woodlark Islanders?[78]

When Raimondi refused to accompany the punitive expedition, the colonial secretary contacted Brother Gennade (Jean-Pierre Rolland), a Marist who had been stationed at Woodlark mission for a number of years prior to Raimondi. But he, too, refused to sail

---

77. In "The Late Massacre at Woodlark Island," *The Empire* (Sydney, 23 June 1856), 4, Colonial Secretary Donaldson is referred to as "Premier." See n. 36 on the use of that title. In view of the deep concern on the part of Mr. St. Julian, the Hawaiian Commissioner, in affording information about the *Gazelle* massacre to the government, and in view of the identical concern on the part of Mr. S. Julien, a friend of Father Salerio (see this chapter, p. 240), the author suggests that these two similar names found in the sources may indicate the same person. For "The Woodlark Murders," see *The Empire* (Sydney, 24 June 1856) 4.

78. PIME: AME 11:617, 602 bis, 602/2, Ambrosoli to Marinoni, 5 July 1856. See also Ambrosoli's additional information in the margin of "Wreck of the Brig *Gazelle*," in PIME: AME vol. 11, fig. op. p. 619. Ambrosoli says that the Woodlark people had murdered Europeans aboard three ships. "Verax" in "Murder Will Out," *The Empire* (Sydney, 20 June 1856), 2, says that they had "slaughtered four ships' companies in cold blood."

aboard the warship, even though he was asked repeatedly to do so. The French Marists, however, did supply information about Woodlark as requested by the colonial secretary.

Finally on 28 May 1858, 102 weeks after Raimondi had arrived in Sydney with news of the *Gazelle* massacre, the twenty-six-gun (all thirty-two-pounders) and 907-ton frigate *Iris* of the Royal Navy left Sydney on a punitive expedition to Woodlark with William Loring in command. He "took along Captain Barrack," Ambrosoli said, "who had been at Woodlark and at Rooke on other occasions, particularly this last time with Raimondi on the *Favourite*." Captain Barrack's chief role on this voyage was to serve as pilot for entering hazardous Guasopa Harbor at Woodlark. H.M.S. *Iris* had many other missions as well and visited Lord Howe's Island, Norfolk Island, and the Isle of Pines in New Caledonia, where "on the reef was the wreck of the *Anne and Jane*, [a] schooner, whose master had been murdered at Tana [Island in New Hebrides]." The *Iris* on 14 June "communicated with the schooner *Clarence*" bound for Sydney and that same day arrived at Port-de-France (now Nouméa) in New Caledonia and "exchanged salutes with the forts . . . During our stay [of one week] at Port-de-France the courtesy and hospitality of the French officers was unlimited." On 25 June it anchored at Aneityum in New Hebrides.

Then on Wednesday, 30 June, the *Iris* anchored off Black Beach, Tana Island, New Hebrides, where "Wan-Attaway, chief of the Wagus tribe, who murdered the captain and part of the crew of the schooner *Anne and Jane*," was seized. On Thursday, 1 July, the *Iris* moved to nearby Wagus, "fired a few rounds of shot and shell to clear the savages from the woods," and then a small-arms party landed under the command of three lieutenants of the Royal Navy and Royal Marines. "The party burnt several villages and destroyed great quantities of cocoanut and bread fruit trees, also banana, yams, etc."

The log extract continues: "Unfortunately Mr. Edward M. Tupper, mate, Captain Barrack and two men were separated in the dense underwood from the main party [and were] surrounded by great numbers of savages. Captain Barrack and one seaman made their way through them and regained the party. Mr. Tupper and Mr. Kennedy, captain of [the] hold, were killed. Mr. Tupper's body was immediately after recovered; Kennedy's we never saw." On 2 July the "landing party again proceeded on shore and continued the work of destruction, the savages not attempting to molest them." Since "the only object was to destroy property and not life," it was "not likely that many were killed. The effect on the islanders, we hear, has been very good; they now dread the visit of a 'fighting ship.'"

On Sunday, 4 July, the *Iris* reached Lifu Island in the Loyalty Islands, where it "anchored in Wreck Bay and communicated with the French missionary priests [namely Marists], formerly stationed at Woodlark Island." On 8 July it anchored in Dillon's Bay at Eromanga Island in New Hebrides, took ashore Wan-Attaway, chief of the Wagus tribe, and placed him in the custody of Captain Edwards.

Here follow in full the notes on the punitive expedition at Woodlark taken from the log of *H.M.S. Iris* and published in the *Sydney Morning Herald* on 7 September 1858, the day after the 131-foot-long vessel returned to Sydney and anchored at Farm Cove.

July 21st [Wednesday]. Arrived at Woodlark Island; going in the ship struck upon a rock; the harbour is dangerous, being full of detached rock, and the passage [is] intricate; for several days the strong tradewind prevented our doing anything.

July 27 [Tuesday]. The landing party under the same officers as at Tana, proceeded on shore, burnt the villages, canoes and other property of the Guasup tribe, as a punishment for the murder of the crew of the *Gazelle* in 1855; the savages offered no opposition. The canoes and houses of the Woodlark Islanders were much superior to [those of] any of the other islanders. It was clearly explained to two of the natives, who understood a little English, the reason [why] this punishment was inflicted.

July 29th [Thursday]. Sailed from Woodlark Island.

The newspaper article containing these and many other details of the voyage was titled: "Notes of a Cruise to Woodlark Island by *H.M.S. Iris*."[79]

When Reina learned on 13 June 1856 from Raimondi of Mazzucconi's death, it meant that he had lost three men or 50 percent of his staff within forty-six weeks. Catechist Corti had died in Rooke on Saturday, 17 March 1855. Father Mazzucconi had been murdered at Woodlark in early September that same year. And Father Salerio, head of the Woodlark mission, had left Sydney on Saturday, 2 February 1856, aboard the *Waterloo* for London, incapacitated for further missionary work. Reina was still entrusted with the two prefectures apostolic of Melanesia and Micronesia, but now his staff consisted only of Fathers Ambrosoli and Raimondi and Catechist Tacchini.

With effort Reina picked up his pen to tell authorities back in Italy what had happened. "We accept everything from the hands of the Lord," he told director Marinoni on 15 June 1856, two days after Raimondi's return from Woodlark.[80] That same day he wrote to Bishop Ramazzotti of Pavia: "The first fruit of our Missions that I present to you is the life and blood of the dearest and best of my companions."[81] And on the following day he informed Archbishop Romilli that "one of the best and most excellent priests" of his Milan archdiocese had died.[82] Father Salerio's voyage on the *Waterloo*, begun in Sydney on 2 February 1856, had taken him around Cape Horn on 9 March and from there to Gravesend in England where he arrived on 14 May.[83] As companion he had a Marist Brother also returning to Europe because of poor health. This condition made it possible for Salerio

---

79. PIME: AME 11:663, Ambrosoli to Marinoni, 11 June 1858; PIME: AME 11:671, 11 September 1858. Practically all details on the various missions of the *Iris* come from "Notes of a Cruise to Woodlark Island by *H.M.S. Iris*" in *The Sydney Morning Herald* (7 September 1858), 4. See also *The Shipping Gazette and Sydney General Trade List* (13 September 1858), which mentions that the *Iris* was anchored at Farm Cove and had arrived on 6 September from a cruise. This publication spells the commander's name "Lohring"; records at the National Maritime Museum in Greenwich, London, spell the name "Loring." Gheddo in *Mazzucconi*, 229, says incorrectly that after Raimondi saw the colonial secretary, "the Sydney Government immediately sent a warship to Woodlark" which returned to Sydney "on 16 September 1856 [sic]."

80. *Beatificationis Positio*, 340, Reina to Marinoni, 15 June 1856.

81. Ibid., Reina to Ramazzotti, 15 June 1856.

82. Ibid., 342, Reina to Romilli, 16 June 1856.

83. RIP: R B-N.2, N.1, Carlo Salerio, "Giornale di Viaggio," 2 February, 9 March, 14 May 1856.

SACRA CONGREGATIO PRO CAUSIS SANCTORUM

OFFICIUM HISTORICUM

1

MEDIOLANEN.

BEATIFICATIONIS SEU DECLARATIONIS MARTYRII

SERVI DEI

IOANNIS BAPTISTAE MAZZUCCONI

SACERDOTIS
PONTIFICII INSTITUTI PRO MISSIONIBUS EXTERIS
IN ODIUM FIDEI, UTI FERTUR, ANNO 1855 INTERFECTI

POSITIO

SUPER INTRODUCTIONE CAUSAE ET SUPER MARTYRIO
EX OFFICIO CONCINNATA

ROMAE - 1969

This is the front cover of the position paper (known as *Beatificationis Positio*) for the cause of beatification for Father Giovanni Battista Mazzucconi.

to travel in easy stages, since he could reside at Marist houses in London, Paris, and Lyon, while en route to Italy. He was hardly recognizable, though, when he arrived in Milan on Sunday, 8 June 1856, a week and four months after leaving Sydney. On Friday that week halfway around the world Raimondi arrived back in Sydney with news of the Woodlark massacre.

It was not until 16 September that year when a brief entry in the records of the Milan Mission Seminary stated that mail had come from Sydney announcing "a first Martyr, that is, the death of Father Giovanni Mazzucconi formerly a Missionary at Rooke."[84] Two days later Bishop Ramazzotti of Pavia pontificated at a Solemn Requiem Mass for the repose of the soul of Mazzucconi in the little church of San Calocero in Milan. It was Thursday, 18 September 1856, and the church was filled with clergy, friends, and Mazzucconi's relatives. Also present was Salerio, who had received his mission cross with Mazzucconi in that very same chapel four and a half years earlier.[85]

In one of the letters that had arrived from Sydney, Reina urged Salerio "to draw all possible good out of our tragedy, principally by proposing the life of Mazzucconi as an example for the students in the Seminary." However, Salerio was to avoid causing too much of a stir about Mazzucconi outside the seminary, Reina said. "If God wants to give him glory, he will know how to do it without us."[86]

On 24 September 1857, two full years after Mazzucconi was killed by a tomahawk, Pope Pius IX introduced at the Holy See the beatification cause of Father Pierre Chanel, a Marist missionary who had been killed by a tomahawk at Futuna in Oceania in 1841.[87] When this news reached Ambrosoli in Sydney, he asked director Marinoni: "Would it not be possible to begin requesting the same thing for our Mazzucconi? For my part I can swear to you that in the three years[88] while I was with him at Rooke, and always close to him . . . , the thought never came to me . . . that he had committed the slightest venial sin."[89]

---

84. PIME: AME 11:211, Reina to Marinoni, 4 January 1856; *Beatificationis Positio*, 367, 548; Tragella, *Missioni estere*, 1:214. Brambilla in *Pontificio istituto*, 1:50, mistakenly says that Salerio returned to Milan in 1855.

85. Tragella, *Missioni estere*, 1:217. Tragella in ibid. supposes that Supriès was in attendance. The accumulated responsibilities which meanwhile had fallen upon the shoulders of Supriès, however, could easily have kept him away. On 10 May 1855 he had become prior of the Carthusian Monastery at Pavia and in 1856 he was named visitor of the Carthusian Monasteries in Italy and co-visitor of La Grande-Chartreuse, motherhouse of the order. See letter of Luc Fauchon, archivist at La Grande-Chartreuse, to Wiltgen, 23 July 1987.

86. *Beatificationis Positio*, 339–40, Reina to Salerio, 14 June 1856.

87. See "Litterae Apostolicae in forma Brevis, quibus permittitur ut Petrus Aloisius Maria Chanel nuncupetur nomine Beati, eiusque reliquiae publicae venerationi proponantur," in *Acta Sanctae Sedis* 22 (1889–90): 259. See also Chanel in Wiltgen, *Oceania*, 588. Chanel was declared blessed on 17 November 1889 and a saint on 12 June 1954.

88. Ambrosoli and Mazzucconi were together at Rooke from 23 October 1852 to approximately 23 January 1855, two years and three months, not "three years" as Ambrosoli says.

89. *Beatificationis Positio*, 364–65, Ambrosoli to Marinoni, 9 February 1858.

Father Giovanni Battista Mazzucconi lost his life in the *Gazelle* massacre at Woodlark Island off the coast of New Guinea in September 1855. Pope John Paul II, at St. Peter's Basilica in Rome on Sunday 19 February 1984, gave Father Giovanni Battista Mazzucconi the title of "Blessed" and declared him to be a martyr of the Roman Catholic Church.
Source: Archives PIME: XIII, 514.

Even before Raimondi had set out to look for Mazzucconi, Ambrosoli had begun sending locks of his hair to Milan missionaries in Central Bengal, India. Explaining how he had obtained the locks, he said that initially Brother Corti had served as barber for the Rooke missionaries. But after Corti took ill, Ambrosoli became the barber. "And when discarding their hair," he said, "I whimsically kept a bit aside. . . ."[90] Then on 5 July 1856 in a postscript to Marinoni he indicated on a rough map sketched by himself the precise location of the *Gazelle* shipwreck and added the place names mentioned in Raimondi's detailed report of the massacre. Ambrosoli may have imagined that his rough map might be used some day for Mazzucconi's beatification process to cast further light upon the circumstances of his death.[91] The last words of Mazzucconi to his mother and father, five sisters, and three brothers, were these: "I have not yet received any letters from you after the one written to me in March of 1853, and I am leaving without knowing when I shall be able to receive some. The earliest opportunity will be at the end of the coming year, that is, at the end of 1856, because at that time a ship will probably come to visit us." He said that he would be boarding the *Gazelle* on the following day, "and on the day after that, Saturday [18 August 1855], I shall already be on the high seas en route to Woodlark."

Thinking of his forthcoming voyage, he described for his family on 16 August what had happened while he was en route from Rooke Island to Sydney earlier that same year.

> We were surprised at sea by a hurricane on Wednesday in Holy Week.[92] It ripped asunder our sails and cordage and broke off the upper half of a mast, driving us aimlessly through the sea for four days. . . . But that God who saved me then will also be with me on this voyage. . . . And as long as he is with me, whatever happens to me will always be a grace, a blessing, for which I must thank him.
>
> If he withdraws in time of danger, or pretends to be asleep in the bow of the ship, I shall go and wake him like the apostles did and make him see my danger. But if he should not want to listen, then I shall say to him: "Lord, command that I come to you." My soul will then walk on the water, it will go to his feet and it will be happy forever. Yes, my dear ones, we have another city, another country, a kingdom where we are all to meet one another, where there will no longer be any more separations or departures, and where the sorrows and dangers of the past will have no other function but to increase our consolation and our glory."[93]

With these sentiments Mazzucconi sailed out of Sydney. With these sentiments he went to his death.

---

90. *Beatificationis Positio*, 374, Albino Parietti to Ambrosoli, 16 April 1856; *Beatificationis Positio*, 363–64, Ambrosoli to Paolo Maestri, 10 November 1856.

91. For Ambrosoli's rough map see PIME: AME 11:602 bis. For a careful adaptation of it, which was used in Mazzucconi's beatification process, see *Beatificationis Positio*, fig. op. p. 304.

92. Wednesday in Holy Week of 1855 was 4 April.

93. Mazzucconi, *Scritti*, 274–75, Mazzucconi to his family, 16 August 1855.

Epilogue

Pope John Paul II on Sunday, 19 February 1984, during a beatification ceremony held at Saint Peter's Basilica in Rome, gave Father Giovanni Battista Mazzucconi the title "Blessed" and declared him to be a martyr of the Roman Catholic Church.[94]

---

94. The decree attesting to "the beatification and martyrdom of the Servant of God Giovanni Battista Mazzucconi" covers six pages in the official organ of the Roman Catholic Church. It summarizes the massacre and reads in part: "They had been expecting Mazzucconi's arrival [at Woodlark]" and "began to carry out their detailed plan to kill the Servant of God, a plan that called for massacring all the sailors as well, so that no one could return [to Sydney] to have the deed avenged.... In fact, a certain man named Avicoar was picked out for this abominable crime by Woodlark Island's leading chief, widely known for his ferocity. On managing to board the vessel—after first being held off by its captain—he went up to the Servant of God, feigned a greeting by taking his hand, and then after withdrawing a tomahawk hidden under his loincloth he struck him down dead with one blow. This was the signal agreed upon to begin the massacre of all...." See "Beatificationis seu declarationis martyrii Servi Dei Ioannis Baptistae Mazzucconi, sacerdotis Pontificii Instituti pro Missionibus Exteris, in odium Fidei a. 1855 interfecti," in *Acta Apostolicae Sedis* 76 (1984) 335. The contents of this document are in Latin.

15

Cuarterón, a Spanish Sea Captain, Offers to Reestablish Reina in Melanesia

9 August 1855

IN EARLY DECEMBER 1855 WHILE RECUPERATING AT TARBAN CREEK NEAR SYDNEY, PREFECT Apostolic Reina pondered over the contents of a recently arrived letter from director Marinoni dated 7 August 1855.[1] The letter contained this extraordinary news: "Providence has arranged that there should still be in Rome an excellent Spanish missionary, Reverend Don Carlos Cuarterón,[2] formerly a sea captain and wealthy shipowner. During his voyages in the Celebes Islands [*sic*] he found a number of pagans who were well disposed to accept the gospel teachings and so he baptized some of them. He returned to Europe, became a priest and a missionary, and is now preparing to return there with two of our members, Father Antonio Riva and Father Ignazio Borgazzi, in order to complete the work so happily begun with divine help. I believe that Propaganda will make very expedient arrangements with him, also on behalf of our Oceania missionaries."[3] Who was Don Carlos Cuarterón, and how did it come about that he entered the pages of Melanesian church history? One might call Cuarterón a second Don Quixote. He was a fabulously gifted man, full of ideals, and he had some impossible dreams. Instead of crossing lands with a horse, a companion, and a sword, he crossed seas with a ship, a compass, and a cross.

---

1. The bulk of Marinoni's letter of 7 August 1855 was treated in chap. 14, pp. 234–35. For Reina's reply of 3 December 1855 see PIME: AME 11:187–88, 387–88.

2. "Quarteron," used here in Marinoni's Italian letter, is an incorrect form of Cuarterón's name. "Quarteron" resulted from Italian rules of orthography and appeared intermittently over the years in correspondence coming from Rome or from Italian church officials elsewhere. Parietti, however, specifically told Marinoni on 24 February 1855 that the proper spelling was Cuarterón. See PIME: AME 13:55. Cuarterón himself always signed his name Carlos Cuarterón. See innumerable original letters of Cuarterón in PIME: AME 29:623–882. See also n. 111 on "Cuarteroni y Fernández."

3. PIME: AME 5:885–86, Marinoni to Mazzucconi, 7 August 1855. This letter, although addressed to Mazzucconi, was opened in his absence by Reina.

CUARTERONI Y FERNÁNDEZ (Carlos) *Biog.* Misionero español, n. y m. en Cádiz (1816-1880), que primeramente siguió la carrera de marina y en 1829 hizo su primer viaje de altura á Manila, como agregado al pilotaje, á bordo del navío *Indiamar*. En 1842 se le concedió el nombramiento de capitán de fragata y el mando de dos buques del departamento de Manila. Compró después la goleta *Mártires del Tonkín*, dedicóse á la pesca de perlas y del carey en los mares de la Oceanía, con lo que llegó á adquirir gran caudal. En 1847, cuando la fortuna le brindaba con todos sus goces, abandonó el mundo y tomó el hábito de los trinitarios, dedicándose á la redención de cautivos, á cuyo efecto empleó una buena parte de su caudal en la compra de buques destinados á tan caritativa obra en las islas del Pacífico. En 1854 recibió las sagradas órdenes de manos del pontífice Pío IX, y presentó varios escritos á la Congregación de Propaganda Fide, solicitando el establecimiento de misiones católicas en la Malasia, lo que le fué concedido. Embarcóse nuevamente para aquellos lejanos países, donde se distinguió mucho por su infatigable actividad en la predicación del Evangelio á los naturales, y rescate de muchos indígenas á costa de arrostrar graves peligros, con indecible y sereno valor. Perdida su salud en aquellas empresas, regresó á su patria en busca de alivio, falleciendo á poco de haber llegado.

Carlos Cuarteroni

This is the article published on Don Carlos Cuarterón in volume 16 of Spain's *Enciclopedia Universal Ilustrada*, page 772.

Cuarterón was born in Spain on 19 September 1816 in the harbor town of Cádiz on the Atlantic coast and early became a seafarer. In 1829 at the age of thirteen he made his first voyage to Manila aboard *Indiamar* assisting the ship's pilot.[4] At twenty-three he was captain of the Spanish mercantile frigate, *Buen Suceso*, and rendered services "to the Royal Navy" of Queen Victoria (1819–1901) "in her war with China 1839–40, and also to her commerce," as he himself said. From 1841 to 1849 he sailed "in a vast area 2500 miles long and 900 miles wide, reaching from the meridian of Singapore to the meridian of the island of Guam, capital of the Marianas Islands, and from the latitude of the islands of Java and Timor to that of Mindanao and Palawan in the Philippines."

It was during this period at the age of twenty-eight that Cuarterón discovered a treasure and became a very wealthy man. As he said, "In the year 1844 . . . I came across an English merchant frigate, laden with valuable cargo, shipwrecked on some rocks in the midst of the China Sea at a distance of about three hundred miles from Labuan [a small island six miles off the northwestern coast of Borneo]. A portion became my property and I gave the rest to the proprietors, as is testified by documents which they in turn gave me and which I have in my possession." In 1844–45 Cuarterón sailed to Oceania aboard the Spanish schooner, *Mártires de Tun-Kin* (Martyrs of Tonkin), which was also "my property and under my command." As for the treasure, "I dedicated my share to God in 1846," he said.[5]

That same year Cuarterón paid a quick visit to Europe and by April 1847 was in Hong Kong. Here he visited Father Antonio Feliciani, a Franciscan priest who was the prefect apostolic of Hong Kong and the procurator (or agent) of Propaganda for dealing with bishops and other ecclesiastical superiors in charge of missions in China and in neighboring countries. Cuarterón explained to Feliciani, with whom he had been in contact at least as early as December 1845,[6] that he wanted to open a mission in Salibaboo (now Salibabu), one of the islands in the Talaor (now Talaud) Archipelago, southeast of the island of Mindanao in the Philippines. Cuarterón had visited Salibaboo for the first time on 22 June 1844 and believed it to be independent from any foreign power.[7]

---

4. See the file card on "Cuarterón" in PIME: File Card Index of Father Giovanni B. Tragella.

5. PF: Acta vol. 219 (1855), f. 818 (pp. 1–2, 12), "Esposizione di una nuova Missione Apostolica, che per la dilatazione e progresso della Religione Cattolica vuolsi stabilire nella Oceania Occidentale; e che per ottenere la necessaria approvazione e legittima autorit . . . , alla S. Congregazione de Propaganda Fide presenta il Sacerdote Carlo Cuarterón." This fourteen-page printed document measuring nine by twelve inches is catalogued simply under f. 818. This author adds in parentheses the printed page numbers of the document to which reference is made. The site of the shipwreck as indicated by Cuarterón points to a vast area in the South China Sea strewn with islets and reefs, called on maps still recently a "Dangerous Area" for navigators.

6. See Cuarterón's letter to Feliciani of 12 December 1845 in PIME: AME 29:623.

7. Carlos Cuarterón, *Spiegazione e Traduzione dei XIV quadri relativi alle isole di Salibaboo, Talaor, Sanguey, Nanuse, Mindanao, Celebes, Bornèo, Bahalatolis, Tambisan, Sulu, Toolyan, e Labuan presentati alla Sacra Congregazione de Propaganda Fide nel mese di settembre 1852 dal Capitano D. Carlo Cuarterón e dedicati a Sua*

As Cuarterón explained to Feliciani, he had found no priests during his voyages through the islands and along the coasts of the Celebes Sea. Consequently he believed that someone—perhaps a layman—should redeem Christian Filipino slaves held captive by the Moros inhabiting those areas. This would make possible the opening of Christian centers where missions could be founded and from which the Roman Catholic faith could spread. Cuarterón stated that he was ready to dedicate himself and his fortune to such a task. "To have a central point for all of my operations, I wanted to establish myself in the port and island of Salibaboo...," he said, "and from there go to the northern coasts of Celebes [now Sulawesi], to Gilolo [now Halmahera], Mortay [now Morotai], Waigiu [now Waigeo] and New Guinea; then to the southern coasts of Mindanao, to the Sulu Archipelago, and to the eastern coasts of the island of Borneo." All of these islands and coasts circled the Celebes Sea.[8]

Realizing that ecclesiastical authorization could be useful and perhaps even necessary for such a project, Cuarterón had come to Hong Kong to ask Feliciani to request it for him from Rome. This Feliciani did, being highly impressed with Cuarterón's plan. Writing to Cardinal Prefect Fransoni on 25 April 1847, he explained the project and said that Cuarterón wished to be considered for all practical purposes an alumnus of Propaganda's seminary in Rome. Feliciani added that Captain Cuarterón also hoped to receive authorization to carry the papal flag on his ship. This would guarantee his personal safety and also allow him to sail wherever he pleased.[9]

In proof of his seriousness about devoting his life to the redemption of captives, Cuarterón while in Hong Kong in May 1847, Feliciani said, received the habit of "the Third Order for the Redemption of Captives." This was the Third Order Secular of the Most Holy Trinity, a society of lay persons living in the world according to the spirit of the Order of the Most Holy Trinity for the Redemption of Captives (O.SS.T.). This order was approved by Pope Innocent III on 17 December 1198, and its unique scope was the redemption of Christians held captive by the Moslems in Spain, North Africa, and the Near East. It was possible for individuals, families and Christian states to ransom the Christian captives. The Trinitarian Order was founded to systematize the ransoming process, to solicit the necessary funds and carry them to Moslem ports, and to provide released prisoners with spiritual, physical, and moral rehabilitation. Besides dedicating his life to this cause,

---

Eminenza Reverendissima il Signor Cardinale Giacomo Filippo Fransoni, Prefetto della medesima, coll'appendice di un vocabolario [Italiano,] Malese, Suluano, Tagalese, una tavola di longitudine e di due carte geografiche sopra le Missioni, pp. vi, 1. This title is given inexactly by Tragella, *Missioni Estere*, 1:xviii, 190; by Rooney, *Khabar Gembira*, 237, 266; and by Glazik, "Kirchenorganisatorische Massnahmen im Indonesischen Archipel," in *Sacrae Congregationis de Propaganda Fide Memoria Rerum 1622–1972*, vol. 3/1, 496 n. 32.

8. PF: Acta vol. 219 (1855), f. 818 (pp. 1f), "Esposizione" of Cuarterón.

9. Feliciani's letter to Fransoni of 25 April 1847 has not been found. Its date and contents have been learned from Fransoni's reply of 22 July 1847 in PF: LDB vol. 336 (1847, Part II), f. 846v–847r, and also from Feliciani's reply to Fransoni of 29 September 1847 in PF: SOCP vol. 78 (1848–56, Part I), f. 264r.

Cuarterón dedicated a good portion of his wealth to it, depositing two thousand pesos with Feliciani.[10]

Wasting no time Captain Cuarterón purchased a small English schooner called *Lynx* and sailed out of Hong Kong in June 1847 under the protection of the English flag for the Sulu Archipelago, "to dedicate myself to the ransom of Christian slaves," as his first purpose. He also intended to seek "the best means for extirpating piracy, so damaging for this vast archipelago, and to explore all those numerous islands in order to be able to establish missions there." En route he was buffeted by a terrible hurricane in the South China Sea and entered a Philippine port to repair his ship. But the Spanish authorities there, noting the English flag, began to harass him and stated that he had no right to undertake a voyage for redeeming captives in Spanish territory. From that port in the Philippines Cuarterón hurried off a letter to Feliciani, indicating how urgently he needed the privilege of flying the papal flag so that he could sail in safety everywhere.

In order not to be taken prisoner, he fled from this Philippine port to the Sulu Archipelago, where at Bally [sic] he found pirates at war with the Dutch. "And so I fled to Salibaboo, which I thought was independent," arriving there on 10 September 1847. But the government of Manila hunted him down like a pirate, claiming that he "had no right to make such a voyage." Eventually he found himself forced to set his *Lynx* afire in the port and island of Salibaboo on 20 April 1848.[11]

It had taken Feliciani's first letter about Cuarterón of 25 April 1847 just three days short of three months to reach Cardinal Prefect Fransoni, who answered it immediately on 22 July. "As for the proposed mission on Salibaboo Island, it is my opinion that all steps whatsoever should be postponed until very exact and reassuring information has been supplied by Don Cuarterón," Fransoni said. "Meanwhile, I cannot but praise his zeal and his concern for the conversion of those abandoned idolaters." Feliciani could see from the files of his predecessor, the cardinal continued, how a similar mission proposed and established in Mindanao had failed because the predecessor had submitted inexact information.[12]

It took only two months and one week for Fransoni's letter to reach Hong Kong, and Feliciani also answered immediately on 29 September 1847. From the beginning, he said,

10. ASV: AN Madrid, Caja 330, Tit. XVI, Rub. 6a, no. 8, Feliciani to Brunelli, 25 May 1849; Tragella, *Missioni Estere*, 1:190 n. 15; PIME: AME 29:660, Cuarterón to Feliciani, 15 February 1850. Cuarterón tells Feliciani that by the time his letter of 15 February 1850 from Cadíz reaches Hong Kong, three years will have passed since he made his deposit. Mail often took three months to arrive. This would mean that the deposit was made in May 1847. All of the source material from ASV: AN Madrid (Secret Vatican Archives, Madrid Nunciature) was discovered by Father Franco Diaz de Cerio, S.J., of the Pontifical Gregorian University, Rome, who kindly shared it with the author of this work. See also "Trinitarians" by Augustine Thomas Walsh, O.SS.T., in *New Catholic Encyclopedia*, 14:293–95.

11. See PF: Acta vol. 219 (1855), f. 818 (pp. 2f), "Esposizione" of Cuarterón; Cuarterón, *Spiegazione e Traduzione del XIV quadri*, pp. vf, 3f; ASV: AN Madrid, Caja 330, Tit. XVI, Rub. 6a, no. 8, Feliciani to Brunelli, 25 May 1849; PF: SOCP vol. 78 (1848–56, Part I), f. 264r, Feliciani to Fransoni, 29 September 1847. Cuarterón's letter from the Philippines was not found, but it is mentioned in PF: SOCP vol. 78 (1848–56, Part I).

12. PF: LDB vol. 336 (1847, Part II) f. 846v–847r, Fransoni to Feliciani, 22 July 1847.

he had realized "that it was not expedient at the moment to make provisions for an uncertain mission about which we cannot know the outcome." However, he had wanted Fransoni to know about the good intentions of Cuarterón, who meanwhile had written to him from the Philippine Islands, saying that he did not want "to accept any other flag but that of the Holy Father" for his ship. "See whether Your Eminence can please him," Feliciani begged, "because it is my hope that this would bring great benefit to our religion."[13]

Three weeks after burning his schooner *Lynx*, Cuarterón on 10 May 1848 wrote from Salibaboo to Feliciani and then left this port and the station which he had been developing there for the previous eight months. On another vessel he fled to Sanguey (now Sangihe) Island, largest of fifty islands in an archipelago of the same name between Mindanao and Manado, Celebes. In Sanguey he was "very well received both by its Rajah . . . and by the natives there," he said.[14] "With the natives of this island I covered the entire stretch of islands between the coasts of Mindanao and Celebes until I reached Manado, after having wandered for eighteen months, counting from the time of my arrival at Salibaboo with the *Lynx*." Two of the islands visited by Cuarterón with the people of Sanguey were nearby Kaluman (now Kalama) and Buquit (now Bukide).[15] After spending "about two months" with the people of Sanguey, he went to Siao (now Siau) Island in the same archipelago but farther south. He finally reached Manado, the port at the northern tip of Celebes, on 4 August 1848 and once again was well received.[16]

Here Cuarterón met Mr. van Olphen, resident of the province of Manado, a part of the Dutch East Indies. Cuarterón told him how he had spent eight months from September 1847 to May 1848 in the Talaor Archipelago. Van Olphen informed Cuarterón that those islands were under his jurisdiction and command, even though they were not occupied by the Dutch. Because of this Cuarterón gave him a census that he had prepared of five islands in the Talaor Archipelago having a population of 37,700 in seventy-nine villages. He listed all of the villages by name, indicating the number of rajahs, men, women, boys, and girls in each village along with its total population. He had made the census in preparation for doing mission work in that area. The following table summarizes his statistical report:

---

13. PF: SOCP vol. 78 (1848–56, Part I), f. 264r, Feliciani to Fransoni, 29 September 1847.

14. PIME: AME 29:643, Cuarterón to Feliciani, 10 May 1848; PIME: AME 29:647–48, Cuarterón to Feliciani, 13 November 1848. Sanguey, the name always used by Cuarterón for the archipelago and island now written Sangihe, is also found in these forms: Sangi, Sangui, and Sanghir. The author thanks the Indonesian government officials of the Sangihe-Talaud Archipelagoes for providing him at the request of Theodorus Hubertus Moors, M.S.C., bishop of Manado, with the modern spellings of these and adjacent islands. The modern spellings do not mean that the forms in vogue at Cuarterón's time were incorrect. Even today there is no uniformity in pronunciation and spelling. For example, sometimes "h" is pronounced like "r" (Sangihe or Sangir), and sometimes "d" is pronounced like "r" (Talaud or Talaur). But Sangihe and Talaud are more commonly used today than Sangir and Talaur. See Letter, Bishop Moors to Wiltgen, 10 August 1989.

15. Cuarterón, *Spiegazione e Traduzione dei XIV quadri*, p. vi. See also Quadro VI between pp. 45 and 46.

16. PIME: AME 29:647f, Cuarterón to Feliciani, 13 November 1848.

Islands	Villages	Population
Salibaboo (now Salibabu)	8	4,550
Kabruang (now Kabaruang)	14	6,450
Karkelong (now Karakelang)	51	23,450
Nanuse (now Nanusa)	5	2,500
Mianguis (now Miangas)	1	750
Total	79	37,700

Cuarterón handed over these census results to van Olphen at Manado on 24 August 1848.[17]

Cuarterón kept Feliciani informed of his movements and activities. He wrote from Manado on 13 November 1848 about how he had gone from Salibaboo to Sanguey, to Siao, and finally to Manado.[18] In his wanderings from island to island he baptized those in danger of death, since there was no Roman Catholic priest in the archipelago. Faithfully he kept a list of the baptized, giving their original name, the name that he gave them in baptism, the date, the village where they had been baptized and also—if it happened before his departure—the date on which they died. His first baptism was at Salibaboo Village on 2 October 1847; his eighteenth and last baptism was at Manado Village in Celebes on 14 January 1849. The ages of those baptized ranged from four months to forty-five years and the baptisms took place in seven villages on six islands.[19]

The time from Cuarterón's arrival with the *Lynx* at Salibaboo on 10 September 1847 until his arrival at Manado on 4 August 1848 amounted to eleven months. Since he said that his "wanderings" had lasted eighteen months counting from his arrival at Salibaboo, he must have continued wandering in the vicinity of Manado for another seven months. In fact, he administered his eighteenth and last baptism there on 14 January 1849, which was five months after he had arrived there. And so it must have been about 10 March 1849 when he boarded the Dutch brigantine schooner *Mercurius* at Manado. This vessel took him to Surabaya in Java and then to Batavia (now Jakarta).

"Here I wrote a memorandum on the islands between Celebes and Mindanao," Cuarterón said. Since resident van Olphen had informed Cuarterón that these islands were under his civil jurisdiction, it meant that they automatically were also under the spiritual jurisdiction of the Roman Catholic bishop at Batavia. Cuarterón therefore gave this

---

17. For the complete census table, see Quadro V between pp. 45 and 46 in Cuarterón, *Spiegazione e Traduzione dei XIV quadri*.

18. PIME: AME 29:647–50.

19. The list of baptisms is in Quadro VI, inserted between pp. 45 and 46 in Cuarterón, *Spiegazione e Traduzione dei XIV quadri*. The eighteen baptisms administered by Cuarterón were at: Dalu Village, five, and Salibaboo Village, three, in Salibaboo Island; Tabukan Village, five, in Sanguey Islands; Nusa Village, two, in Kaluman Island; Tatenquelan Village, one, in Buquit Island; U-lu Village, one, in Siao Island; Port Manado, one, in Celebes Island.

memorandum to Bishop Piet Maria Vrancken (1806–79), coadjutor to the vicar apostolic of Batavia, then serving as administrator of the vicariate. Vrancken, who was Dutch, was Cuarterón's senior by ten years. Previous to receiving Cuarterón's memorandum, Vrancken had had no information so exact regarding the islands between Celebes and Mindanao.

Since Vrancken was responsible ecclesiastically for the islands in which the eighteen baptisms had been administered, Cuarterón also presented his list of those baptized to the bishop with a statement signed on 17 April 1849. In it he said: "To all who were not dead when I left, I presented a card with their [new Christian] name and the date on which they were baptized. Around their necks I placed a small cross made of lead as a symbol of their being a Christian. In this way they would not be confounded with others."[20] Vrancken confided to Cuarterón "his desire to open a mission in southern Borneo at Benjar Massin [now Bandjarmasin]. But for lack of personnel he could not do so." According to Cuarterón this important center had seen no Christian missionaries since 1690, "when by order of the King of Benjar Massin all Christian missionaries were killed. . . ."[21]

Cuarterón sailed from Batavia to Singapore in April 1849. His having been so long in Dutch-controlled territory, however, and his having sailed to Java on a Dutch brigantine seem to have created no problem for him with the Philippine consul at Singapore, who was an official of the Spanish government in Manila. Cuarterón even managed to obtain a passport from the consul for sailing directly to Manila. How explain this sudden change of attitude on the part of Spanish authorities, who only recently had persecuted him? Did Cuarterón perhaps convince the consul that, in view of his good relations with the island peoples between Celebes and Mindanao, he could wean them away from the Dutch and win them for Spain?

In spite of his success in Singapore, Cuarterón decided not to go to Manila. Instead he wanted to deal directly with Her Catholic Majesty, the queen of Spain, about his project. Since his best contact for an entrée to the queen was the papal nuncio in Madrid, and since his best contact for an entrée to the papal nuncio was Procurator Feliciani in Hong Kong, he set sail immediately from Singapore for Hong Kong in May 1849 "in order to report" on his expeditions. This was a voyage of 1,440 miles one way. After his arrival Feliciani wrote a highly complimentary letter of introduction for him on 25 May to the papal nuncio in Madrid, Archbishop Giovanni Brunelli (1795–1861), which began: "I take the liberty of warmly recommending the bearer . . . , Don Carlos Cuarterón of Spain, who is truly an apostolic man. . . ."

---

20. Cuarterón, *Spiegazione e Traduzione dei XIV quadri*, p. vi and Quadro VI between pp. 45 and 46.
21. PF: Acta vol. 219 (1855), f. 818 (pp. 9f), "Esposizione" of Cuarterón.

After receiving this letter Cuarterón lost no time in Hong Kong. "I reembarked in Hong Kong [on 27 May] for Europe," he said, "going via the Isthmus of Suez to England."[22] At this time the Suez Canal was not yet built and passengers crossed the Isthmus of Suez overland.

En route from Hong Kong to the Isthmus of Suez, Cuarterón once again sailed into the port of Singapore, where he arrived before mid-June 1849. Here he met Bishop Jean-Baptiste Boucho (1794–1871), the French vicar apostolic of Malacca (now Malay) Peninsula. On learning of Cuarterón's plans to evangelize islands bordering on the Celebes Sea, Boucher said that repeatedly he had tried to send missionaries to the west coast of Borneo, but could not do so because of opposition from Dutch authorities in Java.[23]

What Cuarterón particularly wanted to discuss with Boucho, whose residence was at Pulo Pinang (now Penang), an island in the Strait of Malacca, was a project suggested by Feliciani in Hong Kong some fifteen days earlier. It concerned the establishment of a central boarding school at Singapore that would provide higher education for mission students in general and also seminary training for those wanting to become priests. Boucho received the proposal enthusiastically and agreed to begin construction at once, when Cuarterón gave him one thousand pesos in cash. It was expected that Bishop Vrancken, vicar apostolic of Batavia, would also join this cooperative effort. Vrancken, Boucho, and Cuarterón were to share construction costs. "The buildings when finished will cost us three thousand pesos apiece," Cuarterón said. "But we shall have the satisfaction of conducting the best college that there is in all of the East Indies."

When informing Feliciani of these negotiations, Cuarterón thanked him for having provided the motivation "for my deciding to contribute toward and to support" this good work. He had written to Bishop Vrancken, he said, explaining the project and inviting him to join it. Once construction was completed, Vrancken, Boucho, and Cuarterón would each pay three or four pesos monthly per boarding student and each could send up to fifty to the school. When informing Feliciani from the Bay of Bengal on 14 June 1849 of his meeting with Boucho, Cuarterón said that construction of the college had perhaps already begun.[24]

---

22. ASV: AN Madrid, Caja 330, Tit. XVI, Rub. 6a, no. 8, Feliciani to Brunelli, 25 May 1849; Cuarterón, *Spiegazione e Traduzione dei XIV quadri*, pp. vi–vii. On page vii Cuarterón speaks of his hurried voyages from Singapore to Hong Kong and back again, but does not indicate the dates. In his Asia/Oceania map appended to his book, he dates his voyages: Singapore to Hong Kong in May 1849 and Hong Kong to Singapore in June 1849. The date 27 May was found by calculating backwards from 30 August 1849, when Cuarterón arrived in Cádiz "after ninety-six days of navigation" from Hong Kong, as he told Feliciani. See PIME: AME 29:653, Cuarterón to Feliciani, 19 September 1849.

23. PF: Acta vol. 219 (1855), f. 818 (p. 10), "Esposizione" of Cuarterón. Here Cuarterón calls Boucho the vicar apostolic of Western Siam; officially he was vicar apostolic of the Malacca Peninsula.

24. PIME: AME 29:651–52, Cuarterón to Feliciani, 14 June 1849; PIME. AME 29:660, Cuarterón to Feliciani, 15 February 81850. Although Cuarterón literally says "the best college that there is in all India," it is clear from the context that the Spanish must be translated: "in all of the East Indies." The author has found nothing in the 14 June 1849 letter of Cuarterón to Feliciani, referred to by Tragella in *Missioni Estere*,

Cuarterón reached Cádiz "on the evening of 30 August 1849 after ninety-six days of navigation, counting from when he had left Hong Kong. In that time he had covered 8,350 miles.[25] Three months later he wrote Feliciani from Cádiz on 29 November 1849 that, armed with Feliciani's letter of recommendation, he was going to Madrid to see Nuncio Brunelli.[26] He was convinced that it would win for him Brunelli's influence with the Spanish government, thus providing "those guarantees which I need to carry forward the enterprise to which I have dedicated myself."[27] Feliciani's letter to Nuncio Brunelli described Cuarterón as "a truly apostolic man afire with a keen interest in redeeming very many unhappy Christians" of the Sulu Archipelago "and of other islands in the Celebes Sea, made slaves by the Moros." He said that Cuarterón had become a Third Order member, explained why he had been forced to set fire to his ship, and pointed out how well he had been treated and honored by the island peoples. "He is now returning to Europe," Feliciani said, "to provide information for the Queen of Spain and to persuade her to civilize those poor Moros and to redeem their unfortunate and unhappy slaves." Feliciani urged Brunelli "kindly to intermediate with the queen so that she may comply with the pious desires of this man, so truly devout and so zealous for the salvation of souls . . ."[28] Spain's queen at this time was eighteen-year-old Isabel II (1830–1904), whose reign (1843–68) was filled with political turmoil and civil war.

After his return from Madrid to Cádiz, Cuarterón on 15 February 1850 sent an optimistic report to Feliciani:

> I presented myself to Most Reverend Brunelli with your letter of recommendation and he received me very well. When I told him about the current status of my project, he promised to assist me in every possible way. I presented myself also to Señor [Lorenzo] de Arrazola [1797–1873], Minister for Justice and Ecclesiastical Affairs, after being recommended to him by friends. . . . He, too, received me very cordially. Both Archbishop Brunelli and Señor de Arrazola asked that I provide them with a memorandum on my voyages, indicating what it was that I proposed to the Government. I was to point out all that I believe advantageous and necessary for the

---

1:190 n. 17, warranting the statement that Boucho was asked to accept some of Cuarterón's students "in the Pulo-Pinang seminary to educate them there for the priesthood." The words "en aquelo punto" in Cuarterón's Spanish letter refer to "Singapore," not to "Pulo-Pinang."

25. PIME: AME 29:653, Cuarterón to Feliciani, 19 September 1849. For the mileage see the navigation charts in *Philips' Modern School Atlas*, 16, 56–57.

26. PIME: AME 29:655, Cuarterón to Feliciani, 29 November 1849. Since Cuarterón was in Cádiz when he wrote this letter of 29 November, and since November has only thirty days, he must be mistaken when he tells Feliciani on 15 February 1850 that he had presented himself to the papal nuncio "in the last days of November" 1849. See PIME: AME 29:659. Coming from Cádiz at the southern tip of Spain, he could not have reached Madrid in the center of Spain in a single day. This is one of the rare instances noted by the author in which Cuarterón errs in his chronology.

27. PIME: AME 29:655, Cuarterón to Feliciani, 29 November 1849.

28. ASV: AN Madrid, Caja 330, Tit. XVI, Rub. 6a, no. 8, Feliciani to Brunelli, 25 May 1849.

good of Spain and for the missions which I shall try to found in all of the archipelagoes in the Jolo [now Sulu] and Celebes seas.

Cuarterón told Feliciani that he was busy drawing up the requested memorandum. "When all this work is finished in the spring, about April or May, I plan to return to Madrid," he said. "And, if possible, I shall also go to Rome in order to see whether once and for all I can complete all arrangements, as I hope, so that I can proceed with founding my Missions." By the time his letter would reach Hong Kong, he said, three years would have passed since his deposit of two thousand pesos had been in Feliciani's hands without having gained any interest. Since he had earmarked this money for the educational institution in Singapore, Cuarterón told Feliciani that it was necessary "from today onwards to be able to obtain the greatest possible amount of interest due to me, in order that I may have available the funds that I need to continue the enterprise which I have begun." He was merely following the advice of Feliciani, who had repeatedly told him to see to it that his money should make more money. Cuarterón said that, if Feliciani wanted to continue using his money, it will be necessary "for you to give me the current rate of interest being offered" in Hong Kong. "And if you should not need this money any longer, I would be very grateful if you were to invest it for me with all possible guarantees, so that it produces something and I can gain some interest."[29]

One year passed, however, and Cuarterón's project made no headway. Nuncio Brunelli, who had been secretary of Propaganda from 1843 to 1847, gave the reason for this lack of success on 9 February 1851 in a letter of recommendation that he wrote for Cuarterón to Cardinal Prefect Fransoni. He pointed out that Cuarterón "has many financial means at his disposal and for a number of years he has thought of using them for the most religious and difficult task of redeeming the many unhappy Christians made slaves by the Moros . . . On returning to Europe he went immediately to Spain to interest the Government in supporting his proposal and his efforts, which are devoid of any design or interest of a political nature. Their only aim is introducing into those places the Catholic Religion with its civilization and obtaining freedom from slavery for a large number of unhappy people."

Brunelli told Fransoni that with pleasure and with dedication he had tried to assist Cuarterón. "But unfortunately I did not find in the Government of Her Majesty that interest, which in the beginning I had expected." And finally when Cuarterón "was counting on the favor of the Duke of Valencia," Lorenzo de Arrazola, "the fall of the ministry headed by him removed every foundation for any hope. This being the state of affairs he [Cuarterón] has decided to go to Rome in order to urge Propaganda kindly to help him and protect him in executing his noble and pious desire."

Like Feliciani in Hong Kong, Brunelli in Madrid praised Cuarterón highly. "From what I could learn in the short time that I have dealt with him, he seems to me to be animated with an excellent spirit and with true zeal for the progress and benefit of Religion. The same

---

29. PIME: AME 29:659–61, Cuarterón to Feliciani, 15 February 1850.

assurance was given me by Father Antonio Feliciani, Procurator of the Missions at Hong Kong, who directed him to me and recommended him warmly. And although he is already furnished with various letters for Your Eminence, written by Vicars Apostolic" in the East Indies, "he has also requested me to accompany him with this letter of mine. Disposed as always to contribute in so far as I can to the greater growth of our Holy Religion . . . , I could not deny his earnest requests." Brunelli was confident, he said, that Fransoni would extend a kind welcome to Cuarterón and would also show sympathy and understanding for his project.[30]

It would seem, however, that Cuarterón was not yet ready to admit defeat in Spain, because after receiving Brunelli's letter of recommendation, he waited another sixteen months before setting out for Rome. By that time he was well aware that the archipelagoes between Celebes and Mindanao, being under Dutch control, would be subject ecclesiastically to the Dutch vicar apostolic in Batavia. This ruled out the possibility that Salibaboo and the fifty islands around it, many of which Cuarterón had visited and studied, might become his mission. Precisely this area had been his first choice.

His second choice was the Sulu Archipelago between northeastern Borneo and southwestern Mindanao. But by August 1851 news must have reached Madrid that Antonio de Urbiztondo y Eguía (1800?–before 1866), captain general and governor of the Philippines, had personally led a campaign against Sultan Mahamed Pulalon of Jolo, largest island in the Sulu Archipelago, obliging him to sign a treaty or capitulation of seventeen articles on 19 April 1851. This treaty was then approved and ratified in Manila on 30 April 1851 by Queen Isabel II of Spain in the person of the governor captain general. This meant that the Sulu Archipelago was now Spanish territory and that the bishop of Cebu, Romualdo Jimeno (1808–72) of the Order of Preachers (O.P.), automatically had obtained ecclesiastical jurisdiction over it. Since it was expected that he would entrust it to the Jesuits, Cuarterón was deprived of what had been his second choice of a mission field. Borneo also bordered on the Celebes Sea and fascinated Cuarterón because it, too, suffered from the Moros. He knew that England had founded a colony on Borneo's northwestern coast, partly to stop piracy, and he reasoned that the two Roman Catholic bishops of Cebu and Batavia could claim no ecclesiastical jurisdiction in English territory. Since no Roman Catholic mission had yet been established there, he believed that Roman authorities might consider entrusting part of the area to him.

It was most likely during the second half of his sixteen-month waiting period that Cuarterón made his voyage from Cádiz to London—a round trip of some twenty-six hundred miles—in order to obtain detailed information on Borneo from Sir Edward Belcher (1799–1877). While in the Sulu Archipelago in 1847, Cuarterón had heard of him and referred to him as "the Commander of the English frigate of war *Samarang*." This naval officer had performed many coastal surveys for the English Admiralty and in 1848 published his *Narrative of the Voyage of H.M.S. "Samarang" During 1843–1846*. It described

---

30. ASV: AN Madrid, Caja 330, Tit. XVI, Rub. 6a, no. 8, Brunelli to Fransoni, 9 February 1851.

his exploration voyages to China, Borneo, the Philippine Islands, and Formosa. Now in need of precise information on Borneo, it was undoubtedly at this time when Cuarterón consulted him personally in London. "Sir Edward Belcher gave me all the information that I wanted," he said.[31]

Cuarterón sailed out of the Bay of Cádiz on 14 June 1852 for Civitavecchia, the port of Rome, where he arrived in ten days. "On the following day, the 25th, I reached the capital of the Christian world," he said. "I presented myself immediately to Propaganda, which received me very well and showed me the greatest affection." He met Cardinal Prefect Fransoni, secretary Barnabò, and undersecretary Buratti; they told Pope Pius IX about him and his many voyages. "They say that the pope wants to get to know me," and so "I am to prepare myself for the moment when His Holiness sends word that he will give me an audience." Cuarterón assured Feliciani that the letter of recommendation written by him had been responsible for this warm reception.

God appeared to be leading Cuarterón toward a stronger commitment and a deeper spiritual life. As he told his friend Feliciani on 9 July 1852: "My chief desire is to make myself a priest in order to be able to serve God that much better in the missions."[32] Earlier on 23 March he had told Feliciani, "I have had the idea of dedicating myself exclusively to the service of God and of contributing toward the growth of His flock by working for the benefit of the missions." Two years earlier he had confided to Feliciani that his spiritual director had ordered him to receive Holy Communion daily in order to nourish his soul.[33]

In September 1852 after the officials of Propaganda had returned from their traditional August holidays, Cuarterón presented them with his "XIV Cuadros" (that is, "Fourteen Reports") in Spanish on islands and archipelagoes known to him where missions could be founded. He had written this lengthy document while in Spain, but Propaganda took no action on it.[34] In this work particular attention was given to Salibaboo. Nevertheless

---

31. Cuarterón, *Spiegazione e Traduzione dei XIV quadri*, p. vii; PF: Acta vol. 219 (1855), f. 818 (pp. 4–5, 11), "Esposizione" of Cuarterón. For the Cádiz-London mileage see *Philips' Modern School Atlas*, 16. See also "Urbiztondo y Eguía," *Enciclopedia Vniversal Ilvstrada Evropeo-Americana*, 65:1401f. The author thanks Father José Barriocanal, S.V.D., for assistance with this and other Spanish source material concerning this chapter. Tragella in *Missioni Estere*, 1:190, when describing Cuarterón's voyage from Java to Rome, says: "From Java he then went to Singapore and from there to Hong Kong. . . . Via England and Spain he finally reached Rome. . . ." Tragella may have been misled by Cuarterón's statement that he "reembarked in Hong Kong for Europe going via the Isthmus of Suez to England." But here Cuarterón is merely giving the farthest distant point to which he sailed. From his correspondence it is clear that he went from Hong Kong via Singapore to Cádiz. In view of the political and ecclesiastical developments described in the present work, it seems probable to this author that Cuarterón went to England in his final months before leaving Cádiz for Rome. Cuarterón does not date his visit to Sir Belcher. See Cuarterón, *Spiegazione e Traduzione dei XIV quadri*, p. vii.

32. PIME: AME 29:675–76, Cuarterón to Feliciani, 9 July 1852.

33. Ibid., 667, Cuarterón to Feliciani, 23 March 1852; ibid., 661, 15 February 1850.

34. PF: Acta vol. 219 (1855), f. 818 (p. 1), "Esposizione" of Cuarterón, 15 February 1855; Cuarterón,

Cuarterón later said that his purpose in becoming a priest was to extend the standard of the cross, not only to Salibaboo, "but to all the islands which I can penetrate with my missionaries in that vast and immense archipelago of Oceania." Although Cuarterón spoke of "my missionaries," he had none at this time.[35]

Cuarterón was thirty-six years of age when he began his studies for the priesthood in October 1852 at the Pontifical Urban College facing the Spanish Square in Rome. Behind the college was the Basilica of Sant'Andrea delle Fratte, where the Blessed Virgin Mary ten years earlier, on 20 January 1842, had appeared to Alphonse Ratisbonne, a twenty-seven-year-old Jew from Strasbourg, France. The basilica was cared for by the Minimi Fathers of Saint Francis di Paola and it was in their large monastery attached to the basilica where Cuarterón took up his lodging. Like Cuarterón, Ratisbonne had also decided to study for the priesthood.

Being a man of means, Cuarterón did not want to be a financial burden on Propaganda, and so he assured its authorities that he himself would cover all the costs for his lodging, studies, and future mission.[36] In fact, only two weeks after reaching Rome he instructed Feliciani to transfer 215 pesos from his Hong Kong account to Propaganda's account.[37] He also supplied the endowment of a benefice for his own support, as Propaganda desired. He did this, he said, "by using other funds that I had in Europe."[38] Later he sent Feliciani a further order to transfer 800 pesos from his Hong Kong account to that of Cardinal Fransoni.[39]

In Cardinal Prefect Fransoni, who reached his seventy-eighth birthday on 10 December 1853, Cuarterón found his principal patron in Rome. But on Christmas Day that year Fransoni was confined to bed because of an open sore on his leg. He was still in bed by 21 January 1854, and all progress on Cuarterón's project had stopped. Although by this time Cuarterón had completed only fifteen months of theological studies, he was

---

Spiegazione e Traduzione dei XIV quadri, p. viii. The original Spanish version of this latter work has not been found; perhaps it was returned to Cuarterón in 1855 for making the translation into Italian.

35. PIME: AME 29:679–80, Cuarterón to Feliciani, 1 October 1852.

36. Both Tragella in *Missioni Estere*, 1:191 n. 21, and Rooney in *Khabar Gembira*, 19, make an issue of whether or not Cuarterón studied at the Pontifical Urban College, because his name appears on no list of students. The fact that he did not live in the seminary and was not supported by Propaganda, but lived across the street from the seminary and paid his own room, board, and tuition, would seem reason enough for his name not appearing on the rosters. As early as 25 April 1847 Feliciani had written to Fransoni that Cuarterón wished to be considered for all practical purposes an alumnus of Propaganda's seminary in Rome. These various considerations make it appear inconceivable that Cuarterón would have made his studies for the priesthood somewhere else. The basilica alongside the monastery where Cuarterón lodged is today known as the Shrine of Our Lady of the Miracle. See Abel, *The Madonna of the Miracle*, 5.

37. PIME: AME 29:671, Cuarterón to Feliciani, 9 July 1852. Cuarterón wrote Feliciani two separate letters on this date. See also PIME: AME 29:675–76.

38. Ibid., 713, Cuarterón to Feliciani, 21 January 1854.

39. Cuarterón's order was dated 21 March 1854, but has not been found. It is mentioned in ibid, 717, Cuarterón to Feliciani, 21 August 1854.

thinking of who might ordain him to the priesthood. He could be ordained by the cardinal vicar of Rome or by some other bishop outside of Rome, he said. But "as long as the Cardinal Prefect of Propaganda is alive," he told Feliciani, "I do not care to be ordained by anyone except by this most virtuous and highly meritorious Prince of the Church."[40]

Meanwhile Archbishop Brunelli's office as nuncio apostolic to Spain had come to an end when Pope Pius IX on 7 March 1853 named him a cardinal. On 31 August 1854, about a month before Cuarterón began his third and final year of studies for the priesthood, the pope appointed Brunelli a member of the Board of Cardinals in charge of Propaganda.[41]

Ten days after Brunelli's appointment, director Marinoni wrote to a friend in Rome, Father Alfieri, secretary general of the Order of Hospitalers of Saint John of God. Because of this priest's "sincere desire—many times expressed—of wanting to be of help," Marinoni requested him to accept the office of procurator (or agent) in Rome for his Institute of Foreign Missions. His task would be to intermediate for Marinoni whenever necessary and "on occasion report back to us what can be of interest to us."[42]

Alfieri informed Marinoni one month later on 16 October 1854 that both Cardinal Prefect Fransoni and undersecretary Buratti had been pleased to learn of his definite appointment as "your Procurator in Rome." But first Alfieri wanted to make something very clear to Marinoni and his men. "If I am to be your Procurator in Rome," he said,

> I want to be in agreement with Propaganda in all things. And if you depend completely upon that Congregation, everything will go along well and the Holy Father will recast the judgment that he made of you when, blinded by fervor . . . , you persisted in choosing Oceania and in not offering the first candidates of your Collegio to the Holy Father, who wanted to send them elsewhere.
>
> My very dear friends, I know that I can make you highly esteemed by Propaganda and by the Holy Father. But for me to do this, you must abandon yourselves to them. They are more eager to provide you in time with particular missions that are all your own, than you are yourselves. And they hope to do this over a brief period of time, forming the two missions of India into two separate vicariates for you. But meanwhile it is necessary for you to make a novitiate there, just like you had to do under the Marists in Oceania.

Marinoni had pointed out to Alfieri that the Marists were insisting that the Milan missionaries must have their own procure or supply center in Sydney. Alfieri assured him that "at its first opportunity" Propaganda shall recommend that the Marists assist the Milan missionaries in realizing this project. His letter, Alfieri said, was "the result of my talk with the Reverend Buratti, who loves you and your Collegio very much . . ."[43] The stage was now set: Cuarterón needed personnel for his mission, and the Milan missionaries

---

40. Ibid., 713–14, Cuarterón to Feliciani, 21 January 1854.
41. Metzler, "Präfekten und Sekretäre," 58.
42. PIME: AME 5:823–24, Marinoni to Alfieri, 10 September 1854.
43. Ibid., 10:65.

needed a new procure or supply center in Oceania, independent from that of the Marists. Earlier Ramazzotti had sent Fransoni a list of ten priests, saying that they were "ready to go to any mission in the East Indies or to any other place where you may wish to send them."⁴⁴ Alfieri's letter had said that the Milan missionaries "must abandon" themselves to Propaganda and accept whatever it offers them. It was clear to undersecretary Buratti and to Procurator Alfieri that Cuarterón's need for personnel could be supplied by the Milan group and that the need of the Milan group for a new procure or supply center in Oceania could be fulfilled by having one in common with Cuarterón.

Consequently when word reached Fransoni that Bishops Carew and Murphy of India were delighted over Rome's offer of priests from Milan, he at once informed Marinoni on 22 November 1854 of their acceptance. In the same letter he said surprisingly, "Perhaps after a short time I shall need two additional fine priests for founding another mission on virgin soil, but in an area well disposed to receive the seed of the gospel." He spoke of "a distinguished Ecclesiastic, well acquainted with the place, who has volunteered to erect the mission." Marinoni's two priests would "practice the sacred ministry" under him. And because of the location of this new mission "with regard to the Missions of Oceania," Fransoni said, "the place in question could provide many advantages for communicating with Prefect Apostolic Reina and for giving him and his companions assistance. I would therefore suggest that you have two of your most experienced and courageous candidates join and collaborate with the above-mentioned Ecclesiastic, provided that you can give me assurance of having them available for this. Meanwhile I shall await your reply. . . ."⁴⁵ Marinoni took no decisive action. He wondered who this mysterious "Ecclesiastic" was, where precisely his mission would be, and what obligations would follow for the Milan Mission Seminary. When sending these questions to Alfieri, he asked what Alfieri might think of withdrawing the Milan missionaries from Melanesia and perhaps offering some of them to Archbishop Polding of Sydney. Polding was in Italy for the forthcoming proclamation of the dogma of the Immaculate Conception of the Blessed Virgin Mary and was soliciting personnel for new missions that he hoped to found in Australia.

Marinoni's letter irritated Alfieri, who replied brusquely on 4 December 1854. "Later I shall write about Polding," he said. "However, it was really imprudent for you to ask whether you should or should not recall your missionaries from Oceania. My dear man! You certainly need someone in Rome to represent you at Propaganda, who is both prudent and cool-headed. And you likewise need two very staid and very prudent counselors."

---

44. PF: CV vol. 43, f. 204r, Ramazzotti to Fransoni, 22 May 1854. See chap. 12, p. 192.

45. PIME: AME 1:141–42, Fransoni to Marinoni, 22 November 1854. Fransoni calls Cuarterón an "Ecclesiastic." In Italian this word can stand for any cleric, even one not yet ordained to the priesthood. Consequently the designation as ecclesiastic is no proof that Cuarterón by this date was already ordained a priest. However it is hard to believe that Fransoni would refer to him in official correspondence as the founder of a proposed mission, if he were not yet ordained a priest.

Alfieri criticized Marinoni for asking "too many useless questions" about things "already under way."[46]

The mysterious "Ecclesiastic" mentioned by Fransoni was, of course, Cuarterón. And because of his great devotion to the Blessed Virgin Mary he was no doubt present in Saint Peter's Basilica on 8 December 1854, when Pope Pius IX during a solemn service proclaimed the dogma of the Immaculate Conception of the Blessed Virgin Mary. Cardinals Fransoni and Brunelli of Propaganda were there. Archbishops Romilli of Milan and Polding of Sydney were there. And Bishop Vrancken of Batavia was also there.[47] By 19 December 1854 no answer had yet arrived in Rome from Marinoni to Fransoni's 22 November request for "two additional fine priests" to be assigned to "a distinguished Ecclesiatic." Alfieri therefore wrote to Marinoni, stressing that Buratti and Vespasiani had charged him to say that "they are waiting for a reply on the new mission, which will be financed completely by the missionary benefactor who proposed it. . . . They told me the name of this person, who recently has become a priest . . . and is the captain and owner of a ship."

Alfieri had further news: "Finally I saw [Archbishop] Polding who received me with great pleasure and told me that he *will be passing through Milan*. So you will be able to reach a better understanding with him in all matters right there on the spot." Marinoni had wanted to give Polding one or two of his priests "to assist him and to serve as procurator" for Reina and the others in Melanesia. Marinoni even wanted Polding "to accept all the others," in case they had to leave Melanesia.

Polding, in fact, already had a mission in mind for them, Alfieri said, not too far from where Reina and his missionaries were working. Alfieri highly esteemed Polding and said that it would be a good idea for Marinoni to collaborate with him. And after discussing the matter with Buratti and Vespasiani, he learned that they also considered it a good idea to collaborate with Polding, who "enjoys much esteem and veneration at Propaganda." As for any young priests who might be assigned to Polding, both Buratti and Vespasiani had told Alfieri that they must study English above all other languages, because it is "a magic key for those places and wins confidence and sympathy from the English people themselves."[48] Christmas and Epiphany came and went, but there was still no word from Marinoni. So Alfieri wrote again on Monday, 8 January 1855. "The enclosed urgent note from Monsignor

---

46. Ibid., 10:69. Marinoni's letter was not found, but its contents are evident from Alfieri's reply.

47. The names of all cardinals, archbishops, and bishops present for the proclamation of the dogma on 8 December 1854 are carved in three slabs of marble in the apse of Saint Peter's Basilica.

48. PIME: AME 10:77, Alfieri to Marinoni, 19 December 1854. Here Alfieri mistakenly speaks of Marinoni's missionaries as being in Polynesia; they were in Melanesia. This letter of 19 December 1854 is the earliest document found by the author which gives a clue to the time of Cuarterón's ordination to the priesthood, since it says that he "recently has become a priest." The precise date is not given and has not been found. See also n. 45. Neither has mention been found in any document of the person who ordained Cuarterón a priest. Because of his close attachment to Fransoni and his stating that he wanted to be ordained by no one else as long as Fransoni lived, it is likely that Fransoni was the ordaining prelate. It was customary for him to ordain heads of new missions. See Wiltgen, *Oceania*, 409. The Spanish work, *Enciclopedia Vniversal Ilvstrada Evropeo-Americana*, 16:772, states without giving any source that Cuarterón was ordained a priest by Pope Pius IX.

Buratti ... obliges me to ask you again: *Do you have two members about whom Father [Carlo] Candiani sent you an explanation?*" (Candiani was secretary to Archbishop Romilli of Milan.) If Marinoni had two such priests, Alfieri said, then he should

> indicate each one's name, age and qualifications, writing at once to me or to Monsignor Buratti, so that an understanding can be reached with Don Cuarterón ... The plan is to call for them immediately, so that for some days in Rome they can become familiar with that mission and with the above-mentioned missionary and apostle, can visit Propaganda together with him, and then can make preparations for leaving together. In two or three days Cuarterón will be returning to Rome from Florence and it will be most unpleasant if he still cannot be assured of receiving personnel. Answer, then, but do so adequately, and not in generic and vague terms like you answered the Cardinal. Could you not have sent me at least a single word?[49]

It was 17 January 1855 when Marinoni finally sent Alfieri the list of missionaries assigned to India and to Cuarterón. Three priests and one lay catechist were assigned to Calcutta; two priests were assigned to Hyderabad; and two more priests were assigned to "an island in Oceania," as the still indefinite mission of Cuarterón was called. The two assigned to Cuarterón were Father Antonio Riva (1823–62) of Lecco, ordained a priest in 1848, and Father Ignazio Borgazzi (1829–78) of Milan, ordained a priest in 1852. All eight missionaries were drawn from a list of ten priests and two lay catechists already submitted to Cardinal Fransoni by Bishop Ramazzotti on 22 May 1854.[50]

By Monday afternoon, 22 January, Alfieri had Marinoni's letter of 17 January and gave it to Buratti and Vespasiani on the following day. Alfieri reported back to Marinoni excitedly on 24 January: "They rejoiced on learning the contents! In their meeting today they will take up the proposal of Cuarterón, who is in Rome. And when I meet him, I shall get him to like you, as if he were one of your own members. Perhaps I can also get him to pass through Milan. But this would be only after his two missionaries have reached Rome and have received all of their instructions, faculties, letters patent and also their Papal Passports (which I can obtain), if such should be useful for them. ..." Since both Propaganda and the pope wanted to keep the Milan missionaries "in Rome for some time to perfect them," Alfieri assured Marinoni that he would "take care of finding them lodging ..."[51]

---

49. PIME: AME 10:79, Alfieri to Marinoni, 8 January 1855. Here Alfieri uses the incorrect spelling "Quarteron" for "Cuarterón." Candiani, as secretary to Archbishop Romilli, may well have accompanied his archbishop to Rome for the proclamation of the dogma of the Immaculate Conception on 8 December 1854 and so would certainly have met Alfieri.

50. For the vague reference to Cuarterón's mission see PIME: AME 11, *Notizie*, Appendix, 1. For the vital statistics of Riva and Borgazzi see PIME: Archivist Angelo Bubani's personnel file and also Tragella in *Missioni Estere*, 1:186. For Ramazzotti's list of missionaries see PF: CV vol. 43, f. 204r.

51. PIME: AME 10:85, Alfieri to Marinoni, 24 January 1855. Alfieri dated his letter simply 24/55, that is,

Alfieri found lodging for the five missionaries destined for India at the international headquarters of his own religious order, the Hospitalers of Saint John of God, on the island in the Tiber River. Riva and Borgazzi, however, were to be lodged at Cuarterón's own expense in the monastery of the Minimi Fathers of Saint Francis of Paola, where he himself was lodged, across the street from Propaganda's headquarters.[52] Things were moving quickly now. Propaganda held a meeting on Father Cuarterón's proposal on 24 January 1855 and on the next day in Lyon, France, the Association for the Propagation of the Faith informed Marinoni that his missionaries going to India would receive the funds requested for their transportation.[53] Marinoni passed on this news to Rome. Then on Saturday, 10 February, Alfieri told Marinoni: "Today—in fact just now I have come back from the Secretariat of Propaganda. While there I also met Monsignor Barnabò for the first time. He together with Buratti and Vespasiani send you greetings. . . ." The two priests assigned to Cuarterón, Alfieri said, would remain in Rome "some days longer" than the missionaries assigned to India.[54]

Three days later, on 13 February 1855, Cardinal Fransoni wrote to Marinoni that, since the good season for sailing was arriving and since funds had arrived from Lyon for the voyage of his missionaries to Calcutta and Hyderabad, he should send them to Rome where final arrangements would be made and where they would receive the necessary instructions. He asked that Marinoni also send along "the two priests, Borgazzi and Riva, who are to join the Reverend Don Cuarterón for the known new Mission. For the duration of their stay in Rome," he said, "they will be lodged at Sant'Andrea delle Fratte alongside Propaganda with the same Don Cuarterón. Thus he can easily converse with them and make the necessary arrangements for their voyage, which will begin after a short while. . . ."[55]

Cuarterón's project was discussed by a small group on 24 January 1855.[56] Most likely at this meeting Riva and Borgazzi were assigned to Cuarterón, and he was given notice to produce quickly an Italian summary of his lengthy mission proposal submitted in Spanish as early as September 1852. Cuarterón completed the summary in three weeks, dedicated it to Fransoni, dated it "15 February 1855" and signed it "The Priest Carlos Cuarterón." Lengthy titles were then in vogue, so he called it: "Description of a new Mission Apostolic, which hopefully will be established in Western Oceania for the spread and progress of the

---

the twenty-fourth day of 1855, or 24 January. The 17 January 1855 letter of Marinoni to Alfieri was not found, but is referred to in Alfieri's reply of 24 January.

52. Ibid., 91, Alfieri to Marinoni (n.d.)

53. Tragella, *Missioni Estere*, 1:185 n. 1.

54. PIME: AME 10:87–88, Alfieri to Marinoni, 10 February 1855. Alfieri first dated his letter 6 February 1855, then changed the 6 into 8, and finally changed the 8 into 10. The Rome postmark is 12 February 1855, and the Milan arrival postmark is 16 February 1855.

55. Ibid., 1:143. This is the first time that Fransoni mentions Cuarterón by name in a letter to Marinoni.

56. Meetings like this were often attended only by the cardinal prefect, the secretary, and that undersecretary who was charged with the geographical area under consideration.

Catholic Religion, now presented by the Priest Carlos Cuarterón to the Sacred Congregation for Propagating the Faith in order to obtain the necessary approval and lawful authority."

On the title page of his summary Cuarterón said that he had not yet been able to present Propaganda with a printed Italian translation of his Spanish work, "not only because I was continually occupied with studying ecclesiastical sciences, but also because the printing press of this Sacred Congregation is busy bringing to light other works recommended with more insistence by His Holiness . . . But now, since the time is approaching for me to be able to go and work in the vineyard of the Lord, I find myself in absolute need of presenting this 'Description' in order to show in a brief synthesis how my thoughts and my undertaking have developed."[57]

Riva and Borgazzi together with the missionaries assigned to India received their mission crosses in a departure ceremony at San Calocero Shrine presided over by Archbishop Romilli of Milan on Monday, 19 February 1855. (This was four days after Cuarterón had completed his summary.) Neither Bishop Ramazzotti nor Father Supriès could attend because of conflicting engagements. In this same shrine Reina and his missionaries had received their mission crosses on 16 March 1852. In the three-year interval no one from the Milan Mission Seminary had been sent to a foreign mission.[58] About 9 p.m. on Ash Wednesday, 21 February 1855, the Milan missionaries left Genoa, sailing via Livorno (also called Leghorn) to Civitavecchia, the port of Rome. Early Friday morning, 23 February, just as the sun was rising, they sailed into port. Alfieri had someone waiting for them at the pier, and by 8 p.m. they reached Rome, where they met Alfieri. He lodged all of them that night at his order's headquarters on Tiber Island.[59]

Father Albino Parietti, eldest in the Milan missionary group, had been named superior by Marinoni. At the end of their first full day in Rome, Saturday, 24 February, he wrote Marinoni that Alfieri had taken all of them that morning to meet Father Cuarterón at the monastery of the Minimi. Riva and Borgazzi took along their baggage and received lodging there. Parietti was greatly impressed by Cuarterón and described him as "a very fine man, about my age, robust in mind and body, having very extensive and exact nautical and geographical knowledge." Parietti, who was thirty-seven years of age at this time, said that Marinoni would be receiving some of Cuarterón's published works.

Alfieri next took the group to Propaganda, "where we were very well received, really very well, first by Monsignor Buratti, next by Cardinal Fransoni and finally by Monsignor Barnabò. They have taken no concrete action yet in our regard," Parietti said, "but will be giving us our assignments in the coming days. One can see, however, that they are most

---

57. PF: Acta vol. 219 (1855), f. 818 (pp. 1, 14), "Esposizione" of Cuarterón. See this chapter, p. 267, n. 5 for the full Italian title of his summary.

58. PIME: AME 11, *Notizie*, Appendix, 1; Tragella, *Missioni estere*, 1:186–87.

59. PIME: AME 13:55, Parietti to Marinoni, 24 February 1855; Tragella, *Missioni Estere*, 1:187. Brambilla in *Pontificio istituto*, 1:146, dates Parietti's letter incorrectly as 24 September that year.

kind. And they rejoiced at seeing this tiny band of missionaries...."[60] By the time Riva and Borgazzi met Cuarterón, he had been in Rome for two years and eight months. Two days after meeting him, Riva wrote that Cuarterón "hopes to have both of us trained in short order as navigators, architects, doctors and whatever else may be necessary to improve the condition of his pagan peoples."[61] Cuarterón was clearly a man of great vision, of decision, of wealth, and a most convincing speaker.

Just eleven days after meeting Cuarterón, Borgazzi called him a man "completely dedicated to God" whose name could well be "the Xavier of Oceania." A few moments of conversation with him were enough "to recognize in him an extraordinary individual called by God to carry out extraordinary feats." He has "noble features, is tall and sturdily built and has a serene expression with no martial airs about him. His beard is long and full and he has a thick head of hair. Behind all of this is concealed a heart schooled in the most loving and sublime virtues." Borgazzi's praise was boundless as he spoke of Cuarterón's "angelic candor, uncommon prudence and cleverness, driving energy, bold sense of enterprise, and being active from morning till night on behalf of his new mission." He is "severe with himself, taking only one meal a day, but with others he is sweet and amiable."[62]

The three-day devotion known as Forty Hours began in the church of the Hospitalers of Saint John of God on Tiber Island on Friday, 2 March 1855, one week after Riva and Borgazzi reached Rome. Archbishop Polding of Sydney was one of the celebrants on the opening day, and all of Marinoni's missionaries were present for his Mass. "Afterwards he granted us half an hour of conversation," Parietti said. "We had already met him at the office of Cardinal Fransoni, where we heard him speak with the cardinal about a new mission that he intended to found in the northern part of New Holland [now Australia] at the Carpentaria headland. When I cautiously inquired whether he intended to recruit priests for this new mission of his, he answered clearly: In Italy, no; in England, yes."

Like Polding, Cuarterón also celebrated Mass on the opening day of Forty Hours and enthusiastically voiced his satisfaction with Riva and Borgazzi. He said that "it was God who sent them to him," Parietti wrote. Yet "Riva and Borgazzi consider themselves even more fortunate" with Cuarterón, Parietti added. "However, they shall not be leaving [Rome] until about Easter [8 April], or even after that, and shall travel via Spain."[63] Marinoni also received a report on his missionaries from Alfieri, who said, "All of them are in good health" and "the conduct of all is most exemplary." He added that Cuarterón was

---

60. PIME: AME 13:55, Parietti to Marinoni, 24 February 1855.

61. Tragella, *Missioni Estere*, 1:191 n. 18.

62. PIME: AME 11:1451–52, Borgazzi to Marinoni, 7 March 1855. Borgazzi says that Cuarterón's name could well be "the Xavier of Oceania," not "the Saint Francis Xavier of Oceania," as Tragella says in *Missioni Estere*, 1:191.

63. PIME: AME 13:57–58, Parietti to Marinoni, 3 March 1855.

highly pleased with his two priests, and "he told me that they really have been sent to him by Heaven."[64]

Parietti had somehow learned that Marinoni entertained the idea of assigning some of his missionaries to Archbishop Polding. Therefore when writing to Marinoni on 8 March, he said clearly that Propaganda "will not permit either Polding or anyone else to deplete the personnel of our seminary," since it was to receive the task of staffing "three vicariates." One of them was to be Hong Kong, he said, and the others were their two new missions in India. Parietti tried his best to make it clear to Marinoni that the Roman officials "want us to be *united* in the diverse duties that are to be assigned to us exclusively . . ." And he added bluntly: "According to my poor insight you ought to beware of making further requests for sending missionaries either with Polding or with others. Propaganda takes it amiss that, after it has conformed to our requests to keep us united, we are now making requests to be separated. . . ."[65]

Marinoni was receiving conflicting advice from Rome: Alfieri had told him that both Buratti and Vespasiani had said that it would be a good idea for him to collaborate with Polding, and now Parietti was telling him the opposite. Alfieri had reflected the views of the two undersecretaries Buratti and Vespasiani. Was Parietti reflecting the views of Secretary Barnabò?

After being in Rome for three weeks, those assigned to India were received in private audience by Pope Pius IX on Wednesday, 14 March 1855. The pope was gentle, affable, and very eloquent, Parietti said, like "a most loving father." He also gave each of them a silver medal and briefed them on the history of their future mission. Three different times he blessed them all and said, "You are at the doors of China." When giving these details to Archbishop Romilli of Milan, Parietti added that his group would be leaving on 21 March for India, whereas Riva and Borgazzi would be accompanying Cuarterón "to the Celebes Islands."[66]

Parietti told Archbishop Romilli the truth about their audience with Pope Pius IX, but not the whole truth. Four days later on 19 March, just two days before he departed for India, Parietti confided the rest of the story to Bishop Ramazzotti of Pavia. He wanted "to tell the unadulterated truth, which can only be advantageous for our Institute," he said.

"We had barely presented ourselves to Propaganda when we heard Monsignor Buratti and especially Monsignor Barnabò state that in general they had little esteem for our most beloved superior, Father Giuseppe Marinoni. They disapproved in particular of his past insistence that additional groups be sent to Oceania, and of his present insistence that contrariwise those already there should be recalled." They likewise disapproved of "his present insistence" on sending candidates from his seminary "with everyone everywhere," especially since originally Marinoni had requested that his personnel be kept as united as

---

64. Ibid., 10:93, Alfieri to Marinoni, 4 March 1855.
65. Ibid., 13:59, Parietti to Marinoni, 8 March 1855.
66. Ibid., 65–66, Parietti to Romilli, 15 March 1855.

possible, even though the missions might be different. This original request had been well received by Propaganda, Parietti said, since it was considered very reasonable.

"When we were received in audience by the Holy Father," he went on,

> the very first words that he said to us were the following: "so here are those sons of mine who have put themselves back onto the road of obedience. That is fine; that is fine! I am greatly pleased about this. It is good to have a spirit which makes one ready to fling himself into the hands of barbarians and so be butchered for Jesus Christ. But it is not good to do so without having a very impelling motive. True virtue consists not so much in facing the greatest dangers, but rather in being disposed to go voluntarily where the Superior decides. Your other companions wanted to go to Oceania. May God bless those poor fellows; they are saints! They piously insisted [on going there] and they also wanted my blessing for Oceania. But it would have been better, if they had allowed themselves to be directed elsewhere. . . ."[67]

With the pope's words still ringing in his ears, Parietti hastened to Propaganda, where he met Monsignor Buratti and thanked him for obtaining the audience with the pope. "I told him how heavy our hearts had become on hearing the pope's words quoted above. I also spoke favorably to him about Reina and his companions and also favorably about our Superior [Marinoni], describing their very correct and holy intentions and stating that their hearts were prompt to obey without limit." Monsignor Buratti, however, was "already aware of everything, as also seems to be the case with Monsignor Barnabò and even with His Eminence, Cardinal Fransoni. They all maintain that Reina and the others did not err in their hearts, but that they did err in their thinking! They should not have wanted virginal territory, because in fact they were all still new. Nor should they have shown such great resistance toward allowing themselves to be placed under the direction of experienced missionaries. Nor should they have chosen a place from which others had withdrawn."

Buratti had requested Parietti "to make no further mention to Marinoni of what was past, so as not to sadden him further." In fact, Parietti went on, "We were to forget these remarks and we were to speak no more about them," since both sides had now given one another "very sufficient explanations and had reached a mutual understanding." Parietti's own conclusion to the embarrassing situation was: "What has happened belongs to the past and before God no one is at fault. There is nothing but merit and this consoles us." Parietti told Ramazzotti that he had renewed "in the most explicit and solemn manner" the institute's complete, absolute, and unlimited dedication to the pope and to Propaganda. They in turn had expressed their deep satisfaction over this. Parietti was convinced that, "if our Institute had obtained only the Oceania Mission, it would most infallibly have foundered." Propaganda "has great responsibilities" in store for the Milan seminary, he said, be-

---

67. Pius IX had suggested Corfu in Greece as a first mission. See chap. 5, pp. 69–70.

cause three vicariates—as he had told Marinoni eleven days earlier—were to be entrusted to them: Central Bengal, Hyderabad, and much later Hong Kong.[68]

Three days after Parietti and the other India missionaries had left Rome, Cardinal Fransoni wrote director Marinoni that the departure of Riva and Borgazzi with Cuarterón for their "important destination" was still in a preparatory stage. Meanwhile he wanted Marinoni to know that "the vastness of the enterprises and the multiplicity of the missions" that Propaganda had in mind for his institute, and from which it intended to begin drawing personnel more frequently and in larger numbers, "makes us desire a more rapid and extensive development of the seminary itself." Fransoni said that he was doing what he could to urge the bishops of Lombardy and of Veneto to collaborate in achieving this goal. He had even approached the patriarch of Venice in an effort to win more personnel for the seminary.

Since Fransoni had learned that Marinoni was going to Parma and to Piacenza, he said that "it would please Propaganda," if in its name Marinoni were able to interest all of those bishops "in assisting a work so holy and so eminent by sending to the seminary of Milan" candidates from their clergy who might wish to do missionary work. Fransoni said that Marinoni could "at the same time assure them that this would provide the greatest pleasure to Propaganda and to the Holy Father. . . ."[69]

The letter from Fransoni must have encouraged Marinoni. But the cardinal by this time was seventy-nine years of age, and since he continually grew weaker, there was talk in Rome about his successor. Four days after he had written so positively to Marinoni, Borgazzi wrote negatively to Father Eugenio Biffi at the Milan Mission Seminary, saying that really the only one in Rome with little confidence in Marinoni was secretary Barnabò. "But on the other hand it is true," he added, "that Propaganda is practically reduced to its Secretary, who—it is said—will quickly become a Cardinal and then also Prefect of the same Congregation. What will happen then?"[70]

Marinoni, however, took no heed of warnings received. For example, Parietti on 8 March 1855 had told Marinoni on the basis of what he had learned in Rome, that Propaganda (that is, Barnabò) "will not permit either Polding or anyone else" to take personnel from the Milan Mission Seminary. On 24 May, eleven weeks later, Marinoni wrote as follows to Fransoni: "I had the good fortune in these days of meeting the Most Reverend Archbishop [Polding] of Sydney. He spoke to me of a mission that could be established at Port Curtis, about four hundred leagues [or twelve hundred miles] from Sydney, saying that it would have the added advantage of being able to serve as a procure for our missions in Oceania." Port Curtis, next to modern Gladstone, served as the port of Rockhampton. But since Polding "did not offer the necessary financial assistance," Marinoni continued, "and since he had not taken the necessary counsel with Your Eminence upon whom we absolutely

---

68. PIME: AME 13:61–62, Parietti to Ramazzotti, 19 March 1855.
69. PF: LDB vol. 346 (1855), f. 248v–249r, Fransoni to Marinoni, 24 March 1855.
70. PIME: AME 11:1455–56, 28 March 1855, Borgazzi to Eugenio Biffi.

depend, I was content with asking all such details, which could provide me with useful information for the future. Besides, I know that Your Eminence in view of letters received from our missionaries in Oceania, considers any decision immature [at this time]. And it seems to me that no one could fail to praise this position."[71] Did Marinoni not realize that this letter would quickly reach the desk of secretary Barnabò and could only exasperate him further?

When officials of Propaganda asked Cuarterón to make an Italian summary of his lengthy Spanish manuscript, they must have complimented him on his detailed and valuable study of the twelve islands mentioned in his title. Evidently this prompted him, once the Italian summary was done on 15 February 1855, to finish translating the complete Spanish text into Italian.[72]

Cuarterón informed Marinoni on 28 April 1855 that he was still "very busy" working on his book. But he was not too busy to praise Riva and Borgazzi. He said that they "are highly esteemed and greatly appreciated" and "both are adorned with the most recommendable endowments for being my two disciples and apostolic collaborators in the vineyard of Our Lord Jesus Christ."[73] On the following day Borgazzi informed Marinoni: "Our most beloved Don Carlos left us yesterday morning. He is returning to Milan and shall pay a visit to Our Lady of Loreto en route."[74] The translation of Cuarterón's lengthy Spanish work was finished on 15 May 1855, and he presented the manuscript to Propaganda's printing press.[75] By that date, however, the press had not yet printed his Italian summary of the Spanish text, which he had completed three months earlier on 15 February 1855. In fact, the summary was not yet printed by mid-July, five months after it had been presented to the press. Evidently other printing jobs were still being given priority.

Cuarterón, Borgazzi, and Riva paid Cardinal Fransoni a visit on Sunday, 22 July 1855. "We found him so deprived of strength," Borgazzi said, "that I fear his life is like a lamp about to be extinguished." Twelve days later he reported that "Fransoni for a week now has been confined to bed and it is feared that he will not recover."[76]

This was the state of Fransoni's health when director Marinoni wrote to him on 4 August 1855, forwarding Father Mazzucconi's letter from Sydney of 20 April. In this letter Mazzucconi strongly suggested that the two missions of Rooke and Woodlark be abandoned.[77]

---

71. Ibid., 5:874, Marinoni to Fransoni, 24 May 1855.

72. PF: Acta vol. 219 (1855), f. 818r (pp. 1–2, 5–6, 8–14), "Esposizione" of Cuarterón; *Spiegazione e Traduzione dei XIV quadri*, pp. iv, viii.

73. PIME: AME 29:721, Cuarterón to Marinoni, 28 April 1855.

74. Ibid., 11:1462, Borgazzi to Marinoni, 29 April 1855.

75. For this date see Cuarterón, *Spiegazione e Traduzione dei XIV quadri*, p. iv.

76. PIME: AME 11:1465–66, Borgazzi to Marinoni, 3 August 1855.

77. Ibid., 795–97, Mazzucconi to Marinoni, 20 April 1855.

With Mazzucconi's letter were copies of letters written by Reina, Ambrosoli, Raimondi, and Salerio. Marinoni told Fransoni that he was submitting these letters at Bishop Ramazzotti's suggestion, and that he would make no comment, so that "Your Eminence will see the true state of affairs and will take those steps which you in your great wisdom consider the most opportune." He called special attention to Mazzucconi's letter, saying that it "asks of me a prompt reply, which I entrust completely to the hands of Your Eminence." Commenting, however, on Prefect Apostolic Reina's letter addressed to Ramazzotti, Marinoni said that it "explains his view that the best means for converting these islanders would be colonization. In it he also speaks of the project of evangelizing New Guinea." This letter had been included for the sake of completeness, Marinoni said, "although it treats of matters that at the moment are more theoretical than practical."

Marinoni likewise informed Fransoni that Father Rocher, the Marist priest in Sydney who chartered ships for the Milan missionaries and bought their supplies, "writes me that if it should happen again that he does not obtain funds [from me] on time, he would be forced to leave our missionaries at the mercy of the natives." Marinoni's missionaries still had seven hundred pounds sterling on hand, he said, but "at least 500 of these will be needed to charter the ship which must go and visit them and which will probably transport them to Sydney, where they may have already arrived by this hour." The balance of that amount would then be needed to pay for their lodging in Sydney, since everything there was "expensive, very expensive." He therefore requested Fransoni to send his missionaries some additional funds.[78]

The enclosures amounted to twenty-eight pages. They, along with Marinoni's accompanying letter of three pages, were sent to Riva. He received this package on 8 August and both he and Borgazzi—following special instructions received from Marinoni—read all of the letters and extracts to Cuarterón. "He was so moved by them," Riva told Marinoni, "that his eyes filled with tears. Certainly, if he was interested before in those poor missionaries, he is doubly so now." The letters were then carefully sealed and arranged in the sequence indicated by Marinoni, whose letter to Fransoni was placed on top of the others. "We did exactly as you had indicated," Riva assured Marinoni.[79]

That afternoon, 8 August, the day on which the packet had arrived, Riva and Borgazzi went with Cuarterón to Cardinal Fransoni's residence across the street from their lodging. Cuarterón presented the packet to the cardinal, saying, "These are confidential letters for you." Throughout their conversation Fransoni held onto the closed packet.[80]

Cuarterón got little sleep that night because the contents of the letters had disturbed him deeply. On the following day he tried to ascertain "a very fitting and safe method" for coming to the aid of the Melanesia missionaries. All of their letters had stressed the impossibility of making any headway at Rooke and Woodlark. They told how the missionaries

---

78. PF: SC Oceania vol. 5 (1853–57, Part II), f. 795rv, 812r, Marinoni to Fransoni, 4 August 1855.

79. Marinoni's letter and the many enclosures are in ibid., f. 795r–812r.

80. PIME: AME 11:1851, Riva to Marinoni, 9 August 1855.

were constantly afflicted by fevers, swellings, sores on their legs, inflammation of the lungs, and other disorders. And Mazzucconi's letter suggested that all of them be removed from Rooke and Woodlark and be sent instead to a place where their services would be appreciated, where they would have some hope of success.

Late Thursday afternoon, 9 August, just twenty-four hours after Cuarterón had handed over the packet of letters to Fransoni, he happened to have an appointment with secretary Barnabò regarding his own mission. Feigning ignorance about conditions in Oceania, he asked whether there was any news from Rooke. "Yes, but it is very bad," Barnabò said. "The expedition is unfortunate!" He told Cuarterón repeatedly how much he had opposed entrusting this mission to the Milan seminary. However, he admitted that he had not yet read the packet of letters given to him by Cardinal Fransoni. "And what did Propaganda intend to do for those poor missionaries?" Cuarterón asked. "Nothing," Barnabò said, "because we are completely ignorant about conditions in Oceania. Therefore we shall wait until your own mission is founded and operative. After that we shall see if and how you might be able to help this other mission as well."

It was at this point, Borgazzi said, that Cuarterón "let his heart speak out on the need for taking prompt measures to alleviate such great sufferings, to avoid such useless dangers and to prevent such extraordinary isolation." Cuarterón told Barnabò that he was planning "to present a memorandum on this matter and that with this in mind he had already printed a geographical chart."[81] In fact, he was in a position "to furnish the necessary information for successfully launching that mission." And he assured Barnabò that it would soon become "one of the most flourishing missions."

Finally Cuarterón admitted to Barnabò that he was acquainted with the contents "of those moving letters" presented to Fransoni. He felt strongly impelled, he said, "to make every sacrifice to come to the aid of this ruined and collapsed mission." His lively conversation ended with Barnabò telling him: "Submit your plans to Propaganda along with your report and we shall examine your proposal. If it should prove feasible, as no doubt it will, we shall approve it and issue orders accordingly. Without first having the necessary information, however, Propaganda cannot take a definite stand."

Borgazzi sensed the importance of Cuarterón's offer, realizing that it might well save the Melanesia mission and cause it to prosper. His letter to Marinoni containing the conversation between Cuarterón and Barnabò had therefore become "a bit long," he admitted. But as he told Marinoni, he had purposely given so much detail "because I want my report to be historical." He also gave assurance that Cuarterón would continue to press for the acceptance of his proposal until it was adopted by Roman authorities.

---

81. The geographical chart referred to is no doubt Cuarterón's "Chart of Asia and Oceania . . ." Copies of this map are in Cuarterón, *Spiegazione e Traduzione dei XIV quadri*, op. p. 224; PF: Acta 219 (1855), f. 819v, "Esposizione" of Cuarterón.

When Cuarterón, Riva, and Borgazzi visited Fransoni on Sunday evening, 12 August 1855, they found him "filled with the greatest anguish" over what had happened to Reina and his missionaries. The cardinal said again: "This poor mission has come to an end."[82]

Cuarterón's reason for visiting Fransoni on 12 August may have been to inform him that his "Description of a New Mission," presented to the press six months earlier on 15 February, was now finally in print. On this occasion he most likely presented Fransoni with the very first copy. In printed form it amounted to fourteen pages measuring nine by twelve inches. Generally only one copy of a proposal was submitted and that in manuscript form. But Cuarterón had decided to print and pay for numerous copies of his "Description of a New Mission."[83] On the following Sunday afternoon, 19 August 1855, secretary Barnabò presented a copy of Cuarterón's printed summary to Pope Pius IX.[84]

After describing his checkered career in this document, Cuarterón said that he had wanted to dedicate himself "to ransoming Christian slaves." But problems arising from both civil and ecclesiastical jurisdictions had made it impossible for him to realize this aim in the Sulu Archipelago, now subject to Spain, and in the archipelagoes between Manado and Mindanao, now subject to the Netherlands. In the latter archipelagoes, he said, "a mission could be founded in any one of these islands: Salibaboo, Sanguey, Siao and Tagolanda [now Tagulandang]," as well as in Manado. Similarly missions could be founded in Bahalatolis, Sandakan, and Tambisan, islands on the northeastern coast of Borneo. But these three islands along with the Sulu Archipelago had fallen under Spanish domain as a result of the 19 April 1851 treaty or capitulation initiated and signed by Captain General Urbiztondo. Thus the bishop of Cebu automatically obtained ecclesiastical jurisdiction also over them.

Cuarterón said that "a third mission [could be founded] in the Island of Labuan and on the entire northwestern coast of Borneo" reaching from Tanjong Api in the southwest to Tanjong Sampanmangio in the northwest. ("Tanjong" was a local word for "point.") Included in this area were the northwestern coasts of modern Sarawak and Sabah, now parts of Malaysia, and the State of Brunei coast.

"The great and important island of Borneo" was "larger than Spain," Cuarterón said, and was believed to have "more than five million inhabitants . . ." However, there were Moro pirates in the area, who robbed and killed and also sold prisoners as slaves in public marketplaces on Borneo's coasts. He explained that Commander George Rodney Mundy

---

82. PIME: AME 11:1469–70, Borgazzi to Marinoni, 13 August 1855.

83. For the full Italian title of Cuarterón's "Description of a New Mission," see this chapter, p. 267, n. 5.

84. Scurati says that the date was 19 August 1855, a Sunday. See PIME: AME 35-04 Scurati, *Memoria del Sacerdote di Lecco, Antonio Riva, Missionario Apostolico a Labuan, poi ad Hong-Kong*, 12–13. Now Sunday was the day on which Barnabò regularly had his biweekly business audiences with the pope. Borgazzi writing on 31 August is less precise, saying that the presentation to the pope was made "fifteen days ago." See PIME: AME 11:1473, Borgazzi to Marinoni, 31 August 1855.

(1805–?) of the frigate of war *H.M.S. Iris* had been sent by England to take possession of Labuan Island and did so on 24 December 1846 with the purpose of founding a British colony. (This twenty-six-gun, 907-ton vessel in 1858 would be sent to Woodlark on a punitive expedition prompted by the *Gazelle* massacre.) Labuan on 28 May 1847 was ceded to England by treaty as a base for suppressing piracy. That same year Queen Victoria (1819–1901) named James Brooke (1803–68) governor general of Labuan and consul general for English bases on the Borneo coast. Wishing to take advantage of the civilizing effect of religion, Brooke asked the London Missionary Society to found a mission in Borneo, and three of its members were appointed for the task. "In Borneo you find Protestant churches, Mohammedan mosques, Jewish synagogues, Chinese pagodas and pagan temples," Cuarterón said, "but not the religion of our redeemer and savior Jesus Christ. . . ."

Cuarterón suggested that the headquarters for his mission ought to be "on the island of Labuan, which is under English authority," since this was "safer" than being on the mainland. Labuan lay six miles off the northwestern coast of Borneo, commanding the entrance to Brunei Bay. It had an area of thirty-eight square miles and enjoyed a deep and well-sheltered harbor on its southeastern coast. If he and his missionaries were successful, they would "press eastward," he said, "until we reach and unite with the Vicariates Apostolic of Melanesia and Micronesia." This was precisely the area entrusted to Prefect Apostolic Reina. No obstacles could prevent northwestern Borneo from being declared a new mission by Rome, Cuarterón said, because its territories either were subject to England or were independently ruled by rajahs or pirates. Consequently neither the bishop of Cebu nor the bishop of Batavia could claim ecclesiastical jurisdiction over it. Cuarterón also had a personal reason for wanting Labuan as part of his mission territory. "Since my other enterprises were not successful," he said, "I felt that I should rather labor in Labuan, that is, the place closest to where God had me find the means to work in his vineyard." The "means" to which he referred was the treasure that he had found in 1844 "on some rocks in the midst of the China Sea at a distance of about three hundred miles from Labuan." This island, he said, "was occupied two years later by the English at about the same time when I offered my fortune to God."

During his voyages Cuarterón had constantly been in contact with missionaries, "transporting them on my ships and living with them in their residences in the missions." This had given him an abundance of mission experience, he said, and was also what had prompted him to suggest that a new mission be founded on the northwestern coast of Borneo. He had also obtained two priests from the Milan Mission Seminary, which was dedicated to Oceania missions. And since director Marinoni "is eager to have the faith spread everywhere," he "willingly agreed to my wishes and desires and has assigned to me Father Ignazio Borgazzi and Father Antonio Riva as the candidates of his institute best suited to help me. I wish to depart with them as soon as possible." Cuarterón was generous. "I shall pay all expenses for these two missionaries from my fortune," he said, "maintaining them and giving them all that they need. And if they get sick, or if we cannot found a mission, I shall bring them back to Europe. Or I shall deliver them wherever Propaganda orders, if it should want them to work elsewhere in those seas, perhaps in other missions. If on the contrary God should bless my new mission, then in order to obtain additional personnel I shall establish in this center of Catholicism a college for training as priests those who express the desire to work in this new mission, whether they be Europeans or natives." It was up to Propaganda, however, "to name as head or superior of this new mission that one of the three priests [Cuarterón, Borgazzi, or Riva] in whom it places the greatest confidence." In addition Cuarterón promised "to build churches in the mission and to found and establish a source of income for their continuance."[85]

Pope Pius IX was particularly pleased on learning from Barnabò during his audience granted on 19 August 1855 that Cuarterón, in addition to founding and funding a mission of his own, intended to come to the rescue of the Milan missionaries in Melanesia. When the pope asked how this rescue operation would be financed, Barnabò said that Cuarterón himself would provide all the funds. The pope then "raised his eyes and his hands to heaven, blessing God for not having set limits to his generosity."

It was a Sunday when Barnabò had this audience with the pope. During the remaining days of that week Cuarterón along with Riva and Borgazzi distributed additional printed copies of his "Description of a New Mission" to all thirteen cardinal members of Propaganda. "The three of us went to visit them at their residences," Borgazzi said, "and we provided them with those clarifications which they wanted to have. All of them received us with effusive cordiality and showed deep interest, especially [Gabriele] Cardinal Ferretti [1795–1860], the Grand Penitentiary, who is truly a Good Shepherd . . . ."[86]

Normal procedure required that the cardinal members of Propaganda should first discuss and approve a project in a General Meeting before its presentation by the secretary to the pope for ratification, but in this case Barnabò had presented the project to the pope first. Only after obtaining his full and enthusiastic support did he present it to the cardinals for their vote at a General Meeting on Monday, 27 August.

What had caused Barnabò to go contrary to protocol in this case? Certainly it was the packet of letters received by Fransoni from the Milan missionaries in Oceania. Those letters prompted Propaganda to take every means available to free the Melanesia missionaries as quickly as possible from their unbearable predicament. Proof of this is Fransoni's letter to director Marinoni of Tuesday, 21 August 1855, written only two days after Barnabò's audience with the pope. "When I received your letter of the fourth of this month with its enclosures from the missionaries of Oceania," Fransoni said, "I flatteringly told myself that they would contain some favorable news about that mission. It was therefore with

---

85. PF: Acta vol. 219 (1855), f. 818 (pp. 1–14), "Esposizione" of Cuarterón. In this work Cuarterón uses the local word "Tanjong" in place of "Point." In his Asia/Oceania map appended to this work Cuarterón uses "Point" in place of "Tanjong." For the punitive expedition to Woodlark, see p. 256–59.

86. See PIME: AME 11:1473–74, Borgazzi to Marinoni, 31 August 1855.

genuine displeasure that I found such sad reports on the most painful situation in which those missionaries find themselves, not to mention the insuperable difficulties that exist there, at least at present. This prevents them from obtaining any fruit whatsoever from their indefatigable labors." Mazzucconi's enclosed letter of 20 April 1855 had made it clear, he said, "to what a miserable state those in Woodlark have been reduced, as well as the others in Rooke." Therefore "one cannot but approve the plan" of Mazzucconi, who wants to profit from "a ship about to leave Sydney by making use of it to transport all of those praiseworthy missionaries to Australia. They can thus recover somewhat from the sickness and infirmity with which they have been afflicted, while they wait there for further orders from the Holy See." Fransoni requested that Marinoni "inform Father Reina, also in my name, that their suggested departure is approved and that new instructions will be issued as soon as possible . . . ."

Hinting at what these "further orders" and "new instructions" might be, Fransoni said that news of their wanting to leave Rooke and Woodlark had reached Rome "at a most opportune time," because Cuarterón, Riva, and Borgazzi were preparing to leave for their "new mission." Marinoni was to tell Reina that "an agreement" was being worked out in Rome "for facilitating the enterprises" of both Cuarterón and Reina. "More suitable locations will be assigned to the missionaries of Father Reina, a common supply center will be created, and useful contacts and communications between the two prefects and their respective missionaries will be established for their mutual benefit and support."

Fransoni also specified that during their stay in Australia they were to take up whatever work Archbishop Polding of Sydney might give them. However, they were to keep in mind that this activity in no way was to prove an obstacle to the realization of their main project about which they would soon receive instructions. Fransoni said that they should get in touch immediately with Cuarterón by mail, should await his arrival in Sydney, and should work harmoniously with him. "I reserve to myself," he told Marinoni, "sending them further orders" at the departure of Cuarterón from Rome.[87]

Cardinal Prefect Fransoni could write a letter like this six days before the cardinals met to create a mission for Cuarterón, only because Pope Pius IX had given his approval in principle for founding such a mission two days earlier to Secretary Barnabò.

The reaction of Cuarterón, Barnabò, Fransoni, and Pius IX to save the Melanesia missionaries from their predicament could hardly have been more expeditious. But even this exceptionally quick action made possible by overturning protocol would prove too late for some of the missionaries. Catechist Corti had been lying in his grave at Rooke Island for five months by this time. And Mazzucconi, whose letter was chiefly responsible for Rome's speedy action, was aboard the *Gazelle* en route from Sydney to Woodlark for his encounter with death. He had set sail just three days before Fransoni wrote his letter. And while Fransoni was writing it, the remaining Melanesia missionaries were aboard the *Phantom*

---

87. Ibid., 1:153–54, Fransoni to Marinoni, 21 August 1855.

in the immediate vicinity of Port Macquarie, sailing southward along the coast toward Sydney, where they would arrive two days later.[88]

Cuarterón's "Description of a New Mission" was to be discussed and voted upon by the cardinals of Propaganda at their General Meeting of Monday, 27 August 1855. This was eight days after the proposal had been approved by Pope Pius IX. Of the thirteen cardinals visited by Cuarterón and his two missionaries in the previous week, nine attended the meeting. They were Cardinals Fransoni, Ferretti, Brunelli, Altieri, Barberini, Marini, Mattei, Patrizi, and Roberti. Fransoni from the beginning had shown himself most sympathetic toward Cuarterón's proposal. Ferretti had received the trio with exceptional cordiality. And Brunelli, a cardinal member of Propaganda since 31 August of the previous year, had supported Cuarterón's proposal from the time when it was presented to him as nuncio apostolic in Madrid in December 1849, almost six full years earlier.

Since the pope had already approved of Cuarterón's project on 19 August, its acceptance by the cardinals was a foregone conclusion. Using delegated authority from the pope they created the "Prefecture Apostolic of Labuan and Its Dependencies" and contemporaneously named Cuarterón its prefect apostolic "under the conditions expressed by him." This meant that his prefecture apostolic consisted of the Crown Colony of Labuan and those English bases on the northwestern coast of Borneo subject to it. Excluded was all the rest of Borneo.

The cardinals, however, provided for the prefecture's geographical extension in time. Cuarterón, namely, was to be informed "that, if God blesses his efforts, he may extend his apostolic ministry to independent Borneo." He had spoken of "coasts subject . . . to other Sultans" and on his accompanying map of northwestern Borneo had designated as "The Independent Coast of the Pirates" the coastal area reaching southward from Brunei to approximately Tanjong Sirik. Brunei he called "Borneo proper." The cardinals made yet another favorable stipulation which read, "Furthermore, as often as circumstances may require him to enter such parts [of Borneo] which are under the spiritual jurisdiction either of the Vicar Apostolic of Batavia or of the Bishop of Cebu, he should inform Propaganda of this in advance so that it can make the opportune arrangements." The cardinals in their concluding statement urged that Cuarterón "strive to keep Propaganda informed regarding his results by writing as frequently as he can."[89]

Together with his "Description of a New Mission" Cuarterón had given to the pope, Cardinal Prefect Fransoni, and all cardinal members of Propaganda, a printed map prepared by himself portraying the northwestern coast of Borneo. The caption on this map

---

88. For the location of the *Phantom* see RIP: R B-N.2, N.1, Carlo Salerio, "Giornale di Viaggio," 21 and 23 August 1855.

89. For the text of the decision of the cardinals see PF: Acta vol. 219 (1855), f. 820r. For the geographical data see Cuarterón's two maps in ibid., f. 819Ar, 819v.

read as follows: "Map of the Northwestern Coast of Borneo situated between the points Tanjong Api and Tanjong Sampanmangio, where Propaganda can establish Missions because the greater part of it is independent and also because many spots along that coast belong to Great Britain. Presented to the Congregation mentioned above and Dedicated to His Eminence, the Cardinal Prefect, by the Priest Carlos Cuarterón in the year 1855." After the creation of the new prefecture apostolic, Cuarterón made a new printing of this map, changing only the caption to read: "Map of the Prefecture Apostolic of Labuan and Its Dependencies Etc., created by the Sacred Congregation for Propagating the Faith during its General Meeting of 27 August 1855 and entrusted to the Reverend Don Carlos Cuarterón, who was declared contemporaneously Prefect Apostolic of that same Prefecture."[90] On 31 August, four days after the General Meeting, Borgazzi joyfully told Marinoni that the cardinals had "fully approved" the project of Cuarterón, "erecting into a Prefecture Apostolic all areas at the disposition of Propaganda, that is, the Island of Labuan with the entire (independent) Northwestern Coast of Borneo." Borgazzi, however, was overenthusiastic and incorrect, basing his statement no doubt on the text of the map printed by Cuarterón, which he had helped distribute to the thirteen cardinals. In order to be exact Borgazzi should have said that the prefecture included Labuan and those parts of the northwestern coast of Borneo which politically were dependent upon the English Crown Colony of Labuan. Then, as the decree of the cardinals read, if God were to bless Cuarterón's efforts, "he may extend his apostolic ministry to independent Borneo."

Borgazzi further told Marinoni that Propaganda at a later date would decide whether the prefecture apostolic should also include "the other two parts [of Borneo] which had been represented by Don Carlos as abandoned and as nominally dependent upon the Bishop of Cebu and the Vicar Apostolic of Batavia." The parts of Borneo referred to here were modern Kalimantan, then under Dutch jurisdiction and consequently under the ecclesiastical jurisdiction of the bishop of Batavia, and the northeastern coast of Sabah, then under Spanish jurisdiction and consequently ecclesiastically dependent upon the bishop of Cebu. If these two parts should later be included, Borgazzi said, "this would put us in communication with Micronesia and Melanesia. Now they are preparing our papers and faculties and afterwards we can leave when we wish. This coming Sunday [2 September 1855] the printed book on those regions written by Don Carlos will be presented to the Holy Father. I shall send a copy of it at once to our seminary in Milan."[91]

Cuarterón's book had cost him painstaking research and much more time than he had anticipated. It was titled: *Explanation and Translation of XIV Reports on the Islands*

---

90. For the map with the caption beginning: "Map of the Prefecture Apostolic of Labuan . . . ," see ibid., f. 819Ar. For the map with the caption beginning: "Map of the Northwestern Coast of Borneo . . . ," see Cuarterón, *Spiegazione e Traduzione dei XIV quadri*, op. p. 224.

91. PIME: AME 11:1474, Borgazzi to Marinoni, 31 August 1855. The printed book was bound prior to the decision reached by the cardinals on 27 August 1855; consequently the detailed map of Cuarterón's territory contained in this work is the one with the caption beginning: "Map of the Northwestern Coast of Borneo. . . ."

of Salibaboo, Talaor, Sanguez, Nanuse, Mindanao, Celebes, Bornèo, Bahalatolis, Tambisan, Sulu, Toolyan, and Labuan, presented to the Sacred Congregation for Propagating the Faith in the month of September 1852 by Captain D. Carlos Cuarterón and dedicated to His Eminence, the Most Reverend Cardinal Giacomo Filippo Fransoni, Prefect of the same congregation, containing an appendix with a vocabulary in [Italian], Malay, Sulu, Tagalog, a Table of Longitudes and also two geographic charts showing the Missions.

The book was an elaborate piece of work with gilded edges and red binding. It was written in Italian, measured nine and one-half by eleven inches, contained a dedication to Cardinal Prefect Fransoni, had an 8-page introduction and 227 pages of text, which was divided into fourteen chapters called "Quadri" or "Reports." The first six were translated directly from the original Spanish. "In the remaining eight I added more details," Cuarterón said. The lengthy table of longitudes gave latitudes as well of place names listed in alphabetical order. This made it possible to locate easily on his two accompanying maps the innumerable place names found throughout his book. The vocabulary was 14 pages long with words in Italian in alphabetical order in one column and the corresponding translations in Malay, Sulu, and Tagalog in parallel columns. The book was printed by Propaganda's press, and all costs were borne by Cuarterón. He had also produced the two maps.[92] The industriousness and munificence of the book's author and the comprehensiveness and exactness of his work must have impressed Pope Pius IX and all authorities at Propaganda.

Borgazzi's letter bringing good news to Marinoni carried some bad news as well regarding their missionaries in Melanesia. "We believed that we would be able to transport them immediately to a better area," he said, "but Propaganda wants us to become established first." Cuarterón nevertheless was still optimistic that the congregation would alter its position on the Melanesia missionaries after seeing from the report that he was writing and from the new geographical chart that he was preparing, how a mission of such great promise could come into being at such little cost.[93]

Since this letter brought Marinoni his first news about the creation of the Labuan Mission, he sent it to his missionaries in Oceania. He also told them about the common supply center for their mission and Cuarterón's which was to be founded at Ternate, an island off the western coast of Gilolo (now Halmahera) at the far west end of New Guinea. In the same letter he enclosed a copy of Cardinal Fransoni's letter of 21 August 1855 telling them to await further instructions from Cuarterón and—if they were in Sydney—to place themselves meanwhile at the service of Archbishop Polding.[94] Marinoni gave repeated study to what Fransoni's letter of 21 August had to say about Cuarterón and Polding. But

---

92. Cuarterón, *Spiegazione e Traduzione dei XIV quadri*, pp. iv, viii. For the full Italian title of this work, see this chapter, p. 267, n. 7.

93. PIME: AME 11:1474–75, Borgazzi to Marinoni, 31 August 1855.

94. Ibid., 5:943, Marinoni to his Oceania missionaries, 6 September 1855. This archive record merely outlines the points touched upon in the letter.

the more he studied it, the more disturbed he became. And so on 11 September 1855, five days after having sent his Oceania missionaries a copy of the letter, he asked Borgazzi a host of questions.[95]

Borgazzi had wanted his answers to be as correct and complete as possible, he said, "in order to dissolve whatever doubts or uncertainties may have been caused by the letter of Propaganda." And so it was 22 September 1855 before he replied, about a week after Marinoni's letter had arrived. "First of all I can assure you that the link, which Propaganda intends to set up between our very dear members in Oceania and Don Carlos Cuarterón, is not a fusion. Much less will it make them subject to him. Nor will any change be made which might alter in the least their pristine independence. Instead there is to be a link for communications as well as for mutual support and assistance, something which should contribute to the progress and prosperity of both groups."

As for the link with Archbishop Polding, Borgazzi said that Fransoni's words were intended merely as a directive for Marinoni to have his missionaries contact Polding "in order to receive from him some temporary occupation." Propaganda had written to Polding on its own initiative, recommending "our missionaries to him and placing them at his disposal, so to speak, until new orders should arrive." Therefore it would appear that Marinoni's concerns had all been provided for, Borgazzi said. But for good measure he had nonetheless inquired "whether it might be possible to obtain" for the Oceania missionaries a special letter of recommendation from Cardinal Fransoni. "We were told, however, that in addition to it being difficult for a superior to issue recommendations to an inferior, it actually would be useless, because the letter of Propaganda is more than sufficient for them to obtain from the most worthy archbishop whatever concern and support they may need. . . ."

Cuarterón was convinced, Borgazzi added, that little Maria "certainly will have obtained the gift of faith for her parents and for her village, and that the small group of neophytes at Woodlark by this time will also have become Christians in large numbers. He consequently believes that our members will not have abandoned their positions. Propaganda also thinks the same way. If this should be the case, then our Don Carlos would write to Milan for a new group [of missionaries] instead of writing to Sydney." Getting this new group established in a better location in Melanesia, Borgazzi said, "could be of assistance to us and also to [our missionaries in] Woodlark and Rooke." Propaganda persisted in its decision, however, "about not wanting to take any more risks. It wants to act safely and therefore wants to see us established first. Don Carlos must have the lodgings for the others prepared in advance."[96]

---

95. Marinoni's letter to Borgazzi of 11 September 1855 has not been found. The date is given in Borgazzi's reply of 22 September.

96. PIME: AME 11:1477–79, Borgazzi to Marinoni, 22 September 1855. Borgazzi here speaks incorrectly of little Maria as being at Rooke; she was at Woodlark. See chap. 12, p. 199.

Meanwhile Propaganda had issued a decree on 4 September 1855, announcing that it had created the Prefecture Apostolic of Labuan and Its Dependencies on 27 August 1855 and contemporaneously had named Cuarterón its prefect apostolic. To the prefecture "will be added other independent regions in Borneo Island as called for by circumstances of both time and place and by the spread of the faith; subsequently they will be duly designated."[97] A second decree also issued on 4 September approved Cuarterón's choice of a Spanish priest, Father Diego Burrueco, to serve as his agent or procurator with Propaganda. The decree identified Burrueco as a member of the "Order of the Most Holy Trinity for the Redemption of Captives," called also Trinitarians (O.SS.T.), and praised him for his "prudence, experience in handling affairs and zeal for religion." Burrueco lived nearby in a monastery adjoining a church on Via Condotti cared for by the Trinitarians. Since Cuarterón had joined the Third Order Secular of the Most Holy Trinity in May 1847 in Hong Kong, it was a natural development that he should find a Spanish Trinitarian in Rome to be his procurator.

Apparently Bishop Vrancken of Batavia had reacted negatively to Cuarterón's invitation that he collaborate in founding an educational institution in Singapore, because meanwhile Cuarterón had decided to found a college or seminary of his own in Rome. (He may have discussed the matter with Vrancken personally when he was in Rome in December 1854 for the dogma of the Immaculate Conception.) Cuarterón had informed Propaganda that his institution would provide Catholic training and education for youths coming from his mission to make advanced studies or to study for the priesthood. He had chosen Burrueco to be its administrator, and the second decree of 4 September also ratified this choice.[98]

Secretary Barnabò officially informed Cuarterón of the decisions taken at the General Meeting of 27 August by letter of 11 September 1855. He said that the cardinals present were "extremely pleased" with his project and that "they praised your piety and your zeal in offering both your work and your fortune for undertaking and realizing the proposed task. . . . It is furthermore recommended that you take a lively interest in the Mission of Melanesia and Micronesia and that you likewise provide assistance—according to the agreements reached—to that Prefect Apostolic and his collaborators, who will be waiting

---

97. PF: LDB vol. 346 (1855), f. 653rv. There is much confusion over this decree. Glazik in "Kirchenorganisatorische Massnahmen," 497 n. 34, says incorrectly that Cuarterón's appointment as prefect apostolic "followed on 4 May 1855." Tragella in *Missioni estere*, 1:193, says incorrectly that the appointment "followed on 4 September." And Rooney in *Khabar Gembira*, 20, says incorrectly that Cuarterón "received his formal appointment on 5 September 1855." The date on the letters patent stating that Cuarterón was prefect apostolic and that Riva and Borgazzi were missionaries apostolic was 9 September 1855. See PIME: AME 29:727, Cuarterón to Marinoni, 22 September 1855.

98. PF: LDB vol. 346 (1855), f. 654rv.

for your views and your instructions in Sydney." Barnabò presumed that the missionaries would be in Sydney because three weeks earlier, reacting to Mazzucconi's letter, Fransoni had told Marinoni to inform Father Reina and his missionaries "that their suggested departure [from Rooke and Woodlark] is approved...."

Enclosed with Barnabò's official letter for Cuarterón were: (1) the decree announcing that the Labuan Prefecture had been created and that Cuarterón had been named its prefect apostolic, (2) a list of faculties for Cuarterón with a notice that others would be added once he reached his mission and learned which ones he still needed, and (3) letters patent for himself and for his two missionaries declaring that he was the prefect apostolic of Labuan and Its Dependencies and that Riva and Borgazzi were missionaries apostolic.[99]

When formally acknowledging the receipt of this important letter from Barnabò, which marked the culmination of eight and a half years of efforts by Cuarterón to obtain some official status for doing missionary work,[100] he addressed his reply to Cardinal Prefect Fransoni. He had been officially advised, he said, that the cardinals at a General Meeting[101] had established the prefecture proposed by himself and had entrusted it to him. "I was also highly pleased with the recommendation expressed so vigorously by Your Eminence and the whole Sacred Congregation," he said, "that I should interest myself in the Mission of Melanesia and Micronesia, working in accord with its Prefect Apostolic and his missionaries, who are waiting for my instructions in Sydney." He promised that he would do "everything possible for the advancement and prosperity of that mission."[102]

Bishop Ramazzotti of Pavia surprised Don Carlos Cuarterón with a first-class relic of his patron saint, Charles Borromeo, a former archbishop of Milan who had died there in 1584. After thanking Marinoni on 22 September 1855 for forwarding the relic, Cuarterón said: "I suppose that you already know through your dear sons, Don Antonio and Don Ignazio, with what enthusiasm both the Sacred Congregation for the Evangelization of Peoples and also His Holiness welcomed my report, which describes and proposes the founding and establishing of a New Mission in Western Oceania. The decision was taken at a General Meeting on 27 August and they named me the Prefect Apostolic of the Mission. . . . Furthermore, Propaganda has recommended to me the Missions of Melanesia and Micronesia, which belong to your San Calocero College. I am to help those missions flourish."[103]

By the time Cuarterón wrote this letter to Marinoni, he had finished his geographical chart of a part of Asia and Oceania, showing where the common supply center for his

---

99. Ibid., f. 660rv, Barnabò to Cuarterón, 11 September 1855. Cuarterón, of course, had learned the results of the General Meeting long before this official notice was written.

100. Cuarterón had officially approached Propaganda through Feliciani in Hong Kong as early as 25 April 1847. See this chapter, p. 268, n. 8.

101. Here Cuarterón incorrectly gives 17 August as the date of the 27 August General Meeting.

102. PF: SC Oceania vol. 5 (1853–57, Part II), f. 829r–830v, Cuarterón to Fransoni, 19 September 1855.

103. PIME: AME 29:726–27, Cuarterón to Marinoni, 22 September 1855.

mission and Reina's would be. But he still had to write his accompanying short report as requested by Barnabò, showing how his mission would assist the Mission of Melanesia and Micronesia.[104] The full title of his second map was: "Chart of a part of Asia and Oceania, between 10 degrees south latitude and 25 degrees north latitude and from 87 degrees 30 minutes longitude to 117 degrees 30 minutes East of the Meridian of Rome, for learning the location of European colonies and the points where our Catholic Religion is established, as well as the voyages made from 1841 to 1849 by Captain Don Carlos Cuarterón, now presented by him to the Sacred Congregation for the Evangelization of Peoples and dedicated to the Cardinal Prefect, His Most Reverend Eminence." If Cuarterón had used the prime meridian of Greenwich, as is common today, instead of the prime meridian of Rome, the longitudes of this map would have read 100 to 130 degrees east longitude, that is, from the Strait of Malacca in the west to the Ceram Sea (now Seram Sea) in the east.

His map measured twelve by sixteen and a half inches, was printed in black and white, and had color codes indicating the areas of influence of four colonial powers: red for England, yellow for Spain, green for Portugal, and blue for the Netherlands. Ternate, the spot chosen by Cuarterón for the common supply center, was colored blue. Besides showing the routes of all voyages made in the area by Cuarterón from 1841 to 1849, the map indicated the dates of those voyages and also the tacking. In the center of the map was Borneo.[105]

Cuarterón had worked hard and long to produce this printed map and the earlier one of northwestern Borneo, hoping in this way better to acquaint the authorities in Rome with that part of the world. The Asia/Oceania map also made clear how a supply center at Ternate, situated at the western end of New Guinea, would open up a shorter and safer supply route for Father Reina and his missionaries in Melanesia. Alfieri nevertheless foresaw "the troubles and dangers" that Reina and his men "will have to endure and the great efforts which they will have to make in order to succeed, in spite of the nautical experience, riches and [personal] connections of Cuarterón."[106]

Since Cuarterón and his two missionaries had received all of their official documents, it was now possible for them to have their farewell audience with Pope Pius IX and leave for their new mission. Secretary Barnabò took the three of them in his carriage from the Spanish Square to the Vatican. No doubt this was on Sunday, 14 October 1855, when he had a private business meeting with the pope. During this meeting he told the pope, "The priests Don Carlos Cuarterón, Don Antonio Riva and Don Ignazio Borgazzi, assigned to the new mission of the Island of Labuan and its Vicinity in Western Oceania, before leaving for those places make bold to implore humbly from Your Holiness on behalf of their relatives by blood and by marriage" a number of favors, which were listed under four

---

104. See ibid., 11:1479, Borgazzi to Marinoni, 22 September 1855.

105. This Asia/Oceania map is in PF: Acta vol. 219 (1855), f. 819v, and in Cuarterón, *Spiegazione e Traduzione dei XIV quadri*, op. p. 224.

106. PIME: AME 10:111, Alfieri to Marinoni, 23 October 1855.

categories. The pope granted all of them. While Barnabò was discussing private matters like this with the pope, the three departing missionaries no doubt were in an antechamber waiting for the moment when they would be called into the presence of Pope Pius IX.[107]

When giving Marinoni details of their audience, Borgazzi said that the pope had expressed deep interest in their missionaries in Oceania and had asked for news about them. Then after Barnabò gave him the latest news, the pope said: "Those poor fellows! They left in a rush with true zeal and God will reward them. Saint Francis Xavier also had to withdraw from some islands because he was not able to realize his holy purpose. Let us hope that from now on things will improve." By the end of the audience Borgazzi was certain that "the Holy Father now looks upon our strong and holy brethren with sentiments of admiration and esteem," he said. But Propaganda "persists in its resolve of wanting to take no more risks, and hence wants to see us established first. It also wants Don Carlos himself to prepare the way for them by providing their lodging, so that their mission can get off to a better start. Only then is he to write to Rome and to Sydney to summon our members. This is something that will really take a long time."

Since Cuarterón's "Chart of a Part of Asia and Oceania" was ready for distribution by this time, he no doubt presented a copy of it personally to the pope during the audience. Borgazzi would seem to confirm this, because in his last letter from Rome describing the audience he tells Marinoni that the chart "is finished and was presented to the Holy Father and to the cardinals, all of whom gave their approval, praising the author's vision and his proposals for the development of those missions." Borgazzi added that many copies of Cuarterón's Asia/Oceania map would be sent to their San Calocero Seminary in Milan

---

107. For Barnabò's business meeting with the pope on 14 October 1855 see PF: Udienze vol. 122 (1855, Part II), f. 2450rv. The author, however, has had to determine the date of the papal audience granted to the three missionaries. His reasons for giving the date as 14 October 1855 are the following: (1) Borgazzi told Marinoni on 22 September 1855: "We hope to present ourselves to the pope on the feast of the Most Holy Rosary. But nothing is certain." See PIME: AME 11:1479. This feast was on Sunday, 7 October 1855, but the author has found no statement in the archives by Borgazzi or by anyone else either at PF or at PIME indicating that the audience actually took place on 7 October. (2) Father Josef Metzler, O.M.I., prefect of the Secret Vatican Archives, made a search for the author in all sections of those archives where documents or information on the audience could be found, but in vain. The author consulted the two remaining archives in the Vatican that might have had the information, those of the Prefecture of the Pontifical Household and those of the Office for Pontifical Ceremonies, but in vain. See Letter, Metzler to Wiltgen, 17 November 1987, Protocol 17.639. (3) Since it is an established fact that Secretary Barnabò had a business audience with Pope Pius IX on Sunday, 14 October 1855; and since documentation shows that at this audience he requested favors for the relatives of Cuarterón, Riva, and Borgazzi; and since Barnabò states that the three missionaries had not yet left Rome, it is most probable that their audience with the pope also took place on 14 October. Still today, according to Brother Stanislaus McGuire, C.F.C., of the Prefecture of the Pontifical Household, it is customary for officials first to conduct their business with the pope and afterwards to present to him attendants who have been waiting in an antechamber. Barnabò here does not use the official name of the prefecture, but instead describes it as "the new mission of the Island of Labuan and its Vicinity ["adiacenze"] in Western Oceania."

together with some copies of Cuarterón's printed book, as well as copies "of his other map of our new Prefecture of Labuan."[108]

This "other map" was identical to Cuarterón's earlier one called northwestern Borneo, except for the caption which had been changed to read: "Chart of the Prefecture Apostolic of Labuan and Its Dependencies, etc., created by the Sacred Congregation for Propagating the Faith in its General Meeting of 27 August 1855 and entrusted to the Reverend Don Carlos Cuarterón, declared contemporaneously its Prefect Apostolic."[109] Before Riva's and Borgazzi's departure ceremony in Milan, Alfieri had told Marinoni that they would be staying in Rome "some days longer" than the missionaries going to India. Indeed, the India missionaries stayed in Rome four weeks; Riva and Borgazzi stayed there eight months. During all this time Alfieri had been not only their agent, "but rather a brother, one might even say a father," as he himself expressed it. For example, when he learned that Propaganda requested free transportation from French steamers only in the case of missionaries traveling to the Orient, he found another way for Cuarterón's group to reach France without charge. Alfieri's good friend, Archbishop Eduardo Hurmuz (1799–1876), was an Armenian monk based in Rome, where he ordained Armenian clerics. Since Hurmuz in turn was a good friend of the Ambassador of France, Alfieri asked Hurmuz to intercede with the ambassador.[110] As a result Cuarterón, Riva and Borgazzi were given free passage aboard the French navy's large steamer *Éclaireur*.

The three missionaries left Rome at 7 p.m. on 19 October and arrived overland at Civitavecchia—the port of Rome—at 5.30 a.m. the next day. Their voluminous baggage was taken aboard, and at 6 a.m. on Sunday, 21 October 1855, they sailed to the French military port of Toulon, where they arrived in thirty hours. The missionaries were treated like staff officers while aboard. In nearby Marseille during the night of 24 October they transferred to a small Spanish steamer, *Mercurio*, which took them to Sète in France and then to the Spanish ports of Barcelona, Valencia, Alicante, Cartagena, Almería, Málaga, Algeciras, and finally Cádiz near the southern tip of Spain, where they arrived on 7 November. There Riva and Borgazzi received a small apartment from Cuarterón's family.[111]

---

108. This last letter of Borgazzi from Rome to Marinoni, found in PIME: AME 11:1457–79, carries no date. When assembling the volume of letters in which it is contained, the late archivist, Father Giovanni B. Tragella, added the date 20 April 1855 in pencil. But internal evidence shows that this date cannot be correct, because Borgazzi describes the papal audience as having already taken place. And he adds: "On Friday evening we shall leave for Civitavecchia." They actually did leave Rome on Friday evening, 19 October 1855. The letter therefore was written some days prior to that date.

109. PF: Acta vol. 219 (1855), f. 819Ar.

110. PIME: AME 10:111, Alfieri to Marinoni, 23 October 1855. Archbishop Hurmuz was born in Constantinople on 22 January 1799 and became a member of the Mekhitarist Order of Venice, Italy. He died in Rome on 22 October 1876. See Letter, Yorgi Kefalidis, archivist at the Armenian Catholic Exarchate in Athens, Greece, to Wiltgen, 14 May 1989.

111. PF: SC Oceania vol. 5 (1853–57, Part II), f. 1210rv, Cuarterón to Fransoni, 23 October 1855; PIME: AME 11:1481, 1484, Borgazzi to Marinoni, 10 November 1855; PIME: AME 11:1458, Borgazzi to Marinoni (n.d.); PIME: AME 10:111, Alfieri to Marinoni, 23 October 1855. In this last mentioned letter of 23 October

Meanwhile Marinoni had received a second letter written by Mazzucconi in Sydney on 12 May 1855, which contained three Marist reasons that Rooke and Woodlark should be abandoned.[112] Seeking counsel on what he should do about it, Marinoni sent Mazzucconi's letter to Father Taglioretti on 28 October,[113] exactly one week after Riva and Borgazzi had sailed from Civitavecchia for Spain. Taglioretti, who had worked closely with the first group of missionaries sent to Oceania, replied on Sunday, 4 November 1855, apologizing for his delay: "You asked me to prepare something and it seems that you wish to know my thoughts on the resolution to be taken regarding the missions of Woodlark and Rooke. At this hour I suppose that the question has already been decided."

The reasons given by Mazzucconi and the Marists, Taglioretti said, "seem to be irrefutable." Mazzucconi's presentation was "logical, sensible and at the same time generous." If there are many abandoned peoples, and if it is necessary to make a choice, then missionaries ought to go to those who are closer to the truth, Taglioretti said. He had quoted these words of Mazzucconi "because they seem to me a categorical answer to the question."

But if the Milan missionaries should decide to remain at Rooke and Woodlark, he said that first they ought to contact the officials of the Association for the Propagation of the Faith in France and ask whether they "would be content if their funds, destined for helping the missions, were to be squandered by making such enormous and useless expenditures . . ." Mission funds "always belong in some way to those who provide them," Taglioretti

---

1855, Alfieri calls Cuarterón "the son of a Milanese father and a Roman mother," which would mean that he was an Italian. This is repeated by Tragella in *Missioni Estere*, 1:189, and by Rooney in *Khabar Gembira*, 18. The following considerations, however, lead the author to believe that Alfieri's assertion must be unfounded and incorrect: (1) Alfieri seems confused about Cuarterón's origin. He told Marinoni on 8 January 1855 that Cuarterón "is from Barcelona and not a Frenchman." See PIME: AME 10:79. (2) Spanish usage gives a person two family names, the first being the name of one's father and the second being the maiden name of one's mother. Generally a person uses both names, but there are exceptions. The first family name of Don Carlos as used by himself was "Cuarterón." See n. 2. The Spanish encyclopedia states that Cuarterón was born in Cádiz in 1816 and died there in 1880. See "Cuarteroni Y Fernández (Carlos)" in *Enciclopedia Vniversal Ilvstrada Evropeo-Americana*, xvi:772. (3) Cuarterón's second family name according to the Spanish encyclopedia is Fernández, a typical and very common Spanish name. This leads Tragella to say in *Missioni Estere*, 1:189 n. 14: "This in fact would mean that his mother is neither a Roman nor an Italian." 4) Nicolás Fernández Cuarterón of Cádiz, Spain, a nephew of Don Carlos Cuarterón, informed Propaganda by letter of his uncle's death in 1880. See PF: LDB vol. 376 (1880), f. 221r, Simeoni to Nicolás Fernández Cuarterón, 7 May 1880; PF: LDB vol. 376 (1880), f. 397rv, Simeoni to Nicolás Fernández Cuarterón, 29 July 1880. From the nephew's two family names it is clear that his father was a Fernández and that his mother was a Cuarterón. She was the sister of Don Carlos and had married someone called Fernández, a name very widespread in Spain. (Her first family name after marriage was identical to her second family name before marriage.) Since the second family name of the nephew of Don Carlos is "Cuarterón," the Spanish encyclopedia cannot be correct in giving the first family name of Don Carlos as "Cuarteroni."

112. For details on the contents of this letter, see chap. 13, pp. 212–14.

113. Marinoni's letter of 28 October 1855 to Taglioretti has not been found. But its date and content are referred to in Taglioretti's reply of 4 November 1855.

said. And so "those who provide them always have some kind of right to insist that it is our obligation to use their funds according to their wishes." If this is not done, perhaps the donors will not insist "on their right regarding funds already granted." But they could well decide to use their right in the future, he said, by giving their funds "to those who respect their wishes. Administering funds capriciously for a pious cause disenchants benefactors, whose number then silently and secretly decreases."

It seemed to Taglioretti that the only objection that one might make, "or let me rather say the only rebuttal," would be to ask: "Then why were these missionaries so obstinate as to want as their field of activity these lands, which are hopelessly impossible to cultivate? Were they not warned?" Taglioretti said that Mazzucconi would answer like this, and he quoted him: "Perhaps the Lord directed us here to try us out, to let us experience our own misery, so that humiliated by suffering and by the futility of our efforts, we would be better suited for taking up his ministry again elsewhere."

This aspect was "a sufficient explanation" for the missionaries having asked that their superiors assign them to "the poor islands which they now renounce," Taglioretti said. "But here I gladly take the opportunity to do justice, I believe, to those very dear young men. I feel that they are being wrongfully accused of having asked for those islands with stubborn insistency. What they asked for was virgin territory—only this—and they preferred the islands of Micronesia. By coincidence the Marists were taking steps at that time to find someone to take their place in that field, where they already had had their share of unfortunate experiences. It seemed that successors to the Marists were being offered by Providence and so our missionaries were sent off to Woodlark and Rooke. This mandate, which corresponded to their aspirations for virgin missions and for Oceania, they then accepted and cherished." They obeyed Rome, Taglioretti said; they did not choose. "Was it rash for them to desire in a general way virgin missions in Oceania? Was it obstinacy to want this wish granted?"

According to Taglioretti, "one has to respect certain hidden tendencies" in a missionary. "Therefore let no one judge . . . the conduct of another who has taken to the altar of sacrifice all that he owns, all his love, his very life." It would be disgusting and insulting, he said, if someone were to say to "these victims of charity and apostolic zeal: You wanted it, then stick to it! And let your life be consumed by the privations and sicknesses in that useless and impossible undertaking into which you have ventured so thoughtlessly."

Taglioretti apologized to Marinoni for his letter having become so long and quickly concluded:

> Sentinels marked for death . . . Yes, that was the password used by Father Supriès in bidding farewell to those young men, sentinels marked for death. But the cry of those sentinels, so resolute and so magnanimous, and the sight of their sufferings and of their death, will arouse ardor in the breasts of many more sentinels. And so the original enterprise that has been launched, or at least the holy examples that have

been given, will make future sentinels abound with success and will bring them the blessings of God.[114]

Taglioretti errs, however, when he says that the Milan missionaries "were sent off to Woodlark and Rooke" in view of a "mandate" from Rome, which they then "obeyed." Rome did not give them a mandate to go "to Woodlark and Rooke." It sent them to "the Missions of Melanesia, or of Micronesia, or of some other mission in Oceania," including the easier missions of Fiji and Samoa. Cardinal Fransoni had urged them to accept Fiji. But Reina's group, as he said himself, had ruled out the easier mission of Fiji even before leaving Milan. Then at Tarban Creek near Sydney, Reina chose Melanesia and Micronesia. And it quickly became clear to the veteran Marists at Woodlark, after Reina's arrival there, that he wanted Woodlark Island—which the Marists had intended to keep for themselves—as well as Rooke. For both of these islands and for the rest of the Mission of Melanesia and Micronesia, Reina accepted responsibility from the Marists within a few days after arriving in Woodlark. Rome, however, had repeatedly given orders that no such transfer of authority was to take place until the young and inexperienced missionaries had completed their period of training under the Marists.[115]

Marinoni, of course, was greatly relieved at seeing that Taglioretti agreed with Mazzucconi and the Marists, but he took no action. Then in early December, one month after receiving Taglioretti's letter of 4 November, Marinoni received two letters written by Reina on 3 September 1855, one for himself and one for Cardinal Fransoni. They explained: (1) how isolated and sickly Reina and his missionaries had been in Woodlark and Rooke; (2) why Mazzucconi had left Rooke for Sydney in January 1855; (3) how Corti had died on 17 March that year; and (4) why Reina and the rest of his personnel had left Melanesia, arriving in Sydney on 23 August 1855, just five days after Mazzucconi had left Sydney for Woodlark. In great detail Reina explained to Marinoni why he and his missionaries had decided to abandon both Rooke and Woodlark.[116]

Almost immediately Marinoni on 5 December 1855 wrote to Borgazzi in Cádiz, enclosing a copy of the letter received from Reina, so that Borgazzi could inform Cuarterón of the whereabouts of the Oceania missionaries whom he was supposed to help.[117]

One week after Marinoni wrote to Borgazzi, Alfieri in Rome picked up a copy of the Milan newspaper *Amico Cattolico* (Catholic Friend) and was surprised to learn from

---

114. PIME: AME 4:573–76, Taglioretti to Marinoni, 4 November 1855.

115. See pp. 90–92, 134, 136–37, and 150–51.

116. PIME: AME 11:155–58, Reina to Marinoni, 3 September 1855; PIME: AME 11:151–54, Reina to Fransoni, 3 September 1855.

117. Marinoni's letter of 5 December 1855 to Borgazzi has not been found, but its date and contents are mentioned in Borgazzi's reply. See PIME: AME 11:1487–92, Borgazzi to Marinoni, 31 December 1855.

its pages that all the missionaries of Rooke and Woodlark had returned to Sydney. On Wednesday, 12 December 1855, when visiting Monsignor Buratti, Alfieri learned that Propaganda knew absolutely nothing about the missionaries being in Sydney. On the following day he wrote to Marinoni: "I said that it had been rumored, without saying that I had learned it from *Amico Cattolico*."[118]

Marinoni naturally showed both of Reina's letters, the one addressed to the cardinal as well as the one addressed to himself, to Archbishop Romilli and to Bishop Ramazzotti, so that they could receive as complete an account as possible about what had happened and why. It was precisely for this reason that Reina never sealed his letters to Fransoni. They were always sent to Rome through Marinoni, so that he and other Milan church authorities could read them. Thus Reina did not have to repeat in a letter to Marinoni what he had already said in a letter to Fransoni. The time needed by Romilli and Ramazzotti to study the letters must have been what caused the delay in this latest news about Reina and his missionaries reaching Rome. Only on 8 December did Marinoni write to Cardinal Fransoni and forward the letter that Reina had addressed to him.[119] Reina's letter assured Fransoni that in a short time he and his missionaries would be "ready once again for another assignment" and would "remain in Sydney to await further orders from you and from Propaganda."[120]

In his letter to Marinoni, Reina went into great length about his unilateral decision to return to Sydney and then added: "We hoped that Propaganda's decision would already have been made before news of the procedure followed by us would reach Europe."[121] Reina's wish was fulfilled because Fransoni on 21 August 1855 had informed Marinoni that his missionaries were free to leave Rooke and Woodlark and go to Australia to recuperate in preparation for taking up work once again in Melanesia with the help of Don Carlos Cuarterón.[122] Two days later, on 23 August 1855, the *Phantom* with Reina and his missionaries aboard dropped anchor at Sydney about noon.

The news about Rooke and Woodlark being abandoned was contained in Reina's letter addressed to Fransoni, which was forwarded by Marinoni with a letter of his own dated 8 December 1855, meaning that the official news reached Rome three months and three weeks after the missionaries coming from those islands had reached Sydney. Marinoni's accompanying letter phrased the issue not only diplomatically, but also enigmatically enough to confuse historians for the next 135 years. This is what he said: ". . . Prefect Apostolic Don Paolo Reina returned with his colleagues to Sydney according to the mind already ex-

---

118. Ibid., 10:125, Alfieri to Marinoni, 13 December 1855.
119. PF: CV vol. 43, f. 247rv, Marinoni to Fransoni, 8 December 1855.
120. PIME: AME 11:153, Reina to Fransoni, 3 September 1855.
121. Ibid., 157, Reina to Marinoni, 3 September 1855.
122. See ibid., 1:153, Fransoni to Marinoni, 21 August 1855.

pressed by Propaganda. . . . Although the decision of Propaganda had not yet been known to him, he did not err in anticipating it."[123]

Reina's words quoted above—"We hoped that Propaganda's decision would already have been made before news of the procedure followed by us would reach Europe"—show that it is misleading and incorrect to say, as has been done, that the departure of Reina and his missionaries from Rooke and Woodlark was ordered by, suggested by, or desired by Propaganda, or that the departure took place according to the mind already expressed by Propaganda.[124] Reina's decision to leave Rooke and Woodlark, in fact, was in no way prompted by Propaganda.

Here is the sequence of what happened:

1. Reina and Ambrosoli left Rooke on 10 May 1855.

2. Reina and his missionaries left Woodlark on 10 July 1855.

3. Propaganda on 21 August 1855 granted approval for Reina and his missionaries to recuperate in Sydney on the basis of Mazzucconi's letter and instructed them to return to Melanesia after consulting with Cuarterón.

4. Two days later, on 23 August 1855, Reina and his missionaries arrived in Sydney.

5. After being in Sydney for three months Reina and his missionaries received Rome's letter of 21 August 1855. This letter, written by Fransoni, merely approved the action that had already been taken by Reina; it did not prompt that action.

Fransoni on Christmas Eve 1855 thanked Marinoni for his letter of 8 December with the one from Reina enclosed. "I am happy over the news of his arrival and that of his companions in Sydney," he said, "where they can recover from their labors and sufferings" while awaiting further instructions from Don Carlos Cuarterón, "with whom the necessary agreements were reached." The cardinal hoped that by this time Marinoni had already passed on to Reina and his companions "the precise instructions" received from Propaganda. Marinoni in fact had done so. "In any event," the cardinal continued, "you could repeat these instructions for them."[125]

---

123. PF: CV vol. 43, f. 247rv, Marinoni to Fransoni, 8 December 1855.

124. This has been maintained by contemporaries of Reina and by authors misled by them: (1) Ripamonti writing to Reina's brother Angelo on 3 January 1856 says that "the reason why they left Rooke was to comply with the desire" of Propaganda. See PIME: AME 11:210e. (2) Marinoni writing to Fransoni on 8 December 1855 says that Reina returned with his colleagues to Sydney "according to the mind already expressed by Propaganda." See PF: CV vol. 43, f. 247rv. (3) Maestrini in *Mazzucconi*, 163, 169–70, says in three places that the missionaries left because Rome had suggested it. (4) Noel Gash in "Christ Comes to New Guinea," 2, says: "In 1855 the Holy See ordered the mission to be relinquished."

125. PIME: AME 1:163, Fransoni to Marinoni, 24 December 1855. Fransoni's letter to Marinoni of 21 August 1855, which contained "the precise instructions" for Reina, is in PIME: AME 1:153–54.

Also on Christmas Eve the cardinal thanked Reina for his letter and expressed joy that he and his companions were now able to recuperate in Sydney from their "grave and long sufferings and toils, so that you can resume your evangelical career—as I hope—with more success." Propaganda "has fully approved," he said, "of the decision that you have already made to withdraw from those areas, which in spite of your most industrious care and prolonged labor gave no indication—not even remotely—of producing the slightest results." Fransoni added that director Marinoni must already have sent word that Propaganda "did not want to abandon completely this [Melanesia-Micronesia] undertaking" and so it had decided "to profit from the favorable occasion offered by the departure of the Reverend Don Carlos Cuarterón, who has been designated Prefect Apostolic for another mission on the coast of Borneo."

Hopefully Cuarterón would be able to help reactivate Reina's work, Fransoni said,

> in a better way and in more suitable and healthier places, since he has had very much experience in those gulfs and archipelagoes, is very willing and is also in a position to offer you every assistance and support. Therefore appropriate arrangements have been made with Don Cuarterón about his sending you word—after his arrival in a suitable place—to come there. Thus the two of you could meet one another and decide upon his and your activities and projects by mutual agreement and consent, and also help one another by establishing regular means of communication and contact.
>
> There may still be a bit of delay before the Prefect Apostolic of Labuan arrives at the place to which he intends to invite you, both for consulting with him on the steps to be taken and for giving you all the cooperation and help that you may need.

In the meantime Reina could expect to receive from Cuarterón "the most precise instructions and directions concerning this matter, to which you then should faithfully conform." The cardinal also expressed the wish that Reina's "new enterprise" with God's help might produce "the most consoling results."

In his letter Fransoni had addressed Reina formally as "Prefect Apostolic of Melanesia and Micronesia," thus indicating clearly where his "new enterprise" would be located. He also encouraged Reina to look upon "the unhappy outcome of the first efforts of your ministry as a test from the Lord for your constancy. Far from despairing over the undertaking," Fransoni said, Reina ought to take courage and "go forward valiantly."[126]

Propaganda's Commission of Cardinals for Economic Affairs held a meeting on 19 December 1855, just five days before Fransoni wrote to Marinoni and Reina. At this meeting the commission took notice that Cuarterón, then in Cádiz, had contributed the huge sum of Lire 5,136.20 by way of endowment. The 5 percent interest that his money would gain annually was to be used "for founding a college in Rome for the benefit of the Mission of Labuan and Its Dependencies."[127] Cuarterón had already begun to provide for the present and the future needs of his mission.

---

126. PF: LDB vol. 346 (1855), f. 819v–820r, Fransoni to Reina, 24 December 1855.

127. See PF: LDB vol. 376 (1880), f. 397v, Cardinal Prefect Giovanni Simeoni to Nicolás Fernández

Finally Propaganda's careful plans could go into effect. Nor was there need for Fransoni to be concerned about whether Reina had learned of those plans, because he already was in possession of Marinoni's letter describing them.[128] As for Cuarterón, he was busy in Cádiz making preparations for his voyage to Borneo.

Cuarterón, 29 July 1880.

128. See this chapter, pp. 265, 267. Reina had Marinoni's letter about Cuarterón by 3 December 1855, because he answered it on that day. See PIME: AME 11:187–88, 387–88.

16

Polding, Pompallier, and Bataillon Compete for the Milan Missionaries

27 July 1856

DON CARLOS CUARTERÓN HAD NOT YET SET SAIL FROM CÁDIZ WHEN DIRECTOR MARINONI'S letter reached Borgazzi with the news that Reina and his missionaries had left Rooke and Woodlark and had gone to Sydney to recuperate. As Borgazzi told Marinoni on New Year's Eve 1855, he read this letter and an accompanying one from Reina to Cuarterón and they "enkindled again in that generous heart all the interest, compassion and affection, which he had for those poor fellows, who up to now have been most unfortunate."

Since a mail carrier regularly sailed from Cádiz for the South Pacific on the fifth day of each month, Cuarterón hurriedly sent off a letter to Reina on 4 January 1856.[1] He called his letter "an official communication or instruction" on what Reina should do if he was not engaged in opening a mission for Archbishop Polding in northern Australia. Since the two missions of Rooke and Woodlark had "collapsed completely," he said that Propaganda "had wanted to abandon this part of the globe entirely" and to reassign Reina and his missionaries to another mission already well established. But Cuarterón feared that Reina's abandonment of Oceania might well jeopardize the progress and even the very existence of the Milan Mission Seminary, which had been founded principally for missions in Oceania. Enjoying the confidence of Fransoni, Barnabò, and Buratti, Cuarterón therefore "had advised and had implored them to suspend their order of abandoning completely the Melanesia and Micronesia Missions so that a new attempt could be made." He urged the officials "to wait and see what results this might produce."

Cuarterón was convinced "that all missions dedicated to evangelizing that part of the globe had been managed rather badly, because no consideration had been given to the political, mercantile and commercial aspects of all those peoples." He maintained that circumstances such as these were advantageous "for penetrating countries that one wishes

---

1. PIME: AME 11:1487–88, Borgazzi to Marinoni, 31 December 1855.

to evangelize." In fact, he had presented these ideas in writing to secretary Barnabò, 'showing him and proving to him that, if missions in Oceania were to succeed, they must start from the west and go east. Starting from the opposite direction, as was the case of Your Reverence, causes them to be isolated and abandoned."

His concrete plan had been approved by Propaganda, he said, namely, to establish a supply center "in Ternate, one of the Molucca Islands [between Celebes and New Guinea]. From that point one can keep in contact with Europe and with all of the missions in Melanesia and Micronesia established up to the present time." He said that the sultans of Ternate and of the nearby island of Tidore both resided in Ternate. "They dominate the most important and most populated parts of the area over which Your Reverence has jurisdiction. From Ternate Island your mission work can then expand, since you will be assured of support from these two heads. Even though they are Moslems, they will not object to your preaching the Gospel to the innumerable idolatrous and pagan tribes within the boundaries of their dominion, since liberty of religion is allowed and is tolerated among those peoples."

From Ternate it would be possible for Reina to extend his missionary work "in three different directions: 1) eastward toward Papuasia, 2) southeastward toward the Aru Archipelago and other islands, and 3) northeastward toward the Palau Archipelago and the Caroline Islands." Cuarterón wanted to point out, however, that Ternate was "an island subject to and governed by the Dutch." And since their nation was "very solicitous over its colonies, it might show some opposition." But even if this were the case, he said, "we still have Manado [in northeast Celebes], Makasar [in southwest Celebes], and Kupang [in southwest Timor]. These three places are also Dutch, but they are free ports in which any foreigner who goes there may settle."

In case Reina was ready "to abandon those coasts" where his vocation "had been so severely tested," Cuarterón urged him "to come immediately with your missionaries to Singapore or to Manila to meet us. We shall then reach an understanding orally on the more important points about which Your Reverence must be concerned, if you are to obtain results from your work and so expand the flock of Our Lord Jesus Christ." If Reina did not find Cuarterón in either Singapore or Manila, the letter said, he would find written instructions waiting for him in Singapore at the residence of the Paris Foreign Mission Seminary and in Manila at the residence of the archbishop.[2]

In Reina's "official" transcript of the same letter, Cuarterón said that he had been authorized by Propaganda to instruct Reina to set out with his missionaries

> for Singapore or for Manila, whichever is easier and more economical . . . I would hope (please God) to arrive in Singapore at the beginning of the month of May and in Manila at the beginning of the month of June. These are the places in which we

---

2. PIME: AME 29:731–32, Cuarterón to Reina, 4 January 1856. This is a "confidential" transcript made by Reina of Cuarterón's letter. Regarding the "confidential" and "official" transcripts made by Reina see Tragella, *Missioni estere*, 1:234 n. 6.

shall meet and join forces. From there I myself shall conduct and accompany Your Reverence and your missionaries to the new places to be occupied in Oceania. I hope that you will be helped there by the grace and mercy of the Lord, so that you can thus fulfill your wishes and your hopes by propagating the true religion of Our Lord Jesus Christ also in that part of the uncivilized world.[3]

One of Cuarterón's many gifts was the ability of making his two missionaries feel that they enjoyed his complete confidence. He discussed with them the contents of his letters to Reina, probably because they translated them for him into Italian. And just as in Rome he had taken them along on Sunday afternoons to visit Cardinal Prefect Fransoni, now he took them every Sunday afternoon to visit the bishop of Cádiz. Convinced that he kept no secrets from them, they esteemed him all the more. As early as 26 November when they were not yet three full weeks in Cádiz, they wrote that Cuarterón had been obliged to flee to the countryside because the people of Cádiz "were honoring him like a saint."[4] Without restraint Borgazzi shared with Marinoni the numerous details that he and Riva had learned from Cuarterón about his plans. Borgazzi said that Riva and he would be building their mission stations in Borneo, while Cuarterón took Reina's group to new places in their territory. This prompt action by Cuarterón would also "remove the danger" of their colleagues at Sydney "being sent to another mission, abandoning Micronesia and Melanesia perhaps forever . . ." And if Cuarterón's idea about Ternate could be realized, then both Reina's group and Cuarterón's "would be able to keep in very close touch with one another."

The reason that Cuarterón wanted to go first of all to Ternate with Reina's group, Borgazzi explained, was that "a Catholic governor and many wealthy Catholic merchants (some of whom he also knows) are located there." And so they "will be received with open arms, since no Catholic priest is based there. And if the Dutch government tolerates them, they will be able to establish a flourishing supply center. From there they could then sail elsewhere to found missions, making use of local merchant vessels. And if they cannot get established" in Ternate, Cuarterón would then take them "to Gebe, an independent area on the route of numerous merchant vessels.[5] From there they could go to Dorei, capital of Papuasia and residence of the Moslem chiefs who are in command of nearly all the islands of Melanesia." Gebe, largest of the Gebe Islands, was on the equator in the Halmahera Sea. Merchant vessels regularly used the Djailolo Passage, which lay between Gebe and Halmahera (formerly Gilolo). In 1842 Cuarterón himself had used this passage. Cuarterón "keeps repeating that a missionary among savages must enjoy the protection and guar-

---

3. PIME: AME 29:729–30, Cuarterón to Reina, 4 January 1856. This is an "official" transcript made by Reina of Cuarterón's letter.

4. On the flight of Cuarterón to the countryside, see PIME: AME 10:125, Alfieri to Marinoni, 13 December 1855.

5. "Gebe" is found in the sources in many forms: Guebe, Geba, Gibi, Giby, Cebi, Ceby, Gavi, Qavi, Javi, Jevi, Xevi. For Cuarterón's 1842 route passing Gebe, called Giby by him, see his "Chart of Asia and Oceania . . ." in Cuarterón, *Spiegazione e Traduzione dei XIV quadri*, op. p. 224; or PF: Acta vol. 219 (1855), f. 819v.

antees of the chiefs in order to be able to exert his influence and practice his ministry," Borgazzi said. "Otherwise he will be looked upon as a brigand, will be held in contempt and will be despised. They will tolerate him as long as he serves their private interests." Cuarterón "has heard a most esteemed priest of the Society of Jesus say repeatedly that, humanly speaking, not even Saint Francis Xavier would have been able to make so many converts among the savages, if he would not have had the backing of the Portuguese. Their protection, at least in the beginning, made him respected."

This was also the reason, Borgazzi pointed out, that Cuarterón "believes that one ought to follow the direction of vessels when founding missions, going from west to east, since this spares expense, obtains influence and support, and also avoids that terrible abandonment and isolation which our poor colleagues experienced at Rooke and Woodlark. This will also guarantee the livelihood of the missionaries in the mission country itself. And as a result there will no longer be any need, or only very little need, of funds from Europe." Borgazzi hoped that all of these plans might be realized so that "two flourishing missions," that of Cuarterón and that of Reina, "might spring up in the heart of Oceania." But Marinoni would have to continue providing support for his own missionaries now in Sydney, Borgazzi said, "because at present Cuarterón can occupy himself only with his own mission...."[6]

Seven weeks earlier Marinoni had sent Reina six thousand francs as the first installment of twenty thousand francs allotted to the Oceania missionaries by the Association for the Propagation of the Faith in France. Enclosed with these funds was a "Letter of Introduction" for Reina and his missionaries written by Archbishop Romilli of Milan and addressed to Archbishop Polding of Sydney.[7]

Polding had set sail from Liverpool, England, on 23 October 1855, and reached Melbourne, Australia, on 18 January 1856. There he had a long conversation with James Alipius Goold, O.S.A., the Irish Augustinian who was bishop of Melbourne. Polding told Goold that he intended to propose to Rome that an extensive territory to the north of his Archdiocese of Sydney should become a diocese named Moreton Bay.[8] Port Curtis, the mission to which Polding hoped to send the priests from Milan, was included in this territory and was nearly three-fourths as far north of Moreton Bay as Moreton Bay was north of Sydney. Fourteen years earlier Polding had succeeded in obtaining some Italian members of the Congregation of the Passion of Jesus Christ (C.P.), popularly known as Passionists, to found a mission among the Aborigines at Moreton Bay near modern Brisbane. That mis-

---

6. PIME: AME 11:1488–89, Borgazzi to Marinoni, 31 December 1855. Tragella incorrectly gives the year of this letter as 1856 in *Missioni estere*, 1:234 n. 3.

7. See PIME: AME 5:913, Marinoni to Barnabò, 23 October 1855; PIME: AME 4:579–80, Marinoni to Reina, 9 November 1855.

8. Henry Norbert Birt, *Benedictine Pioneers in Australia*, 2:225–26.

sion was opened on 24 May 1843. But due to friction between Polding and the Passionists, and due to inherent difficulties in the mission itself, it lasted only four years.⁹

During January 1856, about the time when Polding reached Melbourne, Reina received two letters announcing that arrangements had been made by Rome on his behalf with Cuarterón. One of them was Marinoni's letter of 6 September 1855, which told him about the common procure or supply center to be established at Ternate for his mission and for that of Cuarterón. The other was a copy of Cardinal Prefect Fransoni's letter of 21 August 1855 to Marinoni containing instructions for Reina and his missionaries to stay in Australia and "await further orders from the Holy See." Meanwhile, if they were well and if Archbishop Polding of Sydney wished to avail himself of their services, they were "to present themselves" to him for whatever work he might offer them. This work, however, was not to interfere with "the subsequent project" that Propaganda had in mind for them. Giving assistance to Polding, as Fransoni's letter pointed out, would help guarantee the success of their new project, because their services would "render that praiseworthy archbishop even more benevolent and well disposed" toward them.¹⁰

In view of the orders received from Rome via Marinoni, Reina was baffled one day when he learned from the Marist procurator, Father Rocher, that he had met Polding in Sydney and that the archbishop was eager to send Reina and his missionaries far up the coast to Port Curtis to found a mission there. Polding had told Rocher "that the matter had already been arranged" with Marinoni, that Reina "had to go" to Port Curtis with Cuarterón, that Polding himself "had already spoken with the governor about providing the necessary land for establishing missions, and that the governor's reply had been favorable."¹¹

Marinoni's letter of 9 November 1855 containing the letter of introduction from Archbishop Romilli reached Reina about mid-February 1856. Since Salerio had left Sydney for Europe on 2 February, Reina hastened to tell him what happened: "As soon as I received the letter from the Archbishop of Milan for Archbishop Polding, I went to present it to him and to discuss at the same time the Port Curtis question...." Rocher accompanied him and they were en route to Sydney when they met Polding aboard a steamer. He was returning to Sydney from Subiaco at Parramatta. Polding addressed Rocher first, expressing his great disappointment that Reina and his missionaries would not be leaving immediately for Port Curtis. He then turned to Reina and said: "The whole matter has been taken care of with

---

9. For more information on the Moreton Bay Mission of the Passionists, see Wiltgen, *Oceania*, 358–67, 375–81.

10. For the two letters received by Reina see PIME: AME 1:153–54, Fransoni to Marinoni, 21 August 1855; PIME: AME 5:943, Marinoni to the missionaries in Sydney, 6 September 1855. These letters arrived about mid-January 1856 because Reina answered them on 28 and 29 January. See PIME: AME 11:213–15, Reina to Fransoni, 28 January 1856; PIME: AME 11:221–22, Reina to Marinoni, 29 January 1856.

11. The author has not found explicit mention of this preliminary exchange of ideas between Polding and Rocher, but it is implied because Reina said later that Polding brought up this matter "again" to Rocher, this time in Reina's presence. See PIME: AME 11:231, Reina to Salerio, 23 February 1856.

your Superior. He simply wanted me to take up the matter with you, because he wishes to have your consent as well. . . ."¹² Reina was about to reply when they arrived at the wharf.

Since Polding had to hurry off to another engagement, Reina gave him the letter from Archbishop Romilli and a copy of the 6 September 1855 letter from Marinoni, which also included a copy of Fransoni's letter of 21 August 1855. Reina told Salerio that in Fransoni's letter "the latest orders of Propaganda for us are clearly expressed." Those orders specified that Reina was to offer Polding temporary assistance, but at the same time he was to give priority to the arrangements being made by Rome with Cuarterón. On parting at the wharf Polding asked Rocher to extend an invitation to Bishop Bataillon, then at Tarban Creek, to spend Lent at Subiaco, where the Benedictine nuns were eager to have someone celebrate daily Mass during that holy season.¹³

Bataillon did not accept Polding's invitation, because he had come to Sydney to print some books in the language of his vicariate, a task that required his personal supervision. Reina then offered himself "for the needs of the diocese," as instructed by his superiors, and Polding assigned him to Subiaco. Here Reina offered daily Mass for the nuns and taught Italian. Rocher had said that Polding found Reina's refusal to accept the Port Curtis Mission reasonable, but the archbishop could not understand why no one had written to Reina about the arrangements made in Milan. Reina told Salerio, however, that there must have been some misunderstanding at the Milan meeting, during which Marinoni and Polding spoke French, "because I have noticed that he [Polding] understands only a little French. That is, he has to reflect too long on the words in order to get some sense out of them. And in an ordinary conversation many things escape him."

Reina was meanwhile being treated like a celebrity at the convent, although he was obliged to live like a hermit. "I speak only with the Superior, who knows French," he said. "And then I have one hour of class a day, teaching two novices who are studying a bit of Italian. . . . This is all the company that I have." Reina also told Salerio that he hoped to settle the Port Curtis question soon because Polding "comes here every week" to hear the sacramental confessions of the nuns.¹⁴

Four days later, on Wednesday, 27 February 1856, Polding arrived at the Subiaco convent to hear confessions, and "I was able to have a good talk with him," Reina said. He sent the details to Director Marinoni on the following day, adding that his enclosed letter for Salerio would explain how he had come to Subiaco. He had offered Fathers Raimondi and Ambrosoli to Archbishop Polding as well. "In fact, I told him that both of them know English better than I. But he said that he wants to have them, not only for the moment,

---

12. On Polding's meeting with Marinoni, see chap. 15, pp. 288–89.

13. For Reina's meeting with Polding see PIME: AME 11:231, Reina to Salerio, 23 February 1856. For Marinoni's letter to Reina of 6 September 1855, actually addressed to "The Missionaries in Sydney," see PIME: AME 5:943. For Fransoni's letter to Marinoni of 21 August 1855, see PIME: AME 1:153–54.

14. Ibid., 11:231, Reina to Salerio, 23 February 1856.

but forever, so that he can send us to Port Curtis." Reina then detailed for Marinoni his conversation with Polding, saying that the archbishop had wanted him to consent to accept the mission of Port Curtis.

> I replied that my Superiors without asking my opinion or my consent had determined where my mission would be; that I had no other duty but to obey; that I was Superior over my companions regarding our mission work, but not regarding the choice of a mission; and that if I were to receive the least command or wish from my Superiors [favoring Port Curtis], I would most willingly oblige. He then told me that he had arranged everything, both with the Evangelization Congregation in Rome and with you, Reverend Superior, and that he was surprised that we have received no word about the matter up to the present time....
>
> He also told me that you, Reverend Superior, had wanted to give him some personnel for this purpose at once, but that he had refused them for the moment, pointing out that it was expedient to have everything well prepared and that four or five would be sufficient for a start. He then explained for me the ease of the enterprise in view of the fact that the government is seeking all possible ways of civilizing the Aborigines. The measures that we would have to take—they are the same proposals and the same principles that Bishop [Rudesindo] Salvado gave us in Rome—are these: obtain financial assistance from the Government and from Catholic colonists in Sydney, facilitate communications, etc.[15] He also asked me and just about ordered me to write and tell you the advantages of making such a choice, not only as far as the project itself is concerned, but also for us. That such a choice would be advantageous for the Diocese of Sydney, I also agree. That it would be advantageous for us, I do not know. This I shall let my Superiors decide. Therefore act with complete freedom, Reverend Superior, knowing that we are prepared for anything. Then this time at least we shall be able to have the consolation of saying: We have obeyed.[16]

Just one year earlier, on 2 March 1855, Polding strangely enough had told Father Parietti in Rome that for a new mission in northern Australia at the Carpentaria headland, he intended to recruit priests in England, but not in Italy. Parietti mistakenly interpreted these words to mean that Polding wanted no Italian priests for any mission at all. But ten weeks earlier in Rome, Polding had enthusiastically told Alfieri that he had a mission in mind for Marinoni's priests in northern Australia with a location that could also serve as

---

15. For further details on Bishop Salvado, see Wiltgen, *Oceania*, 604.

16. PIME: AME 11:233, Reina to Marinoni, 28 February 1856. Hugh M. Laracy in "Italians on the Pacific Frontier," published in *The Italians in New Zealand and Other Studies*, 6, says that Reina and his group "were urged by Polding to re-open the Aboriginal mission" of the Passionists at Stradbroke Island (see Laracy, *The Italians in New Zealand and Other Studies*, 3), "but—mindful of the Passionists' experience—they refused." The Passionists' experience, however, was not the reason for refusing Polding's offer. He had offered the Milan missionaries Port Curtis, not Stradbroke Island. Raimondi saw great possibilities in the Port Curtis Mission. See this chapter, p. 327, n. 53.

a supply center for the Melanesia-Micronesia mission. Then in mid-May 1855 Polding visited Marinoni in Milan and offered him the Port Curtis mission.[17]

Besides being solicited by sixty-one-year-old Archbishop Polding of Sydney, the services of Reina and his missionaries were being solicited by 54-year-old Bishop Pompallier, administrator apostolic of the Auckland diocese in New Zealand. As the bishop explained to Director Marinoni, "It was during a week's sojourn in Sydney in April 1856, that Divine Providence had me come to learn about the excellent apostolic work being done by your seminary of Milan. . . ."

During that week, Pompallier said, "I met some missionary priests from Melanesia who had been obliged because of sickness to quit their missions and come to Sydney in order to restore their health. All of these missionaries were from your seminary. Their superior saw how necessary it was for himself and for his companions to take up work in another climate, like that of New Zealand. On learning that here people are eager to embrace our holy faith, he accepted with joy my suggestion that he come to my diocese with two or three of his colleagues. It was understood, however, that everything concerning this matter would have to be communicated" to the superior of the Milan seminary "and also to His Eminence, the Cardinal Prefect of Propaganda. . . ." Pompallier assured Marinoni that he had already written to Rome in order to obtain the views and consent of the cardinal prefect.

In this same letter Pompallier informed Marinoni that, in case of a positive reply, he would like to receive two priests at once and then three more. He said that "in addition to Maori, the language of our local people," they would have to learn English, which "has become practically indispensable here, because the Whites colonizing this country nearly all come from the British Isles." Marinoni would also have to try to obtain funds for his priests from the Association for the Propagation of the Faith in France, Pompallier said, for covering the cost of their voyage from Europe to New Zealand and also for their support for two or three years until his diocese would be able to provide for them.[18]

The services of Reina and his priests were also being sought by 46-year-old Bishop Bataillon, the Marist Vicar Apostolic of Central Oceania, with whom they had been residing at Tarban Creek. Just as he had asked Mazzucconi on 15 August 1855 to inform Marinoni of his desire to have priests for the Fiji Islands, so now he tried to interest Reina in going to that mission.[19] "I cannot tell you how much three bishops are competing with one another in order to win us over," Raimondi wrote on 27 July 1856 to treasurer Ripamonti at the Milan Mission Seminary. "They are using all possible means to convert us! But Father Paolo [Reina] is as strong as a column of soldiers and he stands immovable in the face of

17. See chap. 15, pp. 281, 285, and 288.
18. PIME: AME 28:755–56, Pompallier to Marinoni, 7 September 1857.
19. For Bataillon's negotiations with Mazzucconi on the Fiji Islands Mission, see chap. 13, pp. 226–27.

all their attacks. The Archbishop of Sydney is offering us a beautiful mission at Port Curtis. Bishop Bataillon wants to give us the Fiji Islands. And Bishop Pompallier is inviting us to New Zealand.

"But Father Paolo answers them: I have received no orders from my Superiors. [Then they reply:] But why do you want to go back to those islands? They send you no personnel; you have no money; and you are not healthy. I have to go where my Seminary sends me. But, you have no vows and so you can leave your Seminary. I have no reason to complain about my Superiors and I dearly love my Seminary." Raimondi called Reina intrepid in replying to the bishops. And what was the result? "This unselfishness, this attachment to his Superiors and to our Seminary astonished the Archbishop of Sydney, Bishop Pompallier, Bishop Bataillon, Father Rocher, the Benedictines, Marists, Catholics and Protestants." Reina, in fact, had become quite a personage in Sydney, Raimondi said.[20]

The bishops, however, were persistent. After giving Polding such a lengthy explanation at the Benedictine convent on why he could not accept the Port Curtis mission, Reina wrote Marinoni seven weeks later that the archbishop "continues talking to me about Port Curtis and asks me to write and tell you that there is a great need for priests here."[21] Bishop Bataillon sailed for Europe in May 1856 and before his departure requested Reina to give him a letter of introduction to Marinoni. And Bishop Pompallier, who earlier had written from New Zealand to Bataillon for the addresses of Reina and Marinoni, was still taking action. In spite of all this, Reina waited patiently for further orders from Rome and from Milan.[22]

Cuarterón had planned to leave Cádiz for Singapore and Manila on 31 January 1856,[23] but his voyage had to be postponed one month. The delay was caused by unfinished work on the clipper ship, the *Guadalupe*, which Cuarterón had booked passage for himself, Borgazzi, and Riva. It was a new type of vessel built to compete with steamships for speed, and this was to be its maiden voyage. As Borgazzi told Marinoni on New Year's Eve 1855, it had been tested by a furious storm on 19 and 20 December. The clipper had arrived back at Cádiz on 21 December, and at the end of the month the coppersmiths were still at work and so were the interior decorators.

"The ship is magnificent, the best that there is on this route," Borgazzi told Marinoni. "It is a 1,200-ton vessel, 210 feet long and only 35 feet wide in the middle." The owner, Don Ignazio de Castro, a wealthy businessman in Cádiz, took the three missionaries aboard for a preview. He had named his ship *Guadalupe* after his daughter, who had died only a few months earlier. The captain was the nephew of the owner, and both he and the first pilot were good friends of Cuarterón. While touring the clipper the missionaries met the captain and also the shipbuilder, who proudly said that the *Guadalupe* had raced along "at fourteen

---

20. PIME: AME 11:1031–32, Raimondi to Ripamonti, 27 July 1856.
21. Ibid., 239, Reina to Marinoni, 15 April 1856.
22. Ibid., 245–46, Reina to Marinoni, 14 May 1856.
23. See ibid., 29:730, Cuarterón to Reina, 4 January 1856.

miles and even at sixteen miles an hour (like a good steamer)." And so "in about seventy days," Borgazzi said, "it should bring us to Singapore." The cabin chosen by Borgazzi and Riva was separated from those of the passengers and was located near the pilots, "so that we can be instructed in nautical science by them and at the same time be near the sailors, whom we shall try to catechize."[24]

Before embarking at Cádiz on the night of 27 February 1856, Borgazzi sensed "the duty and the need" to send Marinoni greetings. "We are now going directly to Manila," he said, "where we expect to find" Reina and his companions. Manuel, a brother of Don Carlos Cuarterón, was also a sea captain and was to be placed in command of a ship that Don Carlos hoped to purchase in Manila. Manuel would then take his brother's missionaries to the Labuan mission, or he would accompany Reina's group to their mission, "whichever seems the better thing to do, since nothing can be decided definitely now."[25] The *Guadalupe* finally sailed from Cádiz on 28 February 1856.[26]

Cardinal Prefect Fransoni's letter of 21 August 1855 to director Marinoni, which was forwarded to Reina on 6 September, contained the following words: "More suitable locations will be assigned to the missionaries of Father Reina. . . ."[27] These words apparently were understood by Reina to mean that Rome intended to remove him and his missionaries from the Prefecture of Melanesia, because in his reply to Fransoni he spoke of Rome's plan to give him "a new task in another land."[28]

Borgazzi was under a similar impression, because he had informed Marinoni from Cádiz that "the danger" exists that Reina and his companions "may be sent to another mission, abandoning perhaps forever Micronesia and Melanesia."[29] Subsequently Cardinal Fransoni sent word to Milan that Pope Pius IX had given his blessing to Reina and his companions. As Fransoni told Marinoni in his letter, he hoped that this blessing would be "a forecast of happy results in their new enterprise."[30]

Marinoni wrote right back to Fransoni on 8 March 1856, seeking clarification on Reina's destination. "I would like to know," he said, "whether our missionaries in Sydney, as was written to me from Cádiz, have been called to Singapore to join the Prefect Apostolic of Labuan, Don Carlos Cuarterón, in order to be taken to a new mission. The last letter

---

24. Ibid., 11:1490, Borgazzi to Marinoni, 31 December 1855.

25. Ibid., 1495–96, Borgazzi to Marinoni, 27 February 1856.

26. Borgazzi wrote from Angers (now Anjer Lor) in northwest Java on 31 May 1856 that the voyage to this point from Cádiz had taken ninety-three days. See ibid., 1497, Borgazzi to Marinoni, 31 May 1856. Counting backwards from 31 May, while remembering that 1856 was a leap year and that Borgazzi and the others had embarked on the night of 27 February, one gets a departure date of 28 February. The sailing date of 25 February 1856 given by both Tragella in *Missioni estere*, 1:234, and Rooney in *Khabar Gembira*, 20, cannot be correct, because Borgazzi wrote a letter to Marinoni from Cádiz two nights later.

27. PIME: AME 1:153, Fransoni to Marinoni, 21 August 1855.

28. Ibid., 11:213, Reina to Fransoni, 28 January 1856.

29. Ibid., 1488, Borgazzi to Marinoni, 31 December 1855.

30. PF: LDB vol. 347 (1856), f. 133v., Fransoni to Marinoni, 1 March 1856.

from Your Eminence seems to hint at this, because it informs me of the graciousness with which the Vicar of Jesus Christ…implored upon our missionaries in Sydney the blessings of heaven for the new undertaking to which they have been assigned." Marinoni said that his only motive for putting this question was the necessity in which it would place him "of passing on this information immediately to the Association for the Propagation of the Faith in Lyon, since it would have to give me another 14,000 francs for those missionaries. Nor would there be any time to lose in sending the said amount to Sydney."[31]

Fransoni wrote back: "As to your doubts about the destination" of your missionaries in Sydney, "I assure you that there has been no change as a result of the agreements reached with Don Carlos Cuarterón. These agreements have no other purpose but to facilitate for them a more suitable location in their Mission, and to establish between them and the Prefect of Labuan, as well as with his collaborators, such contacts which will make possible easy and opportune exchanges, correspondence, mutual assistance and support." Fransoni hoped that these new arrangements would bring them "greater success than their previous attempts." He also urged Marinoni to send quickly to his missionaries the funds which he had mentioned.[32]

Three weeks later Fransoni died on 20 April 1856 at the age of eighty, having served as prefect of Propaganda for twenty-one years. According to Alfieri, "The angel, Cardinal Fransoni, died like an angel…at 10 a.m. after two and a half days of sickness. You cannot imagine what sorrow this has caused among his closest friends."[33] At the time of Fransoni's death Cuarterón and his two missionaries were en route to Manila. And Raimondi, whom Reina had sent in search of Mazzucconi, was just six days out of Sydney en route to Woodlark.

In Rome all were convinced that fifty-five-year-old Barnabò, who had been serving Propaganda so well as pro-secretary and then as secretary for the past nine years, would become its next prefect. But knowing how opposed he was to accepting the office, Pius IX bided his time. Then one day about two months after Fransoni's death the pope invited Barnabò to the Vatican. While the two of them were engaged in conversation, the pope had a securely tied bundle placed in his carriage and he made Barnabò promise not to open it until he reached his residence. On opening the bundle Barnabò found the regalia of a cardinal! He rushed back to the Vatican, threw himself at the pope's feet, and tearfully begged him not to carry out his plan. But the pope said that all arrangements had been made and they were irreversible. A few days later, on 19 June 1856, Barnabò was elevated to the rank of cardinal and was named a cardinal member of Propaganda. On 20 June he became its prefect. Barnabò was a hard worker. Almost always he was the first one to arrive in the office. Taking no holidays himself, he substituted for others on vacation, even for copyists

---

31. PF: SC Indie Orientali vol. 15 (1855–56), f. 952rv, Marinoni to Fransoni, 8 March 1856.

32. PIME: AME 1:167, Fransoni to Marinoni, 27 March 1856. This letter, perhaps due to a secretarial error, refers to Reina and his companions as "missionaries of Micronesia."

33. Ibid., 10:159, Alfieri to Marinoni, 21 April 1856.

and clerks. He remained in office until his death in 1874 and once said that ever since he had been in office, no letter had been sent out by Propaganda that he had not read. He was surprisingly quick in reaching decisions and also frank and abrupt in expressing his opinion to others. From 12 February 1812 to 26 July 1814, when eleven to thirteen years of age, he had been sent by Napoleon's occupation forces from his hometown of Foligno near Assisi to the military academy at La Flèche, France. After thirteen months, he became a corporal, the only one in his class of thirty-eight to receive this promotion. Later in life he often said, "Once I was a soldier and I still am a bit."[34]

On 21 April 1856, the day after Fransoni's death, Alfieri informed Marinoni that he would be leaving Rome in four or five days for Verona, Italy, because he had been elected prior of his religious community's hospital there.[35] When appointing Alfieri as procurator or agent in Rome on 10 September 1854, Marinoni had asked that he designate a deputy "worthy of yourself and of our trust," whenever he might not be able to perform the office himself.[36]

Therefore Alfieri took counsel with Buratti at Propaganda regarding a possible candidate to serve as his successor. The two were discussing the issue when Father Diego Burrueco arrived and "graciously volunteered to take upon himself" the task. Burrueco was "already the agent for Father Cuarterón," Alfieri informed Marinoni, "being in charge of his endowment for founding a college in Rome for missionaries." He was also "a great friend" of Riva and Borgazzi and of the others from Milan who had left for India, and also of Father Carlo Bolis, their professor of theology, whom Marinoni had invited to accompany his missionaries to Rome. Alfieri added that Burrueco was highly respected at Propaganda and at the Vatican secretariat of state. "You should therefore write him an official letter, thank him, formally appoint him and also entrust him with ample powers," Alfieri urged. "Then afterwards write about this to Secretary Barnabò and say that because of my departure you are giving him my office."[37]

Marinoni did write to Barnabò, saying that because of Alfieri's departure "we at his advice have turned to the Most Excellent Father Diego Burrueco, a Spanish Trinitarian and great friend of the Reverend Prefect Apostolic of Labuan, Don Carlos Cuarterón. In his goodness he has shown himself most ready to assist us." Marinoni added that Burrueco's being "accepted and esteemed by your Sacred Congregation has been the principal motive

---

34. Metzler, "Präfekten und Sekretäre," 38–39, 41–43.

35. See PIME: AME 10:159, Alfieri to Marinoni, 21 April 1856; Tragella, *Missioni estere*, 1:208.

36. See PIME: AME 5:823–24, Marinoni to Alfieri, 10 September 1854.

37. PIME: AME 10:161, Alfieri to Marinoni, 23 April 1856. Tragella consistently but incorrectly uses "Barrueco" for "Burrueco" in *Missioni estere*, vol. 1. Cuarterón, who had an exceptionally clear handwriting, writes "Burrueco" in addressing mail to him. Burrueco is also the name of a locality in the province of Albacete in Spain, which perhaps gave rise to this family name.

prompting us to take advantage of his kind offer."[38] Another motive prompting acceptance of the offer was Burrueco's friendship with Cuarterón.[39]

After a voyage of ninety-three days the clipper *Guadalupe* reached the small town of Angers (now Anjer Lor) at the northwest corner of Java, some eight leagues from Batavia. A stop there had become necessary to take on provisions, Borgazzi said, "because there are more than three hundred mouths to feed every day...." They were still six hundred leagues from Manila. On reaching Manila, he said, "We hope to embrace our venerable colleagues from Rooke and Woodlark."[40] But on arriving there two weeks later (16 June 1856) they found no trace of their colleagues and no mail from them. And on 2 July, when their mail addressed to Singapore was forwarded, there was still no letter from them. Bewildered by this silence Borgazzi wrote Reina "two lines in order to get some news" and sent his note of 5 July with a ship leaving for Sydney on the following day. He thought that "perhaps they have already made some other decision."[41]

Cuarterón's letter to Reina of 4 January 1856, telling how the two men could get in touch with one another, had taken an exceptionally long time to reach Sydney from Cádiz and arrived in Reina's hands only on Friday, 9 May.[42] Since it brought the news that Cuarterón expected to reach Manila at the beginning of the month of June, Reina wrote to him there that very same day in care of the archbishop, as he had been instructed, and explained why he was being held back in Sydney. Since a voyage from Sydney to Manila took at least six or seven weeks, Reina's letter might arrive in the archbishop's office by the end of June.

Reina also wrote to the cardinal prefect of Propaganda on 14 May, explaining that Cuarterón's letter "invites us in the name of Your Most Reverend Eminence and of Propaganda to set out immediately for Singapore or for Manila, from which points he will then take us to the most suitable places in our mission." Nine months of rest and recuperation in Sydney had made Reina and his missionaries fit for work again, he said, and so "we wanted to obey your orders at once. Two reasons, however, prevent us from fulfilling this duty and desire of ours. The first is that Father Timoleone Raimondi left us this past 14 April for Woodlark Island to search for Father Giovanni Mazzucconi." He was expected back about 14 June. "The other reason is that we do not have the necessary funds to pay the cost of a voyage from Sydney to Manila." But he pointed out that two months earlier Marinoni had announced that funds were en route "and with them we shall be in a

---

38. PIME: AME 6:39–40, Marinoni to Barnabò, 13 June 1856.
39. Ibid., 35-01 Scurati, *Memorie dell'Istituto*, 431.
40. Ibid., 11:1497–98, 1500, Borgazzi to Marinoni, 31 May 1856.
41. Ibid., 1501, Borgazzi to Marinoni, 5 July 1856.
42. In PIME: AME 11:245, Reina tells Marinoni on 14 May 1856 that he received Cuarterón's letter "on the ninth day of this month." In PIME: AME 11:611, Ambrosoli tells Marinoni on 17 May 1856 that Cuarterón's letter arrived "on the tenth of this month." Tragella uses Ambrosoli's date in *Missioni estere*, 1:232. Reina—better than Ambrosoli—must have known when it was that he received Cuarterón's letter.

position to carry out the wishes of Your Most Reverend Eminence." The news being sent to the cardinal prefect, Reina said, had also been sent to Cuarterón in Manila, so that "he will know better what decisions to make."[43]

Raimondi arrived back in Sydney on 13 June 1856 with the news that Mazzucconi and the entire *Gazelle* crew had been massacred at Woodlark. During that first week Raimondi and Reina held "great discussions," Ambrosoli said, "but I do not yet know what will come of them. Reina is in favor of Manila; Raimondi is in favor of Port Curtis; and I am a bit for one and less for the other."[44] Already two months earlier Raimondi was convinced that he and the others "had been assigned to work among the Protestants and the Aborigines in northern Australia."[45] Apparently this discussion arose because Prefect Apostolic Reina did not share with his colleagues the official correspondence that he received from Milan and Rome. Eventually, however, he made it clear to Raimondi that their orders were to sail to Singapore or Manila, meet Cuarterón for discussions, and then go to a better location in their Melanesia-Micronesia mission.

Although Ambrosoli had disembarked with the others at Sydney on 24 August 1855, his recovery at Tarban Creek had lasted until 3 May 1856, when he was assigned to the Saint Vincent Convent of the Sisters of Charity at Wooloomooloo. His health at this time was still very poor, and his only responsibility at the convent was to celebrate daily Mass for the nuns.[46] After being at the convent for two months he wrote in a rather discouraged vein to director Marinoni: "Reina wants to leave for Manila, and I believe that I shall not be wanted. So what shall I do? Nothing at all! If Reina wants me, I shall go; if not, I shall stay. And then I shall do what you yourself tell me to do, if I should still be alive."[47]

Reina booked passage to Manila aboard the *Granite City*, a large vessel of 710 tons. But only two of his original six companions were sailing with him because Catechist Corti was dead, Father Mazzucconi was dead, and Father Salerio was in Milan recuperating. "And poor Ambrosoli," Raimondi said, "who so much wants to go with us to the islands, cannot do so. His spleen and liver have been severely attacked. . . . His entire body is covered with scabs and boils. He suffers much, especially from severe pains in the upper stomach. And so he can do nothing. . . . He will therefore stay here one more year. Then if he gets well, he will come to join us. But I do not think that he will last more than a year. The doctor says that although his lungs have not yet been affected, there is great danger that they will be attacked soon, since his entire body has wasted away and has been ruined

---

43. PIME: AME 11:241–42, Reina to the cardinal prefect, 14 May 1856. Reina apparently was not aware that Cardinal Prefect Fransoni had died on 20 April 1856 and that by 14 May no successor had been appointed.

44. Ibid., 615–16, Ambrosoli to Marinoni, 21 June 1856.

45. Ibid., 1030, Raimondi to Ripamonti, 27 July 1856.

46. Ibid., 611, Ambrosoli to Marinoni, 17 May 1856.

47. Ibid., 618, Ambrosoli to Marinoni, 5 July 1856. Ambrosoli was transferred for one day in mid-August 1856 to the Benedictine convent in Subiaco and then back again the next day to the convent in Wooloomooloo. See ibid., 620, Ambrosoli to Marinoni, 23 August 1856.

by fevers." When Raimondi wrote this on 27 July 1856, Ambrosoli had been recuperating for eleven full months.[48]

Passage was booked also for Puarer of Woodlark, who had been staying with the Milan missionaries at Tarban Creek all this time. Raimondi was full of admiration for this young man, saying that "he gave up his country and his relatives in order to stay with us forever, being ready to go wherever we shall go. He wishes to remain with us like a brother, 'Like Luigi,' as he himself puts it." Puarer referred in this way to Catechist Luigi Tacchini, whom he knew and admired. In Raimondi's eyes Mazzucconi's death had been responsible for saving the soul of Puarer. "I am instructing him," Raimondi said, "and as soon as he is sufficiently prepared, I shall baptize him.... Puarer will then give up his name and take on the name Giovanni, because this was the name of our companion [Mazzucconi]."[49]

Puarer had become a celebrity in Sydney, Raimondi said, being extolled as the one who had unveiled the massacre aboard the *Gazelle*. "His name had appeared in the newspapers together with a description of his stature, physique, etc. And a French painter sought permission to make a portrait" of him. Raimondi sent Salerio, who had known Puarer so very well at Woodlark, a six-page letter telling how he had taken Puarer on a walk through Sydney's streets and for a ride on a steamer to Subiaco. At length he described the reactions of Puarer to all that he had heard and seen.[50]

"We shall be leaving for Manila in ten days, or fifteen at the most," Raimondi wrote to treasurer Ripamonti in Milan on 27 July 1856. But he could not say whether Reina's group and Cuarterón's would constitute a single mission with Cuarterón as superior, "because I do not yet know the particular decisions made by Rome, nor those of Don Cuarterón." The little that he knew was from letters of Cuarterón, Borgazzi, and Riva, that had arrived from Cádiz.

"Don Cuarterón, namely, intends to take us back again into the Vicariate of Melanesia and Micronesia,"[51] Raimondi said. "He recommends two missions in Melanesia, namely, the Aru Islands and the northern coast of New Guinea. But from the little that I know, the natives of these two places differ very little from those of Woodlark and Rooke. And those on the northern coast of New Guinea would be the same ones who destroyed the Dutch fort, obliging the Whites to leave."[52] He suggests further that "another mission for us could

---

48. Ibid., 1031, Raimondi to Ripamonti, 27 July 1856.

49. *Beatificationis Positio*, 360, Raimondi to Salerio, 20 June 1856. Giovanni is the Italian form of John.

50. PIME: AME 11:1034–35, Raimondi to Salerio, 1 August 1856.

51. Here Raimondi incorrectly uses an earlier name for the mission; it had meanwhile been reduced to prefecture status.

52. Raimondi is misinformed in speaking of a Dutch fort on the northern coast of New Guinea. The fort was a British logwood stockade called Fort Coronation. It was built in 1793, was located at Dorei Bay near the present site of Manokwari in the Vogelkop, and was abandoned in 1795. In 1828 at Triton Bay on the southwest coast of New Guinea the Dutch founded a colony called Merkusoord. Here they built Fort du Bus, which was abandoned in 1835. Both forts suffered attack by the local people and both had deadly climates, causing many to die from malaria and beriberi. For more details see Souter, *New Guinea*, 20–22. His map opposite p. 32

be the well-known Palau Islands in Micronesia. But these islands, it seems, have very little communication with Europe because, as Borgazzi's letter says, it is seldom that ships arrive there twice a year."

When writing from Milan to Oceania, Ripamonti regularly lavished praise upon the Milan missionaries working in Madras, India, calling attention to their success. "Those of us in Oceania will also be sending back good news in time," Raimondi told him on 27 July 1856. "Some months ago I believed that we had been assigned to Northern Australia to work among Protestants and Aborigines. If this had happened, I could have promised you five or six dozen converts a year, at least if I may judge from the many conversions that I see here. But in the midst of savages, the scene changes." He pointed out that it had taken from five to twelve years for missions in Western and Central Oceania to obtain three or four hundred converts.[53]

On 4 July 1856, just six weeks before the missionaries were to set sail for Manila, Raimondi informed director Marinoni that Reina's health was in a "precarious state." And he added: "We need new personnel, otherwise we shall have to abandon Melanesia and Micronesia a second time!"[54]

Reina left his post at the Benedictine convent in Subiaco near the end of July 1856 and went to the Marist Center at Tarban Creek. Here, he told Marinoni, "Raimondi, Tacchini and I shall make a bit of a retreat in order to prepare ourselves for our new mission." Treasurer Ripamonti had asked Reina whether he had ever thought about what people might say because of his abandoning the Rooke and Woodlark missions. Reina sent his reply to Marinoni: indeed he had feared "causing displeasure" for his superiors "and doing something contrary to their wishes, since I certainly aimed to please them." In fact, he said, "I thought much about this and it was one of my principal reasons for hesitating. . . ." But as far as others were concerned, those who were not superiors, "I did not even give them a thought. . . . In three years at Rooke we baptized three children. These are our results! Oh well, there is nothing more to say. . . ."[55]

Since the *Granite City* passengers had been instructed to board ship on Thursday afternoon, 14 August 1856, the Milan missionaries earlier that day went to take leave of Ambrosoli at Saint Vincent Convent in Wooloomooloo. "Today we shall go aboard ship and sleep there," Reina wrote to Marinoni. "And tomorrow, God willing, we shall leave. We are now at Ambrosoli's place and in a few hours we shall be leaving him."[56]

---

shows the location of Dorei Bay and Triton Bay, each at approximately 134 degrees 15 minutes east longitude.

53. PIME: AME 11:1030-31, Raimondi to Ripamonti, 27 July 1856. This letter of Raimondi, which refers to the Port Curtis mission as having both Protestants and Aborigines, must have been overlooked by Tragella who in *Missioni estere*, 1:229, speaks only of missionary work among Aborigines at Port Curtis. This incompleteness by Tragella may have misled Laracy. See this chapter, p, 318, n. 16.

54. PIME: AME 11:1025-26, Raimondi to Marinoni, 4 July 1856.

55. Ibid., 273, Reina to Marinoni, 23 July 1856. Reina had been at Rooke two and a half years, not three.

56. Ibid., 293, Reina to Marinoni, 14 August 1856.

The ship, however, did not sail as scheduled on 15 August, which was a Roman Catholic feast known as the Assumption of the Blessed Virgin Mary. Both Reina and Raimondi celebrated their Masses aboard ship that morning, and that afternoon Ambrosoli arrived with a newspaper announcing that the *Waterloo* had reached London "on 13 May."[57] This was very good news for the missionaries because Salerio, who had taken along important mail for their superiors in Milan and in Rome and also for their families, had sailed aboard that very ship to Europe, leaving Sydney on 2 February. Ambrosoli, however, had some bad news for Reina, Raimondi, and Tacchini. He told them that letters happened to arrive for them from Milan and Rome that very day. "I saw them in Father Rocher's mailbox," he said. "But since it was a feast day," Rocher did not come to his office "and I was unable to get at the letters." Ambrosoli promised to forward them with the next ship leaving for Manila.

On Saturday morning, 16 August 1856, after the Milan missionaries had been in Sydney for one week less than a year, their ship sailed out of Port Jackson en route to Manila. "Imagine my chagrin," Ambrosoli told Marinoni, "when one hour after their departure I found Father Rocher standing at the door. . . ." Two days later someone arrived with an additional packet from Father Ripamonti "containing letters from the relatives of Father Reina written on 30 April." By this time the letters had been en route three and a half months and it would take at least another one and a half months for them to reach Manila. "Three days later," Ambrosoli said, "the French Consul gave me a letter from a Spaniard written on 27 April in Rome in Spanish (but I could not make out the name). Enclosed was also a letter from Alfieri for Borgazzi and Riva," as well as other letters, "all directed to Cuarterón via Reina. I shall send them to Manila with the first ship that will be sailing there. . . ."[58]

It is not difficult to figure out that the Spaniard who wrote the Spanish letter dated 27 April 1856 in Rome was Father Burrueco, the procurator or agent at the Vatican for Don Carlos Cuarterón. He was no doubt sending Cuarterón the news that Cardinal Prefect Fransoni had died one week earlier. Burrueco may also have informed Cuarterón that he had volunteered to serve as procurator or agent for the Milan Foreign Mission Seminary and that Alfieri, formerly holder of that office, had recommended him highly to director Marinoni in the past few days.

Four days before Reina sailed out of Port Jackson, Bishop Pompallier wrote to him from Auckland, New Zealand, requesting Marinoni's address. Pompallier wanted to write to Marinoni directly about getting priests from his seminary for New Zealand. In Reina's absence Ambrosoli opened the letter and supplied the address on 15 September 1856.[59] On

---

57. Salerio in RIP: R B-N.2, N.1, "Giornale di Viaggio," says that the pilot came aboard on 13 May, but that they reached Gravesend only on 14 May 1856.

58. PIME: AME 11:619, Ambrosoli to Marinoni, 23 August 1856. The *Granite City*'s sailing date is incorrectly given as 10 August 1856 in *Beatificationis Positio*, 388 n. 4.

59. See PIME: AME 28:756, Pompallier to Marinoni, 7 September 1857. Pompallier's letter of 12 August 1856 to Reina, referred to in this letter to Marinoni, has not been found.

the following day, 16 September, the news finally arrived in Milan that Mazzucconi had been killed.[60] By this time Reina had completed one full month of his six-week voyage to Manila. Would he still find Cuarterón waiting for him there?

---

60. Tragella, *Missioni estere*, 1:214.

17

Reina and Cuarterón Meet in Manila to Discuss Plans
1 October 1856

THE CLIPPER *GUADALUPE* WITH PREFECT APOSTOLIC CUARTERÓN AND FATHERS RIVA AND Borgazzi aboard reached Manila in the Philippines on Monday, 16 June 1856, 109 days after leaving Cádiz, Spain. Three days later in Intramuros, Manila, the missionaries obtained lodging in Convento de San Pablo, called also Convento de San Agustín, a monastery founded in 1571 which is still standing today. It belonged to the Order of Saint Augustine (O.S.A.), whose members are called Augustinians, and served as the central house for the Augustinian province in the Philippines. One of Cuarterón's brothers was an Augustinian priest in this province. During their first days in Manila, Cuarterón, Borgazzi, and Riva visited the city's captain general and also Archbishop José Aranguren Orsa (1801–61), who had been placed in charge of the Manila archdiocese on 19 January 1846.[1]

While waiting for Prefect Apostolic Reina to arrive from Sydney, Cuarterón received a letter dated 22 July 1856 from Father J. M. Beurel, a member of the Paris Foreign Mission Seminary. He resided in Singapore and was pro-vicar general for the Vicariate Apostolic of Western Siam. Father Ambrosoli, left behind in Sydney, had sent a letter in care of the Paris Foreign Missionaries of Singapore meant for Father Riva and had addressed it to "The Prefect Apostolic of Labuan." Beurel wanted to know from Cuarterón whether that was his exact title. "We also have jurisdiction over this island," he said. "And how far does your jurisdiction extend?" Beurel would be pleased, he said, to receive a few words on this matter.

About this time Cuarterón received another shock. His old friend Captain Don Rafael Castro, a Spanish sea captain whom he had last met in Cádiz the previous December, had arrived in Manila and one of his passengers had been Bishop Piet Maria Vrancken, vicar apostolic of Batavia (now Jakarta). When speaking with Castro about Cuarterón, Vrancken

---

1. PIME: AME 11:1501, Borgazzi to Marinoni, 5 July 1856; PF: SC Oceania vol. 5 (1853–57, Part II), f. 1136r, Cuarterón to Fransoni, 5 August 1856. Data on the monastery comes from letters to Wiltgen of Father Isacio Rodriguez, O.S.A., Valladolid, Spain, 20 March 1972, and of Father Restituto Suarez, O.S.A., Intramuros, Manila, 7 April 1972.

had said that neither he nor the Dutch government would ever permit Cuarterón to enter within the limits of their jurisdictions.

Beurel's query and Vrancken's statement so disturbed Cuarterón that he immediately sent off a letter to Cardinal Prefect Fransoni on 5 August 1856. "With great displeasure" he reported what Bishop Vrancken had told Captain Castro and also what he himself had been asked by Beurel. He begged Fransoni and the entire Propaganda Fide to contact the two vicars apostolic of Batavia and of Western Siam "as soon as this letter arrives." In addition, he urged Propaganda not only to advise the two vicars apostolic of its decision to create the new Prefecture Apostolic of Labuan "and Independent Borneo," but also to indicate for each of them the extent of jurisdiction of his new prefecture apostolic. "If you do not do this," he said, "the French missionaries will drive us out when we arrive in Labuan, and the same will happen later when we go to Borneo, where the Dutch will drive us out. And so we shall have to wander, not knowing where to go, after our having made so many and such great personal and financial sacrifices to extend the domain of the Church."[2]

On the same day Cuarterón wrote to secretary Barnabò, saying that the French missionaries of Singapore and the vicar apostolic of Batavia were attacking his mission, as could be seen from his enclosed letter addressed to Fransoni. Cuarterón pleaded with Barnabò: "It is necessary that Your Excellency should not abandon me in these critical circumstances in which I find myself. I shall be completely overpowered by my strong adversaries, if these two Vicars Apostolic declare themselves opposed and if you do not give me your protection. I can find no other protection but in God's mercy and in the justice of Propaganda, which must know that I did not try to deceive it or to surprise it."[3]

Cuarterón sent still another letter that day to Fransoni, explaining that it was impossible to find a ship sailing from Manila to Labuan. The ports for reaching Labuan were Hong Kong and Singapore, he pointed out. But sailing to either of those two ports from Manila was very costly. "Therefore," he said, "I am repairing my ship, the schooner *Mártires de Tun-Kin*." He planned to sail with it directly to Labuan and had placed it "under the command of one of my brothers."[4]

Having received no word from Reina up to this time Cuarterón, like Borgazzi and Riva, began wondering whether Reina had meanwhile decided to go to some other mission.[5] Finally on 17 August 1856, two months and one day after his arriving in Manila, Cuarterón received Reina's three-month-old letter of 9 May sent in care of the archbishop of

---

2. PF: SC Oceania vol. 5 (1853–57, Part II), f. 1137r–1138v, Cuarterón to Fransoni, 5 August 1856. Cuarterón here misrepresents his mission, most likely intentionally, calling it the Prefecture Apostolic of Labuan "and Independent Borneo." On Cuarterón's earlier contact with Vrancken, see chap. 15, pp. 271–73.

3. PF: SC Oceania vol. 5 (1853-57, Part II), f. 1142r, Cuarterón to Barnabò, 5 August 1856.

4. Ibid., f. 1136r, Cuarterón to Fransoni, 5 August 1856. Tonkin, a former independent kingdom, today is part of Vietnam. Cuarterón already owned *Mártires de Tun-Kin* in 1844–45. See chap. 15, p. 267.

5. Borgazzi suggested this possibility when writing to Marinoni on 5 July 1856. See PIME: AME 11:1501.

Manila. It gave assurance that Reina and his group would set out for Manila after Raimondi had returned from his search for Mazzucconi and after funds had arrived from Europe to make possible the voyage from Sydney to Manila.[6] By the time Cuarterón received this letter, Reina and his companions were en route aboard the frigate *Granite City*, having left Sydney for Manila on 4 August.

Cuarterón followed up his 5 August 1856 letters to Fransoni and Barnabò about Beurel and Vrancken with further letters on 3 September in case those of August might go astray en route.[7] Having done this he continued with his original plans as if nothing had happened.

In mid-August Cuarterón visited the Government Navy Yard "at Cavite City seven miles from Manila Bay." There he saw two feluccas for sale, each "about fifteen tons." "Considering them very useful for our mission, since they would make it possible for us to go up the large and extensive rivers found in the Island of Borneo, I decided to buy them . . . ," he told Fransoni. He added that he was having them "almost completely remodeled so that they no longer will be called feluccas, but cutters."[8] The Navy commander general had assured Cuarterón that he would be allowed to use the Spanish flag for traveling safely to his destination.

Riva was put in charge of the cutter called by Cuarterón *Refugium Peccatorum* (Refuge of Sinners), and Borgazzi was put in charge of the one called *Consolatrix Afflictorum* (Consoler of the Afflicted). These titles in honor of the Blessed Virgin Mary came from the Litany of Loreto made popular at the House of Loreto in Italy, a shrine visited by Cuarterón in early May 1855.[9] In addition to having a small but comfortable cabin for the missionary

---

6. PF: SC Oceania vol. 5 (1853–57, Part II), f. 1194r, Cuarterón to Fransoni, 6 October 1856. Cuarterón in this letter to Fransoni says that Reina's letter to him was dated 4 May. But Reina by that date did not yet have Cuarterón's letter of 4 January 1856 from Cádiz, to which he was replying. Proof of this is Reina's telling Marinoni on 14 May 1856 that he had received Cuarterón's letter from Cádiz "on the 9th of this month," that he had answered it at once—this would mean the same day—via the archbishop of Manila, and that he had given two reasons that he could not leave at once. See PIME: AME 11:245, Reina to Marinoni, 14 May 1856. Reina may have written "4" May mistakenly, being misled because he was answering Cuarterón's letter of "4" January. Or Cuarterón may have misread Reina's "9" May as "4" May, being misled by Reina's minute script or because Reina was answering his letter of "4" January.

7. PF: SC Oceania vol. 5 (1853–57, Part II), f. 1159rv, 1165r, Cuarterón to Fransoni, 3 September 1856; PF: SC Oceania vol. 5 (1853–57, Part II), f. 1160rv, Cuarterón to Barnabò, 3 September 1856.

8. A felucca was a small swift vessel propelled by triangular sails; a cutter was a single-masted, fast sailing vessel normally having no more than four sails. The tonnage for the feluccas is given variously by the Milan missionaries. Reina tells Marinoni on 7 October 1856 in PIME: AME 11:299, that they were "14 to 20 tons" each, and on 1 December 1856 he tells Ramazzotti in PIME: AME 11:313, that they were "16 to 20 tons" each. Borgazzi's figure is "30 tons" in Tragella, *Missioni estere*, 1:242 n. 37. But on 5 June 1857 in PIME: AME 11:1518, he tells Salerio that the two feluccas were "about 20 tons each." The author uses "about fifteen tons," which is the tonnage as stated by Cuarterón, buyer of the vessels, in his letter to Cardinal Prefect Fransoni of 18 September 1856, in PF: SC Oceania vol. 5 (1853–57, Part II), f. 1176rv, where he announces his purchase of the feluccas. See also this chapter, p. 341, n. 28.

9. On Cuarterón's visit to Loreto see chap. 15, p. 289.

aboard, each cutter was to be provided with "a chapel for celebrating the Holy Sacrifice [of the Mass], making possible this consolation [for a missionary] when he is sailing on the rivers and is not able to celebrate the Holy Sacrifice on land." Cuarterón added that remodeling the feluccas would cost him five thousand francs apiece.[10]

After spending three and a half months in Manila, Cuarterón was finally able to write Cardinal Fransoni on 6 October 1856: "On the first day of the current month at 2 PM the said Prefect [Reina] presented himself to me in this city together with the priest Don Timoleone Raimondi, telling me that they had arrived that very morning [1 October] in this bay aboard the English frigate *Granite City*, and that the Catechist Luigi Tacchini and a catechumen from Woodlark Island [Puarer] had remained aboard the vessel." Reina had likewise confirmed "the news of the assassination of the priest Mazzucconi and of the captain together with the entire crew of the English schooner [*Gazelle*]...."[11]

Cuarterón succeeded in obtaining lodging for Reina, Raimondi, Tacchini, and Puarer at the same Augustinian monastery where he was lodged with Riva and Borgazzi. This made it convenient for the two prefects apostolic, Cuarterón and Reina, to discuss strategy for relaunching the Melanesia mission. After five days of talks, Cuarterón sent Cardinal Prefect Fransoni his report on 6 October 1856. He was unaware that Fransoni had died five and a half months earlier and that since then all mail addressed to Fransoni was being given to Barnabò, whom Pope Pius IX had named cardinal prefect of Propaganda two months after Fransoni's death. First Cuarterón explained how he had met Reina in Manila and then he described their plans. *Mártires de Tun-Kin* had been careened and was ready to sail, he said. And once the two cutters were remodeled, all three vessels would sail to distant Labuan, southwest of Manila. The southwest monsoon was still blowing, however, and this represented a contrary wind for their voyage. But the winter monsoon beginning in November would bring a favorable wind from the northeast, making it possible for them to sail. "On arriving in Labuan, I shall see whether I can settle there," Cuarterón said. If he

---

10. PF: SC Oceania vol. 5 (1853–57, Part II), f. 1176rv, Cuarterón to Fransoni, 18 September 1856.

11. Ibid., f. 1194r, Cuarterón to Fransoni, 6 October 1856. The sources give various dates for the arrival of Reina in Manila, but 1 October as given by Cuarterón in this letter to Fransoni must be taken as correct. In PIME: AME 11:295, Reina tells Barnabò on 7 October 1856 that he arrived in Manila on 31 September and Tragella repeats this date in *Missioni estere*, 1:232. But 31 September is an impossible date, because September has only thirty days. If Reina meant the day following 30 September, this would coincide with 1 October, which was the date given by Cuarterón. The problem is complicated because on 7 October 1856, the same day on which Reina told Barnabò that he arrived in Manila on 31 September, he told Marinoni that he arrived on 30 September. See PIME: AME 11:299. Reina was very sick on reaching Manila, Cuarterón said, so this could have accounted for his confusion of dates. Reina's letter in PIME: AME 11:295, containing the date 31 September, is a contemporary copy of Reina's original letter, which was forwarded to Barnabò. The original in PF: SC Oceania vol. 5 (1853–57, Part II), f. 1196rv, is of no help on checking the date, however, because in the past 135 years a vertical tear has been made in the paper through the digit following "3," making it illegible, although it resembles "1." Since the page most likely was not torn when the copy was made 135 years ago, it can be presumed that Reina's original letter had 31 September like the copy shows. Tragella in *Missioni estere*, 1:235, says that Reina and his party arrived in Manila on 3 September; this cannot be correct.

could not, he would try to settle in Brunei City, the capital of Borneo Kingdom properly so-called; or in Kuching, the capital of Sarawak District, which included "the states and residence of the Englishman, Sir James Brooke; or in Tampassuk City [near modern Kota Belud], the residence of a Sultan with that same name on the northwest coast of Borneo."

After becoming established in one of these locations "with the hope of being able to continue there," Cuarterón said, "I plan to leave Antonio Riva behind with *Refugium Peccatorum* and also Father Ignazio Borgazzi with *Consolatrix Afflictorum*. I shall then set sail with Prefect Apostolic Father Paolo Reina [along with Father Raimondi, Catechist Tacchini, and the Woodlark catechumen] aboard my schooner *Mártires de Tun-Kin*. And if this vessel cannot make the voyage, I shall replace it with another vessel." He intended to sail first to Menado on the northeastern tip of Celebes (now Sulawesi) and from there to Ternate off the west coast of Halmahera. But he would set sail "only after reaching an agreement both with [Prefect Apostolic] Reina and with Bishop Vrancken, Vicar Apostolic of Batavia, so that the latter causes no opposition to this voyage. Only then would it be possible for me to negotiate with Dutch and Moslem authorities regarding the establishment of a procure in one of those two places, whichever is better located and better suited for supplying the needs" of the missions to be founded. "We would then proceed to the Gebe Islands [at Djailolo Passage in the Halmahera Sea] and to the northern part of New Guinea, particularly to the Port of Dorei on that coast, in order to determine in which of these places the Prefecture Apostolic of Melanesia and Micronesia could be established."

Cuarterón pointed out to the cardinal prefect, however, that Reina's health had "suffered very much." And since there was "no hope at all that the priest Ambrosoli can recover and come from Sydney, Father Timoleone Raimondi will find himself alone and isolated, if Prefect Reina should become completely incapacitated." Cuarterón therefore asked for "some new missionaries, so that this mission will not turn out to be a disaster again." If His Eminence were to approve of sending some personnel, he said, "It is my opinion that for the moment no more than two should come. . . . One of these could stay at Menado or Ternate as procurator and the other could accompany Prefect Reina and Raimondi [to the mission]. Then in case one of those in the mission should get sick, he could leave for recuperation, taking over the office of procurator. . . ." And the one serving until then as procurator could take over the vacated place in the mission. "Should Your Most Reverend Eminence decide to assign two missionaries to Prefect Reina's mission," Cuarterón said, "you could send them via the Isthmus of Suez to Singapore. From there they could leave for Labuan, where we shall all meet. . . ."[12]

On the very day after Cuarterón posted his letter to "Prefect Fransoni," not realizing that he was dead, Reina wrote to Barnabò saying that Marinoni had sent "the consoling news" of his having been named a cardinal and prefect of Propaganda. "And although I know that I have been an occasion of displeasure to the heart of your Most Reverend Eminence in the past," Reina said, "I also know that clemency is not the least of your vir-

---

12. PF: SC Oceania vol. 5 (1853–57, Part II), f. 1194r–1195v, Cuarterón to Fransoni, 6 October 1856.

tues." After describing Cuarterón as "that excellent missionary whom we can now call our guide and our father," Reina repeated the program outlined by Cuarterón in his own letter to Fransoni of the previous day, but without mentioning Menado in Celebes. When Riva and Borgazzi were established, he said, Cuarterón would take him and his missionaries "to the island of Ternate in order to win the support of the Sultan there and of the Sultan of Tidore." Gebe, Dorei, and other islands in the vicinity, which had been suggested by Cuarterón for mission stations, were tributaries and dependencies of these two sultans.

This news must have pleased Barnabò, because as secretary under Fransoni he had repeatedly insisted that Cuarterón's mission must become established first, and only afterwards were Reina and his missionaries to be taken to a new location in Melanesia or Micronesia.

Reina also called to the attention of Barnabò the problem regarding Bishop Vrancken, vicar apostolic of Batavia. He "could obstruct this project because of his right of jurisdiction over those lands, since the Sultans mentioned are tributaries to the Dutch." But it was Reina's understanding that Cuarterón had written in detail on this matter to Rome and that Propaganda "in its wisdom will do what it shall judge proper." With the help of God, Reina said, he was "ready to obey..., no matter what orders" he might receive from Barnabò.[13]

Writing to director Marinoni in Milan that same day, 7 October 1856, Reina was far less optimistic than in his letter to Barnabò, which he enclosed for Marinoni to read and forward. From his letter to the cardinal, Reina said, Marinoni could see that Cuarterón's preference "would be Dorei in northern New Guinea. But all depends on whether or not the Vicar Apostolic of Batavia claims jurisdiction. There is also the Palau Archipelago," Reina said, "but those islands are not very good because their inhabitants have already attacked various ships and killed their crews. Furthermore..., the Spaniards call themselves rightful patrons over all of the Caroline Islands and the Archbishop of Manila in turn extends his jurisdiction wherever the Spanish Government extends its power." Reina said further that Protestant missionaries had already become established at Ponape and Ualan in the Caroline Islands.[14] It would also be possible to open missions in "the Aru Islands and in those nearby; a [supply] center could be founded for them... at Banda. But Prefect Cuarterón seems to be more in favor of Dorei."

Reina also told Marinoni about the schooner, which would take them to Labuan, and the two cutters that would be used for keeping the various mission stations on the Borneo coast in contact with one another. "We missionaries shall be captains of the ships," Reina said, because Cuarterón "starts with the principle that missionaries will be more respected and listened to, if they present themselves in the beginning as captains rather than as missionaries." Cuarterón himself "intends to give us lessons as sailors."

---

13. Ibid., f. 1196rv, Reina to Barnabò, 7 October 1856.
14. On the foundation of the Ponape and Ualan missions, see chap. 10, p. 148.

By listening carefully to what Cuarterón, Borgazzi, and Riva had to say about Propaganda and about Marinoni, Reina during his first week in Manila sensed that something very serious had happened. Delicately he presented the matter to Marinoni: "I asked what it was and they told me the full story, describing the opinion which Propaganda and especially Monsignor Barnabò had of me and—what is worse—also of you, my Reverend Superior." What was said at the audience granted by Pope Pius IX to Father Parietti and the other Milan missionaries going to India, as well as its sequel, had all come to light.[15]

"What purpose is there in being mysterious about this?" Reina asked. "We did not drink the chalice which the Lord gave us to drink. We did not have enough charity. . . ." He said that when Don Cuarterón mentioned these opinions "which Rome had regarding both me and you, Reverend Superior, opinions which were bound to influence him, I tried to excuse myself only by stating factually that I had placed myself completely in the hands of Propaganda when it was discussing the question of sending us to Hong Kong. . . . But what could I say to justify you? Nothing! Tears came to my eyes and the Lord knew what was then in my heart."[16]

When Raimondi learned of Rome's having severely criticized both Marinoni and the pioneer missionaries of Oceania (to whom he himself belonged), he hurried off a cheerful letter to Marinoni:

> It is true that until now this son of yours has given you nothing to compensate for the concern which you and the seminary have shown him. But who knows if he may mature a bit more and become wiser as he gets older? Look, my good Superior! Up to now I have been nothing but a vagabond wandering here and there, spending money and sending you nothing but bad news. Poor old Oceania, right? But if I may judge from what I have heard, you, too, Reverend Superior, have suffered a good deal because of our mission, and all of this because of us. Perhaps you fear that you might sadden us, if you were to order us to pull out [of Melanesia]. Oh! Have no fear of offending us, because missionaries must be ready for everything. And that missionary who might complain even in the least about an order coming from his superior is of no value [for our San Calocero Seminary]! Therefore, if you should notice that our superiors in Rome still wish us to go elsewhere—to India, to America, to Africa, or wherever else they may like—write immediately and tell us to go there because, as you can see, we are used to traveling. . . . You have suffered enough for us, excellent Superior, so be of good cheer and do not weep! Nor should you be sad when you receive news that your sons are suffering. Instead sing a lusty *Te Deum* [in thanksgiving] and drink a toast to our good health![17]

---

15. On the papal audience and its sequel see chap. 15, pp. 286–87.

16. PIME: AME 11:299–300, Reina to Marinoni, 7 October 1856.

17. Ibid., 1039–40, Raimondi to Marinoni, 3 November 1856. See also Tragella, *Missioni estere*, 1:237. Note that Tragella incorrectly dates this 3 November letter as "3 December" in his text, but gives the date correctly in his footnote.

After spending two months with Cuarterón in Manila, Raimondi described him for his close friend Salerio, giving first what he considered characteristics of a Spaniard: "Many words, but few deeds. Many ceremonies, but little heart. Exteriorly devout . . . , but very bad behavior. Always begging like a thief, but dressed like milord . . . Behold, here you have the Spaniard. . . ." To tell the truth, he said, "I have not found the great man whom I had imagined. Yes, there is something extraordinary about him. But so what? I had more confidence in him before I came to know him.

Raimondi added:

> He has done little up to now, and judging from the little that he says about the nature of his missions, I have very little hope that he will enjoy quick success. He is fortunate in getting Labuan, an English colony. But as for Borneo . . . , he wants to baptize some people before they are converted. He talks much, has many projects, but I see that he has little practical mission experience. For the rest his relationship with his missionaries is completely different from ours with Father Paolo [Reina]. There is something of the Spaniard's aristocracy about him. . . . He often deceives himself and makes mistakes. Enough of this! I tell you frankly that, if earlier I had a great desire to work under him, I now have very little desire to do so. And I long for the moment when we can leave for our own mission. He treats me very well, however, and he exercises no authority over me. But I would not like to be in the shoes of [his two missionaries] Riva and Borgazzi.[18]

Meanwhile back in Italy, just five days after Barnabò was named cardinal prefect of Propaganda, Father Alfieri had written from Verona advising director Marinoni "to cultivate" a friendship with the cardinal's private secretary. And he begged him "for goodness' sake" to avoid "expressing or proposing" in his correspondence directed to the cardinal any doubts or alternatives whatsoever regarding decisions already taken by Rome.[19] Following Alfieri's earlier suggestion Marinoni on 13 June 1856 had named Burrueco his procurator or agent in Rome "because of his friendship with Cuarterón and because of the esteem which he enjoyed in Propaganda." Burrueco had replied on 11 July accepting the office.[20]

Reina informed Barnabò on 7 October 1856 of the latest arrangements that had been made for his mission by Prefect Apostolic Cuarterón. The cardinal was pleased and expressed the hope to Marinoni that the mission entrusted to Reina "can now be reactivated in a better way and with happier results," thanks to Cuarterón's direction and support. Barnabò also told Marinoni, who had forwarded Reina's letter, that he would appreciate receiving further news "on the outcome of the voyage which Father Reina shall be making together with Prefect Cuarterón, and also on the types of contact that they establish

---

18. PIME: AME 11:1043–44, Raimondi to Salerio, 7 December 1856.
19. See Alfieri to Marinoni, 25 June 1856, in Tragella, *Missioni estere*, 1:213.
20. PIME; AME 35-01 Scurati, *Memorie dell'Istituto*, 431.

between themselves for promoting the greater good and mutual assistance of their two missions...."[21]

Marinoni did send Barnabò further news on 8 January 1857 drawn from the 7 October letter that he himself had received from Reina. Eleven days later Barnabò wrote back saying, "Please inform me about the types of contact traced out for you" by Father Reina, "since these could serve as a norm for Propaganda."[22] By this Barnabò meant that the pattern of mutual support between the two prefectures apostolic of Cuarterón and Reina could be used as a model by Propaganda for other missions around the world.

Although Reina labored under a defeatist attitude, he did give Bishop Ramazzotti of Pavia a rather detailed account on 1 December 1856 of what plans there were at that moment for relaunching his Melanesia mission. "Prefect Don Carlos Cuarterón has decided upon nothing except a gradual plan," he said,

> which is far too general to allow me to make any conjectures or have any hopes. He plans to go to Labuan and then by using various methods he intends to reach the interior of Borneo. But will the English at Labuan not be opposed to this? They are on bad terms with the natives on the Borneo coast and also with the Dutch, who claim earlier rights to that large land. And what about the Moslems on the coast? These difficulties should not stop a missionary, of course, but often they do delay him. So he will go first [to his own mission] and stay there until one of his priests has become established in Labuan and another in Borneo. Then he will take us to our mission. But where will that be? He does not yet know himself! He seems to favor Dorei in northern New Guinea....

But Cuarterón was not eager to tie himself down to a fixed program, Reina said, "because he wants to act in view of circumstances and by taking into account what he finds on the spot."

Cuarterón had told Reina that Propaganda would send him no new personnel until he was well established in his mission and had some hope of success. Reina insisted in this letter to Ramazzotti, however, that "some additional companions are necessary in order for us to get established." There was little hope that Ambrosoli could join him, "because when I left him in Sydney, he was worse than I. And should he come to the mission, he would be a house-bound missionary." Raimondi, of course, was "good and strong and of good will. But he would not like it very much, he says, if he has to be alone." Reina had no other priest besides Raimondi, however, and he also considered it his duty to avoid "leaving a missionary isolated in the midst of savages." As for his own health, "I cannot rationally or humanly promise myself much," he said. "I am not confined to bed, but neither am I strong. I have a cough in my lungs and it seems that I always want something to eat, except when I have a bit of fever." He had applied a poultice to his left arm a few days earlier, hoping that it

---

21. Ibid., 1:185, Barnabò to Marinoni, 30 December 1856.

22. Ibid., 187, Barnabò to Marinoni, 19 January 1857. Marinoni's letter of 8 January 1857 was not found, but is mentioned by Barnabò.

would cure some sores like those "which I had on my legs for two-and-a-half years and which were cured in Sydney."

Reina ended his letter to Ramazzotti with a postscript: "One day after I wrote this letter, I received a letter from Ambrosoli in Sydney in which he has these words: 'I believe it will be very difficult for us to meet in the mission and I have a foreboding that it absolutely will not happen.'"[23] Boldly Reina wrote to Barnabò on 3 December 1856:

> Prefect Apostolic Carlos Cuarterón has informed me that it was the will of Your Most Reverend Eminence to send no new companions to assist me until after we have become established in some part of our mission and have some guarantee of success. I submitted fully to this decision and made it my own because it was that of my superiors. But now, not because of my own will, but because of the will of God who arranges all things, it seems that I may be allowed to present to Your Most Reverend Eminence a request for some new companions to assist me. Therefore I humbly explain the reasons obliging me to do this.

First, he said, Ambrosoli's health had not improved, and he had written from Sydney to say that he could not join Reina in his new mission. Second, Reina himself after reaching Manila had been afflicted with "a severe cough and a general sluggishness, which makes me doubt that I shall be able to last long in this mission . . ." Third, Cuarterón's plan called for "placing priests in some important places to provide the necessary contacts for my missionaries with Europe and with one another. But this is something that I cannot do because we are only two priests, I and Father Timoleone Raimondi." He begged Barnabò to "believe that these assertions of mine are true." He also gave assurance that no matter what the cardinal's decision might be, it would be looked upon "as coming from the will of God."[24]

Perhaps the happiest day for Reina and his missionaries since leaving Melanesia occurred two days after Christmas 1856, when Puarer of Woodlark was baptized in Manila. Ever since Raimondi had taken Puarer to Sydney, he had been giving the lad religious instructions. Raimondi had even written a catechism in the Woodlark language for Puarer, regretting though that the catechism was "only for one person." But he consoled himself with the thought that "a single soul is well worth the trouble of producing a catechism in one of the island languages." It was Raimondi's dream that Puarer might become a well-trained catechist who would return to Woodlark at some future date to win over his people to Christianity. Repeatedly Puarer had begged Prefect Apostolic Reina to baptize him. Since his instructions for baptism were now completed and since he was to be called Giovanni or John "in memory of poor Mazzucconi," as Reina pointed out, he was baptized on Saturday, 27 December 1856, the feast of Saint John, Apostle and Evangelist.[25]

---

23. Ibid., 11:311–13, Reina to Ramazzotti, 1 December 1856.
24. Ibid., 315, Reina to Barnabò, 3 December 1856.
25. Mazzucconi's baptismal name was John Baptist. See *Beatificationis Positio*, xxxv. Consequently his name day would have been 24 June, the Nativity of Saint John the Baptist, and not 27 December as given by Tragella in *Missioni estere*, 1:241.

Because all rooms of the Augustinian monastery were needed for a provincial chapter, Cuarterón and Reina together with their missionaries had to seek lodging elsewhere in late November and became guests of the Franciscans. Some received lodging in a Franciscan monastery in Manila and the rest in a Franciscan parish just one mile outside of the city. In that same parish church Puarer was baptized by its pastor, a former provincial superior of the Franciscans in Manila. Present for the baptism were Reina with Raimondi and Tacchini and Cuarterón with Riva and Borgazzi. Catechist Tacchini had the honor of being Puarer's godfather. Afterwards Raimondi continued giving Puarer religious instructions on penance or reconciliation and the other sacraments to prepare him for receiving them.[26]

Cuarterón had reached Manila on 16 June 1856, but by 1 December it still was not definite when he would leave for Labuan. A shortage of laborers in the shipyard and problems with Spanish government authorities had caused further delay. The labor shortage was caused by "five large three-masted vessels anchored along the shore since 27 October," all in need of repair. Numerous cargo vessels in the bay were also waiting to be serviced. "This circumstance," Reina said, "has increased the cost of laborers and has made it difficult to obtain them." It even brought the construction work aboard the two feluccas to a halt. "It seems that the government wants to create some difficulties [for Cuarterón] as well," Reina said. "I do not know whether he may decide to leave everything here and purchase his supplies in English colonies. If he should make the first choice, we would be able to leave soon. Otherwise we need patience." Cuarterón at this time was on retreat, enjoying a brief period of retirement for spiritual reflection. "Afterwards he will make his decision," Reina said.[27]

By 7 January 1857, however, Spanish authorities had issued the necessary passports for Cuarterón, Reina, and their missionaries. At this point nothing else needed tending, Reina said, except to finish work on the feluccas, which "might take another fifteen days." He therefore instructed Marinoni to send all future correspondence to Labuan either via Singapore or via Hong Kong.

Meanwhile a new element had entered into Cuarterón's plan. He had learned, namely, that it was possible for him to purchase in Hong Kong at the ridiculously low price of five thousand scudi an English schooner called *Pacifico*. It was "registered at 146 tons," was insured and was ready to set out to sea.[28] The same vessel in Manila would cost about

---

26. PIME: AME 11:317, Reina to Marinoni, 7 January 1857; PIME: AME 11:313, Reina to Ramazzotti, 1 December 1856; Tragella, *Missioni estere*, 1:236. A provincial chapter is a gathering of officials and representatives from one province of a religious order, which in session represents the entire province and is its highest extraordinary internal authority. The chapter examines and regulates affairs within its competence, both spiritual and temporal, touching upon the entire province.

27. PIME: AME 11:313, Reina to Ramazzotti, 1 December 1856.

28. In ibid., 317–18, Reina tells Marinoni on 7 January 1857 that the *Pacifico* is an English schooner "registered at 146 tons." Tragella in *Missioni estere*, 1:242 n. 37, without giving a source, says that Reina ascribes this tonnage to the Spanish schooner *Mártires de Tun-Kin*. But in the above letter of 7 January to Marinoni, Reina calls this latter vessel "a small schooner." Tragella's same note 37, again without giving the source, states that Borgazzi said *Mártires de Tun-Kin* was "about 100" tons. But in PIME: AME 11:1507, Borgazzi tells his parents on 2 May 1857 that each of the two schooners was "200 tons." It would therefore seem that the only reliable

twenty thousand scudi, Reina said. "The war between the English and China," had interrupted commerce, thus causing English shipowners to relieve themselves of vessels at any price, rather than run the risk of seeing them captured by the Chinese. Cuarterón therefore had instructed his agent in Hong Kong to purchase the vessel. If Cuarterón's order were to reach Hong Kong in time, it would raise his total of vessels to four: two cutters and two schooners. Writing to Marinoni, Reina asked, "Why so many ships?" He then proceeded to answer his own question. According to Cuarterón these four vessels were necessary in view of his mission method. "He plans to keep his missionaries amphibious, so to speak. The feluccas [or cutters] shall accompany his missionaries along the river that leads to the interior and—as we believe—ends at a large lake whose perimeter is populated by infidels." The schooner, *Mártires de Tun-Kin*, "will remain stationary either at the mouth of the river or in Labuan itself and will serve" as a depository or storehouse. "In case of need it will also sail along the coast of Borneo, since it is too old and unsteady to withstand the high seas for a long time," Reina said. The *Pacifico*, however, would serve "as a communications link with cities in English and Spanish colonies, and with Europe as well, as Don Carlos told me."

Reina commented to Marinoni: "You see, the idea is beautiful! Blessed be Don Carlos for having the money to carry it out." And then he added: "The circumstances in which I have found myself until now have never been such as to awaken within me any desires of this sort. And if they were to arise, it would take little effort on my part to get rid of them as being out of place and useless."

Since Reina knew that Cuarterón planned to use the *Pacifico* to take him and his missionaries to a new site in Melanesia, he feared that he might be expected to pay part of the vessel's cost. In fact, Cuarterón had asked what Reina thought about the plan. "I told him that I was in no position to take this step," Reina replied, "and that I could not assure him of my being able to cover the future costs which his [mission] method entailed." Cuarterón graciously made it clear, however, that the *Pacifico* would become the property of his own mission and that it was simply being used for the benefit of Reina's mission, without Reina having any property rights. "It pleased him when I said that I felt obliged to pay him a chartering fee, because it was so advantageous for me to be served by a mission vessel. This meant that I would have much more liberty than by using a vessel belonging to a stranger, whose only purpose would be to make money."

So this is "the agreement that we have reached for now," Reina told Marinoni. "I am hopeful that we shall always have such a harmonious relationship, because I am deeply convinced that Don Carlos will always be 'more than reasonable' in these matters." Reina also assured Marinoni that he and his missionaries would do everything possible to avoid displeasing Cuarterón. "He is good and I like him. If one overlooks some small defects, which he himself does not try to conceal," Reina said, one notices that Cuarterón is a man

---

tonnage for the *Pacifico* is that indicated by Reina, which is used by the author in his text. See also this chapter, p. 332, n. 8.

"of good faith and simplicity... One can do nothing but praise him and thank the Lord for him."[29]

Six weeks later Reina and his missionaries were still in Manila. By this time they had been loitering there for nearly five months, and Reina began wondering if they would ever reach Melanesia. "Who knows how long we shall be staying in Labuan?" he said. "And who knows if we shall perhaps even stay there forever? We might die there. Or we might be added to the personnel of Don Cuarterón."[30]

Raimondi enjoyed good health and was very active in Manila. By the end of February 1857, that is, in five months' time, he had written an Italian-Malay dictionary there. He had taken up language studies in Manila, he said, in order "to be ready to do something in Labuan and Borneo during the time that we shall spend waiting in the mission of Don Carlos." Raimondi's dictionary was so good that Cuarterón wanted to submit it to Propaganda under his own name. But Raimondi held off, preferring to send the dictionary to his Milan Mission Seminary as a token of his love for it. The seminary in turn could present the work to Propaganda as something that it had produced.

Besides knowing Malay better than the others, Raimondi also knew English better than the others because of his earlier studies in Australia. This made it possible for him to serve as chaplain for English-speaking sailors in the port of Manila. He also studied tropical medicine under the Hospitalers of Saint John of God in Manila. And since there were no English-speaking priests attached to their hospital, he looked after Catholic and Protestant patients who knew only English. Besides being very intelligent, he had a strong character, a cheerful personality, an open mind, and an iron will. In addition he was also persevering and courageous.[31]

Catechist Tacchini reported optimistically on 17 February: "We are eight persons leaving Manila for Labuan: Prefect Cuarterón, Riva, Borgazzi, Reina, Raimondi, myself, Puarer and a Spanish lad from Manila.... Since this is the good season, we hope to arrive there in twelve or thirteen days...."[32]

But twenty-three more days would pass before the miniature fleet of three ships led by *Mártires de Tun-Kin* could finally sail out of Manila Bay for Labuan on Thursday night, 12 March 1857. Aboard were Prefect Apostolic Cuarterón, his missionaries Riva and Borgazzi, his brother Manuel serving as captain, ten sailors, a cook, a servant, and two Filipino boys aged nine and ten presented to Cuarterón by their parents in Manila. Besides these eighteen persons there were Prefect Apostolic Reina, his two missionaries Raimondi and Tacchini, and also Puarer of Woodlark. Ten additional sailors manned the two cutters, which were towed by *Mártires de Tun-Kin* because unassisted they could not proceed at the same speed as the schooner.

---

29. PIME: AME 11:317–18, Reina to Marinoni, 7 January 1857.
30. Ibid., 319–20, Reina to Ripamonti, 20 February 1857.
31. Tragella, *Missioni estere*, 1:236, 238.
32. PIME: AME 18:27, Tacchini to ?, 17 February 1857.

While sailing along the western coasts of Mindoro and Panay, two large islands of the Philippines, they encountered a dreadful storm. The sailors in the two cutters shouted through the howling wind that even in tow their cutters could not keep pace with the schooner.³³ During the storm the cutters became uncontrollable and crashed into the schooner, causing considerable damage to the cutters. This required a stopover of fourteen days for repairs at Port San José at the southern end of Panay. While the vessels were being repaired, Cuarterón took aboard new supplies. The miniature fleet finally set sail from San José on Saturday, 4 April 1857. Meanwhile five more youths aged fifteen to eighteen, who had been offered to Cuarterón as laborers by their parents, had joined the party. This increased the number of those traveling to Labuan to thirty-seven. The three vessels headed southwestward across the Sulu Sea to North Borneo.³⁴

Ten days later on Easter Tuesday, 14 April 1857, Cuarterón and his fleet reached Port Victoria at Labuan Island on the northwest coast of Borneo. His two missionaries, Riva and Borgazzi, had left the Milan Mission Seminary on 19 February 1855 and had been en route to their mission for two years and two months. "Exactly at noon on 14 April we were anchored in the port of Labuan," Borgazzi said. "Together in our cabin we intoned the Ambrosian hymn of thanksgiving."³⁵

Cuarterón's Labuan mission could now begin.

33. Ibid., 11:1507–9, Borgazzi to his parents, 2 May 1857.

34. Tragella, *Missioni estere*, 1:242.

35. PIME: AME 11:1511, Borgazzi to his parents, 2 May 1857. Like Borgazzi, Reina in PIME: AME 11:321, tells Marinoni on 1 May 1857 that they arrived at Labuan "on the Tuesday after Easter at midday." Cuarterón no doubt giving technical data said: ". . . We dropped anchor at 4 AM at the meeting point northeast of this island [of Labuan] and at 2 PM we happily entered Port Victoria. . . ." See PF: SC Oceania vol. 5 (1853–57, Part II), f. 1376rv. This letter of Cuarterón was addressed to Burrueco, who translated it into Italian for presentation to Barnabò. But his translation mistakenly gives "4" April as the arrival date instead of 14 April, although on the following page the translation says that all disembarked on the "15th" at midday. This shows that "4" April was an oversight, because those aboard would not have spent eleven consecutive nights aboard ship after arriving in the harbor. One night was not uncommon. The arrival date is given incorrectly in Rooney, *Khabar Gembira*, 21, as 8 May 1857.

18

Reina Leaves Labuan for Dorei Bay in New Guinea
25 February 1858

It was midday of 15 April 1857 when Father Carlos Cuarterón, prefect apostolic of Labuan, and Father Paolo Reina, prefect apostolic of Melanesia and Micronesia, disembarked with their missionaries at Port Victoria in Labuan. "We were . . . very well received by the Governor," Cuarterón said, and he "promised to give me land so that I could build a church, a house for my missionaries and schools." Cuarterón presented letters of recommendation that he had received from the French ambassador in Manila and from the English general consul there, as well as his credentials from Rome as prefect apostolic of Labuan. The inhabitants of Labuan numbered about two thousand, including the troops. The island had a chapel for Christians, a mosque for Moslems, and a Chinese pagoda. Most of the fifty Roman Catholics in Labuan were Filipino slaves, he said, and there were "no Protestants to impede or oppose our projects."[1]

Two weeks after their arrival Reina explained to Cardinal Prefect Barnabò that at Cuarterón's suggestion he had written to Bishop Vrancken of Batavia, asking "for his permission to found a supply center with a priest in charge at one of the following places: Manado, Ternate, Banda, Timor Kupang, or Ambom." Banda was an island port in the Banda Sea north of Timor; Kupang was a port in Timor; and Ambom or Amboina was an island port to the north of the Banda Sea. All five ports were west of New Guinea. He had been assured by Cuarterón that the requested permission would be "very readily granted to me." The supply center was to serve Reina's Melanesia-Micronesia mission since—as Cuarterón had pointed out—without such a supply center "we would be reduced to the position in which we found ourselves in our first mission, that is, deprived of communications and deprived of help."[2]

---

1. PF: SC Oceania vol. 5 (1853–57, Part II), f. 1376r–1377r, Cuarterón to Burrueco, 6 May 1857. This letter along with others from Cuarterón in PF: SC Oceania vol. 5 (1853–57, Part II), 1376r–1379v, were all addressed to Burrueco and were translated by him into Italian for the benefit of Cardinal Prefect Barnabò.

2. Ibid., f. 1363r, Reina to Barnabò, 1 May 1857. Here Reina says: "We arrived at Labuan on the 14th of the current month. . . ." When he wrote this part of his letter, it was no doubt still April 1857. But on completing

Reina sent this letter to director Marinoni in Milan that same day, 1 May 1857, asking that he read it and forward it to Rome. "During these months of waiting here in Labuan," he said, "I would have preferred to go to Batavia in order to discuss this matter" with Vrancken personally instead of merely writing him a letter. But Cuarterón was opposed to this, "and I do not want to go counter to his feelings. I believe that he does not consider me mature enough to conduct such affairs."[3]

Less than four weeks after Cuarterón's arrival in Labuan the European and Filipino children there were to be solemnly baptized at a service scheduled for Sunday, 10 May 1857. "But perhaps I shall not be present for that service," Cuarterón said, "since as soon as weather permits I shall be going with all three ships to negotiate the ransom of more than one thousand Filipino Christians in Borneo." In that case he intended to commission Reina to conduct the services in his place.[4] Cuarterón in fact did miss the solemn celebration, since he set sail for Borneo City, on Friday, 8 May, with his schooner, *Mártires de Tun-Kin*, and with his two cutters. Father Riva accompanied him because the area being reconnoitered was to become his mission. Father Raimondi also joined them and reported that by evening they were already "on the wide river that leads to Borneo City."[5] Reina reported that Borneo City was "about thirty miles from Labuan" and that it had a population of forty-six thousand, of whom five thousand were Filipino slaves. "All are Christians," he added, "but unfortunately only in name...." Reina said that they had been "captured by Moors and Moslems in North Borneo and were sold" in Borneo City as slaves.[6]

It took four days to go up the river to Borneo City, called also Brunei Town, where Cuarterón dropped anchor in front of the house of the British consul, Spencer St. John. This official assisted in obtaining authorization from the sultan for Cuarterón to open a mission at Barambangan, a site about one mile from Borneo City.[7]

During a preliminary audience the sultan wanted to know Cuarterón's purpose in coming to Borneo. Spencer St. John replied that Cuarterón and his companions were missionaries, that they had been sent by the head of the Christian religion in Rome, and that their purpose was exclusively religious. The sultan's reply, delivered by one of his ministers to the consul on the following day, was that if the proposed foundation was not against the clauses of the treaty that he had made with the British, they could remain and open churches and schools. Otherwise they could not. When Spencer St. John gave assurance that their foundation was in accord with that treaty, the sultan granted his permission.[8]

---

the letter he placed the date 1 May 1857 at the end. Writing to Marinoni also on 1 May 1857, he said that they had reached Labuan "on the Tuesday after Easter," namely, 14 April.

3. PIME: AME 11:321–22, Reina to Marinoni, 1 May 1857.
4. PF: SC Oceania vol. 5 (1853–57, Part II), f. 1377v, Cuarterón to Burrueco, 6 May 1857.
5. PIME: AME 11:1059, Raimondi to Salerio, 29 May 1857.
6. Ibid., 321–22, Reina to Marinoni, 1 May 1857.
7. Rooney, *Khabar Gembira*, 21.
8. Tragella, *Missioni estere*, 1:245–46.

Rome had made it clear that Cuarterón had to found his own mission of Labuan before taking Reina and his missionaries to some new place in Melanesia. Cuarterón therefore decided to reconnoiter another possible location for a mission station at Mengkabong (also spelled Mankabung and Mankabon), which lay some eighty miles north of Labuan at Gaya Bay in modern Sabah. Before ordering Riva to settle permanently at Barambangan near Borneo City, Cuarterón decided to take him and Father Raimondi to examine the Mengkabong area. Their departure date was set for 30 May, and Reina was to remain at Labuan with Borgazzi. Cuarterón promised that on his return he would take Reina and his missionaries aboard the first ship leaving Labuan for Hong Kong. There they would transfer to the *Pacifico* and sail to a new location in Melanesia. "But no one knows when this will happen," Reina wrote to director Marinoni, "because we have no regular contact with Hong Kong, like we have with Singapore."[9]

Borgazzi was looking forward to teaching classes and to giving catechism instructions at the Labuan mission, once he knew the language. "Meanwhile," he said, "there is nothing to do but pray, study and have patience...." He described Mengkabong as "a more difficult and exposed" area, which Cuarterón intended to care for himself. It had been foreseen, however, that the two cutters would serve as a link between the various mission stations and would visit them from time to time. The missionaries could also make use of the *paralins*, which were small ships "of the local people which come and go between Labuan and Borneo for commerce."[10]

Cuarterón set out from Labuan on 1 June 1857 for Mengkabong, where he was well received by its rajah and by his brother, the rajah of nearby Mangatta. Mengkabong had a well-protected harbor called Gaya Bay. Cuarterón lost no time in choosing a picturesque inlet with a hilly hinterland for building his mission station. One day he and Raimondi climbed to the top of the highest hill, where they raised a cross and carved into a nearby rock the date and the two Latin words *Propaganda Fide*, that is, Propagating the Faith. Raimondi became well acquainted with one of the local men and together with him visited two villages, where he was allowed to enter the dwellings of the people. Before leaving Mengkabong he also succeeded in persuading a Filipino, who had been made a slave in his youth and had always lived as a Moslem, to accept the Christian faith.[11]

One month and ten days later while still in Gaya Bay, Cuarterón wrote to Father Luigi Ambrosi of Hong Kong, who had succeeded Father Feliciani as procurator for Propaganda and as prefect apostolic of Hong Kong. Ambrosi—not to be confused with Ambrosoli of Sydney—now had charge of the funds which Cuarterón had deposited earlier with Feliciani.[12]

---

9. PIME: AME 11:331, Reina to Marinoni, 29 May 1857.

10. Ibid., 1517–18, Borgazzi to Salerio, 5 June 1857.

11. Tragella, *Missioni estere*, 1:246–47. The words *Propaganda Fide* came from what was then Propaganda's official Latin title: *Sacra Congregatio "de Propaganda Fide."*

12. For details on these funds of Cuarterón, see chap. 15, pp. 268–69.

Cuarterón explained to Ambrosi that he had commissioned his brother Manuel to purchase a brigantine in Hong Kong, and he asked that Ambrosi give funds from his account to his brother for this purchase. "Today [10 July 1857] I shall leave this bay on the northwest coast of Borneo and shall sail to Labuan Island," he said. "And from there I must embark again with the missionaries of Oceania in my company, whom I shall locate and establish in Papuasia in the northwestern part of New Guinea."[13]

Two days later Cuarterón arrived back in Labuan with Riva and Raimondi.[14] For three full weeks Reina and his missionaries waited in Labuan, but no vessel arrived aboard which they could sail to Hong Kong and transfer to the brig *Pacifico*. Cuarterón therefore wrote to Procurator Ambrosi again on 1 August 1857, telling of his predicament and stating that in his judgment it would no longer be possible to make the voyage to New Guinea that year.[15] Cuarterón also sent orders to his brother, whom he had named captain of the *Pacifico*, that he should arrive in Labuan by the end of November, so that they could proceed directly from Labuan to Singapore, Ternate, and New Guinea.

Director Marinoni did not forward to Cardinal Prefect Barnabò Reina's forceful letter of 3 December 1856, in which he listed many reasons that Rome should change its policy and should send him new personnel.[16] Instead Marinoni diplomatically stated on 26 February 1857 that Reina on 6 December 1856 had commissioned him to present his problem. "Perhaps some new provision by Propaganda will be necessary," Marinoni said, "so that the attempt to open a new mission [in Melanesia] with the help of the Most Reverend Don Carlos Cuarterón can take place." He also pointed out that the number of priests for the Melanesia mission had been "reduced from five to only two" because Mazzucconi had died, Salerio had returned to Europe, and Ambrosoli had to remain in Sydney because of ill health. He added that Reina himself was in poor health and was "most ready to die in his mission."[17]

Cuarterón also had written to Rome that Reina "would like to receive some new missionaries." He suggested, however, that not more than two be sent for the time being, one to serve as procurator in Manado or Ternate and the other to accompany Reina and Raimondi to their mission.[18] Burrueco, the Spanish Trinitarian priest in Rome serving as procurator simultaneously for Cuarterón and Marinoni, on seeing that each of them had made

---

13. PIME: AME 29:737, 740, Cuarterón to Ambrosi, 10 July 1857. Cuarterón, who always wrote in Spanish, clearly writes "noroeste," that is, "northwestern" New Guinea. Tragella in *Missioni estere*, 1:247, translates this into Italian incorrectly as "nord-est," that is, "northeastern" New Guinea. He repeats this error in *Missioni estere*, 249. Cuarterón called his Hong Kong vessel a brigantine; the Milan missionaries had been calling it a schooner.

14. PIME: AME 29:741, Cuarterón to Ambrosi, 1 August 1857.

15. Tragella, *Missioni estere*, 1:248.

16. For the contents of this letter see chap. 17, p. 339.

17. PF: CV vol. 43, f. 282rv, Marinoni to Barnabò, 26 February 1857.

18. PF: SC Oceania vol. 5 (1853–57, Part II), f. 1195r, Cuarterón to Fransoni, 6 October 1856.

a similar request, approached Propaganda's officials with a proposal. He was, after all, an official consultor.[19] His opinion was that Ambrosoli in Sydney should become procurator for both Cuarterón and Reina either at Ternate or at some other post. Burrueco was then commissioned to instruct Marinoni that he should "inform Cuarterón that Propaganda does not consider it prudent to send further missionaries to assist Reina as long as he has not become established somewhere." Burrueco added that "Propaganda believes it opportune for Ambrosoli to remain at Sydney until some day when he can be employed as procurator for both Reina and Cuarterón."[20] That same day, 1 April 1857, Burrueco wrote to Ambrosoli in Sydney.[21]

Ambrosoli on 18 July wrote to Reina that Burrueco had informed him that Rome had not granted Reina any new missionaries and that Cuarterón had requested "to make me his Procurator and Rome has agreed." Since all of this was news to Reina, he read Ambrosoli's letter to Cuarterón, who replied "that he knew nothing about all of this and that he had only written requesting two companions" for Reina. Cuarterón even insisted "that he had not said a word about Ambrosoli, whom he considered to be lost for the mission," Reina said. "Nor could he explain how this could have come about."

Passing on this news to Marinoni on 9 September 1857, Reina added: "Whatever the case may be, I am writing to Ambrosoli in agreement with Don Carlos Cuarterón, asking that he leave Sydney and come immediately to Singapore, where he will reside at the Procure of the French Missionaries of Paris. . . . We shall go there to pick him up with the *Pacifico* as soon as it arrives from Hong Kong, which will be about the end of November."[22]

Since Burrueco wrote to Marinoni in Milan and to Ambrosoli in Sydney on the same day, 1 April 1857, informing each of Propaganda's decisions, it seems most unlikely that he would tell Marinoni that Ambrosoli was "to remain in Sydney until some day when he can be employed as procurator for both Reina and Cuarterón," and that he would tell Ambrosoli that Cuarterón had requested to have him as his own procurator and that Rome had agreed. Was Ambrosoli misinterpreting, or intentionally misrepresenting, the decisions of Propaganda that he had learned from Burrueco?

Two days after writing to Marinoni, Reina on 11 September 1857 sent orders to Ambrosoli to leave Sydney for Singapore. And on the following day he informed Father Rocher, head of the Marist Center in Sydney, that he was ordering Ambrosoli to leave aboard the first vessel sailing to Singapore. He also authorized Rocher to give Ambrosoli

---

19. See PF: LDB vol. 348 (1857), f. 186v, Barnabò to Burrueco, 7 April 1857, where Barnabò formally addresses Burrueco as "Consultor" of Propaganda.

20. PIME: AME 35-01 Scurati, *Memorie dell'Istituto*, 433.

21. The author has not found this letter of Burrueco to Ambrosoli, but Reina quotes Ambrosoli as saying that he had received word on these matters from Burrueco in a letter "dated 1 April." See PIME: AME 11:335, Reina to Marinoni, 9 September 1857.

22. For the contents of Burrueco's letter of 1 April 1857 to Ambrosoli and of Ambrosoli's letter of 18 July 1857 to Reina, see ibid., 335–36, Reina to Marinoni, 9 September 1857.

for his passage the one hundred pounds sterling left in reserve at the Marist Center. From Singapore Reina intended to take Ambrosoli to Dorei in New Guinea.[23]

But on 16 June of that same year Archbishop Polding had written to Rome about the good work that Father Ambrosoli was doing in his Archdiocese of Sydney, stating that his departure would cause great harm for the many Catholic Italians receiving spiritual assistance from him.[24] Archbishop Gaetano Bedini (1806–64), secretary of Propaganda at this time, replied on 10 September 1857 that Polding could profit provisionally from Ambrosoli's work, "but in such a way that the priest, as is just, will remain at the disposal of his superior in Milan."[25] On the following day Burrueco informed Marinoni that he had heard from Ambrosoli, that Propaganda had notified the priest that he could remain in Sydney for the present, and that it would take up this matter with his superiors at some future date.[26] Thus Ambrosoli's wish had been fulfilled and Reina's staff was reduced to one priest (Raimondi) and one catechist (Tacchini).

Before receiving word of these negotiations Ambrosoli had told Marinoni that he greatly feared taking on once again the heavy responsibility of doing missionary work in Melanesia.

> I know how much one would have to suffer and I also know how disinclined I am to crucify myself. No one will ever be able to tell you how much we had to suffer at Rooke. Nor will anyone ever be able to tell you the desperation that I experienced there. And why did we endure all of this? We had no results at all! Nor was there even the slightest ray of hope. Poor Mazzucconi had always been in favor of those missions up to a certain point. But afterwards he changed in a way that really made me wonder, because he began to say so much against them. According to him all our time, money, physical and mental energy had been wasted.

He also said that "the time had not yet come for those poor peoples, whereas there were others who were in such great need of help."

Apparently Reina now intended "to go to the other end of New Guinea opposite from the one where Rooke is located," Ambrosoli said. "One may certainly hope that he will find some advantages there. But I do not expect much more to be found there than what we found at Rooke and Woodlark. Just last week I heard that in [New] Caledonia they are having no results at all. And the poor superior there, [Father Pierre] Rougeyron, is losing courage even though the French government is there with soldiers and warships. He has

---

23. Reina's letter of 11 September 1857 to Ambrosoli was not found, but is referred to in ibid., 641, Ambrosoli to Marinoni, 19 December 1857. Also Reina's letter to Rocher of 12 September 1857 was not found, but is referred to in PIME: AME 28:824, Rocher to Marinoni, 10 December 1857.

24. For the date and summary of Polding's letter, see PF: LDB vol. 348 (1857), f. 569v, Bedini to Polding, 10 September 1857.

25. Ibid., f. 569v–570r. Bedini was a titular archbishop at this time; in 1861 he was named bishop of Viterbo.

26. PIME: AME 35-01 Scurati, *Memorie dell'Istituto*, 434.

lost almost all of his neophytes because they have been eaten, have died or have run away." At the Isle of Pines, however, "things have turned out a bit well, but only after the corvette, *La Dayonnais*, had been there and had killed their most villainous chiefs."[27]

Some two months after writing this, Ambrosoli received Reina's letter ordering him to take the first ship leaving for Singapore. "I felt no attraction whatsoever" for those orders, he told Marinoni. "I then talked to the archbishop here about it and he told me that I had to remain until he received a reply from Rome to the letter which he had written about me. It would be tantamount to an act of open disobedience to Rome on my part, he said, if I were to leave prior to the arrival of the decision that he had requested. So I promised him that I would remain here and wait for the arrival of the next two mail carriers. One of them was due yesterday [18 December], but it has not yet arrived. The next one is due in early January [1858]." If Archbishop Polding should receive nothing from Rome by then, he said, "I shall set out for Singapore on the first favorable occasion."

Ambrosoli repeated that he did not have any inclination to go to Melanesia. In fact, nothing attracted him. "Nor do I have even the slightest hope of doing some good there. And I hope for nothing at all: neither physical health for myself, nor conversions, nor founding successful mission stations. I can only see myself facing expenses and the loss of lives and men." But since going there would not be his responsibility, he would not hesitate even for one moment, he said. "If I should succeed in baptizing some dying children, say one or two, I shall be satisfied. I cannot hope for anything more."[28]

Father Rocher, director of the Marist Center in Sydney, also wrote to Marinoni, stating that Ambrosoli was "still chaplain for the Benedictine Sisters at Subiaco," but was not robust enough for missionary work in Melanesia. "And in view of a conversation that we had," Rocher continued, "it seems to me that he would not be very desirous of leaving Sydney." Therefore, if his present work and his membership in the Foreign Mission Seminary of Milan "could be combined with his permanent sojourn in Sydney, I believe that for the moment he could not be more content."[29]

Reina, after spending five and a half months in Manila and five more months in Labuan, began to believe that Cuarterón's plan for reestablishing him and his missionaries in New Guinea would never be realized. He felt that he had to speak out clearly, and this he did on 9 September 1857, pointing out for director Marinoni in a long letter the serious "difficulties" which stood in the way of realizing Cuarterón's plan:

1. Propaganda as early as 21 August 1855 had issued an order "that between me and Don Carlos Cuarterón there should be mutual support, help, etc.," Reina said.[30] "Now this order . . . was written" in view of the plan which Cuarterón had at that time. "According to

---

27. PIME: AME 11:639-40, Ambrosoli to Marinoni, 10 October 1857.

28. Ibid., 641, Ambrosoli to Marinoni, 19 December 1857.

29. PIME: AME 28:824-25, Rocher to Marinoni, 10 December 1857.

30. See PIME: AME 1:153, Fransoni to Marinoni, 21 August 1855. This letter contains the orders meant for Reina, who received a copy from Marinoni while he was in Sydney.

what Prefect Cuarterón himself told me, his plan was to place some missionaries at Labuan, others on the east coast of Borneo and still others beyond those shores at Salibaboo and Sanguey. From these places he wanted to keep in contact with us, because his men stationed at Salibaboo and at Sanguey were to have a common procure [or procurement center] with us. But Rome named him Prefect [Apostolic] of Labuan and of Independent Borneo, that is, of the Northwest Coast" of Borneo. "Furthermore, Cuarterón was instructed by word of mouth to begin mission work at Labuan. And if he might wish to go beyond that territory, he was to write to Rome and it would arrange matters with the Vicar Apostolic of Batavia." But now Cuarterón "says that he does not wish to reach out any farther, because the Vicar Apostolic of Batavia will not allow him to do so, and he adds that he has enough to do on the [northwest] coast and in the interior of Borneo. Consequently the procure must now serve my mission alone and the expense of establishing and maintaining a procure—no matter how small it may be—will always be immense for my pocketbook."

2. Moreover, if Reina financially were able to establish and maintain his own supply center, there was still no assurance that the Dutch government would allow it. "The Vicar Apostolic of Batavia," he said, "sent me a very beautiful letter . . . and said that for his part he was pleased [with my proposal], but he did not know whether the government would be pleased. Therefore he forwarded my petition in my own name to the government and he told me that it would send me its reply. But up to now no reply has arrived." Cuarterón, Reina said, would like him to get into Dutch territory and "is also certain that the ports of Manado and Ternate are free ports (which in fact they are)." Because of this anyone may go there and may remain there "without depending upon the general government in Batavia," provided that he has obtained permission from the local governor of a particular port. But Cuarterón "suspects that the Vicar Apostolic of Batavia acted like this because the general government . . . , being opposed to Catholics, sent a notice to the local governor not to receive us. For my part I do not know what to say. It is certain that the letter written to me is most courteous." When Reina had pointed out to Cuarterón that the Dutch government might not permit him to send a priest to take charge of the supply center, Cuarterón had answered that in Ternate or elsewhere Reina could always find a good businessman who would gladly serve as his procurator.

3. "There is still another difficulty," Reina said, "and it is this: Don Carlos cannot give me assurance that there is a ship which regularly, at least once a year, makes the voyage from the place where the supply center might be located to Dorei or to another place nearby.[31] If there is none, it would be necessary to charter one. The only guarantee which we have is that the Sultan's *paran* sails from Ternate to Dorei every year to collect tribute. But judging from what Don Carlos Cuarterón has been able to learn about the Sultans, one cannot put too much trust in them."

---

31. In this context Tragella in *Missioni estere*, 1:248, says incorrectly that the supply center was to be opened "in Dorei or in Ternate." The supply center, however, was to be opened in Manado or in Ternate; Dorei or Gebe was to be the site of the mission station.

4. One more difficulty, Reina said, was that an Englishman arriving in Labuan from Singapore "assures us of having read in a newspaper that the Dutch government has already sent two Calvinist missionaries to Dorei."

In spite of these obstacles, however, Cuarterón had insisted "that we have to go and give it a try," Reina said. "If the Lord gives us the grace, we shall go. Then whatever happens, let it happen." Reina told Marinoni that he had wanted "to write these things to Rome in order to let it know that its plan cannot be realized and that my mission will remain just about as isolated as it was before. But is it up to me to do this? Don Carlos maintains that he has already done so and he says that I should keep silent about this matter. In any case if you believe it would be well to inform Propaganda of this, then do so also in my name."[32]

Reina, of course, could not verify what the Englishman had said about Protestant missionaries being sent to Dorei. But basically the information was correct. Two Protestant missionaries in 1855 had arrived at Mansinam, a small island in Dorei Bay off the coast of modern Manokwari.[33]

Marinoni followed Reina's suggestion and through Procurator Burrueco called Rome's attention to the various "difficulties." Perhaps wishing to avoid a clash with the two Protestant missionaries reportedly sent to Dorei, Marinoni asked Burrueco "whether it might not be better to go to Ponape" in Micronesia.[34] Apparently he was not aware that the Congregational Church from the United States of America had already founded a Protestant mission in Ponape as early as September 1852, the very month and year in which Reina and his missionaries had left Sydney for Woodlark.[35]

Just three weeks after sending Marinoni his "difficulties," Reina was wondering whether in conscience he could go to such an isolated spot as Dorei in New Guinea, since the only order that he had received from Rome was "to establish a common supply center" for keeping in touch with both Cuarterón and Marinoni. Since there was no longer to be a common supply center for his mission and that of Cuarterón, he asked, "Would it not be my duty to wait for new instructions from my superiors before I move elsewhere?" The thought then came to him that Cuarterón could have received "faculties, either in writing or by word of mouth, enabling him to do with my mission whatever he saw fit." And so before deciding not to go to Dorei, Reina made known his doubts to Cuarterón. He did so in writing because he lived some two miles inland on a plain, whereas Cuarterón lived on the coast with his sailors, where he was supervising the construction of a shed for housing the gear of the two cutters.

---

32. PIME: AME 11:336–38, Reina to Marinoni, 9 September 1857. Under the first point of this letter Reina follows the example of Cuarterón, calling the mission incorrectly the Prefecture Apostolic of Labuan "and Independent Borneo." See chap. 17, p. 331.

33. Gavin Souter, *New Guinea: The Last Unknown*, 23, 263. But see chap. 19, p. 362, n. 11.

34. PIME: AME 35-01 Scurati, *Memorie dell'Istituto*, 435–36, Marinoni to Burrueco, 9 November 1857.

35. See chap. 10, p. 148.

Cuarterón replied by citing the few lines of instruction that he had received in writing from Propaganda, namely: "It is furthermore recommended that you take a lively interest in the Mission of Melanesia and Micronesia and that you likewise provide assistance—according to the arrangements reached—to that Prefect Apostolic and his collaborators, who will be waiting for your views and your instructions in Sydney."[36] Because of the circumstances, Cuarterón pointed out, he had been authorized to do whatever he could "for the advancement and welfare of this same mission." And he added: "I was able to obtain from this same Propaganda [the guarantee] that it would not abandon the missions of Micronesia and Melanesia, provided that I would direct them and would pay their costs from my own pocket until they were established." Propaganda's officials had made this concession to him, he said, "inasmuch as they did not want to make any further expenses and sacrifices for the benefit of a mission, which they considered to be practically incapable of making any progress." The interpretation given by Cuarterón to Reina's note was that Reina feared to go to Dorei because he knew that Cuarterón had never been there and even had no certain knowledge about the place. Cuarterón also believed that Reina had created this new problem because he wished to remain permanently in the prefecture apostolic of Labuan. He pointed out to Reina that he had given Rome his word of honor that he most certainly would take Reina and his missionaries back to New Guinea. Consequently, if Reina and his men did not want to go, he threatened to transfer to New Guinea instead Fathers Riva and Borgazzi, since they were also members of the same Foreign Mission Seminary of Milan.

"The whole matter has been concluded quickly to the satisfaction of all," Reina told Marinoni on 30 September 1857. He had assured Cuarterón, namely, that he had written in good faith, that he had no desire to remain in the Labuan prefecture, and that he had no fear of going to Dorei in New Guinea. And as regards the "difficulties" mentioned by him in a letter earlier that month, Reina told Marinoni that they were "no longer valid" in view of the promise made by Cuarterón to Propaganda that he would cover all costs until the Melanesia Mission was established.

"And so it is not up to me to search for one island rather than another, for a place which has contacts rather than one which is isolated, for one race of people rather than another, for a healthy place rather than an unhealthy one," Reina said. "Nor am I even to assume any role in this matter. What I have to do is to let myself be led to the place. And then, when—thanks be to God—I have arrived there, I must abandon myself very peacefully to Divine Providence, just as now I must abandon myself to the hands of others. I assure you, I am truly happy." Life was filled with waiting, Reina told Marinoni. "We wait for letters, we wait for news, we wait for personnel, we wait for our departure, and finally we wait to see our mission. Then there will be nothing else to do, but wait for Paradise."[37]

Reina's financial worries dwindled, but those of Cuarterón increased and he began to complain. He had so many expenses on behalf of his missionaries, he told Prefect Apostolic

36. For the context of this citation see chap. 15, pp. 300–301.
37. PIME: AME 11:341–43, Reina to Marinoni, 30 September 1857.

Ambrosi in Hong Kong, that little money was left over for building churches, schools, and houses.[38] One month later he learned from his brother Manuel then in Hong Kong that the *Pacifico* was in good condition. But there were a number of things that had to be repaired or replaced, like the rigging. So Manuel requested authorization from Don Carlos to make additional expenditures.[39]

Cuarterón's attitude toward the Milan missionaries also changed. On 25 October that year he wrote to Father Burrueco, his procurator in Rome, saying that the Milan missionaries "wanted to take over my Labuan Mission." But he had received "confidential orders from His Eminence not to give them Labuan under any pretext whatsoever," he said. With his letter to Burrueco he enclosed the note from Reina revealing his hesitancy in going to such an isolated mission as Dorei in New Guinea.[40]

Because Captain Manuel and the *Pacifico* were detained in Hong Kong, and because Cuarterón's sailors were all well and could work, he decided to found a third mission and church on the northwest coast of Borneo "before leaving this island to take the missionaries to New Guinea."[41] He left Labuan and sailed for Mengkabong on 2 November 1857,[42] taking along Fathers Reina, Borgazzi, and Riva. While there, he built a chapel and also a house for two servants from Manila, whom he left behind as guards. According to Reina it was Cuarterón's intention "to establish in that place a village of men and women from Manila along with others from the [nearby] mountains, who are infidels." Cuarterón also "gave orders to cut down the jungle and to prepare the ground for a village." He drew up a plan "for a wharf reaching to the port," selected a spot for a dockyard, and gave orders to prepare the land for this purpose.

Reina said that Cuarterón had arrived among these people "in grandiose style with his armed cutters, which they considered to be frigates or warships." He was "generous in paying his laborers" and gave the unspent money to the *pangiran* or local rulers. "Besides causing admiration, this also put a bit of fear" into the people, which was advantageous for Cuarterón. Reina explained that "this method of his is necessary because he wants to promote the emancipation of Christian slaves, who are very numerous. Let God be the judge if he should succeed in this venture. His intentions could not be more sincere."

But Reina could never follow Cuarterón's example, he said,

> because I do not have the money for it. And besides, I am not very favorably disposed toward it either by sentiment or by character, even though intellectually I recognize it as necessary. A few times I mentioned to Don Carlos that I, too, would do the same

---

38. See Cuarterón to Ambrosi, 23 September 1857, in Tragella, *Missioni estere*, 1:248–49.
39. See PIME: AME 11:345, Reina to Marinoni, 22 October 1857.
40. Cuarterón's letter of 25 October 1857 to Burrueco was not found. For its contents see PF: SC Oceania vol. 5 (1853–57, Part II), f. 1379r, Cuarterón to Burrueco, 8 March 1858.
41. PIME: AME 29:745, Cuarterón to Ambrosi, 13 October 1857.
42. See PIME: AME 11:356, Reina to Salerio, 3 January 1858, where Reina says that they left Labuan "on the day of the dead," that is, 2 November 1857.

thing if I could. He expressed great pleasure on hearing this and imagined that he had converted me. Furthermore, he is convinced that our missions did not do well because we had presented ourselves as poor men. So now I do not know what to do. But I hope that God will help me—and I am certain that He will—in whatever circumstances I shall find myself.[43]

Cuarterón had planned to remain at Mengkabong for only two weeks and then return to Labuan. But instead he stayed two months, and after the first month the wine for Mass ran out. "So this year I spent the Christmas holidays without even saying or assisting at Holy Mass," Reina said. And on Christmas day, "I recited the Rosary with the sailors in the new chapel, which has a picture of the Madonna wrapping the Babe in swaddling clothes." To celebrate the feast of Christmas, "I fired the two canons which Don Carlos had ordered to be brought to shore. . . ."[44] It was Tuesday, 29 December 1857, when Cuarterón arrived back in Labuan with Reina, Borgazzi, and Riva, "after an excursion of fifty-eight days" along the coast of Borneo, as he informed Burrueco on the following day.[45]

Surprisingly while Cuarterón was founding his elaborate mission station at Mengkabong in December 1857, a Spanish colony was being founded at Balabac Island in the Balabac Strait on the northernmost fringe of his Prefecture Apostolic of Labuan. And although Cuarterón reported the founding of this Spanish colony to Roman authorities only on the twentieth anniversary of the founding of his own mission at Labuan, he easily could have been aware that the Spanish colony was being founded while he was founding Mengkabong mission. Did he dedicate so many of his funds to founding this station because he anticipated receiving protection from the Spanish colony in case of need?[46] Father Raimondi had been placed in charge of the Labuan mission when Cuarterón sailed to Mengkabong on 2 November with Reina, Borgazzi, and Riva. Catechist Tacchini and Puarer were also left behind. Because of his fluency in English and because he had learned Malay in Manila, Raimondi was able to begin hearing confessions in those languages im-

---

43. Ibid., 350, Reina to Marinoni, 2 January 1858.

44. Ibid., 353, Reina to Ripamonti, 2 January 1858; see also ibid., 356, Reina to Salerio, 3 January 1858.

45. See Cuarterón's letter to Burrueco, which Burrueco translated into Italian and dated "20 December" 1857, in PF: SC Oceania vol. 5 (1853–57, Part II), f. 1377v. But "20 December" cannot be correct because Reina on 3 January 1858 told Salerio that they had left Labuan for Mengkabong on "the day of the dead," namely 2 November, and that they had spent Christmas there. See PIME: AME 11:356. The translation of Cuarterón's letter dated "20 December" says that he had arrived back in Labuan on the previous day. His arrival, however, must have been on 29 December, because counting from 2 November to 29 December would give "an excursion of fifty-eight days," which Cuarterón himself indicated in this same letter as the length of his absence. Consequently Cuarterón's letter was in fact written on 30 December 1857, even though Burrueco's translation of it is dated 20 December.

46. For the map of Cuarterón's prefecture containing his entry by hand announcing the founding of a Spanish colony at Balabac Island in December 1857, see PF: SC Oceania, vol. 11 (1877–78, Part I), f. 153r. This map accompanied Cuarterón's letter to Cardinal Prefect Franchi of 14 April 1877 in PF: SC Oceania, vol. 11 (1877–78, Part I), f. 151r–152v. It was identical to the map printed by Cuarterón in Rome in 1855. See chap. 15, pp. 296–97, 302.

mediately upon arrival in Labuan. The Christians there included some from Madras in southern India, a converted Hindu baptized by Cuarterón, Indian soldiers, and a Protestant English family. Raimondi also visited Christian slaves from Manila, attempting to arouse them from their religious indifference. By mid-September 1857 he had begun preaching in Malay. And by Christmas Day he considered his neophytes—three adults and two young men—sufficiently instructed to receive Baptism. This raised the number of practicing Catholics in Labuan to sixty-two. "What a shame that the population here is not numerous," he said.[47]

After Reina's return from Mengkabong to Labuan, he admitted to Salerio that he would have much to suffer during the long voyage to New Guinea, "because in merely going back and forth to Mengkabong, I did nothing but vomit."[48]

At this time Reina sent Marinoni a letter marked confidential. "For a long time," he said, something had been bothering him that he had never revealed to anyone, but which he now wanted to explain to Marinoni. Because of what had happened to him, his missionaries, and his mission, and because of what had happened even prior to his leaving Italy for his mission—did he mean the letter of reprimand received from Cardinal Prefect Fransoni?—he believed that now he was held in low esteem by both Propaganda and by his own seminary in Milan. In view of this Reina proposed that it might be well for him to resign as prefect apostolic and to work as a simple missionary instead, once his mission would be reestablished in New Guinea.

Marinoni should not be disturbed by this proposal, he said. "It is not that I would like to unburden myself of this task, which really weighs on me." Nor did he want to cast away what was considered an honor in the eyes of the world. "Nor is it because I am tired of the troubles that I have had and because I want to live in peace. My only reason is this: As long as I am in charge, my mission will suffer because of me. Under another superior, however, it would profit more." He was going to present the same doubts to Bishop Ramazzotti, he said, and he hoped that Marinoni and the bishop might help him "by providing frank and immediate counsel." But before taking this step, he said, "I shall also ask the view of Don Carlos Cuarterón, who ought to know how I stand with Rome better than anyone else."[49] He asked Marinoni to send him all future letters in care of Father Beurel, "Catholic Clergyman, Singapore."

Reina in late May 1857 had told Marinoni: "I have one check for 1840 scudi and I shall now be writing to Manila to have them send me the check for 11,000 francs, which I hope you have already sent to Matheson and Company, our London banker." From experience,

47. Tragella, *Missioni estere*, 1:244.

48. PIME: AME 11:356, Reina to Salerio, 3 January 1858. Tragella in *Missioni estere*, 1:247 n. 53, incorrectly gives the date of this 3 January letter to Salerio as 2 January. In fact, much of the information contained in n. 53 actually comes from a 2 January 1858 letter of Reina to Marinoni found in PIME: AME 11:349–50, which Tragella fails to mention.

49. PIME: AME 11:351, Reina to Marinoni, 2 January 1858.

however, Reina knew that allocated funds were never sufficient. "Therefore, if you have some other small funds for my mission, I would ask that you send them to me," he said. "I do not know what you will think about this request of mine, because I know that people say—and with reason—that my mission has cost much money." But he did have needs, he said, and so it was necessary to ask for funds. "I am sending you a blank sheet signed by myself, so that in my name you can write to Lyon whatever you consider advisable to say, giving them a budget for my present and future expenditures. You could also give them news about Labuan, taking it from the [enclosed] letters written by myself and by Raimondi to Salerio.... Since I am so awkward, I do not know what kind of letter to write and I am also afraid of doing more harm than good."[50]

Reina's letter requesting funds was well received in Milan, even though Marinoni waited until 4 January 1858 before contacting the directors of the Association for the Propagation of the Faith in Lyon. He stated that Reina was en route to New Guinea and that it was Don Carlos Cuarterón, prefect apostolic of Labuan, "who had pointed out to Propaganda the usefulness of this mission, promising to introduce our missionaries there himself in view of his experience on those shores. You will understand that our missionaries must reimburse Father Cuarterón, Prefect Apostolic of Labuan, for the expenses that he has made for them. They must also found a supply center in some island located on the routes of commerce, so that they can maintain communication with Europe and provide for their needs." Marinoni also said that Reina "has to increase the number of his missionaries."

He enclosed a letter written by Reina—probably that of 29 May 1857—and also a second sheet which "explains to you the needs of the Oceania mission."[51] This second sheet was no doubt the blank sheet bearing Reina's signature, which meanwhile had been filled in by Salerio, more than likely, who was in Milan at this time and had been in New Guinea. Reina had requested that the budget should call attention to his "present and future expenses."[52] "The Budget of Expenses to be made during 1858 for the Melanesia Mission" was submitted on 4 January 1858 and read as follows:

1) Founding what is actually a new mission in New Guinea: house, boat, agricultural and carpenter tools.   Francs 7.000

2) Supply Center or Procure to be founded in Ternate or nearby with two priests and one layman.   Francs 4.000

3) Voyage of Father Ambrosoli to Singapore from Sydney, his present location.   Francs 1.500

---

50. Ibid., 330–31, Reina to Marinoni, 29 May 1857.

51. PIME: AME 6:151–52, Marinoni to the directors of the Association for the Propagation of the Faith in Lyon, 4 January 1858.

52. PIME: AME 11:331, Reina to Marinoni, 29 May 1857.

4) Voyage of two missionaries from Milan to their destination.	Francs	5.000
5) Provisions for five priests and two laymen.	Francs	4.000
6) Debt to be paid to the Reverend Cuarterón for transportation from Manila to Labuan, from Labuan to Singapore, and from there to Ternate and to New Guinea.	Francs	15.000
Total:	Francs	36.500

Under number 4 the "two missionaries from Milan" were most likely Salerio and Ripamonti. Under number 5 the "five priests" were most likely Reina, Raimondi, Ambrosoli, Salerio, and Ripamonti, and the "two laymen" were most likely Catechist Tacchini and Puarer from Woodlark.[53] About the same time—it was January 1858—Cuarterón and Reina accompanied Father Riva to Borneo City, where they helped him become established at his mission station.[54] "I was with Riva in Borneo and stayed with him up to the last moment," Reina told Marinoni. "If he remains healthy and good like he is now, he will accomplish great things, since he will have much work to do for people, poor people."[55]

Meanwhile the *Pacifico* purchased in Hong Kong by Captain Manuel Cuarterón had arrived in Labuan. Don Carlos Cuarterón's early plan, Reina said, was to load the vessel with the goods of a Chinese merchant, thus helping to pay the costs for the voyage to Singapore, "where we shall take aboard provisions and then go from there to our mission."[56]

"Today the brigantine of Don Carlos Cuarterón is finally leaving," Borgazzi wrote Marinoni from Labuan on Thursday, 25 February 1858, as the *Pacifico* prepared to sail out of Port Victoria en route to Singapore and northwest New Guinea.[57] Aboard were Don Carlos Cuarterón, his brother Manuel as captain, Reina, Raimondi, Tacchini, Puarer, and the crew. "I am alone here," Borgazzi said, "because Father Antonio [Riva] has been at his mission in Borneo for one month already."[58]

Thus Reina and his missionaries had set off once again for Melanesia, this time to make a new start. They departed from Labuan six years after having left Milan, two years and seven months after having left Woodlark for Sydney, and nearly one year and five months after having met Cuarterón in Manila. All arrived safely in Singapore on Saturday evening,

---

53. PIME: AME 6:243, "The budget of expenses... for the Melanesia Mission." The budget is not dated, but was enclosed in Marinoni's letter of 4 January 1858.

54. The date of the opening of this mission station cannot be determined more precisely. Borgazzi writing to Marinoni on 25 February 1858 from Labuan simply states that Riva "has been at his mission in Borneo for one month already." See PIME: AME 11:1520.

55. PIME: AME 16:484, Reina to Marinoni, 6 March 1858.

56. PIME: AME 11:343, Reina to Marinoni, 30 September 1857.

57. Tragella in *Missioni estere*, 1:249, mistakenly says that the *Pacifico* left Labuan for "Hong Kong" and "northeast" New Guinea. See also this chapter, p. 347, n. 13.

58. PIME: AME 11:1520, Borgazzi to Marinoni, 25 February 1858.

6 March 1858, after completing the first leg of their voyage to Dorei in New Guinea. But unexpected news from Rome would catch up with them in Singapore and would radically change all their plans.

19

Reina Reaches Singapore en route to Dorei Bay
6 March 1858

"We arrived in Singapore this evening after eight days of navigating," Prefect Apostolic Reina wrote to director Marinoni on Saturday, 6 March 1858. "And I shall be taking advantage of the mail steamer which leaves tomorrow in order to let you know where your sons are. . . ."[1] He and his missionaries had found lodging in the residence of Father Beurel, pro-vicar apostolic of Malacca-Singapore, a member of the Paris Foreign Mission Seminary. Although Cuarterón had been invited to lodge there as well, he preferred to remain aboard his ship *Pacifico*.[2]

"I do not know how much time we shall be spending here," Reina told Marinoni that Saturday evening.

> It seems to me that it will take about two months for making some necessary repairs on our ship, for the business matters which Prefect Apostolic Cuarterón has to look into, and for doing everything else that he has been talking about. After that we shall leave for Surabaya, a Dutch colony [in eastern Java]. Here Don Carlos [Cuarterón] hopes to find a Catholic governor and to obtain from him some information, not only about our mission, but also about the Dutch government. It is necessary to do this because the Vicar Apostolic of Batavia has not written to me, contrary to what he had promised. It is my guess that he has not yet received a reply from the government. From Surabaya we shall move on to Manado for the same purpose and also to see whether we can find some good businessman there who might become our co-missionary. Don Carlos has many friends there.[3]

From Manado in northeastern Celebes (now Sulawesi) they intended to sail to Ternate in the nearby Molucca Islands, Reina said, "in order to visit the Sultan there and to request

---

1. PIME: AME 16:483, Reina to Marinoni, 6 March 1858.
2. Ibid., AME 35-01 Scurati, *Memorie dell'Istituto*, 473.
3. Cuarterón had spent seven months in Manado and its vicinity starting on 4 August 1848. See chap. 15, pp. 271–72.

him—after showering him with gifts—to lend us his support for Dorei, where Don Carlos is absolutely determined to bring us. Don Carlos himself does not know whether Misory Island and the other islands nearby enclosing the bay [of Dorei] belong to the Sultan. Should they not belong to him, we would be completely free" to open missions there.[4]

Ten years earlier (1848) the Dutch government had defined its frontier on the northern coast of New Guinea to be 141 degrees 47 minutes east longitude. That same year it placed the northwest coast of New Guinea under the nominal rule of the sultan of Tidore, near Ternate, but retained sovereign rights for itself. This meant that the Vogelkop of northwest New Guinea, the area chosen by Cuarterón for Reina's mission, was in territory then considered by the Dutch to be under their domain.[5]

That evening while Reina was on shore writing to director Marinoni in Milan, Cuarterón was aboard his ship writing to his agent in Rome, Father Burrueco. Cuarterón said that he had just arrived in Singapore with Reina, Raimondi, Tacchini, and Puarer. It was 6 March, and he expected to arrive in New Guinea with all of them by May. En route he wanted to have Prefect Reina meet not only Dutch Catholics based at Manado and Ternate, but also "the Sultan of Tidore, who is in command of the northwest coast of [New] Guinea."

Cuarterón told Burrueco that taking these many precautions would make it possible for Reina "to found the new Mission of Micronesia and Melanesia" just as successfully as he himself, Cuarterón, had founded his own mission in Labuan and on the coast of Borneo. By previously reaching an accord "with the English Protestant Governor and the Mohammedan Sultan," Cuarterón said, he had subsequently received from both of them whatever he requested. This had made it possible for him "to establish his mission without any difficulty" in three places: on the island of Labuan; in Brunei, the capital of Borneo; and in Mankabung farther north along the coast. On closing his letter Cuarterón admitted that he was very tired from the voyage and also sick with fever.[6]

That same day, 6 March 1858, Cuarterón also wrote to Father Luigi Ambrosi (1819–67) in Hong Kong, who held the double office of prefect apostolic of Hong Kong and procurator of Propaganda for the Missions of China and Neighboring Kingdoms. Cuarterón informed Ambrosi of his arrival in Singapore and gave his destination as Dorei in northwest New Guinea.[7] The reader should not confuse Father Ambrosi with Father Ambrosoli. Ambrosi of Hong Kong was not a member of the Milan missionaries, but a member of the diocesan or secular clergy of Verona, Italy. Ambrosoli was a member of the Milan missionaries and

---

4. PIME: AME 16:483–84, Reina to Marinoni, 6 March 1858. This route indicated by Reina from Labuan to Dorei via Singapore, Surabaya, Manado, and Ternate shows that Tragella in *Missioni estere*, 1:249, errs when he says that Reina was en route to Hong Kong and that from there he would go to northeast [sic] New Guinea.

5. See Souter, *New Guinea*, 22–23.

6. The original of this letter of Cuarterón to Burrueco of 6 March 1858 was not found, but only an Italian translation of parts of it made by Burrueco for Barnabò. See PF: SC Oceania vol. 5 (1853–57, Part II), f. 1378r.

7. PIME: AME 29:751. Cuarterón sent this letter via the steamer *Cádiz*. See also Tragella, *Missioni estere*, 2:91.

had been left behind by Reina in Sydney because of ill health. By coincidence March 1858, when thirty-three-year-old Reina arrived in Singapore, was the very same month in which thirty-five-year-old Alfred Russell Wallace (1823–1913) settled on the shores of Dorei Bay. Wallace was an English naturalist who resided among the people at Dorei for four months with four Malayan servants. He went here and there in the forests every day collecting insects. "In fact," he said, "I was unarmed and completely in the power [of the local inhabitants], if they had wanted to attack me."[8]

One month earlier that year, in February, while Wallace was in the nearby Moluccas or Spice Islands, "there suddenly flashed upon me," he said, "the *idea* of the survival of the fittest." Wallace then proposed to the scientific world his theory on the origin of species through natural selection, not being aware that Charles Robert Darwin (1809–82) for some years had been preparing for publication his own theory on the origin of species. The Linnaean Society then arranged to have Wallace's theory presented together with Darwin's at its meeting of 1 July 1858 in a joint paper containing writings by both men. Contrary to Darwin, Wallace insisted that man's higher mental capacities could not have arisen by natural selection, but that some nonbiological agency must have been responsible.[9]

Lieutenant Bruijn Kops of the Netherlands in 1850 had already said that the Dorei inhabitants "give evidence of a mild disposition, of an inclination to right and justice, and strong moral principles."[10]

In 1855, the year in which Reina and his missionaries had abandoned Rooke and Woodlark, the Reverend Johann G. Geissler and the Reverend C. W. Ottow, two German Protestant missionaries, arrived at Mansinam Island in Dorei Bay. They were members of the "Gosznerscher Missionsverein" (Goszner Mission Society) and had received their training in Berlin from the Reverend J. Goszner himself. It was his philosophy that missionaries should provide an independent livelihood for themselves within the area assigned to them.[11]

Since Cuarterón had informed Rome that he would establish Reina and his missionaries on the northwest coast of New Guinea by May 1858,[12] Reina was destined to meet missionaries Geissler and Ottow, who were then working on Mansinam Island in Dorei Bay, as well as naturalist Wallace, who was then on the mainland at Dorei. The observa-

---

8. See PF: SC Oceania vol. 13 (1880–81), f. 527rv, Giovanni Cani to Cardinal Simeoni, 26 April 1879. See also Souter, *New Guinea*, 23–24, 263.

9. See "Alfred Russell Wallace" in *The New Encyclopaedia Britannica, Macropaedia*, 19:530–31.

10. Souter, *New Guinea*, 128. See also PF: SC Oceania vol. 13 (1880–81), f. 526r–527r, Giovanni Cani to Cardinal Simeoni, 26 April 1879. Here Cani reports that the usages and customs of the Dorei inhabitants "are less barbarous than what might have been expected . . ." In confirmation of this he gives two pages of quotations from the writings of Lieutenant Bruijn Kops.

11. Paul W. van der Veur, "Dutch New Guinea," in *Encyclopaedia of Papua and New Guinea*, 1:281. Van der Veur calls Geissler and Ottow "German missionaries"; Souter in *New Guinea*, 23 and 263, calls them "Dutch missionaries."

12. See also this chapter, p. 361, n. 6.

tions and experience of these three men would certainly be of great profit for Reina and his missionaries and would seem to indicate that Cuarterón had done well in choosing Dorei as the location for Reina to relaunch his Melanesia-Micronesia mission.

Although technically Father Ambrosoli was still a member of Reina's missionary group, the longer he remained in Sydney, the more convinced he became that Australia would be a highly suitable field of activity for the Milan Mission Seminary. He therefore informed director Marinoni on 11 February 1858 that a mission station was needed in Moreton Bay near modern Brisbane, another at Maitland, another at Gouldbourne, and still another at Bathurst. In addition Archbishop Polding was eager to have the Milan missionaries open a house in Sydney to serve as a center from which they could give parish missions throughout his archdiocese. If the Sydney project should succeed, Ambrosoli pointed out, similar centers could be opened in Melbourne, Adelaide, and Hobart Town.

Stating that this was "one of the most important letters that I could write to you," he explained to Marinoni that it was Archbishop Polding himself who three or four months earlier "had manifested to me his desire of having here a house for missionaries." They would give retreats and parish missions like the Congregation of the Missionary Oblates of Rho in the Milan Archdiocese,[13] "or like the Rosminians in England, or like the Marists in various dioceses of France." Archbishop Polding would give them a parish, Ambrosoli said, "and running it would provide them with something to live on . . ." All that Marinoni needed to do was send three priests; Ambrosoli himself would be the fourth. The center for parish missions in the Sydney archdiocese could then begin at once. After discussing this project with the Marist priest Poupinel and finding him enthusiastic about it, Ambrosoli had informed Reina that he "probably would not be leaving quickly for Singapore." He also told Marinoni this and added that Father Burrueco in Rome had instructed him to remain in Sydney.

"You would not have to spend a single penny for all the missionaries that you send to Australia," he told his superior in Milan. "On the contrary I believe that in a few years we would be able to obtain large sums of money for conducting a mission in the islands, if we had one. The Methodists in Sydney collect thousands of pounds sterling for their missionaries in Fiji and Tonga every year. Why should we not be able to do the same?" He suggested that Marinoni for the moment postpone reopening the Melanesia-Micronesia mission, because it would always be readily available to them. "I believe that in a few years the Solomon Islands will no longer be like they were ten years ago," he said. "They are now being visited continually by ships of commerce from Sydney and are therefore becoming civilized in some way. I even dare to state that there is now more communication with the Solomon Islands than there was with Wallis, when Bishop Bataillon went there twenty

---

13. See chap. 2, p. 20.

years ago."[14] Bataillon had arrived in Wallis for the first time on 1 November 1837 when still a priest.[15]

At this time Ambrosoli had the habit of writing to Marinoni on the eleventh day of each month. On 11 June 1858 he wrote that Captain Dalmagne had left Sydney with the *Phantom* "in order to found a commercial establishment for Mr. Joubert in the Solomons."[16] Since Dalmagne and Joubert had been long-standing business friends of Roman Catholic missionaries with a base in Sydney, Australia, Reina no doubt could have relaunched his Melanesia-Micronesia mission in the vicinity of Joubert's "commercial establishment" in the Solomon Islands, if only he had not left Australia. It is true that being near a successful "commercial establishment" could in some ways prove disadvantageous for missionary work. But the experience of the Marists and of Reina and his missionaries had proven that it was simply impossible for them to exist in such isolated spots as Woodlark and Rooke.

En route to Ambrosoli at this time was a disappointing reply from Marinoni stating that he was not interested in opening a center for parish missions in Australia.[17]

Reina by his own admission was a very poor and slow writer.[18] He was still laboring over his letter to Marinoni of 6 March telling of his arrival in Singapore, when the *Valigia di Europa* sailed into Singapore on Sunday, 7 March, bringing mail.[19] Reina had almost reached the bottom of page two, when without changing the date he said, "I was writing this letter when Father Beurel gave me three consecutive letters from Milan." The most important one was from Marinoni, and it brought Reina the surprising news—as yet unofficial—that he and his missionaries were being transferred by Propaganda from the Melanesia-Micronesia mission to a new mission in Hong Kong. Without questioning his orders, he said, "I shall go to Hong Kong as soon as possible with Raimondi, Tacchini, and Puarer." And he added that "immediately" he would advise Ambrosoli "to remain in Sydney provisorily."[20]

It was necessary for Reina to advise Cuarterón without delay regarding the new instructions that he had received from Marinoni, but Cuarterón was not satisfied with merely a vocal report on the contents of such an important letter. He wanted to see it with

---

14. PIME: AME 11:647–50, 651–54, Ambrosoli to Marinoni, 11 February 1858. This eight-page letter is misnumbered in the archives. Pages 651–54 are actually pages one to four of the letter, and pp. 647–50 are pages five to eight. *Beatificationis Positio*, 364, confuses the issue further by incorrectly giving pp. 647–50 the date 9 February 1858. That date should read 11 February.

15. For Bataillon's arrival in Wallis on 1 November 1837, see Wiltgen, *Oceania*, 158.

16. PIME: AME 11:663, Ambrosoli to Marinoni, 11 June 1858.

17. See ibid., 669, Ambrosoli to Marinoni, 11 September 1858. Here Ambrosoli says that Marinoni's negative decision on a center for parish missions was dated 16 May 1858.

18. See PIME: vol. 11 (Oceania), 187–88, Reina to Marinoni, 3 December 1855.

19. Both the name of the mail ship, *Valigia di Europa*, and the date of its arrival in Singapore, 7 March, were noted by Cuarterón and sent by him to Ambrosi in Hong Kong on 10 March 1858. Ambrosi in turn passed on this information to Barnabò on 30 March 1858. See PF: SC Cina vol. 17 (1857–58), f. 787v.

20. PIME: AME 16:484–85, Reina to Marinoni, 6 March 1858.

his own eyes and make ample extracts from it, since it reversed completely what he had been authorized to do by Propaganda in Rome.

Greatly disturbed over what had happened, he vented his feelings on Monday, 8 March, in a letter to his agent in Rome, Father Burrueco. "I was surprised beyond all belief," he said, "by the letter which Prefect Reina received yesterday from his superior dated 12 January. It refers to a letter received from you dated the 2nd of that same month. Here let me quote a passage from your letter." He then quoted what Burrueco had written to Marinoni on 2 January 1858 regarding the transfer of Reina and his missionaries from the Melanesia-Micronesia mission to Hong Kong. Now Burrueco was agent at Propaganda not only for Cuarterón, but also for Marinoni. "If I had realized prior to my departure from Rome that Propaganda might have been able to change its mind and send the apostolic workers appointed for New Guinea to some other mission . . . ," Cuarterón continued,

> then in no way would I have compromised my reputation with that Sacred Congregation by promising to take them to New Guinea to get them established there. After having made so many efforts and sacrifices on behalf of that mission in vain, I shall now find no one prepared to reimburse me for my numerous expenses. I shall also get a bad name and shall be discredited with both the Sacred Congregation and the Seminary of Milan. Neither did I fulfill my promise, nor did I live up to the obligations that I have by contract, because now I am prevented from completing the task of winning over those peoples to whom I was en route.[21]

Two days later, on 10 March, Cuarterón informed Prefect Apostolic Ambrosi that Reina had received a letter from his superior in Milan changing his destination from Melanesia to Hong Kong. He added that Reina had been instructed "to transfer to Hong Kong in the capacity of Vice Prefect and Vice Procurator."[22]

Reina on 13 March sent his reaction to Cardinal Prefect Barnabò "on the news communicated to me by my most beloved Superior of Milan regarding my new destination . . ." He and his missionaries, he said, were "ready to go wherever the voice of obedience" might call them, even though they were now at the threshold of New Guinea, a mission which they had loved "for such a long time." He wanted Barnabò to know of his deep gratitude to Cuarterón for the assistance received from him "up to now at the cost of so many sacrifices and with such great charity." He requested that Barnabò reward Cuarterón accordingly. "I have also written to the Most Reverend Prefect Apostolic Ambrosi," he said, "expressing to

21. Cuarterón's original letter to Burrueco of 8 March 1858, written in Spanish and containing extracts from Burrueco's letter of 2 January that year to Marinoni, has not been found. But the author did find an Italian translation of parts of that letter made by Burrueco for Barnabò. See PF: SC Oceania vol. 5 (1853–57, Part II), f. 1378r–1379v, Cuarterón to Burrueco, 8 March 1858.

22. Cuarterón's letter to Ambrosi with this information was dated 10 March 1858, as Ambrosi told Barnabò on 30 March 1858. See PF: SC Cina vol. 17 (1857–58), f. 787v. Cuarterón points out details in his letters to Burrueco and Ambrosi that Reina completely overlooks. Reina's letter of 6 March 1858 to Marinoni makes it sound as if he received word of his transfer on 6 March, the day on which he reached Singapore. See PIME: AME 16:484–85, Reina to Marinoni, 6 March 1858.

him our sentiments of submission and affection, indicating the . . . state of my former mission and requesting that he send me at his convenience his orders regarding our departure for Hong Kong."[23]

Reina wrote to Marinoni again on Sunday, 20 March 1858. "From your letter Number 3 of 12 January 1858," he said, "in which you send me a transcript of a letter received from Don Diego Burrueco, it follows that I must wait for a letter from Propaganda before I go to Hong Kong because, as you say, your letter is merely preliminary information. But if Prefect Apostolic Ambrosi should call for me, I believe that I would have to obey. This would be a proof that no difficulty stands in the way. Difficulties will arise once we are on the spot."

He then presented Marinoni with a list of questions:

> What plan must I follow regarding expenses for the personnel of my former mission? What kind of relationship should we have with the Prefect Apostolic [of Hong Kong], with the Franciscans, with the French, etc.? Besides observing the work being done in the Procure and in the Mission, must we also make a survey of local conditions, as you yourself suggest? I hope that Propaganda will be sending me instructions on this matter. In case it should not, you might write me in a confidential manner, telling me all that you know. You could also ask Don Diego [Burrueco] about the wishes of the Sacred Congregation in this matter and then send me the information. . . .[24]

The transfer of Reina and his missionaries from Melanesia to Hong Kong would fulfill a wish expressed in writing to director Marinoni on 20 April 1855 by the late Father Mazzucconi. He had suggested that Melanesia be abandoned in favor of a more promising mission. Two months later, in June 1855, while his letter was still en route to Italy, Rome's Particular Congregation on the Missions of China and Neighboring Kingdoms decided to entrust the Hong Kong mission to the Milan Mission Seminary.

Most likely Reina and his staff would have been sent to Hong Kong already in that year, except for Cuarterón's offer two months later (August 1855) to reestablish the missionaries in Melanesia at his own cost. According to Cuarterón, Propaganda had wanted to abandon the Melanesia-Micronesia mission at this time. But he had succeeded instead in convincing Secretary Barnabò to accept his plan for conducting Reina and his missionaries to a healthier place in Melanesia.

What was it, then, that had made Rome suddenly drop Cuarterón's plan and decide to send Reina and his missionaries to Hong Kong?

---

23. PIME: AME 16:491, Reina to Barnabò, 13 March 1858.

24. PIME: AME 16:497-98, Reina to Marinoni, 20 March 1858. Here Reina says that Marinoni's letter announcing his imminent transfer to Hong Kong was dated 12 January. But writing on 6 March to Marinoni, Reina says that the letter was dated 14 January. See ibid., 484, Reina to Marinoni, 6 March 1858. But Reina was often inexact in his writing. Cuarterón, who was precise with dates, examined this letter from Marinoni, made extracts from it, and reported that it was dated 12 January 1858. This is the date accepted by the author. See PF: SC Oceania vol. 5 (1853-57, Part II), f. 1378r, Cuarterón to Burrueco, 8 March 1858.

20

Why Barnabò Sends Reina to Hong Kong
1850 to 1858

WHY DID CARDINAL PREFECT BARNABÒ ON 9 JANUARY 1858 TRANSFER THE MILAN missionaries from Melanesia to Hong Kong? The decision to send missionaries from Milan to Hong Kong had been maturing for many years and was made possible at this time by a peculiar set of circumstances in Rome, Milan, Melanesia, and Hong Kong. This decision, however, was bound to postpone indefinitely the evangelization of Melanesia and Micronesia to their detriment. Hence it is necessary and proper to inquire into the reasons that seemingly justified this postponement.

During the Opium War (1839–42) between Great Britain and China, the British troops retired to Hong Kong Island. China on being defeated by the British signed the Convention of Chuenpi on 20 January 1841, ceding the island and harbor of Hong Kong to the British Crown. Three months later on 22 April 1841 Propaganda issued a decree stating that Pope Gregory XVI had created the Prefecture Apostolic of Hong Kong Island in order to provide for the spiritual needs of Catholics and to foster the spread of Christianity.[1] Pope Gregory XVI named Father Théodore Joset (1804–42), a Swiss secular priest, the first prefect apostolic of Hong Kong Island. Previously he had been at Macao, forty miles to the west of Hong Kong, serving as Propaganda's procurator or official agent for dealing with the Missions of China and Neighboring Kingdoms. Without losing this office, he moved to Hong Kong on 3 March 1842 to take up his new assignment as prefect apostolic, but he died there five months later at the age of thirty-eight.[2]

Joset's successor in both offices was Father Antonio Feliciani, O.F.M., the Italian Franciscan priest with whom Don Carlos Cuarterón had been in contact before leaving

---

1. For the decree establishing the Prefecture Apostolic of Hong Kong Island, see PF: LDB vol. 325 (1841), f. 388v–389r.

2. Fortunato Margiotti, O.F.M., "La Cina cattolica al traguardo della maturity...," in *Sacrae Congregationis de Propaganda Fide Memoria Rerum 1622-1972*, 3(1) 1815–1972, 527. Joset died on 5 August 1842 and is identified as a Swiss secular priest on his tombstone. For the tombstone text see PIME: AME 35-01 Scurati, *Memorie dell'Istituto*, 485.

Hong Kong to study for the priesthood in Rome. But Feliciani, who never liked his two jobs as prefect and procurator, suggested in 1845 that Rome entrust the "well deserving" Paris Foreign Mission Seminary "with the spiritual care of Hong Kong Island." Pope Pius IX then proposed that Feliciani be asked whether his work as procurator might hinder him from being prefect apostolic of the mission. If so, he was to "name another Italian missionary as his Vicar with the title of Vice Prefect." He would thus have the final word on decisions regarding the prefecture, but not the work load connected with it. But Feliciani did not make use of this faculty.[3]

Next Feliciani suggested that his Franciscan assistant, Father Girolamo Mangieri, should be named prefect apostolic of Hong Kong Island, and that his other assistant, secular priest Luigi Ambrosi, should be named procurator of Propaganda for the Missions of China and Neighboring Kingdoms.[4] Feliciani's proposal was en route to Rome only four days, however, when Propaganda itself found an unexpected solution. Théodore-Augustin Forcade, a member of the Paris Foreign Mission Society, had been named vicar apostolic of Japan and Neighboring Islands with the task of bringing the Catholic Church back to Japan. On Sunday, 3 October 1847, pro-secretary Barnabò requested Pope Pius IX to entrust Forcade in addition and provisorily with the spiritual care of the Prefecture Apostolic of Hong Kong Island. The reason for this was Forcade's suggestion that Hong Kong was the best jumping-off place for his missionary work in Japan.[5] The request was granted by the pope, and on the following day Propaganda issued a decree stating that Forcade for the reasons just mentioned had been entrusted with the administration of the Prefecture Apostolic of Hong Kong Island and was named "pro-prefect."[6]

Forcade became involved immediately with a proposal of Bishop Emmanuel-Jean-François Verolles, also a member of the Paris Foreign Mission Society and vicar apostolic of Manchuria. Verolles while in Rome had proposed to Pope Pius IX on 22 August 1847 that it was time for the hierarchy to be established in China and in its adjoining kingdoms. Rome welcomed the proposal, but obstacles arose and divergent positions were taken by Feliciani and Forcade, causing Rome to postpone the proposal indefinitely.[7] Feliciani continued to complain about Forcade and finally suggested that the prefecture apostolic of Hong Kong Island should be taken away from him and given to Italian Jesuits (officially the

---

3. PF: Acta CP vol. 24 (1850–56), f. 29r.

4. PF: SOCP vol. 78 (1848–56, Part I), f. 264v–265r, Feliciani to Fransoni, 29 September 1847. Scurati in PIME; AME 35-01, *Memorie dell'Istituto*, 486, incorrectly gives Mangieri's name as Geremia (Jeremiah). Mangieri himself signs his name Girolamo (Jerome) in PF: SC Cina vol. 17 (1857–58), f. 571r, Mangieri to Barnabò, 28 November 1857.

5. PF: Acta CP vol. 24 (1850–56), f. 4r.

6. PF: LDB vol. 336 (1847, Part II), f. 1259v–1261r. See also the decree of 24 August 1850 in PF: LDB vol. 339 (1850), f. 744v.

7. Margiotti, "Cina cattolica," 522–23.

Society of Jesus) or to Bishop Lodovico Besi of Italy,⁸ who had earlier served as administrator apostolic of the Nanking Vicariate in China.

After serving as pro-prefect of Hong Kong Island almost two full years, however, Forcade wrote to Cardinal Prefect Fransoni on 20 September 1849 that he wished to be relieved of this office so that he could dedicate himself more completely to making preparations for entering Japan. Fransoni remarked to several cardinals that the arrival of Forcade's resignation was "fortunate" and that "not a minute was lost in taking him at his word." Forcade was informed by letter of 11 January 1850 that his wish would be fulfilled at the first meeting after the return of Pope Pius IX from Portici near Naples, where he was in exile.⁹

The pope arrived back in Rome on 12 April 1850. But the first Particular Meeting on China, which was held on 28 May, did not discuss Forcade's case. It was postponed until the next Particular Meeting on 27 July.

During the interval, Bishop-Elect Ramazzotti of Pavia arrived in Rome on 15 June 1850 to be ordained a bishop by Cardinal Prefect Fransoni. Ramazzotti used this opportunity to request a particular mission field for the new mission seminary that he was promoting and which Pius IX had approved on 21 February that year. But when Ramazzotti informed Fransoni that the preference of the seminary's candidates was Micronesia, he was told that the decision on the matter would be postponed to a later date.¹⁰ Unknown to Ramazzotti, the cardinal prefect in those very weeks was offering the Micronesia mission to the Congregation of the Sacred Hearts of Jesus and Mary (SS.CC.) and to the Oblates of Mary Immaculate (O.M.I.).¹¹

As chairman of the Particular Meetings on China which were then being held, Cardinal Prefect Fransoni was disturbed about the rapid turnover of personnel in Hong Kong. And now, after having had three different prefects apostolic in office for a total of only nine years, he was once again looking for another candidate. The Feliciani-Forcade affair had also shown that having two officials of different nationalities and of different missionary orders in such a small area simply did not work. At some point the cardinal became convinced that a solution for his Hong Kong problems would be to give Ramazzotti's new mission seminary the responsibility for providing Italian candidates from the secular clergy for the offices of procurator and prefect apostolic. With time the seminary could also be made responsible for providing whatever personnel these officials might need.

---

8. Besi signs his name Lodovico, not Ludovico as given by some authors. See PIME: AME 27:11–12, Besi to Marinoni, 8 February 1853.

9. PF: Acta CP vol. 24 (1850–56), f. 4r–5r; PF: Acta CP vol. 24 (1850–56), f. 53r–54r, Forcade to Fransoni, 20 September 1849.

10. Suigo, *Pio IX*, 91–92.

11. For more details see chap. 4, pp. 49–50, and Wiltgen, *Oceania*, 535–39.

This was the plan conceived by Cardinal Prefect Fransoni and secretary Barnabò, which undoubtedly was discussed with Ramazzotti. Lest there be any doubt in Ramazzotti's mind, however, Propaganda's chief clerk, Father Buratti, was instructed to put the cardinal's wish in writing and personally present it to Ramazzotti.[12] This memorandum urged the new bishop "to provide one excellent priest, or better two, to serve in Hong Kong as procurator of the Sacred Congregation de Propaganda Fide for the missions of China." The priest chosen for this office, the memorandum said, was also to be named ecclesiastical superior over Hong Kong "with the rank of prefect apostolic."[13]

The next Particular Meeting on China was held on 27 July 1850, three weeks after Ramazzotti's departure from Rome. At this meeting the cardinals decided to request Pope Pius IX to accept Forcade's resignation.[14] Consequently a new prefect apostolic had to be named for Hong Kong Island. During the meeting six candidates were proposed by Cardinal Prefect Fransoni—namely, Feliciani, Ambrosi, Buffa, Libois, Besi, and "some fine priest of the secular clergy." Feliciani, the Franciscan priest holding office as procurator, was ruled out in view of his "very mediocre capacity" for the task, "although for the rest he is very zealous and a fine religious and missionary." Regarding the priests Luigi Ambrosi and Francesco Buffa, then assisting Procurator Feliciani, "the news at hand . . . is likewise not reassuring as regards their ability to succeed Father Feliciani," Fransoni said.

The next candidate was Father Napoléon-François Libois (1805–72), a member of the Paris Foreign Mission Society like Forcade. He had been procurator for his own society for ten years, first in Macao and then in Hong Kong. But one of the resolutions taken by the cardinals was that "a new Italian Prefect should be named." This excluded Libois, because he was French.

The retired Bishop Besi of Nanking, the next candidate, was a member of the Italian secular clergy. He could provisorily be named administrator of the prefecture apostolic, Fransoni said, and could also be "placed in charge of reorganizing the poorly managed Procure." And if the Synod of Bishops of China and Neighboring Kingdoms were to take place in Hong Kong, he could be named its president.

But if the Besi solution "for some reason were to be excluded," Fransoni continued, "I should think that we ought to assign and send there some fine priest of the secular clergy (since it would be fitting to have such a person as Procurator), and that he be entrusted with the task of running both the Prefecture and the Procure. He should also be given the faculty of delegating a substitute" for his role as prefect apostolic. The reason for giving one person both offices of procurator and prefect was that "inconveniences result for both the Procurator and the Procure," if the prefecture happens to be under someone else's jurisdiction. The procurator-prefect was therefore expected to delegate someone as his vice prefect

---

12. *Beatificationis Positio*, 95.
13. Ibid., 92.
14. Decree of 24 August 1850 in PF: LDB vol. 339 (1850), f. 744v–745r.

to administer the prefecture apostolic. As is evident from this proposal by Fransoni, it is the very project outlined three weeks earlier in the memorandum given to Ramazzotti.

Fransoni then pointed out that if the latter proposal were to be adopted, "Father Feliciani could again receive the Prefecture until the person being sought should arrive." The resolution eventually adopted by the cardinals stated that Father Feliciani in addition to his office as procurator "should return to office and run the Prefecture as in the past" until "a new Italian Prefect can be named, to whom in time opportune instructions shall be given."[15] All of this was approved by Pope Pius IX on 11 August 1850, and the essence of it was published by Propaganda in a decree dated 24 August 1850.[16]

Fransoni waited until 30 September 1850 before informing Feliciani of the pope's action. He said that a new prefect apostolic was to be chosen among Italian missionaries, but added that Feliciani by order of the pope was to accept the office of prefect again until a substitute could be found. The cardinal assured him that this burden would be "of short duration" and added that Feliciani was free to name a vice prefect immediately. In order to lighten his burden Propaganda would also begin using extensively Father Luigi Ambrosi for the affairs of the procure, Fransoni said. But Feliciani was to remain in charge of both the prefecture and the procure.[17] Meanwhile the Micronesia mission had been politely rejected by the Congregation of the Sacred Hearts of Jesus and Mary on 4 June 1850, and also by the Oblates of Mary Immaculate on 25 July.[18] But Roman authorities sent no word about this to Ramazzotti. Apparently Propaganda was more interested in Hong Kong's receiving whatever personnel the small mission seminary might have to offer.

Father Supriès, great promoter of Micronesia as a choice mission for the fledgling seminary, was perplexed by Rome's silence. He wrote to Father Taglioretti on 16 October 1850, wondering why Rome "has not yet taken a stand regarding the area to be assigned to the new missionaries." He urged Taglioretti "to keep Rome abreast of what is happening" with the hope that this would cause Rome to write some letters.[19]

---

15. PF: Acta CP vol. 24 (1850–56) f. 1r, 4r–7r, 22v–23r, 28Arv, 28A+2rv, 29r. There are over four hundred pages of minutes covering the Particular Meetings on China of 28 May, 27 July, and 3 August 1850. The minutes are presented in such a way that it is generally impossible to determine what business was discussed at which meeting. But since the cardinals at the Particular Meeting of 27 July 1850 (see p. 370, n. 14) decided to request Pope Pius IX to accept Forcade's resignation, it follows logically that the discussion of possible successors for Forcade took place at the same meeting.

16. See p. 370, n. 14.

17. PF: LDB vol. 339 (1850), f. 836r–838r, Fransoni to Feliciani, 30 September 1850. The episodes and deliberations just described show that the Italian missionaries referred to by Propaganda in this early stage and desired for Hong Kong, were definitely those of Ramazzotti. Unaware of the documentation found by the present author, Tragella in *Missioni Estere*, 1:265, merely suggests that Milan missionaries may have been the ones under consideration. However, he is uncertain and at once lists other possibilities like individual Italian diocesan priests, Italian priests of the College of the Holy Family in Naples, or members of other missionary orders.

18. See Wiltgen, *Oceania*, 537–39, for more details.

19. See chap. 4, p. 50.

The mission seminary had opened its doors to the first priest candidates on 30 July 1850. Having received no word from Bishop Ramazzotti, Fransoni on 21 November sent an appeal to Father Luigi Sturla, an Italian secular priest working as a missionary at Aden in the Arabian Peninsula. "Propaganda for a long time had been urged by Father Antonio Feliciani," the cardinal explained, to relieve him of the two offices of prefect and procurator in Hong Kong, "which he has held for many years. Propaganda has conducted many inquiries for the purpose of finding a zealous priest who might want to volunteer for the above tasks...." Sturla's qualifications, the cardinal said, were known to him, and they "give me full confidence that you would know well how to conduct" both offices.[20] In reply Sturla wrote two letters to Fransoni, one accepting the two offices and one refusing them. These he sent to a priest friend in Genoa, Father Giuseppe Frassinetti, a moral theologian, asking him to send Rome the one which "in the Lord" he considered to be the more opportune. Frassinetti sent Rome the refusal.[21]

On 26 November 1850, which was five days after Fransoni had asked for Sturla's help, director Marinoni of Lombardy's Seminary for Foreign Missions and his first five candidates drew up a petition. It requested the bishops of Lombardy to urge Propaganda to designate a specific mission field for their seminary, preferably the archipelagoes of Micronesia. Two days later while gathered in session the bishops of Lombardy made this proposal their own, but dependent upon Rome's decision. The official papers of this meeting were then submitted by Bishop Ramazzotti to Cardinal Prefect Fransoni. They included the Act of Foundation of the mission seminary dated 1 December 1850 and nearly an entire page of reasons that it was necessary for Rome to designate a specific mission field without delay. Ramazzotti added that the field to which the candidates wished to dedicate themselves was Micronesia.[22]

Prefect Fransoni and Secretary Barnabò must have been disappointed that Hong Kong was not even mentioned in the certified copy of minutes describing the meeting held by the bishops of Lombardy on 28 November. But Hong Kong was mentioned in an accompanying letter of Ramazzotti to Fransoni dated 5 December 1850. He had made efforts, he said, to find someone "capable of taking on at Hong Kong the functions of Procurator of the Missions in conformity with the commission given me by this Sacred Congregation when I was in Rome." But he did not indicate in writing the results of his efforts because, as he said, director Marinoni himself would personally present the official documents regarding the seminary and at that time would also make a verbal report on Ramazzotti's efforts regarding Hong Kong.[23]

---

20. PF: LDB vol. 339 (1850), f. 968rv, Fransoni to Sturla, 21 November 1850. Tragella in *Missioni estere*, 1:266 n. 24, incorrectly dates this letter 29 November.

21. Tragella, *Missioni estere*, 1:265–66.

22. PF: CV vol. 43, f. 152r–153v. See also chap. 4, pp. 53–55.

23. PF: CV vol. 43, f. 158v, Ramazzotti to Fransoni, 5 December 1850. This Ramazzotti letter of 5 December

Director Marinoni drafted the Hong Kong section in the above 5 December 1850 letter of Bishop Ramazzotti. He had made an earlier and much longer draft which began like this: "All of my attention has been centered as well on another proposal," namely, to obtain one or two priests for Hong Kong. "Hopefully I have found for you two altogether irreproachable priests of solid piety and mature judgement, who lack neither talent nor learning and who are also endowed with great ability in managing temporal affairs. . . ."

The two unnamed priests were thirty-five-year-old Ripamonti and twenty-four-year-old Mazzucconi. Ripamonti had been ordained twelve years earlier and was currently serving as treasurer for the fledgling mission seminary. Mazzucconi, ordained only half a year, had not yet received his first assignment.

The earlier draft indicated that Ramazzotti was willing to add a third priest who, being younger, could learn Chinese better and so might serve as interpreter for the other two. Rome was requested, however, to provide more information on the duties to be performed and to indicate when the priests should arrive in Rome for their departure to Hong Kong. Evidently something had happened at the seminary, making this generous offer in the earlier draft inadvisable. But Marinoni must have taken it along to Rome as a memorandum for himself when speaking with authorities there. Actually the student body by this time had made it clear that their choice of a foreign mission was Micronesia, and the bishops of Lombardy at their meeting of 28 November had supported this proposal. The generous offer in the earlier draft was therefore revised and presented in a much weaker form.[24]

Marinoni had not yet reached Rome with the documents when Father Saison, prior of the Carthusian Monastery in Pavia to which Father Supriès was attached, sent surprising news from Rome (where he was on business) to Archbishop Romilli of Milan on 9 December 1850. Saison said that Rome wished to assign some of the new Lombardy missionaries to the Vicariate Apostolic of Colombo in Ceylon (now Sri Lanka).[25]

Colombo, being an English-language port on the route to Hong Kong, perfectly suited Rome's plan for the mission seminary of Lombardy. In distance about forty-five hundred miles from Italy and three thousand miles from Hong Kong, it could serve strategically as a forward base of the seminary, having the function of providing practical mission experi-

---

is the one regarding Hong Kong that Suigo failed to find in Propaganda's archives. See *Beatificationis Positio*, 92. See also n. 24 below.

24. For Marinoni's earlier draft in his own handwriting, which was not incorporated in the 5 December 1850 letter of Ramazzotti, see PIME: AME 5:327–28. This inclusion in a volume dedicated to correspondence and texts by Marinoni from 1830 to 1855 suggests that the first two pages of Ramazzotti's letter of 5 December 1850 were also drafted by Marinoni. For the content of the first two pages see chap. 4, p. 55. See Suigo's study on the longer unused Marinoni draft regarding Hong Kong in *Beatificationis Positio*, 92, 94–95, which he mistakenly identifies as "an extract from a letter of Bishop Ramazzotti to Cardinal Giacomo Filippo Fransoni" written "without doubt in August-September 1850." See also n. 23 above. Scurati in PIME: AME 35-01, *Memorie dell'Istituto*, 469, gives the names of the candidates as Ripamonti and Mazzucconi.

25. See PIME: AME 4:337–40, Taglioretti to Marinoni, 4 January 1851; PIME: AME 4:341, Taglioretti to Ramazzotti, 10 January 1851.

ence for the candidates and fluency in the English language. But on learning of Rome's proposal to send them to Ceylon, the missionary candidates unanimously voted against it, stating that Micronesia was their only choice.[26] This vote also confirmed their exclusion of Hong Kong, and there is no evidence that the names Ripamonti and Mazzucconi were actually presented to Rome.

Fransoni nevertheless thanked Ramazzotti on 16 January 1851 for his efforts in "procuring for me some fine priests for the Prefecture Apostolic of Hong Kong with the understanding, moreover, that this Mission and Prefecture Apostolic in time could be entrusted exclusively" to the members of the Lombardy Foreign Mission Seminary, "once their numbers and their good success permit it . . ."[27]

In an accompanying letter of the same date addressed to Archbishop Romilli of Milan, Fransoni replied to the official request made by the bishops of Lombardy for the Micronesia mission. The wishes of those in the mission seminary "will be completely fulfilled," he said. In fact, circumstances had made it possible "to designate at this moment already, and for them exclusively, the desired and vast Missions of Melanesia and Micronesia."[28]

Ramazzotti replied four weeks later that negotiations would continue "for obtaining a suitable person for Hong Kong," and he also gave assurance that "Your Eminence will be kept informed most assiduously."[29] Nearly six months passed without Fransoni receiving word about candidates for Hong Kong. Then one day Reina and Salerio arrived in Rome with a letter of 29 July 1851 from Director Marinoni for Cardinal Fransoni, stating that both of them were "ready to sail with four companions to Oceania whenever it should please Your Eminence."

Surprisingly Reina was called into a Particular Meeting on China during this stay in Rome and was asked explicitly in the presence of both Cardinal Prefect Fransoni and secretary Barnabò whether he was ready to go to Hong Kong. As he later said, he expressed readiness to go wherever Propaganda might wish to send him.[30] But on 21 August, the very day on which Reina and Salerio had their audience with the pope, Fransoni wrote to Superior General Colin of the Marists that he would entrust to "the recently founded Seminary for Foreign Missions in Milan" either Micronesia or Melanesia, whichever the Society of Mary did not wish to retain.[31] On 17 December 1852, nine months after Reina and his missionaries had left Milan for Oceania, Marinoni informed Fransoni that he hoped "soon to have found two priests for Hong Kong, provided they are able to settle cer-

---

26. See chap. 4, pp. 56–57.

27. PF: LDB vol. 340 (1851), f. 40rv. Rome was already planning by 16 January 1851 to entrust Hong Kong to the Foreign Mission Seminary of Milan. Brambilla in *Pontificio istituto*, 1:175, mistakenly says that Rome did so only in May 1856.

28. See chap. 4, pp. 58–59.

29. PF: CV vol. 43, f. 165r, Ramazzotti to Fransoni, 13 February 1851.

30. See chap. 5, p. 67.

31. See chap. 5, pp. 67–68.

tain family problems."[32] Two weeks later Fransoni replied: "I wish to thank Your Reverence for still being interested in benefiting the Mission of Hong Kong. In due time I shall profit in good measure from the alumni of your seminary, which could look after that same mission. Now I am busy improving its organization...."[33] By this time two and a half years had passed since Rome's original request for a priest or two.

Some weeks later Marinoni described for Bishop Besi in Rome a certain candidate for the office of procurator. Besi replied on 8 February 1853: "The other evening I went to see Cardinal Fransoni and told him what you had written me regarding the priest whom you propose for the Hong Kong Procure. He was greatly pleased and said that he will speak of this in their next meeting and that he will then inform you by letter of the decision reached."[34] But again nothing came of this.

Time and again Milan had informed Rome that more missionaries were ready to leave for Oceania, but the answer was always the same: the Oceania Mission is not yet giving signs of success and consequently no additional personnel may be sent. When Rome answered in this way for the eleventh time, Fransoni asked Ramazzotti whether the missionaries might be ready to go "to some other less difficult and less dangerous mission, like Eastern India, for example." Ramazzotti replied by sending Fransoni on 22 May 1854 a list of ten priests and two catechists, all of whom were ready to go wherever Rome might want to send them. Ten of these were assigned to eastern India.[35] Thus Propaganda's original plan for sending personnel from Milan to an English-speaking territory on the route between Italy and Hong Kong was at last realized. Once trained in eastern India, the personnel could be transferred to Hong Kong and beyond.

Propaganda's plan was confirmed by Canon Bertinelli, agent in Rome for the bishops of Lombardy. Director Marinoni had sent him news of these latest developments on 31 May and again on 12 and 26 June. Referring to the unsuccessful missionaries of Melanesia, Bertinelli replied on 12 July 1854 that Cardinal Fransoni "has been undecided for some time as to whether he should send them to China. However, I am of the opinion that once the situation in that Empire has quieted down [a war was in progress], those being sent to India will be transferred from there either to China or to Japan. But you must not say a word about this to anyone," Bertinelli warned, "since this is an opinion of mine which I have deduced from conversations that I have heard."

Bishop Corti of Mantova, one of the bishops of Lombardy then in Rome, wrote that same day to Bishop Ramazzotti about his visit with Fransoni. The cardinal had said that if

---

32. PF: SC Oceania vol. 4 (1848–52), f. 1024rv.

33. PIME: AME 1:83–84, Fransoni to Marinoni, 31 December 1852.

34. Ibid., 27:11–12. Besi's reply does not give the name of the priest proposed by Marinoni. Nor has the archivist at the P.I.M.E. Generalate in Rome been able to locate a draft of what Marinoni wrote to Besi. There was also no trace of the reply promised by Fransoni.

35. See chap. 12, pp. 192–93.

no good news at all should arrive from the Melanesia mission, then "the proper thing to do is to send" the missionaries who are there "to other harvests."[36]

Eight months later on 14 March 1855, Pope Pius IX blessed the first group of Milan missionaries leaving for eastern India and said, "You are at the gates of China!"[37] Certainly he had been briefed by Cardinal Prefect Fransoni or Secretary Barnabò and must have meant that their work in eastern India would be a preparation for taking up work some day in Hong Kong. Father Parietti, superior of the group, was informed that Propaganda was negotiating about Hong Kong with Canon Ortolda, director of the Association for the Propagation of the Faith in the Diocese of Turin in northern Italy. Most probably in the following month of April, he learned, Ortolda would be sending three missionaries to Hong Kong. But this was merely a temporary measure, he was told, because Propaganda had the intention of assigning Hong Kong—but after some time—to his Foreign Mission Seminary of Lombardy.[38]

Meanwhile Rome was receiving word now and then that Father Feliciani was not the right man for the two offices that he held. He "was causing ever more harm and was obstructing both the development of the [Hong Kong] Mission and even more so the business of the Procure. And whereas the mission for all practical purposes always remained in a stagnant position or in its infancy, the Procure was daily on the verge of total ruin."

Bishop Francesco Saverio Maresca, former administrator apostolic of Nanking, arrived in Rome in June 1855 to report on the mission and procure of Hong Kong. He highly praised Father Luigi Ambrosi, who for some years had been serving as vice procurator under Feliciani.[39] Ambrosi, a secular priest from Verona, Italy, knew English, French, and Portuguese, in addition to his native Italian. In view of Maresca's recommendation and that of Feliciani, who had praised Ambrosi repeatedly for being prudent and experienced in financial matters, Propaganda decided "to hasten the substitution" of Feliciani.[40] Losing no time Fransoni wrote to Feliciani that same month, addressing him for the last time as prefect apostolic of Hong Kong and procurator of China and Neighboring Kingdoms:

> We have maturely considered your wise remarks and do not wish to postpone any longer the fulfillment of your Paternity's often expressed desire of being exonerated from the two-fold burden mentioned above. You have borne it for so many years and have performed its functions zealously. The Sacred Congregation has therefore judged it fitting to follow the very suggestion made by your Paternity ... and is choos-

---

36. See chap. 12, pp. 193–94.

37. See PIME: AME 13:65, Parietti to Romilli, 15 March 1855.

38. See ibid., 59, Parietti to Marinoni, 8 March 1855; ibid., 62, Parietti to Ramazzotti, 19 March 1855.

39. PF: Acta CP vol. 24 (1850–56), f. 406v–430rv. Margiotti in "Cina cattolica," 527, mistakenly calls Ambrosi of Hong Kong a member of the Milan Foreign Mission Seminary. He confuses him with Ambrosoli of Sydney, a member of the Milan seminary.

40. Tragella, *Missioni estere*, 1:262, 267. For Feliciani's praise of Ambrosi see PF: LDB vol. 346 (1855), f. 417r, Fransoni to Ambrosi, 20 June 1855.

ing the Reverend Luigi Ambrosi as your substitute for the office of Procurator. He is also being entrusted with the office of Prefect Apostolic in order to avoid clashes that might arise, if the two offices are not united in the same person. This is being done in view of the forthcoming reorganization planned for Hong Kong.

He added that the missionary staff would also come from the institute that would provide the prefect and procurator.[41]

Although the "twofold office of Prefect and Procurator" formerly held by Feliciani was given to Ambrosi on 20 June 1855, it was Propaganda's intention already at that time "to send as soon as possible some other priest, whom the Seminary of Milan for Foreign Missions will soon be able to supply. Later it will also be easy to obtain from it as many good missionaries as one may need."[42]

Ambrosi received all of Feliciani's faculties as well as "all burdens, honors and privileges . . ."[43] He was also given instructions "to occupy himself at once with the greatest zeal to reorganize both the mission and the procure and to submit as soon as possible a distinct plan and a detailed report on each regarding their state, needs, etc., along with pertinent observations . . ."[44] The combined offices of prefect apostolic and procurator were such a burden for Ambrosi, however, that he submitted his resignation to Rome twice during his first nine months in office, but Rome did not accept it. After making extensive reforms regarding "things that, as they were, could not help but turn out badly," he began receiving compliments from vicars apostolic. But those whose affairs were managed from Shanghai complained bitterly and insisted: "It is altogether necessary to establish a Vice Procure, or even the Procure itself, in Shanghai."

Ambrosi did not agree. He told secretary Barnabò that "at least for some years to come the Procure . . . cannot be transferred there. Although Shanghai is gaining some importance as a place . . . , it is nonetheless too far out-of-the-way. Hong Kong on the contrary is growing by gigantic steps. Of all ports open to commerce, it is the principal one. And it has become, so to say, a rendezvous for sailing vessels and steamers alike, which come and go constantly from all points and to all points, thus facilitating our contact with all places. It is moreover the center for all of our missions."[45]

---

41. PF: LDB vol. 346 (1855), f. 415v–416v, Fransoni to Feliciani, 20 June 1855. Feliciani later left Hong Kong for Shantung where he taught in a minor seminary for three years. He then went to Shansi, where he became pro-vicar general, and died in 1866. See Tragella, *Missioni estere*, 1:267.

42. Cardinals at the Particular Meeting on China of 21 January 1856 were informed of these June 1855 plans. See PF: Acta CP vol. 24 (1850–56), f. 406v–407r.

43. PF: LDB vol. 346 (1855), f. 434rv, Decree of 20 June 1855.

44. PF: Acta CP vol. 24 (1850–56), f. 406v–407r, Particular Meeting of 21 January 1856. See also PF: LDB vol. 346 (1855), f. 416v–417r, Fransoni to Ambrosi, 20 June 1855. Tragella in *Missioni estere*, vol. 1, op. p. 272, mistakenly calls Ambrosi the "first" prefect apostolic of Hong Kong.

45. PF: SC Cina vol. 16 (1855–56), f. 749rv, 763r, 765r, Ambrosi to Barnabò, 9 May 1856. The folios of this letter are scattered as indicated.

After Cardinal Prefect Fransoni died on 20 April 1856, Pope Pius IX named secretary Barnabò a cardinal on 19 June that year and on the following day appointed him prefect of Propaganda Fide.[46] In the intervening month of May, director Marinoni had sent treasurer Ripamonti to Rome with a new group of missionaries en route to India. Ripamonti informed Marinoni that he had heard in the offices of Propaganda that "the mission of Hong Kong was to be transferred definitively" to their mission seminary.[47] Father Burrueco of the Trinitarians was invited by director Marinoni to be his agent in Rome. When accepting the invitation on 11 July 1856, Burrueco urged Marinoni "to prepare and train for the Procure in Hong Kong at least three missionaries with administrative talent. After they have obtained some knowledge of English," he said, "they are to be sent to Rome to learn here at least the fundamentals of Chinese. Then they will be sent to that office [the Hong Kong Procure] *in perpetuity*."[48]

Marinoni answered Burrueco on 27 July 1856 that he was considering Fathers Ripamonti and Salerio as candidates for the Hong Kong positions. But Salerio had arrived back in Milan from Oceania completely broken in health on 8 June, only seven weeks earlier. Consequently "time and the blessing of God are needed for him to recuperate," Marinoni said. "But it does not seem that this proposal was accepted by the Sacred Congregation," writes Father Giacomo Scurati, secretary to director Marinoni, in his unpublished history of *The Prefecture Apostolic of Hong Kong in China*. Ripamonti, however, one of the two priests concerned, corrected Scurati's manuscript in his own hand by adding, "The proposal regarding the two [priests] was disapproved in the house."[49]

So once again there was a delay and Milan had disappointed Rome, which as early as June 1850 had requested one or two priests for Hong Kong. Six full years had passed without a single candidate going there. Ambrosi begged Barnabò on 29 December 1856 "kindly not to forget" the Hong Kong procure, and he also described what it was like being procurator without an assistant. "From the time when I took over the management of the Procure," he said,

> I have not had a peaceful night. And I am always sad to hear the bell calling me to work the next morning. I must compose, and not a little. I must make copies. I must travel by land and by sea to make purchases, not only for ourselves, but also for the Spanish procures in Manila and Macao, and also for the Jesuits.... Finally I must do

---

46. For details see chap. 16, p. 322.

47. PIME: AME 35-01 Scurati, *Memorie dell'Istituto*, 431, 469–70. It was not in May 1856 when the Propaganda offices spoke about this for the first time. See p. 374, n. 27.

48. PIME: AME 35-01, *Memorie dell'Istituto*, 470; see also 431. Scurati in these passages quotes Burrueco as saying "at least three missionaries" were to be trained for Hong Kong. Tragella in *Missioni estere*, 1:351, inexactly puts the number at "two or three." For more details on Burrueco see chap. 15, p. 300, and chap. 16, p. 323.

49. Compare Scurati's final manuscript draft in *Memorie dell'Istituto*, 470, with the earlier draft, 432, which also contains the correction in Ripamonti's own hand. On Salerio's return to Milan see Tragella, *Missioni estere*, 1:214.

all of these things with this head of mine which is forever aching. And I am almost always distracted. . . .

Imagine, Your Eminence, when there are two, three, or at times four steamers providing occasions all at once for contacting different places, and I have to write to all of them, or to the majority of them, keeping copies of what I write, because the matters are important. Imagine, I say, the whereabouts of my poor head! How can I possibly do well all the things that have to be done? . . . We are men and we are mortals. And here we are in a climate which does not permit us to do everything, that you perhaps can do there [in Rome]. Our climate also greatly shortens our lives because generally we have little appetite.

Ambrosi reminded Barnabò that in his previous letter of 14 December he had pointed out the extreme and urgent personnel needs of the Hong Kong prefecture.[50]

Barnabò replied on 19 September 1857 that he was very much aware of Ambrosi's need for personnel and that "a more appropriate and radical provision for this Prefecture and Procure" had to be made. He promised to keep in mind Ambrosi's "various suggestions," but at the same time he begged Ambrosi to take note that very many difficulties stood in the way of realizing the plans that Propaganda had made. "Therefore you must not be surprised over my not having been able to satisfy, so quickly as I would have liked, your repeated and also just desires regarding this particular matter." Barnabò assured Ambrosi that he was totally absorbed in reorganizing the Hong Kong mission "as soon as I possibly can and in a way that conforms with your plans and ideas." Barnabò promised that "there will be no delay except for complications that we may meet in carrying out this plan."[51] By this time seven years had passed since Rome had requested help from Milan for Hong Kong.

Barnabò's encouraging letter to Ambrosi was still en route when Ambrosi wrote to Barnabò in exceptionally vigorous terms: "For the love of God, Your Eminence, do not forget this Mission, which I told you many times is still in swaddling clothes! This condition will continue as long as other measures are not taken, which I need not repeat here to your and my great annoyance. We keep waiting here—always and endlessly—for the two promised missionaries, one English-speaking and the other Portuguese-speaking, who are really so very necessary." Ambrosi insisted, "You must send me the two missionaries referred to above and you must order the Reverend [Francesco] Buffa to return [to Europe]." Twelve weeks earlier Ambrosi had said that Buffa, a secular priest from Ovada in northern Italy, "needed a change more for his soul than for his body."[52]

Ambrosi had also complained to Barnabò on 25 July 1857 about his vice prefect, a Franciscan named Father Girolamo Mangieri from Sant'Arsenio, Italy. This priest was very

---

50. PF: SC Cina vol. 16 (1855–56), f. 1100rv.

51. PF: LDB vol. 348 (1857), f. 537rv.

52. PF: SC Cina vol. 17 (1857–58), f. 495rv, Ambrosi to Barnabò, 15 October 1857; PF: SC Cina vol. 17 (1857–58), f. 468v, Ambrosi to Barnabò, 25 July 1857.

sensitive, did not like being dependent upon Ambrosi, and was eager to take up work again in a Franciscan mission. Ambrosi was prepared to release him because, as he said, "making someone stay in a mission who does not like to, and who besides accomplishes nothing or very little, does not seem proper to me."[53]

Barnabò wrote back that oversensitive Mangieri should be released, just as Ambrosi had wished, but not immediately. Mangieri had been named vice prefect precisely so that Procurator Ambrosi could be relieved of most of the responsibilities flowing from his additional office as prefect apostolic of Hong Kong Island. Mangieri therefore was to remain in office, Barnabò said, "at least until the Prefecture could be provided with the necessary personnel."[54]

Enclosed with Barnabò's letter for Ambrosi was one of the same date (19 September 1857) for Mangieri, which officially addressed him as "Vice Prefect of the Mission of Hong Kong." It also restored to Mangieri "the government of this mission so very dear to the Sacred Congregation" and gave him all of Ambrosi's faculties for the spiritual development of Hong Kong. Nevertheless Barnabò assured Mangieri that in time he would be freed from office, as he himself had requested.[55]

It was coincidental that, ten days before Barnabò wrote his two important letters of 19 September 1857 to Ambrosi and Mangieri, Reina in Labuan on 9 September had written an equally important letter to director Marinoni in Milan. In it Reina described the "four difficulties" that were blocking the realization of Cuarterón's plan for getting him and his missionaries to Melanesia. This letter reached Marinoni within two months, and on 9 November, following Reina's suggestion, he forwarded a copy of it to Rome, sending it to his agent Burrueco. In it Reina had suggested that it might be better for him and his missionaries to go to Ponape in the Caroline Islands of Micronesia than to Dorei in Melanesia.[56] Originally Supriès had suggested that their Oceania mission ought to start in Ponape.

Burrueco as Marinoni's agent carefully read Reina's letter. On learning of the "four difficulties" blocking the realization of Cuarterón's plan for reinstating the Milan missionaries in Melanesia, and on seeing Reina's suggestion that he and his missionaries be sent to Ponape in Micronesia instead, Burrueco approached Barnabò with a proposal of his own. Since all of Rome's requests for personnel to be sent directly from the Milan seminary to Hong Kong had been fruitless, Burrueco urged Barnabò simply to transfer the Melanesia

---

53. Ibid., f. 468rv.

54. PF: LDB vol. 348 (1857), f. 537rv, Barnabò to Ambrosi, 19 September 1857.

55. Ibid., f. 538v–539r, Barnabò to Mangieri, 19 September 1857.

56. Scurati in PIME: AME 35-01, *Memorie dell'Istituto*, 435–36, when presenting the content of the 9 November 1857 letter of Marinoni to Burrueco, does not say that the letter of Reina being forwarded to Burrueco was that of 9 September 1857 as found in PIME: AME 11:335–38. But comparing the extracts given by Scurati with the actual letter of Reina of 9 September 1857 to Marinoni shows that this is the letter in question. For more details on the "four difficulties" see chap. 18, pp. 350–52.

missionaries of the Milan seminary to Hong Kong. Remembering that Cardinal Prefect Fransoni already in 1854 had suggested that the seminary's unsuccessful Melanesia missionaries might well be sent to Hong Kong, Barnabò accepted Burrueco's proposal and at once began making plans for the transfer.

For seven years and four months, at times patiently and at other times impatiently, Barnabò had been waiting for the Milan Foreign Mission Seminary to send two or three priests to Hong Kong, but this never happened. Even now Barnabò decided not to order the seminary to send personnel there. Rather he asked Burrueco diplomatically to urge and persuade Marinoni to send his surviving Melanesia missionaries to Hong Kong.

Burrueco therefore informed Marinoni on 9 December 1857 that Rome wanted to transfer the remnant of his Melanesia missionaries to Hong Kong.[57] Only a small staff of four or five would be needed, he said, and costs would be minimal. He also stressed the importance of this Hong Kong assignment, because great prestige would follow from being entrusted with managing Propaganda's procure located there. And since Hong Kong was "connected with the name of a primary mission," namely China, public esteem for the Milan Mission Seminary was bound to increase. Burrueco told Marinoni that he had "urged the Sacred Congregation to send there immediately two or three" of his missionaries.[58]

As for Prefect Apostolic Reina, director Marinoni knew that he would readily accept an appointment to Hong Kong, because he had said so when writing from Manila in October 1856. Raimondi, too, writing from Manila in the following month, had expressed his readiness to go wherever Propaganda might wish to send him.[59]

Marinoni, however, seeking advice on accepting the mission, hurried off a letter to his good friend Bishop Besi traveling in northern Italy. Besi was well acquainted with Hong Kong, having visited there while serving in China as a vicar apostolic. In fact, the late Cardinal Fransoni in 1850 had considered Besi the most suitable provisory candidate for the offices of prefect and procurator in Hong Kong, and in 1853 at Marinoni's request Besi had personally discussed with Fransoni one of the candidates proposed by Marinoni for the office of procurator.[60]

Marinoni's letter reached Besi in Bologna just as he was boarding a carriage taking him south to Florence. "During the journey I thought much of the affair about which you requested counsel from me," Besi replied. "After considering it from all sides, I can see nothing but the greater glory of God in your acceptance of the Hong Kong Prefecture that is being offered to you. . . . But keep in mind that you will need personnel endowed with the *greatest zeal*, with much knowledge and with very much—note that I say very much—

---

57. In PIME: AME 35-01, *Memorie dell'Istituto*, 471, Scurati says that the Sacred Congregation "had in mind the remnant of the Oceania Mission . . ."

58. Ibid., 436, 470, Burrueco to Marinoni, 9 December 1857. This is Scurati's summary of Burrueco's important letter; the original cannot be found.

59. See chap. 17, p. 336.

60. For more details on Besi, see this chapter, p. 370.

prudence." He reminded Marinoni that "the Portuguese are there, as well as the French Lazzarists [called also Vincentians] and those from the Paris Foreign Mission Seminary.... These people are all *touchy* and *exacting*."

Besi's reply was written on 20 December in Florence. "Tomorrow," he said, "I leave for Rome. I shall wait for your letter and your orders there."[61]

Burrueco, who was Marinoni's official procurator in Rome, soon became aware that information was being channeled to Cardinal Barnabò about which he knew nothing. He called this to Marinoni's attention on 9 December and again on 23 December, stating that all transactions were to be channeled to Propaganda only through him, because he was the seminary's "faithful representative." Although in office only seventeen months, he said that he was prepared to resign, if necessary.[62]

About this time Cardinal Prefect Barnabò received a letter from Bishop Pompallier, administrator apostolic of the Auckland diocese in New Zealand, dated 2 September 1857. Enclosed was a second letter dated 7 September in which Pompallier requested director Marinoni to send him two priests immediately and three more later. The bishop asked Barnabò to support his request. The cardinal wrote back on 29 December assuring Pompallier that he was indeed forwarding the enclosed letter to Marinoni, "even though there is hardly any hope of a happy outcome for your request, since this institute is still in an adolescent stage."[63] Having waited so long to receive a few missionaries for Hong Kong, Barnabò now was not about to encourage Marinoni to send his limited personnel to New Zealand.

By Saturday, 9 January 1858, Cardinal Prefect Barnabò's plan for Hong Kong was ready for action. He addressed Ambrosi formally as prefect apostolic of Hong Kong and said:

> The information that I am about to give you will surely not be displeasing to you, since I am now perhaps able to satisfy your repeated requests for launching a well planned and durable arrangement for your Prefecture Apostolic and also for giving you help in your office as Procurator.
> Having in fact continued taking the steps already known to Your Reverence for achieving this purpose, it was suggested to me that we assign for this purpose those missionaries of Milan, who earlier were charged with caring for the Oceania Mission of Melanesia and Micronesia. The insuperable difficulties which they have encountered there have unfortunately obliged them to withdraw from that place and they are now with the Reverend Don Carlos Cuarterón, Prefect Apostolic of Labuan, trying to launch their enterprise anew with his guidance and assistance.

---

61. PIME: AME 27:13–14, Besi to Marinoni, 20 December 1857. Scurati gives the date of this letter incorrectly as 10 December in PIME: AME 35-01, *Memorie dell'Istituto*, 436. Marinoni's subsequent letter with orders for Besi has not been found.

62. PIME: AME 35-01 Scurati, *Memorie dell'Istituto*, 436–37.

63. PF: LDB vol. 348 (1857), f. 733v, 735rv, Barnabò to Pompallier, 29 December 1857. See chap. 16, p. 319. See also PIME: AME 28:755–57, Pompallier to Marinoni, 7 September 1857, a three-page letter.

But in view of reports given by the above-mentioned Cuarterón, there does not appear to be any hope for a better outcome at present. I have therefore willingly accepted the proposal [referred to above] and I have already issued the necessary directives for the missionaries in question to be sent and escorted by Cuarterón to Hong Kong instead, so that they can there provide you with their services. I also informed them of my having given Your Reverence similar information immediately. . . . The missionaries referred to above are the Reverend Don Paolo Reina, who headed the said Mission of Melanesia and Micronesia with the rank of Prefect Apostolic. With him are some other assistants and some catechists. It is therefore the wish of Propaganda that Your Reverence for the present should avail yourself of the services of the said Reverend Reina. He should also learn the English language so that you could later entrust to him the office of Vice Prefect and of being your assistant in conducting affairs of the Procure. This would take place as soon as you find him suitable for the above-mentioned tasks and capable of performing them.

Similarly the work of his other companions will help provide for the needs of the mission, since one of them can learn the Portuguese language and one of the catechists can serve in the hospitals or in the schools, etc. Then when you notice that with their help the mission has been sufficiently provided for and organized, Father Mangieri and the Reverend Buffa will be recalled.

Furthermore, whenever reinforcements or new priests are needed for future stages of development, they can easily be supplied by the Seminary of Milan. In this way the stability of the mission and its desired progress will be provided for. In order to hasten the arrival of the above-mentioned missionaries and to guarantee their arrival—just in case Propaganda's letter [to Cuarterón] might get lost or delayed—it would be helpful if Your Reverence in my name were to send to the Reverend Don Carlos Cuarterón at the Island of Labuan your own invitation and expression of concern. . . .[64]

On the following day, Sunday, 10 January 1858, Burrueco as instructed by Barnabò sent Cuarterón at Labuan word that he was to take Reina and his missionaries to Hong Kong.[65] But the letter would not reach Labuan in time because Cuarterón had left with the Melanesia missionaries for Singapore and Dorei on 25 February.

More important was Burrueco's earlier letter of Saturday, 2 January 1858, to Marinoni informing him of Rome's determination on who the leader of the group should be. "Propaganda's choice," Burrueco said,

still favors the person of Father Reina. This outstanding priest can now go to the mission in question in the capacity of Vice Prefect and Vice Procurator. There he will receive his instructions and will acquire the necessary knowledge in order afterwards to become, as is proper, the Prefect and Procurator. Your most illustrious Reverence

---

64. PF: LDB vol. 349 (1858), f. 12v–14r, Barnabò to Ambrosi, 9 January 1858.

65. PIME: AME 35-01 Scurati, *Memorie dell'Istituto*, 438, Burrueco to Cuarterón, 10 January 1858. The general contents of this letter were learned from the letter of Barnabò to Ambrosi of the previous day. See this chapter, n. 64 above.

will write to Reina at once that he should go to this new destination. And you should also send him for his journey the subsidies which Your Reverence has obtained from the Association for the Propagation of the Faith in Lyon.

These subsidies had earlier been earmarked for the Melanesia-Micronesia mission.

Burrueco added that Propaganda would "inform Father Ambrosi to expect the arrival of these missionaries." Once the Hong Kong project began developing, he said, the Milan Mission Seminary "will have a fixed point of operations for relaunching the Mission of Melanesia and Micronesia at whatever spot it considers most opportune. The Milan missionaries, now scattered in diverse missions, will then be able to come together" in Hong Kong. Burrueco urged Marinoni "to accept the project just mentioned with the certainty that it will keep alive the Institute and will be the pride and glory of the Milan missionaries." He added that Father Ambrosoli, left behind by Reina to assist Polding in Sydney, would be allowed "to remain (but always in a provisory capacity) where he is."[66]

Barnabò wrote personally to Reina on 29 January 1858, suggesting that he might already have heard from Marinoni in Milan or from Ambrosi in Hong Kong of Rome's decision in his regard. However, in order to remove all doubts, he said, "I give you official word of the decisions taken not long ago by Propaganda regarding yourself and your collaborators." Propaganda "has pondered all the circumstances and difficulties which at the moment are blocking the project of resuming with some happy success the evangelical ministry in the abandoned regions of Melanesia and Micronesia. And this is happening in spite of all the cooperation given by the excellent Prefect Apostolic of Labuan."

As a result Propaganda "has decided to use your work and that of your companions for another mission, but with the thought that it would still be possible for you in your new position to give a helping hand to the enterprise in the areas of Oceania just mentioned. It was therefore decided that Your Reverence and your collaborators should go to Hong Kong in order to render your services to this important Prefecture Apostolic, which Propaganda has always wanted reserved immediately to itself."

Particular instructions had already been given to Prefect Apostolic Ambrosi of Hong Kong, Barnabò said, regarding Reina's becoming acquainted with the skills needed for fulfilling the responsibilities and functions in both the mission and the procure. Barnabò continued:

> Then later if the need arises, and supposing that you are able adequately to fulfill both tasks, Propaganda will be able in the future to govern that same Prefecture and also assure good progress for its Procure with the exclusive help of missionaries from the Milan Seminary, as it has planned. Furthermore Your Reverence will discover in Hong Kong how easy it will be, by taking advantage of communications and commercial contacts found in that place, to find better ways for reestablishing the Prefecture Apostolic and Mission in Melanesia and Micronesia. You will also send

---

66. PIME: AME 35-01 Scurati, *Memorie dell'Istituto*, 437, 471–72. For details on Ambrosoli's extended stay granted on 10 September 1857, see chap. 18, pp. 348–49.

some well-trained missionaries to the most favorable and safest place there, after having arranged the necessary contacts and guarantees for their desired success.

Now hurry off to Hong Kong with your companions and let yourself be directed by the above-mentioned Don Luigi Ambrosi for the purpose which we have in mind. In order to prevent oversensitiveness in the missionaries, whom you will find assigned there now in a provisory manner, you should keep our plan confidential, conducting yourself toward them in the most prudent way. I shall wait to hear from you after you have reached your new destination. Meanwhile I beg God to grant you every good gift.[67]

This letter from Barnabò with precise instructions and information for Reina was sent unsealed by Burrueco to director Marinoni. He was to read it, seal it, and forward it to Reina.[68]

Marinoni should have noticed that Burrueco's letter to him was substantially different from Barnabò's letter to Reina. Burrueco's letter said that Reina "can now go" to Hong Kong "in the capacity of Vice Prefect and Vice Procurator." Barnabò's letter said not a word about Reina's being vice prefect or vice procurator, and Reina was addressed by Barnabò simply as "Revdo. Sig. Don Paolo Reina," like a common priest. He was not addressed as vice procurator or vice prefect of Hong Kong, and not even as prefect apostolic of Melanesia and Micronesia. In the eyes of Barnabò he was simply an ordinary priest being given a new assignment. Did Burrueco make a mistake? It seems so. If not, then Marinoni must have misinterpreted what Burrueco said. Barnabò, not Burrueco, was the one in authority.

On 30 January 1858, the day after writing to Reina, Cardinal Barnabò sent a second letter to Prefect Apostolic Ambrosi. First he called attention to the astonishing speed of Ambrosi's letter of 28 November 1857 from Hong Kong, which had reached Rome "about 14 January, therefore in about 46 days."

Ambrosi's news was that Mangieri had received his appointment from Barnabò as vice prefect of Hong Kong, but had requested again to be relieved of that office. Barnabò insisted, however, that Mangieri was to remain in office as vice prefect until the Milan missionaries "and especially the Reverend Don Paolo Reina will be in a position according to the judgment of Your Reverence to be designated Vice Prefect. At that time Father Mangieri will be given permission to return to his province, as he has so often requested." Buffa, however, could already be sent back to Italy.[69]

Meanwhile Bishop Besi had been following developments closely. "I am very happy that your seminary has accepted the Prefecture of Hong Kong," he wrote Marinoni from Rome on 9 February 1858. "It is a very important post in every respect and is the only

---

67. PIME: AME 1:195–96, Barnabò to Reina, 29 January 1858. Tragella in *Missioni estere*, 1:249 n. 64, gives the month for this letter incorrectly as November.

68. PIME: AME 35-01 Scurati, *Memorie dell'Istituto*, 438, 472.

69. PF: LDB vol. 349 (1858), f. 55v–56v, Barnabò to Ambrosi, 30 January 1858. Curiously enough Barnabò did not include in this same volume of letters in Propaganda's archives a copy of his letter of the previous day to Reina, perhaps because Reina no longer held any office. For the source of Reina's letter, see n. 67 above.

link joining Europe to China. That mission will grow to gigantic proportions if the Anglo-French armada defeats the Chinese, which is more than likely. In fact, it is certain! . . . If ever you or your seminary are in need of something from those in Rome, write to me about it with the liberty of a friend. Rest assured that you will be doing me a favor. And know that I in turn shall serve you with concern. . . ."[70]

Besi wrote again near the end of that month assuring Marinoni that he had taken care of the problems concerning his two priests in Colombia. They had been accused of insubordination toward Father Juan Bautista Aragón, a Spaniard and member of the Order of Discalced Carmelites (O.C.D.), whom Pope Pius IX had named their immediate superior. Referring to Burrueco's manner of handling this case, Besi said: "If I may speak to you frankly, I am displeased . . . that he is your Procurator." Besi mentioned that he had heard "the great news" about Bishop Ramazzotti of Pavia being named patriarch of Venice by Pope Pius IX.[71]

Burrueco's suspicions were therefore correct about Marinoni using someone else as an intermediary with Propaganda. He had also learned that the "someone else" was Besi. Burrueco therefore on 20 March 1858 told Marinoni that he was resigning as procurator in Rome for the Foreign Mission Seminary of Milan, that he was informing the pope of this, and that Marinoni should indicate for the pope who the new procurator would be. Marinoni wrote back on 19 April defending himself and begging Burrueco not to become an adversary of the Milan Mission Seminary. At the same time he thanked Burrueco for his past services. Then on 15 May, Marinoni expressed his regrets to Cardinal Barnabò over Burrueco's resignation.[72]

Meanwhile Procurator Ambrosi had received authorization from Rome to open a subsidiary procure in Shanghai as he himself had proposed. But not yet having learned of Reina's transfer to Hong Kong, Ambrosi wrote to Barnabò on 27 February 1858 stating that he urgently needed an assistant for the Hong Kong Procure and another for the Shanghai Procure.[73] As early as 9 May 1856 he had told Barnabò that the one chosen for Shanghai ought to be a secular priest, since a secular would be "more impartial than someone belonging to one or other of the two orders" governing the missions in that area. The candidate also "ought to be provided with a good dose of patience and shrewdness and with the capacity and disposition for learning the necessary languages, which are no less than English, French, Spanish, and a bit of Chinese, not to mention Italian and Latin. Finding

---

70. PIME: AME 27:16.

71. Ibid., 23, Besi to Marinoni, 26 February 1858. See also ibid., 1:200, Barnabò to Marinoni, 10 June 1858.

72. See PIME: AME 35-01 Scurati, *Memorie dell'Istituto*, 438, 441.

73. Ambrosi's 27 February 1858 letter was not found. For information from it see PF: SC Cina vol. 17 (1857–58), f. 765v, Ambrosi to Barnabò, 14 March 1858.

a priest there [in Italy] equipped with these languages certainly is not at all easy," Ambrosi said. "But if he should know at least French, he could manage."[74]

Since Cuarterón had kept his funds at the procure in Hong Kong for over ten years, he had become well acquainted with Ambrosi. It was therefore natural for him to inform Ambrosi on 6 March 1858 of his arriving in Singapore that day. He sent along greetings from the "missionary priests" aboard, but he did not say who they were or where they were going.[75]

Barnabò's letter to Ambrosi of 9 January 1858 with the news that Milan missionaries were being transferred from "the Oceania Mission of Melanesia and Micronesia" to Hong Kong, reached Ambrosi on 14 March. That same day he replied to Barnabò, sending his "infinite thanks" for "the real concern which you are displaying for this Prefecture Apostolic by sending us help now in the person of Father Reina and his companions, who I hope will turn out excellently. I must say, however, that there are only two priests and one catechist all told, a very insufficient number for our needs." Ambrosi continued, "As your Eminence said, I may employ Father Reina in such a way that afterwards I can entrust to him, if he proves suitable, the office of Vice Prefect. But entrusting to him in addition the role of being my collaborator in conducting affairs of the procure, is not at all possible, no matter what my predecessor may have written, said or repeated about it." Working for the procure was a full-time job, Ambrosi insisted, one altogether incompatible with being vice prefect of Hong Kong. In fact there was so much work in the procure, that in spite of all his goodwill the procure was very much in disorder. Added to this was a great tiredness and a strange heaviness in his head that bothered him constantly. But a good and faithful Chinese layman named Joseph Soliben was assisting him by copying all the documents in four different languages and he was doing this well.[76]

Cuarterón again wrote to Ambrosi on 10 March 1858, repeating that he had arrived in Singapore on 6 March en route to New Guinea. But then the vessel *Valigia di Europa* arrived in Singapore on 7 March with a letter for Reina from his superior in Milan with instructions for him "to transfer to Hong Kong in the capacity of Vice Prefect and Vice Procurator."

Ambrosi passed on this information to Cardinal Barnabò on 30 March with these comments: "It is therefore useless for Your Eminence to have recommended in your letter to me of 9 January that I must arrange matters in such a way that the missionaries of Milan will not cause the others to be oversensitive, and that I should also keep confidential the purpose of their mission." Ambrosi now had to find "some expedient . . . so that blood will not rush too quickly to the head of Father Girolamo [Mangieri]." Since this priest had received his reappointment as vice prefect of Hong Kong from Barnabò only four months

---

74. Ibid., vol. 16 (1855–56), f. 749rv, 763r, 765r, Ambrosi to Barnabò, 9 May 1856. The folios of this letter are scattered as indicated.

75. PIME: AME 29:751. The letter was sent to Hong Kong via the steamer *Cádiz*.

76. PF: SC Cina vol. 17 (1857–58), f. 765rv, Ambrosi to Barnabò, 14 March 1858.

earlier, Ambrosi knew that he would not appreciate learning that a second vice prefect, namely Reina, was due to arrive shortly.

"Letting missionaries know in advance more or less what the scope of their mission in a particular place will be," Ambrosi said, "has never produced good results." He recalled two such cases for Barnabò in which the candidates for office had "failed in their posts and had to return to Europe."[77]

The French commander of the steam-powered warship *Catinat* in Singapore, scheduled to leave for Hong Kong on 29 or 30 March, granted passage to Reina, but not to the rest of his group. Via the steamer *Aden*, leaving at once for Hong Kong, Cuarterón sent word to Ambrosi that Reina would be arriving aboard the *Catinat* within a few days.[78]

Reina boarded the *Catinat* on 31 March 1858. His letter of introduction from Cuarterón addressed that day to Ambrosi identified the bearer as "Paolo Reina, Prefect Apostolic of Melanesia and Micronesia..., whom I was conducting in the brigantine *Pacifico* to the northwest coast of New Guinea for establishing his mission there. But here [in Singapore] he received orders from his Superior... regarding a decision taken... in Rome that he go to Hong Kong in the capacity of Vice Prefect and Vice Procurator. He is sailing to Hong Kong today aboard the French steamer of war, *Catinat*, in order thus to comply with the mandate of his Superior. He places himself entirely at the service and disposition of Your Reverence...."[79] According to the plan of Cardinal Prefect Barnabò, Hong Kong was to become the central mission of the Milan Foreign Mission Seminary. From here Reina was expected to send a new group of missionaries to evangelize Melanesia and Micronesia. As Reina sailed out of Singapore, however, he had not yet received the 29 January 1858 letter from Cardinal Prefect Barnabò containing these plans.

---

77. Ibid., f. 787v, Ambrosi to Barnabò, 30 March 1858. Cuarterón's letter of 10 March 1858 was not found, but its contents are given in this Ambrosi letter of 30 March to Barnabò.

78. PIME: AME 29:753, Cuarterón to Ambrosi, 26 March 1858.

79. Ibid., 755. Here Cuarterón calls the warship *Catinac*; on 26 March he calls it *Cartinac* (see n. 78); and Marinoni writing to Barnabò on 15 May 1858 calls it *Catinet* (see PIME: AME 6:166). The warship was named after Nicolas de Catinat (1637–1712), field marshal of France. Tragella in *Missioni estere*, 1:252, incorrectly says that Cuarterón took Reina and Raimondi to Hong Kong. Rooney repeats this in *Khabar Gembira*, 21.

21

Barnabò Suppresses the Melanesia-Micronesia Mission
11 December 1858

PREFECT APOSTOLIC AMBROSI WAS AT THE PIER WAITING FOR REINA WHEN HE ARRIVED in Hong Kong on 10 April 1858. The letter of introduction handed by Reina to Ambrosi had been written by Cuarterón, who presented Reina as prefect apostolic of Melanesia and Micronesia, vice prefect of Hong Kong, and vice procurator for the Missions of China.[1] Reina was bound for trouble, however, because in the eyes of Cardinal Prefect Barnabò, he held none of these titles.

That evening Reina wrote to director Marinoni in Milan: "Here I am in my mission and in my house. May the Lord be blessed!" He had been treated very well aboard the French warship, *Catinat*, he said. "As soon as its anchor had dropped, the Reverend Prefect Apostolic Ambrosi came aboard to get me" and "cautioned me not to tell Father Girolamo Mangieri that I was Vice Prefect and Vice Procurator."[2] Actually Mangieri, appointed in virtue of an official document by Cardinal Prefect Barnabò, was the vice prefect of Hong Kong at this time. Ambrosi had received official instructions from Barnabò that Reina was to be named vice prefect after he had been trained and found suitable for office. Barnabò would then remove Mangieri from office.[3]

Ambrosi that first day read to Reina part of a letter from Barnabò indicating why the Milan missionaries had been transferred from Melanesia to Hong Kong. As Reina told Marinoni, Rome had arrived at this decision "because of difficulties with founding the New Guinea Mission, submitted to it by Don Carlos Cuarterón. I did not know that Don

---

1. For the contents of this letter see chap. 20, pp. 382–83.
2. PIME: AME 16:499, Reina to Marinoni, 10 April 1858.
3. See chap. 20, pp. 379–85 passim. See also Mangieri's business letter of 13 April 1858 in PF: SC Cina vol. 17 (1857–58), f. 879r, where he adds under his name the title "Vice Prefect Apostolic," thus leaving no doubt as to who was holder of that office.

Carlos had written in this way," Reina said, "and I am pleased that everything has been done independently of me."[4]

Cuarterón had also been told by Ambrosi why Barnabò had transferred the Milan missionaries to Hong Kong. "In your letter to me," Cuarterón replied, "you write that what prompted Propaganda to send the missionaries to Hong Kong was the number of difficulties that I had expressed about opening a mission in New Guinea at this time. But I mentioned no difficulties to Propaganda . . . , because I know and am thoroughly convinced that in Papuasia one can open and establish missions as good as, or even better than, in Borneo."[5]

It is true, Cuarterón did not present difficulties directly to Barnabò. But he did present them directly to Reina, who sent them to Marinoni on 9 September 1857. Marinoni in turn sent them to Burrueco, who presented them to Barnabò.[6] So Cuarterón had presented the difficulties to Barnabò indirectly. And because of Reina's role in this matter, he could not correctly say that "everything has been done independently of me."

Two days after Reina's arrival in Hong Kong, Ambrosi thanked director Marinoni "for your goodness in wanting to send your missionaries to help us in this Prefecture Apostolic." He also requested additional personnel, specifically Fathers Carlo Salerio and Angelo Ambrosoli, and expressed the hope that with Marinoni's collaboration "we shall finally get this Prefecture organized."[7]

Ambrosi also wrote to Cardinal Prefect Barnabò that same day, requesting that Mangieri be removed from office as vice prefect of Hong Kong. Meeting Reina, he said, had filled him with "favorable expectations," and he requested the cardinal to assist him in obtaining additional personnel from Marinoni.[8]

When Father Raimondi and Catechist Tacchini arrived with Puarer in Hong Kong on 15 May 1858, Vice Prefect Mangieri was in charge of all missionary work. He made Raimondi superior of the seminary and of its seven Chinese candidates for the priesthood. He was also to be their professor and spiritual director and was to study Chinese. The mission already had two Chinese priests, one of whom had been educated in Rome. Among the seventy thousand Chinese within the boundaries of the Hong Kong prefecture, only five hundred were Catholic. Of these only a small number had become Catholics in Hong Kong

---

4. PIME: AME 16:499-500, Reina to Marinoni, 10 April 1858. For p. 3 of this letter see PIME: AME 11:389. On Reina presenting his own doubts to Cuarterón about Dorei, see chap. 18, p. 352.

5. PIME: AME 29:757-59, Cuarterón to Ambrosi, 21 April 1858.

6. See chap. 18, p. 350, and chap. 20, pp. 380-81. See also PIME: AME 11:338, Reina to Marinoni, 9 September 1857; PIME: AME 11:341-42, Reina to Marinoni, 30 September 1857.

7. PIME: AME 16:399, Ambrosi to Marinoni, 12 April 1858.

8. Ambrosi's letter of that day, 12 April 1858, to Barnabò was not found, but its contents are indicated in PF: LDB vol. 349 (1858), f. 423v-424r, Barnabò to Ambrosi, 26 June 1858.

itself; the others had emigrated from various provinces of China.[9] Recently Mangieri had opened Saint Francis Hospital, and he named Tacchini its superintendent. Puarer, who was manifesting good conduct, was assigned to some menial tasks there.[10] The baggage of Raimondi and Tacchini was opened on their arrival, and Prefect Apostolic Ambrosi "disposed of those things which could be of use to this mission," Reina told Marinoni. "I said nothing because Rome had told me to place myself completely under his orders."[11] After observing Raimondi and Tacchini at work for one week and Reina for five weeks, Ambrosi wrote to Barnabò: "I give God infinite thanks for sending me personnel like this."[12]

Meanwhile Cuarterón, who had remained in Singapore, kept wondering whether he was to blame for Rome's transferring the missionaries from Melanesia to Hong Kong. As he told Ambrosi, "The only thing that I wrote to the Sacred Congregation was that my task and responsibilities would come to an end as soon as I had reestablished their mission in a good and safe place. . . ." From then on it would be up to Rome and Milan "to provide for and to maintain the new mission. . . ." Cuarterón thought that "this did not please them."[13] He was wrong about this, however, because the financial arrangement was no factor in prompting Rome to transfer Reina and his missionaries from Melanesia to Hong Kong. Like so many others, Cuarterón was unaware that Rome ever since 1850 had been requesting missionaries for Hong Kong from the Lombardy Mission Seminary.[14]

Still seeking an answer for Rome's sudden and inexplicable change in policy on Melanesia, Cuarterón came closer to the mark when he told Ambrosi: "I suppose that Propaganda has changed its mind . . . because of the lack of missionaries in China. But no matter what the cause may be, let us give thanks to God for everything and conform ourselves to his most holy will, since he always arranges matters for his greater honor and glory." Cuarterón assured Ambrosi that "in the missionary priest Father Timoleone [Raimondi] you will find a robust man who has become accustomed to missionary work

---

9. PIME: AME 16:509, Reina to Marinoni, 20 May 1858; PIME: AME 16:513, 515, Reina to Marinoni, 21 July 1858. See n. 12, below, on the arrival date.

10. PIME: AME 16:515, Reina to Marinoni, 21 July 1858; PIME: AME 35-01 Scurati, *Memorie dell'Istituto*, 497.

11. PIME: AME 16:509, Reina to Marinoni, 20 May 1858.

12. PF: SC Cina vol. 17 (1857–58), f. 884r, Ambrosi to Barnabò, 22 May 1858. Since Ambrosi says in this letter of 22 May that Raimondi and Tacchini had arrived "exactly one week ago," their arrival date must have been 15 May.

13. Ibid., 29:757–59, Cuarterón to Ambrosi, 21 April 1858.

14. See the Spanish version of the financial agreement reached by Fransoni, Barnabò, and Cuarterón in PIME: AME 11:342, Reina to Marinoni, 30 September 1857. Tragella in *Missioni estere*, 1:250, misled by Cuarterón's false assumption mentioned in his 21 April letter to Ambrosi (see n. 13, above), leads readers to believe that there was a financial misunderstanding between Cuarterón and Rome.

and is well experienced in it. He will provide you with a good opportunity for opening the Formosa [now Taiwan] Mission, that you said you are already planning."[15]

On being reminded by Cuarterón, Ambrosi wrote to Cardinal Barnabò on 22 May 1858, saying that the island of Formosa, or at least the western part of it, was a good location for a mission. It was two or three days by ship from Hong Kong, he said, and the Foreign Mission Seminary of Milan could easily send some priests there. "The local people are already in contact with foreigners from every nation, to whom they sell their abundant rice. . . . So it would be good if Your Eminence were to interest the Superior at Milan in sending a rather large number of priests to establish a kind of route from Hong Kong to Formosa and, if possible, also to Shanghai.

"But before everything else," Ambrosi insisted, "let us think about this Prefecture of Hong Kong. Then, if the matter regarding Shanghai does not become practical soon, we can think about Formosa. I am confident that greater results will be obtained there—and also more quickly—than in New Guinea or perhaps even in British India."[16] But Rome did not react to Ambrosi's proposal. Since he had been clamoring so long for personnel for Hong Kong, Barnabò saw little point in sending to Formosa or to Shanghai the few priests now available for Hong Kong.

Reina by this time had received his official transfer of 29 January 1858 from Barnabò[17] and replied on 2 May 1858. "I have had the honor of receiving your venerable letter of 29 January of this year," he said, "in which Your Very Reverend Eminence kindly announces to me the official order to go to Hong Kong with my companions and to give our services to that important Prefecture Apostolic. I am to occupy myself with performing tasks both of the mission and of the procure, always letting myself be directed by the Most Reverend Prefect, Father Luigi Ambrosi, and not provoking the sensibilities of the other missionaries located there." He added that Ambrosi "has placed me under the orders of Father Girolomo Mangieri and now, in addition to studying Portuguese, I am busy ministering especially to the English in the mission."

Barnabò had asked Reina to look into the possibilities of contacting Melanesia and Micronesia from Hong Kong and had suggested that in Hong Kong he should be able "to find better ways for reestablishing the Prefecture Apostolic and Mission" in Melanesia and Micronesia. Reina was also to send some well-trained missionaries "to the most favorable and safest place there." But Reina knew of no such place. To his knowledge no other ships but whaling vessels frequented the islands in question, and consequently a direct

---

15. PIME: AME 29:757–59, Cuarterón to Ambrosi, 21 April 1858.

16. PF: SC Cina vol. 17 (1857–58), f. 878v, 884r, Ambrosi to Barnabò, 22 May 1858.

17. PIME: AME 1:195–96, Barnabò to Reina, 29 January 1858. See the contents of this letter in chap. 20, pp. 384–85.

and regular contact with Hong Kong did not exist. However, he had learned that "in the Caroline Islands there are American Protestant ministers at Ponape or Ascension Island and at Ualan."

If in spite of this Barnabò still wished to found a new mission in Melanesia, Reina made the following proposal: "Annually small ships go from Sydney to the Solomon Archipelago to engage in commerce for turtle shells." The same was true for other ships which leave Sydney "for Fiji, for the Navigators, for Tahiti, and for other parts of Central and Eastern Oceania. They always stop at the first islands of this archipelago, namely, those called New Georgia." He felt certain that such contacts would continually increase, "since a French colony has been established in New Caledonia and since information about those seas is being gleaned little by little." For this reason New Georgia seemed like "a fitting place to open a mission" in case Rome might wish "to evangelize those places." He added that "Sydney could be the communications point, since it is distant from that archipelago by a voyage of only eight to fifteen days."[18]

In view of Reina's proposal it is unfortunate that he himself did not choose to found a mission station at New Georgia in the Solomon Islands. While en route from Sydney to Woodlark and Rooke islands in 1852, his ship made a stopover at New Georgia, as did his supply ships later. Had he opened a mission there, he would not have been so isolated as in Woodlark and Rooke and could have received supplies from Australia frequently and at lower costs.

Six weeks after Reina mailed this proposal to Cardinal Barnabò, Father Ambrosoli of Sydney informed director Marinoni that Captain Dalmagne had recently left Sydney aboard the *Phantom* "in order to found a commercial establishment for Mr. Joubert in the Solomon Islands."[19] Dalmagne and Joubert were friends of the Catholic mission and could have facilitated a foundation in New Georgia. Cardinal Barnabò sent Reina thanks for his letter of 2 May 1858, which contained "the suggestions for my information that you have provided on reestablishing—when it should please the Lord—the Melanesia and Micronesia Missions. In the future I shall be happy to receive whatever additional news you will be able to provide for me, so that I may profit from it when needed."

By this letter of 7 August 1858 Barnabò made it clear to Reina that his only obligation toward his former missions was to supply Rome with information about them. Since Reina had no jurisdiction whatsoever in Melanesia, Micronesia or Hong Kong, Barnabò addressed him simply as "Missionary Apostolic of Hong Kong." This was his only title.[20] Barnabò's earlier letter to Reina of January had been sent to him through Marinoni; this later one was sent to Prefect Apostolic Ambrosi for reading, sealing, and presenting to

---

18. For the original text see: PF: SC Cina vol. 17 (1857–58), f. 838rv, Reina to Barnabò, 2 May 1858. For a copy, see PIME: AME 16:505f.

19. PIME: AME 11:663, Ambrosoli to Marinoni, 11 June 1858.

20. PF: LDB vol. 349 (1858), f. 603r, Barnabò to Reina, 7 August 1858.

Reina. Thus Ambrosi also received official word of Reina's status. He was simply a missionary priest at work in Hong Kong like Raimondi and the others.[21]

After his arrival in Hong Kong, Reina told Marinoni, "I had wanted to send back to Rome my credentials" for Melanesia and Micronesia. But when Marinoni passed on these words to Barnabò on 6 July 1858, he said that Reina "believed that his original appointment had ceased completely, but this was before he received the official letter from Your Eminence."[22]

"The official letter" referred to by Marinoni was that of 29 January 1858 sent by the cardinal to Marinoni for him to read and then to forward to Reina. Marinoni evidently was misled by this letter because on 27 August 1858 he wrote to the president of the Association for the Propagation of the Faith in Lyon that Reina had been ordered to go to Hong Kong "without however renouncing his office as Prefect Apostolic of Melanesia and Micronesia, of which he shall have care as soon as circumstances permit him . . ."[23] But Reina in the 29 January letter had been asked merely to give "a helping hand to the enterprise," not to be in charge of it.[24]

Meanwhile director Marinoni had received from Singapore Reina's 13 March 1858 letter addressed to Cardinal Prefect Barnabò. It said:

> At a meeting of Propaganda held in August 1851 and presided over by His Eminence Cardinal Fransoni of holy and dear memory, I was asked whether I was ready to go to Hong Kong. Answering in the name of my seminary as well, I said that we placed ourselves completely in the hands of His Most Reverend Eminence and were ready to go wherever the voice of obedience might call us. With these same sentiments I have now received the news communicated to me by my most beloved Superior in Milan on my new destination. . . . Yes, it is the Lord who calls me and I go in His name.[25]

---

21. See ibid., f. 602r, Barnabò to Ambrosi, 7 August 1858. For the previous letter of Barnabò to Reina, see chap. 20, pp. 384–85.

22. See PIME: AME 6:177, Marinoni to Barnabò, 6 July 1858, which contains the extract from Reina's letter.

23. Ibid., 201, Marinoni to the president of the Association for the Propagation of the Faith in Lyon, 27 August 1858. For the itemized budget referred to by this letter of Marinoni, see chap. 18, pp. 357–58. No doubt it was also on the basis of the "official letter" from Barnabò, that Marinoni on 21 May 1858 had written to Paris about Reina "now going to Hong Kong, but without abandoning the care of these poor islands of Oceania." See PIME: AME 6:167, Marinoni to the President of the Association for the Propagation of the Faith in Paris, 21 May 1858.

24. See chap. 20, pp. 384–85. Later Raimondi, when in charge of Hong Kong, would be asked by Rome to send Cuarterón's mission some personnel. But this did not imply that Rome was giving Raimondi any jurisdiction over Cuarterón's mission. Similarly Reina's being asked to "send some well-trained missionaries to the most favorable and safest places" in Melanesia and Micronesia did not mean that he was being given any jurisdiction over the area.

25. PIME: AME 16:491, Reina to Barnabò, 13 March 1858. For other details contained in this letter see chap. 19, p. 366.

Marinoni forwarded this letter of Reina to Barnabò on 15 May 1858, explaining that he had informed Reina "privately of the intentions of Propaganda" as soon as he had been informed of them by Father Burrueco. He did this in order that the news of Reina's transfer might reach him "prior to his imminent departure for New Guinea. The letter, in fact, did reach him on time in Singapore," Marinoni said, "and soon after that he must have received the letter from Your Eminence." Marinoni was full of hope that Reina "will concur with the confidence manifested in him by Propaganda and will open up a beautiful field of labor for our missionaries in the Hong Kong Mission."[26]

Expecting his missions in India as well as this new mission in Hong Kong to absorb all of his available personnel, Marinoni on that same day, 15 May 1858, wrote to Archbishop Polding of Sydney. He was not in a position, he said, to accept his "gracious invitation" to send "three or four or five priests" who "would live together in community, have a parish, and at the same time take turns traveling throughout the diocese giving missions. I can see the beauty of this project, but I would not have the personnel to spare for it. . . ." He suggested that Polding contact "some other congregations" which could fulfill his wish more readily.[27] On the following day, 16 May, Marinoni informed Ambrosoli in Sydney of his negative decision regarding Polding's project. He also requested Ambrosoli to forward his enclosed letter to Polding.[28]

Cardinal Barnabò must have been pleased with the way his plan was evolving for the Milan missionaries to take over from Father Ambrosi the Prefecture Apostolic of Hong Kong and Propaganda's procure office for the Missions of China. Relations between Rome and Milan had finally been healed, it seemed. But then a letter from Ambrosi reached the desk of Barnabò along with two other letters from Marinoni and Reina. The information contained in them disrupted the relations between Rome and Milan once again.

The letter from Ambrosi informed Barnabò that Reina had been instructed by his superior in Milan "to pass over to Hong Kong in the capacity of Vice Prefect and Vice Procurator." This information, Ambrosi said, had been sent to him by Don Carlos Cuarterón on 10 March from Singapore.[29] Barnabò at once sensed that something had gone wrong with his plans, because he had never named Reina to the office of vice prefect of Hong Kong or vice procurator of Propaganda. He replied first to Ambrosi addressing him on 5 June 1858 with his formal titles of procurator and prefect apostolic.

"Having received some word of the departure of Father Reina and his companions from Borneo for Hong Kong," the cardinal said,

---

26. PIME: AME 6:165, Marinoni to Barnabò, 15 May 1858.

27. Ibid., 163, Marinoni to Polding, 15 May 1858. Ambrosoli had sent Polding's proposal to Marinoni on 11 February 1858. For more details on the proposal, see chap. 19, pp. 363–64.

28. Marinoni's letter of 16 May 1858 to Ambrosoli was not found. But see chap. 19, p. 364, n. 17.

29. See PF: SC Cina vol. 17 (1857–58), f. 787v, Ambrosi to Barnabò, 30 March 1858.

and in order to avoid any misunderstanding whatsoever, I repeat the following: It is the plan of the Evangelization Congregation to make use of their work on behalf of the mission in question. And in case you should recognize that Father Reina is a suitable candidate, he could be designated afterwards by Your Reverence as Vice Prefect. You could also engage him as your assistant in the Procure Office.

Nevertheless there is no intention of making a decision in this matter at the present time. The above-mentioned missionaries must therefore consider themselves to be simple missionaries, dependent upon Your Reverence as their Superior in everything and for everything. Then when the time comes and in view of the experience that you will have had with him [Reina], and according to what Your Reverence judges to be the most expeditious way of going about it, the plan for which we are preparing will be carried out.[30]

Barnabò next reacted to the 15 May 1858 letter from Marinoni and to Reina's accompanying letter of 20 March. This 20 March letter was addressed to Marinoni and touched upon very delicate matters concerning administration and conduct in Hong Kong.[31] Rather naively Marinoni had enclosed a copy of it as proof for Barnabò of Reina's readiness to obey all orders received from Rome. The cardinal, however, looked upon Reina's queries as an unwarranted and premature intrusion in internal affairs of the Hong Kong prefecture.

In reply to Marinoni's letter of 15 May, Barnabò wrote on 10 June:

Reina manifests a lively desire to have special instructions from you on the demeanor that he ought to have toward the Reverend Father Ambrosi, Prefect Apostolic of Hong Kong and Procurator of the Sacred Congregation. Besides this I have noticed that you prematurely made known to him the confidential plan of this Sacred Congregation, which had been communicated to you by Father Burrueco. This plan was to be implemented in due time, provided that he first worked satisfactorily in an auxiliary capacity and subsequently succeeded as well in fulfilling the duties of the Prefect and Procurator mentioned above.

Therefore in order to avoid conflicting impressions for the missionary personnel already there, and to clarify what perhaps are ill-conceived ideas in the minds of the priests from Milan mentioned above, let this be the task of Your Reverence: You shall make them aware that for the time being they must not consider themselves anything else but simple collaborators and missionaries, dependent like other missionaries in everything and for everything on the above mentioned Superior [Ambrosi] and on his Vice Prefect [Mangieri]. Meanwhile the Sacred Congregation remains free to make such decisions later which in its prudence it judges to be the most fitting for the good of that same mission.

Barnabò then lashed out at Marinoni: "I cannot believe that the method of education in use at [San] Calocero Seminary tends toward instilling and cultivating in its alumni a

---

30. PF: LDB vol. 349 (1858), f. 376rv, Barnabò to Ambrosi, 5 June 1858.
31. See chap. 19, p. 366, for the delicate matters concerned.

spirit of independence toward all authority. Unfortunately such a spirit is manifesting itself in its alumni."³²

If there was anything that Barnabò demanded from missionaries around the world, it was deference for and submission to those in authority. This insistence flowed from his character and from the military training that he had received as a youth. French occupation forces had chosen him along with thirty-seven other youths from the Italian nobility to spend two and a half years at Napoleon Bonaparte's (1769–1821) military academy in La Flèche, France. Barnabò entered on 12 February 1812, three weeks before his eleventh birthday. He was the only one in his class promoted after thirteen months to the rank of corporal. "I was once a soldier," he used to say, "and I still am a bit of one."³³

Marinoni was grief-stricken for weeks by this harsh letter of 10 June from Barnabò. Father Giacomo Scurati, Marinoni's secretary, called it a "humiliating lecture."³⁴ Frustrated over this new impasse with Cardinal Prefect Barnabò, Marinoni sent a copy of the cardinal's letter to Patriarch Ramazzotti in Venice and requested advice on what to do about it.

Ramazzotti replied through his secretary, Don Federico Salvioni, that neither Marinoni nor his missionary candidates "should be discouraged by it," but instead should obey the wishes of Propaganda in all matters, always and everywhere. "For the rest resign yourselves in silence, accepting these painful tests as a means which God uses to better sanctify the institute, its Superior and its members. Oral or written justifications will serve no purpose at all," he said. "Obedience and suffering are such beautiful virtues, that it is worth the trouble to aspire toward them and to practice them to an heroic degree."³⁵

On 21 July 1858, the day after Salvioni mailed Ramazzotti's comforting words to Marinoni, Reina also wrote to Marinoni. ". . . It seems to me that I must tell you that I am neither Vice Prefect nor Vice Procurator. On this day my Very Reverend Prefect Apostolic read to me part of a letter that he had received from Propaganda. Among other things it contained these words: 'The two priests, whom you will receive, are simple missionaries who must be completely subject to you.' I believe that this letter of Propaganda," Reina continued, "is a reply to one that Prefect Ambrosi wrote to Rome when he learned that I was Vice Procurator and Vice Prefect."

In spite of "Prefect Ambrosi's having very much work as Procurator," Reina said, "he does not give the impression that he wants to have an Assistant." But Reina admitted that

---

32. PIME: AME 1:199–201, Barnabò to Marinoni, 10 June 1858.

33. Metzler, "Präfekten und Sekretäre," 41.

34. PIME: AME 35-01 Scurati, *Memorie dell'Istituto*, 503. Here Scurati, referring to Barnabò's letter of 10 June 1858, mistakenly dates it 16 June, which was the date on which it arrived in Milan. He repeats this error in PIME: AME 35-01 Scurati, *Memorie dell'Istituto*, 441, 499. See dates 10 and 16 June on the original letter in PIME: AME 1:199 and 201.

35. PIME: AME 35-01 Scurati, *Memorie dell'Istituto*, 443, 502, Salvioni to Marinoni, 20 July 1858.

he himself was "completely occupied with the mission" and that Ambrosi was doing the right thing by having him work among the people,

> because the need is truly great. We have 70,000 Chinese and among them there are only 500 Catholics, who—except for a few—were not converted here, but have come from various provinces.
>
> The Chinese priest whom we have here was educated in Rome and is talented, but he is not as zealous as one might wish. We have another Chinese priest who was newly ordained a few weeks ago. He serves as house procurator, since it is very difficult for Europeans to deal with the Chinese, who would even cheat the pope. In the southwest of this island and in the interior there are villages of 5,000 and 8,000 people.

Catechist Tacchini and Puarer from Woodlark were both working in Saint Francis Hospital, he added. "It has been opened just recently by Father Girolamo [Mangieri] against the wishes of Prefect Ambrosi.... Puarer is showing good behavior."[36]

That same day, 21 July, Reina also wrote to his colleague in Milan, Father Ripamonti, procurator at his seminary in Milan. "It is necessary that you get out of your head the many false ideas that you have about me," he said. "I am neither Vice Prefect nor Vice Procurator...." Ripamonti had written that Reina "in time would also become both Prefect and Procurator." Reina answered: "The time is not at all near!"[37]

If Reina had seen Ambrosi's letter to Barnabò of the following day, 22 July 1858, he would have been more cheerful. "With a heart full of joy," Ambrosi wrote, "I have the pleasure of telling Your Eminence that these men, the Reverend Father Reina and his companion, Father Raimondi, work hard and zealously in this small vineyard, which still needs pruning. Consequently there is not a minute left over for them to be able to help me with anything in the Procure.... I believe that we shall work sufficiently well together," either here or elsewhere. Raimondi by this time had been in Hong Kong nearly ten full weeks and Reina, nearly fifteen full weeks. Ambrosi also informed Barnabò that Marinoni was ready to send him two or three additional priests.[38] Unknown to Reina, Ambrosi as early as 12 April 1858 had requested authorization from Barnabò to dismiss Mangieri. Barnabò obliged by return mail, sending Ambrosi the following instructions on 26 June together with a letter for Mangieri. "After sealing it," he said, "you will give it to him as soon as you see that it will be possible for him to leave without causing harm to the mission."[39] By arranging for Mangieri's removal from office, Barnabò was actually preparing the way for Reina to succeed him as vice prefect of Hong Kong.

---

36. PIME: AME 16:513, 515, Reina to Marinoni, 21 July 1858.

37. Ibid., 511, Reina to Ripamonti, 21 July 1858. Tragella in *Missioni estere*, 1:270, calls Reina the "cryptic-vice-prefect" of Hong Kong. However, only his own missionary community gave him the title of vice prefect along with Cuarterón, who had quoted from Marinoni's transcript of a Burrueco letter.

38. PF: SC Cina vol. 17 (1857–58), f. 1010rv, Ambrosi to Barnabò, 22 July 1858.

39. PF: LDB vol. 349 (1858), f. 423v–424r, Barnabò to Ambrosi, 26 June 1858.

Reina completed five full months in Hong Kong on 11 September 1858. That same day Ambrosi informed Barnabò that Mangieri would be leaving Hong Kong on the following day in a happy frame of mind. Mangieri's term of office as vice prefect of Hong Kong had come to an end three weeks earlier on 22 August.[40]

Already on the following day, 23 August, Reina complained to Marinoni that he had not been named to succeed Mangieri as vice prefect of Hong Kong. He also complained that Ambrosi was not using him as vice procurator, but intended instead to prepare one of the new priests coming from Milan for that office.[41]

As early as 30 January 1858, that is, seventy days before Reina arrived in Hong Kong, Barnabò had instructed Ambrosi to release Mangieri from office when Father Reina would be "in a position to be deputized as Vice Prefect . . ."[42] But the cardinal's letter of 5 June to Ambrosi had postponed Reina's appointment indefinitely. And five months later, on 13 November 1858, the cardinal informed Ambrosi that this postponement was to remain in force.[43] Apparently Barnabò was in no rush and wanted concrete proof of Reina's submission to authority before naming him as vice prefect of Hong Kong. Back in Europe it was 6 July 1858 when Marinoni finally summoned up sufficient courage to reply to the 10 June letter of Barnabò. What prompted his action was the arrival of a letter from Reina for Barnabò dated 2 May 1858, which contained new proofs of Reina's submission to authority. Marinoni in a letter of his own said to Barnabò that he had indeed accepted the resignation of Burrueco as his agent in Rome, but only after mature consideration and after receiving counsel from many. As for the training given to his missionary candidates, he had always "insistently" prescribed the spirit of obedience and the spirit of sacrifice. But now he was ready to resign from office, he said, because evidently he did not enjoy "the confidence of Propaganda."[44]

Barnabò's reply of 31 July remained silent about Marinoni's offer to resign. As for the letter enclosed from Reina of 2 May 1858, Barnabò expressed gratitude to Marinoni "for the sentiments that it contains and also for his full and unlimited deference to decisions made by higher authority." Barnabò added that he was sending his reply to Reina through Prefect Apostolic Ambrosi, "to whom I do not doubt he will continue to show himself always dependent, no less than his other companions about whose arrival I have learned . . ."[45]

---

40. PF: SC Cina vol. 17 (1857–58), f. 1080r, Ambrosi to Barnabò, 11 September 1858.

41. PIME: AME 35-01 Scurati, *Memorie dell'Istituto*, 501f.

42. PF: LDB vol. 349 (1858), f. 56r, Barnabò to Ambrosi, 30 January 1858. For more details on this letter, see chap. 20, p. 385.

43. PF: LDB vol. 349 (1858), f. 925v, Barnabò to Ambrosi, 13 November 1858. Barnabò feared that his 5 June letter to Ambrosi had gone astray, but as early as 22 July Ambrosi had informed Barnabò of its arrival. See PF: SC Cina vol. 17 (1857–58), f. 1010r, Ambrosi to Barnabò, 22 July 1858.

44. PIME: AME 6:177, Marinoni to Barnabò, 6 July 1858; PIME: AME 35-01 Scurati, *Memorie dell'Istituto*, 443.

45. PF: LDB vol. 349 (1858), f. 552v–553r, Barnabò to Marinoni, 31 July 1858. For the 7 August 1858

On becoming aware in August of the 10 June 1858 reprimand sent to Director Marinoni by Cardinal Barnabò, Reina tried to console his superior:

> As for the question of your having made known to me my destiny to be Vice Prefect and Vice Procurator, I do not know what to say. I also feel that I am in good faith, like you, and I also understand that it is necessary to accept these adverse incidents with a humble and patient spirit. The Lord will know how to draw good out of these things, if we conduct ourselves in a manner worthy of him and of his example. It does not seem fitting for me to write again to Rome after my letters of 12 April and 2 May. You know that in Rome they do not want words, but deeds. In fact, I can say with a completely good conscience that up to now, insofar as it appears to me, my superiors here are satisfied with both me and Father Timoleone [Raimondi]. I also know for certain that the Very Reverend Prefect Ambrosi has written favorably to Rome regarding us.[46]

Prefect Apostolic Ambrosi informed Cardinal Barnabò on 13 October 1858 that Reina on arriving in Hong Kong had requested "his Superiors to contact Your Eminence in order to learn what should be done with those few funds left over from his previous mission. He is of the opinion, as I am, that he should use them in this mission, which can be called his new mission, especially since the costs for rebuilding the church and later also the parish house will be rather high." Ambrosi added that Reina's superior in Milan was apparently of the same opinion, because he had instructed Reina to have transferred from Sydney "the 500 pounds sterling" left behind there at the Marist procure and to use them here in his new mission.[47]

---

reply to Reina sent by Barnabò through Ambrosi, see PF: LDB vol. 349 (1858), f. 603r. For Barnabò's letter to Ambrosi of the same date see PF: LDB vol. 349 (1858), f. 602r.

46. PIME: AME 35-01 Scurati, *Memorie dell'Istituto*, 501f, Reina to Marinoni, 23 August 1858. The misunderstanding between Barnabò and the Milan missionaries resulted from a discrepancy in the orders initially received from Rome through agent Burrueco under date of 2 January 1858 and those subsequently issued directly by Cardinal Prefect Barnabò. The original orders from Burrueco were understood or interpreted by director Marinoni to say regarding Reina: "This outstanding priest can now go to the [Hong Kong] mission in question in the capacity of Vice Prefect and Vice Procurator." But orders sent by Cardinal Barnabò himself that same month and also on later occasions to Reina, to Marinoni, and to Prefect Apostolic Ambrosi indicated clearly and unequivocally that Reina had not been given either of those two offices, but instead was to be trained for them. No confrontation can be made with Burrueco's original letter of 2 January 1858, because this important document cannot be found in the PIME archives. Nor has a complete copy been found. The author has had to work with partial copies of a copy. Had there been a real discrepancy in Burrueco's text, and not merely a misinterpretation drawn from it, one wonders why this was not pointed out to Barnabò. Were the words of Burrueco perhaps misinterpreted by Marinoni and so transmitted to Reina? For Burrueco's letter of 2 January 1858 to Marinoni, see chap. 20, p. 384. Burrueco was Marinoni's agent in Rome and not an official of Propaganda. He could have erred in transmitting information to Marinoni.

47. PF: SC Cina vol. 17 (1857–58), f. 1116v, 1122r.

Barnabò answered Ambrosi on 11 December 1858 about "the balance of money and items" earlier destined for the Melanesia-Micronesia mission. "Since the time for reactivating the mission in question is not very near," he said, "I approve and agree fully that both the funds and the items should be donated and transferred to your Prefecture. I also authorize Your Paternity to withdraw and make use of the funds and items mentioned above. Inform Father Reina of this decision and also say that I received the page which he sent. Meanwhile I reserve for myself making other provisions in good time for the new needs that will arise when we again take up the project of the Oceania Mission."[48]

Prefect Apostolic Ambrosi then drew up and signed the following official receipt for Reina:

> I, the undersigned Procurator of Propaganda for the Missions of China and Prefect Apostolic of Hong Kong, declare and certify that I have received from the Reverend Paolo Reina the sum of three thousand seven hundred and three *(S 3703) pezze forti, that is, Roman scudi*, which formerly belonged to his previous Mission of Melanesia and Micronesia. According to the instructions and decision of the above mentioned Propaganda dated 11 December of the past year [1858], this sum is hereby incorporated in and appropriated by this Prefecture Apostolic of Hong Kong.

One pound sterling at that time was equivalent to approximately 5 Roman scudi; the 3703 Roman scudi were therefore equivalent to approximately 740 pounds sterling. Reina had neither requested nor received a receipt from Ambrosi for the sacred vessels and vestments, books and clothing, which had belonged to his former mission. These also became property of the Hong Kong prefecture apostolic at this time.[49] Ambrosi informed Barnabò on 15 March 1859 that he had transferred the funds and goods as instructed. And he added, "I thank you cordially for this and also for the personnel that you are trying to obtain for us."[50] The Mission of Melanesia and Micronesia, earlier called the Prefecture

---

48. PF: LDB vol. 349 (1858), f. 1028rv, Barnabò to Ambrosi, 11 December 1858. For a photocopy of this letter, see PIME: AME 24:17–21.

49. PIME: AME 35-01 Scurati, *Memorie dell'Istituto*, 505f. Scurati here says that the Sacred Congregation "in the beginning of March 1859" ordered Ambrosi to make the transfer. But Rome's order was issued on 11 December 1858. Scurati in PIME: AME 35-01 Scurati, *Memorie dell'Istituto*, 506, says that Reina's Prefecture Apostolic of Melanesia and Micronesia by virtue of the transfer of funds was incorporated in the Prefecture Apostolic of Hong Kong. But crediting the remaining funds of a dying prefecture apostolic to one that is thriving, is not the same as incorporating one prefecture in the other. Scurati's title for chapter 4 in PIME: AME 35-01 Scurati, *Memorie dell'Istituto*, 495, is therefore incorrect: "Incorporation of the Prefecture of [Melanesia and] Micronesia in the Prefecture of Hong Kong." Tragella in *Missioni estere*, 1:250, speaks of Reina's former mission "being practically entrusted to, rather than united to, the promising mission of Hong Kong." But Ambrosi was the Prefect Apostolic of Hong Kong or holder of jurisdiction and he was never entrusted with Reina's former mission. Tragella in *Missioni estere*, 1:249, says that "Reina did not cease to be prefect" of his Melanesia-Micronesia mission and therefore "it was not suppressed." As proof he refers to Barnabò's letter to Reina of 29 January 1858 (he writes 29 November 1858), which actually did relieve Reina of office as prefect of the Melanesia-Micronesia mission, but did not suppress the mission.

50. PF: SC Cina vol. 18 (1859–60), f. 138rv, Ambrosi to Barnabò, 15 March 1859.

Apostolic of Melanesia and Micronesia, was suppressed by the 11 December 1858 letter of Cardinal Prefect Barnabò. As early as 29 January of that year this ecclesiastical territory had been deprived of its ecclesiastical superior, when Prefect Apostolic Reina was relieved of office and transferred by Barnabò to Hong Kong with the rank of a simple missionary. The Melanesia-Micronesia mission continued to exist until 11 December 1858, but without a superior.

Slowly but surely Prefect Apostolic Ambrosi as ordered by Cardinal Prefect Barnabò was organizing the Hong Kong prefecture and was preparing Reina for the office of vice prefect. He was also waiting for additional personnel from Milan, whom he had requested both from Marinoni and from Barnabò as early as 12 April 1858, just two days after Reina had arrived in Hong Kong. Marinoni reacted to his request by informing Barnabò on 12 June that five priests were ready to leave for Hong Kong.[51]

One might well expect that Barnabò would have been pleased with Marinoni's offer and would have sent the five priests to Hong Kong without delay. But Marinoni's 12 June offer of personnel and Barnabò's "humiliating lecture" of 10 June had crossed in the mail. The cardinal consequently did not even reply to Marinoni. Instead he wrote to Ambrosi on 26 June as follows: "You can rest assured that I shall make great efforts to obtain additional reinforcements. But I must call to your attention that it is necessary to wait for the Milan College to be in a position to provide them. The candidates must be tested most diligently in order to find those who are suitable for this mission."[52] While Barnabò's letter was still en route, Ambrosi sent him a further request for personnel on 22 July 1858, announcing that Marinoni was ready to send him two or three more priests.[53] Ambrosi wrote again on 13 October, complaining that the cardinal had not yet sent Hong Kong any additional priests.[54] Barnabò reacted positively on 11 December 1858, "As regards the new personnel for which you have again asked me to show concern, I only need to receive from Father Marinoni . . . a few clarifications before they can be sent, which I hope will be soon."[55]

One month later on 13 January 1859 Barnabò informed Marinoni that Ambrosi was "waiting anxiously for two or three additional missionaries as reinforcements." He mentioned not a word, however, about the "few clarifications" which Ambrosi had been told were needed. Instead the cardinal urged Marinoni to hurry off to Hong Kong those whom he judged best "for the purpose of organizing well and consolidating that important Mission and Procure."[56] Marinoni in turn on 22 March informed the presidents of the Central

51. PIME: AME 6:171f, Marinoni to Barnabò, 12 June 1858; see also PIME: AME 35-01 Scurati, *Memorie dell'Istituto*, 441.

52. PF: LDB vol. 349 (1858), f. 423v-424r, Barnabò to Ambrosi, 26 June 1858.

53. PF: SC Cina vol. 17 (1857-58), f. 1010v.

54. The original of the 13 October 1858 request was not found, but its contents are indicated in PF: LDB vol. 349 (1858), f. 1027v, 1028v, Barnabò to Ambrosi, 11 December 1858.

55. Ibid.

56. PIME: AME 1:213.

Councils of the Association for the Propagation of the Faith in Paris and Lyon that "the Sacred Congregation for Propagating the Faith has approved sending three missionaries to the island of Hong Kong," for whom he requested funds to cover their transportation.[57]

It had taken Marinoni one full year to learn his lesson. From this time onward in his official correspondence he made no further reference to the Prefecture Apostolic of Melanesia and Micronesia, nor to Reina as if he were still its prefect apostolic. Fathers Gaetano Favini, Giacomo Scurati, and Simeone Volonteri were assigned by Marinoni to Hong Kong. They finally arrived there on 7 February 1860 after a year's delay.[58]

Tacchini and Puarer had been working in Saint Francis Hospital in Hong Kong for three months when Vice Prefect Mangieri was relieved of office. The hospital rapidly declined, and Prefect Apostolic Ambrosi, who had never been in favor of it, decided to close it. No other work could be given to Tacchini, as Reina told Marinoni on 12 November 1858, "because whites do not do menial work" in Hong Kong. Nor did Reina know where to send him. Tacchini himself did not want to return to Europe because, as he said, he had given up his home once and for all. So Reina asked Marinoni for a decision regarding Tacchini's future.

He pointed out to Marinoni also that he had a problem with Puarer, "whom we have always treated well. In order to obtain money he began selling to sailors not only his own things, but also those which he would steal from [his godfather,] Tacchini. And if you reprimand him, he makes such an innocent face that you yourself are filled with remorse." Reina therefore had decided to send Puarer back to Australia, since Prefect Apostolic Ambrosi had given his approval. "When he arrives in Sydney," Reina told Marinoni, "Ambrosoli and Father Rocher will take measures for sending him to the New Caledonia Vicariate or to the Vicariate of Central Oceania. Either in one place or in the other he can do good and can save his soul, if he wants to. We cannot keep him here because it is too easy to steal inside the house. And in the city it is too easy to get into trouble."[59] Six months later Reina informed Marinoni that he had received a letter from Sydney dated 23 February 1859 with the news that Puarer had arrived and that "Bishop Bataillon is taking him along to his Central Vicariate." Father Ambrosoli sent the news and also informed Reina that the Marists would be pleased to have Tacchini come back to them, since he had proved so helpful at the Marist Center after his return from Woodlark. All of the carpenter work at Woodlark mission had been done by him. Reina did not send Tacchini, however, thinking

---

57. Ibid., 6:259.
58. Tragella, *Missioni estere*, 1:270, 363.
59. PIME: AME 16:529–30, Reina to Marinoni, 12 November 1858.

that he could be employed in Hong Kong by the Brothers of the Christian Schools, who were expected to arrive shortly.[60]

But Catechist Tacchini soon disassociated himself from the Milan missionaries and on 14 April 1862 married Balbina Ong-an-Pereira, a young Catholic woman in Hong Kong of Chinese-Portuguese extraction.[61] Eight years later on 24 May 1870 at the age of forty-five, Tacchini died in Hong Kong.[62]

The wandering Father Francesco Buffa, a diocesan priest from Genoa, Italy, also discontinued serving the Hong Kong mission. For some years under Prefect Apostolic Feliciani he had been vice prefect.[63] But Prefect Apostolic Ambrosi wanted to have nothing to do with him. Buffa met Don Carlos Cuarterón in Manila and sailed with him aboard the *Pacifico* to Hong Kong, where they arrived on 22 November 1858.[64] From there Buffa wrote to Barnabò that he had received the cardinal's letter in August with the suggestion that he offer his services to Cuarterón. He made the offer, he said, but Cuarterón considered him too old for the Labuan mission. So now Ambrosi was sending him to Archbishop Polding in Sydney.[65] Ambrosi wrote to Barnabò that same day, 30 November 1858, saying that it was not he, but Reina, who had suggested Sydney to Buffa, who liked the idea. "But let us see how many excuses he will find before he sails," Ambrosi said.[66] Some six weeks later Ambrosi informed Barnabò: "Buffa is finally leaving, not for Sydney, but for Europe, just like I said he would. He is going aboard now."[67]

The staff of the Prefecture Apostolic of Hong Kong nevertheless continued to grow. In addition to the three missionary priests who had arrived on 7 February 1860, one more arrived two months later, bringing the number of priests from the Milan Foreign Mission Seminary in Hong Kong to six.

Giuseppe Burghignoli was the sixth priest, and he arrived in this way: Prefect Apostolic Ambrosi had informed director Marinoni that he needed six Italian nuns immediately and also a priest to accompany them. On receiving this information Marinoni left Milan for Venice, where he interceded with Patriarch Ramazzotti, who had Canossian Daughters

---

60. Ibid., 554, Reina to Marinoni, 4 May 1859.

61. PIME: AME 35-01 Scurati, *Memorie dell'Istituto*, 3, 498. The author has used the form Ong-an-Pereira rather than On-an-Pereira, the form as given by Scurati, because linguist Father Richard Hartwich, S.V.D., says that "Ong-an" is Mandarin, but that "On-an" is not.

62. See "Tacchini" in PIME: Archivio Onomastico Schede.

63. PIME: AME 35-01 Scurati, *Memorie dell'Istituto*, 486.

64. See PF: SC Oceania vol. 6 (1858–60), f. 360rv, Cuarterón to Barnabò, 30 November 1858. See also PF: SC Cina vol. 17 (1857–58), f. 1166r, Ambrosi to Barnabò, 30 November 1858.

65. PF: SC Cina vol. 17 (1857–58), f. 1164r, Buffa to Barnabò, 30 November 1858.

66. Ibid., f. 1166r, Ambrosi to Barnabò, 30 November 1858.

67. Ibid., vol. 18 (1859–60), f. 43r, Ambrosi to Barnabò, 15 January 1859.

of Charity (F.d.C.C.) in his patriarchate. Marinoni succeeded in obtaining six nuns. From Venice on 2 November 1859 he informed Barnabò that he had obtained the nuns and that Burghignoli was ready to accompany them to Hong Kong and to remain there as a missionary.[68] The group arrived in Hong Kong on 12 April 1860, and one month later the nuns already had forty girls in their school. By October that year they had eighty.[69] In the midst of the jubilation over the rapid growth of personnel in the Hong Kong prefecture in 1860, Reina's health continued to deteriorate. Doctors diagnosed his malady as going in the direction of pulmonary tuberculosis. "Consequently I was obliged to have a change of air and I have come to Macao, a Portuguese colony forty miles from Hong Kong," Reina said. When giving this news on 4 May 1860 to Gaspare Dezza, his priest friend in Melegnano, Italy, he added: "Life and death, health and sickness, are all in the hands of the Lord and we have nothing to do but conform ourselves with our whole heart to his holy will. . . . As you say, we shall see one another in heaven."[70]

Three weeks later Reina wrote to Marinoni: "I had to leave Macao because I got worse instead of better. I have been back in Hong Kong for six days now and I have regained a bit of strength. But I cannot offer Mass yet." He added that to all appearances Ambrosi wanted "to choose Burghignoli as his Vice Procurator . . ."[71] This was six weeks after Burghignoli's arrival.

Reina became worse with each new day. Before another month had passed Prefect Apostolic Ambrosi felt obliged to send him back to Italy on Friday, 22 June 1860. It was feared that he might die en route.[72] By this time Reina had been in Hong Kong two years, two months, and twelve days. Barnabò had not yet named him vice prefect of Hong Kong, a title that he would never receive.

"After fifty-four days of continuous travelling," Marinoni reported, Reina arrived in Milan "in a condition which filled us with the gravest fears." There is no record of the date on which he reached Milan. However, since it is known that he left Hong Kong on 22 June 1860, and since Marinoni says here that he arrived in Milan "after fifty-four days of continuous traveling," the date of arrival can be calculated as 14 August.

Marinoni waited until 3 September before informing Barnabò of Reina's return, because he wanted to learn first what the doctors had to say. For a long time Reina had been "gravely afflicted by a slow general inflammation which affected particularly his lungs and his intestines, reducing the sick man to extreme emaciation," Marinoni told Barnabò. But

---

68. PIME: AME 6:293, Marinoni to Barnabò, 2 November 1859. The Canossian Daughters of Charity are still at work in Hong Kong today. Their foundress, Marchesa Maddalena di Canossa (1774–1835), was declared a saint by Pope John Paul II on 2 October 1988 in Rome.

69. Tragella, *Missioni estere*, 1:270, 277.

70. PIME: AME 16:586, Reina to Dezza, 4 May 1860. Tragella in *Missioni estere*, 1:379, n. 1, mistakenly gives the year for this letter as 1861.

71. PIME: AME 16:587, Reina to Marinoni, 24 May 1860.

72. See PIME: AME 35-01 Scurati, *Memorie dell'Istituto*, 514.

doctors were caring for him, and there had been "a visible improvement. His fever has gone down, the dysentery has diminished, and each day there is more hope of his recuperating. Certainly much time will be needed . . . , because his sickness has been neglected far too long and is therefore greatly advanced."[73] Would Reina ever return to Hong Kong?

---

73. PF: CV vol. 43, f. 302r, Marinoni to Barnabò, 3 September 1860.

22

Decline of Cuarterón and His Labuan Mission
21 October 1859

PREFECT APOSTOLIC CUARTERÓN ISSUED THE FIRST OFFICIAL STATISTICS OF HIS LABUAN mission on 28 August 1858. By that time the Mission of Our Lady of the Assumption in Labuan with Father Borgazzi in charge totaled nineteen baptisms. The first was held on 26 May 1857, and the last on 7 February 1858. The Mission of Our Lady of Grace at Brunei on the mainland, where Father Riva was in charge, had four baptisms from 25 June to 20 July 1858. And at Looc-Porin, a port near Gautizan on the northwest coast of Borneo, the Mission of Our Lady of Bethlehem with Cuarterón in charge had three baptisms by 28 August 1858. All told there were twenty-six baptisms in the Prefecture Apostolic of Labuan after sixteen months of activity.[1]

It may have been these statistics that prompted Borgazzi's warning letter of 10 October that year to director Marinoni in Milan: "Do not expect to hear great things very soon about this mission in Labuan and Borneo. I believe that for many, many years, unless there should be some miracle of grace, we shall have nothing but sparse and small groups of Christians. The same will be true, I believe, for the missions now being founded on the coast of Borneo, where the population is completely Mohammedan." Filipinos were "in abundance" there, he said, "putting in six or eight years of slavery."

Precisely because of these Filipino slaves Cuarterón had been attracted to this part of the world. He intended to launch Christian missionary work by paying the required ransom for captive Filipinos, thus making it possible for them to gather freely in places where Christian missions were being founded. Then from these centers Cuarterón expected the Roman Catholic faith to spread to other peoples in Borneo. His plan was bound to succeed, he thought.[2]

---

1. PF: SC Oceania vol. 6 (1858–60), f. 686r.
2. See PIME: AME 11:1523, Borgazzi to Marinoni, 10 October 1858. See also chap. 15, pp. 267–68.

Nearly always on the move Cuarterón spent long periods of time outside of his own mission territory. In Singapore he had learned on 7 March 1858 of Rome's transferring Reina and his missionaries from Melanesia to Hong Kong. Cuarterón did not transport them, though. He was still in Singapore, or had returned there, by 21 April.[3] In May 1858 he returned to Labuan for a brief stay, but left again at the end of June.[4] He was at his own mission of Looc-Porin on 28 August, when he issued his statistical report.[5] He was in Manila on 10 October 1858 and may have remained there until 12 November, when he sailed for Hong Kong, where he arrived on 22 November.[6] He was still in Hong Kong on 12 December 1858 when Reina wrote: "I do not know when he will leave. He would like to sell the *Pacifico* and buy another vessel somewhat larger. But if he does this, he will have to remain here a long time."[7] And in 1859 he wrote letters to Barnabò from Manila in February, April, and May. On 29 May he left Manila for Labuan, where he arrived on 7 July after an absence of a year and one week.[8] Cuarterón had written to Cardinal Prefect Barnabò from Hong Kong on 30 November and 15 December 1858.[9] He systematically numbered all of his official letters to Rome and regularly sent them in duplicate or even in triplicate, using different routes to make sure that one copy at least reached its destination. These letters he wrote meticulously in his own hand, using many a flourish. He also used good quality paper with a distinctive printed letterhead displaying in Italian in the upper left-hand corner the title of his mission: "Prefecture Apostolic of LABUAN and ITS DEPENDENCIES ETC. in Eastern Malaysia." Equally distinctive was his large, legible, and ornate script.[10]

In reply to Cuarterón's November and December letters from Hong Kong, Barnabò pointed out that occasionally he received bits of news about the Labuan mission from

---

3. Cuarterón wrote to Ambrosi from Singapore on 21 April 1858. See PIME: AME 29:757. On the arrival of Father Raimondi and Brother Tacchini in Hong Kong, see chap. 21, p. 390.

4. See PIME: AME 11:1527, Borgazzi to Reina, 18 May 1859; PIME: AME 11:1532, Borgazzi to Marinoni, 3 September 1859.

5. See p. 407, n. 1 above.

6. Cuarterón himself gives these two dates, and Ambrosi also says that Cuarterón arrived in Hong Kong on 22 November. See PF: SC Oceania vol. 6 (1858–60), f. 360r, Cuarterón to Barnabò, 30 November 1858; PF: SC Cina vol. 17 (1857–58), f. 1166r, Ambrosi to Barnabò, 30 November 1858. For the date 10 October 1858, see PF: SC Oceania vol. 6 (1858–60), f. 684r.

7. PIME: AME 16:533, Reina to Ripamonti, 12 December 1858. Reina is incorrect here in stating that Cuarterón arrived in Hong Kong on 26 November. See n. 6 above.

8. See PF: SC Oceania vol. 6 (1858–60), f. 683r–690r.

9. See PF: LDB vol. 350 (1859), f. 119r, Barnabò to Cuarterón, 26 February 1859, which acknowledges the receipt of Cuarterón's two letters of 30 November and 15 December 1858. For the text of the 30 November letter, see n. 6 above.

10. For a very large collection of Cuarterón's letters starting with 12 December 1845 and ending with 18 January 1873, see PIME: AME 29:623–882. Cuarterón's distinctive handwriting and stationery make it a simple matter to recognize his many letters dispersed among thousands of others all bound in volumes in the SC Oceania archives of Propaganda in Rome.

Father Burrueco, Cuarterón's agent in Rome. "Nevertheless I would be pleased if from time to time you also sent me directly a concise report on your mission," the cardinal said. "Keep me informed of the actual state of the mission itself and omit all superfluous details."[11]

During the lengthy absences of Cuarterón from Labuan, Borgazzi and Riva visited one another on alternate months. These visits alleviated their isolation and made it possible for them to receive from one another the Sacrament of Reconciliation.[12]

Father Paolo Reina in Hong Kong also wrote to them occasionally. Borgazzi thanked Reina for his letter of 21 March on 18 May 1859. It had arrived "with the *Black Diamond* on the 12th of this month," Borgazzi said, and then he acquainted Reina with his situation: "At the end of the coming month it will be one year since Don Carlos left Labuan. Englishmen here say that he seems to be tired of staying in his mission. He himself wrote me from Manila on 6 April [1859] that he was detained there because of the grave illness of his brother," an Augustinian friar, whom he had taken to Manila to be cured.

Cuarterón was still there, Borgazzi said, "waiting for the arrival of his brother Manuel, so that he can come back here with him."[13] They returned to Labuan in separate ships, Don Manuel Cuarterón as captain of the English brigantine *Pacifico*, and Don Carlos Cuarterón as captain of his smaller ship, the Spanish schooner, *Mártires de Tun-Kin*. They had sailed via Palawan and Balabac and arrived in Labuan on 7 July 1859.[14]

At times during his voyages Cuarterón earned funds for his mission by transporting goods for Chinese merchants. He may have suffered financially from some of these business ventures, because he never did purchase the larger vessel that he had hoped to obtain in Hong Kong. In fact, from the time of his return to Labuan on 7 July 1859, he and his brother Manuel had begun spreading word about Don Cuarterón's financial problems and even about his intending to give up the Prefecture Apostolic of Labuan.

Borgazzi was greatly pleased with the arrival of the *Pacifico*, at Labuan on 7 July, because it had aboard a shipment of tiles from Hong Kong for the roof of his church. "I had been building it for a year," he told Marinoni, "and only a little work still had to be done before putting on the roof." But "the new church was struck by lightning during a terrible storm on the night of 3 August, causing nearly half of its walls to collapse. . . ." Nevertheless within a week of the disaster Cuarterón had generously authorized Borgazzi to sail on the *Pacifico* to Singapore with his brother as captain to purchase new materials and to hire better workmen. They reached Singapore on 23 August 1859, and on 29 September they arrived back in Labuan.[15]

---

11. PF: LDB vol. 350 (1859), f. 119rv, Barnabò to Cuarterón, 26 February 1859.

12. Tragella, *Missioni estere*, 1:252.

13. PIME: AME 11:1527–28, Borgazzi to Reina, 18 May 1859.

14. PF: SC Oceania vol. 6 (1858–60), f. 690r, Cuarterón to Barnabò, 23 July 1859.

15. Ibid., f. 743r, Cuarterón to Barnabò, 21 October 1859; PIME: AME 11:1531–32, Borgazzi to Marinoni, 3 September 1859.

When writing to Rome about this on 21 October, Cuarterón also told Barnabò that the local governor had become indignant with Borgazzi over his insisting on having a certain document needed for baptizing a child. "I ordered Missionary Borgazzi not to be obstinate with the governor and not to press the matter," Cuarterón said, "since it could result in the complete ruin of our mission. The matter will surely take care of itself and all will be resolved with time."[16]

Borgazzi thought it strange that while en route to Singapore, Captain Manuel Cuarterón kept making vague references about the expenses and financial losses suffered by his brother, Don Carlos.[17] While in Singapore Borgazzi found an opportunity to write confidentially to Reina in Hong Kong and reported that Cuarterón was "bad off financially" and intended "to abandon his mission."[18]

Evidently Reina did not take seriously Borgazzi's remarks about Cuarterón until he received similar information from Father Raimondi. Because of his knowledge of English, Raimondi had been sent by Prefect Apostolic Ambrosi to Manila to collect funds for rebuilding Hong Kong's leading Catholic church. It had burned down in 1859, the same year in which Borgazzi's church had been struck by lightning.

"I have heard terrible stories about Don Cuarterón," Raimondi told Reina, "and I had to tell the Augustinians here repeatedly that I am no longer associated with him." Cuarterón owed the Augustinians money and had also taken money from the Hospitalers of Saint John of God, who had become fascinated with him. Both religious orders had written "to Rome for their money," Raimondi said, "but they were told that Cuarterón no longer had a penny there."

When passing on this information to director Marinoni, Reina said that Cuarterón—ever since they met—had always spoken very badly about Rome's administration of his funds. In view of Cuarterón's financial condition, Reina advised Borgazzi and Riva not to spend all of their private funds and also not to make debts in their own names, because no one knew "what might happen."[19]

Later Raimondi sent Reina more news about Cuarterón. He said that Father Marcantonio, former provincial superior of the Augustinians in Manila, whom he himself and Reina had met in October 1856,[20] had received a letter from Cuarterón "in which

---

16. PF: SC Oceania vol. 6 (1858–60), f. 743rv, 745r, Cuarterón to Barnabò, 21 October 1859.

17. Tragella, *Missioni estere*, 1:252.

18. This letter of Borgazzi to Reina was not found, but extracts are quoted in PIME: AME 16:561, Reina to Marinoni, 15 December 1859. In his usual careless way of referring to source material, Reina does not give the date of Borgazzi's letter, which he is quoting, but simply states that "some months ago Father Ignazio Borgazzi wrote to me in all confidence."

19. Raimondi's letter to Reina was not found, but extracts from it are contained in PIME: AME 16:561, Reina to Marinoni, 15 December 1859. Here Reina uses the word "Fratelli" to refer to the Hospitalers of Saint John of God, who in Italian are known as the "Fate Bene Fratelli." Reina again fails to give the date of this important Raimondi letter about Cuarterón. See n. 18 above.

20. On the circumstances of this meeting, see chap. 17, pp. 333–35.

he said that he was thinking of resigning soon from his mission." Raimondi also learned that Captain Manuel had informed his brother-in-law in Manila, Don Velasco, that Don Carlos "had written to Propaganda about his decision to resign" and was "merely waiting for Rome's reply before doing so."[21]

Reina, superior of the Milan missionaries in Hong Kong, therefore wanted to know from director Marinoni, "What do we do now?" Rome might insist that Cuarterón remain in his mission, or it might accept his resignation and offer the Labuan prefecture to the Foreign Mission Seminary in Milan. "If that should happen," Reina said, "our seminary would be obliged to accept it." But he warned Marinoni that Cuarterón's mission was costly, that it had been "founded incorrectly," and that it would have little success because it was located in Moslem territory. "Use these ideas of mine in whatever way you wish," Reina said. "But for the love of God I beg you not to mention my name, if you write to Rome. This would ruin everything and would put me in an embarrassing situation."[22]

Cuarterón on 21 October 1859 wrote a letter to Cardinal Prefect Barnabò designating it in Spanish "Reservado," that is, "Confidential." It was a long letter containing his resignation from office and his reasons for resigning. It was one of two letters that he wrote to Barnabò that day.

"Up to today I have not been a prefect apostolic except in name," Cuarterón wrote, "because these two missionaries have not wanted to do anything that I have ordered. I have been simply a procurator, obtaining for them all that they have requested and have needed." Since leaving Rome, "I have already spent 100,000 francs for founding and supporting these missions and I have used another 100,000 francs for ships." It was necessary to have ships in order to maintain communications with his missions, Cuarterón said, but now he was running the risk of losing his ships. Cuarterón wrote:

> Since I am not in agreement with these missionary Fathers about the method which each of them wants to use for evangelizing, and since I do not want to have subject to me individuals who do not want to obey me, it is necessary for us to separate. I did not send them back to Europe because I did not want to cause scandal. . . . If Your Very Reverend Eminence believes that I am unfit to manage and conduct this mission, then let Propaganda take charge of it and relieve me of my office as prefect apostolic. But if Propaganda should be pleased that I continue in office as I have up to now, by supporting this mission and by paying its costs from my own funds, then may Your Very Reverend Eminence please indicate the place to which I am to send

---

21. This letter of Raimondi to Reina also was not found. The extracts from it come from PIME: AME 16:577, Reina to Marinoni, 14 March 1860.

22. Ibid., 577–78. Reina does not explain why the Milan Foreign Mission Seminary "would be obliged to accept" Cuarterón's mission.

these missionary Fathers. I shall then be able to fulfill for the mission what I contracted to do for Propaganda in the report which I presented to it on 15 February 1855.[23] At the same time kindly authorize me to look for missionaries who will obey me and who will go along with my ideas. Then let us see whether they together with me can reorganize these missions and make them prosper.

His letter of resignation ended with these words: "Nor can I permit it to be said that, while I was in charge, the missionary Riva was killed in Borneo and Borgazzi was removed from Labuan, because they were overly zealous, intolerant and indiscreet, not taking into consideration that we are living in the midst of Protestants, Mohammedans and savages."[24]

How would Cardinal Prefect Barnabò of the Evangelization Congregation react to this letter from Cuarterón, which seemed like an ultimatum? Would he expel the two priests, who constituted Cuarterón's entire missionary staff? Or would he attempt to reason with them and with Cuarterón? On 20 November 1859, one month after Cuarterón had written his letter of resignation, Riva's Mission of Our Lady of Graces was attacked. It was located on the mainland at Barambang on the Borneo River near Brunei. The reason given by Cuarterón for the attack was Riva's allowing one Filipino slave, who had not been ransomed, to join his mission. That slave's owner arrived at the mission with a band of armed men to take back his slave. Since it happened to be a Sunday, numerous Christian slaves whose ransom had already been paid were on the premises. The armed band kidnapped all of them, leaving behind only the unransomed Filipino slave whose joining the mission had allegedly given rise to the attack.

Riva and the local British consul submitted a protest to the sultan of Brunei, who maintained that he did not have on hand sufficient forces to keep the brigands in check. He therefore suggested that the Catholic mission, to be on the safe side, should pay a fee of five hundred francs for each person attached to the mission station. The sultan, however, was worried that some European nation might be angered over what had happened. He therefore wished to discuss personally with Cuarterón what might be done about the slaves, and he urged Riva to advise Cuarterón of his wish immediately. Riva set out at once for Labuan. He arrived there on 30 November 1859, ten days after his mission station had been attacked, and gave Cuarterón a detailed report.

Unknown to Riva, Cuarterón wrote to Cardinal Barnabò about the kidnapped slaves on 5 December 1859. He said that Riva "had admitted having allowed one Filipino slave to join his mission," and that armed brigands had carried away all the other slaves whose ransom had already been paid, "because Riva did not oppose them." Cuarterón blamed Riva for the incident, but took little action himself other than writing a letter. "Knowing

---

23. The report referred to here is Cuarterón's "Description of a new Mission Apostolic . . ." See chap. 15, p. 283, where he promises Propaganda to transport his missionaries to whatever place Propaganda wishes, if for some reason they are not to remain in his mission.

24. PF: SC Oceania vol. 6 (1858–60), f. 817r–818r, Cuarterón to Barnabò, 21 October 1859.

the treachery of these people, and not having authority from any nation to make a contract, and not having arms to enforce it," as he told Barnabò, he could do nothing else but send a letter to the sultan of Brunei through Riva.²⁵

Cuarterón's letter explained for the sultan how he had learned "from the missionary of Barambang, Antonio Riva, that some who called themselves owners of slaves had attacked with an armed force those people who voluntarily had settled in Barambang," forcing them to return to the places where they had been previously. "But you and other Pangeranes [that is, officials] had granted me permission to build our houses and a Roman Catholic church. Without this authorization and these guarantees I would never have made a foundation in this place," Cuarterón said. He added that it was not possible for him to engage in the purchase and sale of slaves at Barambang. Juridically for him they were "subjects only of Her Catholic Majesty, the Queen of Spain, because they were born in the Philippines and had been removed forcibly from there by pirates."²⁶ At this time Isabel II (1830–1904) was queen of Spain.

Two weeks later on Sunday, 18 December 1859, Cuarterón hastily wrote four letters. One was for Borgazzi based at Labuan, who was addressed with the title: "Missionary Apostolic of Borneo." "I must leave this Isle of Labuan today," Cuarterón said,

> in order to visit the mission which I have established on the Northwest Coast of Borneo. Furthermore, I have already consulted with Propaganda as to whether or not these missions are to be continued. Now since the English are discussing their abandoning of this Isle of Labuan and since I have decided to resign from these missions, I consider it fitting that Your Reverence for the present should suspend your work on the church. You should also make no new expenses as long as we receive no definite word from Rome advising us with full certainty whether or not this mission is to be continued. Thus we shall avoid making superfluous and unnecessary expenses in case we have to abandon all of this work.²⁷

Cuarterón also wrote to Riva, addressing him as "Missionary of Brunei." After referring to the Christians of his mission who were taken captive by the brigands, Cuarterón said, "I consider it fitting that Your Reverence for the present should not allow any slave to settle in your mission, until some Catholic European power reaches an agreement with the sultan there on this matter and on the freedom of the foresaid captives."²⁸

In a second letter addressed to Riva that day, Cuarterón said he had heard that the British consul general was leaving Brunei for Europe and also that Mohammedans were displeased with Riva's Barambang mission, "because their slaves are going there." If a further attack were to be made on Riva's mission, Cuarterón said, he was to take the following

---

25. See ibid., f. 841rv, 852rv, Cuarterón to Barnabò, 5 December 1859, letter no. 68.

26. Ibid., f. 807rv, Cuarterón to the Sultan of Brunei, no date. The letter must have been written in December 1859, since Riva had reached Labuan on 30 November of that year.

27. PF: SC Oceania vol. 6 (1858–60), f. 847rv, Cuarterón to Borgazzi, 18 December 1859, letter no. 4.

28. Ibid., f. 845r, Cuarterón to Riva, 18 December 1859, letter no. 5.

steps: "After sending a protest to the sultan and making him responsible for the damages to your mission . . . , Your Reverence shall abandon it immediately and shall come to this island of Labuan."[29]

Cuarterón's fourth letter informed Barnabò that he had to make a voyage and that consequently he had given "appropriate instructions" to his two missionaries. "But fearing that these instructions shall not be observed," and that in his absence "something sinister might happen," he enclosed for Barnabò copies of the letters that he had written to his missionaries in order to relieve himself "of all responsibility." He also told Barnabò about his ordering Borgazzi to discontinue rebuilding the Labuan church, because the English engineer had said that the church must be rebuilt completely, whereas Borgazzi wanted to repair only the damaged part. Cuarterón added that it was impossible for his mission of Labuan to continue, or even for it to make any progress at all, "because of the absolute lack of subordination" of his missionaries.[30]

Cuarterón sent these four letters of 18 December 1859 to Cardinal Prefect Barnabò through the "Consulate of Spain in Singapore."[31]

In spite of the little success that his mission method was having, Cuarterón remained convinced that the best means for promoting the spread of the Catholic faith in his territory was his original plan, namely: "The ransom of that multitude of Christian slaves from the Philippines, either indigenous or Spanish, who are found here and who are now under the yoke of Mohammedan Princes."[32]

Cuarterón apparently had come to believe that he needed the help of some European power in order to be successful in his mission. And since his mission method involved the ransom of Filipino slaves kidnapped from what then was considered Spanish territory, the European power upon which he was forced to rely was Spain. He had made this clear when he described the slaves at Barambang for the sultan of Brunei as "subjects only of Her Catholic Majesty, the Queen of Spain, because they were born in the Philippines and had been removed forcibly from there by pirates."[33]

Cuarterón believed that his aim could be realized only if Her Catholic Majesty's government were to make a treaty with sultans located in his mission territory, and were to place his mission in charge of ransoming the slaves. The ransom of so many Catholics and families from slavery would give his mission stability and considerable growth, he said, and also a well-founded hope for the conversion of Moslem rulers.

While in Manila the previous year, Cuarterón had presented the governor general of the queen of Spain with his project for the Christianization of Labuan and Borneo and with a cover letter dated 10 October 1858. Subsequently Cuarterón informed Barnabò that

---

29. Ibid., f. 846r, Cuarterón to Riva, 18 December 1859, letter no. 6.
30. Ibid., f. 831v, Cuarterón to Barnabò, 18 December 1859, letter no. 70 [sic].
31. PF: SC Oceania vol. 6 (1858–60), f. 848v.
32. ASV: AN Madrid, Caja 370, Cartella No. 20, Sez. IX, Tit. 5, no. 8, Barnabò to Barili, 20 March 1860.
33. PF: SC Oceania vol. 6 (1858–60), f. 807rv, Cuarterón to the sultan of Brunei. See p. 413, n. 26.

the governor general had not only expressed great pleasure over his project, but had also given assurance that he personally would bring it to the attention of Her Catholic Majesty's government in Madrid. The governor general had stated further that he would request the government of Spain to grant Cuarterón all necessary faculties and instructions, so that his proposal might be realized.[34]

As for the treaty to be signed by Spain and by sultans on the west coast of Borneo, Cuarterón was particularly interested in the conditions to be agreed upon regarding the ransom of Christian slaves. In fact, he hoped to be invested personally by the Spanish government with authority to enforce the observance of the agreements reached. As a help in performing this duty, he intended to request from Her Catholic Majesty's government a steam-powered warship.[35] But he said nothing about a warship to Barnabò.

But then unexpectedly the governor general in Manila informed Cuarterón that he was unable to expedite the project as he had promised. Undaunted, Cuarterón decided to enlist the services of the nuncio apostolic to Spain. He wrote to Barnabò from Manila on 8 April 1859, explained what had happened, and requested that Barnabò approach the nuncio apostolic to Spain on his behalf. He also enclosed for Barnabò a copy of the draft treaty that he had presented to the governor general in Manila. For some unknown reason Cuarterón had delayed mailing this letter for nine months, sending it in a packet together with six others all addressed to Barnabò and all written at Manila or at Labuan in the period from 24 February to 9 August 1859. The packet reached the cardinal bearing these three postmarks: Singapore, 22 January 1860; Foreign Countries via Suez—Marseilles, 26 February 1860; and Rome—by Sea, 1 March 1860.[36]

Letter number 59 containing Cuarterón's draft treaty was dated 8 April 1859 and consequently was almost a year old when it reached Barnabò. It nevertheless captivated the cardinal's attention and at once he wrote on 20 March 1860 to Archbishop Lorenzo Barili, nuncio apostolic to Spain. Pope Pius IX had created the Prefecture Apostolic of the Island of Labuan and Its Vicinity, he said, and had entrusted its government "to the distinguished Spanish priest, the Reverend Don Carlos Cuarterón, and to several collaborators. For some years this praiseworthy prefect apostolic has been applying all his zeal to establish and progressively develop his mission." Barnabò further stated that Cuarterón provided "a rare

34. The date 10 October 1858, when Cuarterón presented his proposal to the governor general, is in PF: SC Oceania vol. 6 (1858–60), f. 684r, Cuarterón to Barnabò, 8 April 1859. All other details are taken from Cardinal Prefect Barnabò's letter of 20 March 1860 to Nuncio Apostolic Barili in ASV: AN Madrid, Caja 370, Cartella No. 20, Sez. IX, Tit. 5, no. 8. A misleading note found on this Barnabò letter summarizes it as: "A project of the Vicar Apostolic of Labuan." But "Vicar Apostolic" should read "Prefect Apostolic." A further note added to the folder containing Barnabò's letter reads: "Project for establishing a Vicar Apostolic in the Island of Labran [sic] and Its Vicinity in Borneo near the Philippines (1860)." However, there is nothing in this correspondence that even remotely suggests raising the prefect apostolic of Labuan (Cuarterón) to the rank of vicar apostolic. For a more accessible copy of Barnabò's letter to Barili see PF: LDB vol. 351 (1860), f. 174r–175r.

35. On the steam-powered warship see Tragella, *Missioni estere*, 1:254.

36. PF: SC Oceania vol. 6 (1858–60), f. 684rv, Cuarterón to Barnabò, 8 April 1859. For the postmarks see PF: SC Oceania vol. 6 (1858–60), f. 687v.

example by dedicating not only his own person [to this task], but even all of his considerable wealth."

Cuarterón had experienced some success, Barnabò said, and "had become aware that the most efficacious means for facilitating the progress of religion and for promoting greater development in his new mission" was to ransom "that multitude of Christian slaves from the Philippines, either indigenous or Spanish, who are found here and who are now under the yoke of Mohammedan Princes."

Barnabò also informed Nuncio Barili of Cuarterón's audience in Manila with the governor general of Her Catholic Majesty. Cuarterón's plan "could be realized," Barnabò said, "if the Government of Her Catholic Majesty were to make a treaty with the sultans in the area, authorizing the mission to take upon itself the obligation of paying a ransom for the slaves." Cuarterón had already presented the governor general in Manila with a draft for such a treaty, Barnabò said. The treaty would bring stability to his mission and would foster its growth. There was even hope that leading Moslems in the area would be converted to the Christian faith. Barnabò further told the nuncio that Cuarterón's project "had pleased the Governor General, who had assured the Prefect Apostolic that he would make it known to his government and would request from it the faculties and instructions needed for carrying out" the plan.

"When presenting me with all this information," Barnabò said, Cuarterón requested "that I cooperate in achieving a happy outcome for his proposal by making use of the valuable intercession of Your Excellency with Her Majesty and with the ministers responsible for issuing appropriate directives to the Governor General in Manila." Barnabò promised the nuncio that he would write to Cuarterón, instructing him "to transmit to Your Excellency an exact report of the proposal as presented to the aforesaid Governor General, along with all additional information, clarifications and remarks that may be of use to you, so that you may be fully informed and could also make use of the data as the need arises.

"In all earnestness," Barnabò concluded, "I request you to show the greatest interest in and concern for bringing about a favorable result for the project mentioned. In order to achieve this goal use the most efficacious means and the greatest diligence. I shall look forward to the courtesy of a reply from Your Excellency after some time. Meanwhile from my heart I offer you my very best wishes. . . ." The letter was signed by Cardinal Prefect Barnabò and by his secretary, Archbishop Gaetano Bedini.[37]

Four days later Barnabò warmly thanked Cuarterón for his packet of letters, particularly for letter number 59 of 8 April 1859 with the text of his proposed treaty "for redeeming Christian slaves on the West Coast of Borneo." He said: "I cannot but approve and praise your plan. And I promise you that for my part I shall extend all the cooperation that I possibly can, so that this project of yours will turn out well." He assured Cuarterón that he would request the assistance of Nuncio Barili in Madrid. He had in fact already done so four days earlier.

37. These details come from Barnabò's letter of 20 March 1860 to Barili. See p. 415, n. 34.

Changing his tone Cardinal Barnabò said:

> With the greatest regret I noticed from your pages that the two priests, Borgazzi and Riva, given to Your Excellency to help you in the task of implanting and progressively developing your mission, instead of cooperating with your well-known zeal and constant efforts, have almost not at all complied up to now as regards their sacred duties. On the contrary they have shown themselves little concerned with the salvation of souls. And being perhaps less animated by a spirit of deference to and dependence upon your loving admonitions, directions and suggestions, they during your short absence have caused incalculable harm for the mission as regards both the spiritual and temporal welfare of their respective mission stations. Thanks to your solicitude and work, these stations had been happily launched and had already given promise of consoling progress.

Barnabò said that he had given director Marinoni orders to admonish Riva and Borgazzi and he hoped that they would reform. But if they were "to continue this reprehensible behavior both in the exercise of their ministry and toward you, and if they damage rather than promote the mission, then let me know and I shall remove them at once from the mission." As for new personnel, he authorized Cuarterón to enlist the services of priests whom he wanted, "who are more zealous and enjoy your full confidence."[38]

That same day, 24 March 1860, Cardinal Barnabò wrote to director Marinoni in Milan. "Always hoping to spare you this displeasure," he said, "I have abstained up to now from informing you that the two missionaries, Borgazzi and Riva, given as collaborators to the Reverend Don Carlos Cuarterón, Prefect Apostolic of Labuan and Its Vicinity, have not conducted themselves in an altogether praiseworthy manner, especially as regards the required deference toward and dependence upon their commendable superior...." Barnabò insisted that Marinoni must admonish his two missionaries "most energetically and efficaciously" to obey Cuarterón. Otherwise they would be "removed from the mission."[39] What had Cuarterón told Barnabò about Borgazzi and Riva in those other "pages" to elicit such a blistering reaction from the cardinal prefect of Propaganda?

Letter number 58 of 24 February 1859 from Cuarterón, written in Manila, said that large amounts of funds were needed by Riva and Borgazzi for building their two churches at Barambang and Labuan. Cuarterón was sending his brother Manuel with the English brigantine *Pacifico* to purchase and to deliver the food and other supplies that the priests needed, as well as the building materials that they had ordered for their two churches.

Letter number 61 of 23 May 1859 written in Manila said that Cuarterón's brother Manuel had returned from his voyage and had made delivery of all requested materials to Riva and Borgazzi for their two churches. Cuarterón announced that "they had decided to

---

38. PF: LDB vol. 351 (1860), f. 182r–183r, Barnabò to Cuarterón, 24 March 1860.
39. PIME: AME 1:251–52, Barnabò to Marinoni, 24 March 1860.

build them of stone, and not of wood as I had ordered them in my instructions.... It would have been more economical to use wood." Cuarterón pointed out that the English had been in Labuan for twelve years "and have only one building of stone. The others are all made of boards, of cane and of palm trees." In addition to their churches his two missionaries still had to build a residence and a school.

Cuarterón's letter number 62 of 23 July 1859 written in Labuan, which was Borgazzi's mission, said that "during the one year that I was absent from it, there were no more than two Baptisms." Cuarterón was setting out with supplies aboard his Spanish schooner, *Mártires de Tun-kin*, for Riva's mission at Barambang near Brunei. "From what I hear," Cuarterón said, "that missionary priest is building a cathedral instead of a mission chapel." Cuarterón had initially promised Barnabò that he would pay all costs for his mission and for his missionaries, something that was becoming a very great drain on his financial resources. He asked Barnabò, "How can all these costs be covered?"

Letter number 63 of 7 August 1859 written in Labuan told how Cuarterón had gone up the River Borneo "to the capital Brunei and to the spot which the local people call Barambang." He arrived there on 25 July and delivered the supplies that Riva had requested. To his surprise and consternation he found a church under construction which was more like a basilica, "imitating Trinity Church in the Mountains" at the top of the Spanish steps in Rome. Like that basilica in Rome, adjacent to the square where Barnabò had his office, Riva's church also had three naves, two towers, and an outside platform upon which the church doors opened. There was also a flight of steps leading up to it. Cuarterón estimated that it would cost another thirty thousand francs to finish the church. This would amount to 30 percent of what he had already spent on his entire mission.

Letter number 64 of 9 August 1859 written at Labuan described Cuarterón's leaving Brunei on 4 August and his arrival on the following day in Labuan, where he found Borgazzi's new church in ruins.[40] As Borgazzi himself said, "I had been building it for a year and only a little work still had to be done before putting on the roof." But then "the new church was struck by lightning during a terrible storm on the night of 3 August, causing nearly half of its walls to collapse...."[41] Cuarterón had his brother take Borgazzi to Singapore to purchase more building materials and get better workmen. As Cuarterón's debts mounted, his fortune dwindled. These letters from Cuarterón had all arrived on Barnabò's desk in a single packet and so had a cumulative effect on him.

Cuarterón meanwhile was anxiously waiting in Labuan for Cardinal Barnabò's reply to his letter of resignation of 21 October 1859. But Cuarterón's letter must have been misdirected, because it took nearly six full months to reach Barnabò. On 18 April 1860 he wrote:

---

40. For letters numbered 58 to 64 of Cuarterón to Barnabò, see PF: SC Oceania vol. 6 (1858–60), f. 683r–694v.

41. See PIME: AME 11:1531–32, Borgazzi to Marinoni, 3 September 1859.

I have just now received your confidential letter . . . telling of the imminent risks to which your two missionaries, Riva and Borgazzi, are exposed. One is in danger of being killed and the other of being expelled from Labuan, all because of their intolerant and indiscreet zeal as well as their insubordination and capricious bearing toward local authorities. These authorities have become extremely indignant toward them.

You therefore ask me either to remove them from the mission, since there is no hope for their reformation, or to relieve you from the office which was entrusted to you. I am far from being able to adhere to your proposal that you retire from that Mission, for which you have already made such great sacrifices and have borne so many hardships with true zeal, thus providing great satisfaction for Propaganda.

"In my previous letter [of 24 March], however, I declared to you that I was ready to recall these missionaries on receiving further word from you that they had not given certain proof of reform and of full submission to your orders and directions. Should that be the case, I would then authorize you at the same time to obtain for yourself other collaborators in whom you have full confidence. . . . In this way I hope to avoid, if possible, a misfortune of this kind or the total ruin of the mission.

At the same time I send you full faculties for yourself, giving you authorization to have the two missionaries leave Labuan as soon as you judge it necessary. In that event send them provisorily to Hong Kong and inform that Prefect Apostolic in advance. Or if there is need, send them to Italy, taking care at the same time to provide yourself with other priests who will help you to reorganize dutifully and to coordinate permanently this mission. . . . Simultaneously I shall inform the director of the seminary at Milan of this decision. . . ."[42]

Keeping his word Barnabò wrote that very day, 18 April 1860, to Director Marinoni, reminding him of his previous letter of 24 March containing complaints against Riva and Borgazzi. He then mentioned Cuarterón's sending a confidential letter in which the prefect apostolic "has manifested to me the absolute necessity of removing the above mentioned missionaries from that mission or of permitting him to abandon the undertaking completely. Matters having reached such a state, there is danger of his becoming a witness to the killing of Riva and to the expulsion of Borgazzi by local authorities.

"These authorities are indignant toward them as a result of their imprudent steps and their capriciousness, joined to indiscreet and intolerable zeal," Barnabò said. "They also give no signs of reforming themselves. Trying to avoid such a disaster by arriving on time, I am at once sending word to the prefect authorizing him to prevent it in this case by having the two missionaries depart either for Hong Kong or—if there is need—even for Italy. I hereby forewarn you of what shall be happening, so that you are notified and can take steps accordingly. I nevertheless still hope to receive better and reassuring reports. . . ."[43] In those days a letter from Rome to Milan took one week. However, Marinoni was so

42. PF: LDB vol. 351 (1860), f. 232r–233r, Barnabò to Cuarterón, 18 April 1860. This letter incorrectly gives 21 November 1859 as the date of Cuarterón's "confidential letter." It should be 21 October 1859. See p. 412, n. 24.

43. PIME: AME 1:253, Barnabò to Marinoni, 18 April 1860.

stunned by the tone of Barnabò's two letters of 24 March and 18 April 1860 that he delayed replying until 12 June. On that date he gave Barnabò assurance that he had sent both Riva and Borgazzi strong admonitions.

Cardinal Barnabò replied on 27 June, praising Marinoni for his admonitions and expressing hope that they might arrive in Labuan on time to resolve the difficulties. He also quoted Cuarterón as saying that Riva and Borgazzi were "lacking in true zeal" and "at the same time had committed acts of imprudence of such a nature as to compromise the very existence of the nascent mission."[44]

Meanwhile in Labuan Riva and Borgazzi were unaware that Cuarterón was sending letters of complaint about them to Barnabò, and that Barnabò in turn was sending letters of complaint about them to Marinoni. Nor was Cuarterón as yet aware of Barnabò's reaction to his letter of resignation.

As late as July 1860, Cuarterón was still confiding in Riva about the collaboration that he hoped to receive from Spanish government authorities in Manila for realizing his plans. He would be given a warship, he said, to supervise the ransom of captives and to help him bring the slaves together in special places. Without such protection Cuarterón believed that his mission would collapse, since the English government had taken no stand against the attack made on the Barambang mission.

Meanwhile Cuarterón's ship *Pacifico* was paying many visits to Balabac, the new Spanish colony founded off the northern tip of Borneo. Balabac was not too far distant from Cuarterón's own Mission of Our Lady of Bethlehem at Port Looc-Porin near Gautizan. From this port he wrote to Riva on 3 July 1860 and again on 22 July about voyages being made by the *Pacifico* to Balabac.[45] Did Cuarterón perhaps envision Balabac and Gautizan as places where he could gather together the slaves that he might set free with the help of authority bestowed upon him by the Spanish government?

About this time Riva's life was threatened at Barambang mission and so, in obedience to Cuarterón's written instructions, he left at once for Labuan. While there he together with Cuarterón and five others signed a protest dated 4 August 1860 and addressed to the sultan of Brunei and to other authorities regarding this threat and other matters.[46]

Ten days later, on 14 August 1860, Cuarterón drafted a formal letter in Labuan addressed to Queen Isabel II of Spain. It stated that he, Don Carlos Cuarterón, prefect apostolic of Labuan and Its Vicinity, prostrated himself at her feet "in order to ask for justice, refuge and protection, not for himself, but for very many unfortunate subjects of Your

---

44. Ibid., 257, Barnabò to Marinoni, 27 June 1860. Marinoni's letter to Barnabò of 12 June 1860 was not found, but its date and content were learned from the 27 June reply of Barnabò.

45. PIME: AME 29:789, 791, Cuarterón to Riva, 3 and 22 July 1860.

46. PF: SC Oceania vol. 6 (1858–60), f. 1124r–1125v, Cuarterón and others to the sultan and other authorities of Brunei, 4 August 1860.

Royal Majesty found within the limits of his ecclesiastical jurisdiction," who were being oppressed under the yoke of the most excruciating slavery.[47]

The following day was the patronal feast of the mission station founded in Labuan. It was 15 August 1860, feast of the Assumption of the Blessed Virgin Mary. It should have been a very happy day because some three years and four months earlier, on 14 April 1857, Cuarterón had arrived there with Riva and Borgazzi to launch the new prefecture apostolic. However, Prefect Apostolic Cuarterón chose this patronal feast in 1860 as the day on which to expel both Riva and Borgazzi from his mission.

Cuarterón wrote to Cardinal Prefect Barnabò, justifying their expulsion in these words: "In view of Your Most Reverend Eminence's decision contained in your communication of 18 April 1860, No. 2, I today am sending the Reverend Missionary Father Antonio Riva," who was in charge of the Brunei mission, "to the Prefecture Apostolic [of Hong Kong], as Your Reverend Eminence orders me." Cuarterón was sending him "aboard an English warship leaving for Singapore and Hong Kong. The Reverend Missionary Father Ignazio Borgazzi, who was in charge of this mission of Labuan, is also accompanying him for the reasons which I gave . . . in my previous letter."[48]

Cuarterón wrote a second letter that day, 15 August 1860, to Prefect Apostolic Ambrosi of Hong Kong and gave it to Riva and Borgazzi for personal delivery. It read:

> His Eminence, the Cardinal Prefect of Propaganda in Rome, told me under date of 18 April of the current year to send provisorily to the city of Hong Kong the Reverend Fathers and Missionaries, Antonio Riva and Ignazio Borgazzi, with word that they are under your orders and at your disposition. In view of this superior decision I have arranged for them to embark today on the English steam-powered warship *Victoria*, which is to leave [Labuan] for Singapore. From that port they will proceed at the earliest opportunity to their new destination in order to fulfill the orders of His Eminence. In case Your Reverence has received no news from Rome, rest assured in virtue of this communication of mine that I have here the original order of the Cardinal Prefect.[49]

Meanwhile Nuncio Apostolic Barili of Madrid, after receiving Barnabò's request of 20 March 1860 regarding Cuarterón's project of ransoming slaves with the assistance and the authority of the Spanish government, wasted no time. He obtained an audience on 2 May 1860 with the competent government official in Madrid, Director General "de Ultramar," the minister in charge of all Spanish colonies. Barili presented a summary in Spanish of Barnabò's Italian letter, which described Cuarterón's project, and the two men discussed the matter. The nuncio explained what action Cuarterón had already taken with Spanish officials in Manila and then ended his petition as follows:

---

47. Ibid., f. 1126r–1127v, Cuarterón to the queen of Spain, 14 August 1860.
48. Ibid., f. 1132rv, 1137r, Cuarterón to Barnabò, 15 August 1860, letter no. 81.
49. PIME: AME 29:793–94, Cuarterón to Ambrosi, 15 August 1860.

The Nuncio of His Holiness has been commissioned to recommend this proposal and desires to know whether Her Majesty's Government in Manila has sent word of the project described above. The Prefect Apostolic will no doubt send clarifications and observations on this particular subject to the Nuncio, so that he may then be able to provide this information to Her Majesty's Government. In this way the Nuncio hopes to attract the government's attention to the great concern of this priest, who spares no effort for the good of his mission and also tries to improve the lot of Spaniards, his co-nationals.[50]

That same day, 2 May 1860, Barili received this written reply: the director general "has the honor of informing you that the Government of Her Majesty has not received from authorities in the Philippine Islands the project presented by the Labuan Missions in Borneo."[51]

To all appearances Cuarterón never sent Nuncio Barili any of the details requested by Cardinal Prefect Barnabò. Consequently the nuncio never again approached Her Majesty's Government on the matter.[52] Cuarterón was now alone. He had dismissed his two-man staff, and his project for obtaining financial assistance and authority from the Spanish government had proved an idle dream. But he still had his other dream of a multitude of ransomed Christian slaves gathered together in one or more places, who would thus hopefully give vigor and growth to his Prefecture Apostolic of Labuan and Its Vicinity. But now he had no one with whom to share this dream. Would he be able to persevere? He did have one ally: his age. He was only forty-four years old, appeared to be in the best of health, and always had new ideas.

Borgazzi from Singapore, on 24 August 1860 while en route to Hong Kong, sent Director Marinoni in Milan his latest news. "At the beginning of this month we received an order from Rome to go to Hong Kong," he said. "It was sudden and unexpected, since we did not know what had led up to it. However, we keep consoling ourselves with the hope that we have in no way contributed to the abandonment of that mission. . . ."[53]

Riva also wrote that day from Singapore, telling Marinoni that their orders to go to Hong Kong were contained in a letter from Barnabò addressed to Cuarterón. He had read a part of that letter to them and then "suddenly suspended the missions." Riva said that Cuarterón, however, had never manifested any displeasure toward him throughout the entire time that he had been in Borneo. Nor was Riva aware that he had ever caused Cuarterón any displeasure. In fact, on the day before they left Labuan, Cuarterón had ordered him to draw up a detailed report indicating all of the incidents in which Moslems had used

50. ASV: AN Madrid, Caja 370, sez. IX, Tit. 5, No. 8, Barili to director general "de Ultramar," 2 May 1860.
51. Ibid., director general "de Ultramar" to Barili, 2 May 1860.
52. The archives of the Nunciature Apostolic of Madrid up to 1903 are now part of the Secret Vatican Archives. Rome's Father Franco Diaz de Cerio, S.J., discovered the Barili data in these archives and kindly shared it with this author. He gave assurance that nothing further on Cuarterón and his project is to be found in this Vatican source.
53. PIME: AME 11:1543–44, Borgazzi to Marinoni, 24 August 1860.

their power to damage his mission station at Barambang. Cuarterón had told Riva that he wanted to present this information to Manila "in order to try to obtain from the Queen of Spain herself the steam-powered warship about which he had already spoken so often. But only after making a treaty with the sultan," Cuarterón said, "would it be possible to open the mission again."[54]

While Borgazzi and Riva were en route from Singapore to Hong Kong, director Marinoni on 3 September 1860 contacted Cardinal Prefect Barnabò. He said that Prefect Apostolic Ambrosi of Hong Kong needed one or two additional priests to take the place of Reina, who had returned to Milan.[55] Then six days later on 9 September, as if in answer to Ambrosi's need, the two priests Riva and Borgazzi arrived in Hong Kong aboard the warship *Victoria*. They handed Prefect Apostolic Ambrosi the 15 August letter of Cuarterón with the surprising news of their official transfer from the Labuan prefecture apostolic to that of Hong Kong.[56]

Borgazzi from his Borneo Mission had often informed Reina about the activities of Cuarterón. On learning now that Reina had left Hong Kong on 22 June for Milan on sick leave, Borgazzi quickly wrote to him. "We learned here that we have been withdrawn from the [Labuan] Mission and have been sent to this one because we were incorrigible." But Cuarterón, he added, only "wanted to justify himself and protect himself by unloading on the two of us the responsibility for his decision to abandon those missions. May the Lord bless and help him, so that he may be able to save his soul and we, ours!"[57] After Reina's departure from Hong Kong, Raimondi had become superior of the Milan missionaries there. Consequently two days after the arrival of Riva and Borgazzi, Superior Raimondi tried to explain for Director Marinoni what had happened. "To tell the truth," he said, "I do not know how to reconcile the bad reports about our two missionaries, which were sent to Rome, with the facts that I know and with the official letters written to them by Don Carlos Cuarterón, which I have read. Don Carlos Cuarterón had assured his friends in Manila already last year [1859] that he wanted to abandon his mission, not because he was discontent with his missionaries, whom he praised, but rather because of money matters." Civil authorities in the Labuan mission, Raimondi said, had taken a dislike to Cuarterón, and this dislike had then branched out to include his missionaries. Consequently "as soon as the two missionaries had to stand firm in defense of their Christians, the authorities were on their backs."

---

54. Ibid., 1869–71, Riva to Marinoni, 24 August 1860. Tragella in *Missioni estere*, 1:254, n. 78, mistakenly dates this letter as 20 August. Riva clearly writes 24 August 1860 at the end of his letter and says they had to embark in two hours. Borgazzi also wrote to Marinoni on 24 August. See p. 422, n. 53.

55. PF: CV vol. 43, f. 302r, Marinoni to Barnabò, 3 September 1860.

56. See PIME: AME 11:1547–48, Borgazzi to Reina, 12 September 1860; PIME: AME 29:793–94, Cuarterón to Ambrosi, 15 August 1860.

57. PIME: AME 11:1547–48, Borgazzi to Reina, 12 September 1860.

"God will judge the case," Raimondi said. After carefully reflecting on it himself, making his own investigations, and keeping in mind various things that he had heard in Manila about Cuarterón's mission, Raimondi told Marinoni that he had reached this firm opinion: "Don Carlos Cuarterón was already determined to abandon his mission more than a year ago, that is, before these unpleasant incidents had occurred between the missionaries and the civil authorities. But in order to have a reason to resign honorably, he seized upon this occasion and wrote to Propaganda, perhaps without being aware that he was describing the affair much darker than it was in reality."[58]

For the rest of that month Riva, who had been Cuarterón's confidant, pondered over his plight and then put his thoughts in writing on 28 September: "As for the letters from Rome, they do not disturb me, because I really believe in conscience that in Borneo I have done the best that I could do. I always believed that I was in perfect rapport and harmony with my superior. The many letters that I still have from him are proof of this. So if he spoke to me and wrote to me in one way, and wrote to Rome in another way, that is his business."[59]

Hardly two months after Riva and Borgazzi arrived in Hong Kong, Raimondi reported to director Marinoni that Prefect Apostolic Ambrosi was "highly pleased" with his two new missionaries from Labuan.[60]

Ambrosi himself for six more weeks closely observed his two new priests and on 30 December 1860 sent this testimony to the treasurer, Father Alessandro Ripamonti, at their headquarters in Milan: "Whatever may have been said about the Reverend Fathers Riva and Borgazzi, I have nothing but praise for them. They work in the vineyard of the Lord like good missionaries. For my part I shall not fail to profit from circumstances as they arise, in order to make some things known to Propaganda. I am satisfied equally well with all the others, who labor with no less ardor in fulfilling their various tasks." On the next day, New Year's Eve, Ambrosi added a postscript to his letter, saying: "I took advantage of an opportunity to write to the Cardinal Prefect about Fathers Riva and Borgazzi. And what I said about them is true."[61]

What did Ambrosi say to Barnabò about them? He said that from Milan he had received word that there was no hope of Father Reina coming back to Hong Kong. "However, I must give abundant thanks to the Lord, because after his [Reina's] departure the two priests from Labuan and Borneo came to me in his place, the Reverend Fathers Riva and

---

58. Ibid., 16:621–22, Raimondi to Marinoni, 11 September 1860.

59. PIME: AME 35-04 Scurati, *Memoria del Sacerdote Riva*, 29. This manuscript work of Scurati makes direct quotations from Riva's 28 September 1860 letter, but fails to indicate to whom the letter was sent. Nor was the PIME archivist able to locate the original letter.

60. PIME: AME 16:627, Raimondi to Marinoni, 15 November 1860.

61. PIME: AME 16:421–22, Ambrosi to Ripamonti, 30 December 1860.

Borgazzi. I cannot be anything but highly pleased with their zeal and activity and goodness." It was New Year's Eve, 31 December 1860.[62]

By the end of the following year, 1861, the number of Catholics in the Prefecture Apostolic of Hong Kong was calculated as 3,000 in a total population of approximately 1 million. There were two Chinese priests and eight European priests attached to the prefecture, as well as nuns who conducted schools. There were six churches or chapels, two schools with 100 girls, four schools with 150 boys, and a minor seminary with 12 candidates. Two orphanages had a total of 100 orphans.[63]

Father Riva's active missionary career in Labuan and Borneo had lasted three years and four months. In Hong Kong it would last only one year and four months. He was plagued with some strange malady in January 1862 that local doctors could not diagnose. Borgazzi assisted Riva often during his five-month illness and was also at his bedside when he died with a smile on his face at three o'clock in the morning of 27 May 1862. Riva was thirty-eight years old and his last words were, "Jesus, Mary and Joseph, I give you my heart and my soul."[64]

Father Reina had arrived in Milan on 14 August 1860, the day before Cuarterón expelled Riva and Borgazzi from his Labuan prefecture. But Reina had consumption, and by this time it was so far advanced that physicians could do nothing to save him. He died on 14 March 1861 at the age of thirty-six, exactly seven months after his arrival in Milan. His funeral took place on Saturday, 16 March, at 9.30 a.m., in the church of San Calocero. From here he and his six companions had left for Oceania after receiving their mission crosses at a departure ceremony held nine years earlier to the day and to the hour.[65]

Director Marinoni informed Cardinal Prefect Barnabò on 19 March 1861 that Reina had died. The cardinal replied a month later, saying it was "a great displeasure" for him to learn of the death "of the excellent missionary Father Paolo Reina. And although in view of your remarks he may well be considered as enjoying already the blessed lot of the just, I did not forget to pray for him at Mass as you had suggested and requested." Much earlier Reina had been relieved of his office as prefect apostolic of Melanesia and Micronesia. And since he had received no new office in Hong Kong, not even that of vice prefect nor that of vice procurator, the cardinal referred to him with no other title but simply that of a missionary priest.[66]

---

62. PF: SC Cina vol. 18 (1859–60), f. 1094rv, Ambrosi to Barnabò, 31 December 1860.
63. Tragella, *Missioni estere*, 1:278.
64. PIME: AME 35-01 Scurati, *Memorie dell'Istituto*, 518–20.
65. Tragella, *Missioni estere*, 1:380.
66. PIME: AME 1:265, Barnabò to Marinoni, 18 April 1861.

In 1860, the year before Reina died, there were already six Marist priests and three Marist brothers stationed at three mission stations in the Fiji Islands. Cardinal Prefect Fransoni had early recommended the Fiji Islands as a mission field to Reina, but he and his missionaries prior to their departure for Oceania had voted against accepting these islands. By 1861, when Reina died, there were already some three thousand catechumens in the Fiji Islands mission. Then on 1 March 1863 the Prefecture Apostolic of the Fiji Islands was created by Pope Pius IX. By that time there were ten thousand to twelve thousand catechumens and sixteen hundred baptized Christians.[67] The Protestant Mission in Northwest New Guinea, founded on Mansinam Island in Dorei Bay, suffered a severe earthquake and tidal wave in 1864, which destroyed all buildings on the island. It was this area to which Cuarterón had wanted to take Reina and his missionaries in 1858. Four Protestant mission stations were then founded on the adjoining mainland as additional missionaries arrived, but they were plagued with "epidemics of both smallpox and dysentery." And "after twenty-five years . . . the number of missionaries and family members who had died in [Northwest] New Guinea exceeded the number of natives baptized."[68] By sending the Milan missionaries instead to Hong Kong, Rome had unwittingly saved them from calamities awaiting them in Dorei Bay.

In April 1861, one month after Reina's death, Father Alfieri was back in Rome and once again began serving Marinoni as procurator. "On the 24th I saw His Holiness [Pope Pius IX]," he told Marinoni, "and he blesses you and your missionaries. . . ." On April 27 he saw Cardinal Prefect Barnabò. He "asked me to greet you and your members. He added that he has nothing against you, but he wants you to give much thought to the formation of your candidates in the spirit of abnegation, submission and humility. These [qualities], he said, are particularly necessary for success in the missions, so that there will be no further incidents like those in Nueva Granada, those under Cuarterón, and those in India. What is important is not building a house which one believes to be more beautiful, more useful, etc., but rather doing the will of God [as manifest] in the decisions of one's own lawful and direct superiors."[69]

Marinoni and his mission seminary continued to enjoy the services of Alfieri as their procurator in Rome, even after he was elected superior general of the Hospitalers of St. John of God in 1862 and also after he was reelected in 1872. These services Alfieri ren-

---

67. Brief of Pius IX, "Non sine arcano," 27 March 1863, in *Jus Pontificium*, vol. 6, part 1 (Rome 1894), 387–88; PF: LDB vol. 354 (1863), f. 147v–148r, Decree of 27 March 1863. These two documents state that Pope Pius IX created the Prefecture Apostolic of the Fiji Islands on 1 March that year. See also PF: SC Oceania, vol. 15 (1885–86), f. 508r–509r, Memorandum of 9 October 1885 on the Prefecture Apostolic of the Fiji Islands, sent to Propaganda by Marist Procurator General Claude Nicolet, S.M. Regarding Fransoni's recommending the Fiji Islands and their being turned down by Reina's group, see chap. 9, pp. 133–34.

68. Souter, *New Guinea*, 23.

69. PIME: AME 10:177, Alfieri to Marinoni, 28 April 1861. Nueva Granada is near Cartagena in Colombia.

dered until shortly before his death on 3 August 1888 at the age of eighty-one.[70] Director Marinoni himself would die at the age of eighty, but two and a half years later.

Six months and ten days after Reina's death, Ramazzotti also died. Rome had promoted him to the highest ecclesiastical office in Italy, that of patriarch of Venice, on 15 March 1858. Then on 10 August 1861 he was informed by Giacomo Cardinal Antonelli (1806–76), Secretary of State, that Pope Pius IX would raise him to the rank of cardinal at the forthcoming secret consistory. Ramazzotti received this news on his deathbed. He indicated his formal acceptance of the honor on 22 August, but died on 24 September 1861, three days before the cardinalate was to be bestowed.[71]

Archbishop Romilli of Milan, who had worked closely with Ramazotti in founding the Milan Foreign Mission Seminary, died two years earlier on 7 May 1859. Bishop Luquet of France, based in Rome, died on 3 September 1858. It was from Luquet that Romilli and Ramazzotti had learned in November 1847 that Pope Pius IX wished to see founded in Lombardy a mission seminary modelled after the Paris Foreign Mission Seminary. Luquet had correctly predicted disaster if the Milan missionaries, instead of choosing Ceylon, were to accept Melanesia and Micronesia. They would not produce "abundant fruit," he said, and there would be "many losses . . . in Missionaries, in effort, in money, in everything . . ."[72]

Father Ambrosi remained prefect apostolic of Hong Kong and procurator of Propaganda for the Missions of China until his death in Hong Kong on 11 March 1867. His predecessor in office, Father Feliciani, the good friend of Cuarterón, had died in China in 1866. Father Burrueco, who had served as procurator for Cuarterón and also briefly for the Milan Foreign Mission Seminary, had meanwhile died in Rome.[73]

Father Salerio had been sent back to Italy from Sydney, Australia, in February 1856 because of ill health, and he remained in Italy for the rest of his life. In 1859 he founded the Sisters of Reparation to the Sacred Hearts of Jesus and Mary Immaculate, whose headquarters in Milan, Italy, are on a street named in his honor: Via Padre Carlo Salerio. When he sensed that his death was approaching, he asked to be moved into the room in which Father Reina had died nine years earlier. Salerio died there on 29 September 1870 at the age of forty-three.[74]

Bishop Pompallier, administrator apostolic of the Auckland diocese in New Zealand, had requested personnel from Marinoni in vain on 7 September 1857. Ten years later his diocese was so much in arrears that he left New Zealand for good on 18 February 1868

---

70. Marinoni, *Scritti vari*, 303.
71. Bassan, *Da Avvocato a Patriarca*, 132, 187; Tragella, *Missioni estere*, 1:389–90.
72. For the Luquet quotation see chap. 5, pp. 61–62.
73. See chap. 1, p. 14. See also PIME: AME vol. 24, part 2, p. 25, Raimondi to Barnabò, 14 March 1867.
74. Tragella, *Missioni estere*, 1:380; Suigo, *Pio IX*, 77.

and sailed for France. The following year he retired from office as bishop of Auckland, was given the honorary title of archbishop, and took up residence in the village of Puteaux near Paris. When his health failed, the nuncio apostolic of Paris brought him the blessing of Pope Pius IX on 20 December 1871. Pompallier died on the following day, just ten days after his seventieth birthday.[75]

Archbishop Polding of Sydney and Bishop Bataillon, vicar apostolic of Central Oceania, had also sought personnel from Marinoni in vain. Both were acquainted with most of the Milan missionaries sent to Oceania. Polding died in Sydney on 16 March 1877, and Bataillon died less than one month later in Wallis on 10 April.

Father Supriès was the Carthusian monk who had envisioned a flourishing mission in Micronesia for the Foreign Mission Seminary of Milan, whereas the student body chose Melanesia instead. He outlived five of the seven missionaries who were sent to Melanesia. During his lifetime Supriès held some of the highest offices in his order, being prior at Pavia from 1855 to 1869 and at Rome from 1869 to 1877. While in Rome he was also procurator general of his order. He was co-visitor of La Grande-Chartreuse in 1856 and also visitator of all Carthusian monasteries in Italy in 1856, 1863, and 1866.

At the Carthusian General Chapters of 1856, 1863, and 1869, Supriès was one of the priors on the Board of Definitors. This board for the duration of a General Chapter has supreme powers for regulating affairs of the order. The Board of Definitors also decides whether the minister general and the priors of the order are to remain in office. Supriès was transferred from Rome in 1877 to the Carthusian Monastery of Saint Mary's for the Aged at Mougères near Caux (Herault) in southern France. Here he died on 20 November 1888 at the age of eighty-eight, just seven months before his fiftieth anniversary in vows as a Carthusian monk.[76]

Queen Isabel II of Spain was dethroned on 26 September 1868, two weeks before her thirty-eighth birthday. On being expelled from Spain, she took up residence in Paris, where she remained until her death on 9 April 1904. Those who still had roles to play in this drama were Pope Pius IX, Cardinal Barnabò, Bishop Bataillon, Don Carlos Cuarterón, director Marinoni, and Father Raimondi. Nearly all other actors had been carried off by the Grim Reaper, who would soon return to seek out and find those whom he had missed.

---

75. Lillian G. Keys, *The Life and Times of Bishop Pompallier*, 355, 361, 366, 377–78, 381.

76. Letter, D. Luc Fauchon, archivist of La Grande-Chartreuse, to Wiltgen, 23 July 1987, accompanying p. 148 of "Catalogue des Religieux," which contains a full-page entry titled: "153. Dom Thaddée SUPRIÈS." The author expresses his indebtedness for these precise vital statistics. Suigo in *Pio IX*, 75, gives the date of death for Supriès incorrectly as 20 September 1888, and Didinger in *Bibliotheca Missionum*, 8:63, gives the date incorrectly as 20 October 1888. Supriès died on 20 November 1888. He was born on 20 October 1800 at Cotignac (Var) in the Diocese of Fréjus.

23

Bataillon Tells Barnabò: Send Elloy to Micronesia
1 May 1870

LOUIS-ANDRÉ ELLOY (1829–78), A FRENCH MARIST PRIEST, ARRIVED IN THE VICARIATE Apostolic of Central Oceania at the age of twenty-six to take up missionary work. Later he wrote: "Samoa is the archipelago where I have worked as a missionary since 1856 and where the good God has deigned to bless my efforts." He was so successful there and so well-liked by his bishop and by his fellow missionaries that Pope Pius IX on 9 August 1863 named him titular bishop of Tipasa and coadjutor to the vicar apostolic of Central Oceania. Elloy at that time was thirty-three years old. His office as coadjutor meant that he would succeed Bishop Pierre Bataillon, also a Marist, his senior by nearly twenty full years, who was then vicar apostolic of Central Oceania.[1]

Bataillon had been in the first group of Marists who accompanied Bishop Pompallier to his Vicariate Apostolic of Western Oceania.[2] In November 1837 he was assigned to Wallis or Uvea island located in the very center of four clusters of islands known as the Samoa (or Navigators) Archipelago, Ellice Islands (now Tuvalu), Fiji Islands, and Tonga (or Friendly) Islands. When this entire area became the Vicariate Apostolic of Central Oceania on 8 August 1842, Bataillon was chosen to be its first vicar apostolic.[3] He was then thirty-two years old.

Victor Poupinel, also a Marist priest, was visitator of Marist missions in Oceania since 1857. He informed Cardinal Prefect Barnabò of Propaganda Fide on 24 November 1863 that Marist Missionaries of the Central Oceania vicariate were highly pleased "over the news of the elevation of the Reverend Father Elloy to the episcopacy." This was fifteen weeks after Elloy's appointment. Poupinel said that

---

1. PF: SC Oceania vol. 9 (1869–72, Part I), f. 263r, 264v, Elloy to Barnabò, 21 June 1869. Elloy was born on 29 November 1829, and Bataillon was born on 6 January 1810.

2. On the origins of the Vicariate Apostolic of Western Oceania, see Wiltgen, *Oceania*, chap. 6.

3. On the origins of the Vicariate Apostolic of Central Oceania, see ibid., chap. 14.

this young prelate, whose zeal and other apostolic virtues I have often admired, knows how to win for himself the confidence and affection of missionaries and of neophytes. For two months he has been in Sydney, where he was sent by Bishop Bataillon to complete the composition of texts in the Samoan language, which the mission urgently needs, and to have them printed quickly. We all hope that this momentary absence of Bishop Elloy from the theater of his labors will prove to be of great profit for the mission. . . .[4]

After completing this task in Sydney, Elloy returned to the Central Oceania vicariate and was assigned by Bataillon to a post in the Tonga Islands. But this was not at all to Elloy's liking. "I could not continue to remain at that secondary post, being nothing but a replacement for a simple missionary at the parish of Maofaga in Tonga," he told Cardinal Barnabò. "There I had only nominal authority over the rest of the archipelago. This would lower the episcopal dignity in the eyes of the local people and would greatly reduce the influence of a bishop in those islands for both the present and the future. When I called this to the attention of Bishop Bataillon, he sent me to Sydney as director of an agricultural school in Clydesdale. . . ."

This transfer proved to be "a surprise and a scandal for people [in Sydney]," Elloy said, "when they saw that a bishop just one year after his consecration had come back [to Sydney] to take charge of buying and selling, busying himself with all of the innumerable details involved in putting to good use a large property. . . ." And since the population of Sydney was English and to a large extent Protestant, Elloy felt that "the episcopal character" was being compromised even more, as he told Cardinal Prefect Barnabò of Propaganda on 21 June 1869. In fact, coadjutor Elloy considered Bataillon's treatment intolerable enough and unreasonable enough for him legitimately to separate himself from the Vicariate Apostolic of Central Oceania to which he had been assigned by Rome.[5]

Barnabò did his best to reconcile the two bishops, explaining to Bataillon as early as 22 March 1866 that Elloy had been given to him as coadjutor "by the Holy See in order to assist Your Excellency in conducting your episcopal ministry. I believe, however, that his work could be of greater help to you, if you were to allow him to administer—under your direction—some part of your mission. . . ."[6]

Bataillon replied that precisely this type of arrangement, which Barnabò was asking him to adopt, was the kind that he in fact had already introduced. "I gave my coadjutor a separate territory, the Archipelago of Friends [or Tonga Islands], which is the most important territory after the area in which I myself work." Elloy had accepted this arrangement, Bataillon said, and had even requested it. "But he threatened me that he would leave, if I

---

4. PF: SC Oceania vol. 7 (1861–64), f. 970rv, Poupinel to Barnabò, 24 November 1863.

5. Ibid., vol. 9 (1869–72, Part I), f. 264v, Elloy to Barnabò, 21 June 1869. Elloy was in Rome when he wrote this letter.

6. These extracts from Barnabò's letter of 22 March 1866, are quoted in ibid., f. 455v, Bataillon to Barnabò, 25 August 1869.

did not give him the Navigators [or Samoa] Archipelago."⁷ This particular archipelago, however, Bataillon had wanted for himself.

Already in the previous year on 9 July 1868, Bataillon had complained to Barnabò about Elloy and also about Father Poupinel, who had been sent to Oceania by Superior General Favre to make an official visitation of Marist missions.⁸ Barnabò had replied on 30 October 1868:

> Although I see that relations between you and your missionaries and the Society [of Mary] have worsened after the visitation, there is nothing better that I can do but give you the following advice:
>
> Busy yourself with settling all these quarrels by means of your kindness and prudence, and grumble no more about them. Strive also with all your zeal to achieve the one goal of putting the minds of your missionaries at rest, so that they may experience their original peace and concord with you, which is so necessary for propagating the Catholic faith.

Bataillon himself, Barnabò said, had stipulated that Elloy "be ordained a bishop" and had also "attested to his good spirit and to his zeal for preaching the faith." Therefore,

> I judge it best that he [Elloy] should receive the government of that part of the Central Oceania Vicariate which was cut off from your vicariate by decree of 20 August 1850 and was erected into a new vicariate with the name Navigators Archipelago. Its administration had earlier been handed over to Very Reverend Douarre, your other coadjutor.⁹
>
> But by decree of 20 August 1851, its administration was again entrusted to Your Excellency after he [Douarre] returned to his Vicariate of New Caledonia. I judge that full administration should now be given to your above-named coadjutor, the Most Reverend Elloy, precisely in the same way as was done with the Most Reverend Douarre. Thus you will be relieved of the excessive burden of caring for both vicariates [of Central Oceania and of the Navigators] and he [Elloy], in his part of the Lord's vineyard, could apply himself fully. I shall wait for a categorical reply from Your Excellency to the above matter.¹⁰

One year and nine days later Bataillon sent Barnabò his reply from Sydney halfway around the world.

---

7. PF: SC Oceania vol. 9 (1869–72, Part I), f. 455v, Bataillon to Barnabò, 25 August 1869.

8. The date and substance of Bataillon's letter of 9 July 1868 are found in PF: LDB vol. 360 (1868, Part II), f. 1191r, Barnabò to Bataillon, 30 October 1868. Favre had succeeded Colin in office as superior general of the Marists on 10 May 1854.

9. For details on Douarre and on the founding of the Navigators or Samoa Vicariate Apostolic, see Wiltgen, *Oceania*, 425–31, 511–21. See also the present work, chap. 3, pp. 40–42, 43, and 45.

10. PF: LDB vol. 360 (1868, Part II), f. 1191r–1192r, Barnabò to Bataillon, 30 October 1868.

I had asked for the Reverend Father Elloy as my coadjutor because he had been a person full of ideas and full of ardor, who often had given evidence of his attachment to me and of his confidence in me. But since his ordination [as bishop] he has seemed to grow cold in my regard.... He declared to me in formal terms that if I did not resign, he himself would resign.... My coadjutor disappeared and went to Sydney under the pretext of looking after some business. From there he informed me that he would not return to the mission again and that he had written to the Superior General of our Society, placing himself at his disposal.

Subsequently, however, Elloy did return to the Central Oceania vicariate, Bataillon said, "and I agreed to assign a separate area to him so that he could give expression to his zeal there. But the condition was that he would not refuse me his services, whenever they were needed for another part of the vicariate.... The entire matter seemed to be resolved and I sent him to see Father Poupinel [in Sydney] to put a number of things in order ... and to get this entire affair settled.... He went. But when he got there, he changed his mind and left for Europe."

Bataillon assured Barnabò that he was eager to go to Rome himself in order to settle his difficulties. If the cardinal were to send back coadjutor Elloy, Bataillon said, he would hand over to Elloy the management of the vicariate. As for himself, he would go to Rome and would also take part in the Vatican Council, which was scheduled to begin in Saint Peter's Basilica thirteen months later on 8 December 1869.[11]

Cardinal Prefect Barnabò on 30 October 1868 had asked Bishop Bataillon for a categorical reply on the Navigators Archipelago. Six months and six days later Bataillon submitted the following summaries of his previous letters and called them his categorical reply:

"My idea, my wish and my request," he said, "would be that for the following reasons I should not at all be dispossessed of the Navigators Archipelago:

- "1. After I surrendered the Fiji Islands, the Navigators Archipelago became the principal and most important part of my mission. As I see it, I became entitled to the Vicariate of the Navigators Archipelago after giving up Fiji, since otherwise only a modest fragment of Central Oceania would have been left over for me."
- "2. Moreover," he said, "his residence and his principal buildings, properties and schools, all of which had been built by himself at great expense, were all located in the Navigators Archipelago.
- "3. The very heart of communications for the isolated islands of Central Oceania, which are to remain in my territory," he said, "is located in the [Navigators] Archipelago..., since only here do regular opportunities exist for correspondence ... and transportation by ship.
- "4. Ceding the Navigators, which Your Eminence now proposes to me, is what my coadjutor earlier wished to impose upon me by threats and pressure." If Cardinal

---

11. PF: SC Oceania vol. 9 (1869–72, Part I), f. 445rv, 446v, Bataillon to Barnabò, 8 November 1869.

Barnabò were now to take that same position, Bataillon said, Elloy would win out and Bataillon's authority would suffer, because all of his missionaries knew about Elloy's earlier threats.

"5. The main reason, however, is that ceding [the Navigators Archipelago] does not seem necessary to remedy the existing evil. The reason alleged by my coadjutor for putting me at a distance from him is that he cannot stand me. Would it not then be simpler and more fitting, that he should agree to put himself at a distance from me?"

Bishop Bataillon then made this concrete proposal: Cardinal Barnabò should send Bishop Elloy back to the Tonga Archipelago because of his knowledge of the language there. This was also the largest archipelago in Bataillon's vicariate after the Navigators. "All powers would be given to him to operate there freely," Bataillon promised. "In addition this would be a temporary arrangement, since in view of my age [fifty-nine years] and my infirmities, it will not be long before he has everything." Bataillon added that Elloy in the past had considered his receiving the Tonga Archipelago as the solution for everyone's problems. "To me it still seems to be so," Bataillon said. This was the categorical reply prepared for Barnabò by Bataillon.[12]

Meanwhile Bishop Elloy had arrived in Rome and in May 1868 presented a report to Pope Pius IX and a copy to Cardinal Prefect Barnabò. It contained his reasons for feeling obliged to leave the Central Oceania vicariate. Cardinal Barnabò "graciously and favorably accepted these reasons . . . ," according to Elloy, "thus making legitimate" his departure from the Central Oceania vicariate.

When in Rome again thirteen months later, Elloy on 21 June 1869 assured Barnabò that he would submit "to all decisions that Your Eminence wishes to make." He nonetheless pointed out

> that the difficulties of the past will begin again, if I am to return and place myself at the disposition of Bishop Bataillon without Your Eminence having determined the field in which I am to work. I ask for neither the Navigators Vicariate, nor for that of Central Oceania.
>
> But if I am to be at some distance from our islands, the only thing that I hope for is that I might be sent to a part of the Vicariate of Central Oceania, where the gospel has not yet penetrated. I wish to mention the archipelago known as the Gilbert Islands or Kingsmill Islands, which is situated on the equator and numbers more than sixty thousand inhabitants. Many of the local people from this archipelago have already been baptized at Samoa, where they were brought by a Dutch ship. So we could more or less count on a good reception in many of these islands, since we are known there without having gone there. If I were to be entrusted with this archipelago, where nothing as yet has been done, we could perhaps avoid causing pain for Bishop Bataillon.

12. Ibid., f. 453r–454r, Bataillon to Barnabò, 6 May 1869.

> If on the other hand Your Eminence should want to accede to the wishes of the Superior General of the Society of Mary and assign the Navigators Vicariate to me, as you yourself had intended to do in the beginning, I would then ask that the Gilbert Islands be included, since their contacts... are mostly with Samoa. I have spoken of this project with Reverend Father Favre. He himself was supposed to write to Your Eminence, requesting that you join the Kingsmill Islands [or Gilberts] to the Navigators in case this vicariate is to be entrusted to me.... May I request a definite decision from Your Eminence?[13]

Three days later on 24 June 1869, Bataillon, as if perceiving Elloy's thoughts by telepathy, sent the following note to Cardinal Barnabò from his far-off residence in Samoa: "I would be so grateful, if Your Eminence were to allow me to choose the territory or that part [of my mission], which is to be given to my coadjutor. But should you wish to assign it to him yourself, I submit myself... to your decision..., whatever it may be."[14]

Besides receiving this letter from Bataillon, Cardinal Barnabò also received one from Superior General Favre dated 17 September 1869 expressing great fear that the Navigators Vicariate would be ruined, if it were to remain entrusted to Bishop Bataillon.[15] Seven weeks later on 7 November, Favre repeated his warning, saying that letters arriving from Bataillon's vicariate "only confirm my fears and my sad forebodings. All missionaries, even the most holy ones, complain of the conduct of Bishop Bataillon and declare him to be intolerable." Favre then proceeded to list their complaints: "The difficulties encountered by the bishop in his administration have not made him more moderate, more indulgent, or more merciful. Instead they have soured his character, which by nature is already cold, egotistical and imperious. As a result his method of administration has become harassing and truly despotic. The bishop has a passion for authority—a blind passion—which instead of safeguarding his authority, compromises it and makes it detestable." All Marist missionaries, Favre said, "are clamoring for Bishop Elloy, who founded the Samoa Mission and who alone can raise it from its ruins and make it flourish once again."

Favre was "profoundly afflicted by the sad conditions in the Central Vicariate" and hoped that Barnabò "might provide an efficacious remedy for them as soon as possible." These evils, Favre maintained, resulted from "a character fault of the prelate and from his bad administration. This is proven by the fact that our missionaries in New Zealand, Fiji

---

13. Ibid., f. 263r–265v, Elloy to Barnabò, 21 June 1869. Here Elloy considers identical the Gilbert Islands and the Kingsmill Islands. An *Atlas*, however, designates as the "Kingsmill Group" a number of islands at the southeastern end of the Gilbert Islands, whereas a *Year Book* designates these as belonging to the Gilbert Islands. See the *National Geographic Atlas of the World* map, p. 140, and the names of individual Gilbert Islands in *Pacific Islands Year Book and Who's Who*, p. 204. See also this chapter, p. 451, n. 65.

14. PF: SC Oceania vol. 9 (1869–72, Part I), f. 273v, Bataillon to Barnabò, 24 June 1869.

15. Favre's letter of 17 September 1869 was not found. But its contents are referred to in ibid., f. 417r, Favre to Barnabò, 7 November 1869.

and New Caledonia, are not at all asking to leave their missions. Similarly the vicars apostolic in those places do not at all complain" about their missionaries.[16]

One month later the Vatican Council was to begin in the right transept of Saint Peter's Basilica; its first meeting was scheduled for 8 December 1869. Pope Pius IX had named Cardinal Prefect Barnabò a member of the Central Preparatory Commission and also president of the Commission on the Missions. It thus became Barnabò's responsibility to prepare a *schema* or preliminary draft for a document on missionary activity.

Bishops from mission lands—thanks to Barnabò—were invited to participate in the Vatican Council, something not provided for by church law. As a result mission territories with the rank of vicariates apostolic were represented by their vicars apostolic. These were titular bishops, not bishops in charge of full-fledged ecclesiastical territories called dioceses. Coadjutors of vicars apostolic, like Elloy, being also titular bishops, were invited to participate as well. This was the Twentieth Ecumenical Council in the history of the Roman Catholic Church, better known from its location as the Vatican Council.[17]

France had earlier favored Propaganda "by transporting its missionaries free of charge to lands in the East." Since 1860, however, France had "refused to transport them to the [East] Indies and to China; but New Caledonia . . . was an exception." This caused "immense expenses" for Propaganda, which had always looked upon France "as a Catholic power proud of being protectress of missions in the East . . ."

The Austrian Lloyd Line, however, had begun to make "very broad concessions." In fact, "It not only continued to transport free of charge two missionaries every week to missions in the West, but from 1860 onward it also began providing the same service for missions in the East." To this permanent favor, "extraordinary ones are continually being added. No wish is ever refused when transportation is requested for more missionaries than the two already agreed upon, or if transport is requested for nuns, regardless of whether persons are assigned to missions in the West or in the East."

When Pius IX convoked the Vatican Council, the Lloyd Line "offered free passage to all bishops and to their retinues, who sailed to Rome from ports touched by Lloyd ships." This liberality pleased the pope "so highly, that he decided to express his good pleasure by decorating with knighthood the Catholic board members" of the Lloyd Line and "by giving a precious gift to its top director, Baron [Elio] Morpurgo [1804–76], a Jew." Director first and since 1865 president of the administrative board of the Austrian Lloyd shipping company, Morpurgo supervised Austria's transition to propeller-driven iron steamers.[18]

16. See ibid., f. 417r–417v, Favre to Barnabò, 7 November 1869.

17. Metzler, "Präfekten und Sekretäre," 47. Since the Twenty-First Ecumenical Council (1962–65) also took place in the Vatican, it has been called from the beginning the Second Vatican Council. From that time the Vatican Council of 1869–70 has been referred to as the First Vatican Council. A titular bishop is given a titular diocese, that is, a diocese where the Roman Catholic Church once flourished, but which now exists only in name or title.

18. PF: LDB vol. 377 (1881), f. 188rv, Pro Memoria, 7 April 1881. On Morpurgo and his renowned family see *Österreichisches Biographisches Lexikon 1815–1950*, pp. 378–81, and *Encyclopedia Judaica*, vol. 12, col.

Vicar Apostolic Bataillon had also received an invitation to attend the Vatican Council. But eight and a half months before it was to begin, he informed Cardinal Prefect Barnabò from Apia that, if Elloy did not come back, he would take this to mean that he himself had been dispensed from attending.[19]

Three months later on 24 June 1869, Bataillon wrote again from Apia to Cardinal Prefect Barnabò: "Lo and behold! It is time for me to get started on my way to Rome, if I am to arrive there on time for the council. But having no news of the return of my coadjutor, nor of the arrival of any missionary reinforcements, I believe it is reasonable for me to interpret this to mean that the intentions of the Holy Father and of Your Eminence are that I should remain at my post. . . ."[20] Two months later on 25 August 1869, Bataillon repeated this. Then on 3 October he sent further excuses for not having set out for Rome.[21]

Six days after the opening of the Vatican Council, Bishop Elloy wrote from Rome to Cardinal Barnabò: "For over two years I have been waiting for a solution . . . ," he said.

> I ask for neither the Navigators Vicariate, nor the Central Oceania Vicariate, nor Tonga, nor any of the islands already evangelized. I permit myself to express nothing else but my one and only desire to be sent to a land still entirely pagan, namely, to the *Kingsmill Archipelago*, where a population of sixty thousand souls seems ready for sowing the Gospel.[22] I would like to arrive there before Protestants get there ahead of us. . . .
>
> Your Eminence had proposed entrusting to me the Navigators Vicariate. And the Superior General of the Marists had accepted this arrangement enthusiastically. . . . I myself would also accept it with complete obedience. However, I would dare to request—in case you sanction giving me this vicariate—that Your Eminence add to the Navigators the Kingsmill Archipelago and the Tokelau Group, countries which are still pagan. These islands are in contact with the Navigators Archipelago and not at all with other islands in the Central Oceania Vicariate. This is true at least for the Kingsmills Islands. . . . Please make a decision without having recourse to Bishop Bataillon once again, because otherwise this would mean a delay of another year. . . .[23]

Elloy took active part in the Vatican Council, and Father Ferdinand Vitte, a professor of theology at Marist headquarters in Lyon, was sent to Rome to assist him and to look

---

348–50.

19. See PF: SC Oceania vol. 9 (1869–72, Part I) f. 449rv, Bataillon to Barnabò, 23 March 1869.

20. Ibid., f. 273r.

21. Ibid., f. 455r, 456r, Bataillon to Barnabò, 25 August 1869. For Bataillon's letter of 3 October 1869, see the reference to it in PF: LDB vol. 363 (1870, Part I), f. 123v, Barnabò to Bataillon, 18 February 1870.

22. When Elloy speaks of "a population of sixty thousand souls," one must look upon this figure as a rough estimate, perhaps even as a pious exaggeration, meant to draw attention from authorities and mission aid societies in Rome and France. In 1963 there was still no exact count. "The estimated native population" of the sixteen islands which made up the Gilbert Islands was given in that year as 35,630. See *Pacific Islands Year Book*, 204. See also this chapter, p. 434, n. 13, and p. 451, n. 65 on Elloy identifying "the Kingsmill Archipelago" with the Gilbert Islands.

23. PF: SC Oceania vol. 9 (1869–72, Part I), f. 1385rv, Elloy to Barnabò, 14 December 1869.

into matters regarding the Marist rule. On 17 November 1869, just two days after arriving in Rome, Vitte informed Superior General Favre of Barnabò's urgent wish to confer personally with him in Rome. This was three weeks before the Vatican Council was to begin. Barnabò had been able to deal directly with Elloy on the Navigators Vicariate question and now also wanted to discuss it and the Marist rule directly with Favre. But three weeks passed and Favre did not appear. So Barnabò had Vitte send reminders to him on 8 December (the opening day of the Vatican Council) and again on 14 and 18 December. Because of Barnabò's insistence Favre eventually left Lyon for Rome on 3 January 1870.[24] He remained in Rome for the rest of January and, at the suggestion of Barnabò, wrote to Bataillon in the course of that month.[25]

Cardinal Barnabò followed up Favre's letter to Bataillon by writing one of his own on 18 February 1870. He reminded the bishop that the Vicariate of the Navigators had been given to him "temporarily for governing" some "twenty years earlier," when Bishop Douarre returned to New Caledonia.[26] Barnabò did not want to impose on Bataillon his own solution for the problems, he said, nor did he wish to accept Bataillon's solution for them, since it was too difficult "to deal with such grave matters by letter.... I believe it would be best for you to make a voyage to Rome. Then here in the presence of the Superior General you can make those declarations from which Propaganda can learn the causes of the evils as well as the remedies to be adopted...."

"It will also prove advantageous for Your Excellency to be present at the Ecumenical Council," Barnabò said. "On that occasion you will be able to tell Propaganda much about the needs of your Mission." He further assured Bataillon that the administration of his vicariate would suffer no harm. "In order to prevent this," he said, "I shall send your coadjutor back to the mission and he will meet you in Sydney. Therefore upon receiving this letter of mine, put your vicariate in order immediately and begin your journey...."[27]

On the very day that Barnabò sent his instructions to Bataillon, 18 February 1870, the Twenty-Seventh General Congregation of the Vatican Council took place in Saint Peter's Basilica. Under discussion was the "schema" or draft called "The Constitution on a Concise Catechism." The second speaker that Friday morning was Bishop Elloy, coadjutor of the

---

24. See *Origines maristes (1786–1836)*, 3:172 nn. 3 and 5.

25. See PF: SC Oceania vol. 9 (1869–72, Part I), f. 784v, Favre to Barnabò, 19 February 1871. Here Favre gives the month and year (January 1870) of his letter to Bataillon, but not the particular day.

26. To be precise, Douarre returned to New Caledonia on 5 April 1851. For more details see chap. 3, pp. 40, 42, and 43.

27. See PF: LDB vol. 363 (1870, Part I), f. 123v–124v, Barnabò to Bataillon, 18 February 1870. This is the version that was sent to Bishop Bataillon. A more forceful version bearing the same date, but differing in several respects from the LDB version, is found in PF: SC Oceania vol. 9 (1869–72, Part I), f. 447rv. This latter version may well have been submitted by Elloy or Favre after a conversation with Barnabò. Such proposed drafts for official letters, however, are seldom found in Propaganda's archives.

Central Oceania vicariate. Being of the opinion that the "Concise Catechism" should be identical for the entire Catholic world, Elloy preferred to call it a "Universal Catechism."

His address to the Council Fathers was drawn up, no doubt, with the help of Father Vitte. Bishop Elloy spoke of "the usefulness and quasi moral necessity of a universal catechism." Some Council Fathers wanted a very short catechism containing only those doctrines necessary for salvation. Elloy said that such a catechism "would be sufficient for the uneducated and for small children," but for everyone else there ought to be a larger catechism containing "an explanation of doctrines along with proofs for them." These explanations and proofs, he added, ought to be the same or similar all over the world.

"As regards peoples recently converted from paganism, and especially as regards inhabitants of Oceania . . . ," he said,

> they have been living in the greatest ignorance and many of them have been accustomed to cannibalism. But in those islands where forty years ago there were no Christians, there are now more than 50,000 Christians. And I can testify from my own experience that the island peoples of Oceania—at least those who have received the faith at an early age or were born into it—are in no way inferior in their knowledge of Catholic doctrine, either to children or to young people of the same age in my own country of France, who have received the usual [catechetical] instructions. Consequently there is no obstacle to their having the same catechism as other Christian peoples. In fact, the introduction of such a catechism will very greatly assist us in our preaching, when we testify that it is the very same catechism being used by the entire Catholic world.

In his introduction Elloy had placed particular emphasis on the universal aspect of the catechism. "Venerable Fathers," he had said,

> what would it be like if someone could say: The doctrine that I teach and the words that I use are identical to those of bishops and priests, not only in this diocese, but in our Church all over the world! If this were the case, would that person not enjoy greater authority, and would his words and doctrine not be received with greater obedience and veneration? . . . For our neophytes and for the inhabitants of our islands in Oceania, Venerable Fathers, the fact of there being only one catechism which comes, so to say, from the hand of the Supreme Pontiff and from this Sacred Assembly, would beyond doubt be a very strong argument for the truthfulness of our doctrine. It would also lend great weight to the authority of those who preach the doctrine of Christ's Church in the midst of infidels.[28]

Superior General Favre's visit to Rome in January 1870 was followed in April by a visit from Father Poupinel, visitor of the Marists in Oceania. Writing from Rome to Cardinal Prefect Barnabò on 8 April 1870, Poupinel thanked him profusely for his letter of 18 February ordering Bataillon to leave for Rome immediately. "I cannot but thank God

---

28. For Elloy's complete intervention in the original Latin, see Ioannes Dominicus Mansi, *Sacrorum Conciliorum Nova et Amplissima Collectio*. . . . (Arnhem (Pays-Bas) & Leipzig, 1924), vol. 50, col. 781–86.

on learning that Propaganda has taken this step," he said. It was necessary "if one wishes to prevent the very probable ruin of the Central Oceania Mission." Nor would Bataillon's absence harm his mission. "On the contrary," Poupinel suggested, "his absence will prove to be a great relief for his priests, who have been suffering for such a long time. This will also make it possible to provide a remedy for evils which have lasted far too long."

But on asking himself whether Bataillon would obey Barnabò's order to come to Rome, Poupinel told Barnabò: "I would hope so, but I do not at all expect that he will. Those who know the prelate well, know also that he is endowed with a singular power of resistance. I shall be very surprised if he does not find reasons—according to him compulsory ones—for not leaving the mission until he receives new orders." Poupinel insisted that matters in the Central Oceania Vicariate and above all in the Archipelago of Samoa were "continually getting worse," even though "some years ago the mission was making such rapid progress."

Being well acquainted with the misery experienced by missionaries working under Bataillon, Poupinel added: "I am astonished that they have borne up with it to this day. But the best of them can no longer hold out there. . . . Bishop Elloy's return would restore confidence and courage to both the neophytes and the missionaries. . . ." Elloy besides was "gifted with rare qualities for the ministry and he enjoys great influence over the local people," Poupinel said. "Still, if he has to go back and be dependent upon Bishop Bataillon, far from causing good, his return to the Central Oceania Vicariate would cause evil. And the causes which had forced him to leave, would revive without delay. . . ."

Poupinel had high hopes that Elloy would be sent back to Oceania "as soon as possible." Yet he cautioned Barnabò: "One must foresee the very probable case of Bishop Bataillon not leaving his mission. Your Eminence earlier informed him that in this case his vicariate would be divided into two parts and that the Samoa Archipelago would be entrusted to his present coadjutor. This at least was the wish of Your Eminence. Samoa's remaining under the Most Reverend Vicar Apostolic [Bataillon] would ruin the mission in this archipelago." Poupinel's foreboding letter contained a concrete proposal as "a means of terminating promptly and as peacefully as possible this pernicious conflict." He suggested that Barnabò present Elloy on his departure from Rome "with a letter for Bishop Bataillon." In this letter Barnabò would state that Bishop Elloy "had been placed in charge of the Samoa [or Navigators] Archipelago." However, a special clause would point out that "this letter shall remain secret" if Bishop Bataillon "sets out for Rome."[29]

Barnabò did not adopt the proposal. He believed that his own letter of 18 February 1870 was strong enough and that it would surely have the desired effect of causing Bataillon to set out for Rome.

Fifteen days after Father Poupinel wrote to Cardinal Barnabò, Bishop Elloy wrote in a similar vein to Pope Pius IX. "In the audience which Your Holiness deigned to grant me several days ago," he said, "I informed Your Holiness of some of the reasons why it is neces-

---

29. PF: SC Oceania vol. 9 (1869–72, Part I), f. 451r–452v, Poupinel to Barnabò, 8 April 1870.

sary to make provisions so that I may return to the Navigators Archipelago, where the mission is going to ruin." Vicar Apostolic Bataillon, he said, was devoting himself "completely to material projects which he directs, namely, making paths, building fences—only to tear them down again after some months—and digging ditches. For six years these have been the principal occupations of the bishop."

Bataillon's missionaries "receive no spiritual direction," Elloy added, "and the retreats held in common have not taken place for five years. Nor are theological conferences held any more by the missionaries. The bishop avoids bringing them together, because then he would have to listen to them and introduce uniform measures. . . ." The missionaries were also often transferred from one place to another. "And finally, Most Holy Father, the Samoa Mission is headed for extinction." Elloy's letter was dated 23 April 1870 and stated that the pope had given him reason to hope that he would be entrusted "with the administration of the Samoa Archipelago."[30]

Eight days later as if being aided by telepathy again, Bishop Bataillon wrote to Cardinal Prefect Barnabò from Wallis (or Uvea) Island, requesting that Bishop Elloy be kept out of the Samoa Archipelago permanently, that he be relieved of his office as coadjutor, and that he be sent instead to launch the Vicariate Apostolic of Micronesia, a mission that earlier had been entrusted to the Marists. He was suggesting, namely, that Elloy be named vicar apostolic of Micronesia.

"I believe that I must . . . give Your Eminence some news on the islands of Micronesia which are close to my mission," Bataillon said.

> When our Vicar Apostolic, Bishop Pompallier, arrived in Oceania thirty-three years ago, he at first thought of starting his mission in the Caroline Archipelago at Ascension Island [now Ponape], about which he had received favorable reports. But circumstances changed his plans and we established ourselves in the southern hemisphere at Wallis, Futuna and New Zealand. Later there was again talk of opening a station on Ascension Island, but this has not yet come about.[31]
>
> Some time later Micronesia was separated from Western Oceania, was erected into a vicariate apostolic and was entrusted to Bishop Epalle. This prelate, also as a result of the good reports which he had obtained about the Archipelago of the Carolines and about Ascension Island in particular, intended to establish himself there. But he was of the opinion that first he ought to go ashore in the Solomon Archipelago, about which he had no news. And there he met his death! Now if he or if others from his mission had pressed forward as far as Ascension Island, there is reason to believe that they would have succeeded and that today they would possess a flourishing mission.[32]

30. PF: SC Oceania vol. 9 (1869–72, Part I), f. 539r, 540r, Elloy to Pius IX, 23 April 1870.

31. For details on Pompallier's interest in Ascension Island (Ponape) see Wiltgen, *Oceania*, 138f, 141–43, 151–57 passim, 160, 215, 250–51, 276–77.

32. For details on founding the Micronesia vicariate and on the death of Bishop Epalle, see ibid., 284–310, 331, 338–41.

In that earlier period difficulties were not lacking, Bataillon admitted, because "the peoples were still savage and there were no means of communication. But today circumstances seem much more favorable for the foundation of a mission in the Caroline Archipelago and in all the islands of Micronesia. An influential House of Commerce based in Shanghai (China) is making capital of the products in these islands. It has made foundations in the principal islands, one of which is Ascension Island, where it keeps a large flotilla for visiting all the islands roundabout. What opportunities this would provide for evangelization!"

Being a Catholic missionary, Bataillon said, obliged him to show interest not only in his own people, "but also in *my neighbor* and in those near to me. But who will speak to Your Eminence about these abandoned peoples, who are so far away, if we who are their neighbors keep silent? I therefore take the liberty of pleading their cause before Your Eminence."

Bataillon then proceeded to give Barnabò a brief historical survey of the missions in Western Oceania and the role of the Society of Mary, which had earlier been responsible for them and "must take up this work again." From the time that the Society of Mary apparently wanted to withdraw from the Oceania missions, he said, it had ceased to grow in France. "Taking up missionary work resolutely would be the best means for it to attract new vocations."

He pointed out that the large archipelago of New Hebrides had also been entrusted to the Society of Mary. And although it "has made great efforts to be relieved of this responsibility, Protestant ministers there have held fast." The Society "had also been active in Melanesia, but later abandoned it," he said. "If it fears these archipelagoes because they are unhealthy and dangerous, it ought to take up work at least in the Vicariate of Micronesia, which is healthy, is frequented by ships and consequently is without any danger, and it can also be easily reached. Protestants have not yet occupied these regions, except for Ascension [Island], where ministers are at work.... It would be necessary not to allow heresy to advance in the other islands, because it constitutes the greatest obstacle for Catholic missions."

Cardinal Barnabò "should request the Society [of Mary] to take up responsibility again for the islands which it has abandoned," Bataillon said, "at least for New Hebrides Islands and above all for the Vicariate of Micronesia." And if a mission superior should be needed, he said,

> I am prepared to give up my coadjutor [Elloy] for the benefit of these new missions. Our characters do not harmonize and it is painful for him to live with me. For everyone's benefit it seems best to entrust him with another mission. I feel certain that he would very much like to be entrusted with Micronesia or with some other mission.
>
> As for sharing with him the little mission that is left to me, it is not worth the trouble. In my original vicariate there were five hundred thousand souls. As a result of the various divisions that have since been made, I have given up all of these except

a population not exceeding sixty thousand souls. I have further reasons for not wanting this territory [of mine] divided.

For a long time Bataillon had wanted to send Barnabò a report on the islands adjoining his mission territory. What prompted his doing so now was information that he had just received from the captain of a ship belonging to a house of commerce with a foundation at Ascension Island (or Ponape) in the Carolines. Explorations already made by that company extended as far as Wallis, where Bataillon was at the moment. He sent Barnabò "these notes made in haste" via that same ship, which was setting out on its return voyage to Ascension Island.[33]

One month later on 1 June 1870, Bataillon further informed Barnabò that he now had "a more certain route" for sending mail. If the Micronesia mission were to be revived, its center "ought to be established in Ascension [or Ponape], the most important island in the Carolines." He said that this island was so important "because it is the center of commercial operations and one can travel from there to all other islands, [even] to the Palaus and Marshalls. The most suitable place for the procure office of these missions would be the city of Shanghai, from which the ships depart" to visit the islands of Micronesia and to engage in commerce.

The Central Oceania vicariate which was assigned to him had been founded on 11 August 1842 and "originally had consisted of four large archipelagoes," Bataillon said.

> They were New Caledonia, New Hebrides, Fiji and the Navigators, containing a population of six hundred thousand.[34] Both New Caledonia and New Hebrides were cut off first, containing three hundred thousand souls. The next section to be cut off was the Fiji Islands, which became a new vicariate with a population of more than two hundred thousand souls. Nothing else was left for me but the Navigators [or Samoa] along with some other islands and ports having a population of sixty to seventy thousand souls. It is not worth the trouble to make still another division.
>
> It would be more worthwhile to subdivide the Vicariate of New Caledonia . . . and make New Hebrides a new vicariate,

Bataillon said. The Society of Mary had had a mission in New Hebrides, "but has left it and is no longer concerned about it . . . I would like to see the Society [of Mary] take up this mission again. If it cannot do so at this moment, then let it resign itself to take charge at least of Micronesia, which offers less difficulties and more chances of success."

In conclusion Bataillon again pointed out that his character clashed with Elloy's and that Elloy had too much to suffer from him. And so Bataillon for the sake of Elloy's happiness readily consented "to be deprived of his services" so that another mission elsewhere "could be assigned to him." And if the Society of Mary "should again take up the missions

---

33. PF: SC Oceania vol. 9 (1869–72, Part I), f. 543r–544r, Bataillon to Barnabò, 1 May 1870.

34. Bataillon's letter of 1 May 1870, written just one month earlier, gave the total population as five hundred thousand, not six hundred thousand. See ibid., f. 544r. Statistics for large islands and archipelagoes at this time were mostly guesswork.

which it originally had, at least that of Micronesia, and if a head for that mission should be needed, "I voluntarily give up my coadjutor for this purpose." Bataillon had one more request for Cardinal Barnabò, namely, that Father Poupinel should not be sent back to Oceania as visitator, but should be replaced.[35] On 20 July 1870, one day after the Franco-Prussian War broke out in Europe, Barnabò informed Bataillon that five months had passed "since I wrote to Your Excellency requesting that you take advantage of your opportunity and come to the [Vatican] Council." He added that Propaganda could make use of his "collaboration and counsel for putting in order the affairs of the vicariates apostolic located in Central Oceania." As for coadjutor Elloy, Barnabò said that for the time being he would be entrusted with the administration of those vicariates.

"Therefore if you have not yet begun your voyage, I approach you once again in the Lord, insisting that upon receipt of this letter you set out immediately, since this is also the will of our Holy Father. Therefore place the care of the Vicariates of Central Oceania and of the Navigators Archipelago in the hands of the Most Illustrious and Most Reverend Bishop Elloy, your coadjutor, and give him full powers for disposing of everything for the happy outcome of those missions. You yourself must get busy and come to Rome as quickly as possible...."[36]

Four months later Bataillon answered Barnabò's letter from Futuna, an island in the Pacific Ocean twelve and a half miles long and three miles wide. "Grave events have happened in Europe," he said, "which shall perhaps delay the return of my coadjutor, something which creates an obstacle for the voyage that you have asked me to make." He was referring to the Franco-Prussian War, and he begged Barnabò to allow him to make one more attempt at improving relations with his coadjutor right there in Oceania after Elloy's return. "If we should succeed, then please dispense me from such a troublesome and costly voyage," he said. But if he should still be obliged to make the voyage, he was resolved in that event to bring their differences "before the tribunal of the Holy See." Should no new letter arrive from Barnabò, however, Bataillon would then take it to mean "that you will let me make another attempt here."

Seven more weeks had to pass before Bataillon finally mailed this letter to Barnabò. In a postscript dated 8 January 1871, he said: "Up to now I did not find a good opportunity to send Your Eminence this letter. Nor did I have an opportunity to make the voyage that Your Eminence requests in your letter written this past February, to which Your Eminence refers in your letter of the month of July [1870]. I forgot to mention above that I never received your letter [of February]. It went astray."

Bataillon added to his postscript that he had received no further news about the return of his coadjutor. This made it impossible for him to leave for Europe, he claimed,

---

35. PF: SC Oceania vol. 9 (1869–72, Part I), f. 593r–594r, Bataillon to Barnabò, 1 June 1870. This letter, like that of 1 May 1870, was written at Wallis (Uvea) Island.

36. PF: LDB vol. 364 (1870, Part II), f. 580v–581r, Barnabò to Bataillon, 20 July 1870.

because he first had to transfer his mission personally to Coadjutor Elloy, since there was no one else to whom the mission could be entrusted.[37]

The Franco-Prussian War (1870–71) hastened Elloy's return to his mission, since it brought the Vatican Council to an abrupt close. A French garrison based in Rome since 1867 had been serving as a bulwark for the temporal power of the papacy. But when allied Prussian and German forces attacked France in 1870, the garrison was recalled to help France protect itself. The 89th (and last) General Congregation of the Vatican Council took place on 1 September 1870 with 104 Council Fathers present. Eighteen days later on 19 September the siege of Paris began, and on the following day the armed movement for the unification of the Italian peninsula captured Rome.

On 20 October 1870, exactly one month after the fall of Rome, Pius IX found himself forced to issue an Apostolic Letter suspending the Vatican Council "until some other more opportune and more fitting time." Due to the Franco-Prussian War and the Italian unification movement, he said, the Council Fathers could not enjoy "the necessary liberty, security and tranquility" required for dedicating themselves to Council matters. Furthermore, dioceses in Europe affected by the war needed to have their bishops in their home dioceses. Therefore the pope "regretfully" suspended the Vatican Council, which was never reconvened.[38] The list of unfinished business contained provisions for a universal catechism. But it would be published 122 years later on 15 November 1992 with a simple title: *The Catholic Catechism*.[39]

One of the Council Fathers not present at the last General Congregation on 1 September 1870 was Bishop Elloy. Following instructions received from Barnabò, he had returned to France, recruited personnel for his mission, and at the end of October 1870 sailed from London to Sydney.[40] After a happy crossing of seventy-six days, "we arrived at the port of Sydney on 18 January 1871 . . . ," he told Barnabò. "I have with me for the Vicariate of Central Oceania and for the Archipelago of the Navigators, two Marist priests, two Teaching Brothers of the Congregation of Petits-Frères de Marie, and six nuns of the Congregation of Notre Dame des Missions."

Elloy knew that Cardinal Barnabò had written to Bishop Bataillon a third time on 20 July 1870, stating, "Upon receipt of this letter you must begin your voyage immediately, since this is also the will of our Holy Father." Barnabò had also ordered Bataillon "to leave the care of the Central Oceania Vicariate and that of the Navigators Archipelago" in Elloy's hands. Elloy had therefore expected to find Bataillon in Sydney, "or at least a letter with instructions from him." But Elloy found neither. And yet Bataillon, "according to the orders

---

37. PF: SC Oceania vol. 9 (1869–72, Part I), f. 716r–717v, Bataillon to Barnabò, 19 November 1870, with a postscript of 8 January 1871.

38. See Mansi, *Sacrorum Conciliorum Nova et Amplissima Collectio*, vol. 53, col. 36, 155–58.

39. *The Catholic Catechism* was published by Pope John Paul II.

40. See PF: SC Oceania vol. 9 (1869–72, Part I), f. 784v, Favre to Barnabò, 19 February 1871. Here Favre says that Elloy took along from Europe five nuns. But Elloy himself says that he took along six nuns. See n. 41, below.

of Your Eminence, must hand over [to me] the administration of his vicariate with full powers," Elloy said. The missionaries themselves, however, feared "that Bishop Bataillon would continue to live in his vicariate in spite of orders received from Your Eminence and our Holy Father, the Pope...."

In this letter Elloy gave Barnabò a dismal view of Bataillon's mission. "I well believe that in many islands of this vicariate we can see the beginning of the end of the mission," he said. "The Samoa Mission in particular, which for the past seven years has experienced such confusion, will soon be no more than a ruin. Many places, in which we had established fervent Christian communities, have already been abandoned and Protestant ministers or their catechists have arrived to regain territory which they had lost. If the mission continues to be so disorganized as it is in this moment, God alone knows how this disaster will end."

Elloy made the following proposal to Barnabò: "All seem to fear that Bishop Bataillon still wants to govern his vicariate in spite of the orders that he has received to go to Rome. If this happens, or if he should not give me any powers on his leaving the vicariate, it would be necessary that I receive my faculties directly from Rome. In this case I would request that Your Eminence send me whatever faculties have been granted to Bishop Bataillon. ... May God grant that this final and extreme measure may not become necessary...." It was in Sydney on 25 January 1871, when Elloy wrote his letter, just three days before Paris capitulated to allied Prussian and German troops after being under siege for four months. "Since our mother house in Lyon is occupied by troops," he said, "would Your Eminence kindly address your letter meant for me to: Marist Fathers, Rue du Bon Pasteur, Toulon. They will send it to Sydney and from there it will be sent to me in the islands of the vicariate."[41]

This letter was sent unsealed by Elloy to Superior General Favre, so that he could read it and then forward it to Barnabò. When Favre forwarded it on 2 April 1871 from Rochefort, France, he told Barnabò: "It is my duty to inform you that the letters which I am receiving from the Central Vicariate [of Bishop Bataillon] indicate that the missionaries are suffering much and are impatiently awaiting a remedy for the evils [afflicting them]...."[42]

Barnabò had meanwhile received Bataillon's proposal of 1 June 1870, suggesting that the Society of Mary revive its missionary activity in New Hebrides or at least in Micronesia. According to Bataillon, Micronesia offered "less difficulties and more chances of success."[43]

In response to Bataillon's proposal, Barnabò on 4 January 1871 sent identical letters to coadjutor Elloy and Superior General Favre. "Recently," he said, he had received a letter from Bishop Bataillon explaining

---

41. Ibid., f. 778rv, Elloy to Barnabò, 25 January 1871.
42. Ibid., f. 779r, Favre to Barnabò, 2 April 1871.
43. Ibid., f. 593r–594r, Bataillon to Barnabò, 1 June 1870.

that there is a very excellent opportunity for sending missionaries again to the islands of Micronesia and New Hebrides. He points out that those territories at present are often visited by merchants and that a maritime society has been established in Shanghai to engage the islands just mentioned in commerce. Consequently it would now be easy to found mission stations in those territories for diffusing the Christian faith among those uncivilized peoples. I am therefore writing about this to you, requesting that you carefully consider these matters together with Father Poupinel, the Visitator, and then let me know what you think about them.[44]

Barnabò sent both letters to Superior General Favre, who forwarded the copy for Bishop Elloy via Sydney, Australia. Eight full months passed before it caught up with Elloy at Apia in Samoa. By this time half a year had already passed since Superior General Favre had sent his reply to Barnabò from Verdelais near Bordeaux. It was dated 19 February 1871, three weeks and a day after Paris had capitulated to Prussian and German troops.

"I have conferred about this important matter with Father Poupinel, Visitator of our missions...," Favre said, continuing:

> Both of us are of the opinion that because of the terrible calamity now afflicting France, which has caused confusion for the majority of our foundations, it would not be possible for us to accept this new mission. We shall even have much trouble supplying the needs of our existent missions, both as regards personnel to be sent out and as regards funds, because allocations from the [Association for] the Propagation of the Faith have been very considerably reduced. I therefore beg Your Eminence kindly to hold us excused.[45]

Cardinal Barnabò reached his seventieth birthday on 2 March 1871 and on 19 March had his first attack of convulsions. His health suffered from his enormous workload. Besides being cardinal prefect of Propaganda, he was also a member of most of the other congregations of the Roman Curia. Each of these had major business meetings of their own, that he as a member was obliged to attend. In addition he was Cardinal Protector for a number of religious communities of nuns. He also spent many hours in the confessional, an activity that he called his recreation. Converts also sought him out, especially for counsel and spiritual direction.

Since Barnabò was approaching complete blindness as well, Pope Pius IX decided to give him an easier task and decided to name him Cardinal Prefect of the Datary, a congregation of the Roman Curia that examines the fitness of candidates for papal benefices. On hearing of this, however, Barnabò begged the pope not to take this step. He would rather give up the cardinalate, he said, than leave the congregation responsible for foreign missions. The pope showed consideration and granted Barnabò's request.[46]

---

44. PF: LDB vol. 365 (1871, Part I), f. 3v, Barnabò to Elloy and to Favre, 4 January 1871.
45. PF: SC Oceania vol. 9 (1869–72, Part I), f. 784rv, Favre to Barnabò, 19 February 1871.
46. Metzler, "Präfekten und Sekretäre," 43.

Barnabò must have recuperated quickly from his convulsions because thirty-four days later, after receiving Elloy's report on his arrival in Sydney, Australia, the cardinal replied immediately:

> I have read the letter of Your Excellency of 25 January of the current year in which you give me much information about the outcome of your voyage and about the Most Reverend Bataillon. I consider it a grave matter that the prelate just mentioned has not yet left his vicariate, nor does he think of leaving it. I am now writing to him again, ordering him to return to Europe and to surrender to you his full faculties, one and all. Now if he should still refuse, I shall consult with the Sacred Congregation on what is to be done.
>
> However, I want you to keep up your good spirits, for I shall never let you down. And if there is something that you might need, do not fail to let me know. I would be most grateful to you, moreover, if you were to draw up a report about that vicariate, especially about the needs with which it is afflicted. Indicate also what would be useful and applicable for propagating the faith. . . .[47]

That same day, 22 April 1871, Barnabò wrote to Bataillon. "I have already written three times to Your Excellency," he said,

> indicating that it is the will of our Most Holy Father and of this Sacred Congregation that you set out immediately for Rome, leaving the administration of your vicariate to your coadjutor together with all necessary and opportune faculties. Furthermore the prelate, whom I have just mentioned, has already arrived in those regions and therefore nothing can any longer keep Your Excellency from boarding a ship and setting out for Europe. I therefore make known to you again the will of our Holy Father and I am convinced that you will obey it immediately. . . .[48]

Barnabò sent his letters for Elloy and Bataillon to Superior General Favre at Rochefort (Gard) in France for forwarding. At the same time he acknowledged the receipt of Favre's letter of 2 April and accepted the reasons given by him for not being able to accept the Micronesia and New Hebrides missions. Barnabò also informed Favre that he was writing again to Bataillon, "ordering him to come to Rome . . ."[49]

In the midst of the Bataillon-Elloy controversy, Father Gioacchino Gata wrote to Cardinal Barnabò on 18 May 1871 from the Central Oceania vicariate. He was not a Marist, but a member of the secular clergy, and consequently served as an impartial witness. Gata had made his studies for the priesthood in Rome at the Urban College of Propaganda and had been assigned to Bataillon's vicariate. In those days graduates of this college were obliged to send a letter every two years to the cardinal prefect of Propaganda about them-

---

47. PF: LDB vol. 365 (1871, Part I), f. 346r, Barnabò to Elloy, 22 April 1871.
48. Ibid., f. 345rv.
49. Ibid., f. 344v–345r, Barnabò to Favre, 22 April 1871.

selves and about their activities.[50] Gata stated that Bataillon was brusque with his priests and that he threatened them and their churches with interdict for the least little thing. Nor was he frank and open with them; instead he always considered his episcopal authority as being jeopardized by them.[51]

Barnabò replied promptly on 7 September 1871: "I read with pleasure your letter of this past 18 May in which you give me an account of the ministries which you have fulfilled up to now. I am acquainted with the difficulties of that vicariate and I am devoting myself to them. You must take care, however, to obey your superiors in all things and apply yourself completely to the conversion of your fellow men, so that the light of Jesus Christ may finally enlighten the tribes in those remote areas."[52]

Two months later Cardinal Barnabò received the long-awaited news from Bishop Bataillon that he had reached an accord with his coadjutor. But since no word arrived from Bishop Elloy, and in view of Father Gata's recent unfavorable report, Barnabò wrote to Superior General Favre on 11 November 1871 inquiring whether he had received news of an accord being reached by the two bishops.[53]

Favre had received no such news and so did not reply until 6 December 1871. On that day he received a letter from Elloy along with a fifteen-page report addressed to Cardinal Prefect Barnabò, to whom Favre wrote: "The truth is that no accord has been reached and that relations are as strained as ever.... Bishop Bataillon's conduct is a mystery to me and the abuse which he makes of his authority is such, that I do not know what to say." Favre insisted once again: "There is urgent need to recall Bishop Bataillon, if one wishes to save the Central Mission from complete ruin...."

He then went into detail: "Our missionaries beg me to help them.... But what do you want me to do? I can do nothing with Bishop Bataillon.... For two years now he has not answered my letters.... Nothing but the authority of the Holy See can provide a remedy for this evil. And unless a remedy is provided, my conscience will not allow me to send any more missionaries to Central Oceania where they are at the mercy of a despot, who treats them like slaves. Instead of directing them, encouraging them and supporting them, he exposes them to murmuring, to rebellion and to the danger of being lost." It pained Favre all the more, he said, to disturb Barnabò and to bring up "once again this sad affair," since the Holy See was in such sorrowful circumstances, due to the Papal States having been invaded.[54]

---

50. Regarding this practice see PF: SC Oceania vol. 9 (1869–72, Part I), f. 333rv, Adulfo Lecaille to Barnabò, 10 September 1869, from Greenough, Western Australia.

51. Ibid., f. 837rv, Gata to Barnabò, 18 May 1871.

52. PF: LDB vol. 366 (1871, Part II), f. 789v, 789Ar.

53. For the date and content of Barnabò's letter to Favre of 11 November 1871, see PF: SC Oceania vol. 9 (1869–72, Part I), f. 1148rv, Favre to Barnabò, 6 December 1871.

54. See ibid. for Favre's letter to Barnabò of 6 December 1871.

Elloy's fifteen-page report explained for Barnabò that he had set out from Sydney on 18 February 1871, had arrived in Tonga on 17 March, and had reached Apia in Samoa on 14 April. Elloy was then under the impression that Bataillon had already left for Europe and that consequently he himself was now in charge. But Bataillon actually was at Futuna Island, where he learned that Elloy was at Apia. Bataillon himself disembarked at Apia on 24 May 1871 and on the following day began transferring missionaries. One month later on 25 June he left for Wallis.[55]

When leaving Samoa for Wallis, Bataillon had informed Elloy that he would return every four or five months to Apia in order to check up on how things were going. This gave Elloy the impression that Bataillon "is not thinking of going to Europe and even less of giving me full powers to administer his own Vicariate [of Central Oceania] or even that of Samoa...." Elloy had been allowed to remain in Samoa, he told Barnabò, but Bataillon "had reserved for himself the administration of our schools and also of the foundation at Apia, which is the center of the mission in this archipelago."[56]

The 22 April 1871 letter from Barnabò ordering Bataillon to "set out immediately for Rome" because it was "the will of Our Most Holy Father and of this Sacred Congregation," was handed to Bataillon personally in Wallis on 30 August by Commander Pouthier of the steam-powered dispatch vessel *l'Hamelin*.[57] In early October a ship coming to Samoa from Wallis brought Elloy the news that Bataillon actually had left for Sydney. "But he wrote neither to me nor to anyone else," Elloy told Barnabò. "So I do not know whether he is actually on his way to Rome.... And I fear to go to Wallis, since the Vicar Apostolic [Bataillon] gave me powers only for the Navigators Islands...."[58]

Barnabò's letter of 22 April 1871 addressed to Elloy reached him at Apia in Samoa by 17 August. This was much faster mail service than usual. "But what today is an extraordinary event will probably soon become a regular means of communication," Elloy said, "because there is talk of a mail service crossing North America and also of steamships going from San Francisco to Sydney. These vessels from now on shall stop at the Navigators Islands every month to take on coal," he said. "This will greatly increase the rapidity and the regularity of our communications with Europe." He added that the same rapid service would be provided for mail going in the opposite direction, moving from Apia to San Francisco and then across the United States of America and on to Europe. This was another marvel of international cooperation which would prove highly beneficial for missionary work in the far-flung Pacific area.[59]

To complete the final section of the first transcontinental railroad of the United States of America, a distance stretching more than halfway across the country, the federal

---

55. PF: SC Oceania vol. 9 (1869–72, Part I), f. 1149r, 1150rv, 1154rv, Elloy to Barnabò, 17 August 1871.
56. See ibid., 1054r–1055v, Elloy to Barnabò, 3 September 1871.
57. Ibid., f. 1054v.
58. Ibid., f. 1056rv, Elloy to Barnabò, 7 October 1871.
59. Ibid., f. 1149r, Elloy to Barnabò, 17 August 1871.

government had chartered the Union Pacific Railroad to move westward from what is now Omaha, Nebraska, and the Central Pacific Railroad to move eastward from the San Francisco Bay area. Both construction teams met on 10 May 1869 at a point in a Utah desert, where the last spike made of California gold was pounded into the last tie made of polished California laurel.[60] Less than two years later, as testified by Elloy, official correspondence from Rome was taking this route to missionary bishops in the South Pacific.

In view of this new mail service Elloy predicted to Barnabò that his current letter of 3 September 1871, being sent via San Francisco, might well arrive in Rome before his previous letter of 17 August, which had been sent via Sydney.[61]

Meanwhile Bishop Bataillon, still seeking a solution for his problems with Bishop Elloy, suggested that Cardinal Barnabò "should request the Society [of Mary] to accept responsibility once again for the islands which it has abandoned, at least for New Hebrides Islands and above all for the Vicariate of Micronesia."[62] He did this by letter of 1 May 1870, which took the rest of that year to reach Rome. And if a mission superior should be needed, he said, "I am prepared to give up my coadjutor for the benefit of these new missions." He added that shipping services in recent years had improved and multiplied greatly in the vicinity of those missions.[63]

But Cardinal Barnabò first wanted to check whether the facts in Bishop Bataillon's letter were correct and whether Bishop Elloy would actually be interested in the kind of mission work being proposed for him by Bataillon. And so on 4 January 1871 he sent an inquiry on this to Elloy.[64] The cardinal's letter, however, traveled via Sydney and reached Elloy at Apia on 3 September that year, after being en route for eight months. The cardinal's following letter to Elloy dated 22 April traveled via San Francisco and was en route only four and a half months.

"It is true," Elloy replied, "that the Solomon Islands, the islands of Micronesia, and also those of New Hebrides, are visited more frequently by merchant vessels today than they were twenty years ago, when attempts were being made to establish missionaries there." Elloy added that New Caledonia was developing into a French colony and that it and nearby New Hebrides "are likewise visited very often" by merchant vessels.

He further reminded Barnabò that he himself had earlier called attention to "a group of islands called the Gilbert Islands, known also as the Kingsmill Islands, where we already

---

60. Luther S. Miller, "History of U.S. Railroads," 166.

61. PF: SC Oceania vol. 9 (1869–72, Part I), f. 1054r–1055v, Elloy to Barnabò, 3 September 1871. Elloy's letter of 17 August 1871 to Cardinal Barnabò was mailed to Superior General Favre in Lyon, France, for forwarding to Rome. It reached Favre on 6 December 1871. See PF: SC Oceania vol. 9 (1869–72, Part I), f. 1148r, Favre to Barnabò, 6 December 1871.

62. For details on Micronesia being entrusted originally to the Marists on 16 July 1844, see Wiltgen, *Oceania*, chap. 17. New Hebrides was part of their Vicariate Apostolic of New Caledonia. See p. 453, n. 70.

63. PF: SC Oceania vol. 9 (1869–72, Part I), f. 543r–544r, Bataillon to Barnabò, 1 May 1870.

64. For the date and content of Barnabò's 4 January 1871 letter, see PF: SC Oceania vol. 9 (1869–72, Part I), f. 1054r, 1055r, Elloy to Barnabò, 3 September 1871.

have Christians who were baptized in Samoa. The people there ask for missionaries persistently. In the Navigators you now find merchant vessels belonging to a German company established at Apia; they regularly visit those islands twice a year." It was on 14 December 1869, just six days after the opening of the Vatican Council, when Elloy presented his request to Barnabò that he attach the Gilbert or Kingsmill archipelago "to the Navigators Vicariate, which you then wanted to entrust to me. Today I renew this request," he said.

Elloy claimed that these islands had "more than sixty thousand inhabitants." And as soon as "the Vicar of Jesus Christ tells us to set foot on these islands," he said, "I shall go there myself with one or two missionaries to establish a mission. I shall also continue visiting them, taking advantage of the ships leaving Apia to go there." He assured Barnabò that Superior General Favre "will not refuse to give us the two or three members whom we shall need for this foundation . . . And if for lack of missionaries it should not be possible to execute this project immediately," Elloy noted, "I could at least get the mission ready for occupancy at the first opportunity. . . ."[65]

Barnabò had sent both Bishop Elloy and Superior General Favre identical letters on 4 January 1871 containing Bataillon's suggestion that the Marists might wish to reconsider doing missionary work in New Hebrides and particularly in Micronesia, because now there was much contact with merchant vessels in that area. Furthermore Elloy could easily be freed to direct this missionary work, Bataillon had said. Favre, however, turned down the proposal categorically on 19 February 1871.[66]

Some eleven months later Barnabò received Elloy's favorable reply, which told of regular contacts with merchant vessels in New Hebrides, New Caledonia, Solomon Islands, and the many islands of Micronesia. He specifically spoke about the Gilbert or Kingsmill Islands and even requested that they be added to the Navigators Vicariate, over which he was administrator. In view of these many positive aspects, Barnabò ignored the refusal presented by Superior General Favre eleven months earlier and now wrote to Favre again on 13 January 1872 as follows:

> In his latest letter, which arrived recently, Bishop Elloy points out—after having been approached by me—that now an easier route has opened up for reaching the Solomon Islands, the islands of Micronesia, and also New Hebrides and the Gilbert Islands. He therefore suggests that the time is opportune for sending new missionaries to those islands and at the same time he requests, if it is at all possible, that the Gilbert Islands be added to his vicariate. Therefore if it seems to you that this could be done, and if you also have ready suitable missionaries for sending to the islands of Micronesia and of [New] Hebrides, kindly let me know soon so that I may be able to make provisions for all of the priests in question.[67]

---

65. Ibid., f. 1054r–1055v, Elloy to Barnabò, 3 September 1871. In this letter Elloy still uses Kingsmill Islands as a synonym for the Gilbert Islands. See this chapter, p. 434, n. 13, and p. 436, n. 22.

66. See this chapter, p. 446, n. 45.

67. Theo B. Kok, archivist at the Marist Generalate in Rome, on 21 January 1993 sent the author a photo-

Unfortunately Barnabò was not so circumspect in making this proposal to Favre, as Elloy had been in making it to Barnabò. Realizing that Favre had little personnel to spare, Elloy had suggested that Barnabò request "two or three" Marists from Favre for the Gilbert or Kingsmill foundation.

Favre waited until 4 May 1872 before replying to Barnabò's 13 January letter: "As Bishop Elloy has written to Your Eminence," it certainly is true

> that a much larger number of ships are now transacting business in those islands. Because of this it would be much easier for missionaries to establish themselves there today. But Your Eminence must be aware that the Solomon Islands and also those of Micronesia, particularly the Gilbert Islands and the Marshall Islands, are not entrusted to our Society.[68] Without a doubt we would be happy to see the preaching of the Gospel brought to the unfortunate inhabitants of those numerous islands. But it would be rash for us to accept responsibility for evangelizing those archipelagoes, since our part of Oceania is already quite extensive.

The New Hebrides Archipelago, however, as Favre pointed out, was part of the New Caledonia vicariate apostolic assigned to his missionary community. "Earlier attempts made by our missionaries in that archipelago have proven unfortunate," he said. "Three of our men died there and the others all returned from there gravely ill. Because of the [blackbirding] trade being practiced in this archipelago by numerous English ships, which have taken away many of the natives, the people there are incensed against Europeans and also against Protestant missionaries, some of whom—including an Anglican bishop—have recently been killed there."[69] Once the Marist missions in New Caledonia become well founded and begin to enjoy lasting peace, Favre said, "we hope to attempt anew the evangelization of New Hebrides. We shall begin by gathering together young people and teaching them in New Caledonia."

Bishop Douarre, coadjutor to Bishop Bataillon, had celebrated the first Mass in New Caledonia on Christmas Day 1843. This was at Mahamata village alongside Port Balade. As early as 27 June 1847, New Caledonia was raised to the status of vicariate apostolic. The French government in 1864 began using New Caledonia as a penal colony. By 1872 the mission was growing rapidly, Favre said, "above all because of the thousands of condemned political prisoners deported there and because of the need to lodge them, clothe them, feed them, direct and supervise them, and keep watch over them. All of this requires a considerable deployment of forces [by the French government] and also a very large number of

---

copy of this Barnabò letter to Favre of 13 January 1872.

68. See chap. 21, pp. 400–401, on the Melanesia-Micronesia mission being suppressed by Cardinal Prefect Barnabò on 11 December 1858.

69. "Blackbirding" meant recruiting native labor for cotton plantations in Fiji and for cotton and sugar plantations in Queensland. Favre here referred to John Coleridge Patteson, the first Anglican bishop of Melanesia, who was killed on 20 September 1871. See *Pacific Islands Year Book*, 9th ed., 422, 430, 432.

administrative personnel. What will become of our poor mission in the midst of this penal colony?" Favre asked.[70]

According to Favre the solution was to appoint as head of the New Caledonia vicariate "a man capable of dealing suitably on behalf of religion with the governor of the colony, with its administrative personnel, and also with the French Government." Father Rougeyron, then in charge, was not suitable for this task and had asked to be replaced by a vicar apostolic. "The French Government would be pleased to have a vicar apostolic named for New Caledonia," Favre said. And the director of colonies in France had also given assurance of this several times. Favre therefore asked whether Barnabò "would agree to such a nomination and whether we may now present for approbation by the Holy See a candidate for this important post . . . ."[71]

Meanwhile Bataillon had written to Cardinal Barnabò from Sydney on 26 February 1872. This was six months *after* he had received his latest orders from Barnabò to "set out immediately for Rome." He reminded Barnabò of his earlier letter stating that satisfactory arrangements had been made with his coadjutor. And after mailing that letter he had written another, asking that he be dispensed from making a voyage to Rome, or at last that it be postponed. But en route his letter had crossed still another coming from Barnabò, he said, which "manifested anew your will and that of the Holy Father for me to leave for Rome." Since Bataillon did not wish "to sadden His Holiness and Your Eminence," as he said, "I am setting out on my way at once. . . . Tomorrow [27 February] I take a ship . . . sailing first to France . . . , where I shall arrive about the end of April. . . . And then, please God, I hope to arrive in Rome in the first half of May. . . ."[72]

Favre had also received word that Bishop Bataillon was leaving Sydney on 27 February 1872 for Rome. He was sailing via the Suez Canal, completed three years earlier, and was expected to arrive in France about the middle of May. "I am happy to report to Your Eminence," Favre said on 4 May, "that Bishop Elloy's return to the islands has been received with great joy . . . According to his latest reports all is now going well in the Central Vicariate. . . ."[73]

On Favre's return to Lyon on 14 June 1872 from a voyage to England, he found Bishop Bataillon waiting for him. "I do not know what proposals Bishop Bataillon will be making to the Holy See . . . ," Favre told Cardinal Prefect Barnabò three days later in a sealed letter to be hand-carried by Bataillon to Rome. "I only know that he wants to return to Oceania to end his days there. . . . However, if Bishop Bataillon should return to Oceania, it would appear altogether necessary to me that his Central [Oceania] Vicariate should be separated from the Navigators Vicariate, and also that this latter vicariate should be entrusted to Bishop Elloy, and also that its full administration should be given to him. If this is not done

---

70. For more details on founding the New Caledonia Vicariate Apostolic, see Wiltgen, *Oceania*, chap. 27.
71. PF: SC Oceania vol. 9 (1869–72, Part I), f. 1296v–1297rv, Favre to Barnabò, 4 May 1872.
72. Ibid., f. 1290rv–1291r.
73. Ibid., f. 1296v–1297rv.

the two bishops will never come to an understanding and the conflict between them will only become malicious, to the great scandal of their missionaries and their neophytes and to the great detriment of the mission."

It seemed to Favre that Bataillon wanted Rome to give Elloy a completely new mission. "But this is not possible," Favre said, "because we do not have sufficient personnel to take over a new mission. Furthermore, removing Bishop Elloy from the Navigators Vicariate, where he was its apostle, instead of relieving the general irritation with Bishop Bataillon, will do nothing else but make Bishop Bataillon more odious and more insupportable. This would bring about the ruin of the mission in this vicariate. . . ."

Favre said that the Central Oceania vicariate of Bataillon without the Navigators Archipelago "would not be of considerable size and would have about thirty thousand souls." But the bishop was sixty-two years old and consequently was said to be "advanced in age and in need of a rest after thirty-six years of apostolic labors . . ." Bataillon was a dedicated man, Favre said, but

> his faults of character unfortunately are reflected in his administration, which often becomes excessively absolute and arbitrary. . . .
>
> Not having enough regard for human weakness and not seeing anything but the rights of his authority, he does not understand that to make this authority acceptable and to obtain filial obedience from inferiors, it is necessary to join both sweetness and goodness to firmness: *suaviter et fortiter*. After causing wounds by the inflexibility of his character, he does not know how to heal them by performing acts full of charity and condescension. . . . And when missionaries make observations to him, which they judge to be necessary, their observations . . . are regarded as acts of rebellion and the result is anger and malcontent on both sides.

Favre signed and sealed his letter to Barnabò, dating it 17 June 1872, and gave it to Bataillon who left for Rome on the following day.[74]

Cardinal Barnabò by this time was seventy-one years old and was growing blind. When he no longer was able to read the many letters bringing him problems and proposals from missions in Oceania, North and South America, Africa, Asia, and parts of Europe, he did not allow this to slow down his pace. He simply had others read the reports to him, and he dictated his replies.[75]

Bishop Bataillon had several audiences with Cardinal Barnabò. During one of them the cardinal presented Bataillon with two letters written by Superior General Favre and with another letter written by Bishop Elloy. He invited Bataillon to present a reply in writing. Bataillon's reply filled thirty-two pages and was dated 29 June 1872. It contained numerous justifications for his actions and was addressed to Barnabò. Bataillon said that he had read the three letters in which Favre and Elloy "with great ability make efforts to

---

74. Ibid., f. 1363rv, 1365rv.
75. Metzler, "Präfekten und Sekretäre," p. 43.

exculpate themselves and to inculpate the Vicar Apostolic... I regret to say that in general all facts reported there are *false*, or considerably *exaggerated*, or *misrepresented*."

Having presented his defense and having given his proposals for the various problems, Bataillon then gave a summary called "Conclusion." Referring to Elloy and to himself in the third person, he begged Barnabò "to maintain the *status quo* at least in appearances. That is, each shall remain in his place and with his titles. But in view of their differences in character and their manner of doing things, each is to have a separate territory." Elloy, he said, should have "the Samoa Archipelago which he desires, as already handed over to him." In addition Elloy was to conduct missionary work in that area "with full liberty to do as he likes, and with complete control as the Holy See shall determine...."[76]

In short Bataillon was suggesting that Elloy retain his title as coadjutor, that he not be named officially or juridically the vicar apostolic of Samoa, but that Rome simply authorize him to act within his territory *as if he were* the vicar apostolic of Samoa. Barnabò, it appears, then requested Bataillon—or more likely instructed him—to present these proposals in detail and in writing. Four days later (3 July 1872) Bataillon submitted such a document to Barnabò.

Bataillon insisted in his rebuttal that his authority as vicar apostolic of Central Oceania had already been compromised far too much by all that had happened and consequently in no way should his territory be formally or juridically divided. The division would be juridical and formal if Elloy were named the vicar apostolic of Samoa. "What I propose here ...," Bataillon said, "seems to satisfy the wishes and interests of all. Namely, it maintains the non-separation juridically and grants the separation in fact." Referring to himself and to Bishop Elloy again in the third person, he explained the matter like this: "Each shall retain his title, but each shall have a separate field of activity. And my coadjutor in the field entrusted to him, shall have full liberty of administration as he understands it, or shall have sole control as regulated by the Holy See."

His coadjutor, Bataillon said, could further receive directly from the Society of Mary his quota of personnel and funds. "This method grants to my coadjutor what he desires, namely, his liberty of action. And it suffices to preserve for the Vicar Apostolic [that is, Bataillon] at least the appearance [of non-separation]." After all, he said, "it is really not worth the trouble" dividing this mission territory once again, because so little of it remains. By retaining the status quo, however, "if one of us gets sick, there is someone who can look after the other's part. And if one should die, the other will inherit everything without the necessity of holding a new election."[77]

Without losing time and without even waiting for Bataillon to submit the above, more detailed proposal dated 3 July 1872, Barnabò had written to Superior General Favre on 2

---

76. PF: SC Oceania vol. 9 (1869–72, Part I), f. 1394r, 1409v

77. Ibid., f. 1454rv, Bataillon to Barnabò, 3 July 1872.

July summoning him to Rome. Not revealing that he had presented Bataillon with two of Favre's letters and one of Elloy's, Barnabò simply told Favre that he had presented "objections" to Bataillon regarding the administration of his vicariate. Bataillon had replied, he said,

> by denying the facts or by explaining matters in a way different from the way in which they had been presented in the objections. Nor does he in any way show himself ready to abdicate the pastoral office. In fact, he has confirmed his wish to die in the territory that was entrusted to him. Therefore in order to settle all of these matters more easily, it would be best if Your Paternity were to come to Rome as soon as possible for a brief amount of time. Then in my presence you could give the necessary explanations, so that this affair may be terminated once and for all. . . .[78]

Barnabò's letter reached Favre in Lyon within four days and he wrote back at once on Saturday, 6 July 1872, saying:

> Your letter of 2 July causes me great embarrassment. On the one hand I would have to leave for Rome immediately in order to respond to Your Eminence's appeal. Yet on the other hand I am held back by important affairs here, which I would not know how to abandon except for some imperious necessity. Finding myself in a situation so difficult, I dare ask that Your Eminence kindly dispense me, if possible, from going to Rome at this moment. Bishop Bataillon certainly gave you my letter of 17 June, in which I presented Your Eminence with my way of seeing things . . . and with the remedy which ought to be applied. . . . If I go to Rome, I shall be obliged in conscience to insist on the full contents of that letter. . . .

Favre was convinced that Bataillon was minimizing the accusations made against him. "But how can he be right," Favre asked, "and everybody else be wrong?" Superior General Favre repeated that it was "altogether necessary" to give Bishop Elloy "the free and complete administration of the Navigators." He begged Barnabò a second time kindly to dispense him from going to Rome, "because at this moment I am so busy with affairs in France. Nevertheless if Your Eminence judges the journey to be absolutely necessary, you need but say the word and I shall obey immediately."[79]

Barnabò replied to Favre as follows: "I understand that you are detained by grave matters preventing you from coming to Rome. The Most Reverend Bataillon shall therefore return to you in order to take care of his affairs. It is especially necessary that both of you discuss the accusations brought against him and that he explain diligently the series of facts which have been made public. He also gave me a lengthy report on this matter." It is impossible, however, "for the truth to become known," Barnabò said, "unless in addition to the allegations presented by him in his favor, the contrary positions should also be indicated."

---

78. PF: LDB vol. 368 (1872, Part II), f. 842rv, Barnabò to Favre, 2 July 1872.
79. PF: SC Oceania vol. 9 (1869–72, Part I), f. 1459r–1460r.

Favre and Bataillon were to discuss the entire matter, Barnabò said, and were also "to reach an agreement on the method to be followed in the future, so that peace can be restored." The cardinal insisted that "in the first place care must be taken that the Mission of the Navigators Archipelago should be separated from the Vicariate of Central Oceania and should be handed over for governing to Bishop Elloy alone." As for that part of the mission "which perhaps will be left over to the Most Reverend Bataillon, he must see to it that in the future his conduct is such that scandal deriving from disagreements shall be altogether avoided...."[80]

These directives sent by Barnabò to Favre on 12 July, as well as other directives given by the cardinal to Bataillon in Rome by word of mouth, resulted in an important document dated 12 August 1872. It was drafted and signed by both Bishop Bataillon and Superior General Favre in Lyon and was addressed to Barnabò. It informed Cardinal Barnabò that they together "had agreed that the administration of the Vicariate Apostolic of the Navigators was to be completely separated from the government of the Central Mission" entrusted to Bataillon, "and that it should be given over completely" to coadjutor Elloy.[81]

Father Giovanni Simeoni (1816–92), secretary of Propaganda since 13 March 1868, presented its proposal for settling the differences between Bishop Bataillon, Bishop Elloy, and Superior General Favre to Pope Pius IX on Sunday, 22 September 1872. Six days later Propaganda issued a decree stating that Bishop Bataillon, vicar apostolic of Central Oceania, "has presented to Propaganda Fide his urgent request to abdicate the administration of the Vicariate Apostolic of the Navigators Archipelago in view of his advanced age. His Holiness, Pope Pius IX, on receiving a report about this matter from the Secretary of the same Sacred Congregation during his audience of 22 September 1872, accepted the resignation just mentioned and decided that the Most Reverend Louis Elloy, [Titular] Bishop of Tipasa in Numidia and Coadjutor of the same Prelate, should be declared the Pro-Vicar Apostolic of the Mission just mentioned...."[82]

These solutions were identical to those insisted upon by Elloy, by Favre, by Poupinel, and by Barnabò. It was Barnabò who single-handedly and after much patience succeeded in persuading Bataillon to accept all of them. As for Bataillon's "advanced age" mentioned in the decree, it was merely a nominal consideration meant to save face. The bishop was only sixty-two years old.

On 28 September 1872, the same day on which the decree was issued, Barnabò wrote separate but substantially identical letters to Bishop Bataillon and to Superior General Favre. He enclosed a copy of the decree for each of them and stated that he had received their signed document of 12 August 1872. He expressed his happiness over that document and then added, "As you will see from the enclosed decree, our Most Holy Father

---

80. PF: LDB vol. 368 (1872, Part II), f. 873rv, Barnabò to Favre, 12 July 1872.

81. For the 12 August 1872 document, see ibid., f. 1227rv, Barnabò to Favre and Bataillon, 28 September 1872.

82. Ibid., f. 1256v–1257r, Decree of 28 September 1872.

has confirmed your proposal by an authoritative decision of his own and has appointed" Bishop Elloy "the Pro-Vicar Apostolic of the Navigators Archipelago." Barnabò informed Bataillon that he himself would see to it that the decree was handed over to Elloy, the new administrator. And in his letter to Superior General Favre, he said: "You will take care of transmitting the [enclosed] decree itself to the new administrator...."[83]

Barnabò also wrote that day to Elloy, having promised him much earlier that he would not let him down. He said: "After the Most Reverend Bataillon, Vicar Apostolic of Central Oceania, had taken counsel with me and also with the [Marist] Superior General on matters concerning his Mission, he made up his mind to abdicate the administration of the Vicariate Apostolic of the Navigators Archipelago and to turn it over to you, insofar as this was in his power, so that it might be governed completely by you...."[84] Superior General Favre forwarded this letter and decree to Elloy as instructed.

This South Seas controversy over ecclesiastical power had lasted nine full years. During that time the Melanesia-Micronesia mission had remained unstaffed. The protagonists of the controversy, Bishop Bataillon and Bishop Elloy, were unaware that they had only five more years to live.

---

83. PF: LDB vol. 368 (1872, Part II), f. 1227rv, Barnabò to Favre and Bataillon, 28 September 1872.
84. Ibid., f. 1228v, Barnabò to Elloy, 28 September 1872.

24

Picpus Missionaries Refuse Melanesia and Micronesia
22 September 1873

Bishop Bataillon drafted his "Report on Oceania for Propaganda" and sent it to Cardinal Prefect Barnabò from Hotel Minerva alongside the Pantheon in Rome on 2 October 1872. As the pioneer missionary bishop in Central Oceania, he was disturbed that the people of Melanesia and Micronesia had no missionary personnel. In fact he considered it his obligation "to take up the interests of these poor abandoned people and to plead their cause with the most vigorous insistence possible before both the Holy Father and Propaganda Fide. That is what I am allowing myself to do by writing this present letter," he said.

According to Bataillon's report, "Oceania properly so-called contains a population of nearly two million, including three or four races and just as many different languages. And these are subdivided into many dialects." There were two missionary congregations active in the area, he pointed out. One was the Congregation of the Sacred Hearts of Jesus and Mary, also called the Picpus Fathers. It occupied Eastern Oceania and had been at work there for forty-six years.[1] Its missionaries currently staffed three vicariates with "a population of about 150,000" belonging to the Polynesian race.

The other congregation in Oceania was the Society of Mary, or Marists. They occupied Central Oceania and had been at work there for thirty-six years. They also staffed a diocese in New Zealand. The population of their missions excluding New Zealand was 500,000, Bataillon said, and they were divided among four vicariates apostolic: (1) New Caledonia with New Hebrides, which had more than 200,000 people; (2) Fiji with 200,000; (3) the Navigators with 40,000; and (4) Central Oceania properly so-called with about 30,000.

Bataillon then made his point. "Two additional vicariates called Melanesia and Micronesia remain unoccupied," he said. "These two vicariates are located in Western and Northern Oceania and have a greater population than the eight vicariates" staffed by Picpus missionaries and Marist missionaries. "Their population must reach close to one

---

1. On the origin of the Congregation of the Sacred Hearts of Jesus and Mary, see Wiltgen, *Oceania*, chap. 1.

million. The Vicariate of Melanesia is the more highly populated of the two, having some 700,000 to 800,000 people. The population of Melanesia is also more savage, more inhospitable, and its climate is less healthy. The Vicariate of Micronesia has a smaller population (I would judge 200,000 to 300,000). The natives there are more peaceful and they are better acquainted with Europeans."

It is "earnestly to be desired," Bataillon said, that Propaganda "should offer these vast missions" of Melanesia and Micronesia "to some missionary organizations before heresy is imposed upon them." If Rome were to "insist with the Society of Mary," he said, "I believe that it would accept . . . , because not many missionaries would be needed to make a beginning and this enterprise would also attract personnel."

An additional reason for the Marists "to reoccupy these shores," Bataillon said, was the fact that the tombs of Bishop Epalle and Bishop Collomb and those of several other Marists were located in Melanesia.[2] "The first missionaries would go there to reconnoitre the area, choose a healthy location . . . , and make a base camp. Then they would learn the language, evangelize, etc., etc. After discovering the first good location, the mission would organize itself and develop." And since the islands of Melanesia "have a number of commercial contacts with Australia," as Bataillon pointed out, "the supply center for this mission could well be located in Sydney. This is yet another reason for the Marists to take charge of them."

Bataillon then spoke at length about Micronesia, saying that its contacts were "with China and with the Sandwich Islands. Therefore Micronesia should be offered to the Milan Missionaries," he said, "who have a procure in Hong Kong." Or it might be better to offer Micronesia "to the good Picpus Fathers," who occupy Eastern Oceania. "From the Sandwich [or Hawaiian] Archipelago where they are already, they could easily branch out to the islands of Micronesia, since the Caroline Islands, which are not very far away, are at the center [of Micronesia].

"In fact the island of Ponape or Ascension could be occupied at once," Bataillon said. "It is a beautiful island, very fertile, and has lovely ports. Its gentle and civilized people have requested missionaries and have been waiting for them for a long time."[3] It was Bataillon's conviction that in this way the Picpus missionaries and the Marists, "the two congregations to which Oceania has been entrusted, could divide among themselves those parts which are still unoccupied."[4] But Barnabò took no action and approached neither the Marists nor the Picpus Fathers.

Bishop Elloy returned to his headquarters at Apia, Samoa, in February 1873, after having visited the islands within his territory. Waiting for him was a letter from Barnabò containing Propaganda's decree of 28 September 1872, declaring him to be the pro-vicar apostolic of the Navigators Archipelago. This was what Elloy had been requesting in person and in writing for years from Pope Pius IX and from Barnabò. But on examining closely the decree and its accom-

---

2. For details on Collomb and Epalle, see Wiltgen, *Oceania*, 589, 592.
3. See "Ponape," in Wiltgen, *Oceania*, 602.
4. PF: SC Oceania vol. 9 (1869–72, Part I), f. 1530rv, Bataillon to Barnabò, 2 October 1872.

panying letter, Elloy saw that the Gilbert or Kingsmill islands had not been included within his jurisdiction, even though he explicitly and repeatedly had requested them from Barnabò.

When acknowledging the receipt of these official documents, Elloy called Barnabò's attention to "the fact that the time seems to have come for beginning a mission in the Gilbert or Kingsmill Islands. We have already been asked by the local people of those islands to come. Many of them have been instructed and some have even been baptized during sojourns made in Samoa. Recently some forty of them landed at Futuna Island, after having escaped from a ship belonging to pirates. By ruse the pirates had taken them aboard to deliver them to Fiji as laborers. We welcomed them, instructed them, and prepared them for Baptism."

Elloy added that a German firm in Hamburg—it was known as Johann Cesar Godeffroy und Sohn—had a warehouse at Apia and that its ships "two or three times a year" visit the islands in the Gilbert Group and those in the Caroline Group. "I would be able to profit from these opportunities," Elloy said, "if I were to be assigned to work for the salvation of those peoples still in the darkness of paganism." He added that "Protestant Presbyterian catechists have already preceded us" and that two years earlier a ship belonging to the Presbyterian mission had already begun visiting those islands.[5]

Elloy further pointed out to Barnabò that the Tokelau (or Union) Group of Islands also had been part of Bataillon's Vicariate of Central Oceania. And so he asked whether they perhaps had now been assigned to him along with the Gilbert or Kingsmill Islands, since one could visit the Tokelau Islands much better from Samoa than from anywhere else.[6]

Barnabò replied as follows on 30 September 1873 to Elloy's query on the Tokelau Islands: "I shall write later." As for the Gilbert or Kingsmill Islands, he did not even mention them.[7] And so the Marists in Lyon were not approached on behalf of Micronesia.

But Micronesia could be offered as well to the Milan Foreign Mission Seminary, Bataillon had said, because they conducted a procure office in Hong Kong. Barnabò knew only too well, however, that the Milan missionaries were short on personnel for the missions which they already had, so he did not approach them either.

Bataillon had also suggested that Micronesia might well be offered "to the good Picpus Fathers" working in the Hawaiian Islands. From those islands, as he had pointed out, they could easily reach out to islands in Micronesia like Ponape and the Carolines. Barnabò now decided to try this approach. In the meantime eleven months had passed since Barnabò had received Bataillon's report of 2 October 1872 containing suggestions on how to find personnel for Melanesia and Micronesia.[8]

---

5. *Pacific Islands Year Book and Who's Who*, 106-7. The firm's name in English is abbreviated to: J. C. Godeffroy and Son.

6. See PF: SC Oceania vol. 10 (1873-76), f. 63r, 64rv, Elloy to Barnabò, 8 March 1873.

7. PF: LDB vol. 369 (1873), f. 507rv, Barnabò to Elloy, 30 September 1873.

8. PF: SC Oceania vol. 9 (1869-72, Part I), f. 1530rv, Bataillon from Rome to Barnabò, 2 October 1872.

N 1.   Rme Pater

Plures jam anni sunt ex quibus populi insularum Melanesiae et Micronesiae destituti operariis evangelicis in miserrimas idololatriae tenebras quibus Christi lux affulgente erui coeperant, reciderunt. Id quidem dolendum sane est praesertim hoc tempore quo inter varias Oceaniae gentes quaquaversus Missionarii adlaborant uberesque fructus referunt. Quae quidem cum accurate consideraverim, cupiens eorum barbarorum quantum fieri potest saluti consulere in eam veni sententiam ut te enixe rogarem ad rem hujusmodi mente revolvendam si forte religiosi viri Instituti tui qui missiones insularum propinquarum dirigunt illuc mitti possent. Qua super re quod sit consilium Paternitatis Tuae quam primum ut significes etiam atque etiam rogo.

Cuperem aliquid scire de missione insularum Sandwich, multum enim tempus elapsum est ex quo nihil a superiore illius christianitatis ad me pervenit.

Interea Deum precor ut tibi fausta quaeque largiatur. Romae ex Aed. S. C. de P. Fide die 4 Septembris 1873.

P.tis Tuae
Addictissimus

A. Card. Barnabò

Rmo P. Euthymio Rouchouze
Sup. Cong.is SS. Cord. J. et M.

Joannes Simeoni Secret.

Cardinal Prefect Barnabò wrote on 4 September 1873 to Superior General Rouchouze of the Fathers of the Sacred Hearts (Picpus), offering him and his missionaries the Melanesia / Micronesia Mission.
Source: Archives SSCC: 1-1-11/ 43.

Barnabò had also done some research of his own. Back in 1864 he had received from Very Reverend Euthyme Rouchouze, superior general of the Picpus Fathers in Paris, a five-page report on their missions. Rouchouze said that the Hawaiian Islands by that time had thirty-six thousand Catholics and that fifty Hawaiian teachers in 150 schools were giving classes to Hawaiian children.[9] This outstanding progress apparently gave Barnabò confidence in contacting the Picpus Fathers, because he wrote to their superior general on 4 September 1873.

"For many years now the peoples of the islands of Melanesia and Micronesia have been deprived of missionaries," Barnabò said,

> and so have fallen back into the miserable darkness of idolatry, a darkness which was being dispersed by the shining light of Christ. This is certainly deplorable, particularly at the present time when in every place our missionaries are at work among the various tribes of Oceania and are reaping rich fruit. After giving these matters careful consideration, and because I am anxious to contribute as much as possible to the salvation of these uncivilized people, I have decided to ask you to reflect earnestly upon this matter and see whether the men of your religious institute, who are directing missions on nearby islands, could possibly be sent there. I request in earnest that you indicate your Paternity's mind in this matter as soon as possible.[10]

Barnabò's one-page Latin letter elicited a four-page Latin reply dated 22 September 1873. It was signed by Father Marcellin Bousquet (1828–1911), who pointed out that Superior General Euthyme Rouchouze, to whom the cardinal's letter was addressed, had died in Paris on 2 December 1869. "In his place I was elected Superior [General] on 5 April 1870. In that same year toward the end of the month of May, Your Eminence kindly received me in Rome as a pilgrim...."

Bousquet had read the letter from Cardinal Prefect Barnabò "reverently," he said. And because of "my respect for your position and for the Holy See, I considered attentively the two-fold proposal contained in that letter. I shall now try to explain my views briefly...."

First Bousquet explained that the original Vicariate Apostolic of Eastern Oceania entrusted to his missionary community had been divided eventually into three vicariates apostolic named after the Tahiti Islands, Marquesas Islands, and Sandwich Islands (Hawaii).[11]

---

9. PF: SC Oceania vol. 7 (1861–64), f. 1063r–1065r, Euthyme Rouchouze to the Evangelization Congregation, 13 February 1864. The word used here for children is *kanakas*, a Polynesian word that has been absorbed into Pidgin English. See Francis Mihalic, *Grammar and Dictionary of Neo-Melanesian*, 54.

10. PF: LDB vol. 369 (1873), f. 474r, Barnabò to Euthyme Rouchouze, 4 September 1873. Rouchouze was born on 15 January 1813.

11. Bousquet says that it was Pope Pius IX who had divided his community's Vicariate Apostolic of Eastern Oceania in 1848 into three vicariates apostolic. Actually Pope Gregory XVI had already divided the original Vicariate Apostolic of Eastern Oceania in 1844, separating from it what became the Sandwich Islands Vicariate Apostolic. Pope Pius IX in 1848 then created the Marquesas Islands Vicariate Apostolic by removing these islands from the still existing Eastern Oceania Vicariate Apostolic. He then changed the name of this latter vicariate apostolic to that of Tahiti Islands. See Wiltgen, *Oceania*, chaps. 18 and 32.

The Vicariate Apostolic of the Tahiti Islands, Bousquet said, included the Tuamoto or Low Archipelago, the Gambier Islands, Easter Island, Cook Islands, and Roggewein Archipelago, "totaling at least one hundred islands scattered over very vast portions of the ocean." These islands were being cared for "by seventeen missionary priests and are producing abundant results. This is true especially for the principal island called Tahiti, the Gambier Islands and the Tuamoto Islands. It has not yet been possible to supply missionaries for the other islands, at least not on a permanent basis." Bishop Florentin-Etienne Jaussen (1815–91) was the one in charge of this vicariate.

Bishop Ildefonse-René Dordillon (1808–88), who had attended the Vatican Council, was in charge of the Marquesas Islands Vicariate Apostolic. "Ten priests of our institute are working under him," Bousquet said.

He then reported on the Vicariate Apostolic of the Sandwich or Hawaiian Islands, where Bishop Désiré-Louis Maigret (1804–82) was in charge. Bousquet called him "a truly apostolic man, whom Your Eminence also met in Rome on the occasion of the Vatican Council." Although he was elderly and had already spent forty years doing missionary work, "he is nevertheless still spry, is very vigilant in his ministry, and zealously fulfills his office." His vicariate had twenty-five priests and "with God's blessing those generous missionaries are gathering a very rich harvest of souls for heaven. . . ." Bousquet added that "the population of the Sandwich Islands is estimated at 60,000 of whom about 25,000 profess the Catholic faith. . . ."

Missionary priests in these three vicariates had innumerable and difficult tasks to fulfill, Bousquet said, "whether it is to overcome idolatry, to expose and refute heresy, to snatch from the filth of depraved customs those unfortunate peoples of Oceania who so easily are inclined to vice, to enlighten children in schools with the truth, and finally to propagate and establish our sacred religion. How great, I say, is the labor that rests upon their shoulders. Words can hardly describe it."

After filling three pages in this way Bousquet added:

> From these remarks of mine Your Eminence must have detected what my view is on this serious matter, which you propose to me. For even though I must give thanks to God for graciously assisting the labors of my priests, and even though great praise must be given to the Association for the Propagation of the Faith for not failing to give appropriate financial assistance to the vicars apostolic, still the missionary priests themselves are too few in number to cultivate sufficiently the entire [mission] field of the Master. They become exhausted prematurely and some have already reached old age.
>
> Furthermore the tasks which we must perform are almost countless and they require many priests and healthy priests, be it in our houses, missions, colleges and parochial schools in South America, or be it in our minor and major seminaries and colleges, and in our own houses in France and Belgium. As a result of wars and civil discord, the number of our novices for some years now has seen only a slight increase.
>
> Consequently after weighing the matter carefully before God, I am forced to confess to Your Eminence that I cannot—at least *at present*—take on such an expanse of islands.

If God were to fill his novitiate once again with novices, Bousquet said, "I shall at once write to Your Eminence on this matter. For I would like to fulfill the wishes of the Apostolic See and so together with my fellow religious give as much glory to God as possible."[12]

Barnabò had been secretary of Propaganda when Melanesia was abandoned by the Marists in 1853 and also when it was abandoned by the Milan missionaries in 1855. In 1856 he was named cardinal prefect of Propaganda. As year after year passed, he became ever more anxious to assign some missionaries before his death to take up the work again in Melanesia and Micronesia. Twice he had approached Superior General Favre of the Marists for personnel, but in vain. And now he had also received a negative reply from Superior General Bousquet of the Picpus Fathers.

Bousquet's reply lay unanswered on Barnabò's desk for four and a half months. Perhaps the cardinal was postponing his reply because he was unwilling to admit to himself that he had failed in obtaining permanent personnel for the two vast Vicariates Apostolic of Melanesia and Micronesia. And now he was blind, sick, and seventy-two years old.

Barnabò on 16 February 1874 suffered a violent and excruciating attack of convulsions. On 19 February, the fourth day of this prolonged attack, Secretary Giovanni Simeoni (1816-92) replied to Bousquet's letter of 22 September 1873 in the name of the agonizing cardinal prefect.[13] Simeoni wrote: ". . . My heart truly rejoices on learning that your members up to now have gathered fruit in proportion to the many and great labors which they have undertaken for the vineyard of the Lord." He also urged Bousquet and his missionaries "to remain forever confident that Christ, who has begun this task, will bring it to completion himself and will also provide a solid foundation for it."

Simeoni then used the following words as if they were coming from the lips of Barnabò:

> I regret very much that up to now no solution has been found for remedying the truly lamentable condition of the peoples of both Melanesia and Micronesia. Nevertheless I cannot deny that very grave reasons prevent the missionaries of your religious congregation, so busily engaged in caring for their present missions, from being able to go and propagate our religion in lands other than those which your congregation already has.
>
> There is, however, one thing more to do: If now you are able to take the light of the Gospel to the peoples [of Melanesia and Micronesia] only by wishful thinking, then pray earnestly that God will always assist your efforts in such a way, that shortly you may be able to take them the light of the Gospel in reality.

---

12. PF: SC Oceania vol. 10 (1873–76), f. 323r–324v, Bousquet to Barnabò, 22 September 1873.

13. Simeoni errs in the first sentence of his letter by saying that Bousquet's letter had reported on the status of the "Central Oceania Vicariates of his Congregation." The three Picpus vicariates, as Bousquet's letter rightly says, had been created from the Vicariate Apostolic of "Eastern Oceania," not Central Oceania. The Central Oceania Vicariate had been entrusted to the Marists with Bishop Bataillon in charge and had also subsequently been divided into several vicariates.

N. 1

Rme Domine

EX ARCHIVO
Dom. princ.
SS. CC.

Litterae Dominationis Tuae diei 22 Septembris anni nuper elapsi ad me pervenerunt, quarum pars statum Vicariatuum Oceaniae Centralis Congregationi tuae commissorum refert, pars vero de negociis religionis in septentrionalibus ipsius Oceaniae regionibus pertractat.

Quod primum attinet, gaudet profecto animus inde intelligere haud imparem tot tantisque laboribus pro vinea Domini exantlatis fructum usque adhuc tuos collegisse. Spero fore ut in incepto curriculo constanter permaneatis fidentes in eo qui incepit opus, Ipse enim illud perficiet solidabitque.

Quod alterum spectat, licet maxime doleat miserandae quidem Melanesiae ac Micronesiae populorum conditioni viam consulendi adhuc latere, attamen non inferior gravissimas extare causas quae prohibent quominus religiosae istius Congregationis Missionarii tot distenti jam curis in praesentiarum ad alias, praeter eas quas obtinet terras, religionis propagandae causa sese conferre valeant.

Qua in re unum superest, Deum videlicet enixe adprecari qui vestra ita semper secundet, ut si nunc in votis tantum remanet ad eos populos lucem Evangelii offerendi, idipsum brevi comprobetur effectu.

Interim Deum precor ut tibi fausta quaeque largiatur.
Romae ex aed. S. C. de P. Fide die 19 Februarii 1874.
Dom. Tuae   Addictus
Pro Emo Card. Praefecto impedito
Joannes Simeoni Secrius

Rmo P. Marcellino Bousquet
Sup. Gnli Congr. ss Cordium
Paris

Cardinal Prefect Barnabò sent this letter on 19 February 1874 to Superior General Marcellino Bousquet of the Fathers of the Sacred Hearts (Picpus). It is in Latin and is signed by Secretary Giovanni Simeoni "for the Most Eminent Cardinal Prefect who is impeded." Five days later Cardinal Barnabò died.
Source: Archives SSCC: 1-1-11/ 46.

The letter closed "Devotedly Yours," was signed "On behalf of His Eminence, the Cardinal Prefect, who is currently impeded," and ended with the signature Joannes Simeoni, secretary.[14]

After eight days of convulsions and six days before his seventy-third birthday, Barnabò's agony came to an end. He died on 24 February 1874. After his first attack of convulsions three years earlier, Barnabò was to be relieved of his post by Pope Pius IX, who wanted to give him an easier assignment. But Barnabò explained that he would rather give up being a cardinal than give up working in Propaganda Fide. His wish was granted by both God and the pope, who allowed him to remain in office until his death.[15]

14. SSCC: 1-1-11/46, Barnabò-Simeoni to Bousquet, 19 February 1874.
15. Metzler, "Präfekten und Sekretäre," 43.

25

Marists Refuse Micronesia for the Third Time
18 June 1875

AT LEAST TWICE IN 1869 AND TWICE IN 1870–71, BISHOP ELLOY REQUESTED CARDINAL Prefect Barnabò to place under his jurisdiction the Navigators Islands and the Gilbert or Kingsmill islands. In 1873 he requested jurisdiction over the Tokelau Islands. In 1874 Elloy sent still another letter to Barnabò, this time requesting that the Gilbert Islands together with the Caroline Islands be placed under his jurisdiction. Elloy made these requests while he was coadjutor to Bishop Bataillon, vicar apostolic of Central Oceania. Because of a unique Samoan commercial venture centered in Apia, Elloy foresaw endless transportation possibilities that were bound to accelerate and facilitate the work of evangelization in these tiny scattered islands of Micronesia.

Nothing came of all these proposals, however, because the Marist superior general was not in a position to supply the personnel needed to staff additional missions. Long before this time, however, Protestant missionary societies had become interested in these same clusters of islands and in others as well. Originally all of these islands were parts of the Roman Catholic Vicariate Apostolic of Central Oceania founded on 8 August 1842 and of the Melanesia-Micronesia Vicariates Apostolic founded on 16 July 1844.[1]

The London Missionary Society (L.M.S.) was founded in 1795 as a nondenominational organization dedicated to spreading the Christian faith in the non-European world. Its primary support came from the Congregationalists, and its first missionary to reach Samoa was John Williams. He landed at Sapapalii, Savai'i, in August 1830 with Charles Barff and with an exiled Samoan of chiefly standing. They had come with a small schooner built at Rarotonga that was named *Messenger of Peace*. Williams was received as a great teacher and was left in charge of Rarotongan and Tahitian teachers, whom he had selected to commence work in Samoa. While Williams made new contacts, Barff worked in Tahiti

---

1. On the origin of these three vicariates apostolic, see Wiltgen, *Oceania*, chaps. 14 and 17.

and Rarotonga, returning to Samoa in 1834 with the first books printed in the Samoan language: "a small reading and spelling book, a small catechism, a small hymn-book," all printed at their own printing press in Huahine.

A permanent staff of six missionaries and their wives arrived in Samoa on 6 June 1836, sent by the London Missionary Society. The new workers were quickly distributed throughout the Samoa Archipelago, and the mission's future by this time was assured. As early as 1840 Samoans themselves were going overseas, taking the gospel to other islands like Niue, Tokelau, Ellice, Gilberts, New Hebrides, etc.[2]

Surprise, a vessel of the London Missionary Society, set sail in June 1871 to take the Christian message from Cape York Peninsula, the northern tip of Australia, to New Guinea Island one hundred miles directly north. Aboard were the Rev. Samuel MacFarlane and the Rev. A. W. Murray. They and the eight teachers with them from the Loyalty Islands began missionary work in the islands of Torres Strait. Then in 1872 under the care of the Rev. Murray and the Rev. Wyatt Gill, six Rarotongan teachers with their wives were placed in coastal stations near Redscar Bay west of Port Moresby.

While in England in 1874, MacFarlane suggested to the London Missionary Society that it should begin placing missionaries on the New Guinea mainland. As a result MacFarlane and also William George Lawes (1839–1907), who had already given eleven years of service at Niue (Savage Island), were assigned to the New Guinea mainland. Lawes and his wife took up residence at Port Moresby on 24 November 1874. Twelve months earlier Rev. A. W. Murray had settled four Polynesian teachers there.

Meanwhile MacFarlane reconnoitered the mainland, making use of a small steamer, *Ellengowan*, for exploration voyages up the Baxter (now Mai Kussa) River and the Fly River. These voyages became widely known because MacFarlane had invited prominent men to accompany him. For the Baxter River voyage he chose Victorian Parliament member James Orkney, explorer Octavius Stone, and engineer Henry Smithurst. For the Fly River voyage he invited magistrate Henry M. Chester of Somerset in the Cape York Peninsula and also the Italian naturalist Luigi Maria d'Albertis (1841–1901). Port Moresby remained the center for the mainland mission, which developed quickly.[3]

The American Board of Commissioners for Foreign Missions, founded by New England Congregational Churches in 1810, was the first foreign missionary society established in the United States. Its missionaries took up work in 1852 in the Caroline Islands of Micronesia at Kusaie and Ponape. Hawaiian members of the Hawaiian Evangelical Association, earlier trained by the American Board, contributed their assistance in the Caroline Islands.

---

2. *Pacific Islands Yearbook*, 95f.

3. Souter, *New Guinea*, 25–29; R. J. Lacey, "Lawes," in *Encyclopaedia of Papua and New Guinea*, 2:629f. See also R. J. Lacey, "Missions," in *Encyclopaedia of Papua and New Guinea*, 2:772.

By 1857 the American Board mission had acquired its own sailing vessel, the *Morning Star*, and decided to expand its work in Micronesia by making new foundations immediately at Ebon in the Marshall Islands and at Apaiang in the Gilbert Islands. Mr. Hiram Bingham Jr. published the Gospel of Saint Matthew in Gilbertese and also a small hymn book. Three converts were received at Ponape in 1860 after eight years of waiting, and new missions were opened in the Gilbert Islands at Tarawa in 1860 and at Butaritari in 1865. Also in 1865 the Hawaiian missionaries opened a new mission at Jaluit in the Marshall Islands.

Ponape teachers were sent in 1871 to two neighboring Caroline Islands called Mokil and Pingelep, and in 1873 three couples from Ponape volunteered to open a mission in the Mortlock Islands three hundred miles southwest of Ponape. By 1875 three churches were organized in the Mortlocks, four more in 1876, and eight more in 1877. In that same year a new mission was opened at Truk by two Ponape volunteer teachers. In 1880 Kusaie became the center for missionary work in the Gilberts and Marshalls, and Ponape became the center for work in the Carolines. Kusaie is one of the most beautiful islands in the South Seas and is the farthest east of the Carolines.[4]

The Rev. George Brown (1835–1917), a member of the Methodist Church and of the Wesleyan Missionary Society (W.M.S.), served as a missionary in Samoa for fourteen years (1860–74), dedicating himself to linguistic, educational, and health work, and to building churches. This experience convinced him that Fiji, Tonga, and Samoa ought to send missionaries to New Britain in the Bismarck Archipelago. He presented his proposal to the Executive Committee of the Board of Missions in Sydney in September 1874 and succeeded in having it accepted.

Brown together with his wife Lydia arrived at Port Hunter in the Duke of York Group of the Bismarck Archipelago with twelve Fijian and Samoan colleagues on 15 August 1875 aboard the Methodist vessel *John Wesley*. Brown's first European assistant arrived three years and three months later on 2 December 1878. By the time Brown withdrew from the mission on 4 January 1881, there were ten mission stations in the Duke of York area, seven in the Gazelle Peninsula in northeast New Britain, and four in New Ireland.[5] That was a total of twenty-one stations founded in five and a half years, and during two of those years Brown was abroad.

---

4. Strong, *American Board*, 3–6, 56f, 231–48 passim. On Ponape, see Wiltgen, *Oceania*, 138f. In the present work, see Kusaie (formerly Ualan Island), chap. 5, pp. 70–71, and Ponape (also called Ascension Island), chap. 10, p. 148.

5. Ian Stuart, "They Didn't Push Their Way in—They Walked Softly," in *Post Courier*, Port Moresby, Papua New Guinea, 7 August 1975, p. 5; R. J. Lacey, "George Brown," in *Encyclopaedia of Papua and New Guinea*, 1:124–27.

Meanwhile Cardinal Prefect Barnabò had died on 24 February 1874, and Pope Pius IX had named Alessandro Cardinal Franchi (1819–78) his successor on 10 March 1874.[6] Months later Elloy saw an obituary of Barnabò reporting that Franchi had been named his successor. By this time Elloy was also aware of the progress being made in Micronesia by the American Board of Commissioners for Foreign Missions, whom he called Presbyterians. Hopeful that the new cardinal prefect might react more energetically to his proposals than Barnabò, Elloy wrote to Franchi in detail. After congratulating him on his new office, Elloy expressed his indebtedness to Barnabò, described his mission and presented his case.

Writing on 14 January 1875, ten months after Franchi had taken office, Elloy introduced himself as a Marist missionary sent to the Navigators Archipelago in 1856. By decree of 22 September 1872 he had been entrusted with the administration of the Vicariate Apostolic of the Navigators Archipelago, he said, while remaining at the same time coadjutor to the Vicar Apostolic of Central Oceania, Bishop Bataillon.

Elloy explained that the Navigators vicariate contained the entire archipelago under that name, also called the Samoa Archipelago. Its total population was about thirty-five thousand with some three hundred Europeans and Americans. Foreigners generally spoke English, he said. A large majority of the local people were Protestants, either Presbyterians or Methodists. "Catholics number about 5,000, all being converted from Protestantism, which was already widespread in the archipelago when the first Catholic missionaries arrived in 1846."

Apia on the north coast of Upolu Island in Samoa was the most important port and also the place most centrally located for communications. As Elloy explained, it was also the spot chosen for the residence of the vicar apostolic. "To visit islands which are 130, 70 or 25 miles away, I usually travel in a small boat with four or five oarsmen. And if there is a wind, I use a sail." The twelve priests at work in his vicariate were all French, he said, and were all members of the Society of Mary.

There was an English school "at Apia for the children of the English, American and German colonists, who are beginning to settle in this archipelago," he pointed out. "The majority of students are Protestants from birth, but all study the catechism and many are preparing for Baptism. The school is run by the Little Brothers of Mary, whose motherhouse is in Lyon. There is no English-language Protestant school in Samoa."

Elloy also had a school for Samoan girls in Apia which was run by Sisters of Our Lady of the Missions. "This school has some forty boarders coming from all parts of the archipelago and approximately fifty non-boarders as well, who come from populated areas nearby." The bishop explained that each village had a resident catechist, if the number of Catholics warranted it. "The catechist is a married man and he presides over the prayers that are said in common in a small chapel built for these reunions. This man also conducts school for children and adults. In addition he teaches all to recite the catechism and gives some explanations. He also teaches children how to read and even how to write."

---

6. For details on Franchi's career, see Metzler, "Präfekten und Sekretäre," 48f.

SACRORUM CONCILIORUM

NOVA ET AMPLISSIMA COLLECTIO

CUIUS

IOANNES DOMINICUS MANSI

ET POST IPSIUS MORTEM FLORENTINUS ET VENETUS EDITORES
AB ANNO 1757 AD ANNUM 1798 PRIORES TRIGINTA UNUM TOMOS EDIDERUNT
NUNC AUTEM CONTINUATA ET DEO FAVENTE ABSOLUTA

CURANTIBUS

Illmo et Rmo D. D. LUDOVICO PETIT

ARCHIEPISCOPO ATHENARUM
E CONGREGATIONE AUGUSTINIANORUM AB ASSUMPTIONE

ET

IOANNE BAPTISTA MARTIN

SACERDOTE, PROFESSORE IN CATHOLICA UNIVERSITATE LUGDUNENSI.

TOMUS QUINQUAGESIMUS

SACROSANCTI OECUMENICI CONCILJI VATICANI
PARS SECUNDA
ACTA SYNODALIA (Congreg. I-XXIX).

ARNHEM (Pays-Bas) & LEIPZIG
MCMXXIV.

SOCIÉTÉ NOUVELLE D'ÉDITION DE LA COLLECTION MANSI (H. WELTER).

This is the title page of Volume 50 of Ioannes Dominicus Mansi's work, completed after his death, containing all texts of the First Vatican Council.

While in Rome at the First Vatican Council, Elloy had spoken out on 18 February 1870 in favor of a universal catechism for the Roman Catholic Church. Such a catechism containing explanations and reasons for the various teachings, he said, did not rule out a simpler form of the same catechism for special audiences. As he told Cardinal Franchi: "In this vicariate we have an abbreviated catechism and another more extensive version, both printed in the local language. There is also a prayerbook in the same language. It contains epistles and gospels for Sundays and feast days, the principal prayers used in church, some prayers from the *Roman Ritual*, and about 100 hymns, all in the local language. At this moment we are printing a translation of a short Bible history covering the Old and New Testaments."

Elloy's letter went into detail about the Gilbert or Kingsmill archipelago with its approximately "60,000 inhabitants," and about the Caroline Islands, whose population he put at twenty thousand. These islands were near the equator, he said, either north or south of it, and ships leaving Apia regularly visited them "two or three times a year." From those archipelagoes many men "have been brought to Samoa as laborers" and in Samoa "they became Catholics, above all on the island of Tafitouevea (Drummund Island). On returning to their own islands they spoke favorably about Catholic missionaries and so we are now wanted in many places. Unfortunately Presbyterian ministers [from the American Board of Commissioners for Foreign Missions] have already preceded us to numerous localities. If we wait too long before sending missionaries to these archipelagoes, heresy will definitely take possession of them. Then in place of reaping," he said, "we shall be able only to glean."

Since the Gilbert Islands as well as the Caroline Islands "have most of their contacts with Samoa," Elloy told Franchi, "I would like to place myself once again in the hands of the Holy See." Elloy urged Franchi to do whatever he judged more fitting "for procuring the glory of God and the salvation of these peoples who have been left abandoned . . ." The bishop realized that his Society of Mary did not have priests enough to be able to take upon itself full responsibility for a new vicariate embracing the Gilberts and the Carolines. But he believed that "perhaps an appeal made on behalf of these islands by a bishop, who might be placed in charge of them, would give rise to new vocations for taking up work in this new field."[7]

If Franchi needed a bishop to evangelize the Gilberts and the Carolines, Elloy gave assurance that he himself was ready to take on the task. "I could still retain Samoa, since Apia is the central point for spreading out to all these places. The reason for this is that two commercial houses are established in this port and their ships monopolize the coconut trade carried on in these islands. I am making no request. But if the task is offered to me, I shall not refuse it."[8]

---

7. Elloy's letter in this context mistakenly calls Rooke Island, where Marist Bishop Jean-Georges Collomb had died, "one of the Carolines." But Rooke Island (now Umboi Island) is between New Britain and New Guinea and was part of the Melanesia vicariate. For details on the death of Bishop Collomb at Rooke Island see Wiltgen, *Oceania*, 483–85.

8. PF: SC Oceania vol. 10 (1873–76), f. 833r–836r, Elloy to Franchi, 14 January 1875.

Dictum quoque fuit: duplex ordinarie est catechismus, unus minimus, in quo continentur ea tantum, quae necessaria sunt ad salutem necessitate medii vel praecepti, qui rudibus et pueris tenerisve aetatis satis sit, alter magis extensus, in quo etiam continentur doctrinae explicationes et rationes. Optime. Sed cur haec aut similia non providentur in catechismo a concilio Vaticano imponendo? Quoad populos recenter ab infidelitate conversos, et praesertim quoad Oceaniae incolas, qui duplici in argumento in hac aula allati sunt, fateor equidem eos in maxima ignorantia versatos fuisse, multosque ex eis anthropophagiae deditos fuisse; sed in istis insulis, in quibus nullus erat christianus 40 abhinc annis, nunc sunt plus quam 50000 christianorum; et nunc pro mea parte testificor insulares Oceaniae, illos saltem qui a iunioribus annis ad fidem venerunt, aut in ea nati sunt, nullo modo inferiores esse in doctrinae catholicae cognitione sive pueris sive iuvenibus eiusdem aetatis, qui instructione communi in nostra etiam Gallia gaudent: ideoque nihil obstat quin eumdem catechismum ac caeteri christiani populi habeant; et immo maximum adiumentum nostrae praedicationi adhibebit introductio catechismi, quem testabimur eumdem esse pro universo orbe catholico.

This extract from Mansi's Volume 50 contains the address given by Bishop Elloy at the First Vatican Council on the importance of a Universal Catechism for his mission in the South Pacific.

Elloy's letter to Cardinal Franchi, dated 14 January 1875, was en route nearly six full months before arriving in Rome on 5 July 1875. By that time Franchi surprisingly had already taken action on the proposal contained in Elloy's letter. This is how it happened: Elloy in 1874, not aware that Barnabò had died, had written yet another letter on his proposal to Barnabò. It arrived in Rome on 13 January 1875. By this time Franchi was already in office for ten full months. As the new cardinal prefect of Propaganda, he opened the letter addressed to Barnabò, read it, liked the idea, and took action on it. This was before Franchi received the letter of 14 January 1875, which Elloy had addressed to him personally.[9]

Franchi had assigned Canon Sambucetti, one of his assistants, to study Elloy's earlier letter addressed to Barnabò. He also had Sambucetti call it to the attention of Father Benoît Forestier, procurator general of the Marists, who resided at the French Seminary in Rome. Sambucetti not only provided Forestier with background information on the Melanesia and Micronesia vicariates apostolic, but also explained what had led up to Elloy's request.

Forestier then passed on this information to Superior General Favre in Lyon and received back from him a reply dated 18 June 1875.[10] A cardinal prefect often uses an intermediary when approaching a superior general with a new project. Whether the reply is positive or negative, the same intermediary usually conveys it to the cardinal prefect.

This is just what happened. Superior General Favre wrote to Forestier, who turn wrote from the French Seminary in Rome on 28 June 1875 to Canon Sambucetti: "I had the honor of communicating to the Very Reverend Superior General of our Society the request made by Bishop Elloy," Forestier said, who wished "that his jurisdiction be extended to include the Kingsmill, Gilbert and Caroline islands." But Superior General Favre has pointed out "that these islands are part of the Vicariates Apostolic of Melanesia and Micronesia, which have been entrusted by Propaganda to the Milan Seminary for Foreign Missions."

Forestier added that Superior General Favre

> charges me to express to His Eminence, the Cardinal Prefect, the regret which he experiences, since his lack of missionaries does not permit him to accept these new missions. You know already that it is not possible to satisfy completely the requests coming from the Very Reverend Vicars Apostolic. Therefore it would seem altogether imprudent on the part of our Society to take on new obligations, as long as Divine Providence does not send us a larger number of missionaries.
>
> In the second place, if Bishop Elloy were placed in charge of evangelizing the islands mentioned above, there is no doubt that His Excellency would be absent for long periods of time from the Navigators Archipelago. He would also take along

---

9. See ibid., f. 836r, for a secretarial note stating that the letter of Elloy of 14 January 1875 was answered in July that year. See also PF: LDB vol. 371 (1875), f. 532v, Franchi to Elloy, 7 July 1875. Here Franchi says that he had received one of Elloy's letters on 13 January 1875 and another "the day before yesterday," which would have been 5 July 1875. Franchi gives the dates on which Elloy's two letters arrived. Contrary to the practice of Barnabò, he does not give the dates of the letters themselves.

10. See PF: LDB vol. 371 (1875), f. 573r. Franchi to Favre, 21 July 1875. Here Franchi explains the procedure that he followed in approaching Favre and also mentions Favre's 18 June 1875 letter to Forestier.

with him many of the better missionaries, whom it would not be possible to replace promptly.

According to Forestier, Superior General Favre was convinced "that the certain harm which would come to the [Navigators] Mission because of this, would not be compensated by the altogether doubtful success of the new foundations."

Finally there was "the fear that Bishop Elloy may very soon be called upon to succeed Bishop Bataillon, whose coadjutor he is. In this case His Excellency [Elloy] would have to provide for the needs of a very extensive Vicariate Apostolic," an area including both Central Oceania and the Navigators. This new burden, if he were to become responsible also for the Gilbert Islands and the Caroline Islands, "would render his task altogether out of proportion." Forestier therefore invited Sambucetti "to submit these reflections to His Eminence, if you judge it useful. . . ."[11]

Forestier's letter to Sambucetti was dated Monday, 28 June 1875. Exactly one week later on 5 July, Franchi received Elloy's letter of 13 January 1875 bringing him congratulations on becoming successor to Barnabò. This was the letter addressed by Elloy to Franchi, which contained Elloy's proposal regarding the Gilbert and Caroline islands.

On 7 July, two days after receiving Elloy's letter, Franchi replied. After thanking Elloy for his congratulations, Franchi said that "orders cannot be given for carrying out the proposal which you made of extending your jurisdiction to the Gilbert, Kingsmill and Caroline islands. Your Congregation's Father General informed me recently that a lack of sufficient missionaries for those missions already entrusted to the Society of Marists makes it impossible for that same Society to accept new missions."

Franchi added that there was only one thing left to do: "Pray that God sends workers into His harvest." He promised Elloy, however, that he personally would take care of sending missionaries to those islands "when the opportunity presents itself."[12]

Franchi did not wait, however, for an opportunity to present itself. Instead he created one. First he asked the Propaganda archivist to verify what Superior General Favre had maintained, namely, that the Vicariates Apostolic of Melanesia and Micronesia had been entrusted by Propaganda "to the Milan Seminary for Foreign Missions." The archivist replied that in 1844 both Melanesia and Micronesia had been entrusted to the Marists, who "in 1852 had requested that they be relieved of responsibility" for them. Members of the Milan Foreign Mission Seminary "were then sent there to collaborate with the Marists. In 1855 Father Reina of Milan, who was called Prefect Apostolic of Melanesia, was allowed to withdraw because there was no hope of making conversions."[13]

---

11. PF: SC Oceania vol. 10 (1873–76), f. 960rv, Forestier to Sambucetti, 28 June 1875.

12. PF: LDB vol. 371 (1875), f. 532v–533v, Franchi to Elloy, 7 July 1875.

13. For the research done by the archivist, see PF: SC Oceania, vol. 10 (1873–76), f. 963v. For the many occasions on which Colin sought to be relieved of responsibility for the Melanesia and Micronesia Vicariates see Wiltgen, *Oceania*, 534–8 passim, 514, 517, 528–32 *passim*, 544, 546.

Since Favre did not become superior general until ten years after the Melanesia and Micronesia vicariates had been created, Franchi decided to clarify for him the juridical state of the question. Perhaps Franchi hoped that Favre might still be persuaded to allow Bishop Elloy to extend his own territory, so that he could care for those Catholic converts made earlier within his territory, who meanwhile had returned to their villages in the Gilbert, Kingsmill, and Caroline islands.

Therefore on 21 July 1875, only two weeks after writing to Elloy, Franchi wrote to Superior General Favre. He explained that Propaganda at its General Meeting of 15 July 1844 had created two vicariates apostolic, "one containing Melanesia and the other containing Micronesia, but in such a way that both missions for the moment were to be governed by one and the same Vicar Apostolic. Now this is the mission that was entrusted to the care of your Society of the Blessed Virgin Mary," Franchi said, continuing:

> And even though later, namely, in the year 1852, missionaries of the San Calocero Seminary of Milan [Italy] were sent there to help the priests of your Congregation, it was never the mind of this Sacred Congregation to remove the Marist missionaries from the forenamed regions, or to force them to leave. This is expressly stated in the letter dated 24 February 1853 addressed to the Reverend Father Frémont, Prefect Apostolic at that time of the forenamed missions.[14]

Franchi pointed out further that the areas in question "have been abandoned for various reasons by the Milan personnel and also by the Marists." He said that Bishop Elloy, "Vicar Apostolic of the Navigators Archipelago, who belongs to your Society," has informed Propaganda by letter of 14 January, "that there exist some islands around the equator called Gilbert, Kingsmill and Carolines. These islands are included within the boundaries of the forementioned Micronesia Mission and already contain some Catholics. Many more people there are inclined to embrace our religion."

But "now they are in rather grave danger of losing their faith or of losing their call to grace," either because of the lack of missionaries or because of the teachings of Protestants, who much earlier entered those areas in order to propagate their religion. Because of this Bishop Elloy is more than ready to extend his pastoral care also to those areas, if it should seem well to the Holy See, but without giving up his own vicariate."

All of this had been explained in general, Cardinal Franchi said, to the Marist procurator, Father Forestier. But now having received Superior General Favre's views dated 18 June 1875, Franchi agreed with Favre

> that your Society cannot accept any new missions because of its lack of missionaries. Therefore, in order that this matter may be taken care of in the best possible way, I request that Your Paternity give me all data whatsoever that you may have on the *status quo* of the forenamed Missions, indicating whether there truly exists genuine

---

14. For further information on this 24 February 1853 letter to Frémont, see chap. 10, p. 165.

hope of converting these peoples to the faith. Kindly indicate as well the most suitable means that one might use in order to achieve this goal. And finally, what are the difficulties which stand in the way of realizing this proposal? I shall await your reply to these questions....[15]

Superior General Favre answered Cardinal Franchi's letter of 21 July on 12 October 1875, almost three months later. He excused himself for not being able to reply at once, because he had been busy visiting Marist houses in Europe. He was also hindered by giving spiritual retreats to his members, "which ordinarily take up the months of August and September." Since his return to Lyon he had made "the necessary research on the important subject which Your Eminence has deigned to submit to me and I now have the honor of transmitting the results to you." The "results" covered eight pages.[16]

"The information that I can give you on the present state of these islands, and in particular on the archipelagoes mentioned by you, is very slight indeed," Favre said. "The islands of Woodlark, Rooke and San Cristóbal, where we formerly had foundations, are included in the Vicariate of Melanesia. The archipelagoes of the Carolines, Gilberts and Kingsmill, on the contrary, are "part of Micronesia where our missionaries have never penetrated."

Explaining in general why the Society of Mary had left the Melanesia-Micronesia missions, Favre said that from 1844 to 1848 his society "had lost by premature death a very large number of its missionaries." Bishop Epalle, the first vicar apostolic, was killed in 1845 "by the inhabitants of Santa Isabel Island. And several of his missionaries were seriously wounded." Father Crey "died of fever at San Cristóbal Island" in March 1847 and in the following month "Fathers Paget and Jacquet along with Brother Hyacinthe Chatelet were assassinated on the same island. Bishop Collomb, successor to Bishop Epalle, died from fever at Rooke on 16 July 1848" and his companion Father Villien "died from the same sickness." Four months later illness forced two other missionaries to leave for Europe.[17]

At this point in his letter Favre claims that twenty-three years earlier Prefect Apostolic Frémont had consulted Superior General Colin on "the appropriateness of withdrawing [from Melanesia], at least for a time, and of joining the missions in Central Oceania where the zeal of our missionaries seems to be more useful." If what Favre claims is true, this would mean that the Marist staff was eager and ready to leave Melanesia.

The late Father Jean Coste of the Marists, however, lists four authentic letters from Frémont to Colin written in 1850–52. And Coste says: "In none of these letters does Frémont consult Colin" on "the appropriateness of withdrawing" from Melanesia. Among the four authentic letters, however, there is an unauthentic copy of Frémont's letter dated 25 June 1852. "It is very unfortunate," Coste says, "since this so-called copy is a free compo-

---

15. PF: LDB vol. 371 (1875), f. 572r–573v, Franchi to Favre, 21 July 1875.

16. See PF: SC Oceania, vol. 10 (1873–76), f. 1009r–1010v, 1013r–1014v, for the eight-page letter. The intervening pages, f. 1011r–1012v, contain another letter.

17. For more details on the deaths of these missionaries, see their names in the index of Wiltgen, *Oceania*.

sition by Poupinel. The paragraph . . . , 'We have been counseled . . . ,' is not in the original and [so] no conclusion may be drawn from it."[18]

The following words found only in Poupinel's copy consequently are unauthentic and are to be ascribed to Poupinel and not at all to Frémont: "We have been counseled, in view of the uselessness of our efforts and the hardness of heart of our savages, to shake the dust from our feet and leave Woodlark in order to carry elsewhere the benefits of the peace of which we are the ministers. . . ."[19]

Superior General Favre used many arguments to convince Cardinal Prefect Franchi that the Marists were no longer responsible for the Melanesia and Micronesia vicariates apostolic. He claimed, for example, that Propaganda by March 1852 had handed over responsibility for both vicariates to the Milan Foreign Mission Seminary. "I found this confirmed by a report in *Annales de la propagation de la foi*, March 1852," Favre said.[20]

The magazine that he cited, however, was not an official organ of Propaganda, but merely a pious mission monthly published in Lyon by a fund-raising society.[21] Favre's March 1852 information was taken from a report on the society's funds distributed in 1851. Page 193 said that "the Prefecture Apostolic of Melanesia and Micronesia (Foreign Mission Seminary of Milan)" had received 12,752 francs. As has been shown in earlier chapters, Rome at this time had not yet designated which territory the Milan missionaries were to receive. Paolo Reina, head of the departing group, was in Lyon in March 1852, when the magazine was published. And on 30 March 1852 by coincidence he wrote to Cardinal Prefect Fransoni from Lyon that it was the wish and mind of Colin "that we should take over the mission of Micronesia and Melanesia."[22]

But what did Colin himself actually tell Cardinal Fransoni about his discussions with the Milan missionaries? Colin's 22 March 1852 letter to Fransoni does not say that the Italian missionaries from Milan "should take over the mission of Micronesia and Melanesia." What Colin says is that he had counseled the Milan missionaries to found immediately two stations in Melanesia, one at Woodlark and the other at Rooke. Then from the Rooke Mission they could easily reach the "important island" of New Guinea.[23]

Cardinal Prefect Fransoni approved Colin's proposal and informed Colin of this by letter on 6 May 1852.[24] Consequently the earlier *Annales* issue of March 1852, by mention-

---

18. See the 4 October 1976 query of Wiltgen to Coste and the 13 October 1976 reply of Coste to Wiltgen in the RW Collection, 13548f. The four authentic letters are in SM: OMM/208.

19. PF: SC Oceania, vol. 10 (1873–76), f. 1009v–1010r, Favre to Franchi, 12 October 1875. Favre's report to Franchi mistakenly dates this 25 June 1852 letter of Frémont as 23 June.

20. PF: SC Oceania, vol. 10 (1873–76), f. 1010r, Favre to Franchi, 12 October 1875.

21. See *Annales de la propagation de la foi*, 24:192f (Lyon, March 1852).

22. See chap. 6, p. 99.

23. See chap. 6, p. 100.

24. See chap. 7, p. 109.

ing in parentheses the Milan Foreign Mission Seminary, could not have meant that this seminary was in charge of both areas. It only meant that a grant had been given to the seminary in 1851 for use in one or the other area. Rome never handed over to the Italian missionaries from Milan responsibility for the two Vicariates Apostolic of Melanesia and Micronesia.

Favre proceeded to describe for Franchi how the Marists had handed over their mission to the Milan missionaries.[25] And he added what he knew about the current state of the Carolines, the Gilberts, and the Kingsmill Islands. He called Hogoleu (now Truk) the principal island in the Carolines and said that it was "about 800 leagues (more than 2,390 Roman miles) distant from Apia, the residence of Bishop Elloy." The majority of the Carolines "are even farther away," he said.

The Carolines actually were "closer to the Marianas Islands and the Island of Guam, with which the local people seem to have had contact." Favre had heard that Spanish Dominicans had a small number of missionaries in the Marianas Islands. But he had never heard "that there are Catholics in the Caroline Islands. American Protestant missionaries, however, have made one or two foundations there," he said.

As for the Gilbert Islands and the Kingsmill Archipelago (the southern half of the Gilbert Islands), they were "respectively 600 and 500 leagues distant from Apia (about 1800 and 1500 Roman miles)," Favre said. "The American Protestants have some foundations in these two archipelagoes, but our missionaries have never penetrated there."

Favre pointed out further that

> some years ago a Protestant German firm opened a warehouse at Apia, which has become the center of its commerce. From there it sends out its ships to surrounding islands, also to those at very great distances. Some local people from the Gilbert Islands and from the Kingsmill Islands have come to Apia aboard these ships. They were charitably received by the Catholic population and received preliminary [religious] instructions. Although it seems doubtful that any of them were baptized, many left for their homeland taking along the seed of our Holy Faith. These beginnings are very rudimentary. Yet this evidently is a favorable circumstance for establishing a Catholic Mission among their fellow countrymen. If only one could find zealous missionaries able to accept this project.[26]

The German firm to which Favre referred was no doubt Johann César Godeffroy (1813–85) und Sohn with headquarters in Hamburg, Germany. By 1837 a branch of this company had been founded in Havana, Cuba. In 1845 another branch was founded in Valparaìso, Chile, and in 1849 a third branch was founded in San Francisco, California. This firm had twelve ships by 1845. By 1856 its fleet had grown to twenty-seven ships, nine

---

25. PF: SC Oceania, vol. 10 (1873–76), f. 1010v, Favre to Franchi, 12 October 1875. Here Favre says that the Milan missionaries "remained at Woodlark until the month of August 1855." They actually left Woodlark on 10 July of that year. See chap. 13, p. 223.

26. PF: SC Oceania, vol. 10 (1873–76), f. 1013rv, Favre to Franchi, 12 October 1875.

of which were built in the company's own shipyards. Godeffroy und Sohn thus became the largest shipping company based in Hamburg.

August Unshelm (?–1864), manager of the Godeffroy branch in Valparaìso, opened a branch at Apia in Samoa in 1856. Although other branches of the company failed to prosper periodically, that in Samoa continued to grow by purchasing or by founding coconut and cotton plantations. Unshelm also opened trading stations in Fiji and at Vava'u in Tonga.

Unshelm died in Fiji in 1864 and was succeeded by Theodor Weber, a man of vision and extraordinary energy. Within a few years Weber had greatly extended the Godeffroy trading enterprise by pushing south, west, and north from Apia. He placed hundreds of traders on hundreds of islands and founded agencies in Fiji, Tonga, Niue, Futuna, Wallis, Tokelau Islands, Gilbert and Ellice islands, Northern Solomons, New Hebrides, New Britain, New Ireland, Nauru, and also in the Caroline, Marshall, and Marianas archipelagoes.

By collecting raw materials from these islands and distributing finished products to them, the Godeffroy ships covered practically the entire central and western Pacific. The company founded yet another large station at Yap in the northwest Pacific, halfway between Samoa and Cochin China, where it early had a copra mill. It was from this vast shipping network that Bishop Elloy wisely had wanted to profit, using it to reach out from Samoa to the Kingsmill, Gilbert, and Caroline islands.[27]

Marist Superior General Favre, however, did not share his vision. It was "easy to understand that Bishop Elloy is grieved over the loss of so many souls," Favre told Franchi, "and that his zeal makes him want to go to their aid. I am compelled to think, however, that his zeal has impeded him from giving sufficient attention to the means needed to execute his proposal. The distance alone would be an insurmountable difficulty, unless he were to sacrifice the interests of his own mission. In spite of all his activity it is not possible," Favre insisted, for Bishop Elloy "at one and the same time to govern [missions in] archipelagoes which are distant some 500, 600 and 800 leagues from his own residence, and are located in seas where the means of communication are so rare and so uncertain."

Further, Favre said,

> Bishop Elloy cannot reasonably hope to obtain the missionaries necessary for these foundations. We are making very great sacrifices in order to continue the missions which have been entrusted to our society and whose needs keep increasing without interruption. It would be impossible for us to increase our responsibilities [in the Pacific] without sacrificing our establishments in Europe. And this would mean eliminating the very source of our vocations.
>
> Bishop Elloy is aware of this and therefore it seems that he is counting on a direct appeal that he personally would make to the clergy of France. But His Excellency already made such an appeal during his last voyage to Europe at the time of the Vatican Council. Its result does not at all justify a second attempt. Besides, this would require

---

27. Kaethe Molsen, "Godeffroy, Ueberseekaufleute und Reeder," in *Neue Deutsche Biographie* (Duncker & Humblot, Berlin, 1964), 6:494f; *Pacific Islands Year Book and Who's Who*, 106.

His Excellency to be absent from his mission for several years, something that would be very dangerous especially at this moment. The Navigators Archipelago, where Protestantism is still dominant, is going through a crisis which is at once political and religious. And it will have important results for the future. It is there that Bishop Elloy's zeal and also his influence, which he has been able to acquire over the local people, will be most needed and most justly put to use.

Favre offered his own solution for the problem: "Therefore, Your Eminence, if a new mission can be launched in Micronesia, it seems to me that some society other than ours ought to be entrusted with it. A very small number of missionaries would suffice as a start, provided that they would be certain of receiving additional personnel later. Then, if they considered it opportune, they could go first to Apia, where they would receive very cordial hospitality from our missionaries." Once there, it would be easy for them to get in touch with the local people from the Kingsmill Islands. The new missionaries could also "learn their language, perhaps train catechists as their assistants, and make foundations in Micronesia as opportunities present themselves. Thus they would avoid the majority of obstacles and nearly all of the dangers to which our first missionaries were exposed."

If Propaganda could not find a mission sending society "able to take charge of this project," Favre said,

> I believe that Bishop Elloy ought to restrict his efforts to bringing together as many young men as possible in order to provide them with a solid education. Depending upon the circumstances he should then train either a local clergy or dedicated catechists, who some day could substitute for the permanent presence of a priest. However, it seems altogether necessary to me that His Excellency should avoid being absent from his mission for a notable period of time. He should also avoid extending his jurisdiction to begin foundations which it would be impossible for us to continue in spite of our desires.

At the end of his eight-page letter Favre told Franchi that the Marist procurator general, "who shall be returning to Rome this coming month," could supply any further explanations that Franchi might desire. In brief Favre's long letter meant that Franchi was free to entrust to other missionary groups any or all of the islands contained in what had once been the two Marist Vicariates Apostolic of Melanesia and Micronesia.[28]

Approximately one month later in mid-November 1875 a glowing report dated 24 August 1875 arrived in Rome for Cardinal Prefect Franchi from Bishop Bataillon of Wallis. His Central Oceania vicariate had once been "very vast," he said, "but today is one of the smallest vicariates in Oceania, because the vicariates of New Caledonia, Fiji and Samoa, have all been separated from it." His Central Oceania vicariate at present consisted of "groups of islands," he said, "of which the principal ones are Uvea [or Wallis], Futuna, Rotuma, Tonga, Haapoi, Vava'u and Tokelau. We have mission stations on all of these islands, but we do not yet have missionaries to send to other less important islands. . . ."

28. PF: SC Oceania, vol. 10 (1873–76), f. 1013v–1014v, Favre to Franchi, 12 October 1875.

The Roman Catholic religion "is flourishing most of all on the island of Uvea or Wallis," Bataillon said. "For this reason it is called the Little Rome of Oceania." It was here thirty-three years ago that the Catholic religion was first implanted, he said. And it was from here that it had spread to the multitude of islands which were then still part of the Central Oceania vicariate. "The Church of Uvea," Bataillon said, "which I with the help of God had the consolation of founding, now numbers more than one hundred encircling daughter churches. This is a very consoling result and one that has been achieved in the space of thirty years."

Bataillon added that his missionaries were "all French and belong to the Society of Mary. I have had only one indigenous priest and he was trained and ordained" at the Urban College of Propaganda in Rome. "This was the first attempt made in Oceania, but the man unfortunately turned out bad. He compromised himself in such a way that we were obliged to put him under interdict and even to separate him from the Church...."[29]

This success story of Bataillon reached Cardinal Prefect Franchi most likely in November 1875.[30] On 15 November that year Jean-Claude Colin, founder and first superior general of the Marists, died at the age of eighty-five. Back in 1852 Bataillon had sent a very distressful letter to Propaganda, announcing that it was Colin's "intention little by little to remove all his subjects from Oceania."[31] But Colin's missionary group did not accept this policy. Due to internal conflict Colin then resigned on 9 May 1854 as superior general and Favre became his successor.[32]

One year and five months after Colin's death, Bishop Bataillon died at Wallis on 11 April 1877. He was sixty-seven years old and was dead only ten months when Pope Pius IX died on 7 February 1878 at the age of eighty-five, which was also the age at which Colin had died. The pope's reign had lasted thirty-one years (1846–78) and included the twenty-five-year period covered by this book. At the conclave convened to elect a new pope, Cardinal Prefect Franchi of Propaganda received the support of Spain and became one of the leading candidates for the papal office. But he himself campaigned for Gioacchino Pecci (1810–1903) and suggested that his own votes be given to that candidate. Pecci was then elected pope on 20 February 1878 and took the name Leo XIII. Two weeks later on 5 March, Leo XIII chose Cardinal Franchi to be his secretary of state. But on 31 July that year, hardly five months later, secretary of state Franchi died at the age of fifty-nine.[33]

Since Bishop Elloy was coadjutor to Bishop Bataillon with right of succession, Elloy automatically succeeded Bataillon as vicar apostolic of Central Oceania. At the same time he retained his other office as pro-vicar apostolic or administrator of the Navigators

---

29. PF: SC Oceania vol. 10 (1873–76), f. 984r–985r, Bataillon to Franchi, 24 August 1875.

30. See ibid., f. 985r. A secretary's note added to Bataillon's letter of 24 August 1875 states that it was answered on 1 December 1875. It no doubt had arrived in November.

31. See Wiltgen, *Oceania*, 547.

32. *Origines maristes*, 4:238.

33. Metzler, "Präfekten und Sekretäre," 49.

Archipelago. Having complete charge now of both vicariates and being full of plans for the future, Elloy hurried back to France to obtain additional personnel and adequate provisions for his expanded mission territory.

After being absent from his missions for more than a year, Bishop Elloy was at Notre Dame de Bon-Encontre near Agen, France, preparing to return to the South Pacific, when suddenly he died on 22 November 1878, one week before his forty-ninth birthday. This was one year and seven months after the death of Bishop Bataillon.

For eight years (1864–72) Elloy and Bataillon had been wishing to be separated from one another. Now both were dead according to God's plan, and neither could profit from the absence of the other.

Contrary to expectations, however, the younger Bishop Elloy died very soon after Bishop Bataillon. Also contrary to expectations was the proposal presented by Superior General Favre regarding their successors. For years he had insisted upon separating the two vicariates apostolic. But now with Elloy and Bataillon both dead, Favre urged Rome to appoint a single successor to be put fully in charge of both vicariates apostolic. They "could be governed well by a single bishop residing at Apia," he said, since it was a port city that served as a maritime contact for the chief islands of both vicariates.

The cardinal members of Propaganda gathered together for a General Meeting in the Vatican Apartments on 28 April 1879 to study the proposals of Superior General Favre. They were told that Favre wanted both offices to be given to a single bishop, "at least for now," since the Vicariate Apostolic of the Navigators was "not very extensive." Even the Central Oceania vicariate had been greatly diminished in size when the Fiji and Ono islands in 1863 were separated from it to become the Prefecture Apostolic of the Fiji Islands.

Father Jean-Amand Lamaze (1833–1906) was the first of three candidates presented by Favre for this new office. He had worked in the Tonga Islands for more than fourteen years. The cardinals chose him as their candidate, and Pope Leo XIII on 7 May 1879 named him vicar apostolic of the Vicariate Apostolic of Central Oceania and administrator apostolic (1879–96) of the Navigators Archipelago.[34]

---

34. PF: Acta vol. 247 (1879) f. 250r–252r, General Meeting of 28 April 1879. See also the fax from Marist archivist Gaston Lessard of 18 October 1994 to Wiltgen for the dates concerning Lamaze.

26

Raimondi Becomes Vicar Apostolic of Hong Kong
4 October 1874

HERBERT ALBERT VAUGHAN (1832–1903) WAS BORN IN GLOUCESTER, ENGLAND, THE ELdest in a family of fourteen children. His father was a colonel, and his mother was a convert to Catholicism. At the age of twenty-two Vaughan was ordained a priest in Lucca, Italy, and in the following year was named vice president of Saint Edmund's College, a seminary for diocesan clergy in Ware, England, just north of London.

Father Vaughan's ecclesiastical superior was Cardinal Nicholas Wiseman (1802–65), archbishop of Westminster. In 1861 while the two were enjoying a drive on the Isle of Wight off the southern coast of England, the young priest turned to the cardinal and said that he would like to be a foreign missionary and train others to follow that vocation. Vaughan had been hesitant, but Wiseman welcomed his proposal and called it an answer to prayer.

As they drove along in their horse-drawn carriage, Wiseman explained to Vaughan that while preparing in Rome in 1840 for his ordination as bishop on the following day, he had spoken with Father Vincenzo Pallotti (1795–1850).[1] This saintly priest made a point of Wiseman's duty to found in England a seminary for the foreign missions because of the many overseas colonies of England. Wiseman promised to do so on his return to England, but he never did. He told Vaughan, "You are the first person who has offered himself for the purpose." For two days Wiseman and Vaughan discussed the matter, and Vaughan then wrote in his diary, "We determined to do nothing for some time but to obtain prayers."[2]

---

1. Pallotti was beatified on 22 January 1950 by Pope Pius XII and was canonized by Pope John XXIII on 20 January 1963. See also Pallotti under "saints" in Wiltgen, *Oceania*, 604.

2. Arthur McCormack, *Cardinal Vaughan: The Life of the Third Archbishop of Westminster, Founder of St. Joseph's Missionary Society, Mill Hill*, 57f. For additional details on the Wiseman-Pallotti meeting, see Hermann auf der Heide, *Die Missionsgenossenschaft von Steyl: Ein Bild der ersten 25 Jahre ihres Bestehens*, 7. The Wiseman-Pallotti meeting is described by both authors, but with discrepancies.

Prefect Apostolic Ambrosi of Hong Kong had long recognized in Father Raimondi a hustling, energetic person ready to carry out any assignment, and so Ambrosi sent Raimondi to Europe in order to find some English-speaking teaching brothers for Catholic schools in Hong Kong. Raimondi's search took him to London where he knocked on the door of Cardinal Wiseman. It was 1861, shortly after Wiseman's carriage ride with Vaughan. When Raimondi introduced himself to Wiseman as a founding member of the Foreign Mission Seminary of Milan, the cardinal repeated the story about Pallotti that he had told to Vaughan a short time earlier. Wiseman then arranged for Vaughan to meet Raimondi, saying that Vaughan could certainly profit from knowledge about the early days of the Milan Foreign Mission Seminary. Vaughan was also able to draw from Raimondi's rich missionary experience in Hong Kong, New Guinea, Labuan, and Borneo.[3] The two men became friends.

Raimondi's search for teaching brothers was to no avail because religious communities themselves had few vocations. Upon arrival in Venice ten months earlier as vice prefect of Hong Kong, Raimondi had written to Milan on 13 August 1861, urging that director Marinoni keep secret the news of his arrival, even from his family. "My mission comes first and then my relatives," Raimondi said. "My mother is the Hong Kong Mission; my brothers and sisters are all the Christians of Hong Kong." In mid-June 1862 he left Venice and returned to Hong Kong.[4]

Raimondi was back in Hong Kong four and a half years when Prefect Apostolic Ambrosi died on 11 March 1867. Three days later Raimondi sent news of his death to Cardinal Prefect Barnabò.[5] By decree of 17 November 1867 Propaganda announced that Raimondi had been named pro-prefect of the Hong Kong mission.[6]

Before dying Ambrosi had requested Raimondi to take charge of the Hong Kong prefecture apostolic and also of the procure office for the Missions of China. A year later Raimondi informed Marinoni in Milan that he had both tasks on his hands. He complained that the records for both were one hopeless conglomeration. "It is difficult for the Prefect [Apostolic] to separate the Procure from the Hong Kong Mission," he said, "because so many things have been bunched together." Maybe with time "this disorder can be avoided, but not now." Propaganda wanted the procure office for the Missions of China to continue in Hong Kong as formerly.

"It would be well if the one named superior of this Mission were for the present also in charge of the Procure," Raimondi said. "He could then delegate someone else to be

---

3. Auf der Heide, *Missionsgenossenschaft von Steyl*, 7.

4. Tragella, *Missioni estere*, 1:279, 388.

5. For Raimondi's letter to Barnabò of 14 March 1867 see PIME: XXIV (Hong Kong), 2:25. Tragella in *Missioni estere*, 2:91, incorrectly says that Ambrosi died on 10 March. Brambilla in *Pontificio istituto*, 1:177, gives the date incorrectly as 5 March.

6. See PIME: XXIV (Hong Kong), 2:31. For a lengthy commentary on this decree and its significance, see Tragella, *Missioni estere*, 2:93–96.

Procurator. The abnormal situation which has existed up to now should not continue..., namely, of having a Procurator for Propaganda, who knows nothing about the Mission, but still is in charge of the Prefecture and then names a vice prefect. I say this because it is necessary for the superior to be a missionary who knows the needs of the mission and has the time to work for and direct the mission."

Raimondi hoped that the one to be placed in charge "will not be an outsider, but that the mission will be given" to the Milan Foreign Mission Seminary. "Otherwise it will be very difficult to get things moving because of various elements, etc." If Rome should happen not to entrust the Hong Kong Mission to the Milan Foreign Mission Seminary, Raimondi suggested to Marinoni that it would be "better for us to wrap up our belongings and leave the place."[7]

From now on Raimondi was frequently in touch with Barnabò, who officially called him "Procurator of the Sacred Congregation of Propaganda" on 13 August 1868 and as early as 27 November 1867 sent him faculties which authorized him as pro-prefect also to administer the procure office.[8]

As procurator he also became Rome's intermediary for forwarding correspondence to Don Carlos Cuarterón, prefect apostolic of Labuan. At the end of a letter addressed to Cuarterón and dated 29 January 1870, Cardinal Prefect Barnabò said, "Taking advantage of this occasion I urgently request that you send me without delay a full report on the Prefecture of which you are in charge. In order that you may compose it more easily, I am including with my letter a copy of the questionnaire which Vicars Apostolic and other Mission Superiors must answer."[9] Vaughan from 1863 until 1865 traveled widely, spreading news of his mission seminary and collecting funds. He celebrated the foundation date of St. Joseph's Missionary Society of Mill Hill (M.H.M.) on 19 March 1866.[10] In October 1868 he bought *The Tablet: A Weekly Newspaper and Review*, which had been founded in 1840 and was published in London. He called it "the oldest established Catholic Journal in Great Britain" and used it to make known St. Joseph's Foreign Missionary College at Mill Hill.

After building St. Joseph's Foreign Missionary College at Mill Hill, he began training priests to be missionaries. In 1870 he decided to visit Rome in order to discuss the canonical status of his newly founded missionary society and to ask Barnabò to entrust a foreign mission to the Mill Hill Fathers.[11]

---

7. PIME: AME 16:683f, Raimondi to Marinoni, 3 March 1868.

8. PF: LDB vol. 358 (1867) f. 948v, Barnabò to Raimondi, 27 November 1867. PF: LDB vol. 360 (1868, Part II) f. 884r, Barnabò to Raimondi, 13 August 1868. Margiotti in "La Cina cattolica," 527, incorrectly says that Raimondi received these faculties only on 3 December 1868.

9. PF: LDB vol. 363 (1870, Part I), f. 56v, Barnabò to Cuarterón, 29 January 1870. The archive copy indicates that this letter was to be forwarded to Cuarterón via Procurator Raimondi.

10. The Vatican yearbook, *Annuario Pontificio per l'Anno 1992*, p. 1429, gives 19 March 1866 as the founding date of the St. Joseph's Missionary Society of Mill Hill.

11. McCormack, *Cardinal Vaughan*, 96.

Vaughan arrived in Rome on Wednesday, 4 May 1870, and went directly to Saint Peter's Basilica to entrust to Saint Peter the happy outcome of the various requests that he wanted to present to church authorities. Rome was a busy place at that time because the Vatican Council was in session. "They were voting on the Little Catechism in the Council," Vaughan said, "and I could hear distinctly the words *placet* or *non placet* or *placet juxta modum*."[12] These were Latin words for three possible ways of voting. The results were 491 affirmative votes, 56 negative votes, and 44 affirmative votes with qualifications.[13]

On the following day Vaughan already met Barnabò, whom he described as being "not a little surprised to see the Photograph [of St. Joseph's Foreign Missionary College] and to find his orders had been so promptly obeyed as to building a College." The other officials at Propaganda were "in very good humor with us." All that month Vaughan was in and out of Rome and used his opportunities for speaking with missionary bishops, hoping to have a mission assigned to his new community of priests. In spite of numerous possibilities he wrote on 19 May: "Nothing is finally settled. . . . Borneo, I believe, will be our mission: and I will try to get a promise of Japan when we are ready for it, making Labuan the condition and the half-way house. Cashmere, etc., is out of the question."[14]

On 25 May Vaughan had good news to report: "I have now at last got faculties to present our students for Ordination *ad titulum missionis infidelium* [under the title Foreign Missions]. Till now we have not been able to ordain them. Soon I hope to get our Fundamental Rules and Oath approved. I am working to have a mission assigned to us. Borneo is not the place you imagine. . . ." It had continuous malignant fevers to deal with, he said, and Mohammedans as well. "China and Japan are preferable: perhaps even the 500,000 Indians of Texas and New Mexico, who have no Priest at all among them."[15]

Lady Herbert of Lea back in England was being kept informed continuously by Vaughan of his successes and failures in Rome. She had become a convert to Catholicism in 1865 as a result of the Oxford Movement and the Catholic revival in the Church of England. In 1866 she met Father Vaughan when he was collecting funds for his mission seminary. Her new religious enthusiasm resulted in her becoming the principal benefactress for his new seminary. Lady Herbert was a niece of Lord Heytesbury, British ambassador to Russia. Her husband, Sidney Herbert, was England's minister for war during the Crimean Campaign, which left Lady Herbert a widow with four sons and three daughters.

---

12. *Letters of Herbert Cardinal Vaughan to Lady Herbert of Lea 1867 to 1903*. Edited by Shane Leslie from the mss. at Courtfield with an introduction by J. Brodrick, S.J., 181.

13. In ibid. Leslie says simply that Vaughan arrived in Rome in May. But it was 4 May because Mansi gives the date of the voting as 4 May 1870. See Mansi, *Sacrorum Conciliorum Collectio*, vol. 51, cols. 501–12. For more details on the "Little," "Concise" or "Universal" Catechism, see chap. 23, pp. 437–38, n. 28.

14. *Letters of Vaughan*, 182.

15. Ibid., 183f.

She was known as a friend and benefactress of Florence Nightingale. Lady Herbert lived until 1911 after being a widow for fifty years.[16]

Vaughan informed Lady Herbert that he had his audience with Pope Pius IX on Saturday, 28 May 1870. "I told the Pope about how much you had done for the Mill. . . . He wrote a blessing for you under a Photo of the College." He was also "very pleased with the *Tablet*. . . ." But nothing had yet been settled about a mission. "The French refuse to give up an inch of Japan," Vaughan said. "I believe we shall end thus: a portion of the Interior of China will be given to us: the most healthy part of the Empire, where there is much to do, and occasional persecution breaking out. This will be a good beginning. People from Borneo tell me that constant malignant fever, scorching heat and Mussulmans [sic] are its characteristics: not a good field to begin upon.

"I have made great friends with the Society of Milan for Foreign Missions," Vaughan told Lady Herbert, "and as we have the same rule, aim and history, for they, like us, spring out of the Oblates of St. Charles, I think we may knit together and good may come out of the union in more ways than one. I think I shall return by Milan in order to see the Superior [Marinoni] at home: he returns there from Rome to-day. *You* gave one of their men, Father Brogazzi, 5 Pounds once in London. Do you remember?"[17]

Borgazzi had been assigned by Marinoni to the Labuan Prefecture Apostolic of Don Carlos Cuarterón. Either Borgazzi or director Marinoni himself must have informed Vaughan about the malignant fever, scorching heat and Moslems.

One year later on 13 June 1871, Vaughan informed Marinoni that he had received two letters from Raimondi offering him missionary work in China. But Vaughan had received no word from Marinoni on this and so was hesitant about taking action. Vaughan said that Raimondi himself "invites me to send out some English Priests to him in Hong Kong. I have kept priests ready to send out, and must not delay much longer in sending them somewhere."[18]

Pope Pius IX eventually saw fit to make Vaughan a bishop. On 16 October 1872 Vaughan told his friends, "Today I received a brief nominating me to be Bishop of Salford." This meant that he would no longer have to seek out a bishop to ordain candidates for the priesthood; he could do the ordaining himself. Being in charge of a diocese, however, he would have less time to devote to conducting his mission seminary. He therefore chose a Belgian priest in his diocese, Canon Peter Benoit (1820–92), to be the new rector of the seminary. Vaughan at this time was forty years old; Benoit was fifty-two.[19]

---

16. Ibid., viif, xiv. The details on Lady Herbert come from Shane Leslie's "Introduction" in ibid., vii-xiv.

17. Ibid., 185f.

18. PIME: AME 29:841f.

19. McCormack, *Cardinal Vaughan*, 128; Rooney, *Khabar Gembira*, 24. Vaughan was born on 15 April 1832; Benoit was born on 1 November 1820.

Cardinal Prefect Barnabò had been appalled on learning from Raimondi that Procurator Ambrosi had left behind a huge debt of three hundred thousand francs.[20] Raimondi's next letter, however, brought good news for Barnabò, who answered at once on 22 May 1867 congratulating Raimondi on having considerably reduced Ambrosi's debt. He regretted, however, that he could not relieve Raimondi of responsibility for the Hong Kong mission, nor for the procure office, "as you request." Barnabò simply did not know whom to name for this office, he said. "So you shall remain in charge!"[21]

Barnabò wrote again on 27 November 1867, stating that it was absolutely necessary for Raimondi to take care of debts in the procure office immediately. "So we decided to put the Procure in charge of a Pro-Prefect who, having faculties for this task, can better satisfy the needs of this administration. I am pleased to say that this office has been given to you, as you will see from the enclosed documents."[22]

From then on the title used by Barnabò for Raimondi was "Prefect of the Mission of Hong Kong" and "Procurator of the Sacred Congregation." One title after another was being given to Raimondi. Barnabò enclosed apologies on 24 November 1871, when he sent Raimondi a rescript regarding his latest title of apostolic prothonotary, which had been granted to him five years earlier in 1866. This new office made Raimondi an honorary prelate belonging to the Pontifical Household. Barnabò assured Raimondi that the "extraordinary delay" in delivering the rescript to him "has nothing to do with your person."[23]

Barnabò had a reprimand for Raimondi and engaged the services of Marinoni for it on 18 April 1871: "I would like you to write something to the Reverend Raimondi, Prefect Apostolic of Hong Kong, in order to calm down his excessively vivacious character. He picks quarrels with everyone and shows himself generally to be contrary to religious order members. Urge him to strive for harmony and peace. I shall do the same when I write to him the next time."[24] Eventually Cuarterón did get around to sending some information to Barnabò about his mission, which he spread over letters numbered 139 to 144, and for which the cardinal thanked him. Much of the cardinal's reply, sent again via Raimondi, was devoted to Cuarterón's funds and what he must do about them. The cardinal explained that Cuarterón's agent in Rome, Father Burrueco, had taken care of the funds until his death.[25] Cuarterón also reported on his bad health and about his need for funds.[26]

On 11 April 1871 Cuarterón had told Barnabò that in his territory there were many Christians who had been taken captive and were living in servitude under the

---

20. See PF: LDB vol. 358 (1867), f. 434r, Barnabò to Raimondi, 10 May 1867; ACTA vol. 242 (1874, Part II, China), f. 589v.

21. See PF: LDB vol. 358 (1867), f. 474rv, Barnabò to Raimondi, 22 May 1867.

22. Ibid., f. 948v.

23. Ibid., f. 1021rv.

24. PF: LDB vol. 365 (1871, Part I), f. 322r–323r.

25. Ibid., f. 346v–347v, Barnabò to Cuarterón, 22 April 1871.

26. Ibid., f. 471v–472r, Barnabò to Cuarterón, 27 May 1871.

Mohammedans. Cuarterón therefore was interested in obtaining men from religious orders, who would be dedicated to redeeming Christian captives living in servitude. Barnabò replied, however, that "in view of the present state of Europe, it seems too difficult an undertaking." He said that religious orders were also experiencing financial difficulties. Certainly, he continued, "it is to be desired that something should be done about so many evils. But the very serious needs pressing upon us at the present time prevent this."[27]

Prefect Apostolic Raimondi sent Cardinal Prefect Barnabò some surprising and pleasant news on 24 October 1871, to which the cardinal replied:

> I learned with great pleasure that you are busy founding a newspaper. How opportune and timely it will be for the place where it comes to light. It will also prove most useful by providing exact information on what is happening in the Churches of the Far East. And it will help this Sacred Congregation to obtain more precise knowledge about local circumstances, something which will be better known nowhere else than right there on the spot. May these considerations serve to encourage you to go forward with this enterprise of yours.[28]

Father Vaughan had gone into great detail when describing for Lady Herbert his meeting with Cardinal Prefect Barnabò on Thursday, 5 May 1870. The cardinal "had that day been giving orders as to a Mission for us, one of great importance: but would say no more," Vaughan said. "The next morning I learnt that this was no other than Labuan and Borneo." But Vaughan was "constitutionally" opposed to taking immediate action "in a matter of such moment," he said.

"I agreed with Secretary [Giovanni Simeoni] that it would be better not to settle the matter definitely without further information." Propaganda therefore decided "to write *at once* to the Prefect Apostolic, Mgr. Cuarterón at Labuan, and obtain details and his consent to receive us. I have been reading over his letters to Propaganda and have a better idea of the place and work than before. It is a highly important position in many ways: and Labuan is a very healthy place."[29]

Vaughan did not leave the matter of obtaining further information up to the Propaganda secretary alone. On 12 May 1870, the very day after writing to Lady Herbert about Labuan and Borneo, he wrote to the Honorable James Pope-Hennessy, governor of Labuan. He sent him a lengthy questionnaire about Labuan, Borneo, and Cuarterón himself. His letter would take nearly three months to arrive.[30]

---

27. See ibid., f. 592rv, Barnabò to Cuarterón, 27 June 1871.
28. PF: LDB vol. 366 (1871, Part II), f. 1114v–1115v, Barnabò to Raimondi, 18 December 1871.
29. *Letters of Vaughan*, 179f.
30. Vaughan's letter has not been found, but its contents are evident from Pope-Hennessy's reply.

Governor Pope-Hennessy's report was dated Government House, Labuan, 8 August 1870. It was a Monday. "I proceed at once to answer the queries in your letter from Rome of the 12th of May," he said.

> The Prefect Apostolic Don Cuarterón is a remarkable man. He combines the spirit of an Apostle and the devotion of a most pious Priest with the roving disposition of a Sailor. He is a Spaniard, and was for some years the Captain of a merchant ship. Doubtless you have heard the story of how he found a great treasure in a wreck in the China Sea and how the Admiralty Court at Hong Kong declared him to be the lawful captor; and how he took the money to Propaganda [Congregation] praying that he may receive Orders [that is, the priesthood] and be permitted to found a Mission in Borneo.
>
> Without occupying your time about the past, it is enough at present to know that the Mission has not succeeded. He has spent large sums of money; I do not know [how] much, but from all I hear I believe considerable sums. He devoted himself almost exclusively to the laudable task of saving from slavery the Christians who had been captured from the Philippine Islands by the Soo Loo [now Sulu] pirates and sold to the Rajahs on the coast of Borneo. But except in spending money there has been little result to these labours. He tells me that a few years ago there were as many as four thousand Christian slaves in the city of Brunei; but that owing, he says, to the apathy of those [who] were formerly Governors of Labuan and Consul Generals in Brunei, he could do nothing to shake the hold of the Mahomedans [sic] upon these poor people.
>
> At present the Mission in Brunei is abandoned. To secure something there in the event of any future effort being made by the Propaganda [Congregation], I purchased [from Cuarterón] for the small sum of one hundred dollars the site of the Mission House and I received from the Sultan of Borneo a grant of a large piece of land including the site in question. Padre Cuarterón with the $100 [sic] built the little atap[31] chapel where we now hear Mass in Labuan. To make the financial part of this story complete, I must add that a Chinaman at Brunei purchased [from me] some bricks and timber from the old site for the same sum I gave the Padre, so that I have the place for nothing except a few dollars I spend on a caretaker.
>
> The Mission at Menkabong, Gaya Bay, about eighty miles to the north of Labuan on the Coast of Borneo, is still nominally in existence.[32] But there are not thirty Christians there.
>
> The Padre spends his time between Menkabong and Labuan, but most of it here.

---

31. Sago palm leaf fronds used for roofing.

32. Cuarterón informed Cardinal Prefect Franchi on 14 April 1877, the twentieth anniversary of his founding the Labuan mission: "We abandoned the Bay of Gaya Mission [that is, Menkabong] in 1873 and we occupied it again in 1876." Pope-Hennessey's words were written on 8 August 1870.

In Labuan the vast majority are Moslems and Chinese. There are ten or a dozen gentlemen who call themselves Church of England (and for whom the poor tax payers here have to provide a Chaplain at 350 Pounds a year). There are some Scotch miners, Freekirk, and a few Baptists. The rest of the Christian population are Catholics. The Catholics are the largest Christian denomination and indeed there is not among the active Christians a single one who is not a Catholic.

I have the greatest affection and respect for Padre Cuarterón, but to *you* I must not conceal my conviction that his devotion to the rescuing of the slaves or half slaves, has checked the progress of the Mission here. He dislikes the Chinese and has thrown away opportunities of securing wealthy converts. When the leading Chinese Traders in Brunei and Labuan found that I was supporting them - making them Magistrates - and giving them politically and socially a position they never had held before - they hinted, I understand, to the Padre their desire to become Catholics.

The Padre told me that their declarations were not genuine - that it was merely a desire to compliment me - and that their only God was the Dollar. So far I believe he rightly estimated their overtures, but, as one of the richest of the Chinamen in question had a family of young children, I ventured to hint that some honest result might possibly be obtained in that quarter. He shook his head saying he doubted the reality of Chinese Christians.

As to other Eastern races here, the Padre completely agrees with me that the Mooruts and other inhabitants of Borneo and of Labuan, who are not Moslems, constitute an admirable field for a Catholic Mission. They are simple, and intelligent, but without any form of religion.

The Kadyans, a valuable agricultural population, who are now coming in good numbers to Labuan, are strict Moslems.

On the whole, then, I am of [the] opinion that there is a fine field for a Mission here.

Long ago I discussed with the Padre the question of Borneo as a field for St. Joseph's College. *The Tablet* is one of the two English newspapers I can afford to take, and when the subscription list for St. Joseph's College[33] first appeared in it [in 1869], I showed it to the Padre and he at once said: "This would be a good place for such missionaries." He spends every Sunday with me, and I believe hardly a week passed since then without some talk about St. Joseph's College.

You can therefore imagine how welcome your letter was to me; and I suppose he has been also very glad (though he has said nothing about it) to hear the intentions of the Propaganda [Congregation].

As to means and property at the disposal of the Mission, it seems to be altogether the Padre's. His money has hitherto supported it. Just now he has commenced a subscription to complete a fine Catholic Church which was nearly [completely] built in Labuan in 1858.[34] He gives $100; a poor official who can ill afford at present to give anything offers $150; and probably there will be twenty or thirty small subscribers.

33. Vaughn's name for his foreign mission seminary at Mill Hill was St. Joseph's College.

34. Father Borgazzi had nearly completed this church when it was struck by lightning on the night of 3 August 1859. See chap. 22, p. 409.

Of course at Brunei the Mission will have a safe site on the land granted to me by the Sultan—though he never would give a grant to the Padre. In fact, the Sultan, though a kindhearted and most peaceful Prince, is a very keen Mahomedan.

In Labuan there would be no difficulty in securing a good estate, the cultivation of which might go far to supporting the Priest.

Schools, and especially industrial schools, would succeed.

The Malay language is easily acquired.

The climate I believe to be the best in the East. Here we have land and sea breezes twice every day—The thermometer ranges from 70 degrees to 90 degrees Fahrenheit in the shade. With temperance, and plenty of exercise, good health is certain to be enjoyed. I have not had a day's illness since I came here (Nov. 67). Brunei and the opposite coast is equally healthy. Within sight of Labuan, about twenty or thirty miles off, are a range of mountains from four thousand to six thousand feet high.

As an industrial pursuit, to support the Mission, I would recommend the Mission to settle down upon some of the grazing lands in Labuan. Our milk, butter and beef have a high reputation in Hong Kong and Singapore, and very justly. There is always a demand for cattle here owing to the ships coming for coal. And if such a charge would not be inconsistent with your rules, it might go far to render the Mission financially independent.

I like this place so much, that I have purchased the Island of Kuramdu, where I am slowly forming a little estate, which in years to come may be valuable; so that whatever promotion I may receive in the Governor's list, I shall always have an interest in Labuan.

Therefore you can imagine how heartily I shall welcome two or three young Priests from your College and how cheerfully I shall give them all the aid in my power.—I am sure they would be equally welcome to the single-hearted and simple-minded Padre.

One good character I can give of the little group of Catholics in this distant region. It contains no pupils of M. Eratry or Mgr. Dupanloup. It is remote from news and even at this date is still waiting with a lively Faith the event of the 19th Century—the definition of Pontifical Infallibility.

Believe me always your faithful

J. Pope-Hennessy

This letter of Governor Pope-Hennessy of Labuan was filled with important details and was twelve pages long. It would be of utmost help to Vaughan in deciding whether or not he should accept the Labuan Mission for St. Joseph's College.[35]

---

35. MHFA: BOR-2-b, Pope-Hennessy to Vaughan, 8 August 1870.

Cardinal Barnabò had made many attempts to obtain a report on the Labuan mission directly from Prefect Apostolic Cuarterón. But he never received a report which came even close to that of Governor Pope-Hennessy. Barnabò wrote to Cuarterón on 2 June 1870 requesting once again "a report about your Mission and about the things that you have done till now for the benefit of the Christian religion."[36] He needed this report for Vaughan, to whom he wanted to entrust the Labuan mission.

Raimondi later informed Barnabò from Hong Kong that "the Italian Government is going to open a Colony on the coasts of Borneo, a mission area entrusted to Father Cuarterón. He has been plagued with sickness for some time now and intends to resign. It would therefore be necessary to take action on behalf of this mission, because the Dutch Government will lose no time in sending people there."[37]

Barnabò replied immediately to Raimondi: "I am most grateful to you for your news on the Penal Colony of Borneo. When that plan has become a reality, I shall take up the matter of how to provide for the welfare of Catholics who may be detained there. Meanwhile I would appreciate having some information from you about the semi-defunct Mission now established there and some suggestions on how to make it come to life again. . . ."[38]

"I know that you have already offered it to the new Seminary [of Mill Hill] in London," Raimondi replied, "but those Gentlemen did not like it. The present Prefect Apostolic is alone. He is also getting old and feeble and it would be well if he were to resign. . . . But the mission should not be deserted. It needs to be entrusted to a [missionary] congregation."

If the Milan Mission Seminary had personnel, Raimondi said, "It would be the best suited group to take over the mission, because being Italians they could in time also care for the Italian colonists. . . . Nor would I have any difficulty in going there myself for some time. . . . Transportation is available and I could go every year for a month or two." But since the Milan seminary has no personnel, "it is useless to think of this possibility. It might be best to give this mission to the Paris [Foreign Mission] Seminary, because it is in contact with Singapore." The Labuan Prefecture could always be divided later, he said, part of it remaining with the Paris Seminary and the other part being given to an Italian congregation. "This is all I have to say on this matter."[39]

Again Barnabò wrote back at once to Raimondi on 27 September 1872. "In your letter of this past 25 July," he said, "I have read what you pointed out about the unhappy state of the Labuan Mission and about the remedies that could be used to reorganize it. But since this concerns a Prefecture that has been established by the Reverend Carlos Cuarterón at his own expense, and one in which he has toiled with such good will, I can well see the

---

36. PF: LDB vol. 363 (1870, Part I) f. 445v–446r.
37. SC Cina vol. 24 (1871–72), f. 691rv, Raimondi to Barnabò, 20 March 1872.
38. PF: LDB vol. 367 (1872, Part I), f. 613v, Barnabò to Raimondi, 14 May 1872.
39. PF: SC Oceania, vol. 10 (1873–76), f. 177rv, Raimondi to Barnabò, 25 July 1872.

necessity of writing first of all to him in this matter. After you have read the contents of my enclosed letter, which I have left unsealed, kindly send it on to him...."[40]

Barnabò used the same date, 27 September 1872, on his enclosed letter to Cuarterón and addressed him as prefect apostolic of Labuan and Neighboring Territories. "Often in your letters to me," he said, "you have spoken of the affairs of your Mission and you have requested that some priests be sent to help you. This would seem even more opportune now, since the Kingdom of Italy is preparing to found a Penal Colony in your area. But before I take further steps, it is necessary that you describe the state of your mission and that you indicate what measures would be more conducive to its growth. I expect to hear from you on this matter as soon as possible...."

Cuarterón had often mentioned in his numerous letters to Barnabò that he needed funds and that he was wondering about his foundation money left behind in Rome. In this same letter Barnabò therefore told him that his funds were currently in the hands of the Italian government and that he needed a special document in Italian signed by the Italian consul in Labuan in order to obtain his funds. "Otherwise we cannot do anything," Barnabò said.[41]

In 1870 the Italian state had confiscated the patrimony of Propaganda, which was the source from which that Congregation drew its funds for missionary work. Since Propaganda was holding Cuarterón's funds, these had been confiscated as well.[42]

This was already the third letter written by Barnabò in 1872 to Cuarterón requesting a contemporary report on his mission, so that it could be entrusted to Mill Hill. Barnabò was nearly blind at this time; he dictated his outgoing mail and had others read to him his incoming mail.

Raimondi, who pleased Barnabò by keeping him so speedily and so well informed, wrote to him again on 5 February 1873: "Father Cuarterón writes to me of his intention to place two catechists in charge of his mission and then he will leave for Manila. From there he will sail to Europe in order to negotiate in Rome the entrusting of his Labuan Mission to some [missionary] congregation. Now this is all very well," Raimondi said, "but in the meantime his mission will be left without a priest." Raimondi enclosed a letter from Cuarterón for Barnabò.[43]

Barnabò wrote right back to Raimondi on 24 March 1873: "Kindly let him know that I shall gladly see him to confer about measures to be taken with regard to his Mission...."[44]

The longer Barnabò worked with Raimondi, the more he liked him. He was already enthusiastic about Raimondi's idea of launching a Catholic newspaper in Hong Kong, which became a reality and has survived down to the present day. Barnabò could not do

40. PF: LDB vol. 368 (1872, Part II), f. 1224r.
41. Ibid., f. 1224v–1225r.
42. Metzler, "Präfekten und Sekretäre," 45.
43. PF: SC Oceania, vol. 10 (1873–76), f. 179r.
44. PF: LDB vol. 369 (1873), f. 109rv.

enough for a good project when he saw one. Raimondi then bombarded Barnabò with letters on 13, 14, and 21 February 1872, which Barnabò received by 9 April, the day on which he answered them. This was a mere six weeks and five days since the last of these Raimondi letters had been mailed from Hong Kong. Time was being whittled away from the seagoing voyages between Rome and Hong Kong.

Raimondi asked Barnabò for a favor. He wanted help from the archbishop of Westminster and the archbishop of Dublin in obtaining teaching brothers of the Christian schools for Hong Kong. He also wanted Barnabò to intercede with the two archbishops on his behalf.

Barnabò called it "a good idea" to get teaching brothers for Hong Kong. "As for the Brothers requested by you," he said, "it would be necessary for you to tell me if you prefer to have those whose nationality is English. It seems to me that this would be more advantageous for Hong Kong. In any case send me word and I shall help the best I know how."[45]

Without revealing to Raimondi what he was doing, Barnabò that same day, 9 April 1872, sent Cardinal Paul Cullen (1803–78), archbishop of Dublin, and Archbishop Henry Edward Manning of Westminster (1808–92), identical letters. Barnabò said that Protestants in the Hong Kong government, according to Raimondi, were causing trouble for Raimondi's college, which was attended by so many students and was so popular. These same officials were also causing trouble for his orphanage. Raimondi therefore wondered whether Cardinal Cullen and Archbishop Manning might be able to take steps with the Superior Government of England in order to defend his schools. Barnabò closed his two identical letters with these words: "I request you warmly to take such action in this matter as prudence may suggest to you on behalf of the above institutes."[46]

Raimondi supplied Barnabò with detailed information on 14 June 1872, which the cardinal decided to forward to both Cullen and Manning. As Barnabò told Raimondi on 5 September 1872:

> I am most solicitous for the schools of Hong Kong, about which you spoke to me also in your letter of 3 July. I have written again to Reverend Filippo, Superior of the Brothers of the Christian Schools, and have requested Irish Brothers for you. But if it is not possible to obtain them, I shall do all that I can in order that your needs will be provided for in some other way. I am sending both Cardinal Cullen and Archbishop Manning a copy of your text and I am recommending the matter of the schools to them.[47]

Barnabò pointed out for both Cardinal Cullen and Archbishop Manning that Raimondi's text explained the dangers menacing the schools of Hong Kong. Barnabò was aware, he said, that both Cullen and Manning would surely do what they could by contacting the

---

45. PF: LDB vol. 367 (1872, Part I), f. 478r–479r, Barnabò to Raimondi, 9 April 1872.
46. Ibid., f. 477v–478r.
47. PF: LDB vol. 368 (1872, Part II), f. 1142r–1143r, Barnabò to Raimondi, 5 September 1872.

British government in order "to hinder the very grave harm which otherwise would result for the [Roman Catholic] Church, if Protestants and non-believers were to keep young people to themselves, and if they were to imbue them with perverse maxims of the present generation."[48]

Barnabò would not let the matter rest. After his letter of 5 September he wrote again on 27 September 1872 to Raimondi, saying that he himself and also the superior of the Milan Missionary Society were doing "everything possible to obtain [Teaching] Brothers." At the moment it seemed as if the Brothers of St. Joseph of Belgium were ready to offer personnel. "I shall advise you at once," Barnabò said, "if this comes true."[49]

Six weeks later on 9 November 1872, Barnabò again contacted Cardinal Paul Cullen, archbishop of Dublin. "In an earlier letter," he said, "I informed you of the extreme need of the Prefect Apostolic of Hong Kong for teachers for the schools of that city." But up to this time none have been found, he said. "It has now been learned that in Ireland there are Brothers of the Christian Schools who are separate from those of France." The prefect apostolic of Hong Kong therefore inquires whether His Eminence of Dublin might kindly approach the Superior of those Brothers and inquire "whether he could favor Raimondi [of Hong Kong] by sending him four or five Brothers who could take in hand the task of teaching there. If you are able to do something in this regard, kindly let me know so that I can inform Raimondi and thus relieve the Prefect Apostolic of his anxiety."[50]

Raimondi had been in Europe for ten months back in 1861–62 and as late as 28 January 1873 had told director Marinoni of Milan, "No one in Europe will ever see my face again." But that same year on 6 September 1873, Raimondi was back in Rome and five days later was received in audience by Pope Pius IX. Raimondi by this time had been serving as prefect apostolic of Hong Kong and procurator of Propaganda for the Missions of China almost seven full years. All business matters and all problems of Propaganda connected with the China missions went through his hands.

Cardinal Prefect Barnabò presented Raimondi with a schedule of appointments for his stay in Europe, giving him numerous tasks to be performed on behalf of Propaganda, China, and Labuan. Raimondi also was seeking teaching brothers for his Hong Kong schools. Barnabò provided him with numerous letters of introduction and sent him off.

Raimondi made a brief stop at Milan and also in Turin, the headquarters of the Salesians founded in 1859. "I saw Don Bosco in Turin," Raimondi said. "What a man! I should rather say: What a Saint! The aim of his priests is the education of youths, precisely what is so necessary in Hong Kong." From there Raimondi moved on to Paris and met the superior of the brothers of Christian schools, but no immediate decision was reached. In early October he left for Brussels and then for London and Dublin, arriving in France in

---

48. Ibid., f. 1144v–1145r.
49. Ibid., f. 1223v.
50. Ibid., f. 1344v–1345r.

November. He returned to northern Italy in December and was back in Rome by January 1874.[51]

Meanwhile the health of Barnabò had steadily worsened until he died in office on 24 February 1874, just six days before his seventy-third birthday. For twenty-seven years he had served as pro-secretary, secretary, and prefect of Propaganda and has been called by a Vatican archivist "one of the most influential men in Rome during the Pontificate of Pius IX."[52] Alessandro Cardinal Franchi (1819–78) succeeded Barnabò in office as prefect of Propaganda on 10 March 1874.

Bishop Vaughan, founder of the Mill Hill missionaries, wrote a letter to Pope Pius IX on 21 April 1874. It informed the pope that the Lazarists through Procurator Raimondi of Hong Kong had offered part of their Chinese mission to Mill Hill and that Mill Hill was willing to accept it.[53]

The letter of Vaughan for the pope was forwarded to Raimondi in Rome by Father Benoit, the new Superior of the Mill Hill Seminary. Raimondi in turn on 5 May 1874 forwarded it to Cardinal Prefect Franchi, successor to Barnabò, saying that he personally supported Vaughan's request.[54] This was one of many ways in which the services of Raimondi were being used.

Raimondi writing from Hong Kong on 25 July 1872 had suggested to Cardinal Prefect Barnabò that the Labuan mission should be offered to the Paris Foreign Mission Society, since he knew that the Mill Hill missionaries did not want it.[55] But no action was taken on the proposal. Now that Raimondi was in Rome another memorandum to the same effect and dated 27 April 1874 appeared on Cardinal Franchi's desk. It must have been the work of Raimondi, since the proposal was identical.[56] This time action was taken.

Propaganda contacted Father Joseph Rousseille, procurator in Rome of the Paris Foreign Mission Seminary, requesting him to inquire whether the seminary's Council would accept the Labuan Mission. Rousseille wrote to Paris on 3 May 1874 and received this reply written on 25 May:

"In the last reunion of the Council, we considered the letter which you addressed to us dated 3 May..., in which you asked us if we would be disposed to accept the post Labuan (Borneo), in case the Sacred Congregation might have the intention of placing it in our charge." It was the view of the Council, however, that this new Mission was "too far away" and that "our Missions are already too far separated from one another... You know that we can hardly fulfill the requests for new missionaries which are addressed to us by

---

51. Tragella, *Missioni estere*, 2:190–93, 233 n. 8.
52. See Metzler, "Präfekten und Sekretäre," 47f.
53. PF: CV vol. 18, f. 432r–433r, Vaughan to Pius IX, 21 April 1874. The Lazarists, also known as Vincentians, are officially known as the Congregation of the Mission (C.M.).
54. Ibid., f. 436r–437r, Raimondi to Franchi, 5 May 1874.
55. PF: SC Oceania, vol. 10 (1873–76), f. 177rv.
56. See the memorandum in Franchi's papers dated 27 April 1874 in ibid., f. 184v.

our various Missions. . . . It would not be prudent to multiply the posts we serve, especially when we are trying by every means to bring all our stations closer together, so as to spare the missionaries of our Society the danger of isolation. . . . The one or two who would be stationed in Labuan, would be isolated . . . , and would have no consolation either from an active ministry or from numerous conversions. . . ."[57] In brief, the Council declined Rome's offer.

Meanwhile talk was circulating in Rome about Hong Kong becoming a vicariate apostolic with a bishop in charge. Raimondi wrote about the matter to director Marinoni in Milan on Monday, 13 April 1874.

> There now remains the question of whether or not to erect Hong Kong into a Vicariate. If I were not the Prefect of the Mission, I would already have convinced them to do so, but it is too delicate a matter for me. The question of the Procure is also connected with this. The proposal that I made was that the Procure Office of Hong Kong should be suppressed, because it is useless the way it is. I would also say it causes damage because the bishops are not pleased to have a priest give them orders and they are right. Therefore let them choose one of the old Vicars Apostolic and give him the authority over the other bishops. But it seems that this proposal does not please Propaganda.
>
> As for the Prefecture [of Hong Kong] I made it clear that Propaganda should not have any regard for me and that they should appoint as Vicar Apostolic the one who they believe is best. [Secretary] Monsignor Simeoni even appeared to be offended on hearing that I wanted to resign. And there the matter rests. I hope that the Congregation's meeting of May will reach a decision.

Raimondi added that Propaganda had been working on a paper about the missions of China for four years. The Holy Father himself had established by Brief a Commission of Cardinals for the Affairs of China. "But it has not functioned for the past seventeen years," Raimondi said. "The *Ponenza* [an elaborated report] has already been given to them and they are studying and discussing it. . . ."[58]

Raimondi was still busy in Rome when he heard some rather startling news which he sent at once to director Marinoni on 29 April 1874. He reported that the English clergy had moved heavily onto the scene and that "Bishop Vaughan of Salford and others were trying to obtain the Hong Kong Mission for the English Mill Hill Seminary."

He had learned this from Monsignor Francesco Nardi (1808–77), a friend of the Milan Foreign Mission Seminary, who had spoken out strongly against the proposal to Cardinal Prefect Franchi. "Some fear that he will give in because he is rather weak." Nardi was an auditor on the Sacred Roman Rota, the ordinary court of appeal for cases from around the

---

57. Ibid., f. 697rv. Rousseille's letter of 3 May 1874 was not found, but its date and contents were learned from the Council's reply of 25 May.

58. PIME: AME 16:1529–33, Raimondi to Marinoni, 13 April 1874.

world appealed to the Holy See. The Rota, which serves as a court of final appeal, is subject only to papal authority. In his younger years Nardi had served as a professor of philosophy and canon law. He was sixty-seven years old now and enjoyed renown as a Catholic journalist as well. Secretary Giovanni Simeoni in confidence had passed on the startling news to Nardi. Nardi in turn passed it on to Raimondi, strongly recommending that he in turn forward it without delay to director Marinoni in Milan.

Raimondi wrote to Marinoni at once and advised him "to write to Cardinal Franchi, plainly telling him what you know about it," defending our seminary energetically. "Do not lose time. If some accusations are being made against our missionaries, find out what they are, but do not give in to intrigue.... And if they have something against me, I am ready to renounce the office. But do not let my companions, who are excellent missionaries, be sacrificed. And do not compromise the honor of our Seminary on my behalf...."[59]

Marinoni was pleased with one part of Raimondi's letter, because it indicated that Rome seemed to want Raimondi for the office of vicar apostolic of Hong Kong. On the other hand he was appalled that Mill Hill should be making overtures in Rome to obtain the Hong Kong mission. He answered Raimondi's letter at once and enclosed a letter for secretary Simeoni written on Saturday, 2 May 1874. He did not write to Cardinal Prefect Franchi, as Raimondi had suggested. Informing secretary Simeoni that he had heard two contradictory rumors, Marinoni said that he was writing to the secretary of Propaganda in order to learn what was true. The first rumor, he said, was that there were plans to raise Hong Kong to the status of vicariate apostolic and that Prefect Apostolic Raimondi was being considered for the office of vicar apostolic and bishop of Hong Kong. This pleased him highly, he said, "because the Prefect Apostolic had already spent twenty-two years working with tireless zeal for the good of the missions, manifesting great intelligence and capability." (Marinoni counted the years from the time when Raimondi left London for Melanesia in 1852.)

The contradictory report, Marinoni said, was "that the Hong Kong Mission is to be taken out of our hands and given to others after so much care had been shown, such great work had been done, and so many sacrifices had been borne by us in order to cultivate this portion of the mystical field given to us...."[60]

Marinoni sent his letter for Simeoni unsealed to Raimondi, so that he could read it and then perhaps give it to Monsignor Nardi unsealed, who in turn could present it sealed to secretary Simeoni. It was mailed from Milan on Saturday, 2 May 1874, and Raimondi already had it in Rome on Monday, 4 May. "It was a beautiful idea to write to Monsignor Simeoni," Raimondi said in his reply to Marinoni that same day. But since it had been precisely Simeoni who passed on in confidence to Nardi the information about Mill Hill,

---

59. Ibid., f. 1545–47, Raimondi to Marinoni, 29 April 1874.

60. PF: Acta vol. 242 (1874, Part II, China), f. 593rv. These extracts are from Marinoni's letter of 2 May 1874 to Simeoni as discussed by the cardinals of the Particular Congregation on China.

and since Propaganda "jealously keeps guard over its secrets," Raimondi thought it wiser to hold onto the letter for the moment.[61]

On the following day, 5 May 1874, Raimondi wrote to Marinoni again saying that Propaganda wanted him to go and take care of some business for it in Paris and Brussels. On 10 May he informed Marinoni that he would be leaving for Paris on the following day.[62]

When in Brussels, Raimondi usually stayed at the general headquarters of the Congregation of the Immaculate Heart of Mary (C.I.C.M.), founded in 1861–62 in the town of Scheut near Brussels. The superior general there, Father François Vranckx (1830–1911), was a friend of Raimondi, and China was the principal mission of the Scheut missionaries. Raimondi had written to Vranckx from Rome in April 1874, saying that he would be paying him a visit before returning to China.

Vranckx was acquainted with Monsignor Dr. Ludwig von Essen (1830–86), who lived in Neuwerk, Germany, not far from the Belgian border. Vranckx had been urging von Essen to found in Germany a foreign mission seminary for training German and Austrian priests for China, and von Essen had written to Rome about it. The matter came to Raimondi's attention in Rome.

Vranckx, who was eager for von Essen's project to succeed, wrote to him on 25 April 1874, saying: "Monsignor Raimondi, Prefect Apostolic of Hong Kong and Fac Totum in China of the Propaganda [Congregation], has informed me from Rome that he . . . intends to come and spend once again a few days with us before his departure for China. I shall be sure to inform you of his arrival. It would be extremely useful for you to make his acquaintance, because much later, when you are negotiating for one place or another in China, he could be of great help to you."[63]

Prior to leaving Rome, Raimondi had changed his mind about holding onto Marinoni's letter regarding the startling rumors. Eventually it was submitted to secretary Simeoni, who wrote to director Marinoni on 30 May: "In reply to yours of 2 May," Simeoni said, Propaganda shall very soon have to deal with the matter "of giving a more stable form to the Hong Kong Mission. I shall not fail to present to the Sacred Body the grave reasons indicated by you, which tend to confirm your Institute's possession of the said mission."[64]

Secretary Simeoni wrote again on 25 July 1874. Since the Hong Kong prefecture apostolic was to be raised to the status of a vicariate apostolic, he said, he needed three names

---

61. PIME: AME 16:1555.
62. Ibid., 1557, 1561.
63. SVD: 2257f, Vranckx to von Essen, 25 April 1874.
64. PIME: AME 1:493, Simeoni to Marinoni, 30 May 1874.

of candidates "so that, if Propaganda should decide to leave this Institute in charge of the Mission of Hong Kong, it could select whom it judges best adapted to govern it."[65]

Director Marinoni became very disturbed on reading that Simeoni would need a list of candidates from the Milan Foreign Mission Seminary, "if Propaganda should decide to leave this Institute [that is, Marinoni's] in charge of the Mission of Hong Kong." This indecision by Rome in July 1874 proved to Marinoni that there was a basis for the rumors heard by Raimondi in April.[66]

In spite of director Marinoni's preoccupations, he lost no time in providing his list of three candidates, sending their names to Cardinal Prefect Franchi on 5 August 1874. "In addition to Italian and Latin," he said, Raimondi "knows English, French, Portuguese, Spanish and the Chinese languages Hakka and Punti." He added that Raimondi for some years had been vice prefect apostolic, prefect apostolic, and procurator for the Missions of China. "I therefore consider him the most suitable of all to be promoted. . . ." The two additional candidates listed by Marinoni were Father Giuseppe Burghignoli and Father Luigi Piazzoli.[67]

Raimondi left Rome on 11 May and took care of the business in Paris that Propaganda had requested of him. The Paris Foreign Mission Seminary had not yet finalized its reply on whether or not it wished to accept Labuan as a mission. It would do so on 25 May 1874, Pentecost Monday.

On 22 May 1874, the Friday before Pentecost, Raimondi arrived at Neuwerk in Germany, and visited the Reverend Dr. von Essen, pastor of St. Mary of the Assumption Parish, while en route to Vranckx at Scheut near Brussels in Belgium. That same day under the dateline Neuwerk, 22 May, von Essen wrote a news story about Raimondi for the local Gladbach newspaper, *Gladbacher Volkszeitung*, which was published on 23 May. The article read: "Today [22 May] the Prefect Apostolic of Hong Kong, China, has arrived in this very place. . . . This high Prelate will spend a few days with his friend, the Prelate of the Pontifical Household and Pastor Dr. von Essen."[68]

Evidently Raimondi had finished his official business with Dr. von Essen on Friday and Saturday, because he wrote an official letter to von Essen on Saturday, 23 May, signing himself: "T. Raimondi, Prefect Apostolic of Hong Kong and Procurator General of Propaganda for All of China." His letter was in French:

> Before leaving Germany, Monsignor, I am pleased to assure you of the good reception given in Rome to your proposal regarding the opening of a Mission Seminary in Germany or in Austria. I have spoken about it with Monsignor Simeoni, Secretary

---

65. Ibid., 497. Secretary Simeoni sent this letter, not Cardinal Prefect Franchi as Tragella says in *Missioni estere*, 2:205.

66. See Tragella, *Missioni estere*, 2:205f.

67. See PF: Acta vol. 242 (1874, Part II, China), f. 605v–607v.

68. Fritz Bornemann, S.V.D., *Der Pfarrer von Neuwerk: Dr. Ludwig von Essen (+1886) und seine Missionspläne*, 65f.

of Propaganda, who testified to me his great satisfaction. I have also pointed out in a document, which I presented to Propaganda, the advantages which would come to the Missions of China by having a Seminary for German Missionaries.

"For my part I shall always be ready to assist you in whatever way I can in order to have German Missionaries in China. I am certain that they will succeed very well both in studying the language and in surmounting the difficulties found in the Missions. I wish you great success in your holy enterprise and I have no doubt that Their Excellencies, the Bishops of Germany and Austria, will support your good desires and will help you to accomplish a task which will bring glory to the Bishops and to the Catholic Clergy of Germany."[69]

From the content and solemnity of Raimondi's letter, and because of his mentioning secretary Simeoni and giving his own complete and official title, it was evident that Raimondi had a special purpose in writing the letter. He wanted to put something in the hands of von Essen, which could be quoted in letters that he might send to the bishops and clergy of Germany and Austria.

On the following day, Pentecost Sunday, Raimondi wrote to Marinoni in Milan, saying that he was spending the feast of Pentecost with "the very good" Monsignor von Essen. "He is thinking of opening a seminary in Germany for the missions. And since I dealt with this matter in Rome, it was necessary for me to speak with him."[70]

That year Dr. von Essen had written to Cardinal Prefect Barnabò on 14 January 1874, asking for authorization to found in Germany a mission seminary, which would prepare Germans and Austrians for missionary work in China. His seminary was to be constituted much like that of the Congregation of the Immaculate Heart of Mary (C.I.C.M.), founded at Scheut near Brussels in 1861–62. This missionary group, also known as the Scheut missionaries, prepared Belgians for missionary work in China.

Vranckx in January 1874 had informed Raimondi in Rome of von Essen's project. Raimondi replied to Vranckx that he had presented the project immediately to Monsignor Simeoni and that the monsignor gave him the advice that von Essen should write officially about it to Propaganda.[71]

Besides contacting Raimondi in Rome on von Essen's behalf, Father Vranckx had also written in January 1874 to his own agent in Rome, Father André-Félix-Chrysostome-Joseph Gennevoise (1835–1901), who replied: "I immediately went to Monsignor Simeoni to speak about the project of founding [a mission seminary] by Monsignor von Essen. He told me that this news gave him great pleasure, but that von Essen before anything else needed to have men and money."

Gennevoise then went to see Cardinal Barnabò, now almost completely blind, and read Vranckx's letter about von Essen to him. "Do reply to Monsignor Vranckx," Barnabò

---

69. Ibid., 203, Raimondi to von Essen, 23 May 1874.
70. PIME: AME 16:1563.
71. Bornemann, *Pfarrer von Neuwerk*, 55, 196.

said, "that I am happy to learn this good news. The time is not very opportune. And will this Bismarck allow such activities to increase? No matter, the project is very beautiful, very consoling. However, I cannot assign a mission [to him], nor can I promise anything, until this new project has become solidly established. It must have resources, it must have some personnel, and it must train them. Then we shall see."

Vranckx told von Essen that he had expected this kind of answer. But since the project was pleasing to Rome, this was "already something." He assured von Essen that if he managed to test "two or three young priests or theologians who would agree to become members" of his congregation, he would "certainly have success."[72]

Von Essen's letter of 14 January 1874 to Barnabò, left unanswered because of the cardinal's death in the following month, was answered by Cardinal Prefect Franchi, his successor, on 8 April 1874. Raimondi was still in Rome when the letter was written.

Franchi's letter said that he had not failed to inform the pope on von Essen's project. "Although His Holiness knows that such a project can hardly be realized now because of the present difficulties, he nevertheless feels obliged to welcome your Reverence's plan warmly, since such an institute can only benefit our holy religion. In order that you may bring this work to a happy ending, His Holiness gives you from his heart his Apostolic Blessing."[73]

Either Vranckx, or Raimondi, or both, must have had a hand in Cardinal Prefect Franchi's writing this letter of praise and encouragement to von Essen.

Cardinal Prefect Barnabò in the last three or four weeks of his life had referred to "this Bismarck," while speaking to Father Gennevoise about von Essen's project of founding a German or Austrian Foreign Mission Seminary. Barnabò meant Prince Otto von Bismarck (1815–98), the Iron Chancellor, founder of the German Empire, the one mainly responsible for inaugurating the *Kulturkampf*. Literally it meant "culture struggle." Actually it was a political struggle in 1872–87 between the German Imperial government and the Roman Catholic Church over attempts by the state to control both educational and ecclesiastical appointments. Cardinal Prefect Franchi had referred to it as "the present difficulties." The *Kulturkampf* would reach its peak in 1875.

It was now May 1874. Bismarck and his government had already closed many seminaries, like the minor seminaries of Fulda and Paderborn, the seminary of Hildesheim, and the major seminaries of Posen-Gnesen, Paderborn, Hildesheim and Trier.[74] The Prussian Landtag's law of March 1872 had subjected all schools to state inspection. In June of that

---

72. Ibid., 197, Vranckx to von Essen, 11 February 1874.

73. Ibid., Franchi to von Essen, 8 April 1874, pp. 63, 200f.

74. Fritz Bornemann S.V.D., *Arnold Janssen: Founder of Three Missionary Congregations 1837–1909: A Biography*, trans. John Vogelgesang, S.V.D., 45.

year all religious order members were excluded from public education in Prussia. On 4 July the Reichstag ordered all Jesuits expelled from the empire within six months, sending more than five hundred Jesuits into exile. When Pope Pius IX protested in December 1872, Bismarck severed diplomatic relations with the Vatican. The Redemptorists, Vincentians, Holy Ghost Fathers, and Religious of the Sacred Heart fell under the same ban as the Jesuits in 1873. That year the Prussian Landtag promulgated a series of laws in May that came to be called the May Laws. They placed priestly training under close government supervision. Clerical appointments by bishops were subjected to government veto, and restrictions were placed on episcopal powers of excommunication and discipline. The archbishop of Cologne and the bishop of Trier were arrested.

In 1874 a second set of May Laws made recalcitrant bishops and priests liable to deposition and exile. During vacancies caused by their removal, their offices were to be administered in accordance with the Prussian government's directives. Civil marriage was made obligatory in Prussia in February 1875 and later in other German states as well. Also in February 1875, Pope Pius IX declared the May Laws null and void. All religious order members, except those engaged in hospital work, were expelled in May 1875. In June all church property was confiscated, and title to it was transferred to lay trustees. By 1877 thousands of parishes had lost their pastors, and nine out of the twelve Prussian bishops were in exile.[75]

This was the atmosphere that had surrounded Raimondi's discussions with von Essen. At the moment there was nothing that von Essen could do. If he opened the seminary for foreign missions in his own parish, it could be confiscated by the government at any time. If he founded it in Belgium, the country where his mother was born, he would have to give up the Neuwerk parish, and the archbishop of Cologne would not be allowed to assign a successor. This dilemma faced Rome, Dr. von Essen, and Raimondi, and Rome expected Raimondi to find a solution. Having found none, he settled the matter by writing his letter of condolence to von Essen on the Saturday before Pentecost, as if he had anticipated departing on that day or on the following day. But then something happened.

A short train ride away from Neuwerk was a small German town called Kempen with an Ursuline Convent whose chaplain was a thirty-six-year-old diocesan priest named Arnold Janssen (1837–1909). He was an ordinary man, the second of eleven children. His father ran a two-horse farm and once a week used the horses for his teamster business, hauling goods between his hometown of Goch in Germany and Nymwegen in the Netherlands, and also to and from Geldern and Straelen in Germany.

Chaplain Janssen was industrious like his father and edited single-handedly a modest eight-page monthly magazine as his contribution in combating Bismarck's *Kulturkampf*. He started publication in January 1874 and called his magazine *Kleiner Herz-Jesu-Bote* (Little Messenger of the Heart of Jesus). His articles were mostly about the foreign missions.

---

75. Hans W. L. Freudenthal, "Kulturkampf," in *New Catholic Encyclopedia*, 8:267–69.

"In May 1874," he said, "I read in the *Gladbacher Volkszeitung* [issue of 23 May] that the Prefect Apostolic . . . of Hong Kong, Monsignor Raimondi, was visiting the Reverend Dr. Ludwig von Essen, pastor at Neuwerk near Mönchen-Gladbach. I visited him in order to become better informed about the missions. I was trying, namely, to stir up interest in the missions through the *Herz-Jesu-Bote* [sic]."[76] Janssen was welcomed by Raimondi and von Essen. When Raimondi learned that Janssen was in favor of a German-language Foreign Mission Seminary like von Essen was promoting, he suggested most energetically that Janssen should found one himself and "join up with Dr. von Essen." Janssen agreed to collaborate in such a venture by publicizing it, but insisted that he could not direct it. But Raimondi, realizing that Janssen was free to take up such a task in a safe neighboring country like the Netherlands, pressed him all the more and would give him no rest. Raimondi explained how he himself had helped found two Foreign Mission Seminaries in Europe, the Italian one in Milan and the English one at Mill Hill. He kept urging Janssen to do the same on behalf of a German-language Foreign Mission Seminary.[77]

Raimondi, von Essen, and Janssen all conversed in French. Janssen had not known of Dr. von Essen's interest in founding a Foreign Mission Seminary, but was highly pleased with this news. He himself was promoting such a seminary in his mission magazine. He was also impressed on learning that von Essen had already corresponded with Rome about the matter and had received good wishes and support from secretary Simeoni, Cardinal Barnabò, Cardinal Prefect Franchi, the nuncio apostolic in Belgium, the archbishop of Cologne, and that he had even received a blessing for his project from the Holy Father himself, Pope Pius IX.

This news was all the more gratifying for Janssen, because in an article lying on his desk back in Kempen, which he had written for the June issue, there were these two sentences about priests and those studying for the priesthood: "Is there not one among them in the whole of Germany who feels called to dedicate himself to the mission cause? How would it be if German priests would work together to organize a German Mission Seminary in some safe place?" On Janssen's return to Kempen he would make an insertion at this spot in his text as follows: "As the writer knows for certain, this would comply with the wishes of Propaganda in Rome and with a wish already expressed by the Holy Father himself."[78]

Before Janssen left von Essen's residence, Raimondi told him vigorously, "I shall come to visit you in Kempen in order to impress upon you even more emphatically the importance of this matter."[79] Raimondi made it his goal to convince Janssen that this project was not only Rome's will, but also God's will. The letters and other documentation from Rome, which were constantly being quoted by Raimondi and von Essen, left no doubt in Janssen's mind about it being Rome's will. But he needed more time to make sure that it was also God's will for him to take the lead as Raimondi was suggesting.

76. Fischer, *Arnold Janssen*, 9, 84.
77. Ibid., 84.
78. Bornemann, *Arnold Janssen*, 46–47, 48–49.
79. Fischer, *Arnold Janssen*, 86.

in die Hand zu nehmen. Da sollte im Jahre 1874 vom apostolischen Präfekten Raimondi eine ausdrückliche Aufforderung dazu an ihn ergehen.

3. Zusammenkunft mit Raimondi.

Msgr. Raimondi war einer der Mitbegründer des Mailänder Seminars für auswärtige Missionen, welches im Jahre 1850 ins Leben trat. Er befand sich unter den ersten Missionaren, welche von diesem Hause nach Melanesien geschickt wurden. Von dort kam er nach Hongkong, wurde dessen erster apostolischer Präfekt und später auch erster apostol. Vikar. Hongkong ist eine ehemalige chinesische Insel, seit 1842 in englischem Besitz und bildet noch immer das Eingangsthor Chinas in seiner südwestlichen Ecke, wo alle von Europa kommenden Dampfer zuerst landen.

Im Frühjahr 1874 besuchte Raimondi für einige Tage den Herrn Dr. Ludwig von Essen, Pfarrer von Neuwerk in der Nähe von M.-Gladbach. Dieser Besuch wurde in der Gladbacher Volkszeitung gemeldet und veranlaßte den Gründer unserer Genossenschaft, den apostl. Präfekten in Neuwerk um eine Unterredung zu bitten. Rektor Janssen hatte zwar fleißig in den Annalen der Glaubensverbreitung studiert, fühlte aber doch das Bedürfnis, sich noch eingehender über das Missionswerk in China und die Art der Missionierung unterrichten zu lassen.

Er wurde freundlich aufgenommen und erhielt auf seine Fragen befriedigende Auskunft. Nachdem er so den Zweck seines Besuches erreicht, sprach er sein Bedauern darüber aus, daß das katholische Deutschland noch kein einziges Missionshaus besitze und deshalb hinter den Protestanten und anderen Nationen zurückstehe, von denen doch schon so vieles in dieser Beziehung geschehen sei.

Die Antwort Raimondis war: „Gründen Sie selbst eins und vereinigen Sie sich zu dem Zwecke mit Herrn von Essen."

„„Aber ich bin schon zu alt, um noch in die Missionen zu gehen!""

In the very first pages of the 25th Anniversary publication on the Foreign Mission Seminary of Steyl, Superior General Arnold Janssen speaks of his providential meeting with Prefect Apostolic Raimondi of Hong Kong. Source: Hermann auf der Heide, *Missionsgenossenschaft von Steyl*, page 6.

Raimondi on 8 June informed Marinoni that his forwarding address for Belgium would be the Scheut Fathers and that for Germany it was Neuwerk near Gladbach, in care of Monsignor von Essen. "I am expecting letters from Germany, where I believe I shall still have to return ...," he said.[80]

Raimondi kept his promise about visiting Janssen and arrived at Kempen on 26 June, a Friday. On the following day *Neues Wochenblatt* (The New Weekly) of Kempen carried a story with the dateline 26 June, Kempen. It read:

> Today [Friday] the Prefect Apostolic of Hong Kong, Monsignor Raimondi, honored our city with a visit to the publisher of the mission magazine *Kleiner Herz-Jezu-Bote*. Hong Kong is a Chinese island that was transferred from China to England in the year 1841. It is the very center of steamship connections for the entire world. ...
>
> The honorable Raimondi is a handsome mission figure. He has a long beard and a face that clearly shows the scars of the missionary work that he has endured. He serves as intermediary for Rome and the twenty-eight Catholic Bishops of China. Under the direction of the Holy See he has visited thirteen of the eighteen Chinese provinces, each one of which has on the average so many people as the entire Kingdom of Prussia ....[81]

One of the "letters from Germany" that Raimondi had been expecting may have been from Father Janssen reporting that he had received the printed copies of his June issue containing the article proposing a new Foreign Mission Seminary for Germany. Issues of the magazine were generally ready for distribution shortly before the end of the month. Raimondi, in fact, had a purpose in mind and was collecting all issues of the magazine starting with the first one of January 1874.

Raimondi visited Janssen a second time in Kempen on 24 July 1874. Once again his visit took place near the end of the month when the *Kleiner Herz-Jesu-Bote* was ready for distribution. From Kempen he informed Marinoni on 24 July 1874 that he was working his way back to Milan by stages. "Borgazzi writes me," he said, "that the Hong Kong matters will not be decided before mid-August and maybe in September."[82]

Monsignor Raimondi had been requested by von Essen to inquire from the bishop of Luxembourg whether it might be possible to build a seminary in Luxembourg for training German priests for the foreign missions. Bishop Nikolaus Adames (1813–87) was away on a Confirmation tour, but his secretary, Father Petrus Hoffmann, answered Raimondi's questions. It would be very difficult to erect a German seminary in Luxembourg, he said. But it would be no trouble at all to receive young candidates from Germany and train them in Luxembourg's seminary, until divine providence made it possible to open a mission seminary in Germany.

---

80. PIME: AME 16:1569f, Raimondi to Marinoni, 8 June 1874.
81. SVD: 136, 200. Photograph of the *Neues Wochenblatt* news story published on 27 June 1874.
82. PIME: AME 16:1589, Raimondi to Marinoni, 24 July 1874.

Neues Wochenblatt
Kempen, Germany

() Kempen, 26. Juni. Heute hat der apostolische Präfekt von Hongkong, Monsignore Raimondi, unsere Stadt mit einem Besuche beehrt und ist beim Herausgeber der von hier aus redigirten Missionsschrift „Kleiner Herz Jesu Bote", abgestiegen. Hongkong ist eine chinesische Insel, im Jahre 1841 von China an England abgetreten. Sie ist der Mittelpunkt der Dampfschiffahrtverbindung der ganzen Welt. Von hier aus gehen ab einerseits die französischen Dampfschiffe, die um Asien herum durch den Suez-Canal nach Marseille fahren, anderseits fahren von Hongkong ab, die großen amerikanischen Schiffe, welche Japan berühren und dann über den großen Ocean nach Californien segeln. Herr Raimondi ist eine schöne Missionargestalt, mit langem Barte und einem Gesichte, das deutlich die Spuren der überstandenen Missionsarbeiten zeigt. Er hat die Vermittelung zwischen Rom und den 28 kath. Bischöfen Chinas und hat im Auftrage des apostolischen Stuhles 13 von den 18 chinesischen Provinzen bereist, wovon jede durchschnittlich so viele Menschen hat als das ganze Königreich Preußen. Gaben für die chinesische Mission nimmt der Redakteur der genannten Zeitschrift Hr. Arn. Janssen entgegen.

The 27 June 1874 issue of Neues Wochenblatt of Kempen, Germany, announces that Prefect Apostolic Raimondi of Hong Kong paid a visit to Father Arnold Janssen, chaplain at the local Ursuline convent. Source: Archives SVD: 136200 Photograph

When Raimondi sent this information to von Essen on 2 August 1874, he added a dire remark: "Divine Providence seems not to want a German Mission Seminary for the Missions of China at this time. Instead one should recruit German candidates for the missions and have them study in seminaries outside of Germany."[83]

Three days after Raimondi reported to von Essen about the possibilities in Luxembourg, Marinoni submitted to Cardinal Prefect Franchi his list of three candidates for the office of bishop and vicar apostolic of Hong Kong. He called Raimondi "the most suitable of all." His second and third candidates were Fathers Giuseppe Burghignoli and Luigi Piazzoli.[84]

One week later on 12 August 1874, Raimondi was at La Grande-Chartreuse in the Alps of France.[85] It was here that French-born Father Supriès, great friend of the pioneer Milan missionaries, had become a novice in 1838 and had received his basic training as a Carthusian monk. Previous to this time he had served as a member of the Paris Foreign Mission Seminary in India, Isle of Bourbon, Nicobar Islands in the Bay of Bengal and in Siam (now Thailand). When Raimondi would return to Rome from his tour through France, Germany and Belgium, he would find Supriès at the age of seventy-three serving as prior at the Carthusian Monastery attached to the Basilica of Saint Mary of the Angels built in 1563–66 by Michelangelo. Supriès held the elective office of prior from 1869 until 1877, serving simultaneously as procurator general at the Holy See for the entire Carthusian Order. A prior is the top superior over a Carthusian monastery. Carthusians have no abbots.[86]

Cardinal Prefect Franchi reprimanded Raimondi by letter on 17 August 1874 because of his impatience over the slow-moving process regarding Hong Kong's becoming a vicariate apostolic.[87] This reprimand came twelve days after Marinoni had submitted Raimondi's name in the first place for bishop and vicar apostolic of Hong Kong.

Nine days later on 26 August 1874, secretary Simeoni wrote even more critically of Raimondi in reply to a letter of 20 August received from director Marinoni in Milan. Some of the concerns regarding Hong Kong which had been manifested in Marinoni's letter, Simeoni said, were the very same that

> were repeated to me by voice and in writing many times by the same Prefect Raimondi. Therefore in reply I must tell you what I have already told the Prefect..., namely, that the Hong Kong question may not be treated in a General Congregation,

---

83. Bornemann, *Pfarrer von Neuwerk*, 81–83, 209.

84. PF: Acta vol. 242 (1874, Part II, China), f. 605v–606r, Marinoni to Franchi, 5 August 1874. RW-14812f

85. PIME: AME 16:1593, Raimondi to Marinoni, 12 August 1874.

86. Letter, archivist Luc Fauchon of the Grande-Chartreuse to Wiltgen, 23 July 1987. The Carthusian Monastery in Rome was abandoned in 1884.

87. See PIME: XXIV (Hong Kong), 2:67.

but must be treated in the Particular Congregation created this year by the Holy Father specifically for the affairs of China. But because of the sickness of the Eminent Cardinal Patrizi, who is the Dean, it has not been possible as yet to hold this Particular Congregation. There are hopes that it will be possible to hold it in this coming month of September.

Please rest assured that in these circumstances we shall not fail to present also the affairs concerning Hong Kong. Moreover Your Reverence ought to reflect that Propaganda must deal with many other affairs equally important and at times even more so, than those concerning the Mission of Reverend Raimondi.... For the rest, as has already been said to the same Raimondi when he was here in Rome, one does not see the necessity of his having to wait in Europe for the outcome of these affairs. Therefore let him return at this time to his Mission....[88]

These two sharp and highly critical letters about Raimondi, one from the prefect of Propaganda and the other from its secretary, hardly augured well for Raimondi's chances of being chosen by the four cardinals for the office of bishop and vicar apostolic of Hong Kong.

The Particular Congregation on China and Adjacent Kingdoms had held its last meeting in December 1859, when it became defunct. Pope Pius IX had reestablished it in 1874, naming as its members the Cardinals Costantino Patrizi, Camillo di Pietro, and Giovanni Battista Pitra, and Prefect Alessandro Franchi.[89] Since Patrizi was the sole survivor from the 1859 Particular Congregation, he as dean was to chair the meeting in which Hong Kong was only one of many important items on the long agenda.

Earlier rumors still rumbled in Rome and caused concern for Marinoni and Raimondi. But Raimondi's way of solving problems was to face them boldly. So in September he left Milan in order to see what he could learn and do in Rome. First of all he assured Propaganda that he was not loitering in Europe, but had been busy collecting funds for his mission and had also obtained Brothers of the Christian Schools (F.S.C.).

He no doubt also explained how he had carried out his commission in Neuwerk. Although Monsignor von Essen was prevented from founding a German Foreign Mission Seminary because of the *Kulturkampf* and the May Laws, there was another German priest named Father Arnold Janssen, he said, who was free to take up the task which von Essen could not perform.

Raimondi's bold approach to Propaganda proved so beneficial for both himself and his mission that he was able to telegraph Marinoni the following message from Rome on 19 September: "AFFAIRS IN GOOD SHAPE STOP RECEIVED VERY WELL STOP MEETING SET 28 THIS MONTH STOP"[90]

---

88. PIME: AME 1:507, Simeoni to Marinoni, 26 August 1874.
89. Margiotti, "La Cina cattolica," 526.
90. PIME: AME 16:1609.

The Particular Congregation on China and Adjacent Kingdoms met nine days later on Monday, 28 September 1874, with Costantino Cardinal Patrizi presiding. The paper regarding Hong Kong's being raised to the status of a vicariate apostolic had been prepared under the direction of Camillo Cardinal di Pietro and covered sixty-two pages. Giovanni Battista Cardinal Pitra and Alessandro Cardinal Franchi, prefect of Propaganda, also were members of this Particular Congregation.[91]

Since Cardinal di Pietro had been responsible for preparing the paper on Hong Kong, which the cardinals had received earlier for study, he now presented the subject and led the discussion, advising the cardinals of latest developments in the matter. He explained that when it became known that the reorganization of Hong Kong was soon to take place, "objections and complaints began reaching Propaganda" from some who did not want the Italian missionaries of Milan to remain in charge. "In view of the great development of that island, particularly under the English," they said, "there ought to be an agreement to take away responsibility for that island from the Italian Seminary of San Calocero [the Foreign Mission Seminary in Milan] in order to give it to English missionaries."

Cardinal di Pietro pointed out that similar objections were received from Bishop Patrick Moran (1830-1911) of Ossory in Ireland. Through his procurator in Rome, Monsignor T. Kirby (1801?-95), Moran had submitted the following proposals:

> All parts of China are now slowly opening up to English Commerce, to traveling businessmen and to others from that nation. And it is the Port of Hong Kong which is the key to that immense and until now unknown country. Therefore it would be a matter of the greatest importance to have in that place a Prefect Apostolic of the English tongue, who is zealous and capable. He could perform an immense amount of good there, certainly more than someone else having a different language and nationality, provided of course that he is devout and has good intentions.[92]

But how did Bishop Moran of Ireland become involved in this question? He had been an agent in Rome for the Irish and the Australian bishops and now was interceding for the English clergy. Born in 1830, he had gone to Rome as a twelve-year-old orphan to study for the priesthood at the Irish College where his uncle, Father Paul Cullen, was rector. Moran was ordained a priest in 1853 and served as vice-rector of the Irish College from 1856 to 1866. His uncle, during his own term as rector of the Irish College from 1832 to 1850, had served as agent at the Vatican for the bishops of Ireland and Australia. Moran spent a total of twenty-four years in Rome and also had become a skilled agent by acquiring the techniques of his uncle.

When Paul Cullen became archbishop of Dublin and in 1866 the first Irish cardinal, he called Moran from Rome to Dublin to be his private secretary. This lasted until 1872 when

---

91. PF: Acta vol. 242 (1874, Part II, China), f. 173r, 214v, 594v. The lengthy historical report on the Missions in China and the adjacent Kingdoms is in PF: Acta vol. 242 (1874, Part II, China), f. 2Av-271r.

92. Ibid., f. 593r.

Moran himself—thanks to Cullen—was named bishop of Ossory in Ireland. As secretary to his uncle and later as bishop of Ossory, Moran continued submitting requests to Rome on behalf of Irish and Australian bishops. He did so through Monsignor Kirby in Rome, who remained rector of the Irish College until 1891. By that time Moran had become the cardinal archbishop of Sydney, Australia.[93]

Cardinal di Pietro, after calling attention to Moran's proposal submitted through Kirby, also called attention to director Marinoni's letter of 2 May addressed to secretary Simeoni. Marinoni had wanted to find out which of two contradictory reports was true, di Pietro said. First he had heard that Hong Kong was to become a vicariate apostolic and that Raimondi was being proposed as vicar apostolic. This had pleased him highly, "because [Raimondi] had worked with tireless zeal for twenty-two years already, and as Prefect Apostolic had shown much intelligence and capability, which contributed to the good of the mission."

Di Pietro then pointed out that on the other hand Marinoni had heard "that the Hong Kong Mission is to be taken out of our hands and given to others after so much care had been shown, such great work had been done, and so many sacrifices had been borne by us in order to cultivate this portion of the mystical field given to us . . ." In reply, di Pietro said, Propaganda had informed Marinoni that the considerations presented by him would be discussed by the cardinals at their meeting.

The cardinal then explained how the procurator for Propaganda at Macao, Father Joset, had been sent to Hong Kong when it became a prefecture apostolic and how the procurator from then on had always held the additional office of prefect apostolic of Hong Kong. Joset was succeeded by Feliciani, who was followed by Forcade, who was followed by Feliciani again.

All of these prefects apostolic had difficulty in obtaining priests for Hong Kong, di Pietro said. So when Ambrosi was given the office of prefect apostolic and needed missionaries, he turned to Propaganda, which in turn approached the Milan Foreign Mission Seminary for personnel. "The Milan Seminary accepted the invitation," di Pietro said, "and from that moment onward the spiritual affairs in Hong Kong began to prosper very much."

In addition, di Pietro said, "when Procurator Ambrosi died in 1867, he left behind a debt of 300,000 francs." Raimondi succeeded him in office as both procurator and prefect, "and still governs that Prefecture." Di Pietero pointed out that Raimondi in the meanwhile "has amortized practically the entire debt" of three hundred thousand francs.

The next topic to come up in the meeting was the terna or list of three candidates for the office of bishop and vicar apostolic submitted by director Marinoni to Cardinal Prefect Franchi on 5 August. It listed Raimondi in the first place and called attention to all the languages that he spoke, including English and two Chinese languages. It also mentioned

---

93. Patrick O'Farrell, *The Catholic Church in Australia—A Short History: 1788-1967*, pp. 150-52, 206.

the various offices that he had held. The cardinals were told that director Marinoni of the Milan Foreign Mission Seminary considered Raimondi to be "the most suitable of all to be promoted..."[94]

Once discussion was completed, the voting by the four cardinals began. "Should the Prefecture Apostolic of Hong Kong be elevated to the rank of Vicariate Apostolic?" The cardinals voted yes. "Should the Hong Kong Mission remain in charge of the Milan Foreign Mission Seminary? Again the answer was yes. "Who is to be vicar apostolic with the rank of bishop?" The decision was: "See the pope on behalf of Timoleone Raimondi."

There was still another important vote to be taken. Raimondi had suggested that the procure office had ceased to fulfill a purpose in Hong Kong and should be abolished. The four cardinals, however, voted to retain the office and they chose Father Giuseppe Burghignoli of the Milan Foreign Mission Seminary to succeed Raimondi as procurator of Propaganda for the Missions of China.

These decisions were all reached on Monday, 28 September 1874, and were submitted by secretary Simeoni to Pope Pius IX on Sunday, 4 October. The pope readily gave his approval, thereby creating the Vicariate Apostolic of Hong Kong, placing it in charge of the Milan Foreign Mission Seminary, making Raimondi both vicar apostolic and bishop, and appointing Burghignoli as procurator of Propaganda for the Missions of China and Adjacent Kingdoms.[95]

Perhaps the most important item treated by this Particular Congregation of four cardinals on 28 September 1874 concerned its position on making preparations leading up to the establishment of the hierarchy in China. Cardinal Patrizi was chairman for this section of the meeting, and he presented the question in the following way: should the vicariates of China and adjacent areas "be divided into regional groups with the aim of preparing the way for the introduction of the Ecclesiastical Hierarchy in those places? And if so, how should the divisions be made?"

The cardinals decided that constituting the Ecclesiastical Hierarchy in China and Adjacent Areas "is not expedient at this time. As for dividing the Vicariates into regions, the reply is yes with qualifications. And the qualification is that we hear the opinion of Prefect Apostolic [Raimondi] of Hong Kong, now in Rome, by inviting him to indicate which of the 1869–70 projects he considers most useful, in view of the condition of the places, the character of the inhabitants, and the diversity of the institutes that run the missions there." The decision of the four cardinals about obtaining the views of Raimondi on which of the several projects he personally considered to be most useful was also presented by secretary Simeoni to Pope Pius IX on Sunday, 4 October 1874. The pope was in favor of their obtaining Raimondi's views.

---

94. PF: Acta vol. 242 (1874, Part II, China), f. 589rv, 593r–594r, 605v–606r.

95. Ibid., f. 587r, 594v–595v. Tragella in *Missioni estere*, 2:206, mistakenly gives the date of this meeting as 4 October, a Sunday. But meetings were always held on weekdays, in this case on 28 September, a Monday. Regularly on Sundays the secretary would take the decisions of Propaganda to the pope for ratification.

Bishop Raimondi was Vicar Apostolic of Hong Kong. Source: Tragella, Giovanni. *Le missioni estere di Milano nel quadro degli avvenimenti contemporanei*. Vol. 2, p. 473.

In 1869–70 the First Vatican Council was in session. Cardinal Barnabò, still vigorous at that time, convoked a meeting on 14 July 1870, attended by thirteen bishops from China. The proposal of creating regional synods was accepted by a majority vote, but two different plans were suggested. One plan called for eight regions and another called for five. Raimondi was personally in favor of five regions as proposed by Vicar Apostolic Louis-Simon Faurie, vicar apostolic of Kweichow, a member of the Paris Foreign Mission Society. Faurie's proposal of five regional synods was also approved by Pope Pius IX on Sunday, 4 October 1874.[96]

Raimondi, of course, was most curious to learn how the four cardinals had voted about Hong Kong at their meeting on Monday, 28 September, since everything had been kept secret. Finally on Friday, 2 October, Raimondi found a reason to present himself in the Propaganda offices, hopeful that in this way he might obtain some information. He wrote a letter to Cardinal Prefect Franchi saying, "I have the honor of sending to Your Eminence the two latest issues of the *Messenger of the Heart of Jesus* of Father Janssen in the Rhineland, Prussia. I had the honor of presenting the previous issues of this magazine to Your Eminence in person."[97] By early Sunday morning, 4 October 1874, Raimondi had ferreted out some information. He hurried off a note to director Marinoni saying, "It seems that the Vicariate Apostolic has been created and that the Vicar Apostolic has been named. This evening the Pope will speak on the matter and make a decision, or rather will confirm [the decision]."[98]

Raimondi's information was correct because on that evening secretary Simeoni brought the decisions of the four cardinals to Pope Pius IX at his residence. The pope ratified them all.

Finally on Tuesday, 6 October, Raimondi obtained the news and immediately sent off a telegram to Marinoni in Milan saying, "HOLY FATHER LAST SUNDAY CONFIRMED CREATION VICARIATE STOP ELECTED RAIMONDI VICAR APOSTOLIC STOP"[99]

That same day Raimondi sent director Marinoni "the Resolutions made by the Congregation of Cardinals and confirmed by His Holiness on 4 October." He expanded on the matter of the Hong Kong procure. "It was decided," he said, "that it is not fitting for the Vicar Apostolic to be Procurator." The cardinals had discussed whether this office should be annulled. "The answer was that it should be kept *for the present* and be entrusted to Vice Prefect, Reverend Giuseppe Burghignoli." Thus, as Raimondi said, also that office was kept in the PIME family.[100]

---

96. PF: Acta vol. 242 (1874, Part II, China), f. 172r–173v. For more details on this initial step in founding the hierarchy of China, see Margiotti, "La Cina cattolica," 525.

97. SVD: 133-091, 133-092 (photographed copies), Raimondi to Franchi, 2 October 1874.

98. PIME: AME 16:1624.

99. Ibid., 1629.

100. Ibid., 1625.

Raimondi thanked Cardinal Prefect Franchi on 8 October 1874 "in the name of the Catholics of Hong Kong for elevating the Prefecture to the rank of Vicariate Apostolic" and also for his being chosen for the office of vicar apostolic. However, he had "one last favor" to request: "To be able to receive my consecration [as bishop] in the city where the Vicar of Christ resides, so that I may always be more united in heart and sentiment to the center of Catholicism." And if he should be able to receive his consecration from the hands of Cardinal Prefect Franchi himself, "this would be an extraordinary favor," Raimondi said, "one which I would never forget."[101]

Papal Briefs—that is, official letters issued in Latin by the pope—regularly announced when ecclesiastical territories were created and when new ecclesiastical superiors were named. Pope Pius IX on 17 November 1874 issued two Papal Briefs, one announcing the creation of "the Vicariate Apostolic of Hong Kong Island in China" and the other announcing the name "of the Vicar Apostolic of Hong Kong Island in China." The Papal Briefs also explained that the vicariate's name, Hong Kong Island, did not mean that the vicariate was geographically restricted to that island.[102]

Cardinal Prefect Franchi had granted Raimondi's request and was the ordaining prelate on Sunday, 22 November 1874, in Propaganda's chapel at Piazza di Spagna. Present for Raimondi's episcopal ordination, besides a number of archbishops, bishops, and prelates, were the ambassador of France, the minister of Portugal, and the plenipotentiaries of Peru and Belgium. One of the co-consecrators assisting Cardinal Franchi was Cardinal Howard of England, a close friend of Bishop Vaughan of Salford. Director Marinoni was occupied with other matters in Milan.

Raimondi and all his guests were invited for a festive banquet at the Generalate of the Hospitalers of St. John of God located on the island in the Tiber River. Raimondi had a standing invitation to take lodging there whenever he was in Rome. Father Alfieri, who was still serving the Milan missionaries as their procurator at the Vatican, was now superior general of the Hospitalers of St. John of God.[103]

Two days after Raimondi's episcopal ordination he was received in audience by Pope Pius IX. On 3 December, missionary feast of St. Francis Xavier, he celebrated a Solemn Mass at his Alma Mater in Milan. On 8 December, feast of the Immaculate Conception of the Blessed Virgin Mary, he celebrated another Solemn Mass, this time in the magnificent cathedral of Milan. Finally on Friday, 11 December 1874, he embarked at Venice for Hong Kong, having

---

101. PIME: XXIV (Hong Kong), 2:677.

102. *Ius Pontificium de Propaganda Fide*, Pars Secunda, vol. 6, part 2, pp. 252f. Brambilla in *Pontificio istituto*, 1:177, says incorrectly that these decisions on Hong Kong were made in 1870. *Guida delle Missioni Cattoliche*, 252, mistakenly gives 17 November 1874, date of the Papal Briefs, as the foundation date of the Vicariate Apostolic of Hong Kong. The foundation date was 4 October 1874, the day on which the pope ratified Propaganda's decision.

103. See PIME: AME 16:1631, Raimondi to Marinoni, 10 October 1874; see PIME: AME 16:1651, Raimondi to Marinoni, no date. See also Tragella, *Missioni estere*, 2:206f.

spent fifteen consecutive months in Europe.[104] He had won the confidence of Propaganda, which had come to prize highly the judgment, energy, and administrative ability of this man.

By coincidence on 11 December, the very day on which Raimondi embarked for Hong Kong, Propaganda issued a decree informing the Catholic world that Father Guiseppe Burghignoli had been appointed procurator of Propaganda for the Missions of China. It had been considered advisable to remove this additional burden from the shoulders of the new vicar apostolic, the decree said. Actually Father Ambrosi, Raimondi's predecessor, had always insisted vehemently on the necessity of separating these two offices.[105]

Eight months later a letter written in French and dated 11 August 1875 at Kempen, Germany, reached director Marinoni in Milan. It was written by Father Arnold Janssen and said:

> Last year Monsignor Raimondi, a former student of your seminary, came on two occasions to see me and to encourage me to found a German seminary for the foreign missions. Without his encouragement I would not have undertaken this task. But being urged on by the Monsignor, I began doing my utmost, especially with my monthly bulletin for propagating the faith. With the help of God, who has provided money and personnel, and with the approval of the Most Eminent Bishops of Germany, Austria and the Netherlands, the time has now arrived to open the seminary this coming 8 September [1875].

It was an honor, Janssen said, for him to pass on this news to Marinoni. But at the same time he requested prayers "so that the good God will make us worthy of our older brothers in Italy, France, Belgium and England." He was referring, of course, to the foreign mission seminaries of Milan, Paris, Scheut, and Mill Hill. Candidates for his seminary would be drawn from Germany, Austria, and the Netherlands, he said. The mission house itself was located in the Netherlands at Steyl, by Tegelen, near Venlo, in the Diocese of Roermond, in the Dutch province of Limburg.[106]

Father Janssen's first two missionaries to be sent abroad were assigned to Bishop Raimondi's Vicariate Apostolic of Hong Kong for two years in order to obtain missionary experience. They arrived there on 20 April 1879.[107] One was German, Father John Baptist Anzer (1851–1903), who later became bishop and vicar apostolic of South Shantung, China, the first mission entrusted by Rome to Janssen's foreign mission seminary. The other missionary was from Austria, Father Joseph Freinademetz (1852–1908), born in South Tyrol, who never left China.

---

104. Tragella, *Missioni estere*, 2:206f. Since Raimondi was in Italy by 6 September 1873 and embarked for Hong Kong on 11 December 1874, he spent fifteen consecutive months in Europe, not fourteen as Tragella says in *Missioni estere*, 2:207.

105. PIME: XXIV (Hong Kong), 2-69, Decree, 11 December 1874.

106. The original Janssen letter was not found, but a copy translated into Italian was published in *Le Missioni Cattoliche*, no. 34 (Milan, 21 August 1875), 402.

107. Bornemann, *Arnold Janssen*, 133.

Arnold Janssen founded the Society of the Divine Word (S.V.D.) in Steyl, Holland, in 1875.

Raimondi and his Italian colleagues had originally worked in the New Guinea area of the Vicariate Apostolic of Melanesia, where they arrived on Friday, 8 October 1852. From Rooke and Woodlark islands they had hoped to reach the New Guinea mainland and win it over to Christianity. But insuperable difficulties forced them to leave this area on 10 July 1855, and eventually Rome reassigned them to Hong Kong.

Forty-one years later in 1896 Rome assigned six of Arnold Janssen's German missionaries to the northeast coast of New Guinea to found the Prefecture Apostolic of Wilhelmsland [sic]. They arrived on 13 August 1896 at Madang (then Friedrich Wilhelmshafen) in what was then called Kaiser Wilhelmsland.

As prefect apostolic of Wilhelmsland, Janssen chose Father Eberhard Limbrock (1859–1931), a German, who sailed to New Guinea directly from China. There he had obtained thirteen years of missionary experience in the Vicariate Apostolic of South Shantung.

Janssen, who died in 1909, lived to see the first twelve years of development of the New Guinea mission and lavishly supplied it with personnel. This was also one of Raimondi's dreams, but he had died in Hong Kong on 27 September 1894.

One hundred years after Janssen had founded the Steyl Foreign Mission Seminary, he was beatified (declared Blessed) by Pope Paul VI at Saint Peter's Basilica on 19 October 1975. Father Joseph Freinademetz, whom Janssen had sent to China, was also beatified with him.

On 5 October 2003, Arnold Janssen, founder of the Society of the Divine Word, and Joseph Freinademetz, the early Divine Word Missionary who labored in China for nearly thirty years, were canonized saints by Pope John Paul II in a ceremony in St. Peter's Square in Rome.

While the membership of many Catholic religious orders declined significantly in the four decades after the Second Vatican Council, the Society of the Divine Word continued to grow and prosper. In 2007 there were over 6,100 Divine Word Missionary priests and brothers serving in more than seventy countries.

27

Mill Hill Will Attempt to Reach New Guinea via Labuan
4 June 1878

CARDINAL PREFECT FRANCHI CONTACTED VICAR APOSTOLIC RAIMONDI OF HONG KONG about Don Carlos Cuarterón on 29 December 1874 and said:

> As you well know, the efforts made by this Sacred Congregation have failed to provide missionaries for the Labuan Mission, which has been reduced to an absolute lack of personnel. Also its Prefect Apostolic cannot remain there much longer because of his advanced age. So there is nothing else left to do by way of a poor substitute than to have Your Excellency send him from time to time some priests from your mission to practice there the sacred ministry in dependence upon that Prefect Apostolic. I have written to the Reverend Cuarterón in this same vein, since it would only be fitting that both you and the Prefect Apostolic reach some agreement on this matter before the project in question is put into effect. . . .[1]

That same day, 29 December 1874, Franchi wrote to Cuarterón in Labuan asking for "a letter on the state of your mission, giving especially your view on how one should contribute to the welfare of the faithful living there and to the propagation of the faith." Franchi suggested that meanwhile Cuarterón could "request some priests" from Raimondi. He added that they would be placed under Cuarterón's jurisdiction and "could administer the Sacraments to the faithful and offer them the nourishment of the Divine Word. . . ."[2]

In the course of 1895 a number of letters from Cuarterón reached Franchi's desk. He acknowledged their receipt on 1 December, saying:

> They were not answered because from them it appeared that you had the intention of coming to Rome. Now although the Catholic population entrusted to your care

---

1. PF: LDB vol. 370 (1874), f. 632r.
2. Ibid., f. 632v–633r.

> is quite restricted and is composed of non-stable elements for maritime reasons, I would still like to see a greater religious development, not only among the local people, but also among the Europeans. I am aware, sad to say, that you are deprived of the means and especially of the personnel needed to realize this goal. Also the difficulties standing in your way are not small, especially since the Spanish Government—as you say—contributes in no way to the efforts that you make. I shall not fail to invoke the assistance of the Nuncio Apostolic in Madrid on your behalf.

Franchi again suggested as he had done one year earlier, that Cuarterón should reach an agreement with Bishop Raimondi in Hong Kong "for obtaining personnel from him and from some other vicars apostolic" for his mission.³

True to his word Franchi that same day, 1 December 1875, interceded with the nuncio apostolic in Madrid. This official was none other than Giovanni Simeoni, former secretary (1868–75) of Propaganda, who had been named nuncio to Spain by Pope Pius IX on 15 March 1875.⁴

"The Prefect Apostolic of Labuan has had recourse to Propaganda," Franchi said,

> to manifest the miserable condition of his mission, his absolute lack of resources, and also the lack of all help that he once received from European Governments, especially from the Spanish Government. Among other things he complains that slaves within his jurisdiction in Borneo are no longer recognized as Spanish subjects by the Philippine Government and that in consequence they become Mohammedans in order to acquire their freedom. He says further that the same Government not only does not contribute the necessary funds, but even prohibits him from asking for alms in order to obtain the money needed to ransom those miserable people.
>
> Now if the Prefect Apostolic mentioned above should resort to the Government [of Spain], as apparently he intends to do, it would be well if he could find the ground already prepared. Your Most Reverend Eminence, knowing how concrete are the miseries of those Christians and also of that mission just mentioned, will have the kindness—I beg of you—to discuss this matter with the Lord Minister of Colonies and through him persuade the Government to come to the help of those unfortunate people. . . .⁵

By this time the pope had also named Simeoni archbishop and cardinal.

Evidently Cardinal Prefect Franchi's letters to Cuarterón and to Nuncio Apostolic Simeoni had some effect, because the Bay of Gaya Mission on the northwest coast of Borneo, which had been abandoned in 1873, was reopened in 1876.⁶

---

3. PF: LDB vol. 371 (1875), f. 892rv.
4. Metzler, "Präfekten und Sekretäre," 49.
5. Ibid., f. 891rv, Franchi to Simeoni, 1 December 1875.
6. See PF: SC Oceania, vol. 11 (1877–78, Part I), f. 152r, Cuarterón to Franchi, 14 April 1877.

W. M. Rodway of England in 1874 became commander of the British troops at Kuching in Sarawak on the northwest coast of Borneo, the third largest island in the world.[7] Two years later, on Sunday, 15 October 1876, his mother, Mrs. Elizabeth Rodway of England, wrote a few lines about her son to Father Henry Benedict Mackey. He was a member of the Order of Saint Benedict (O.S.B.), was attached to Douay Abbey in France, and was the greatest living authority in his day on St. Francis de Sales.

Mackey's sister was a nun, Sister Frances Margaret, at the Visitation Convent, Westbury-on-Trym, near Bristol, England. Commander Rodway of Borneo had a sister in the same convent. She was Sister Mary Thais (1843–1934), known to the world as Rose Rodway, and had entered the Westbury convent in 1869 at the age of twenty-six. The two nuns arranged for the letter of Mrs. Rodway to reach Father Mackey.[8] Her letter to him contained these words: "Out of love for the soul of my son, I wish to request that missionaries be sent to Sarawak. My son has need of the Sacraments so that his soul may not be soiled by sin." His term of office was eight years, she said, two of which he already had completed. She added that he was commander of the British troops in Sarawak and that he was a Roman Catholic.[9]

Father Mackey in turn forwarded Mrs. Rodway's letter of 15 October to the Mill Hill Missionaries along with a letter of his own dated 17 October 1876. He hoped that her request would be well received, he said, and would result in the Mill Hill Missionaries going to Borneo. "You already know," he continued, "that Borneo is an English colony and occupies the seacoast for a length of two hundred miles and a width of one hundred miles. This would be an excellent support area for converting the entire island. It would be a matter of great importance for the Rajah of Sarawak . . . , if you were to make known to him, that the missionaries whom you intend to send are English, and have received their education in England."

Commander Rodway did not desire "to take the initiative in this affair," Mackey pointed out, "not because of indifference, but for fear that this would do more harm than good." The letter was signed "Your servant in Jesus Christ, H. B. Mackey," and also contained the address of the Rajah as supplied by Mrs. Rodway:

---

7. Letter, M. Fleischmann, M.H.M., late archivist of Mill Hill, to Wiltgen, 11 April 1972. Here Father Fleischmann says that the initials for Rodway are W. M. (not W. H. as in Rooney, *Khabar Gembira*, 25).

8. The information on Mackey, on the Visitation Convent, and on the Rodway family, was sent to the author on 26–27 June 1993 by archivist Sister Callender of the Visitation Convent at Waldron, East Sussex, England, where the Westbury-on-Trym community moved in 1959. Mrs. Rodway's maiden name was Allin; her husband's name was Henry. In Rooney, *Khabar Gembira*, Mackey's name is incorrectly given as McKay on p. 25 and Mackay on p. 252 n. 3.

9. PF: SC Oceania, vol. 11 (1877–78, Part I), f. 727rv, Mrs. Rodway to Mackey, 15 October 1876. See also Acta vol. 246 (1878), f. 651r–653r.

H.H. the Rajah of Sarawak
Government House
Kuching, Borneo[10]

Bishop Vaughan, founder of the Mill Hill Missionaries, lost no time in taking action on the petition received from Mrs. Rodway through Father Mackey. On 27 October 1876 he submitted a proposal to Cardinal Prefect Franchi "concerning the Propagation of the Faith in the vast island or rather continent of Borneo." Without mentioning Mrs. Rodway, or her son, or Father Mackey, Vaughan said:

> A few days ago I was indirectly requested by the *Rajah of Sarawak* in Borneo to send some missionaries there. The *Rajah* is an Englishman and is very powerful in those areas. Nor does he have confidence in Protestant missionaries. There is talk that Catholic missionaries under his influence could convert many of the Dyaks, the people of that country, and gain entrance to the interior of that unknown region. I also heard that Father Cuarterón is old and infirm and I believe that he would be content if some English missionaries were to be sent to *Sarawak*.

The Mill Hill College would be able to send two or three missionaries to Borneo, Vaughan said, since the Madras mission in India "asks for only two or three a year. And at present it appears that the Negro Missions in America will perhaps have enough if we send them two every year. Would Your Eminence, then, have the goodness of indicating whether you wish that we try to found a mission in *Sarawak* in Borneo? If you should desire this to happen at once, we can deal directly with the *Rajah* on this matter...."[11] Yes, Vaughan could now deal directly with the Rajah, because Mrs. Rodway had sent him the Rajah's address.

It is difficult to understand how the request of Mrs. Rodway and that of Father Mackey for missionaries can be called by Vaughan an indirect request "by the *Rajah* of Sarawak in Borneo to send some missionaries there." Perhaps he is referring to someone whom he met "a few days ago." He could not be referring to Governor Pope-Hennessy's letter, since it had been written a few years ago, on 8 August 1870. Most likely he is referring to Commander Rodway, whose words Mackey quoted.

The rajah of Sarawak to whom Bishop Vaughan referred was Charles Anthony Johnson (1829-1917), who adopted his uncle's name Brooke on becoming the second white or English Rajah on 3 August 1868. He is known for his forty-nine-year nonoppressive reign. The first white or English Rajah was Sir James Brooke (1803-68), whose dynasty was founded in 1841 and ended in 1941. He died on 11 June 1868.

---

10. PF: SC Oceania, vol. 11 (1877-78, Part I), f. 727v-728r, Mackey to the Mill Hill missionaries, 17 October 1876.

11. Rooney in *Khabar Gembira* incorrectly dates Vaughan's letter of 27 October (p. 25) as 17 October 1876 on p. 237 n. 60, and says that no copy of the letter survives. The author of the present work has found the original letter in PF: SC Oceania, vol. 10 (1873-76), f. 1331v-1332r, Vaughan to Franchi, 27 October 1876, and has made use of it in the text.

At the end of Vaughan's letter of 27 October 1876, either Cardinal Franchi or his secretary added this note: "Wait for the Prefect Apostolic."[12] Six months later Cuarterón had not yet reached Rome. But in May 1877 Franchi was assured by Cavaliere Angelini, a Roman confidant of Cuarterón, that "the Prefect Apostolic shall surely be arriving in Rome."[13]

Franchi waited in vain two more months for Cuarterón's arrival and finally wrote to Bishop Vaughan of Salford on 13 July 1877. Eight and one half months had passed since Vaughan had written to Franchi, so the cardinal replied: "I did not fail to take into consideration what Your Reverence indicated to me in your letter of 27 October of last year on the Borneo Mission. But nothing could be decided because we are waiting from moment to moment for Very Reverend Father Cuarterón, Prefect Apostolic of that island, to arrive. Since it is known that he will soon be in Rome, we shall keep in mind also the proposal made by Your Reverence when we deal with him regarding other affairs."[14]

Cuarterón, however, was in no hurry to reach Rome. Instead he busied himself with writing letters in Labuan, trying to find personnel himself who might want to take charge of his mission.

On Saturday, 14 April 1877, Cuarterón took time out to write a very special letter to Cardinal Prefect Franchi. "Exactly twenty years ago today I took possession of these missions and established myself here," he said. (Had he postponed his return to Rome so that he could reach his twentieth anniversary in Labuan?) The letter was not only a four-page summary of his activities, and a report on the current status of his mission, but also an unveiling of his soul. In order that Cardinal Franchi and Propaganda might obtain "an exact idea" of his Prefecture Apostolic of Labuan, he enclosed a copy of the same map in color which he had published prior to leaving Rome on 19 October 1855 for this mission.

"In my charge there are eight hundred miles of coastline or an area extending for about three hundred leagues," he said. "We restrict ourselves to a circle of ninety miles, that is, thirty leagues, and we are established in Labuan, Brunei, and the Bay of Gaya." The Brunei mission had been destroyed in 1860 when people deliberately burned the church. "We abandoned the Bay of Gaya Mission in 1873, but returned to occupy it in 1876. . . ." Cuarterón referred to Rajah Charles Brooke, the second white or English rajah of Sarawak,

---

12. See PF: SC Oceania, vol. 10 (1873–76), f. 1332r.

13. The information from Angelini is in a note added to Cuarterón's letter to Franchi of 14 April 1877, in PF: SC Oceania, vol. 11 (1877–78, Part I), f. 152v.

14. PF: LDB vol. 373 (1877), f. 316r. Vaughan's letter of 27 October 1876 had spoken of propagating the faith on "the vast island or rather continent of Borneo." And in his reply Cardinal Franchi referred to Vaughan's letter about "the Borneo Mission." The mission in question was Labuan and its Vicinity or Dependencies or Neighboring Territories. The mission did not include the entire island of Borneo, but it did include parts of northwestern Borneo.

as owner of the kingdom of Sarawak and as tributary to the sultan of Borneo. "When we meet, he always asks me for Roman Catholic missionaries for Sarawak," Cuarterón said. "This mission is most suitable for the Augustinian Fathers and could be separated from the Labuan Mission and be supported by their own funds. I am sending a map to their present Provincial [in Manila] and am recommending that he go to Sarawak Mission for the present, even in spite of an Anglican Bishop being there with twenty missionaries...."

His mission was "arid and difficult," Cuarterón said. If Franchi was not satisfied with his "twenty years of work and his having spent thirty-five thousand francs, which the missions in question" had cost him, he begged the cardinal to wait for his arrival in Rome before relieving him of his office.

Cuarterón said that he had already offered his own mission to the provincial superior of the Spanish Augustinians in Manila. He had learned just a few days earlier from one of the Augustinians there that Nuncio Apostolic Simeoni in Madrid had contacted their procurator at the court of Spain "and said they should take charge of these missions." However, the provincial superior in Manila, in spite of Rome and Cuarterón both offering him the mission, said that he did not want it.[15]

After Cuarterón on 14 April 1877 had told Rome that the Spanish Augustinians in Manila did not want his mission, he sent the following information for some puzzling reason to Rajah Charles Brooke of Sarawak on 1 May 1877: "Since various Spanish Roman Catholic Religious of the Order of Saint Augustine wish to come to evangelize in the large Island of Borneo and establish Missions, I would like to know whether Your Highness is agreeable to admit them into your Kingdom of Sarawak. I believe that they will enjoy more security and personal freedom there than in any other part of the said Island of Borneo.... I hope to receive a favorable reply from Your Highness...."[16] Cuarterón may have believed that the provincial superior would change his mind if he saw a letter from Rajah Charles Brooke inviting him and his priests to Sarawak.

Promptly on 8 May 1877 the rajah of Sarawak answered Cuarterón from Kuching:

> I have the honor [sic] to acknowledge the receipt of your letter dated 1st May 1877, in which you request a reply to whether there would be any objection to a Roman Catholic Mission being established in Sarawak country. I am, Sir, unable to reply with any degree of certainty to your proposal without giving the matter further consideration and would lay before you the difficulties and complications that might arise in consequence of the Protestant Mission, which now has been so long established in this country, and which is spread over a very considerable extent of it....[17]

---

15. PF: SC Oceania, vol. 11 (1877–78, Part I), f. 151r-152v, Cuarterón to Franchi, 14 April 1877. Cuarterón's map in color is in PF: SC Oceania, vol. 11 (1877–78, Part I), f. 153r. See also PF: SC Oceania, vol. 11 (1877–78, Part II), f. 1338r-1339v.

16. Ibid., Part II, f. 1313r. Glazik in "Kirchenorganisatorische Massnahmen," 497 n. 36, must be mistaken when he states that in this letter Cuarterón reports "that Spanish Augustinians are working with him as missionaries."

17. PF: SC Oceania, vol. 11 (1877–78, Part II), f. 1314r-1315r.

Cuarterón on 25 May 1877 sent Franchi copies of his letter and of Brooke's reply, which Cuarterón said was not definitive. "But I understand it as being negative . . . ," he added.[18]

Six months later on 27 November 1877, Cuarterón wrote to Franchi again, giving reasons that had hindered him from leaving for Rome. He also mentioned that the last letter to reach him from the cardinal had arrived on 17 July of the previous year.[19]

Pius IX died on 7 February 1878 at the age of eighty-five after serving as pope for thirty-one years and eight months. He was succeeded on 20 February 1878 by sixty-seven-year-old Pope Leo XIII (1810–1903), who chose Cardinal Prefect Franchi of Propaganda as his secretary of state on 5 March 1878. At the same time the new pope appointed sixty-one-year-old Giovanni Cardinal Simeoni, nuncio apostolic to Spain, as the new cardinal prefect of Propaganda. Simeoni was well acquainted with Cuarterón, having been secretary of Propaganda for seven years (1868–75) and having interceded for Cuarterón as nuncio apostolic in Madrid.[20]

When taking office as cardinal prefect, Simeoni found the unanswered letter of 27 November 1877 from Cuarterón to Franchi. Simeoni answered it on 28 March 1878, stating that Propaganda had sent no further letters "because we were expecting you in Rome from moment to moment, since you had promised to discuss with us the affairs of your mission." Simeoni said that he understood the reasons given by Cuarterón for being prevented from coming to Rome. He appreciated as well the negotiations being conducted by Cuarterón "with the Spanish Government on behalf of the Filipino slaves now in Borneo." The cardinal saw "no difficulty," however, in Cuarterón's considering it expedient for his mission, if he were to leave Borneo for Rome. "But in any event before leaving the mission," Simeoni said, "you should provide for its being well cared for in your absence. . . ."[21]

Simeoni's kind letter was en route three months when Cuarterón wrote on 26 June 1878 to his confidant in Rome, Cavalier Enrico Angelini, in a very disgruntled frame of mind and bared his soul. Angelini was currently Cuarterón's agent, who evidently had hurried off to Cuarterón news about Simeoni's appointment as cardinal prefect of Propaganda.

"The Very Eminent Lord Cardinal Simeoni will not remember me and much less will he remember these Missions," Cuarterón solemnly intoned. "As soon as I reach Rome, I believe that he will take away my title as Prefect Apostolic. His Eminence is the same person who went to the Procurator in Madrid of the Augustinian Religious in the Philippines in order to persuade those Religious to take upon themselves the Labuan

---

18. Ibid., f. 1316r.
19. Ibid., f. 1320r.
20. See Metzler, "Präfekten und Sekretäre, 49–51.
21. PF: LDB vol. 374 (1878), f. 130rv, Simeoni to Cuarterón, 28 March 1828.

Mission." (Cuarterón was ready to grant the Augustinians the Sarawak mission, but not Labuan, which he wanted to keep for himself.) "The Eminent Cardinal Franchi, Prefect of the Evangelization Congregation at that time, had wanted me also to hand over to them the Lire 10,000 in alms which His Majesty Alfonso XII [1857–85] had assigned to me, so that I might have something to live on. These alms were granted to the priest Carlos Cuarterón and not to the Mission of Labuan," as Cuarterón carefully pointed out.

> If it should happen that they take away these alms from me and dismiss me, as a reward for all of my sacrifices and services, I shall then present myself to His Holiness. I shall ask that he give me something to eat, since I was ordained under the title of Patrimony, as His Eminence, Cardinal Fransoni, had counselled me, and not under the title of Missionary. I created my own Patrimony or Ecclesiastical Benefice by purchasing bonds issued by the Papal States. However, I have not been paid any interest on them since 1866, the year in which my Procurator, the Reverend Father Diego Burrueco, died there. And I have received no attention from Propaganda since 17 July 1876. I do not know if they are doing this to me out of contempt or perhaps because they are waiting for my return to Rome.

In this letter written on 26 June, Cuarterón said that he would be hindered from leaving for Rome "until the end of August, by which time I shall have completed all my tasks. And those which are not completed, I shall abandon, even though they have cost me 20,000 francs. And if I do not return here, all this money will go to the Devil."[22]

Angelini, thinking that Cardinal Prefect Simeoni should be aware of this letter and its contents, presented him with a copy.

The election of Pope Leo XIII in February 1878 and the appointment of Simeoni as cardinal prefect of Propaganda in March that year, prompted Bishop Vaughan to take up in May once again the matter of the Mill Hill missionaries receiving an independent mission.

More specifically, Vaughan wanted the English colony of Northwestern Borneo currently entrusted to Cuarterón. Vaughan also felt at home with the new cardinal prefect, Simeoni, who had been secretary from May 1870 to March 1875, while Vaughan was urging Propaganda to give him a mission that would be completely in the hands of his Foreign Mission Seminary of Mill Hill. This time he sent Benoit to Rome.

Bishop Vaughan wrote to Cardinal Simeoni on 20 May 1878 that the bearer of his letter was Father Peter Benoit, the one whom he had chosen as rector or superior of the Mission Seminary at Mill Hill. Vaughan had retained office as superior general of the Mission Society of Saint Joseph of the Sacred Heart. He was sending Benoit to Rome "to discuss our interests and to receive your orders . . ." He also presented Simeoni with French

---

22. PF: SC Oceania, vol. 11 (1877–78, Part II), f. 1335rv, Cuarterón to Angelini, 26 June 1878. This copy is a translation of the Spanish original of Cuarterón into Italian, and the translation mistakenly has Angelino for Angelini.

translations of the letters received nineteen months earlier from Mrs. Rodway and Father Mackey.[23]

Since May 1870, when Vaughan had come to Rome seeking an independent mission for the first time, various missions had been given consideration. There had been talk of a territory in China or Japan, but these came to naught. There were discussions on Borneo that were broken off in 1870 and others about Africa that were broken off in 1876. Then Cardinal Edward Howard, a Roman prelate and good friend of Bishop Vaughan, suggested New Zealand in early 1878, but Mill Hill remained cool to this proposal.

After Benoit reached Rome in late May 1878, Cardinal Howard suggested New Guinea as a possibility. But Benoit favored Borneo and supported his choice with good reasons: The English were in Labuan; Lady Brooke, wife of Rajah Charles Brooke, had leanings towards Catholicism (she later became a Catholic); the rajah's troops had a Catholic as commander, W. M. Rodway. Moreover, Benoit believed that Cuarterón's one-man mission would not last much longer. Benoit was received in audience twice by Cardinal Prefect Simeoni and pointed out to him how eager Vaughan was to have a mission that was completely independent. By this he meant having a mission in which the Mill Hill Fathers would not be working under some other prefect apostolic or vicar apostolic, but rather under a prefect apostolic or vicar apostolic who was a Mill Hill missionary.

The Mill Hill seminary was now twelve years old, he said, and had more than sixty members. Sixteen of its priests were working among Negroes in the United States, but in two dioceses under bishops who were not Mill Hill missionaries. Also the twelve priests in Madras, India, were still waiting to have a mission assigned exclusively to them, so that they could be in charge. Cardinal Simeoni then invited Benoit to pick out a mission from all the various mission fields of Propaganda which were unstaffed at that time. This included the Mission of Melanesia-Micronesia and the Diocese of Auckland in New Zealand.[24]

Because the majority of Maori in New Zealand were in the Auckland diocese and needed a bishop and priests, Simeoni was eager for Benoit to accept this mission. But Benoit considered himself authorized to accept only a mission in Borneo, not one in New Zealand with a long history of problems and debts. Simeoni then wrote directly to Bishop Vaughan on 29 May 1878: "It is known to me that Your Excellency would be pleased with a mission for your priests which corresponds to the aims of your pious Society. Now it is probable that the Diocese of Auckland could shortly be available, because it is a vacant see at present for which some negotiations with another Society are pending. I would therefore like to know whether Your Excellency in such a hypothetical situation would consider it opportune for the Mission to be offered to the Society of which you are in charge. Kindly let me know. . . ."[25]

23. Ibid., f. 1361r.
24. McCormack, *Cardinal Vaughan*, 202f.
25. PF: LDB vol. 374 (1878) f. 258v.

Simeoni's letter was in Bishop Vaughan's hands by 5 June when he wrote to Lady Herbert: "I hear from Propaganda to-day that they are willing to offer us the Diocese of Auckland in New Zealand. . . ."[26] But Vaughan, who no doubt was informed by Benoit of the numerous problems connected with the Auckland diocese, formerly headed by Bishop Pompallier, was no more interested in obtaining it than was Benoit. Simeoni offered it to six different missionary groups before he found someone ready to accept it.[27] From this it is clear that Propaganda often had problems finding staff for its missions.

While Simeoni's letter on the Auckland diocese was en route to Bishop Vaughan, Father Benoit was busy in Rome drawing up a lengthy report in French which he called "A Project for a New Mission in Oceania." He dated it 4 June 1878 and sent it with an accompanying letter of the same date, which was addressed to all cardinal members of Propaganda. The letter informed them that he was acting in the name of Bishop Vaughan of Salford, the "Superior General." Benoit said: "There is an opening in Borneo in the area under English influence," and there is also "the hope of winning many souls there, if the area were to be constituted into a prefecture [apostolic] under the direction of the Society of Saint Joseph of the Sacred Heart of London."[28]

After giving some details on the activities and total membership of the Mill Hill missionaries, he mentioned that they were still waiting for a mission and its government to be entrusted to them by Propaganda. "Meanwhile," he said, the Mill Hill Seminary "takes the respectful liberty of placing itself at the disposition of Propaganda for sending some of its missionaries to Borneo with the aim of reaching out later to New Guinea, if God in his goodness blesses their sacrifices." He assured the cardinals that Superior General Vaughan was "disposed to take charge of the Prefecture of Borneo or of a part of this immense Island."

In other words Borneo would be a stepping-stone for reaching New Guinea. This was the very same idea that director Marinoni of Milan had proposed when offering his two priests, Borgazzi and Riva, as assistants to Cuarterón. The two missionaries were expected to provide the services of a procure or supply center for the New Guinea mission.

In a few lines Benoit dismissed the twenty-one years of missionary activity of Prefect Apostolic Cuarterón in Labuan and Borneo. "Some fifteen years ago," he said incorrectly, Cuarterón "went to plant the faith there, but without any success."[29]

---

26. See the letter of 5 June 1878 in *Letters of Vaughan*.

27. The Auckland Diocese was offered to the Mill Hill missionaries, Holy Spirit Fathers, Irish Religious of Saint Isidore, Benedictines at Subiaco, Jesuits, and Friars Minor Conventual. The Conventuals went to Auckland diocese in 1860 and left in 1873.

28. PF: SC Oceania, vol. 11 (1877–78, Part I), f. 728r, Benoit to the Propaganda cardinals, 4 June 1878.

29. Twenty-one years, not fifteen, is the correct figure. Cuarterón arrived in Labuan on 14 April 1857 and was still there on 4 June 1878, when Benoit prepared this letter. See chap. 17, p. 342.

The report was written in French so that the officials of Propaganda would have no trouble reading it. Benoit also enclosed French translations of the October 1876 letters received from Mrs. Elizabeth Rodway and Father Mackey. (It was now June 1878.) He explained that the two letters "implore us to send some missionaries to Sarawak... We did not inform Propaganda about them, because His Eminence [Cardinal Franchi], Prefect of the Congregation, had told us that he was expecting the arrival of Reverend Cuarterón in Rome from day to day."[30]

Father Benoit's 4 June project for a new mission in Oceania was certainly drawn up after he had discussed it with officials of Propaganda, who proved sympathetic to his proposal. But when he returned on Wednesday, 12 June, to inquire whether any decision had been reached, he learned that nothing had been done. After he left that day, a note was added to the official papers by the secretary, which read: "He shall return tomorrow, 13 June [Thursday], thinking that something will be decided at the meeting."[31] But nothing more was decided than to bring up the matter at the next General Meeting scheduled for July.

A summary of Benoit's entire proposal was then prepared, was set up in type, and was printed, so that each cardinal member with a right to attend the General Meeting in July could have his own copy for advance private study. The summary was extensive and pointed out that "the Superior General... is disposed to take charge of the Prefecture of Borneo or of a part of this immense Island."

The summary went on to say that Mill Hill had proposed that the entire coast under English influence could be constituted a prefecture, that is, going north from the equator and consequently containing "the English Colony of Sarawak; the Sultanate of Brunei, which is called Borneo Proper and is under the influence of the English King of Sarawak; and Labuan, which is an English Possession." In addition to these three territories, all of which were under English influence, Benoit called attention to another fact. The Missionary Society of Mill Hill, namely, had a considerable proportion of members who were Dutch by birth. Consequently any territory that was to be given to Mill Hill, Benoit said, could also extend into Dutch possessions in Borneo.

"The Sultanate of Brunei, or Borneo Proper," Benoit added, "is the coast that we want as a Prefecture Apostolic. The Spaniards possess absolutely nothing, insofar as I know, on the shores in question." The conclusion of Benoit's presentation of 4 June was briefly this: Saint Joseph's Society for Foreign Missions "places itself at the disposition of Propaganda to send some Missionaries to Borneo, with the aim of later reaching out toward New Guinea, if the good God wishes graciously to bless their sacrifices."[32]

---

30. PF: SC Oceania, vol. 11 (1877–78, Part I), f. 725r–728r, Benoit to the Propaganda cardinals, 4 June 1878.
31. PF: SC Oceania, vol. 11 (1877–78, Part II), f. 1363.
32. See PF: Acta vol. 246 (1878, Part II), f. 650r–653v.

Everything was moving along splendidly, and a General Meeting was scheduled for July 1878 in order to confer officially upon the Mill Hill Missionaries a prefecture apostolic over which they would have full charge. However, it was presumed that Cuarterón would arrive in Rome prior to that meeting. But when Cuarterón did not appear by 28 June 1878, Cardinal Prefect Simeoni ordered that all preparations for discussing Labuan at the General Meeting be suspended. The numerous papers already prepared for this discussion ended with this notice: "The Cardinal Prefect has ordered the suspension of the *Ponenza* for the decision on Labuan until the arrival of Prefect Cuarterón."[33] For the second time Mill Hill's efforts to obtain part or all of Cuarterón's prefecture apostolic had come to a full stop.

Cardinal Prefect Simeoni had cancelled all preparations for giving Cuarterón's prefecture apostolic to Mill Hill, because he had decided to divide it. This is clear from his letter of 28 June 1878 that he wrote to Cuarterón:

> Your Excellency has requested Propaganda many times to send missionaries to the Prefecture Apostolic of Labuan and its Dependencies, which because of the almost total lack of missionaries has remained as if it were abandoned.... And yet Propaganda has not failed to do its part in order to remedy this deficiency. However, it has had no success up to the present time.
>
> But now the Lord has been pleased to inspire a religious community with members whose nationality is English to offer itself spontaneously to look after the entire portion of the present Prefecture Apostolic of Labuan which is under English rule, while you remain entrusted with that part which is under Spanish rule. This project will be submitted to the judgment of the Eminent Fathers at the next General Meeting, and no difficulties are foreseen regarding its acceptance. You are hereby being informed and I would ask you to have the courtesy of informing me in the shortest possible time of whatever observations you can suggest in order to facilitate the erection of the Prefecture mentioned.

Simeoni was very sorry to learn that Cuarterón had no priests for the Spanish part of his prefecture apostolic. Nor could Simeoni send him any Spanish priests from the secular clergy, "not only because Propaganda is not accustomed to send such missionaries, but much more so because of the scarcity of vocations for such a kind of life."

The only alternative for Cuarterón, Simeoni said, "would be to turn to some Spanish religious community. But one can readily foresee that if a [religious] order were to accept the offer, it would want to be independent in practising the ministry and in directing the prefecture." Simeoni therefore urged Cuarterón "kindly to consider this matter seriously because, as you can well see, it is of the greatest importance. So do let me know your ideas on the subject as soon as possible."[34]

Cardinal Prefect Simeoni's proposal was remarkable. Cuarterón could come to Rome and did not need to fear that he would be stripped of his office as prefect apostolic. He

---

33. PF: SC Oceania, vol. 11 (1877–78, Part II), f. 1364v.
34. PF: LDB vol. 374 (1878), f. 312rv, Simeoni to Cuarterón, 28 June 1878.

would remain prefect apostolic of Labuan and within his former territory would have jurisdiction over all parts that were under Spanish rule. As Simeoni had said in his letter, a new prefecture would be erected for the English missionaries, which would contain all parts of the former Prefecture Apostolic of Labuan, which were under English rule.

Cuarterón himself had suggested to Cardinal Prefect Simeoni that the Spanish Augustinian provincial in Manila could begin work in Sarawak, which was under English rule. He added that this mission without difficulty could be separated from the Prefecture Apostolic of Labuan. What Cuarterón had suggested for the Spanish Augustinian provincial superior would now become part of the new prefecture apostolic containing territories under English rule, which was to be entrusted to English missionaries, namely, those of Mill Hill. One might well ask, however, what territory concretely would be left for Cuarterón, since he was to have as his prefecture apostolic that territory "which is under Spanish rule." Actually the map of Cuarterón's Prefecture Apostolic of Labuan and its Vicinity, which was submitted by him to Propaganda on 14 April 1877, the twentieth anniversary of his arrival at Labuan, indicated in yellow a Spanish colony established in December 1857 at Balabac Island above the Strait of Balabac. No other territory on his map was indicated as being under Spanish rule. Consequently Simeoni—perhaps knowingly, perhaps unknowingly—was indicating that Cuarterón's prefecture would be decreased in size to that of Balabac Island. Cuarterón's map showed English territory in red, Dutch territory in blue, and Portuguese territory in green.

Benoit had indicated in the summary of his proposal that Mill Hill wanted a part of or all of Cuarterón's territory. It may have been this vagueness regarding both the territory to be given to Mill Hill and the territory to be retained by Cuarterón that prompted Simeoni to have Benoit send him a map of Borneo. Benoit did this on 5 July 1878.[35]

Six months after Simeoni had blocked all further negotiations regarding Labuan until Cuarterón's arrival in Rome, Bishop Vaughan's patience gave out and he wrote to Monsignor Rinandini, a friend of his in Rome. Vaughan complained bitterly that no independent mission had yet been entrusted to his Mill Hill missionaries. Rinandini passed on Vaughan's complaints to Cardinal Prefect Simeoni, who then quickly wrote to Vaughan on 14 January 1879.

"Monsignor Rinandini communicated to me a passage from a letter sent by Your Excellency to him," Simeoni said, "in which you refer to the bad impression being created in various people by the fact that a mission among the pagans has not yet been assigned to Saint Joseph's College. It is hinted that this might indicate a lack of esteem on the part of Propaganda for the institute which is promoted by and presided over by Your Excellency

---

35. PF: SC Oceania, vol. 11 (1877–78, Part II), f. 1359r–1360r, Benoit to Simeoni, 5 July 1878. Cuarterón's large printed map of his prefecture apostolic with various political areas in different colors is in PF: SC Oceania, vol. 11 (1877–78, Part I), f. 153r.

with such great zeal and good will. . . ." But Simeoni insisted that there was no lack of esteem at all on Propaganda's part. "The very suspicion of such a thing," he said, "would cause me the greatest displeasure, since this Sacred Congregation on the contrary has no greater desire than to see your institute flourish. . . ." Simeoni assured Vaughan that Mill Hill "enjoys the full confidence of Propaganda Fide."

Simeoni had more to say: "Let me not omit to recall that when the Rector of Saint Joseph's College came to Rome a few months ago, I invited him to pick out from among all available missions dependent upon this Sacred Congregation, that one which he would consider most fitting for his candidates . . ." And since Rector Benoit had "manifested the desire to have his College placed in charge" of the English parts of the Prefecture of Labuan, Simeoni had written about the matter immediately in these terms to Prefect Cuarterón. "But I have not yet received a reply from him," Simeoni said. He assured Bishop Vaughan, however, that Propaganda "wants to see this affair brought to a conclusion in the manner which is so much desired by Your Excellency . . ."[36]

How many more months or years would have to pass before Cuarterón's arrival in Rome? Only then would it become possible for Propaganda to create a new prefecture apostolic for the Mill Hill missionaries, one including all portions of the present Prefecture Apostolic of Labuan that were under English rule. Wanting to show his confidence in the Foreign Mission College of Bishop Vaughan, Simeoni wrote at once offering him a mission in Afghanistan. Vaughan in turn wrote to Lady Herbert on 23 January 1879: "I have just had a letter from Propaganda asking whether we will take Afghanistan and send out three or four priests without delay. . . . I have been desired to telegraph my answer and have telegraphed YES GLADLY."

Mill Hill's priests were to become military chaplains temporarily for service with the British Expeditionary Force in Afghanistan. Once hostilities ended, the priests would be allowed to open a mission. But one of the first three to leave England died of dysentery in three months, and the possibility of opening a mission was never realized.[37]

Simeoni naturally was pleased at receiving the telegram from Vaughan announcing his acceptance of the Afghanistan mission. But he was also disturbed because Cuarterón had not yet replied to his letter of 28 June 1878 and it was now late January 1879. In normal circumstances correspondence between Rome and Labuan would take two months each way. In that letter Simeoni had told Cuarterón that his mission was to be divided at a General Meeting in July 1878 and that he would obtain the territory under Spanish rule, whereas the Mill Hill fathers would obtain the territory under English rule.

Once again Simeoni picked up his pen and wrote to Cuarterón, this time on 26 January 1879. He said: "On 28 June of the year already passed this Sacred Congregation sent you a letter. I am enclosing a copy of it, because I take it for granted that my letter must have got-

---

36. PF: LDB vol. 375 (1879), f. 16r, Simeoni to Vaughan, 14 January 1879.
37. McCormack, *Cardinal Vaughan*, 203; see also the letter of 23 January 1879 in *Letters of Vaughan*.

ten lost. On this occasion I ask you kindly to send me an answer as soon as possible, since this Sacred Congregation is interested in terminating the project referred to."[38]

Rome's task of persuading Cuarterón to hand over his mission or part of it to some other group was still unsettled after nine years of effort on the part of three cardinal prefects: Barnabò, Franchi, and Simeoni. Cardinal Barnabò as early as May 1870 had assured Vaughan that he had already given orders for Cuarterón's mission to be handed over to the Foreign Mission Seminary of Mill Hill. But now Barnabò was dead, and his successor Franchi was also dead. Cuarterón was still very much alive, however, and it had become Simeoni's turn to see if he could persuade Cuarterón to come back to Rome and negotiate.

The process had been slowed down by Vatican diplomacy, which insists upon courtesy being maintained when transferring power from one person to another, especially if the one losing the power was guilty of no blatant evil. The long silence between Cuarterón and Rome was broken on 6 March 1879, when Cavalier Enrico Angelini informed Simeoni that "My distinguished friend," Don Cuarterón, was pleased to learn that the Cardinal Prefect "has a good opinion of him."[39]

That same month in Labuan on 26 March 1879, Cuarterón received Simeoni's letter of 26 January 1879, exactly two months after it was written. With this letter Simeoni had enclosed a copy of his 28 June 1878 letter, which Cuarterón had never answered. It explained that the Mill Hill missionaries were ready to take over responsibility for English territories of the Labuan prefecture apostolic. Cuarterón, who said that he had never received Simeoni's letter of 28 June 1878, replied within five days (31 March) and sent Simeoni a second letter on 18 April.[40]

After receiving the two letters of 31 March and 18 April, Simeoni wrote back on 30 June 1879 saying:

> With displeasure I have learned that you are not very well and for this reason you could not leave. I hope that the condition of your health is better now and I wish you a speedy and complete recovery. . . . I shall be very pleased to see you again here in Rome. Meanwhile I want you to be assured of the esteem which we have here for you and for the well-known efforts which you have made for the advancement of this mission. On the other hand what you tell me about the scarcity of priests in your Prefecture, shows how necessary it is for us to make provisions there—as here we

---

38. PF: LDB vol. 375 (1879), f. 26v.

39. PF: SC Oceania, vol. 11 (1877–78, Part II), f. 1355r, Angelini to Simeoni, 6 March 1879. This reaction of Cuarterón was prompted by an earlier letter of Simeoni, not by that of 28 June 1878 or that of 26 January 1879. These two letters did not reach Cuarterón until 26 March 1879.

40. Ibid., f. 1352rv, Cuarterón to Simeoni, 31 March 1879. The Cuarterón letter of 18 April was not found, but its receipt was acknowledged by Simeoni on 30 June. See ibid., f. 266v, Simeoni to Cuarterón, 30 June 1879.

have already thought of doing—by entrusting the English part [of your Prefecture] to a religious community from England, as I wrote to you on 26 January.⁴¹

Cuarterón meanwhile had taken it for granted that the General Meeting of July 1878, as mentioned in Simeoni's earlier letter of 28 June that year, had taken place and that consequently part of his prefecture apostolic had been given to the Mill Hill missionaries. Consequently in a further letter of his dated 27 May 1879, he expressed surprise that no English missionaries had yet arrived in Labuan to take over part of his mission.⁴²

Early in October 1879, without forewarning, Don Carlos Cuarterón arrived in Rome, broken in health. Twenty-four years earlier he had left Rome on 18 October 1855 en route to Civitavecchia, Cádiz, Manila, and Labuan. The mission that he had tried to found in Labuan and on the Borneo coast had proved more difficult than he had anticipated. In part it was also fruitless. His missionary vocation to a large extent had become giving witness to Christ in a Moslem world, and in doing so he had consumed his health, his wealth, his life.

Monsignor Ignazio Masotti (1817–88), appointed secretary of Propaganda on 19 September 1879, had many tasks during his first thirty days in office. One of them was to book lodging at the Irish Franciscan Monastery of Saint Isidore on the Street of Artists in Rome, a ten-minute walk from the Propaganda offices. Masotti on 10 October wrote to the Superior there: "Since the Prefect Apostolic of Labuan, Don Carlos Cuarterón, has come to Rome and must remain for a short time, the undersigned Secretary of Propaganda requests that Your Paternity kindly grant him lodging in your monastery. . . ."⁴³ Back in May 1870 Vaughan informed Lady Herbert from Rome that Cardinal Prefect Barnabò had just given orders "as to a Mission" for Mill Hill, which was "no other than Labuan and Borneo."⁴⁴ From Rome on Christmas Eve in 1879 Vaughan sent Lady Herbert his latest news on Borneo: Father Cuarterón "is now in Rome . . . and wants to resign, from age and sickness." Vaughan added that "Cardinal [Prefect] Simeoni is most anxious that we should undertake Borneo . . . and if possible New Guinea and New Ireland! I wonder how many other countries he would like to send us to."⁴⁵

Bishop Vaughan may have known, or perhaps he did not know, why Cardinal Prefect Simeoni was "most anxious" that Mill Hill "should undertake . . . if possible New Guinea and New Ireland." Earlier that year Simeoni had negotiated in Rome with Italian-born

---

41. PF: LDB vol. 375 (1879), f. 266v–267r, Simeoni to Cuarterón, 30 June 1879.

42. PF: SC Oceania, vol. 11 (1877–78, Part II), f. 1349r–1350r, Cuarterón to Simeoni, 27 May 1879. This letter of 27 May from Cuarterón crossed Simeoni's letter of 30 June 1879.

43. PF: LDB vol. 375 (1879), f. 443v, Masotti to the Superior of Saint Isidore Monastery, 10 October 1879.

44. *Letters of Vaughan*, 179f.

45. Ibid., 313.

Father Giovanni Cani of Cooktown, Queensland. He had sailed from Australia to Rome in order to convince Simeoni that it was vital to found immediately a Catholic mission on the south coast of New Guinea.

Simeoni then authorized Cani to reconnoiter the south coast of New Guinea and search for a suitable place for beginning missionary work. His Eminence also solicited and obtained funds from the Lyon and Paris centers of the Association for the Propagation of the Faith for Cani's New Guinea mission and for his additional mission of Queensland. Pope Leo XIII, on 22 May 1879, while Cani was still in Rome, had named him pro-vicar apostolic of Queensland. Later Cani became the first bishop of Rockhampton.[46]

Charles de Breil, Marquis de Rays, had his secretary inform Cardinal Prefect Simeoni by letter of 10 October 1879 that the Free Colony of Port Breton was being founded at the southern end of New Ireland in the abandoned Melanesia-Micronesia vicariate, and it needed priests.

Since Vaughan showed little interest in both New Guinea and New Ireland, Cardinal Prefect Simeoni shared all the documentation received from Cani about southern New Guinea, and all the data received from the office of Marquis de Rays about New Ireland, with Father Victor Jouët, procurator in Rome for the Missionaries of the Sacred Heart (M.S.C.). Jouët had told his superior general by 14 March 1881: "I have had two long interviews with His Eminence Cardinal Simeoni who is very eager to have us accept the beautiful and immense Mission of New Guinea and its surrounding islands." Missionaries of the Sacred Heart eventually pioneered in both New Ireland and New Guinea and are still working there today.[47]

On 10 January 1880, three full months from the date on which Cuarterón received lodging in Rome, Vaughan again wrote from Rome to Lady Herbert about his affairs: "Propaganda prepares to give us the endowment and house in Holland. We are discussing the subject. Also Borneo, New Guinea, Cashmere and other projects. The whole question of studies, philosophy and the new regime here . . ."[48]

One month later (16 February 1880) Bishop Vaughan sent off this news: "I believe we shall get a foundation in Holland for the Foreign Missions, but there may be difficulties raised in Holland. We do not intend it to be known in Holland that it is intended to give it to *us* until the preliminary arrangements are made."[49] Like Father Arnold Janssen, Bishop Vaughan also looked upon the Netherlands or Holland as a neutral territory, not affected by the *Kulturkampf*. For him it was rather an area from which he could obtain missionary vocations for Mill Hill. As Vaughan himself said: "From the beginning of our work for

---

46. PF: LDB vol. 375 (1879), f. 239rv, Decree of 30 May 1879 on Cani being named pro-vicar apostolic of Queensland on 23 May 1879. See also in PF: LDB vol. 375 (1879), Simeoni to the president of the Association for the Propagation of the Faith in Lyon, 18 July 1879.

47. Jean Bertolini, M.S.C., *Missio ad Gentes: Genèse de l'envoi missionnaire de notre société*, 50–54, 63–65.

48. *Letters of Vaughan*, 314f.

49. Ibid., 316.

the Foreign Missions, Dutch candidates have come to Mill Hill in order to prepare for the Apostolate among the heathen. They get on so well with our English students, both in the Seminary and on the Missions, that all seem to belong to one and the same country. In order to strengthen still more this Apostolic union between England and the Netherlands, we have decided to erect in the latter country a preparatory Seminary for our Dutch aspirants to the Apostolate." For similar reasons Bishop Vaughan established a third preparatory seminary at Brixen in the Austrian Tyrol.[50]

Cuarterón had been in Rome about three full months when he received the following invitation dated 16 January 1880: "You are requested to see His Eminence, the Cardinal Prefect of Propaganda, tomorrow, Saturday, the 17th, at 10:30 A.M., for the meeting regarding Labuan about which you have been informed. . . ." An identical letter was sent to Bishop Vaughan, founder of the Mill Hill missionaries, who was also in Rome at that time.[51]

Unfortunately no documentation has been found in Mill Hill or Roman archives to ascertain what happened at this important meeting of 17 January. But in view of Simeoni's earlier letters to Cuarterón, one can surmise what happened. Since Cardinal Prefect Simeoni later continues to refer to Cuarterón as prefect apostolic, it is clear that he was not removed from office. Had he been removed from office, Bishop Vaughan and Father Benoit would have been requested at once to present candidates for the office of prefect apostolic, something that did not happen.

In view of Cardinal Prefect Simeoni's previous letters to Cuarterón on this matter, there was a change, but Cuarterón's title was not changed. What was changed was the geographical area over which he had jurisdiction. It had been reduced to areas under Spanish rule.

Simultaneously a new prefecture apostolic was—or was to be—created for the areas under English rule, which up to that time had been a part of Cuarterón's Prefecture Apostolic of Labuan and Neighboring Territories. This new prefecture apostolic was—or was to be—entrusted to Bishop Vaughan and his Foreign Mission Seminary at Mill Hill in London.

One month later on 15 February 1880, Bishop Vaughan, writing from the English College in Rome, informed Father Rector Benoit that "Propaganda wishes to name someone Pro-Prefect Apostolic of Borneo. Who shall we have fit for this office? We ought to send three out to Borneo soon. When will three be fit to go? Sarawak will be their head quarters. Let me know your proposal as to the three to go, without delay."

Vaughan numbered the points in his letter from one to five. In point two he said: "We must turn our attention seriously to getting such men instructed in medicine, and in

---

50. McCormack, *Cardinal Vaughan*, 202.

51. PF: LDB vol. 376 (1880), f. 43r, undersecretary's note to Cuarterón of 16 January 1880, and secretary's note to Vaughan of 16 January 1880.

some mechanical arts, such as mechanics—making sun dials, taking observations—stuffing birds, the elements of botany etc. . . . The way to succeed in Borneo will be to give the natives some natural advantages, such as some of the arts I have referred to. . . ."

Benoit was told in point three: "Do not let it be known in Holland that it is probable we shall have the Seminary there. The proposals I have made are very acceptable at Propaganda, but they will not let the Nuncio in Holland know the *personel* [sic] until the general principles are settled and agreed to by the legal trustees."[52]

On the following day, 16 February 1880, Vaughan was finally able to send Lady Herbert the good news. After ten years of waiting he had nothing more to say than: "Borneo is a *fait accompli*."[53]

Within four months of the 17 January 1880 meeting between Simeoni, Vaughan and Cuarterón, a nephew of Cuarterón, Nicolás Fernández Cuarterón of Cádiz, informed Cardinal Prefect Simeoni of the death of his uncle, Don Carlos Cuarterón. Cardinal Prefect Simeoni wrote back on 7 May 1880 saying: "With great displeasure I learned the sorrowful news of the death of the Reverend Don Carlos Cuarterón, Prefect Apostolic of Labuan and Its Vicinity [sic]. We are greatly indebted to his zeal for suggesting this mission and for founding it. I was truly pleased to learn from the letter which Your Excellency has just written to me, how your city [of Cádiz] has decided to honor in such a worthy manner the memory of that excellent missionary, its fellow citizen. . . ."[54] Cuarterón's nephew had also informed Simeoni that he was deputy executor of the estate of his uncle and that he had appointed Cavalier Enrico Angelini in Rome as his mandatory. Propaganda's Commission of Cardinals for Financial Affairs then discussed this case at its meeting of 11 June 1880 and "decided that the entire amount constituting the patrimony of the late Don Carlos Cuarterón, Prefect Apostolic of Labuan," should be given to Cavalier Enrico Angelini, the mandatory named by the nephew. The total amount was Lire 3,018.38.

When Simeoni informed Nicolás Fernández Cuarterón of this by letter on 29 July 1880, he stated that Don Carlos Cuarterón had given an additional sum, which drew 5 percent interest per year, "for founding a college in Rome for the benefit of the Mission of Labuan and Its Dependencies [sic], as is evident from the meeting of the Financial Congregation of 19 December 1855 . . ." Simeoni said that this additional sum plus the in-

---

52. MHFA: BOR-2-f.

53. *Letters of Vaughan*, 316.

54. PF: LDB vol. 376 (1880), f. 221r, Simeoni to Nicolás Fernández Cuarterón, 7 May 1880. Rooney in *Khabar Gembira*, 22, says that Cuarterón "went to Seville, where he died." What Simeoni quotes from the letter of Cuarterón's nephew, however, seems to indicate that Cuarterón went from Rome to Cádiz, his home city, and died there. The nephew's letter probably contains the date and place of death, but this letter has not been found.

terest on it had amounted to Lire 11,299.65 by 20 February 1880. The cardinal noted, however, that this latter amount could not be given to Angelini since the legal stipulation made by Cuarterón had been *inter vivos*, that is, the property could be withdrawn by Cuarterón only as long as he was alive. But since it had not been withdrawn by him in life, his own legal arrangement signified that the amount "was meant for the Mission of Labuan and Its Vicinity [sic] according to the pious will of the donor himself, Don Carlos Cuarterón..."[55]

Two months later Simeoni was advised under date of 1 October 1880 by the president of the Association for the Propagation of the Faith in Lyon, France, that Bishop Vaughan had requested a subsidy for a mission in Borneo. The president was confused and wondered if perhaps a new mission had been created by Rome, since he knew only of the Prefecture Apostolic of Labuan.

Cardinal Simeoni replied on 29 October 1880 that

> this particular mission is not new, but is the Prefecture Apostolic of the Island of Labuan and Its Vicinity [sic]. Besides the principalities of Sarawak in Borneo, it includes also other lands in the northwest section of that island. This Prefecture is now entrusted to the Society of Missionaries of the Seminary of Saint Joseph of Mill Hill, near London, headed by Bishop Vaughan, its founder. Prefect Apostolic Don Carlos Cuarterón has died, but the new Prefect Apostolic has not yet been named.... Ever since Cuarterón left the mission last year, it has remained without a single priest.... And so you could say that it needs to be reborn....[56]

Since Cuarterón had died, and since Mill Hill had not yet presented a candidate for office as prefect apostolic, the second prefecture including only territories under English rule had not yet been established and, in fact, no longer needed to be. The existing prefecture of Cuarterón, now that he had died, was simply given to the Mill Hill missionaries and their Seminary of Saint Joseph.

Father Rector Benoit was still trying to make up his mind about the candidates to be proposed for the office of prefect apostolic of Labuan and Its Vicinity, when he contacted the Benedictine priest, Father Henry Benedict Mackey, and said that he was interested in obtaining further information about Borneo from Mrs. Elizabeth Rodway. Her letter, which had been written four years and three months earlier on 15 October 1876, had helped reawaken interest in Borneo at the Mill Hill Seminary. To his surprise Benoit received a four-page letter dated 30 January 1881 from a nun, Sister Mary Thais Rodway, of the Monastcry [sic] of the Visitation at Westbury-on-Trym in North Bristol, England. She wrote:

---

55. PF: LDB vol. 376 (1880), f. 397rv, Simeoni to Nicolás Fernández Cuarterón, 29 July 1880.

56. PF: LDB vol. 376 (1880), f. 562v, Simeoni to the president of the Association for the Propagation of the Faith in Lyon, 29 October 1880.

father only 27 hours. Since I entered religion the old Rajah has been succeeded by his nephew and of him I know nothing. The uncle was very favourable to the idea of a Catholic mission in Borneo for he found that the Protestant missionaries were not liked by the natives. The Borneans have been described by my brother as being a noble race and I had been told that he uttered when he visited England two years ago "take precise heed with him." I will send by today's

Sister Mary Thais on 30 January 1881 wrote a four-page letter on Borneo to Father Peter Benoit, rector of the Foreign Mission Seminary at Mill Hill. This is page 2.
Source: Archives MHM: BOR-2-a

I have been informed through Father Benedict Mackey that you would be glad of some information about Borneo. My dear Mother, who could have given you so many particulars about the country, died on the 3rd of this month, surviving my father only 27 hours. Since I entered religion [in 1869], the old Rajah [Sir James Brooke] has been succeeded by his nephew, and of him I know nothing. The Uncle was very favourable to the idea of a Catholic Mission in Borneo, for he found that the Protestant Missionaries were not liked by the natives. The Bornese have been described by my brother as being a noble race and I had been told that he wished, when he visited England two years ago, to take priests back with him.

I will send by today's post for my brother's address and, if you wish, will forward it to you with a note from myself in case you desire to communicate with him direct.

My brother has lived in Borneo for about eighteen years and had, when I last heard, one of the first positions in the island but was, I imagine, the only Catholic there.

If it would be of any service, I would try to procure some letters descriptive of the country and people, which were written by my brother when he first landed in Borneo.

She closed her letter begging Father Benoit's blessing.[57] In a second undated but apparently subsequent letter Sister Mary Thais enclosed a portion of a letter received from her brother with his signature: "W. M. Rodway."[58]

The meeting of Cardinal Simeoni, Bishop Vaughan, and Prefect Apostolic Cuarterón, in which responsibility for the prefecture was transferred to Mill Hill, had taken place on 17 January 1880. The letter of Sister Mary Thais Rodway was dated 30 January 1881, one year and two weeks later. Unfortunately Father Rector Benoit had waited too long, a whole year before directing his queries about Borneo to Elizabeth Rodway.

Bishop Vaughan on 15 February 1880 had informed Father Rector Benoit that Propaganda wished to name someone pro-prefect apostolic of Borneo, and he said: "We ought to send" the missionaries to Borneo soon. But a year and a month passed without Vaughan and Benoit agreeing on who should be named prefect apostolic of the Labuan/Borneo mission. Finally Vaughan on 15 March 1881 "took the matter entirely into his own hands and simply submitted Father Jackson's name to *Propaganda*, knowing well that *Propaganda* would do nothing except appoint his nominee." Cardinal Prefect Simeoni did in fact name thirty-four-year-old Father Thomas Jackson of Preston, Lancashire, England, the prefect apostolic on 19 March 1881. This was two years after Jackson had been ordained a priest.

Jackson had worked in the Mill Hill India mission and had also been assigned briefly to Afghanistan. Others assigned to the Labuan prefecture with him were Fathers Edmund Dunn and Aloysius Goossens. They arrived in Kuching, Sarawak, on 10 July 1881. Prefect

---

57. MHFA: BOR-2-a, Sister Mary Thais Rodway to Benoit, 30 January 1881.
58. MHFA: 13-A-3a.

Apostolic Jackson arrived in Labuan in the following month with Father Daniel Kilty. Bishop Vaughan accompanied Jackson's three young assistants from London to Rome, where they were received in audience by Pope Leo XIII. He dedicated their mission to Saint Francis Xavier and to Saint Michael the Archangel.[59]

Three years later the Mill Hill missionaries held a General Chapter which started on 15 August 1884. Prefect Apostolic Jackson was present. Five days before the General Chapter was to begin, Bishop Vaughan sent Cardinal Prefect Simeoni word about it and also presented a report on the work of his missionaries. "The Mission of Borneo is that which claims the most deepfelt sympathy," he said. "It is one of the most difficult missions on earth. . . . Our missionaries are on the Island 3 years now. At present we have 7 missionaries working there. . . . In the interior they have nothing to eat but rice and plants; they never see bread. . . ."

Vaughan also reported that they had opened four schools, that a good number of children had been baptized so far, and that approximately one hundred Chinese had also been baptized. But no progress had been made among the Moslems.[60]

On learning from Vaughan that Prefect Apostolic Jackson was at Mill Hill for the General Chapter, Simeoni in his reply of 20 August 1884 requested Vaughan to ask "the Prefect Apostolic of Labuan and North Borneo who is about to return to his Prefecture, kindly to contact the Vicar Apostolic of Batavia [now Jakarta] on the boundaries of his Borneo Mission."[61] Simeoni was reacting to a letter of 10 June 1884 that he had received from Bishop Adam Carolus Claessens, S.J. In it the Dutch bishop complained that the Mill Hill missionaries "seem to think that they have all of Borneo. But by far the most belongs to the Batavia Vicariate. . . ." Claessens headed the Batavia vicariate.[62]

Jackson wrote to Claessens from London in September 1884 that Cardinal Prefect Simeoni "has manifested his wish that I take up correspondence with Your Grace in order to arrange in a friendly way the question of borders of our respective missions on the island of Borneo. In the decree received from Propaganda containing his own nomination, Jackson said, his mission was called "Prefecture of Labuan and Neighboring Territories in Borneo Island." In letters received from Propaganda, however, he was called: "Prefect Apostolic of Labuan and North Borneo." Regarding a map made by Cuarterón, he said: "I find that the countries of Sarawak and Brunei, as well as a part of northern Borneo together with Labuan and other islands, are marked as belonging to his [Cuarterón's] jurisdiction.

"As Your Grace will see, this is all very vague," Jackson said. "I should like to know how far the jurisdiction of Your Grace extends. During my three-year sojourn in Borneo, I have built stations at Sandakan in the English part of North Borneo, at Labuan, at Bandar

---

59. Rooney, *Khabar Gembira*, 26–28, 30, 32. The words quoted about Vaughan's choosing Jackson are Rooney's.

60. PF: CV vol. 18, f. 449r-450r, Vaughan to Simeoni, 10 August 1884.

61. See PF: LDB vol. 380 (1884), f. 437r, Simeoni to Vaughan, 20 August 1884.

62. See PF: SC Oceania, vol. 15 (1885–86), f. 454r–455v, Claessens to Simeoni, 10 June 1884.

in the country of Brunei, at Kanowit on the banks of the Rejang River, and at Kuching, the capital of Sarawak."[63]

The Borneo mission continued to develop under the Mill Hill missionaries, although they never did reach out to care for New Guinea. In a report written on 4 June 1888, just seven years after his missionaries arrived in what had been Cuarterón's prefecture apostolic, Bishop Vaughan pointed out that his mission currently was staffed by eleven priests, five nuns, and two brothers, who occupied eight mission stations.

Besides Kuching in Sarawak, where Prefect Apostolic Jackson had his residence, there were three other mission stations in Sarawak, three in Brunei, and a foothold had been made in Labuan. At Kuching, capital of Sarawak, there were about one hundred Christians and in the interior at Kanowit (also in Sarawak) there were about one hundred converts. The queen of Sarawak, an English Protestant woman, had become a convert to the Roman Catholic faith in the previous year, Vaughan said.[64] He was undoubtedly referring to the wife of Sir Charles Brooke, the Rajah of Sarawak, who had been most helpful and cooperative from the time of the arrival of the first priests. The Mill Hill Missionaries have continued working in the territory up to the present time.[65]

Don Carlos Cuarterón was dead and buried eleven years already when Cardinal Prefect Simeoni on 23 December 1891 sent surprising news to Bishop Vaughan, superior general of the Mill Hill missionaries. For Vaughan it was like getting a Christmas present. Simeoni said that

> Don Carlos Cuarterón, former Prefect Apostolic of Labuan and Borneo, who died in 1880, had deposited a sum of money with this Sacred Congregation hoping that it would increase gradually, until it could be sufficient for founding a college for his mission.
>
> The said amount together with the interest that has accrued from it up to and including the current year, amounts to Italian Lire 17,665. Since it can hardly be increased to reach the above-mentioned purpose, it was decided to keep it on deposit until it amounts to Lire 25,000, which is the sum required for an endowment making possible the placement of a student in the Urban College [of Propaganda in Rome], who would then be assigned to this same Prefecture.
>
> An alternative decision was to give the interest to some other college or seminary outside of Rome, where expenses are less, for educating a candidate for the Prefecture. . . .

Simeoni therefore wanted to know whether Vaughan wished to receive the interest on the money deposited by Cuarterón, so that he might educate someone at Mill Hill for the Labuan Mission.[66] When Cuarterón in 1855, thirty-six years earlier, had created this fund,

---

63. PF: SC Oceania, vol. 15 (1885–86), f. 620rv, Jackson to Claessens, September 1884.
64. PF: CV vol. 18, f. 463v-464r, Vaughan's Report of 4 June 1888.
65. For further details see Rooney, *Khabar Gembira*.
66. PF: LDB vol. 387 (1891), f. 920v, Simeoni to Vaughan, 23 December 1891.

the amount that he deposited had a much greater purchasing power than when Simeoni wrote to Vaughan about it in 1891.[67]

Vaughan answered on 28 December: "I thank Your Eminence heartily for the proposal made to me in your kind letter . . . regarding the education of a missionary for the Prefecture of Borneo." Since Mill Hill had to provide priests for that mission, Vaughan said, he would be happy to receive "the interest of the fund deposited with Propaganda, that is, the amount of Italian Lire 17,665, in order to provide missionaries for that mission with greater certainty." However, he considered it advisable not to designate a specific person for whom the interest was meant, "because all are being educated for the missions." Nevertheless the superior of the seminary, Vaughan said, must see to it that all advantages from these funds in the form of trained personnel will be allocated "to the Prefecture of the deceased beloved Cuarterón."[68]

Propaganda's Financial Commission met on 29 January 1892 and decided to honor the proposal as formulated by Bishop Vaughan of Salford. Its orders were—until a different decision might be made—that the annual interest on the sum of Lire 17,665, which was the accumulated capital up to and including the entire past year 1891, was to be used for the purpose indicated by Vaughan. The endowment fund was still earning an interest of 5 percent per year, as was the case when Cuarterón had made his original endowment in 1855. Since that time the fund had increased annually by gaining compound interest. The Financial Commission of Cardinals therefore made available to Mill Hill from then onward the annual interest at the rate of 5 percent or Lire 883 and Centesimi 25, beginning on 1 January 1883.[69]

During the month of January 1892, the very month when the Financial Commission made this decision in favor of the Mill Hill missionaries, Bishop Vaughan of Salford was promoted by Pope Leo XIII to the office of third archbishop of Westminster. In the following year he was decorated with the title of cardinal.

Cardinal Prefect Simeoni died in office that same month, on 14 January 1892, two weeks prior to the decision taken by the Financial Commission. He was succeeded in office on 26 January by Cardinal Prefect Mieczyslaw Ledóchowski (1822–1902).

Cardinal Ledóchowski informed Bishop Vaughan on 8 August 1892 about the decision taken by the cardinals regarding "the application of the Cuarterón fund." The interest had been granted to the Mill Hill College, he said, "for the purpose of educating young missionaries for the Prefecture Apostolic of Labuan and Borneo according to the intentions of the Founder."[70]

Cuarterón's dream of contributing toward the training of priests for his Prefecture Apostolic of Labuan at last was realized—as divine providence would have it—in the Foreign Mission Seminary at Mill Hill after his death.

67. On Cuarterón establishing this foundation in 1855, see chap. 15, page 310.
68. PF: CV vol. 18, f. 485r, Vaughan to Simeoni, 28 December 1891.
69. PF: CV vol. 18, f. 486v, Decision of the Financial Commission, 29 January 1892.
70. PF: LDB vol. 388 (1892), f. 504rv, Ledóchowski to Vaughan, 8 August 1892.

Father Rector Benoit died on 28 August 1892. Two months later on 21 October the Mill Hill missionaries were informed that beginning with the end of that year the full amount of Lire 883 and Centesimi 25, the interest earned during 1892 on Cuarterón's fund, would be granted to them for the first time.[71]

Bishop Timoleone Raimondi continued to serve as vicar apostolic until his death in Hong Kong on 27 September 1894 at the age of sixty-seven. In view of his enterprising manner, linguistic talent, robust health, ability to seek and find solutions, and great success in founding the Roman Catholic Church in Hong Kong, one is tempted to wish that he—and not Paolo Reina (1825–61)—had been named the prefect apostolic of Melanesia and Micronesia.

Father Thaddée Supriès was born in 1800 at Cotignac in the Diocese of Fréjus, France. As a young man he joined the Paris Foreign Mission Seminary and worked in the Nicobar Islands near India in the Bay of Bengal. After returning to France to regain his health, he visited the Carthusian monastery, La Grande-Chartreuse, in the French Alps and decided to join the order on 28 June 1838. Later he became retreat master at the Carthusian monastery in Pavia near Milan, Italy, where he inspired seminarians to take up foreign missionary work. These young men became the first candidates of the Milan Foreign Mission Seminary.

Historians have published two different dates for his birth in 1800 (20 and 30 October) and three different dates for his death in 1888 (20 September, 20 October, and 20 November). Father Luc Fauchon, archivist at La Grande-Chartreuse monastery, has supplied vital statistics on Supriès from that monastery's archives. This official record shows that Supriès was born on 20 October 1800 and died on 20 November 1888 at Saint Mary's Carthusian monastery in Mougères, France. This was one month after his eighty-eighth birthday and in the year of his fiftieth anniversary as a Carthusian monk.

Father Giuseppe Marinoni, director of the Foreign Mission Seminary of Milan (P.I.M.E.), wanting to study for the priesthood as a young man, was not accepted by the Carthusians or Pallottines because he was sickly. He was born on 11 October 1810, lived to be eighty years old, and died on 27 January 1891 in Milan.

---

71. See PF: LDB vol. 388 (1892), f. 786rv, Propaganda to Stotter, 21 October 1892.

Father Giovanni Maria Alfieri of the Hospitalers of Saint John of God, born in Milan on 26 March 1807, rendered yeoman service to the Milan Foreign Mission Seminary down through the years. In addition to being procurator in Rome for his own international religious community, he also served as procurator for the Milan group, helping guide Marinoni and his candidates at the same time with his wisdom in their dealings with Rome. Marinoni's priests from Milan were always welcome at Alfieri's monastery on the Island in the Tiber and were given board and lodging. They were also invited, if in Rome, to solemn liturgical celebrations at the monastery. Although elected as superior general of his order in 1862 and reelected in 1872, he continued serving as procurator for his friends in Milan. He died on 3 August 1888 at the age of eighty-one.

Father Peter Benoit, first rector at Mill Hill, died on 28 August 1892 at the age of seventy-one. His Eminence, Herbert Cardinal Vaughan, archbishop of Westminster, founder of Mill Hill, died on 19 June 1903, also at the age of seventy-one. Both men, founders, superiors, and pioneers, are buried in the cemetery of Saint Joseph College on Lawrence Street at Mill Hill in London. They died eleven years apart.

Rose Rodway became a Visitation nun at the age of twenty-six and chose the name of Saint Thais as her religious name. Thais was a famed Greek prostitute who in the early days of Christianity became a saint by giving up her dissolute life, doing penance in the desert and following in the footsteps of Christ. Sister Mary Thais spent sixty-five years as a Visitation nun and was ninety-one years old when she died at Harrow-on-the-Hill convent in 1934. Her religious community remembers her even to this day as being very talented, especially as regards finance and administration. She was still bursar or treasurer "at the age of ninety," her fellow sisters say, "with every detail at her fingertips." She then caught pneumonia and died.

The Spanish *Enciclopedia Vniversal Ilvstrada* says that Don Carlos Cuarterón was born in Cádiz in 1816 and died there in 1880 at the age of sixty-four.

Could Cuarterón, broken in health, have died also of a broken heart? His dream was to found the Roman Catholic Church in the Prefecture Apostolic of Labuan and to ransom Christian Filipino slaves taken there by the Moslems. He interrupted a successful career as a sea captain to study for the priesthood, which he said would better qualify him to attain his new goals. He was a man of vision, courage, and great determination, who sacrificed his life and his fortune out of compassion for his fellow men.

Abbreviations

TO DESIGNATE THE ARCHIVES AT THE INTERNATIONAL HEADQUARTERS OF A RELIGIOUS ORder, the official Latin abbreviation of the order is used, but without periods.

B   Generalate Archives of the Clerics Regular of Saint Paul, usually referred to as Barnabites. Via Giacomo Medici, 15; 00153 Rome, Italy.

CART   Archives at the foundation of the Carthusians at La Grande-Chartreuse, France.

CP   Generalate Archives of the Congregation of the Passion of Jesus Christ, usually referred to as Passionists. Piazza SS. Giovanni e Paolo, 14; 00184 Rome, Italy.
(CP)SS: A subdivision titled "Provincia Spiritus Sancti, Documenta Fundationis Primaevae, 1842, etc."

CSI   Archives of Saint Isidore College (C.S.I.: Collegii Sancti Isidori), Via degli Artisti, 41; 00187 Rome, Italy.

PF   Archives of the Sacred Congregation for the Evangelization of Nations (PF: "de Propaganda Fide," the traditional and often still used title of the Sacred Congregation). Palazzo di Propaganda Fide; Piazza di Spagna, 48; 00187 Rome, Italy.

    PF: Acta: *Acta Sacrae Congregationis*, i.e., the minutes of General Meetings attended by the cardinal members, giving a full report on the issue up for discussion, the decisions reached, and the position taken later by the pope.

    PF: CP: *Congregazioni Particolari*, i.e., the minutes and the documentation used at Particular Meetings, those at which a committee of cardinals studies a particular question.

    PF: LDB: *Lettere e Decreti della Sacra Congregazione e Biglietti di Monsignor Segregatio*, i.e., a verbatim record of practically all letters written by the cardinal prefect and the secretary as well as copies of numerous decrees issued by the Sacred Congregation.

    PF: SC: *Scritture riferite nei Congressi*, i.e., documents of secondary importance discussed at weekly meetings not attended by the full membership of cardinals.

PF: SOCG: *Scritture originali riferite nelle Congregazioni Particulari*, i.e., incoming letters and reports from bishops, missionaries, royalty, government officials, nuncios, minutes of synods, etc., used as a basis for discussion at General Meetings.

PF: SOCP: *Scritture originali riferite nelle Congregazioni Generali*, i.e., incoming letters and reports from bishops, missionaries, royalty, government officials, nuncios, minutes of synods, etc.

PF: Udienze: *Udienze di Nostro Signore*, i.e., requests of a personal or private nature for faculties, indulgences, matrimonial dispensations, etc., brought to the pope's attention by the secretary because granting them exceeded the powers of the cardinal prefect or of the Evangelization Congregation.

PIME   Generalate Archives of the Pontifical Institute for Foreign Missions (P.I.M.E.: Pontificium Institutum pro Missionibus Exteris). Via F. D. Guerrazzi, 11; 00152 Rome, Italy.

SAC   Generalate Archives of the Society of the Catholic Apostolate, called also Pallottines. Piazza Vincenzo Pallotti, 204; 00186 Rome, Italy.

SM   Generalate Archives of the Society of Mary, usually referred to as Marists. Via Alessandro Poerio, 63; 00152 Rome, Italy.

SSCC   Generalate Archives of the Congregation of the Sacred Hearts of Jesus and Mary, often referred to as the Picpus Fathers (SS.CC.: Congregatio Sacrorum, Cordium Iesu et Mariae). Via Rivarone, 85; 00166 Rome, Italy.

+ This symbol is used in SSCC. It is a substitute for 271.788, the Universal Decimal Classification number for the Congregation of the Sacred Hearts of Jesus and Mary (SS. CC.).

Other abbreviations used are:

AMO   Société de Marie, *Annales des missions d'Océanie*, vol. 1. See the listing in the Bibliography.

OM   *Origines maristes (1786–1836)*. See the listing in the Bibliography.

Bibliography

Annales de la propagation de la foi 24. Lyon: Rusand, 1852.

Annali della propagazione della Fede: racolta periodica. Naples, 1853.

Annuario Pontificio per l'Anno 1992. Vatican City: Tipografia Poliglotta Vaticana, 1992.

Bassan, Alfonso. *Da avvocato a patriarca: Cenni biografici di Mons. Angelo Ramazzotti (1800–1861), Fondatore del Pontificio Istituto Missioni Estere, Vescovo di Pavia, Patriarca di Venezia.* 2nd ed. Milan: Editrice Pontificio Istituto Missioni Estere, 1961.

"Beatificationis seu declarationis martyrii Servi Dei Ioannis Baptistae Mazzucconi, sacerdotis Pontificii Instituti pro Missionibus Exteris, in odium Fidei a. 1855 interfecti." In *Acta Apostolicae Sedis* 76 (1984).

Beatificationis seu Declarationis Martyrii Servi Dei Ioannis Baptistae Mazzucconi sacerdotis Pontificii Instituti pro Missionibus Exteris in odium fidei, uti fertur, anno 1855 interfecti Positio super introductione causae et super martyrio ex officio concinnata. Edited by Carlo Suigo. Rome: Sacred Congregation for the Causes of Saints, 1969. [This is the official document prepared on Father Mazzucconi's virtues and martyrdom, which was used as a basis for discussions and decisions leading to his beatification by Pope John Paul II on 19 February 1984.]

Bertolini, Jean. *Missio ad Gentes: Genese de l'envoi missionnaire de notre societe.* Fontes M.S.C., Series 3, Studia Historica, Vol. 1. Rome: Missionari del Sacro Cuore, 1985.

Birt, Henry Norbert. *Benedictine Pioneers in Australia.* Vol. 2. London: Herbert & Daniel, 1911.

Bornemann, Fritz. *Arnold Janssen der Gründer des Steyler Missionswerkes 1837–1909: Ein Lebensbild nach zeitgen'ssischen Quellen.* Verbum Supplementum 12. Rome: Collegio del Verbo Divino, 1969.

———. *Arnold Janssen: Founder of Three Missionary Congregations 1837–1909: A Biography.* Translated by John Vogelgesang. Manila: Arnoldus, 1975.

———. *Der Pfarrer von Neuwerk: Dr. Ludwig von Essen (+1886) und seine Missionspläne.* Studia Instituti Missiologici Societatis Verbi Divini 8. St. Augustin: Steyler, 1967.

Brambilla, Gerardo. *Il pontificio istituto delle missioni estere e le sue missioni: Memorie.* Vol. 1. Milan: Pontificio Istituto delle Missioni Estere, 1940.

Burce, Willard. Letter to author. 12 January 1966.

Burton, Ivor F., and Douglas Woodruff. "Pius IX, Pope." In *New Encyclopaedia Britannica, Macropaedia.* Vol. 14. Chicago: Encyclopaedia Britannica, 1997.

Calendarium Romanum: Ex decreto Sacrosancti Oecumenici Concilii Vaticani II instauratum auctoritate Pauli PP. VI promulgatum. Vatican: Typis Polyglottis Vaticanis, 1969.

Carobbio da Nembro, Metodio. "La Missione Etiopica nel secolo XVIII." In *Sacrae Congregationis de Propaganda Fide Memoria Rerum: 350 Years in the Service of the Missions 1622–1972.* Vol. 2: *1700–1815.* Rome: Herder, 1971.

Centenaire des missions maristes en Océanie (1836–1936). Lyon-Paris: Vitte, 1936.

The Code of Canon Law in English Translation: Prepared by the Canon Law Society of Great Britain and Ireland in Association with the Canon Law Society of Australia and New Zealand and the Canadian Canon Law Society. London: Collins Liturgical Publications, 1983.

Connole, P. F. *Australia and the Near North: The Commonwealth in the Modern World.* Vol. 2. Brisbane: Jacaranda, 1961.

Cuarterón, Carlos. *Spiegazione e Traduzione dei XIV quadri relative alle isole di Salibaboo, Talaor, Sanguey, Nanuse, Mindanao, Celebes, Bornèo, Bahalatolis, Tambisan, Sulu, Toolyan, e Labuan presentati alla Sacra Congregazione de Propaganda Fide nel mese di settembre 1852 dal Capitano D. Carlo Cuarterón e dedicate a Sua Eminenza Reverendissima il Signor Cardinale Giacomo Filippo Fransoni, Prefetto della medesima, coll'appendice di un vocabolario [Italiano,] Malese, Suluano, Tagalese, una tavola di longitudine e di due carte geografiche sopra le Missioni*. Rome: Tipografia della S.C. di Propaganda Fide, 1855. The author found a well-preserved copy of this rare work in the Evangelization Congregation Library, Pontifical Urban University, Rome [Urban University file number: C3n 243].

"Cuarteróni Y Fernandez (Carlos)." In *Enciclopedia Vniversal Ilvstrada Evropeo-Americana*. Vol. 16. Bilbao: Espasa-Calpe, 1923.

Delbos, Georges. *The Mustard Seed: From a French Mission to a Papuan Church 1885–1985*. Port Moresby: Institute of Papua New Guinea Studies, 1985.

Didinger, Johannes. *Bibliotheca Missionum*. Münster: Aachen, 1916.

Dwyer, Eileen. Letter to author. 5 November 1986.

Enciclopedia italiana di scienze, lettere ed arti. Rome: Istituto della Enciclopedia Italiana, 1949.

Encyclopaedia of Papua and New Guinea. Melbourne: Melbourne University Press in association with the University of Papua and New Guinea, 1972.

Encyclopedia Judaica. Vol. 12. Jerusalem: Keter, 1972.

Fauchon, Luc. Letter to author. 23 July 1987.

Fischer, Hermann. *Arnold Janssen Gründer des Steyler Missionswerkes: Ein Lebensbild. Missionsdruckerei*. Netherlands: Steyl, 1919.

———. *Life of Arnold Janssen: Founder of the Society of the Divine Word and of the Missionary Congregation of the Servants of the Holy Ghost*. Translated by Frederick M. Lynk. Techny, IL: Mission Press, S.V.D., 1925.

Fleischmann, M. Letter to author. 11 April 1972.

Foot, William. Letter to author. 20 June 1989.

Freudenthal, Hans W. L. "Kulturkampf." In *New Catholic Encyclopedia*. Vol. 8. New York: McGraw-Hill, 1967.

Frumento, Francesco. Letter to author. 8 October 1985.

Gash, Noel. "Christ Comes to New Guinea." In Paulian Association Lay Missionary Secretariat, *PALMS Post* (Sydney), April 1970.

Gheddo, Piero. *Mazzucconi di Woodlark: Un martire per il nostro tempo*. 2nd ed. Bologna: Editrice Missionaria Italiana, 1984.

Glazik, Josef. "Kirchenorganisatorische Massnahmen im Indonesischen Archipel." In *Sacrae Congregationis de Propaganda Fide Memoria Rerum 1622–1972*. Vol. 3: *1815–1972*. Freiburg: Herder, 1975.

Guida delle Missioni Cattoliche. Rome: Unione Missionaria del Ciero in Italia, 1935.

Harney, Robert Forest. "Rossi, Pellegrino." *New Catholic Encyclopedia*. Vol. 12. New York: McGraw-Hill, 1967.

Heide, Hermann auf der. *Die Missionsgenossenschaft von Steyl: Ein Bild der ersten 25 Jahre ihres Bestehens*. Kaldenkirchen: Verlag der Missionsdruckerei in Steyl, 1900.

Hilliard, David Lockhart. *God's Gentlemen: A History of the Melanesian Mission 1849–1942*. St. Lucia, Queensland: University of Queensland Press, 1978.

Hosie, John. *The French Mission: An Australian Base for the Marists in the Pacific to 1874*. M.A. thesis, Macquarrie University, 1971.

Ius Pontificium de Propaganda Fide. Pars Secunda. Vol. 6, Part 2.

Jaspers, Reiner. *Die Missionarische Erschliessung Ozeaniens: Ein quellengeschichtlicher und missionsgeographischer Versuch zur kirchlichen Gebietsaufteilung in Ozeanien bis 1855*. Münster: Missionswissenschaftliche Abhandlungen und Texte, 1972.

Kefalidis, Yorgi. Letter to author. 14 May 1989.

Keys, Lillian G. *The Life and Times of Bishop Pompallier*. Christchurch: Pegasus, 1957.

Kimmel, Gerhard. Telephone conversation with author. 17 November 1986.

Kowalsky, Nicolas. *Serie dei cardinali prefetti e dei segretari della Sacra Congregazione "de Propaganda Fide."* Rome: Urbanianae, 1962.

Laracy, Eugénie, and Hugh Laracy. *The Italians in New Zealand and Other Studies*. Auckland: The Society Dante Alighieri, 1973.

Laracy, Hugh M. "The First Mission to Tikopia." *Journal of Pacific History* 4 (1969) 105–9.

———. "Italians on the Pacific Frontier." In *The Italians in New Zealand and Other Studies*. Auckland: Society of Dante Aligheri, 1973.

———. *Marists and Melanesians: A History of Catholic Missions in the Solomon Islands*. Canberra: Australian National University Press, 1976.

———. "Roman Catholic 'Martyrs' in the South Pacific, 1841–55." *Journal of Religious History* 9 (1976–77) 189–202.

"The Late Shipwreck and Murder in the South Seas." *The Sydney Morning Herald*, 18 June 1856.

"Laughlan." *Salem Observer*, 9 May 1846, pp. 2–3. In *American Activities in the Central Pacific 1790–1870: A History, Geography and Ethnography Pertaining to American Involvement and Americans in the Pacific Taken from Contemporary Newspapers, etc.* Vol. 4, pp. 8–11. Edited by R. Gerard Ward. Ridgewood, NJ: Gregg, 1966.

Lessard, Gaston. Fax transmission to author. 18 October 1994.

Leslie, Shane, editor. *Letters of Herbert Cardinal Vaughan to Lady Herbert of Lea 1867 to 1903*. London: Burns & Oates, 1942.

"Letter to the Editor." *The Sydney Morning Herald*, 22 January 1856.

"Litterae Apostolicae in forma Brevis, quibus permittitur ut Petrus Aloisius Maria Chanel nuncupetur nomine Beati, eiusque reliquiae publicae venerationi proponantur." In *Acta Sanctae Sedis* 22 (1889–90).

Lloyd's Register of British and Foreign Shipping: 1855, 1856. London: Gregg, 1856.

"Loss of the Brig *Gazelle*, and Murder of Her Crew by the Natives of Woodlark Island." *The Sydney Morning Herald*, 14 June 1856.

"The Loss of the Sailing Vessel *Gazelle* . . ." *The Sydney Morning Herald*, 15 June 1856. [This report is an extract from the log of the *Favorite* and is signed by "Missionary E. (sic) Raimondi, Captain A. Barrack, Mate J. Bennett."]

"The Lost Missionary." *The Empire* (Sydney, January 1856 [exact date unknown]). The letter itself was dated 17 January.

Love, Lyn. Letter to author. 23 September 1988.

MacKenzie, Iain. Letter to author. 22 May 1989.

Maestrini, Nicholas. *Mazzucconi of Woodlark: Biography of Blessed John Mazzucconi, Priest and Martyr, of the P.I.M.E. Missionaries*. Hong Kong: Catholic Truth Society, [1983?].

Manuel des cérémonies romaines: tiré des livres romains les plus authentiques, et des écrivains les plus récens et les plus intelligens en cette matière. New and expanded ed. Avignon: Fischer-Joly, 1840.

Mansi, Ioannes Dominicus. *Sacrorum Conciliorum Nova et Amplissima Collectio. . . .* vol. 50. Paris: Welter, 1924.

Margiotti, Fortunato. "La Cina cattolica al traguardo della maturita." In *Sacrae Congregationis de Propaganda Fide Memoria Rerum 1622–1972*. Vol. 3: *1815–1972*. Freiburg: Herder, 1975.

Marinoni, Giuseppe. *Scritti vari del defunto Mons. Giuseppe Marinoni*. Edited by Giacomo Scurati. Milan: Tipografia Pontificia di S. Giuseppe, 1892.

Mazzucconi, Giovanni. *Scritti del Servo di Dio: P. Giovanni Mazzucconi*. Edited by Carlo Suigo. Milan: Pontificio Istituto Missioni Estere, 1965. [This critical edition of the writings of Father Mazzucconi lists chronologically all his letters known to exist as well as other writings.]

McCormack, Arthur. *Cardinal Vaughan: The Life of the Third Archbishop of Westminster, Founder of St. Joseph's Missionary Society, Mill Hill*. London: Burns & Oates, 1966.

McGrath, John Joseph. "Faculties (Canon Law)." In *New Catholic Encyclopedia*. New York: McGraw-Hill, 1967

Metzler, Josef. Letter to author. 17 November 1987.

———. "Präfekten und Sekretäre der Kongregation im Zeitalter der neueren Missionsära (1818-1918)." *Sacrae Congregationis de Propaganda Fide memoria rerum 1622-1972*. Vol. 3: *1815-1972*. Freiburg: Herder, 1975.

Mihalic, Francis. *Grammar and Dictionary of Neo-Melanesian*. Techny, IL: Mission Press, 1957.

Miller, Luther S. "History of U.S. Railroads." In *The Encyclopedia Americana*, 23:163-69. International ed. New York: Americana, 1979.

Molsen, Kaethe. "Godeffroy, Überseekaufleute und Reeder." In *Neue Deutsche Biographie*. Vol. 6. Berlin: Duncker & Humblot, 1964.

Monti, Antonio. "Le cinque giornate di Milano." *Enciclopedia italiana di scienze, lettere ed arti*.

Moors, Theodorus Hubertus. Letter to author. 10 August 1989.

"Murder Will Out." *The Empire* (Sydney), 10 June 1856.

National Geographic Atlas of the World. Washington, DC: National Geographic Society, 1963.

New Catholic Encyclopedia. New York: McGraw-Hill, 1967

New Encyclopedia Britannica, Macropedia. Chicago: Encyclopedia Brittanica, 1974.

"Notes of a Cruise to Woodlark Island by *H.M.S. Iris*." *Sydney Morning Herald*, 7 September 1858.

Notizie sull'istituzione del Seminario delle Missioni Estere eretto dai Rev. Vescovi di Lombardia nel 1850: Partenza e prime lettere dei missionari giunti in Oceania. Milan: Boniardi-Pogliani, 1853. [The only copy of this 142-page book known to exist is in PIME: vol. 11 (Oceania)].

Österreichisches Biographisches Lexikon 1815–1950. Graz: Bohlaus, 1954.

O'Farrell, Patrick. *The Catholic Church in Australia: A Short History, 1788–1967*. Sydney: Nelson, 1968.

Origines maristes (1786–1836). Edited by J. Coste and G. Lessard. Vol. 3: *De la controverse . . . l'histoire apres la dèmission du P. Colin*. Rome: Fontes historici Societatis Mariae, 1965.

Origines Maristes, 1786–1836. Vol. 4: *Compléments et index*. Edited by J. Coste and G. Lessard. Rome: Fontes Historici Societatis Mariae, 1967.

Pacific Islands Year Book and Who's Who. 9th ed. Sydney: Pacific Publications, 1963.

"Pavia." *New Encyclopaedia Britannica, Micropaedia*. Vol. 7. Chicago: Encyclopaedia Britannica, 1997.

Petermanns Geographische Mitteilungen. Gotha, 1862.

Pirri, Pietro. "Pio IX, Papa." *Enciclopedia Cattolica*. Vol. 9, pp. 1510-23. Vatican City: Ente per l'Enciclopedia cattolica e per il Libro cattolico, 1954.

Quinn, A. James. "Faculties, Decennial." In *New Catholic Encyclopedia*. New York: McGraw-Hill, 1967.

———. Faculties, Quinquennial." In *New Catholic Encyclopedia*. New York: McGraw-Hill, 1967.

"Radetzky, Joseph, Graf." *New Encyclopaedia Britannica Micropaedia*, 8:372-73. Chicago: Encyclopaedia Britannica, 1997.

Rodolico, Niccolò. "Carlo Alberto." *Enciclopedia italiana*, 9:59-62.

Rodriguez, Isacio. Letter to author. 20 March 1972.

Rooney, John. *Khabar Gembira (The Good News): History of the Catholic Church in East Malaysia and Brunei (1880–1976)*. London: Burns & Oates, 1981.

Roussel, René. *Un précurseur: Monseigneur Luquet (1810–1858) des missions étrangères de Paris*. Langres: Société Historique et Archéologique, 1960.

Scurati, Giacomo. *Memorie dell'Istituto*. Unpublished manuscript in Rome: Archivo Generale Pontificio Istituto Missioni Estere, Archivio Missioni Estere, 35.

———. "Memoria del Sacerdote di Lecco, Antonio Riva, Missionario Apostolico a Labuan, poi ad Hong-Kong." Rome: Archivo Generale Pontificio Istituto Missioni Estere, Archivio Missioni Estere (Vol. 35:04) 1–37.

The Shipping Gazette and Sydney General Trade List. Various dates. Apollo Bay, Victoria: W. & F. Pascoe, 1844–60.

Souter, Gavin. *New Guinea: The Last Unknown*. Sydney: Angus and Robertson, 1964.

Steel, Lexie. Letter to author. 16 March 1989

Strong, William E. *The Story of the American Board: An Account of the First Hundred Years of the American Board of Commissioners for Foreign Missions*. Boston: Pilgrim, 1910.

Stuart, Ian. "They Didn't Push Their Way in—They Walked Softly." In *Post Courier* (Port Moresby, Papua New Guinea), 7 August 1975.

Suarez, Restituto. Letter to author. 7 April 1972.

Suigo, Carlo. *Pio IX e la fondazione del primo instituto missionario Italiano a Milano*. Rome: Direzione Generale Pontificio Istituto Missioni Estere, 1976.

Testore, Celestino. "Perrone, Giovanni." In *Enciclopedia Cattolica*. Vol. 9. Vatican: Ente per l'Enciclopedia cattolica e per il Libro cattolico, 1949–54.

Tragella, Giovanni B. *Le missioni estere di Milano nel quadro degli avvenimenti contemporanei*. Vol. 1. Milano: Pontificio Instituo Missioni estere, 1950.

"Urbiztondo y Eguía." In *Enciclopedia Vniversal Ilvstrada Evropeo-Americana*. Vol. 65. Madrid: Espasa-Calpe.

Van der Veur, Paul W. "Dutch New Guinea." In *Encyclopaedia of Papua and New Guinea*. Vol. 1. Melbourne: Melbourne University Press in association with the University of Papua and New Guinea, 1972.

Verguet, C. M. Léopold. *Histoire de la première mission catholique au vicariat de Mélanésie*. Carcassonne: Labau, 1854.

"Wallace, Alfred Russell," in *The New Encyclopaedia Britannica, Macropaedia*. Vol. 19.

Walsh, Augustine Thomas. "Trinitarians." *New Catholic Encyclopedia*. Vol. 14. New York: McGraw-Hill, 1967.

Ward, Gerald R., ed. *American Activities in the Central Pacific 1790–1870: A History, Geography and Ethnography Pertaining to American Involvement and Americans in the Pacific Taken from Contemporary Newspapers, etc*. Vol. 4. Ridgewood, NJ: Gregg, 1966.

Willeke, Bernward (sic) H. "Die Propagandakongregation und die Erneuerung der japanischen Kirche (1800–1922)." In *Sacrae Congregationis de Propaganda Fide Memoria Rerum 1622-1972*. Vol. 3. *1815–1972*. Freiburg: Herder, 1975.

Willett, B.M. *Philips' Modern School Atlas*. Birmingham: Philips, 1986.

Wiltgen, Ralph M. *The Founding of the Roman Catholic Church in Oceania: 1825 to 1850*. Canberra: Australian National University Press, 1979.

"The Woodlark Murders." *The Empire* (Sydney), 24 June 1856.

"Wreck of the Brig *Gazelle*, and Horrible Massacre of All on Board." *The Empire* (Sydney), 14 June 1856.

Index

NUMBERS IN *ITALICS*
INDICATE FIGURES.

Act of Foundation of the
    Seminary of Foreign
    Missions, 54–55
Adames, Nikolaus, 509
Afghanistan, Mill Hill
    missionaries assigned
    to, 535
Alexander VII
Alfieri, Giovanni Maria, 65
    accepting office of
    procurator for
    Marinoni's Institute of
    Foreign Missions, 279
    advising Marinoni
    on relations with
    Propaganda Fide, 337
    criticizing Marinoni
    for questions about
    Cuarterón's plans,
    280–81
    death of, 426–27, 548
    designating successor for
    himself in Rome, 323
    introducing Calderon's
    missionaries in Rome,
    284–85
    learning of Milan
    missionaries' return to
    Sydney, 307–8
    at meeting regarding
    Cuarterón's
    "Description of a New
    Mission," 296

Alfieri, Giovanni Maria (*cont.*)
    realizing troubles facing
    Reina and his men, 302
    reiterating request to
    Marinoni for two
    priests for Cuarterón,
    281–82
    reporting on meeting
    with Fransoni
    regarding desire for
    more missionaries in
    Oceania, 195–96
Alfonso XII, 529
Ambrosi, Luigi, 346–47, 361–
    62, 368, 370, 371
    assigned dual role of
    prefect and procurator
    for Hong Kong, 376–77
    authorized to open
    subsidiary procure in
    Shanghai, 386
    complimenting Reina and
    Raimondi's work in
    Hong Kong, 398
    death of, 427
    experience of, as Hong
    Kong procure, 378–80
    explaining to Reina reasons
    for Milan missionaries'
    transfer to Hong Kong,
    389–90
    leaving significant debt
    behind, 490

Ambrosi, Luigi (*continued*)
    meeting Reina in Hong
    Kong, 389
    need for nuns at Hong
    Kong, 404–5
    opinions on moving an
    office to Shanghai, 377
    preparing Reina for office
    of vice prefect, 402
    requesting additional
    personnel for Hong
    Kong, 390, 402
    sending Raimondi to
    search for English-
    speaking brothers for
    Hong Kong schools,
    486
Ambrosoli, Angelo, 74
    assigned to convent at
    Wooloomooloo, 325
    believing Australia would
    be suitable field
    for Milan Mission
    Seminary, 363–64
    confusion over role of,
    347–49
    drawing maps of Rooke
    and Woodlark, 143
    fearing responsibility
    and results of more
    missionary work in
    Melanesia, 349–50
    going to Rooke, 153

Ambrosoli, Angelo (*continued*)
  illness of, 199, 211, 217–18, 325–26
  named as missionary apostolic for Oceania, 91
  unsure of Milan missionaries' destination after Sydney, 325
American Board of Commissioners for Foreign Missions, 148, 469–70, 471
Angelini, Cavaliere, 526
Angelini, Enrico, 528, 536, 540
Anliard, Jean-Baptiste, 39, 44–45
Anliard, Michel, 40, 44
Annals of the Propagation of the Faith, 7
Anzer, John Baptist, 519
Apia, 449, 451, 460, 471, 473
Aragón, Juan Bautista, 386
Ascension Island. *See* Ponape
Association for the Propagation of the Faith, 54, 58, 74, 76–78, 97, 101, 144–45, 161, 163, 283, 315, 319, 446, 464, 538
Auckland, Diocese of, 530–31
Augustinians (Order of Saint Augustine [O.S.A.]), 330
Australia
  gold rush in, 140–41
  as potential mission field for Milan Mission Seminary, 363–64

Bagust, H., 254
Balabac Island, 355, 420
Balbi, Adriano, 57
baptism
  of first wives, among local people, 124

baptism (*continued*)
  of infants, 81, 120–21, 124
Barambangan, Cuarterón seeking approval to open mission in, 345–46
Barff, Charles, 468–69
Barili, Lorenzo, 415–16, 421–22
Barnabites (Clerics Regular of Saint Paul [C.R.S.P.]), 49
Barnabò, Alessandro
  apprising Pius IX of situation with New Caledonia and Navigators vicariates, 41–42
  approving additional personnel for Hong Kong, 402–3
  approving of Cuarterón's plan for redeeming Christian slaves, 415–16
  audiences with Bataillon over difficulties with Elloy, 454–55
  clarifying roles of personnel in Hong Kong, 394–97
  confirming proposal to separate Navigators Archipelago from Central Oceania vicariate, 457–58
  death of, 467, 499
  demanding deference and submission from missionaries, 396–97, 399
  in discussions regarding New Caledonia, 34
  giving Cuarterón order to expel Riva and Borgazzi, 417–25

Barnabò, Alessandro (*cont.*)
  granting Cuarterón official approval for his work, 300–301
  having little respect for Marinoni, 286–87, 288
  ill health of, 446, 465
  instructing Bataillon to give Elloy full powers for missions, 443
  issuing faculties to Montrouzier, 121–23
  letters to Favre and Elloy regarding opportunities in Micronesia and New Hebrides, 446
  as mastermind of Propaganda Fide, 165
  named cardinal and prefect of Propaganda Fide, 322–23
  offering Micronesia-Melanesia to Picpus Fathers, 462, 463–67
  promising full cooperation with Lombard seminary, 46
  receiving memorandum regarding mission seminary, 29
  reorganizing New Caledonia, Samoa, and Central Oceania vicariates, 67
  response to Cuarterón's reports about Riva and Borgazzi, 419–20
  responsible for document on missionary activity for First Vatican Council, 435
  stating Propaganda Fide's refusal to help Oceania missionaries, 291
  summoning Bataillon to Rome, 437, 447

Barnabò, Alessandro (*cont.*)
    summoning Favre to Rome regarding Bataillon and Elloy, 455–57
    working on reorganizing Labuan mission, 495–97
Barrack, A., 241–44, 246, 248, 251, 252, 256–58
Bataillon, Pierre, 32, 317, 429
    advice for Reina on choice of missions, 133–37
    audiences with Barnabò, 454–55
    in charge of Central Oceania vicariate until his death, 43
    complaining about Elloy and Pompallier, 431–33
    complaints about, 434–35, 438–40
    death of, 428, 483
    desiring to have Milan missionaries in Fiji, 226
    dispute with Elloy over mission territory in Central Oceania vicariate, 431–58
    Douarre recommending, to lead Navigators Islands mission, 37–38, 39
    glowing report of, on success in his Central Oceania vicariate (1875), 482–83
    meeting missionaries on arrival in Australia, 112
    on naming a vicar apostolic for Navigators Archipelago, 42–43
    recommending splitting off Fiji Islands from Central Oceania vicariate, 43
    "Report on Oceania for Propaganda," 459–60

Bataillon, Pierre (*continued*)
    reporting movement toward Catholicism in Navigators and Fiji archipelagoes, 84
    returning to Rome, 453
    seeking priests for Fiji, 131
    soliciting services of Reina and his missionaries, 319
    suggesting that Elloy be named vicar apostolic of Micronesia, 440
    suggesting that Fiji be cut from Central Oceania vicariate, 133
    transferring headquarters to Navigators Archipelago, 40–41
    as vicar apostolic of Central Oceania, 429–31
    working with Favre on resolution of Central Oceania vicariate issue, 457
Bay of Gaya mission, reopened in 1876, 523
Bedini, Gaetano, 349, 416
Belcher, Sir Edward, 276–77
Benaglia, Gaetano, 12
Benedict XIV, 129
Benoit, Peter, 489, 529–32, 543, 547, 548
Beretta, Pompeo, 10, 13–14
Bergillon, Optat, 60–61
Bernin, Claude-Marie, 32–33, 120n19
Bertani, Father, 49
Bertinelli, Raffaele, 24, 29–30, 193–94, 375
Besi, Lodovico, 161–62, 369, 370–71, 381–82, 385–86
Beurel, J. M., 330
Biffi, Eugenio, 288
Bingham, Hiram, Jr., 470

Bismarck, Otto von, 505–6
Blair, Captain, 203–4, 207, 208
Bofondi, Giuseppe, 15n30
Bolis, Carlo, 323
Borgazzi, Ignazio, 145, 265, 282–85, 293
    arrival in Labuan, 343
    arrival in Manila, 330
    Cuarterón's displeasure with, 417–18
    Cuarterón's instructions to, upon submitting his resignation, 413, 414
    delayed departure from Rome, 303
    esteem held for Cuarterón, 314
    expelled from mission, 421–25
    farewell audience with Pius IX, 302–3
    looking forward to Labuan mission, 346
    on preparations for leaving Cádiz, 320–21
    reporting on territory of Cuarterón's prefecture apostolic, 297
    reporting to Marinoni on Cuarterón's conversation with Barnabò about the Melanesia missions, 291
    transferred to Hong Kong, 423
    visiting Riva on alternate months, 409
    writing to Reina about Cuarterón's financial difficulties, 410
Borneo, 293, 296–97, 492
    Cuarterón, Riva, and Raimondi traveling to, 345–46
    Cuarterón attracted to, 276–77

Borneo (*continued*)
  establishment of mission at, 358
  mission of, developing under Mill Hill missionaries, 545
  mission at Barambang attacked, 412–13
  penal colony of, 495–96
  as stepping-stone for New Guinea, 531
  success of mission in, 407
Borromeo, Charles, 301
Boucho, Jean-Baptiste, 273
Bousquet, Marcellin, 463–65
Bravi, Giuseppe Maria, 56
Brooke, Charles, 526–27
Brooke, James, 293, 525
Brothers of the Christian Schools (F.S.C.), 512
Brown, George, 470
Brown, Lydia, 470
Brunei, 492
Brunelli, Giovanni, 7, 16, 115, 272, 274, 275–76
  meeting regarding Cuarterón's "Description of a New Mission," 296
  named as cardinal and appointed to head up Propaganda Fide, 279
Buffa, Francesco, 370, 379, 385, 404
Buratti, Clemente Maria, 7, 8, 281, 286–87
Burghignoli, Giuseppe, 404–5, 503, 515, 517, 519
Burrueco, Diego, 300, 328
  death of, 427
  expressing Rome's desire to transfer Melanesia missionaries to Hong Kong, 381

Burrueco, Diego (*continued*)
  resigning as procurator for Foreign Mission Seminary of Milan, 386
  volunteering to substitute for Alfieri in Rome, 323–24, 328

Caccia, Carlo, 187n40
Candiani, Carlo, 282
Cani, Giovanni, 537–38
cannibalism, 177, 178
Canossian Daughters of Charity (F.d.C.C.), 404–5
Caret, François-d'Assise, 129
Carew, Patrick Joseph, 192, 197, 280
Caroline Islands, 50, 469, 470
Carthusians, Order of, 3
Cassinelli, Vincenzo, 10, 13, 57
Castro, Don Rafael, 330–31
catechists, role of, in Oceania, 159
catechumens, methods for receiving, 124
Caterini, Prospero, 124–25, 127, 164
Catholic Catechism, The, 444
Cazalis, E., 44
Celebes Sea, Cuarterón's desire to spread Catholic Church through, 268, 270–72
Central Oceania vicariate
  conditions in (1852), 42–43
  consolidated after deaths of Bataillon and Elloy, 484
  as easier first mission for Milan missionaries, 89, 93–94
Certosa di Pavia, 3–5
Ceylon (Sri Lanka)
  mission at, 13, 61–62

Ceylon (Sri Lanka) (*continued*)
  urgently requesting missionaries (1850), 56–57
Chanel, Pierre, 261
Charles Albert, King, 19, 20
Chester, Henry M., 469
Cipolletti, Tommaso-Giacinto, 123
circumcision, on Rooke Island, 177
Claessens, Adam Carolus, 544
Clerics Regular of Saint Paul (C.R.S.P.). *See* Barnabites
Coffey, James, 254
Colin, Jean-Claude, 5–6, 16, 59
  arguing against allowing Douarre to resign as New Caledonia vicar apostolic, 45
  attempts of, to unburned Marists of Micronesia and Melanesia, 100
  death of, 483
  on designating prefects apostolic for Melanesia and Micronesia, 67–68
  fearing conflict between missionaries at Woodlark, 151
  happy at Marists' ending responsibility for Micronesia and Melanesia, 109
  letter to Frémont about staying in Woodlark, 106–7
  on Marists' training of new missionaries, 83–84
  resigning as superior general, 190, 191
  resolving issue of leadership in Navigators Archipelago and New Caledonia, 38

Colin, Jean-Claude (*continued*)
  responding to difficulties at Melanesia, 61
  responding to request for information on Micronesia and Melanesia, 65–66
  sending no more missionaries to Oceania, 136
  subdelegating choices of prefects apostolic, 72–73, 80
  supporting Douarre's desire to retain leadership in New Caledonia, 41–42
  trying to exonerate himself and Marists of responsibility for Micronesia, 72–73
  wishes of, for Milan missionaries before their departure, 98–100
  writing after attack on New Caledonia, 33
Collegio di San Calocero, 64. *See also* Lombardy Seminary for Foreign Missions
Collomb, Jean-George, 18, 33, 71, 83, 183, 200, 214
Company of Saint Francis Xavier, 10
Compendio di geografia (Balbi), 57
confessions, subdelegating faculties for, 126
Congregational Church, 148, 352, 368, 369
Congregation of the Immaculate Heart of Mary [C.I.C.M.], 502
Congregation of the Missionary Oblates of Rho, 20, 53
Congregation of Oblates of Saints Ambrose and Charles, 23
Congregation for the Propagation of the Faith. *See* Propaganda Fide
Congregation of the Sacred Hearts of Jesus and Mary (SS.CC.). *See* Picpus Fathers
Convention of Chuenpi, 367
Corfu, need for missionaries in, 67, 69, 70, 75, 167, 194
Corti, Giovanni, 193, 375–76
Corti, Giuseppe, 97, 185n35,
  death of, 210–11, 236
  going to Rooke, 153
  illness of, 199
Coste, Jean, 478
Crimean War, 204
Cuartéron, Don Carlos, 265, 490–91
  activities in Cádiz, Madrid, and London, 272–77
  activities in Rome, 277–82
  activities in the Talaor Archipelago, 270–71
  arrival in Manila, 330–31
  arrival in Rome (1879), 537–40
  arrival in Singapore, 387
  article from *Enciclopedia Universal Ilustrada*, 266
  attracted to missionary work with Filipino slaves, 407
  beginning studies for the priesthood, 278
  believing he'll be stripped of his title, 528–29
  carrying Propaganda Fide's plans for Reina and his missionaries, 313–14

Cuartéron, Don Carlos (*cont.*)
  changing attitude toward Milan missionaries, 354
  concerns about Reina's health and requesting more missionaries, 334
  death of, 540, 548
  delayed in leaving for Labuan, 340
  "Description of a New Mission," 292, 294, 296
  desiring to open mission in Salibaboo, 267, 276
  desiring to train missionaries as sailors, 335
  devoting life and wealth to redemption of captives, 268–69
  discovering treasure, 267
  disturbed by Reina's transfer to Hong Kong, 364–65
  early work as sailor, 267
  endowment left by, 540–41, 545–46
  on expanding missions in west-to-east fashion, 313, 315
  expelling Riva and Borgazzi from mission, 421–25
  experiencing financial difficulties, 353–54, 409–10, 423
  Explanation and Translation of XIV Reports . . ., 297–98
  eyeing Sulu Archipelago as source for mission, 276
  faith of, in ultimate success of Milan missionaries, 299
  farewell audience with Pius IX, 302–3
  founding his own seminary in Rome, 300

Cuartéron, Don Carlos (*cont.*)
  "Fourteen Reports" document on possible locations for missions, 277
  instilling fear in local peoples, 354
  involving the chiefs in order to do mission work among savages, 314–15
  leaving Rome, 303
  making plans for Reina's new mission in northwest New Guinea, 360–61
  meeting Reina in Manila, 324–25, 333
  meeting staff of Propaganda Fide, 277
  mission experience of, 293
  offered services of Milan missionaries, 279–81
  optimistic about circumstances for Oceania missions, 312–13
  origins of, 305n
  plan for his keeping Labuan and Spanish parts of his prefecture, 533–34
  plans for ransoming Filipino slaves, 407, 414–16
  plans for Western Oceania, 283–84
  praise for Riva and Borgazzi, 289
  preparing to leave for new mission as Rooke and Woodlark missionaries were leaving, 295
  presuming that Mill Hill missionaries were given Labuan, 537

Cuartéron, Don Carlos (*cont.*)
  project for the Christianization of Labuan and Borneo, 414–16, 421–22
  providing financially for present and future mission needs, 310
  providing support for his missionaries, 293–94
  purchasing English schooner to use in missions work, 340–41
  purchasing two cutters for river travel, 332–33
  Raimondi's impressions of, 337
  recommended to take interest in mission of Micronesia and Melanesia, 300–301
  report on occasion of twenty years in Labuan, 526–28
  requesting new missionaries for Reina, 347
  requesting to fly the papal flag, 268, 269
  responding to attack at Borneo mission, 412–13
  responding to conditions of Milan missionaries in Melanesia, 290–91
  Riva and Borgazzi assigned to, 282–85
  Sacred Congregation's attempt to persuade Cuarterón to come to Rome, 535–37
  searching for reasons for change in personnel to Hong Kong, 391–92
  seeking personnel for, 522–23, 526

Cuartéron, Don Carlos (*cont.*)
  spending much time outside his own territory, 408–9
  submitting resignations, 411–12, 537–38
  suggesting mission for Island of Labuan and northwest coast of Borneo, 292
  travel plans, after meeting Reina in Manila, 333–34
  voyages and projects of, 267–72
  wanting to spread church through the Celebes Sea, 268, 270–72
Cuarterón, Manuel, 321, 354, 409, 410, 417
Cuarterón, Nicolás Fernández, 540
Cullen, Paul, 497, 498, 513–14
Curti, Angelo, 145

d'Albertis, Luigi Maria, 469
Dalmagne (Captain), 80, 81, 82, 141, 143, 144, 148–49, 170, 208, 216–17, 219, 224, 227, 242, 364, 393
Darwin, Charles Robert, 362
Davies, M., 102, 103, 104, 105–6
Davis, Henry Charles, 112
de Arrazola, Lorenzo, 274
de Briel, Charles, 538
de Castro, Don Ignazio, 320
de Jessé, Antoine, 78, 101
de Mazenod, Eugène, 14, 50
Devoti, Giovanni, 189
Dezza, Gaspare, 405
di Pietro, Camillo, 512–15
Divine Word Missionaries (Society of the Divine Word [S.V.D.]), 519–21

Djailolo Passage, 314–15
Donaldson, Colonial Secretary, 256
Dordillon, Ildefonse-René, 464
Dorei
    Cuarterón's choice for relaunching Micronesia-Melanesia mission, 363
    Protestant missionaries sent to, 352
Douarre, Guillaume, 16
    death of, 45
    desire to resign as New Caledonia vicar apostolic, 45
    desiring new mission after attack at New Caledonia, 32–33
    desiring to open mission at Tikopia, 39–40
    leadership roles in New Caledonia and Navigators Archipelago, 38–39
    named first vicar apostolic for Navigators Islands, 34–35
    named first vicar apostolic for New Caledonia, 32
    on possibility of mission expanding to Micronesia and Melanesia, 33–34
    preparing for Isle of Pines mission, 36
    request for reassignment to New Caledonia, 36–38
Ducrettet, Eugène-Joseph, 60
Dunn, Edmund, 543–44

Eastern Oceania, Vicariate Apostolic of, divided into three vicariates apostolic, 463
Elloy, Louis-André
    administration of Navigators Archipelago given to, 457
    arriving in Sydney prepared to take over Central Oceania Vicariate and Navigators Archipelago, 444–45
    death of, 484
    dispute with Bataillon over mission territory in Central Oceania vicariate, 431–58
    on need for universal catechism, 473, 474
    petitioning Franchi for involvement in Gilbert archipelago and the Carolines, 473–75, 481
    as pro-vicar apostolic for Navigators Archipelago, 460–61
    reasons for leaving Central Oceania vicariate, 433
    requesting assignment to Gilbert or Kingsmill Islands, 433–34, 450–51
    requesting faculties from Rome to conduct work of the Central Oceania mission, 445
    requesting jurisdiction over Tokelau Islands, 468
    rise of, in Central Oceania vicariate, 429–30
    speaking at Vatican Council on universal catechism, 438
    succeeding Bataillon as vicar apostolic of Central Oceania, 483–84
Epalle, Jean-Baptiste, 14, 50, 66, 115, 153, 440
Errington, George, 104
European commerce, potential influence of, 213
Explanation and Translation of XIV Reports . . . (Cuarterón), 297–98
Eymard, Pierre-Julien, 5–6, 63n6

faculties
    for dealing with local marriages, 124, 128–29
    Frémont's request for, 125–26, 164
    granted to Mazzucconi, 114
    granted to Reina, 114–18
    granted to Salerio, 117
    granted to Vaughn, to present students for ordination, 488
    Marinoni requesting for Milan missionaries, 114–16
    Marinoni's request for, 126–27
    Montrouzier's request for, 120, 121, 123, 129
    subdelegated by Reina, 118
Faré, Paolo, 10, 13–14
Fatati, Giuseppe Gaspare, 120
Faurie, Louis-Simon, 517
Favini, Gaetano, 403
Favre, Julien, 191, 437
    approached about Marists taking over Melanesia and Micronesia, 465
    explaining why Marists had left the Micronesia-Melanesia missions, 478–79
    involvement of, in turning down Elloy's request for extending his jurisdiction, 475–76, 481–82

Favre, Julien (*continued*)
   on opportunities in Solomon Islands and Micronesia, 452
   proposal of, for successors to Bataillon and Elloy, 484
   summoned to Rome regarding Bataillon and Elloy, 455–57
   Superior General, reporting complaints about Bataillon, 434–35, 436, 454
   working with Bataillon on resolution of Central Oceania vicariate issue, 457
feast days, 125
Feliciani, Antonio, 267, 268–70, 273–76, 367–69, 371, 427
Ferdinand I, 14
Ferdinand II, 28–29
Ferretti, Gabriele, 294, 296
Fiji
   assigned as prefecture apostolic, 43
   Bataillon's suggestion for dividing, 106
   Bataillon's desire to have Milan missionaries in, 226
   Colin's ideas of, for new missionaries, 100
   Milan missionaries' lack of interest in, 101
   move toward Catholicism in, 84, 85–86
   recommended as mission field, 426
Five Days of Milan, 19–20
food, of island peoples, 174–75, 178
Forcade, Théodore-Augustin, 368–70

Forestier, Benoît-Jean, 40, 45, 475–76
Formosa, as possible mission location, 392
Fort Coronation, 326–27n52
Fort du Bus, 326–27n52
Frances Margaret, Sister, 524
Franchi, Alessandro, 471, 499, 512–15, 528
   agreeing that Marists could not take on Micronesia and Melanesia, 477–78
   death of, 483
   letter of encouragement to von Essen, 505
   responding to Elloy's requests for extending his jurisdiction, 475–76
Franciscans (Order of Friars Minor [O.F.M.]), 21
Francis Joseph I, 25, 187
Francis Xavier, Saint, 21
Franco-Prussian War, 443–44
Fransoni, Filippo, 16, 17
   against sending second group of missionaries so soon to Oceania, 160, 162, 163
   anguished over conditions for Reina and his missionaries, 292
   approving of Milan missionaries' decision to go to Melanesia, 146
   approving of Reina's choice of a mission, 160
   clash with Supriès, 1
   concerned over personnel turnover in Hong Kong, 369
   considering Reina prefect apostolic only for Melanesia, 146
   Cuarterón's principal patron in Rome, 278
   death of, 322

Fransoni, Filippo (*continued*)
   desiring to send missionaries to India, 192–93
   desiring warm relationship between French and Italian missionary groups, 109
   disagreeing with Colin's plans for Oceania, 73–74
   in discussions regarding New Caledonia, 34
   establishing Micronesia vicariate, 3
   explaining decisions regarding New Caledonia and Navigators vicariates, 42
   giving special instructions regarding Lombard seminary, 63
   granting Micronesia and Melanesia missions to Lombard seminary, 58–59
   hoping Cuarterón would help reactivate Reina's work, 310
   informing Colin of new missionaries coming to Oceania, 68
   on issue of dual prefects apostolic for Melanesia, 165–66
   letter of, accompanying the *Instructions*, 132–33
   letter to Archbishop Polding of Sydney regarding arriving Milan missionaries, 104
   letter of praise to Benaglia, 12

Fransoni, Filippo (*continued*)
letter to Romilli about audience with Pius IX, 30–31
meeting regarding Cuarterón's "Description of a New Mission," 296
on Micronesia and Melanesia being reserved for Lombard mission seminary, 35–36
on necessity of Marists' helping Milan mission to Oceania, 85–86, 88–89
optimism of, regarding beginning of Oceania mission, 78–79
praising Marinoni for treatment of missionaries, 109
praising Supriès's offer of Lombardy clerics for mission, 11–13
producing *Instructions* for Milan missionaries, 85, 87
providing guidelines for beginning Oceania mission, 76–77
reaction to news of abandoning Rooke and Woodlark, 238–39
receiving memorandum regarding mission seminary, 29
on receiving reports from Reina about Oceania mission, 191–92
reluctant to send more missionaries to Melanesia, 192, 195–96
reorganizing New Caledonia, Samoa,

Fransoni, Filippo (*continued*)
and Central Oceania vicariates, 67
responding to Reina about legacy of Lombard ministry, 87
wanting to postpone second group of missionaries, 146
Frassinetti, Giuseppe, 372
Freinademetz, Joseph, 519, 521
Frémont, Pierre-Jean, 60–61, 149
accompanying Salerio to Woodlark, 181
concerned over Milan missionaries' insinuations, 151
elected as prefect apostolic of Mission of Micronesia and Melanesia, 72–73, 80
end of activity in Melanesia and Micronesia, 184–85
first letter to Fransoni as prefect of mission, 108–9
going to found the station at Rooke, 152, 153–54
on inability to infuse morality into people of Rooke Island, 180
on keeping Woodlark for the Marists, 150–51, 160
on Marists leaving Woodlark altogether, 151
on progress of Woodlark mission, 164
on report he desired to go to New Caledonia, 185–86
report to Rocher on state of Oceania missions, 186

Frémont, Pierre-Jean (*cont.*)
request for additional faculties, 125–26, 164
resolved to stay in Woodlark, 107, 108
Fullard, Joseph, 254

Garibaldi, Giuseppe, 188
Garibaldi, Pietro Antonio, 64
Gata, Gioacchino, 447–48
Gautizan, 420
Gaysruck, Karl Gaetan, 6–7, 9, 12, 14
Gazelle
attack on, 248–51
attempts to secure another ship to search for, 239–40
insurance on, 239
local response to loss of, 254–58
murdered crew of, 254
shipwreck of, 243–46
Gebe, 314
Geissler, Johann G., 362
Gennade (Jean-Pierre Roland), 81, 149, 150, 257
accompanying Salerio to Woodlark, 181
end of activity in Melanesia and Micronesia, 184
Gennevoise, André-Félix-Chrysostome-Joseph, 504
German/Austrian priests, mission seminary for, 502–11, 519–20
Gilbert (Kingsmill) Islands, 433–34, 450–51, 461, 470
Gill, Wyatt, 469
Gilligen, John, 254
Godeffroy, Johann César, 480
Goold, James Alipius, 315
Goossens, 543–44
Goszner, J., 362

Goszner Mission Society (Gosznerscher Missionsverein), 362
Gould, Henry, 254
Grant, Thomas, 68
Gregory XV, 1
Gregory XVI, 6, 16, 115, 116, 125, 129
   creation of Prefecture Apostolic of Hong Kong Island, 367
   dividing Eastern Oceania vicariate, 463n11
Guadalupe, 320–21
Guasopa, 60, 61
Guérin, J. F. M., 3n2

Hall, James, 50
Hargreaves, Edward, 141
Hawaiian Evangelical Association, 148, 469–70
Herbert of Lea, Lady, 488–89, 537
Herbert, Sidney, 488
Hoffman, Petrus, 509
Holy Roman and Universal Inquisition (Holy Office), 121
Hong Kong
   Barnabò clarifying roles of personnel in, 394–97
   ceded to British Crown, 367
   giving to English missionaries, 513–14
   growth of mission in, 404
   mission history of, leading up to Reina's transfer, 367–82
   numbers of Catholics in, 390–91, 425
   Reina's transfer to, 364–66
   rising to status of vicariate apostolic, 500–502, 512–13, 518–19

Hong Kong Island, Prefecture Apostolic of, 367
Howard, Edward, 530
Huinima, Solomon, 102
Hurmuz, Eduardo, 303

Immaculate Conception, dogma of, proclaimed, 225, 280, 281
impediments, 116–17
   Milan missionaries assigned to, 282–85
   new missionaries sent to, 207
   plans for sending Lombardy missionaries to, 375
   requests for missionaries to, 192–93, 194, 196
Innocent III, 268
Instructions for the Prefect Apostolic and the Missionaries of the Seminary of Milan Going to Oceania, The, 91–94, 132, 135–36, 165
Instructions, violation of principles in, 153
Invernizzi, Luigi, 145
iron, 151
   importance of, to missionaries' survival, 224
   locals' need for, 154
   as trade item, 141
irregularities, 116–17
Isabel II, 274, 276, 413, 428
Isle of Pines, 32
   progress at, 35, 39
   school opened at, 40
Italy
   revolution in (1848), 28
   war of independence against Austria, 1920

Jackson, Thomas, 543–45
Jansen, Cornelis, 188
Jansenism, 188
Janssen, Arnold, 506–9, 512, 519, *520*, 521
Jaussen, Florentin-Etienne, 464
Jimeno, Romualdo, 276
Johann Cesar Godeffroy und Sohn, 461, 480–81
John XXIII, 5
John Paul II, 264, 521
Johnson, Charles Anthony, 525
Joset, Théodore, 367, 514
Joubert, 204, 208, 214, 364, 393
Julien, S., 240

Kilty, Daniel, 544
King, Robert, 254
Kirby, T., 513
Kleiner Herz-Jesu-Bote, 506
Kops, Brujin, 362
Kulturkampf, 505–6

Labuan and Its Dependencies, Prefecture Apostolic of, creation of, 296–97, 300
Labuan mission, 292–93, 493
   arrival at, 344
   children of, to be presented for baptism, 345
   confusion over jurisdictional issues in, 330–32
   Cuarterón and Reina's groups arriving at, 342–43
   Cuarterón's twentieth anniversary in, 526–28
   determining interest for, in Paris Foreign Missionary Seminary, 499
   official statistics on, 407
   plans for reorganizing, 495–97

Labuan mission (*continued*)
   Pope-Hennessy's report on, 495
   prefect apostolic for, 541
La Grande Chartreuse, 1
Lakemba Island, 84n13
Lamaze, Jean-Amand, 484
Lambruschini, Luigi, 120
language
   local, use of during church services, 129–30
   study of, at Rooke Island, 173–74
   studying in preparation for travels, 12, 37, 43, 87, 89, 102
Laughlan Islands, 81–83, 100, 139
Lawes, William George, 469
Ledóchowski, Mieczyslaw, 546
Leo XIII, 483, 484, 528
Libois, Napoléon-François, 370
Liguori, Alphonsus Maria, 64, 189
Limbrock, Eberhard, 520
Litany of Loreto, 332
living conditions, raising standards of, for locals, 154
Lloyd Line, providing free transportation for missionaries and for transportation to Vatican Council, 435
local marriages, rules for dealing with, 124–26
Lombard missionaries. *See* Milan missionaries
Lombards, involvement of, as foreign missionaries, 7–13
Lombardy
   episcopal conference of (1850), 52–53, 54–55
   memorandum to Pius IX regarding mission seminary at, 29–30

Lombardy (*continued*)
   Supriès's desire for mission seminary at, 12–14
Lombardy Seminary for Foreign Missions
   associating with another congregation, 62–63
   criticized by Austrians in local government, 53
   curriculum of, 53–54, 64
   first missionaries from, 64–65
   founding of, 20–21
   funding for, 51, 62, 64
   granted Micronesia and Melanesia as mission fields, 57–58
   new missionaries from, being recommended for Ceylon, 373
   opening of, 51–52
   preparations for opening, 46–48
   requesting specific mission field, 55–57, 372–74
   rule and daily order for, 51, 53, 63
   transferred to Milan, 54, 64. *See also* Milan Seminary for Foreign Missions
London Missionary Society (L.M.S.), 293, 468–69
Longoni, Giovanni, 145
Loring, William, 258
Luquet, Jean-Félix-Onésime, 15–18
   death of, 427
   discussing with Ramazzotti founding of seminary for Lombardy, 20–21
   warning about conditions in Melanesia and Micronesia, 61–62

MacFarlane, Samuel, 469

Mackey, Henry Benedict, 524, 541
Mai, Angelo, 116
Maigret, Désiré-Louis, 464
mail service, improvement in, 449–50
Mangieri, Girolamo, 368, 379–80, 387, 389, 390–91
   desire to be relieved of office in Hong Kong, 385
   dismissal of, 398–99, 403
Manning, Henry Edward, 497
Marceau, Auguste, 102
Maresca, Francesco Saverio, 376
Marietti, Antonio, 14, 145
Marinoni, Giuseppe, 26
   accepting director position at Lombard seminary, 47, 49
   admonishing Riva and Borgazzi, 420
   alarmed at Colin's vague promise of assistance, 84–85
   apprising Fransoni of conditions in Melanesia, 290
   chosen as Lombardy seminary director, 25–27
   confused after Pius IX's meeting with Reina and Salerio, 69–71
   death of, 427, 547
   on departure proceedings for Milan missionaries, 98–99
   desiring second expedition for Micronesia and Melanesia, 144–45
   grief-stricken at Barnabò's harsh letter, 397
   informing Milan missionaries about

Marinoni, Giuseppe (*cont.*)
Labuan mission, 298–99
involvement in reassessment of Hong Kong mission, 503
learning lesson on dealing with Barnabò, 403
offering first missionaries to Rome, 65
persistence in requesting second group of missionaries, 162–63
preparing for episcopal conference of 1850, 53
presenting Act of Foundation to Rome, 55–56
pursuing pope's approval for second group of missionaries to Oceania, 162, 167
receiving letters regarding abandonment of Woodlark and Rooke, 233
request for faculties, 126–27
requesting faculties for Milan missionaries, 114–16
response to Ramazzotti's instructions regarding Milan seminary, 75
seeking Taglioretti's advice on Milan missionaries, 305–7
on seminary's opening day, 51
thanking Fransoni for *Instructions* and related correspondence, 94–95
urging Colin to settle apprenticeship for Milan's missionaries serving under the Marists, 71

Marinoni, Giuseppe (*cont.*)
urging Fransoni to approve second group of missionaries for Oceania, 161–62
working on details regarding opening of mission seminary, 49
Marists (Society of Mary [S.M.]), 6
Bataillon's reasons for their presence in Micronesia-Melanesia, 460
desiring to be relieved of Micronesia and Melanesia, 49
end of activity in Melanesia and Micronesia, 184–85
giving Milan missionaries supplies for use in the mission, 152
greeting new missionaries to Woodlark, 149–50
influence of, in missions of Oceania, 186
involvement of, in training new missionaries for Melanesia and Micronesia, 67–68
jurisdiction of, considered as obstacle to Lombard mission progress, 86
leaving Micronesia and Melanesia mission, 130
providing no more priests for Melanesia and Micronesia, 61
required to stay in Oceania to train Milan missionaries, 73–74
role of, in Central Oceania, according to Bataillon, 441–43
suggestion of, to temporarily withdraw from missions, 212–13

Marists (S.M.) (*continued*)
Vicariate Apostolic of Micronesia entrusted to, 3
work of, in Oceania, 459
Marist Supply Center (Sydney), 33, 85, 185, 279
Marmoiton, Blaise, 40
Marquesas Islands, Vicariate Apostolic of, 464
marriages, local, faculties for dealing with, 124, 128–29
Marshall Islands, 470
Mary Thais, Sister (Rose Rodway), 524, 541–43, 548
Masotti, Ignazio, 537
May Laws, 506
Mazzucconi, Giovanni Battista, 5, 10–11, 13, 14, 74, 262
against Austria during the revolution, 53
concern over absence of, 233–42
death of, 249–50, 253, 326
departing Sydney, 226–27
describing Tonga-Java for his family, 206–7
discussing with Ramazzotti acceptance into mission seminary, 28
faculties given to, before voyage to Sydney, 114
final correspondence of, to family, 263
final letter of, before missionaries' departure, 102
going to Rooke, 153
heading back to Woodlark, 227–28
ideas for abandoning missions, reported to Marinoni, 208–10
illness of, 199

Mazzucconi, G. B. (*continued*)
  leaving Rooke for health reasons and to report on travels, 205, 206–7
  letter to family upon arrival at Tarban Creek, 113
  on Marists' suggestion to temporarily withdraw from missions, 212–13
  named as missionary apostolic for Oceania, 91
  position paper for beatification of, *260*
  preparing for voyage to Sydney, 114
  proposing to Reina that the missionaries leave Rooke and Woodlark, 200, 205
  receiving news from Marinoni while in Sydney, 225
  receiving title of "Blessed" as recognized as martyr, 264
  reporting "few ideas" of island peoples, 174
  requesting admission to Lombard seminary, 47
  restored to health in Sydney, 225
  search for, 242–52
  on seminary's opening day, 51
  suggested for Hong Kong mission, 373
  suggesting abandonment of Rooke and Woodlark missions, 289, 291
  suggesting that missionaries regroup in Sydney, 215
  suggestion for location of supply center, 213–14

Mazzucconi, G. B. (*continued*)
  upon seeing New Guinea, 154, 155
  working on details regarding opening of mission seminary, 49
Mazzucconi, Giacomo, 10
medicine, practicing, faculty requested for, 122–23
Melanesia
  early deaths of Marists at, 60
  multiple languages of, 140
  named vicariate apostolic, 49
  pessimistic outlook for, after first year, 193–94
  reduced to mission status, 34
  reserved as mission field for Lombard mission seminary, 35–36
  two prefects apostolic for, 164–66
  vicariate of, unoccupied (1872), 459–60
Melanesia-Micronesia mission
  funds left over from first, 400–403
  ideas for reviving, 392–94
  settling questions regarding jurisdiction over, 476–80
  suppression of, 401–2
Melanesia mission. *See also* Milan missionaries
  budget for (1858), 357–58
  lacking funds, 290
  left completely in hands of Milan missionaries, 181
  Reina and Cuarterón's plans for reestablishing, 337–39
Mengkabong, mission site of, 346, 354, 355
Menkabong, 492

Micronesia
  named vicariate apostolic, 49
  pessimistic outlook for, after first year, 193–94
  reduced to mission status, 34
  reserved as mission field for Lombard mission seminary, 35–36
  universally favored as Lombard seminary's first mission in Oceania, 70, 71
  Vicariate Apostolic of, creation of, 3
  vicariate of, recommendation to separate from Melanesia, 18
  vicariate unoccupied (1872), 459–60
Micronesia mission, offered to Congregation of the Sacred Hearts of Jesus and Mary (SS.CC.) and Oblates of Mary Immaculate (O.M.I.), 369
Milan
  founding of Congregation of Saint Francis Xavier in, 7–8
  stormy relations with Rome, 395–97
  under Austrian rule, 6–7
Milan missionaries
  to accompany Frémont to Rooke Island, 150
  awaiting supplies, 203–4
  Bataillon's reasons for their proposed presence in Micronesia, 460, 461
  Central Bengal, Hyderabad, and Hong Kong to be entrusted to, 288

Milan missionaries (*continued*)
cost of initial mission, 95–97
departure ceremony for, 97–98, 101–2
first group of, thanking Fransoni for *Instructions* and related correspondence, 94–95
first group's fate in Melanesia, 147
freedom of, requested in Melanesia and Micronesia, 72
illness among, 170–72
instructed to take up work again in Melanesia with Cuarterón, 308–10
lack of funding for, 181, 196–97, 204, 214–15
leaving Rooke for Woodlark, 218–19, 309
leaving Sydney for Manila, 328–29
linkage to Cuarterón's mission, 298, 299
linkage to Polding, 299
liturgical calendar to be followed by, 115
mail for, 207–8, 214–15
money for, waiting in Sydney, 208
no interest in Fiji, 101
political and theological problems at home, 187–88
preparing for beginning of mission at Woodlark, 140–41
receiving flood of correspondence for support, 194–95
residing at Tarban Creek after leaving Woodlark, 230

Milan missionaries (*continued*)
returning to Sydney for health reasons, 222
second group, 145
traveling to Sydney, 103–6, 110–12
traveling from Woodlark to Sydney, 223–24, 227–28
Milan Seminary for Foreign Missions
charges about, regarding anti-Austrian sentiments, 187–90
curriculum at, 189
responsibility of, for Melanesia and Micronesia, 476–77, 479
Cuarterón's concern for existence of, 312
disappointment of, after Marinoni's meeting with Pius IX, 167
mission of Hong Kong to be transferred to, 378
second expedition from, awaiting news from Oceania, 169
to use Hong Kong as base for relaunching Micronesia-Melanesia mission, 384–85, 388
Mill Hill missionaries
in Afghanistan, 535
general chapter held (1884), 544
origins of, 485–91
prefecture transferred to, 543
receiving new prefecture apostolic, 539
requested to go to Borneo, 524–25
seeking a part of Cuarterón's territory, 531–34

Mill Hill missionaries (*cont.*)
seeking an independent mission, 529–31, 534–37
Mill Hill Seminary, trying to obtain Hong Kong mission, 500–502
Missionaries of Saint Francis Xavier, organization of, 7–10
missionary work, Reina's *Memorandum* on, 180–81
Mola, Cesare, 9, 10, 13, 57
Molteni, Angelo, 24–25, 27, 53
Montrouzier, Jean-Xavier, 44–45, 80, 81, 113
on accompanying Milan missionaries to Rooke, 143
assigned to Woodlark, 150
difficulties of, outside competence of Propaganda Fide, 123–25
producing first Woodlark dictionary, 140
questioning Colin on future of Marist missions, 139–40
reporting on progress at Woodlark, 139
requesting additional faculties, 120, 121, 123, 129
working with Reina on choice of missions, 131–32, 135, 136–37
Moran, Patrick, 513–14
Moreton Bay, mission at, 315–16
Morlacchi, Carlo Gritti, 54–55
Mornico, Alessandro, 49, 74
Morpurgo, Elio, 435
Mulsuce, Gaetano Antonio, 56

Mundy, George Rodney, 292–93
Murphy, Daniel, 192, 193, 197, 280
Murray, A. W., 469

Nardi, Francesco, 500–501
Navigators Archipelago (Samoa)
    Elloy and Bataillon both wanting, 431–34
    move toward Catholicism in, 84
    separated from Central Oceania vicariate, 457
New Britain, 470
New Caledonia, 393
    Anglican presence in, 35, 36
    attack on Vicariate Apostolic of, 32
    Colin's suggestion of, as destination for Marists, 186
    creation of Vicariate Apostolic of, 32
    mission activity in, 452–53
New Georgia, 158, 393
    arrival at, en route to Woodlark, 148
    considering new foundation in, 222
New Guinea, 469, 537–38
    importance of, to Colin, 100
    Protestant mission at, earthquake at, 426
New Hebrides Islands, 34
New Ireland, 537–38
New Zealand, Propaganda Fide's actions in, 83
Northern Oceania, as independent mission, 1
Novasconi, Antonio, 193

Oblates of Mary Immaculate (O.M.I.), 50, 369, 371
Oceania
    Australian revenge for murders in, 258–59
    Bataillon's report on, 459–60
    communication with, 66
    funding mission for, 77–78
    languages of, 174
    Salerio's report on missionary life in, 159
    supplies needed for, 65
    transportation to, 66, 77, 80
oil, using in place of wax, 118–20
Ong-an-Pereira, Balbina, 404
Opium War, 367
Order of Carthusians (O. Cart.), 25
Order of the Most Holy Trinity for the Redemption of Captives (O.SS.T.). *See* Trinitarians
Order of Saint Augustine (O.S.A.). *See* Augustinians
ordinaries, 126
Origo, Spirito, 70
Orkney, James, 469
Orsa, José Aranguren, 330
Ortolda, Canon, 376
Ottow, C. W., 362

Pakò, missionaries' high hopes for, 197–98
Pallotti, Vincenzo, 485, 486
papal states, 28
Parietti, Albino, 284, 285–89, 376
Paris Foreign Mission Seminary, 1
Parkins, Junius, 254
Parkins, William Thomas (W.T.), 239, 242, 254

Particular Congregation on China and Adjacent Kingdoms, 366, 367, 512–15
Passionists (Congregation of the Passion of Jesus Christ [C.P.]), 315–16
Patrizi, Constantino, 296, 512–15
Paul III, 125
Paul VI, beatifying Janssen and Freinademetz, 521
Paul IX, encouraging Reina to be in good spirits, 195
Pecci, Gioacchino, 483
Perrone, Giovanni, 64, 189
Perroton, Francoise, 157
Piazzoli, Luigi, 503
Picpus Fathers (Congregation of the Sacred Hearts of Jesus and Mary [SS. CC.]), 11, 49–50, 129, 369, 371
    activity of, in Oceania, 459
    Bataillon's reasons for their proposed presence in Micronesia, 460, 461
    offered Micronesia-Melanesia mission, 462, 463–67
Pitra, Giovanni Battista, 512–15
Pius IX, 14, 17
    on answers to questions from Montrouzier, 124
    approval of Lombard seminary, 30–31, 46
    blessing missionaries going to India, 376
    blessings to missionaries in Oceania and to Milan seminary, 168, 169
    comforting letter to Reina, 234

572　*Index*

Pius IX (*continued*)
　creating Prefecture Apostolic of the Fiji Islands, 426
　creating Vicariate Apostolic of New Caledonia, 32
　creating Vicariate Apostolic of the Samoa or Navigators Archipelago, 34
　death of, 483, 528
　decisions regarding New Caledonia and Navigators vicariates, 42
　desire to found foreign mission seminary for Lombardy, 20–21
　desire to see Milan missionaries go to Corfu, 167. *See also* Corfu
　in exile, 28–29
　farewell audience granted to Cuarterón, Riva, and Borgazzi, 302–3
　granting audience to Bertinelli and Fransoni regarding mission seminary, 29
　granting faculties to Milan missionaries, 115
　granting Marinoni's request for faculties, 127
　granting private audience to missionaries assigned to India, 286
　hoping for improvement for Milan missionaries, 303
　introducing beatification cause of Pierre Chanel, 261
　issuing Papal Briefs on Hong Kong, 518

Pius IX (*continued*)
　naming Elloy titular bishop of Tipasa and coadjutor to vicar apostolic of Central Oceania, 429
　ordering funding for Lombard seminary, 58
　pleased that Cuarterón would be rescuing Milan missionaries in Melanesia, 294
　pleased with sendoff of Milan missionaries, 110
　private meeting with Reina and Salerio, 66–67, 69
　proclaiming dogma of Immaculate Conception, 281
　protesting *Kulturkampf*, 506
　questioning Feliciani about Hong Kong, 368
　ratifying Ramazzotti's appointment as bishop of Pavia, 48
　response to Frémont's request for faculties, 126
Pius V, 128
Polding, John Bede, 34, 104, 112, 280
　arranging for Milan missionaries to found a mission in Port Curtis, 316–18
　death of, 428
　planning for mission in northern Australia, 318–19
　planning mission for Milan missionaries under Cuarterón, 281
　preliminary plans for mission at Port Curtis, 288–89

Polding, John Bede (*continued*)
　proposing diocese of Moreton Bay, 315
　requesting new missionaries, 395
Pompallier, Jean-Baptiste-François, 3, 16, 116, 429, 440
　death of, 427–28
　requesting more missionaries from Barnabò, for New Zealand, 382
　soliciting services of Reina and his missionaries, 319
　wanting priests from Marinoni's seminary, 328–29
Ponape (Ascension Island), 33–34, 393, 441, 442
　Bataillon's suggestions for mission work at, 460
　as potential headquarters for Micronesia mission, 50
　Protestant mission founded in, 148, 352
Pondicherry, Vicariate Apostolic of, 16
Pontiggia, Pietro, 14
Pope-Hennessy, James, 491–94
Port Balade, Douarre founding mission at, 40
Port Curtis, Milan missionaries instructed to found a mission at, 316–18
Port Moresby, 469
Poupinel, Victor, 196–97, 429–30, 438–39
Pozzi, Francesco, 145
Prada, Giuseppe, 23, 24
Praelectiones theologiae dogmaticae (Perrone), 64

Propaganda Fide
(Congregation for the Propagation of the Faith), 1
  accepting proposal for dividing Pondicherry vicariate, 16
  agreeing to designation of prefects apostolic for Melanesia and Micronesia, 34
  cited as authority for Lombard seminary, 30
  declining more missionaries until Reina's new mission was established, 347–48
  desiring to free Melanesia missionaries from their situation, 294–96
  holding off on associating Cuarterón's mission with Milan missionaries in Melanesia, 298, 299, 303
  intentions of, for Milan missionaries, 287–88
  reason for postponing second group of missionaries, 166
  supporting Milan missionaries, 74
  supporting missions in Oceania, even with difficulties, 194
  transferring Reina to Hong Kong, 364–66, 382–85
Protestant missionaries
  causing trouble in Hong Kong and for Raimondi's college, 497
  interested in Central Oceania, 468–70
  presence of, in Gilbert Islands and Kingsmill Archipelago, 480

Puarer, 153, 223, 252–53, 326
  baptism of, 339–40
  departure from Hong Kong, 403
  describing massacre at Woodlark, 248–51
  in Hong Kong, 391
Pulalon, Mahamed, 276

quinine, supplies exhausted, 170, 172, 185, 203

Radetzky, Joseph, 19, 20, 48
Raimondi, Carlo, 138
Raimondi, Timoleone, 74, 516
  active in Manila, 342
  admiration of, for Puarer, 326
  on bishops competing for services of Milan missionaries, 319–20
  considered for vicar apostolic of Hong Kong, 503
  criticized regarding the process of Hong Kong becoming a vicariate apostolic, 511–12
  death of, 547
  on dismissal of Riva and Borgazzi, 423–24
  episcopal ordination of, 518
  focused on New Guinea, 138
  illness of, 183–84, 215
  impressions of Cuarterón, 337
  involved in search for Mazzucconi, 241–52
  involvement in starting German-language foreign mission seminary, 503–11

Raimondi, Timoleone (cont.)
  knowledge of Cuarterón's plans for Milan missionaries, 326–27
  on Mill Hill seminary trying to obtain Hong Kong mission, 500–502
  multiple titles given to, 490
  named as missionary apostolic for Oceania, 91
  named pro-prefect of Hong Kong mission, 486–87
  placed in charge of Labuan mission, 355–56
  pledge to assist German missionaries in China, 503–4
  questioning if Hong Kong should have vicariate status, 500
  relaying information about Cuarterón, 410–11
  remaining at Woodlark, 153, 154
  responsibilities in Hong Kong, 390
  return to Sydney after search for Mazzucconi, 253–54
  searching for English-speaking teaching brothers, 486, 497
  up for consideration for bishop and vicar apostolic of Hong Kong, 514–15
  upon learning of Rome's criticism of Marinoni and pioneer Oceania missionaries, 336
  wanting Hong Kong mission given to Milan Foreign Mission Seminary, 487

Raimondi, Timoleone (*cont.*)
   working on reorganizing Labuan mission, 495–97
   writing catechism in Woodlark language, 339
Ramazzotti, Angelo Francesco, 20–21, 22
   asked to provide priests to serve as Propaganda Fide's procurators for China, 48
   chosen as new bishop of Pavia, 25
   death of, 427
   furious at Marinoni's letter regarding mission location for seminary graduates, 75
   giving Cuarterón relic of his patron saint, 301
   indicating more missionaries ready for assignment, 191, 192–93
   installed as bishop of Pavia, 52
   meeting with Molteni about seminary, 27
   memorandum of, regarding Lombard seminary, 30
   moving to Saronno to supervise founding of mission seminary, 27–28
   offering house at Saronno for proposed mission institute, 21–23
   ordained as bishop of Pavia, 48
   as promoter and protector of Milan seminary, 86
   requesting Micronesia as mission field, 50

Ramazzotti, Angelo F. (*cont.*)
   requesting mission field for new mission seminary, 369
   requesting specific mission field for Lombard seminary, 55
   response of, to charges against Milan missionaries regarding anti-Austrian sentiments, 188–90
   seeking support of bishops of Lombardy dioceses, 46–47
   on Lombard seminary's opening day, 51
   supporting Marinoni's request for second group of missionaries, 162
   tensions and misunderstandings with Marinoni, 168
   writing memorandum for Pius IX on Saronno plan, 24–25
Ratisbonne, Alphonse, 278
Ravizza, Gaetano, 23, 25
Reina, Paolo, 14, 19–20, 49
   acknowledging unhealthiness of Melanesia, 199–200
   assigned to Subiaco, 317
   against Austria during the revolution, 53
   authorizing Mazzucconi to decide on future of Woodlark mission, 205
   beginning negotiations with Frémont, 150
   on bishops competing for services of Milan missionaries, 320

Reina, Paolo (*continued*)
   booking passage to Manila to meet with Cuarterón, 325–26
   chosen as prefect apostolic, for mission in Oceania, 90–91, 92, 04
   concern about Mazzucconi's delayed return to Sydney, 235–38
   concerned about legacy, 87
   considering opening a third mission station, 153
   convinced that mission should be abandoned, 219–22
   death of, 425
   deaths of half his staff, 259
   deciding on mission for Lombard missionaries, 131–37
   deciding to abandon Rooke, 218
   departure from Hong Kong, 405–6
   desire to open new mission in New Guinea, 205–6
   destination of, uncertain (1855–56), 321–22
   disagreeing with abandonment of missions, 200–203
   doubting potential success of Cuarterón's plans, 350–52, 380–81
   explaining missionaries' desires to serve their superiors, 231
   explaining reasons for abandoning Rooke and Woodlark, 231–32, 307
   expressing gratitude to Fransoni, 88
   faculties granted to, 114–18

Reina, Paolo (*continued*)
  on food supplies, how long they lasted, 235
  gathering supplies for mission, 140
  going to Rooke, 153
  illness of, 211, 217–18, 338–39, 405–6
  impressions of Cuarterón, 341–42
  inability to work in Cuarterón's style, 354–55
  on initial conditions at Rooke, 155–56
  introduced at Hong Kong with false titles, 389
  leaving Labuan for Singapore, 358–59
  on Lombardy seminary's opening day, 51
  making plans to meet Cuarterón, 324–25
  meeting Cuarterón in Manila, 333
  Memorandum on missionary work and relations, 180–81
  on missionaries' decision to accept both Micronesia and Melanesia, 99
  named as prefect apostolic of Melanesia, 165–66
  offering to resign as prefect apostolic, 356
  official title of missionary apostolic of Hong Kong, 393
  opinions on Cuarterón's handling of Labuan mission, 411
  plan for New Guinea, 232
  private audience with Pius IX, 66–67, 69

Reina, Paolo (*continued*)
  questioned about readiness to go to Hong Kong, 374
  questioning Cuarterón on status of the mission, 352–53
  reestablishing mission in New Guinea, 356–58
  reporting Mazzucconi's death, 259–61
  reporting to Salerio on conditions at Rooke, 217
  requesting admission to seminary, 28
  requesting new missionaries from Barnabò, for Cuarterón's mission, 339
  responding to Ripamonti's suggestions for reducing mission expenses, 232–33
  response of, to Frémont's decision for Marists to leave, 151–52
  return to Italy, 405–6
  on Rooke Island natives' limitation of ideas, 180
  sent to Rome upon seminary graduation, 65, 66–67
  suspecting that missionaries would be recalled from Oceania, 221, 222
  transferred to Hong Kong, 364–66
  traveling to Hong Kong, 388
  traveling to Lyon to meet with Marists, 68, 71, 74

Reina, Paolo (*continued*)
  unanimous choice as superior for Oceania mission, 77
  understanding of his role at Hong Kong, 397–398
  waiting to sail to Hong Kong from Labuan, 347
  worried about superiors' opinions regarding decision to abandon Woodlark and Rooke, 235
  writing to Barnabò upon finding out of Fransoni's death, 334–35
  writing to Marinoni on Cuarterón's priorities, 335
  writing to secure approval of a supply center location, 344–45
"Report on Oceania for Propaganda" (Bataillon), 459–60
"Report on Western Oceania" (Barnabò), 34
Rinandini, Monsignor, 534
Ripamonti, Alessandro, 28, 49
  considered for Hong Kong position, 378
  on Lombardy seminary's opening day, 51
  offering suggestions to Reina on reducing mission expenses, 232
  praising work of Milan missionaries in India, 327
  suggested for Hong Kong mission, 373
Ritter Island, 155
Riva, Antonio, 145, 265, 282–85, 293
  arrival in Manila, 330
  arriving in Labuan, 343

576 Index

Riva, Antonio (*continued*)
  Cuarterón's displeasure with, 417–18
  Cuarterón's instructions to, upon submitting his resignation, 413
  death of, 425
  delayed departure from Rome, 303
  esteem held for Cuarterón, 314
  expelled from mission, 421–25
  farewell audience with Pius IX, 302–3
  transferred to Hong Kong, 423
  visiting Borgazzi on alternate months, 409
Rocher, Jean-Louis, 33, 80, 112
  agreement reached with Joubert to deliver goods to missionaries, 204
  on Ambrosoli's status in Sydney, 350
  chartering a schooner to search for Mazzucconi, 241
  chartering ship to bring supplies to Milan missionaries, 225
  reporting negative news to Mazzucconi on mission's future, 207
  working with Reina on choice of missions, 131–32, 134–37
Rodway, Elizabeth, 524–25, 541
Rodway, Rose. *See* Mary Thais, Sister
Rodway, W. M., 524
Roman Catholic doctrine, safeguarding, 121
Romilli, Carlo Bartolomeo, 14, 16

Romilli, Carlo B. (*continued*)
  death of, 427
  discussing founding of seminary for Lombardy, 20–21
  on Lombard seminary's desire for unrestricted mission territory, 86
  meeting with Ramazzotti regarding opening of mission seminary, 47
  on Milan missionaries' attitudes toward Marists and Propaganda Fide, 90
  thanking Colin for wise counsel given to Milan missionaries, 109–10
  thanking Fransoni for help with Seminary for Foreign Missions, 78
Rooke Island (Umboi), 60, 100
  abundance of food in, 159
  Ambrosoli's map of, *142*, *143*
  arrival at, 154–55
  conditions of, in second year, 199–200
  foods of, 178
  gardening on, 179
  high costs of mission at, 212
  illnesses at, 170–73, 199
  languages of, 173–74
  local customs of, 177–81
  medical report on, *176*
  natives' impressions of white people, 175
  parents killing babies, 179–80
  position of, beneficial for the mission, 178
  prayer on, 177
  three great wonders of, 175
  treating sickness on, 177
Rossi, Pellegrino, 28

Rouchouze, Euthyme, 463
Roudaire, Gilbert, 39, 43–45
Rougeyron, Pierre, 36, 453
Rousseille, Joseph, 499–500
rubrics, 120, 121

Sacred Congregation of Rites, 119
Sacred Congregation of the Holy Office, 124
Sacred Roman Rota, 500–501
Saint Michael's Village, 197–99
Saison, Charles-Marie, 23, 27, 28, 53, 56
Salerio, Carlo, 19, 49
  appointed to Woodlark, 152–53, 154
  against Austria during the revolution, 53
  building an altar on the ship to Sydney, 103
  chosen as future superior of Woodlark mission, if Marists left, 151
  concern about Mazzucconi's delayed return to Sydney, 233–34
  considered for Hong Kong position, 378
  convinced that Woodlark should be abandoned, 219
  death of, 427
  early descriptions of Woodlark, 156, 181–82, 204, 224
  embarking on new tactics for mission, 197–98
  faculties given to, before voyage to Sydney, 114
  illness of, 215, 238
  on life of missionary in Oceania, 159
  on Lombard seminary's opening day, 51

Salerio, Carlo (*continued*)
   named as missionary apostolic for Oceania, 91
   planning for educating the locals, 156–57
   preparing for voyage to Sydney, 114
   private audience with Pius IX, 66–67, 69
   reporting on voyage from Woodlark to Sydney, 224–25
   requesting admission to Lombard seminary, 47
   on role of catechists, 159
   sent to Rome upon seminary graduation, 65, 66–67
   sickness of, 184
   on suitable mission field for Lombard seminary, 56–57
   on surrounding islands' mission potential, 157–58
   traveling to Lyon to meet with Marists, 68, 71, 74
   travel to Rooke to give report to Reina, 181
   wanting to discuss mission's future with Reina, 216–17
Salvioni, Federico, 5–6, 14, 63n6, 98
Sambucetti, Canon, 475–76
Samoa Archipelago. *See also* Navigators Islands
   London Missionary Society in, 469
Scheut missionaries, 504
Schwarzenberg (Lieutenant), 47–48, 51–52
Sciomacher, Giulio, 145
Scotti, G. B., 176
Scurati, Giacomo, 378, 397, 403
self-defense, on part of missionaries, 123–24
Serbati, Antonio Rosmini, 67, 189
Shanghai, 377, 386, 392
Signay, Joseph, 128
Simeoni, Giovanni, 457, 465, 501–3, 511, 523, 528–31
   death of, 546
   decision to divide Cuarterón's prefecture, 533–34
   negotiating for founding mission on south coast of New Guinea, 537–38
   responding to Vaughn's impatience, 534–35
Singapore, Cuarterón's plan for boarding school at, 273
Smithurst, Henry, 469
Society of the Divine Word (S.V.D.). *See* Divine Word Missionaries
Society of Mary (S.M.). *See* Marists
Soliben, Joseph, 387
Solomon Islands
   Epalle attacked in, 14
   increasing commercial activity in, 363–64
Sonderbund, 15n30
South Shantung, Vicariate Apostolic of, 521
Steyl Foreign Mission Seminary, 521
St. John, Spencer, 345
St. Joseph's Foreign Missionary College at Mill Hill, 487–88, 493–94
St. Joseph's Missionary Society of Mill Hill (M.H.M.), 487
Stone, Octavius, 469
Sturla, Luigi, 372
Sulu Archipelago, Cuarterón's desire for mission in, 276
Supriès, Thaddée (Paul-Laurent-Marcel), 28, 371, 511
   advice on curriculum at Lombard seminary, 53–54
   in charge of retreats at Certosa di Pavia, 3–5
   clash with Fransoni, 1
   concerned over delay in papal approval of mission seminary, 28, 31
   considering his mission accomplished, 95
   death of, 428 of, 547
   on entrusting Micronesia to Lombard seminary, 50–51, 52
   finding personnel for Micronesia mission, 3, 11
   letters to Fransoni regarding mission seminary, intent of, 15
   matters in common with Luquet, 17
   meeting with Ramazzotti and Prada on Lombardy mission, 23
   pleased with missionaries' arrival in Sydney, 146–47
   on Prada, 23
   pursuing Micronesia as mission field for Lombardy priests, 14
   recognized as originator of Lombard seminary, 57
   reiterating support for Micronesia mission, 62, 63

Supriès, Thaddée (*continued*)
  suggesting affiliation of Lombard seminary with the Marists, 62–63
  trying to restore courage of abandoned missionaries, 195
  vital statistics of, 2, 4
  writing on the opening of Lombard seminary, 49
  writing to Buratti on Marists' behalf, 7
  writing to Fransoni to promote mission to Oceania, 8–10, 11
Sydney, suggested as place of support for missions of Oceania, 163

Tablet, The: A Weekly Newspaper and Review, 487
Tacchini, Luigi, 97, 326
  activity of, at Woodlark, 183
  departure from Hong Kong, 403–4
  illness of, 215
  named superintendent of Saint Francis Hospital, 391
  remaining at Woodlark, 153
Tacconi, Pietro, 13, 56
Taglioretti, Angelo, 20
  convoking meeting of seminary students to discuss mission work in Ceylon, 56
  discussing founding of seminary for Lombardy, 21
  Marinoni seeking advice of, regarding Milan missionaries, 305–7

Taglioretti, Angelo (*continued*)
  on need for missionaries in Corfu, 69–70
  reporting on Lombardy seminary's opening, 52
  reporting to Milan missionaries on Italian impressions of their work, 194
  working on details regarding opening of mission seminary, 47, 49
  writing to Marinoni about being seminary director, 25–27
Tahiti Islands, Vicariate Apostolic of, 464
Tamburini, Pietro, 188, 189
Tarban Creek, 112–13
Ternate, Cuarterón's choice for supply center, 302, 313, 314
Thomassin, Joseph, 60, 80, 82, 149, 150
  end of activity in Melanesia and Micronesia, 184
  having no doubts about abandoning Woodlark, 221
  opening school at Woodlark for thirty boys, 221
  remaining at Woodlark, 152, 153
  treatment of people at Woodlark, 181–83
Tikopia, mission expanding to, 43–44
Tokelau (Union) Group of Islands, 461, 468
Tonga-Java (Lord Howe Group, Luangiua), 205, 206–7
Tosti, Antonio, 48n12

transcontinental railroad (U.S.), 449–50
Trapenard, Pierre, 60, 80, 149–50, 152
Trappists (Cistercian Order of the Strict Observance [O.C.S.O.], 158–59
Trinitarians (Order of the Most Holy Trinity for the Redemption of Captives [O.SS.T.]), 268, 300
Tupper, Edward M., 258

Uaman, mission station at, 60
Univers pittoresque, 62
Unshelm, 481
Urbiztondo y Eguía, Antonio de, 276 l, 292

Valentine, survivor of *Mary* shipwreck, 82
Van Olphen, 270
Vatican Council (First), 435–38, 444, 472, 517
Vatican Council (Second), 521
Vaughn, Herbert Albert, 485–91, 499, 500, 525
  arrangements with the Netherlands or Holland for support for Mill Hill, 538–40
  death of, 548
  losing patience with lack of action on mission for Mill Hill missionaries, 534–37
  naming prefect apostolic for Labuan, 543
  promoted to third archbishop, 546
  promoting St. Joseph's Foreign Missionary College at Mill Hill, 487–88
  receiving Cuarterón's endowment funds, 546

Vaughn, Herbert Albert (*cont.*)
   requesting subsidy for mission in Borneo, 541
   taking up matter of Mill Hill missionaries receiving an independent mission, 529–31
Verguet, C. M. Léopold, 81
Verolles, Emmanuel-Jean-François, 368
Victoria, Queen, 293
Villoresi, Federico, 143
Vimercati, Giovanni, 30, 62
Visconti, Gian Galeazzo, 3
Vistarini, Giovanni, 10, 13, 57
Vitte, Ferdinand, 436–37, 438
Volonteri, Simeone, 403
von Essen, Ludwig, 502, 503–7, 512
Vrancken, Piet Maria, 272, 273, 330–31
   concern over jurisdiction of, 335
   negative reaction to founding an educational institution in Singapore, 300
Vranckx, François, 502, 504–5

Wallace, Alfred Russell, 362
Wan-Attaway, 258
Weber, Theodor, 481
Wesleyan Missionary Society (W.M.S.), 470
Western Oceania establishing hierarchy in, 16
Wilhelmsland, Prefecture Apostolic of, 521
Williams, John, 468–69
Wilson, Henry, 254
Wiseman, Nicholas Patrick, 114, 485, 486
Woodlark Island (Murua), 33, 60, 99
   Ambrosoli's map of, 250
   arrival at, 149
   call for punitive action against, for Mazzucconi's death, 253–58
   catechumenates at, 107–8, 139, 149, 197–98
   daily life of missionaries at, 158
   dictionary for, 140
   difficulties at, 66, 106, 107
   discontent among missionaries at, 60–61
   high costs of mission at, 212
   illness at, 183–84
   internal warfare at, 222–23, 246
   little success at, 81
   massacre at, 236–64
   medical report on, 176
   missionaries at, at time of Reina and Salerio's appointment, 71–73
   mission making progress under Marists, 149–50
   natives' beliefs about death, 183
   new tactics for mission at, 197–99
   people of, struck with famine, pestilence, and war, 182
   plan to annihilate the missionaries at, 216
   preparations at, in advance of Milan missionaries, 138
   rift between natives and missionaries, 182
   sickness striking natives of, 182
   supplies from Sydney indispensable for missionaries, 158
   worsening relations at, 215–16, 218, 220–21
   young men at, recruited by Thomassin, 182–83

Yates, James, 254
yaws (tropical ulcers), 184

www.ingramcontent.com/pod-product-compliance
Lightning Source LLC
Chambersburg PA
CBHW080529300426
44111CB00017B/2651